The Best Of ALABAMA

A • GUIDE • TO

ATTRACTIONS, LODGINGS, RESTAURANTS & EVENTS

D0878249

Birmingham's Fannie Flagg, who wrote the novel,
"Fried Green Tomatoes at the Whistle Stop Cafe,"
is surrounded by stars of the film.
Turn to page 132 for the story of the real cafe
which inspired the novel. You can still eat
fried green tomatoes in the cafe.

The Best Of ALABAMA

A • GUIDE • TO

ATTRACTIONS, LODGINGS, RESTAURANTS & EVENTS

First Edition

Lee Sentell

Ed Hall, Editorial Director

Seacoast Publishing, Inc.
Birmingham, Alabama

The Best of Alabama: A Guide to Attractions, Lodgings, Restaurants & Events
Copyright 1993 by Lee Sentell

Library of Congress Cataloging-in-Publication Data

The Best of Alabama

       Includes index
       1. Alabama - Descriptions and travel - 1993
-Guide Books. I. Sentell, Lee

ISBN: 1-878561-16-2

First edition, First printing
Printed in the United States of America

Design by Joel McWhorter of Paler/McWhorter Marketing
Production services by Janet Shults of Baker & Baker Design
Color separations by Graphic Color
Printing by Ebsco Media

Published by: Seacoast Publishing, Inc.
                P.O. Box 26492
                Birmingham, AL 35226

Acknowledgments

A book this comprehensive would not be possible without the support and help of travel professionals and the advice of family and friends. The author is indebted to those who were generous with their advice, time and answers.

The people listed are some of the hospitable Alabamians who provided information on their areas: Alex City: Martha Kelly; Anniston: Cindy Bailey, Paige Moreland; Auburn: Pat Dakin, Bob Lowry, David Housel; Athens: Bob Dunnavant, Jenny Brownlow; Birmingham: Ed Hall, Dilcy Hilley, Sarah Fuller, Dave Godber, Elma Bell, Pat Lynch, Marie Belcher, Betty Scharf, Johnie Sentell; Childersburg: Al Mathis; Clanton: Connie Bolton; Decatur: Cathy Wahl, Julian Walker, Chris Bell, Jerry Paasch, Doug Maze; Demopolis: Jane Gross; Dothan: Don Fabiani; Eufaula: Betty Sutton, Doug Purcell; Eutaw: Sibyl Banks; Florence: Virginia Gilluly, Winford Turner, Steve Antley; Fairhope: Kolleen Krandall; Foley: Linda Michelson; Fort Payne: Gaynelle Pitts, Sherry Whitten; Gadsden: Lloyd Wagnon, Peggy Rary; Gulf Coast: Maggie Hennessy, Jim Ackis, Herb Malone, Liz Wade, Susan Pafford; Greensboro: Randy Rhodes; Haleyville: Debra Hood; Huntsville: Judy Ryals, John Rison Jones, Harvie and Lynn Jones, Daniel Little, Lamar Higgins; Mobile: Caldwell Delaney, Gertrude Malbis, Eva Golson, Sue Lyons, Terry Monteith, Abby Gilman, JoAnn Cox; Montgomery: Marianne Thompson, Andy Britton, Patti Mullen, Patty McDonald; Betty Jenkins, Starr Smith, Sarah Findley, Blake Guthrie, Margaret Butcher, Tonya Tucker, Tina Hutchison, Ami Simpson, Gary Leach; Monroeville: Peggy H. Jaye; Kimberly Moore; Scottsboro: Rick Roden; Selma: Edie M. Jones, Alvin Benn; Scottsboro: Rick Roden; Stevenson: Patsy Jones; Sylacauga: Warren Jones, Virginia Coleman; Talladega: Frank Hubbard, Jim Freeman; Tuscaloosa: Leon Maisel, Jan Adams, Marvin Harper; Tuscumbia: Glenda Butler, Dick Cooper; Tuskegee: Deborah Gray.

A word of appreciation to Ed Hall, Edward O. Buckbee, Robin Stone, Mrs. Opal Traylor, Bob Ward and Jim Siegle.

Photo credits: U.S. Space & Rocket Center, Selma Chamber of Commerce, Bob Gathany, Alabama Bureau of Tourism & Travel, Alabama Shakespeare Festival, Greater Birmingham Convention & Visitors Bureau, Alabama's Constitution Village, Gary Ellis and Compass Marketing.

Introduction

This guide was written to assist people contemplating a trip to Alabama as well as those already here and wondering where to go and what to do. It contains recommendations for getaway weekends for couples and families and group itineraries for those spending a couple of nights in Alabama en route to other Southern destinations.

It is aimed at the detailed planner as well as the spontaneous traveler.

Alabama is a state that offers a remarkable variety of landscapes, history and experiences. You can splash in the waves of the Gulf of Mexico, and climb the craggy rocks of Mount Cheaha. Peer thousands of years into the past at DeSoto Caverns, and be an astronaut for the day at the U.S. Space & Rocket Center. Clap to the cadence of hill music at "Looney's Tavern" near Cullman, and applaud the artistry of the Alabama Shakespeare Festival players in Montgomery. Munch on superb barbecue served on a paper plate at Chicken Comer's, and spread a crisp napkin across your lap and savor sophisticated regional food on Birmingham's Southside. Snuggle under a feather comforter in a B&B, and relax in the privacy of a modern hotel room.

Towns celebrate their uniqueness with parades and festivals, from the giant peanut blowout in Dothan to the devil-may-care frivility of Mobile's Mardi Gras, from Eufaula's historic pilgrimage to Birmingham's City Stages. Many events are centered around people, too. The legacies of Helen Keller and W.C. Handy are celebrated in the Shoals, while the Alabama Band raises money for Fort Payne area schools with a huge musical celebration.

Some Alabama towns remember the state's rich antebellum heritage and showcase the handsome plantation houses which dot the landscape of the Black Belt. Others honor the blacks who forced a change in the nation's discrimination laws, and, at the same time, remember their own ancestors.

If you've never traveled here, you probably have an incomplete awareness of Alabama. You might not know that:

- A black scientist in Tuskegee pioneered the nation's agriculture research,
- A Tuscaloosan who eradicated malaria in Panama was knighted by the king of England,
- Scientists in Huntsville developed the rockets which put astronauts on the Moon,
- Auburn scientists invented McDonald's MacLean sandwich patty,
- A state agency financed the largest golf development in history,
- Birmingham, a world leader in heart transplants, hosts the world's oldest continuous arts festival.
- And, the favorite bit of Alabama trivia: The first Mardi Gras in the New World was in Mobile, *not* in New Orleans.

What sets Alabama apart from the other 49 states, however, are the memorable people you might encounter on a journey through the Cotton State: such as Sarah Penny, the cheerful Huntsville cook at Alabama's Constitution Village; hotelier Tom Scott at Twin Pines; Anne Waldo, the genteel B&B hostess in Montgomery; "ghost lady" Kathryn Tucker Windham of Selma; preservationist Marvin Harper of Northport; knowledgeable tourism planners Frances Smiley and Patti Mullen; "Inspiration Oak" guide Stan Foote, and chatty Perdido Beach sales rep Maggie Hennessy. Chances are you'll find your own "beautiful people."

How to use this book

This guide is divided in four sections, with a major city in each, representing the geographical regions: North Alabama and Huntsville, Central Alabama and Birmingham, South Alabama and Montgomery, and Gulf Coast and Mobile.

The cities and larger towns have short summaries listed under the place name. After the descriptions of attractions come recommendations of lodgings and restaurants, with some of the annual events in each vicinity. Because of space limitations, it is not possible to include every sizable town.

Hotel rates

Most listings for hotels and motels include rates which should be used as a guideline for comparision purposes. For reservations, call the phone number listed in bold and ask for the lowest available rate for the night(s) you need. Ask about discounts. Rates quoted do not include lodging taxes.

The hotels and restaurants selected by the author were among many visited without any mention of this guide research, although they were contacted subsequently for details. No free meals or lodgings were solicited or accepted in order that the reader might have an honest and objective view of the establishments. No establishment paid to be listed.

Restaurant ratings are indicated by the following:
*Above average; **Very good; ***Excellent; ****Outstanding

Other details

All Alabama phone numbers begin with Area Code (205).

Motorcoach groups should begin planning for Alabama tours by contacting the Alabama Travel Council, P.O. Box 210729, Montgomery, 36121. Phone 271-0050.

For general state information, contact the Alabama Bureau of Tourism & Travel at 1-800-ALABAMA.

While every care has been taken to assure the accuracy of the information in this guide, the passage of time will always bring change, and consequently, the author cannot accept responsibility for those that occur.

It is hoped that "The Best of Alabama" will lead you to discover many special moments in this beautiful state and that your "goodbyes" will be met with, "Y'all come back to see us."

Lee Sentell
700 Monroe Street
Huntsville, Ala.

ALABAMA

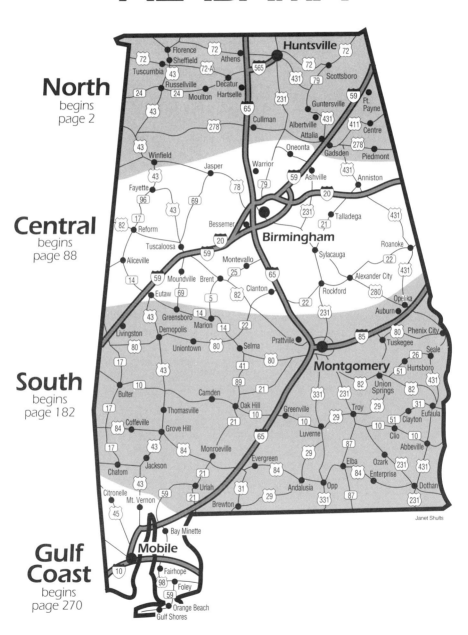

North
begins
page 2

Central
begins
page 88

South
begins
page 182

Gulf Coast
begins
page 270

Janet Shults

Table of Contents

NORTH ALABAMA

Few people outside the state are aware that the engines and boosters which launch the Space Shuttle are designed in Huntsville. In other words, Cape Canaveral gets credit for what Huntsville does. Here, the Pathfinder shuttle rests atop an external tank and solid rocket boosters at the **U.S. Space & Rocket Center**, *Alabama's leading attraction.*

ATHENS

- **Claim to fame:** Athens State College
- **Don't miss:** Fiddlers festival in October
- **Population:** 16,901
- **Tourist information:** Chamber of Commerce, P.O. Box 150, Athens, 35611. Phone 232-2600.

Pull off I-65 into downtown Athens to see an attractive courthouse square surrounded by dogwood trees and thriving businesses. **Athens State College**, the state's oldest institution of higher learning, and a number of antebellum homes are just a couple of blocks away.

Founded in 1818, Athens was an important education and commerce center prior to the Civil War. The town square, tree-lined streets and Greek Revival homes still display the charm and dignity of that era. Athens was the first major Alabama town to be occupied during the Civil War. In May of 1862, soldiers looted and pillaged when the Union's commanding officer, Col. John Turchin, said, "I will close mine eyes for one hour."

The **Limestone County Courthouse**, crowned by a dome in the French Second Empire style, dominates the business district. It was built in 1916 on a design by Birmingham architect Bem Price who was influenced by Palladio's Villa Rotund.

The best time to visit is spring when dogwoods bloom or early October during the **Old Time Fiddlers Convention**.

North of Athens near Ardmore is the **Fromargerie Belle Chevre**, which any student of French will explain means "cheese factory of the beautiful goat."

While in Saudia Arabia, Leone Ashbury watched goats being herded through the streets each morning to eat the town's garbage. After returning to Alabama and unsuccessfully attempting a goat dairy on her Limestone County farm, she decided in 1988 to try a fromargerie. She excelled. Her "beautiful goat" cheese is now sold at the South's finest groceries and is even available in Macy's main store in New York.

Milk arrives by truck each morning from nearby goat farms from late winter to mid-fall. It is pasteurized and poured into long vats where the curd is separated, bagged and left to drain for a couple of days. Garlic, chives or other spices are added for flavor. Then, an extruder forms the cheese curd into logs which are cut to size and wrapped. Workers dip the cheese in olive oil and wrap in cellophane or place it into small jars for labeling and shipping.

The cheese has received medals from the American Dairy Goat Association. It is great as a holiday dip or salad garnish. You can find it at Vincent's Market in Birmingham, the Johnston Street Cafe in Decatur and the Market Place in Huntsville. It is also sold across the state line at the Ardmore cheese plant store. Phone 423-2238.

ATTRACTIONS

ATHENS STATE COLLEGE, founded in 1822, is the state's only senior level college. **Founders Hall** was built in 1843-45 as Athens Female College and is a notable example of Greek Revival architecture. On the second floor in a small chapel is a hand-carved altar depicting scenes from the New Testament. Enrollment is about 3,000. Phone 232-1802.

Getting there: Take U.S. 31 into town and go west to Beaty between Pryor and Bryan streets.

BROWNS FERRY ENERGY CONNECTION uses videos, interactive games and scale models to explain how the Tennessee Valley Authority generates power at one of the world's largest nuclear plants. Using a personalized green card, you can learn TVA history, give your opinions on energy issues, play electronic games such as balancing the supply and demand for power generation and try hands-on quizzes. Open Mon.-Fri., 10-5; Sat.-Sun., 1-5. Free. Phone 729-2000.

Getting there: It is located southwest of Athens on the Tennessee River. Take U.S. 72 west to either Brownsferry Road or Shaw Road and follow the signs.

DONNELL HOUSE, a two-story Greek Revival frame house, was built in 1845 and named Pleasant Hill by Cumberland Presbyterian circuit rider Robert Donnell. He retired to Athens after preaching 40 years in the mid South. Yankee Col. Turchin camped his troops here when his troops looted Athens in 1862. After 1870, the house was used by several schools as a boarding house. It became a museum and library in 1970. Rev. Donnell's Bible is displayed. The **Limestone County Historical Society** stages an annual pilgrimage to benefit the museum.

Getting there: 601 Clinton St.

HOUSTON MEMORIAL LIBRARY is housed in the circa 1835 home of George Smith Houston, a congressman who left his seat in Washington in 1861 when Alabama left the Union. At the close of the war he was elected to the U.S. Senate but was not allowed to serve. He served as governor (1874-78) after wresting control of the state government from radical Northern carpetbaggers. Antiques and period documents are displayed. Open Tues.-Fri. and Sat. morning. Phone 233-8770.

Getting there: 101 Houston St. at Market.

WHERE TO STAY IN ATHENS

Days Inn, 1322 U.S. 72 E., has 95 rooms featuring some mini-suites and executive suites with refrigerators and microwaves. Outdoor pool. **Phone 233-7500** or 1-800-325-2525.

Welcome Inn, intersection of U.S. 31 and U.S. 72, is just west of I-65. It has 80 rooms, restaurant, pool and cable TV. **Phone 824-6834.**

ANNUAL EVENTS

Second or third Saturday in April
Athens Pilgrimage - Tours of several 19th-century homes near the courthouse square are sponsored by the Limestone County Historical Society. Phone 233-6404.

First weekend in October
Tennessee Valley Old Time Fiddlers Convention - Athens State College - The sounds of professional fiddling fill the campus as musicians of all ages fiddle off for championships and about $9,000 in prizes. Musicians compete for titles of fiddle king and classic old-time fiddler, a style meant for dancing, not performing. They also play mandolins, bluegrass banjos, harmonicas and other stringed instruments.

Most of the performances are from the lawn of **Founders Hall**, the main building on campus. If you're serious about devoting hours to hearing the finest fiddling around, bring a folding chair and arrive very early. When you're ready to stretch your legs, go behind the building to browse among more than 100 arts and crafts booths. The impromptu practice sessions among "pickup" groups are a delight.

The convention has been a hand-clapping, toe-tapping hit since the first event in 1967 was held to revive traditional or non-amplified fiddling. It has become the largest fiddling competition in the country and draws upwards of 20,000 persons over the weekend. Proceeds from the conventions have generated more than $150,000 for scholarships and other needs. Entry is on Beaty at Pryor streets. Free parking is available along adjacent streets and behind the First Baptist Church. Activity is moved inside the gym in case of rain. Admission. Phone 232-1802 or 233-8204.

BOAZ

- **Claim to fame:** Scores of factory outlets
- **Nickname:** Shoppers' Paradise
- **Population:** 6,928
- **Shopping information:** Boaz Chamber of Commerce, P.O. Box 563, Boaz, 35957. Fax 593-1233. Phone 593-8154.

Everything you've heard about Boaz shopping is true. It is among the three or four largest outlet centers in the nation and discounts range from so-so to great. What began as a Vanity Fair factory outlet in 1982 has mushroomed into shoulder-to-shoulder shopping centers featuring nearly every imaginable label at bargain prices.

Chamber of Commerce Volunteer Executive Chalmus L. Weathers was responsible for getting the early outlets to locate. Before long, the rest were begging to come. At last count, Boaz had 140 stores in five malls, with most of the nation's manufacturers which operate outlet stores already in Boaz.

It's not unusual for 15,000 people a day to shop. The concentration of shoppers and stores is so heavy that shuttle buses circle the various strip centers so shoppers don't have to move their cars. No longer does the Chamber of Commerce need to promote Boaz as a "shopper's paradise." Boaz's reputation has spread nationwide, attracting more than five million shoppers a year who leave more than $180 million in the stores' cash registers. Of the town's municipal budget of $4.5 million, $3.3 million comes from sales tax.

An article in *The Los Angeles Times* has noted, "People stop through here from all over the country to buy everything from hats to shoes, carpets to teacups, all at discount prices. In the South, if shopping's your game, Boaz is the name. The town's residents are used to seeing tour buses crammed with shoppers who can knock themselves out during the day and rest the night at a motel across the street from the stores."

On Saturdays, fleets of motor coaches - many from Atlanta - descend on the outlets. Parking lots are packed right before Easter and Christmas. Getting around is very easy. Unlike the outlets at Pigeon Forge, Tenn., which are linked by stairs and hills, Boaz is flat. The Boaz outlets are located within a square framed by Mill Avenue on the north, U.S. 431 to the east, Billy Dyar to the south, and Lackey to the west. The stores are just west of 431, about 50 miles south of Huntsville and 19 miles north of Gadsden. Shopping tip: Mondays and weekdays after 4 p.m. are the best times to shop without crowds.

SHOPPING CENTERS

Boaz has grown steadily over the years and is constantly adding new stores. Some manufacturers occasionally merge several shops into one. The following is a lineup of the outlets (subject to change).

Tanger Factory Outlet Center has Barbizon, Allen Edmonds, Cape Isle, Unisa, Jordache, OshKosh, Dansk, Liz Claiborne, Mikasa, Stone Mountain Handbag, Samsonite, Eddie Bauer, Geoffrey Beane, Bugle Boy, Reebok, Chaus, Barbizon and Leslie Faye. Exit U.S. 431 onto Hwy. 168 West, which becomes Billy Dyar Blvd.

Boaz Outlet Center, with 68 shops, is the heart of the action. Located across Hwy. 168 from Key West Inn motel, it is a good place to park because it's within walking distance of all but the Vanity Fair area and downtown stores. The WestPoint Pepperell anchor is at the lower end. Turn off U.S. 431 at McDonald's Hamburgers and follow the traffic. Some of the stores: Sewell Factory Store, Bass Shoes, Leather Loft, Welcome Home, Polly Flinders, Capezio, Wembly Tie, Jerzees, Oneida, Burlington, Henson, Langtry, Toy Liquidators, Gitano, Coring/Revere, Donnkenny, Childcraft, Hushpuppies, Old Mill, Knife Factory, Judy Bond, Jockey, Van Heusen, Carter's Childrenwear, Today's Child, Everything's a $, Creekwood, Garment District, Famous Brands, Socks Galore, Naturalizer, Fieldcrest Cannon, L'eggs, Hanes & Bali, Jaymar, Top of the Line Cosmetics, Sergio Valente, Izod/Gant, Swank, Farah, Libby Glass, Aileen, Boot Factory, Hanes Activewear, Maidenform, Kitchen Collection, Royal Doulton, Sarah Coventry, Just About Perfect, Euro Collections, Paragon Decors and Pfaltzgraff.

A section closer to the main highway has Reading China and Glass, Ducks Unlimited, Athletes Foot, Westport Limited, USA Jewelry, Brass Outlet, Missy Sportswear, Rack Room, and 9.99 Stockroom. Stores open Mon.-Sat., 9-9; Sun., 12:30-5:30. Phone 593-9306.

Fashion Outlets is adjacent behind the Oneida/Bass side of the Outlet Center complex. Stores are Polo/Ralph Lauren, London Fog, Anne Klein, Toy Town, J.H. Collectibles, J. Crew, Dollar Time, S&K Menswear, Shoe Place, Famous Footwear, Jones Jewelry Outlet, Duckhead, Clothestime, Arrow Shirts, Leathers, Strasburg Lace, Perfumania, T's, Specials (Levi Strauss), Bon Worth, Dress Barn, Nike, Book Warehouse, Sweet Shoppe, Eagle's Eye, Boston Trader Kids, Factory Connection, Totes, L&S Shoes and Benetton.

Vanity Fair Factory Outlet at East Mill Avenue (Hwy. 168) and Lackey Street is closer to downtown. Move your car around behind VF to park and shop VF. The 12 shops in the 118,000-square foot VF building are American Tourister, Banister Shoes, Black & Decker, Evan-Picone, Jewelry Outlet, Jonathon Logan, Paper Factory, Prestige Fragrance, Danskin, Vanity Fair Activewear, Vanity Fair Clearance, Vanity Fair Factory Outlet (anchor), Your Toy Center. Note: VF Outlet does not accept credit cards. Open Mon.-Thur., 9-6; Fri.-Sat., 9-9; Sun., 12:30-5:30. Phone 593-2930. Follow Bill Dyar from 431 and it will intersect the main street near VF.

Downtown features covered sidewalks and a variety of locally owned discount stores, notably, **Hammer's**, and **Unclaimed Baggage**, where you can pick among items in luggage that the airlines lost. Most locally owned stores are open weekdays, 9-5.

WHERE TO STAY

The **Key West Inn**, across Mill Avenue (Hwy. 168) from the major complex of stores, permits easy shopping without moving your car. Each of the 41 rooms on two floors has two double beds and cable TV. Coffee bar and continental breakfast. Free shopping coupons for the outlet center. Fax 593-9100. Double rate: $42-$48 plus tax. **Phone 593-0800** or 1-800-833-0555.

Days Inn, with 60 rooms and a lounge, is south of the intersection of 431 and Billy Dyar Blvd. **Phone 593-0000** or 1-800-325-2525.

Best Western Inn, U.S. 431, has 120 rooms. Phone 593-8410.

WHERE TO EAT IN BOAZ
*Mrs. Tupper's buffet by Morrison's is in the outlet center opposite the Key West Inn. Phone 593-6901.

ANNUAL EVENT
First weekend in October
Harvest Festival - Various locations - The canopied sidewalks of downtown Boaz become the setting for a giant sidewalk sale of handmade arts and crafts. There are musical acts, an antique car show and plenty of bargains at the factory outlet stores. The harvest festival, which dates from 1965, is sponsored by the Boaz Chamber of Commerce. Phone 593-8154.

BRIDGEPORT

ATTRACTION
RUSSELL CAVE NATIONAL MONUMENT chronicles thousands of years of inhabitation and is one of the nation's most important archaeological sites.

The focal point is an overhanging cave shelter continuously occupied by various cultures for approximately 8,000 years. It is part of a larger cavern that reaches about 7 miles into the side of a limestone mountain. The tools, bones, campfire charcoals and other debris tell the story of the people who were sheltered by the cave from approximately 7000 B.C. to A.D. 1000. Artifacts found here detail the progress from Archaic humans through Mississippian period dwellers, who used pottery and more sophisticated weapons and tools. The people developed a primitive form of agriculture and buried their dead in mounds. Using objects recovered from the excavations, the visitor center portrays these prehistoric people. Interpreters periodically demonstrate the Archaic people's tools and weapons.

The cave was excavated in 1953 by the **Smithsonian Institution** and the **National Geographic Society**, whose resulting magazine coverage made the site famous worldwide. After studies were completed, the Society donated 310 acres to the state in 1961. The National Park Service now administers the cave and staffs a visitor center with static exhibits on the excavation. You should spend 5-10 minutes looking at the exhibits before proceeding to the cave mouth.

You may be disappointed by the limited access of the cave itself. A chain link fence inside the entrance restricts viewing to only the mouth of the cave. However, you can see the exposed cave stratigraphy as it has been revealed through excavations. A short audiovisual program shown in the cave shelter highlights the occupation site and excavations.

Hiking trails are marked. Russell Cave is primarily recommended for the serious student of history and not for young children who might not be interested in the site. Among the 27,000 people who visit each year are school children on field trips and RV-roving retirees.

The best time to visit is during **Indian Day** held on the third Saturday in April. Demonstrators make and fire pottery, explain how to use herbs and plants, and discuss the history of masks. Open daily, 8-5. Closed Thanksgiving, Dec. 25 and Jan. 1. Free. Phone 495-2672.

Getting there: It is 7 miles from U.S. 72. Just south of Hardee's on U.S. 72, turn west on County Road 91 and go to County 75 and follow the signs.

CULLMAN

- **Claim to fame:** German heritage
- **Don't miss:** Ave Maria Grotto
- **Special event:** "Looney's Tavern" outdoor drama
- **Eat at:** Orange rolls at All Steak Restaurant
- **Nickname:** Poultry capital of America
- **Population:** 13,367
- **Tourist information:** Jimmy Gilley, Executive Director; Cullman Co. Area Chamber of Commerce, Convention & Visitors Bureau, P.O. Box 1104, Cullman, 35055. Phone 734-0454.

In the era following the Civil War, a German immigrant named John Gottfried Cullmann envisioned a cooperative agricultural colony of his countrymen 30 miles south of the Tennessee River. Acting as land agent for the Louisville & Nashville Railroad in 1873, he recruited families from Cincinnati and other Midwestern cities. Within a year some 123 families were carving a town with 100-foot-wide streets from the wilderness.

Col. Cullmann had been exiled from his homeland because of his alleged involvement to assassinate the Russian czar. (Russians dominated his native Landau.) He survived an attempt against his own life in 1874 when a man, hired by thugs opposed to the town, stabbed him twice in the forehead. The attacker was later hanged for horse-stealing in Macon, Ga.

European varieties of grape and cereals did not transfer well to the rocky soil, although the immigrants grew potatoes and strawberries through the 1950s. Poultry and manufacturing have become important in recent years.

Because the area grew little cotton, which needed cheap labor for harvests, the town traditionally has had few black residents. In fact, prior to civil rights legislation, a sign at the depot warned blacks not to be in Cullman after dark.

Cullman County currently ranks as the nation's top poultry producer. Alabama is second only to Arkansas in broiler production, with 17 million broilers processed a week. The average American eats 74 pounds of chicken a year compared to 64 pounds of beef and 61 pounds of pork. The Alabama Poultry & Egg Association's annual meeting in Birmingham holds the unofficial state record for the number of people sitting down to dinner in one room. Guess what they eat?

The western edge of town is brushed by I-65, giving Cullman the largest number of motel rooms on the interstate between Nashville and Birmingham.

ATTRACTIONS

AVE MARIA GROTTO is a remarkable religious legacy linked to Cullman's German heritage. The grotto consists of 125 small stone and cement structures on a hillside at St. Bernard Abbey, built over a 40-year period by a Benedictine monk. With photos for reference, Bavarian-born **Brother Joseph Zoettl** transformed the 500-foot-long hillside using dioramas depicting biblical events and miniatures of famous cathedrals, buildings and shrines from many parts of the world. Most range from two to four feet in size.

Brother Joseph arrived in 1892 at the newly founded abbey at age 14. A construction injury which left him hunchbacked shattered his dream of being an ordained priest.

In his spare time from shoveling coal to feed the power plant, he began a hobby of creating tiny masterpieces. He used donated and cast-off materials, such as cement, marbles, stained glass, shells, colored tile, costume jewelry, cold cream jars and Alabama marble. For example, an old birdcage is the frame for the dome of St. Peter's in Rome and its famed four-acre plaza is scaled to eight feet wide while retaining remarkable details. The largest object is the 27-foot-high grotto (cave) honoring the Virgin Mary. Within the main grotto is a nine-foot altar. The six-foot statue of Mary is of Ravaccione marble and weighs more than a ton.

Not all of Brother Joseph's creations are religious subjects. One of the largest is "Hansel and Gretel visit the Temple of the Fairies," featuring a whimsical dragon chained, so as not to scare young children. Others are patriotic, including a tribute to the Statue of Liberty and a 48-marble American flag. He originally placed his creations of **Little Jerusalem** in the Abbey gardens and moved them to the present site in 1934 because of large numbers of visitors.

He was 80 when he completed a 1/75 scale of the Basilica of Lourdes in France in 1958. He died on Oct. 15, 1961.

Today, the slightly weathered miniatures draw about 65,000 visitors a year from around the world. The grotto is especially popular with senior citizens because of the colorful environment of thrift, azaleas, holly and towering pine trees. The west-facing miniatures are best photographed in early afternoon. The ideal time to visit is in April during the Bloomin' Festival.

Don't miss such treasures as Noah's Ark and the Hanging Gardens of Babylon, complete with elephants. After you've toured, walk past the parking lot to the small cemetery where Brother Joseph is buried. Plan an hour. Open daily, 8-sunset, except Christmas. Adults $3.50, children 6-12 $2, senior citizens over 61 $3. For group rates, write 1600 St. Bernard Dr. SE, Cullman, 35055. Phone 734-4110.

Getting there: Take I-65 exit 308 to U.S. 278 and follow signs through downtown. It is 3 miles east of the interstate.

CLARKSON COVERED BRIDGE is the largest covered bridge in the state. It is 296 feet long and was built in 1904 in the truss style. Reproductions of a pioneer dogtrot log cabin and a grist mill are nearby. Free.

Getting there: Go 9 miles west on U.S. 278. Phone 739-3530.

CULLMAN COUNTY MUSEUM is housed in a replica of the home that town founder John Cullmann built. It features a recreated 19th-century street scene of display windows holding antique clothing, Indian artifacts and other items representing German heritage and rural identity. Thumb through the stacks of scrapbooks of newspaper clippings which document the many personal stories of the town suggesting that the town is really one large family.

A life-size bronze statue of the town's founder is on the north side of the house. A time capsule, which is to be opened in 2073 as part of Cullman's bicentennial celebration, is buried nearby. Open Mon.-Wed. and Fri., 9-noon and 1-4; Thurs., 9-noon; Sun., 1:30-4:30. Closed major holidays. Admission. The **Chamber of Commerce** also has offices on the second floor. Phone 739-1258 or 734-0454.

Getting there: When you leave the Ave Maria Grotto, turn right on Second Avenue and go several blocks to 211 Second NE. It's the large yellow house opposite the municipal building.

"INCIDENT AT LOONEY'S TAVERN" is an outdoor musical drama of the true story of a Winston County school teacher who fought to keep Alabama in the Union and out of the Confederacy.

The two-hour production is performed by local people and staged at an amphitheater carved out of a sloping hillside overlooking the beautiful Bankhead Forest not far from the tavern site. The isolation sets an evocative mood against which author Lanny McAlister's story is played. Music, dance and humor are mixed with the political theme to deliver a memorable evening.

The premise of *Looney's Tavern* runs counter to the *Gone With the Wind* image that all Southerners favored leaving the Union. The story: The remote hill people of Marion and Winston counties of 1861 have few slaves and grow almost no cotton. They have little sympathy for the Black Belt plantation owners who stand to lose their labor supply when "black Republican" Abraham Lincoln is elected president. Therefore, they oppose leaving the Union.

In the race for delegate to the secession convention in Montgomery, Christopher Sheats is elected over a prominent slaveholder and unsuccessfully debates fiery secessionists at the State Capitol. Jailed as a traitor to the state, Sheats is eventually permitted to return home where he chairs a debate at Bill Looney's Tavern on July 4, 1862, over whether Winston County should secede from Alabama.

From the decision to remain neutral comes the county's nickname "The Free State of Winston." Although many people believe that the county withdrew from the state, in fact, it did not.

President Ulysses S. Grant appointed Sheats as U.S. consul to Denmark and Sheats later was elected to Congress. He retired to Decatur and is buried nearby.

Despite being based on a story little known outside North Alabama, the play has been successful beyond most expectations. More than 20,000 people see the production annually.

Promoters have added other elements to keep patrons at the site longer. Pre-theater musical entertainment involves the audience to create a friendly, folksy feeling. Visit the separate 300-seat theater to watch *Dual Destiny*, a 40-minute musical production featuring robotic characters performing Civil War songs of the North and South. Several craft shops, selling handmade dolls, quilts, antiques and souvenirs, provide other air-conditioned distractions. An 18-hole miniature golf course is themed on the play.

To more completely enjoy the trip, take a late afternoon dinner cruise aboard *The Free State Lady*, Looney's 60-passenger riverboat. The boat cruises Smith Lake from the amphitheater dock while a narrator spins yarns of the region. For reservations, phone 489-3500.

The nearest motel accommodations are in Cullman. Consider eating before you leave for this remote location. Sister Sarah's Kitchen at the theater has a long line prior to the start of the play and does not take reservations. Cokes and other snacks are sold at a separate concession stand. Other gift shops and food shops are convenient.

Performances run several nights a week through the summer and Saturdays into October. For dates, write P.O. Box 70, Double Springs, 35553. Phone 489-5000 and reserve tickets with a credit card.

Getting there: The very isolation which gave rise to the story makes the location distant from even the nearest towns of Cullman and Decatur. You can easily get lost trying to cut through Bankhead National Forest. While the theater is close to Double Springs, the most reliable route is from Cullman via U.S. 278 West. It's 26 miles from I-65. The hills are very dark when the play is over. Returning home via 278 is strongly recommended.

WHERE TO STAY IN CULLMAN

The **Ramada Inn** on I-65 was an interstate landmark for decades while it was a Holiday Inn, and it's still a well maintained motel. The 125 rooms have cable TV. It has a restaurant and a heated indoor pool that overlooks the patio and a wing of rooms. Leave I-65 at Hwy. 69 at the Cullman-Good Hope exit. **Phone 739-4126.**

Howard Johnson Lodge, I-65 exit 308 on U.S. 287, has 97 rooms with cable TV, HBO. Discount at Jerry's restaurant. Fax 734-8336. Double rate: $32-$40 plus tax. **Phone 739-4603** or 1-800-446-4656.

WHERE TO EAT

**All Steak Restaurant - *Save room for the orange rolls*
414 Second Ave. Phone 734-4322
Mon.-Wed., 6:30 a.m.-9 p.m.; Thurs.-Sat., 6:30 a.m.-10 p.m.; Sun., 6:30 a.m.-4 p.m.

The All Steak has served excellent prime rib steaks, seafood and desserts in downtown Cullman since 1934. The clean white interior, furnished with metal tables and chairs, may seem a bit sterile, but the floor is clean enough to eat on. Like any solid local restaurant, the civic clubs eat upstairs and the local customers sit in the rear dining room. You may go through the lunch buffet line upstairs any day except Saturday.

The waitresses are the old fashioned kind: efficient and friendly. Owner Charles Dobson's sweet orange rolls served hot in cupcake wrappers after the meal are delicious. (If you order a dozen to go, the waitress will provide instructions for re-heating them.) Open every day except major holidays. The average breakfast costs $3-$5, lunch runs $4-$7 and dinner, $5-$16.

*The Creamery - *A restaurant located in a former creamery*
402 Fifth St. SW. Phone 739-3131
Mon.-Wed., 11 a.m.-2 p.m. for lunch; 5-9 p.m. for dinner. Thurs.-Sat., 5-9 p.m.

The Creamery, located next door to the Civic Center, is popular for its lunch casseroles (chicken and broccoli, ham and asparagus). At night, the menu offers chicken cordon bleu ($9) as well as 12-ounce ribeye ($14), strip steak ($13) and broiled, fried or blackened catfish fillet ($8). The pastel decor is attractive and the service is prompt and friendly.

*The Rabbit Hutch - *Try not to think of the Easter Bunny*
West of Cullman off U.S. 278. Phone 747-1043.
Open Fri.-Sat., 4-9 p.m.; Sun., 11-6. Groups by reservation.

When the Rabbit Hutch is first mentioned, some people think it is a spin on the old snipe hunting "gottcha," but Mr. and Mrs. Fred Venzes have been raising and frying rabbit for years at their rural house-turned-restaurant. Bunny art covers the walls, fuzzy toy rabbits of all colors and sizes hang from the ceiling, and plaster bunnies are centerpieces on your table. If you can't handle the thought of baked bunny over rice (average check $10), the Hutch also has catfish, shrimp and barbecue. From I-65 exit 308, go west on 278 for 9.5 miles and turn left. Go 4.5 miles and look for the lattice porch.

WHERE TO SHOP

Cullman's downtown remains an active and viable retail district. Large shopping centers flank downtown on both ends of U.S. 31. The **Jim Norman Antique Mall** contains many rooms and is well worth a stop. It is located on the southern approach to downtown on Second Avenue (U.S. 31). **New Directions Gallery** in the Stiefelmeyer Building at 102 Second St. SE just off First Avenue East sells handcrafted pottery, wooden crafts, jewelry and other regional work. Phone 737-9933.

A Touch of German, 218 First Ave. SE, is a delightful shop crammed with ornate beer steins, blue deft, glass Christmas ornaments and the largest collection of costumed nutcrackers you've ever seen. A wall full of cuckoo clocks sounds a cheery melody on the hour. European willow baskets hang from the rafters and racks display the traditional German clothing you'll need for Oktoberfest.

Workers often dress in cheerful German costumes and enjoy discussing the merchandise. The success of the shop demonstrates how lovingly this town treats its German heritage. It's a half-block off U.S. 278 (Third Street) east of the railroad tracks. Open Mon.-Sat. 9:30 a.m.-5:30 p.m. Phone 739-4592.

ANNUAL EVENTS

Second or third weekend in April
Bloomin' Festival - St. Bernard campus - The St. Bernard Preparatory School's annual arts and crafts festival attracts thousands of locals who shop among the scores of booths to buy food, pottery, clothing, woodwork and jewelry. Raffle tickets are sold for such items as cars, trips and savings bonds. The timing coincides with the anticipated peak of azaleas blooming inside Ave Maria Grotto which offers discounted admission during the festival. Phone 734-6682 or 734-4110.

First week in October
Oktoberfest - Various locations - The town settled by Germans celebrates its heritage with daily German lunches and dinners, Bavarian music, a crafts show, historic tours and a ball. A burgermeister presides over the festivities. The only thing missing is German beer; the town is "dry." Phone 739-4592 or 734-0454.

DECATUR

- **Claim to fame:** Chemical industry, hot-air balloon races
- **Don't miss:** Point Mallard, Mooresville
- **Best souvenir:** 'Cotton Country Cooking' cookbook
- **Eat at:** Simp McGhee's, Gibson's, Court Street
- **Nickname:** City of Opportunity
- **Population:** 48,761
- **Tourist information:** Jerry Paasch, Executive Director; Decatur Convention & Visitors Bureau. P.O. Box 2349, Decatur, 35602. Fax 350-2054. Phone 1-800-524-6181 or 350-2028.

The Tennessee River at the city's northern edge has played a pivotal role in the community's history, recent industrial growth and recreational opportunities.

The 1820 settlement where Dr. Henry Rhodes operated a ferry across the river evolved into the modern, industrialized city of Decatur, but not without a colorful heritage of struggle against war, epidemic and economic depression.

The first boost to the town's strength was political. With the help of other valley representatives jealous of Huntsville's prominence, Decatur was selected in 1832 as the site for the Tennessee Valley branch of the State Bank of Alabama and an imposing building was erected 3 blocks from the river, but financial mismanagement plagued operations and the statewide system was finally crushed in the early 1840s.

While Decatur was not large enough to be a political target during the Civil War, the presence of the Memphis & Charleston Railroad bridge over the river gave it great strategic significance. The railroad was known as the "backbone of the Confederacy" and the army which controlled the bridge owned the line in the vicinity.

As a result of periodic conflict over the bridge, virtually every building near the river not essential to military operations was burned by Union soldiers to prevent an ambush from the south by Confederates. Only the Burleson-McEntire House, the bank, the Dancy-Polk House and the McCartney Hotel (now demolished) survived the ravages of war.

In some instances, the Reconstruction was as painful as the war wound it was supposed to heal. It was not until a group of Northern businessmen bought land south of Lee Street and promoted a new population center in 1887 did Decatur rise from the ashes of defeat. The census figures for Decatur listed 606 residents in 1850. The town had only 671 in 1870 and climbed to 1,063 in 1880.

The development of the adjacent town of New Decatur attracted 3,565 from 1887 to 1890 while only 2,765 were living in "old" Decatur at the decade's end. Separate only by the railroad along Lee Street, intense rivalry sprang up between the two towns and each had its own business center and residential district.

In an effort to gain a more distinct identity, voters of the new town decided in 1916 to change the name to Albany in honor of the New York city left by a number of the Northern transplants. In 1920, Albany had a population of 7,652 and Decatur had 4,752. A number of consolidation efforts failed and a state legislator finally authored an act in 1927 to merge the twin cities.

Had it not been for a terrifying epidemic of yellow fever in 1888, New Decatur might have become the industrial hub which it sought to be. Just as the town was gaining momentum, the epidemic caused hundreds to flee overnight and many never returned, including some of the major stockholders in the land improvement company which fostered the boom.

A few years later came the Nashville & Decatur Railway to give Alabama a rail outlet to the north. It was incorporated into the Louisville & Nashville Railroad by the businessman who would become better known for building Sloss Furnaces in Birmingham. A sprawing complex of shops serviced the trains bound for the small mining town of Birmingham. In the early 1930s, many of the 2,000 railroad shop workers went out on strike, which prompted the management to move the shops and put many hundreds more out of work during the Great Depression.

The city was forced to diversify into industry and agriculture. Promoting the availability of labor and easy access via river, rails and highways, the city landed a tubing plant in 1947 and chemical operations (**Monsanto, 3M** and **Amoco Chemicals**) several years later. The city which was nearly abolished by war, plague and depression was finally on solid footing. It was here that Chemstrand (now Monsanto) researchers invented **Astroturf**.

Abundant electrical power provided by the Tennessee Valley Authority made possible those plants and the ones which followed. Today, Decatur has 17 manufacturing plants affiliated with Fortune 500 companies.

Decatur was the scene of a racial trial which drew international attention in the 1930s. Eight black boys were convicted in Scottsboro of assaulting two white girls who hopped a freight train in 1931. Northern communists and liberals took up their case and successfully appealed to the U.S. Supreme Court. The convictions by all-white juries were overturned in a landmark decision on the grounds that qualified Negro jurors had been systematically excluded from serving.

When the case moved to Decatur under intense worldwide press attention, an all-white jury again found the **Scottsboro Boys** guilty, and a national radio commentator who noticed that a copper statue of Justice outside the courthouse was missing her scales said that the fairness of justice was missing inside the courtroom as well. Judge James E. Horton went against popular sentiment and dismissed the conviction. A TV mini-series which portrayed the judge as a courageous hero was filmed (in Georgia) in 1973 following his death at age 95.

The site of the now-demolished courthouse where the trial was held is an attractive park named **Cotaco Square** in front of the current Morgan County Courthouse. The statue of Justice still stands on the same spot facing Ferry Street, but is restored, with scales intact.

HISTORIC DISTRICTS

The **Old Decatur** Historic District, between the Tennessee River and Lee Street, is a Victorian neighborhood nestled under towering oaks and framed by old sidewalks. The National Register district occupies the site of the original town of Decatur settled in 1820 and destroyed by Union soldiers in 1862-64. The neighborhood contains 19th-century homes, the historic **Bank Street** commercial district and the restored 1833 **Old State Bank**. Turn off Sixth Avenue (U.S. 31) onto Walnut at the **Chamber of Commerce** and admire the Old Decatur houses on the cross streets of Ferry, Line, Oak, Canal and Bank.

The **Albany Heritage** district contains fine examples of Queen Anne, shingle and Eastlake styles along Gordon Drive, Sherman and Jackson streets. The most notable is the Chenault House, a turreted grande dame on the corner of Jackson Street and Eighth

Avenue. Delano Park, which defines the southern boundary of the district, was included in the 1887 plans.

WELCOME CENTER

The **Decatur Convention & Visitors Bureau** welcomes visitors at a Victorian house on U.S. 31 a couple of blocks north of McDonald's. The bright yellow two-story building at 719 Sixth Ave. SE is open Mon.-Fri. 8-5. Phone 350-2028.

DECATUR ATTRACTIONS

COOK'S NATURAL SCIENCE MUSEUM began as an employee education program of Cook's Pest Control and evolved into a free museum enjoyed by school kids on field trips and adults as well. It contains numerous mounted displays of wildlife, an extensive insect exhibit, snakes, coral and a rock collection. Cook's Pest Control is a Decatur-based, family-owned company that is among the South's fastest growing exterminating firms. Wildlife films are shown in a small auditorium. Allow a half hour. Open Mon.-Sat., 9-noon and 1-5; Sun., 2-5. Closed Thanksgiving, Dec. 24-25 and New Year's Day. Free. Phone 350-9347.

Getting there: Turn west off U.S. 31 to llth Street and turn left at the next intersection. Follow the signs within the Cook's complex to the museum at Fourth and 13th Street.

The OLD STATE BANK is a classical porticoed, two-story brick building which opened in 1833 as a branch of a statewide system. The president of the bank and his family lived on the second floor. During the Civil War, the bank served as a military hospital. The oldest bank building in the state was given to the American Legion after World War II for a museum and later donated to the city. The most interesting feature is the original vault on the ground floor behind the teller cage. Open Mon.-Fri., 9:30-noon and 1-4:30. Closed major holidays. Free. Phone 350-5060.

Getting there: North end of Bank Street. Turn west off U.S. 31 at Church Street and drive to Bank Street.

POINT MALLARD is a sprawling 749-acre recreation park east of Decatur where Flint Creek flows into the Tennessee River. Its wave pool - the first in the nation - draws thousands of swimmers and sunbathers daily between Memorial Day and Labor Day. In the same aquatic complex are an Olympic diving pool and diving tower, kiddie pool, squirt factory, sky pond, three-flume waterslide, picnic grounds, playground, sand beach and 18-hole miniature golf course.

Point Mallard's aquatic center was developed in the early 1970s after Mayor Gilmer Blackburn saw enclosed "wave-making swim pools" in Japan and thought one could become a tourist attraction in the U.S. Ohio manufacturer J. Austin Smith worked with the city to design and install the pool in 1970. It has been a popular attraction for North Alabama families ever since, with various water rides added. Between 130,000 and 180,000 visit each summer, making it one of the state's most popular seasonal attractions.

For the most enjoyment in the pool, bring or purchase a raft so you can ride over the rolling waves rather than swim to stay above the bobbing surf. Adults and children 12 and up $10, children 5-11 $5; senior citizens $7. For special discount nights, phone 350-3000 or 351-7777.

Bring a picnic lunch and stake out a table in the shade near the backwaters of the Tennessee River. The name of Point Mallard is derived from the wildfowl which winter within the **Wheeler National Wildlife Refuge** which surrounds the park.

An outdoor ice rink, a rarity this far south, is open from November to mid-March. The 18-hole championship golf course and 25-acre campground are open year round.

Point Mallard hosts a number of special events each year, including the **Alabama Jubilee** hot-air balloon races and the **Spirit of America Festival** on the Fourth of July.

Getting there: Turn east at McDonald's on U.S. 31 onto Eighth Street SE and follow the signs.

PRINCESS THEATER is the venue for local theatrical productions, touring shows and concerts. The theater was built in 1887 as an elegant stable for the Casa Grande Hotel and was a vaudeville house and movie theater before being remodeled in 1941 in the popular art deco style. It was the last surviving downtown movie theater before closing in the early 1970s. The city bought it in 1978 and restored it in 1983 for live productions once again. The vertical neon sign atop the marque dazzles at night when a performance is under way. Phone 350-1745.

SIDE TRIP TO MOORESVILLE

MOORESVILLE is a charming, tree-shaded village, with homes dating from the 1820s and 1830s. It was settled by cotton planters about 1805 and, after Mobile, is the oldest town in Alabama. The village never grew beyond its one-square mile boundary because the early residents would not permit a railroad to pass through town. Instead, it went 2 miles north, near the mansion built by Alabama's second governor.

The entire town of 54 people, including some fifth-generation residents, is listed on the National Register of Historic Places, but only the 1840 **Post Office** is open to the public.

Park your car just off the highway near the brick building that houses the Alabama Mountain Lakes Tourist Association, the regional promotion agency which provides tourism and outdoor recreation details on the 16 northernmost counties of the state (Mon.-Fri., 8:30-5. Phone 1-800-648-5381). Then, investigate the town on foot. Towering magnolia and cedar trees and blocks of white picket fences give the tiny town a special charm. Walk to the tiny wooden **Post Office** (Mon.-Sat., 7:30 a.m.-1:15) and visit with Postmaster Barbara Coker. She'll show you the original 48 call boxes used since 1840 and give a bit of history on the remarkable village that time forgot.

(When the postal service put Mooresville's tiny post office on a "hit list" for closure, Mayor Dorcas Harris rallied the state's congressional delegation and U.S. Sen. Howell Heflin personally intervened to save the state's oldest post office.)

Walk around the brick 1839 Cumberland Presbyterian Church where a psychic minister preached and go over to the 1854 frame church where **James A. Garfield** preached when he was a Union general during the Civil War. He later was elected president. One of the oldest buildings is the reddish, two-story frame building perpendicular to the highway. This tavern and stagecoach inn, built about 1825, is awaiting restoration.

When **Andrew Johnson** was a young man, he apprenticed at the Sloss tailor shop here. The two-story frame house where he stayed is at the southwest corner of town just off Piney Street. The imposing brick residence in the center of town is not a period house, but was built in 1927.

Mooresville remains undisturbed despite its proximity to a major interstate highway interchange and being sandwiched between the growing city limits of Decatur and Huntsville.

Getting there: From I-65, swing east to I-565 and take the first exit (Mooresville-Belle Mina). Mooresville is a long block to the south. A mile north of I-565 stands the privately-owned, magnificent **Belle Mina Hall** mansion built in 1826 by **Thomas Bibb**, second governor of Alabama. A row of six white stuccoed Doric columns supports a simple portico on the red brick facade which incorporates features used by Thomas Jefferson at the University of Virginia. The bricks were formed and fired at a creek about a mile from the house. An old slave story is repeated that Bibb had so many slaves on his 2,500-acre plantation that they simply lined up and passed the bricks by hand, fire-brigade-style. The house stayed in the Bibb family until 1941. A heavy growth of trees and boxwoods makes it difficult to see the front of the house from the road.

SIDE TRIP EAST OF DECATUR

WHEELER NATIONAL WILDLIFE REFUGE, which spreads over 34,500 acres, surrounds the middle third of Wheeler Lake between Decatur and Huntsville. Alabama's largest wildlife refuge, it winters the state's largest concentration of ducks and Canada geese. Its diversity of habitat, including pine uplands, mudflats, tupelo swamps, bottomland hardwoods and agricultural fields, provides a refuge for a wide variety of wildlife, particularly waterfowl.

Canada geese, which usually arrive the third week of September, and several species of ducks spend their winters on the Wheeler refuge. The largest concentrations from late December to early January are near Limestone Bay, Garth Slough and Flint Creek. Stragglers stay until the end of February. There are no resident geese in the spring and summer. The refuge hosts the National Audubon Society's annual Christmas Bird Count in late December.

During the winter, the visitors center and observation building are open seven days a week. Other times they are closed Mon.-Tues. The Wildlife Visitor Center, on Hwy. 67 between Decatur and I-65, houses wildlife displays that describe the role of the refuge. Nature films are shown on weekends. The refuge has foot trails, a wildlife observation building, a waterfowl observation platform and a boardwalk that extends into one of the tupelo swamps.

The best time to visit is just before sunset in December or January when the largest concentration of waterfowl touches down to feed in front of the observation building. You can sit behind the large, one-way glass in the observation building to watch and hear (thanks to a hidden microphone) the ducks and geese splashing and quacking away. Grounds are also open for picnicking, boating, hunting and fishing. Permits are available. Free. Phone 350-6639. From I-65, go 2 miles west on Hwy. 67 and look for the signs on the south side of the road.

To visit the 1837 **Somerville Courthouse**, the oldest in the state, go east on Hwy. 67 to Somerville. The Morgan County Sheriff's Department now occupies the second story.

SIDE TRIP WEST

Visitors who notice references to the **Wheeler National Widlife Refuge** and **Wheeler Dam** might well wonder, "Who was this Wheeler?" Sixteen miles west on

Hwy. 20 is the tiny community of the same name where **Gen. "Fighting Joe" Wheeler** lived following an illustrious career in the Confederate cavalry.

Born in Georgia, the diminutive West Point graduate commanded a Confederate brigade at Shiloh at age 26 and later planned and executed some of the most daring cavalry raids of the Civil War. He was in 500 skirmishes and commanded in 127 battles. After Appomattox, he settled in rural Lawrence County on the plantation where his wife was born and he became a cotton planter. He also served in the U.S. Congress for 18 years. During the Spanish-American War, when Wheeler was 62, President McKinley appointed him a major general and he was involved in combat in Cuba.

It was during the Civil War that Wheeler's troops camped on the Jones plantation where the young widow Daniella Jones Sherrod lived. A romance ensued. He returned after the war and proposed to her 10 days later. Their marriage produced four girls and two sons.

Wheeler, who died in 1906 at age 70, was survived by a daughter who was a nurse during the war in Cuba. Miss Annie, as she was affectionately known, helped run the estate. Widely respected as a hard worker, the matriarch often walked to Decatur to shop and walked home with her purchases, refusing rides from motorists who offered to take her home. She died in 1955.

Although one of the two homes on the **Wheeler Plantation** dates to 1820, the houses are less remarkable for their architecture than for the furnishings and clothing which remain as they were when the last resident died. Rather than dispose of the house and dispurse the heirlooms, descendants have for decades had family retainer C.A. Turner welcome visitors and give tours.

To learn more about this interesting family, turn off Hwy. 20 and drive up to the white frame house surrounded by mature boxwoods. The homestead represents three generations of Southern life: first, Col. Richard Jones, who established the plantation; second, the postbellum period of Jones's daughter and her husband, Joe Wheeler; and third, the Wheelers' four daughters and two sons.

A tour of the two-story house Wheeler built in 1884 is like going through a time warp. There are no ropes or barriers to restrict the movements of guests. It is as though the family is still living in the present. While hearing stories about the general's military exploits, you can handle his sword and study his medals and uniforms (West Point, 1854-59; Confederate, 1861-65; and U.S. Army, 1898). While Turner talks about Miss Annie, you can open her wardrobe and pull out her dresses, nurse's uniform and riding habit. Another eerie note: her calling cards are still on a table in her bedroom.

A collection of china includes a cabinet full of Blue Willow pattern that the Wheelers received as a wedding present and another set that was buried during the Civil War so that Yankee soldiers couldn't find it.

Unfortunately, the small income collected over the years from the tours hasn't generated sufficient funds to maintain the house. After preservationists began a fund, descendants agreed to give the plantation houses to the state historical commission. Open daily, 8 a.m.-4:30 p.m. Admission. Phone 637-8513.

Getting there: Go west from Decatur on Hwy. 20 for 16 miles. Look for the two historical markers on the left.

WHERE TO SHOP

River Oaks Center on the Beltline (Hwy. 67) is the retail center for the area south of the Tennessee River. Mall anchors are **Parisian**, **Rogers**, **Castner-Knott** and **Sears**.

Check out antiques and collectibles in the three-story **Old Town Antique Mall** on historic Bank Street off Hwy. 20 West. **Hudson's Antiques**, north on U.S. 31 near Tanner, has numerous booths with silver, furniture, rugs, guns and paintings. Roam through a number of small rooms in **Jim Norman's Antique Mall** in Hartselle at 209 U.S. 31 N. to shop for primitives, glass and silver. Norman stages auctions on Memorial Day and Labor Day in a large warehouse just east of the railroad track in downtown Hartselle. Phone 773-6878.

A TREAT FOR THE LADY

If you're looking for the ultimate gift for a wife, mother or girlfriend, make arrangements to give her "a day of beauty" at Deloain's New York Salon de Beaute on Johnston Street.

For a mere $150, she will be pampered beyond compare. The salon staff begins by cutting and styling her hair, then, she moves to other stations for a manicure, pedicure, facial, scalp and hair treatment.

After a lunch from the Johnston Street Cafe (it's included), she receives a complete makeup application and is unveiled to the world.

To gild the lily, she can continue downstairs to the Carriage House where Jimmy and Marella Adams display some of the state's most beautiful clothes for discriminating women and select a new ensemble.

WHERE TO STAY IN DECATUR

Amberley Suite Hotel on Bank Street offers a central location for browsing through the Old Decatur historic district and provides the comforts of home in a suite arrangement (with kitchen) at an attractive price. Turn west off U.S. 31 at the Holiday Inn to Hwy. 20. Go to the second traffic light and turn left behind the Old Bank. The Amberley is next door. **Phone 355-6800**.

Dancy-Polk House is a bed and breakfast in a landmark building dating from 1829. The two-story frame house built by town founder Col. Frank Dancy was a boarding house when Pam and Ned Anderson bought it in the 1970s. They operated an antique shop here before making it their home and a B&B. One of the rooms contains a bed which Ned bought from the estate of "Miss Kate" Lackner, whose notorious house of ill repute stood a couple of blocks away on the bank of the river. The Dancy-Polk House is behind the Old Bank and the Amberly hotel, and faces the railroad tracks. Located at 901 Railroad St., a block off Hwy. 20 West. **Phone 353-3579**.

Days Inn at 810 Sixth Ave. NE (U.S. 31) has 118 rooms arranged in a box shape around a courtyard with large outdoor pool. Rooms have cable TV. Rate includes free breakfast, newspaper and coffee. Room service. The Days Inn is 2 long blocks from the Tennessee River and near the Chamber of Commerce. Fax 355-7213. Double rate: $40-$48 plus tax. **Phone 355-3520** or 1-800-325-2525.

The **Holiday Inn**, largest of the city's motels with five stories, is at the corner of U.S. 31 and Hwy. 20. Some of the 227 rooms have a view of the Tennessee River. Rooms have coffee makers and guests receive passes to Gold's Gym. A concierge floor offers extra amenities. The Holiday Inn is a **Holidome** and features an indoor swimming pool. *Louie's, a full-service restaurant with daily breakfast and lunch buffets, specializes in Italian and American entrees. A bar is attached. Double rate: $58-$65 plus tax, weekends: $48-$55. Golf, romance and safari packages are available. **Phone 355-3150.**

WHERE TO EAT

Big Bob Gibson's Barbecue has been the standard for North Alabama barbecue since 1925 when Gibson began cooking out of a pit. Big Bob's serves shredded meat from pork shoulders and burns hickory wood over an open pit. The barbecue sauce is a thin tomato mixture with vinegar that sits well with the pork. What might be overlooked, however, is the barbecue chicken. It's the best in the state. Plus, the homemade pies are simply not to be missed. The two Gibson's in Huntsville owe their lineage to Big Bob. From I-65, go west to U.S. 31. Open daily, 6:30-9. Phone 353-9935.

Court Street Cafe serves gourmet sandwiches, soups, pastas and fish and beef entrees at the most reasonable prices in town. The atmosphere is friendly and casual. The cozy surroundings feature exposed brick walls hung with antique quilts. You can eat in the main dining area, a private party room in the back, the bar or dine outside in the courtyard. Highly recommended. Open every day. Corner of Moulton Street (Hwy. 24) and Second Avenue downtown. Phone 350-5777.

McCollum's Seafood, on Hwy. 24 West, was opened in 1961 by Allen and Marie McCollum. It has such a following that the dining room has been expanded twice. McCollum's serves excellent catfish, shrimp, scallops and deviled crab. Oysters on the half shell are as good as you'll find anywhere this far from the Gulf. Barbecue is popular, too. The combination fried seafood platter, served with the trademark giant slice of onion, is an excellent value. The waitresses are cheerful and efficient and the average check is $5. Open Tues.-Sat., 8 a.m.-9:30 p.m. Closed Fourth of July week and Dec. 24-Jan. 2. Phone 353-9321.

Roberts' Catfish, near where I-565 leaves I-65 north of the river, serves excellent traditional Southern catfish and barbecue in a large building, surrounded by cotton fields. The management encourages guests who visit during harvest season to venture out into the cotton field to pick a cotton boll or two to take home. Located at I-565 exit 2. Phone 350-4009.

Rockin' McDonald's on the Beltline is a cross between a fast-food restaurant and the Hard Rock Cafe. The decor is vintage 50's, with tin toys, Boy Scout patches, Elvis artwork, period collectibles, juke boxes and Howdy Doody puppets literally covering the walls. "I Love Lucy" and other sitcoms and old movies play on the television. The most remarkable feature is a restored Corvette or other classic auto parked *inside* the restaurant. Other McDonald's have adopted the style, but none has done it better. It is on Danville Road across Hwy. 67 from River Oaks mall. Phone 350-7083.

Shelley's Iron Gate is a pleasant luncheon spot in a two-story painted brick house constructed for Probate Judge Skeggs around the turn of the century. Noted for its casseroles and congealed salads, Shelley's also serves prime rib sandwiches and vegetable lasagna. The poulet de Normandie (chicken and dressing baked in a cheese mushroom sauce) is another favorite. You can sit on the enclosed front porch and watch traffic headed downtown or enjoy your meal in one of the large rooms decorated in pastels and trimmed with natural wood. Cindy Sensenberger purchased the tea room from Betty Shelley. Located at 402 Johnston St. SE. Phone 350-6795.

***Simp McGhee's** on historic Bank Street serves North Alabama's best Cajun or blackened fish dishes. Located in an old two-story commercial building down the street from the Old Bank, the restaurant gets its name from the riverboat captain whose girlfriend was Kate Lackner, the turn-of-the-century madam. The atmosphere is enhanced by antiques, occasional live piano entertainment and a well-stocked bar. Whether you're having stuffed oysters, blackened amberjack or shrimp, plan on three givens: it'll be spicy, it'll be delicious and it'll be a while. Simp's is one of the state's undiscovered classic restaurants. Entrees range from $12-$16. Phone 353-6284.

CULTURAL ACTIVITIES

Cultural activities include a wide range of theatrical and musical events, with many centered at the **Princess Theater**. The **Bank Street Players** usually produces three plays a season. Phone 353-1200. **Dream Weavers** Children's Theater uses child and adult amateur actors in three productions a year geared toward children. Phone 350-1745. **Decatur Civic Chorus** is a community group of singers which performs locally. **Decatur Concert Association** is a concert subscription program which brings three or four top professional musical performers each season. For information, phone the Princess Theater at 350-1745.

ANNUAL EVENTS

Third or fourth Sunday in April
Spring Tour of Homes - Citywide - Historic and contemporary homes are open for afternoon tours. Phone 350-2028.

Memorial Day weekend
Alabama Jubilee Hot-Air Balloon Classic - Point Mallard -The Mid South's largest hot-air balloon competition attracts more than 50 entries from throughout the nation. First flown in 1978, the race is renowned for its warm hospitality toward guests, high-flying and earth-bound alike. Thousands arrive at Point Mallard by 6 a.m. to watch the colorful balloon envelopes inflate, take shape and rise slowly into the morning sky. Afternoon flights are also heavily attended. Events include the "hare and hound," where a balloon which leaves first is chased by the rest. The "bean drop" requires balloonists to fly into the park and drop a weighted bag near a large X on the field. Antique car shows, softball competitions and other events fill the calendar Sat.-Mon. Check *The Decatur Daily* for schedules. Free. Phone 350-2028 or 353-5312.

Fourth of July
Spirit of America Festival - Point Mallard - One of Alabama's largest Independence Day celebrations features children's parades, sports tournaments, games and enter-tainment during the day and a patriotic program climaxed by fireworks at night.

The top patriotic award is named for a movie star, **Audie Murphy**, whose first claim to fame was being the most decorated soldier in World War II. He had agreed to accept a patriotism award in 1971 shortly before he died in a plane crash. Since then, the Audie Murphy Patriotism Award has been presented annually to honor outstanding service to the nation. Previous recipients include Gen. Omar Bradley, track star Jesse Owens, Secretary of State Alexander Haig, astronauts and politicians.

The festival was started in 1967 to counter criticism of U.S. involvement in Vietnam. When President Ronald Reagan attended in 1984, he told the crowd, "When people were burning the flag, you were waving it. I don't know if a president has ever thanked you for that. Please accept my gratitude."

Girls from throughout Alabama compete for the title of Miss Point Mallard, a preliminary to the Miss Alabama contest. Winners in 1977, '82, '85 and '91 became Miss Alabamas. Teresa Cheatham, the '77 winner, was first runner-up to Miss America. Phone 350-2028 or 353-5312.

Labor Day Weekend

September Skirmish - Point Mallard - Several hundred costumed Civil War re-enactors set up camp and conduct battles and skirmishes in the fields near the Spirit of America stage. Candlelight tours, living history camps and battles offer closeup looks at military history. Historical displays in the T.C. Almon Recreation Center feature statues, books, prints and some items for sale. Phone 350-2028.

Late September

Racking Horse World Celebration - Valley Sports Coliseum - For 10 nights in late September, thousands of horse fans from 30 states gather at the indoor arena to watch the breed's best 2,000 horses compete in various classes. The highlight comes late on the closing Saturday night with the crowning of the world's grand champion. Celebration of the racking horse, the official state horse, began in 1972 and has grown to become the state's largest equestrian event. A "rack" is a bi-lateral four beat gait. Motels in Decatur, Hartselle and Cullman are usually filled during the final nights of the event. Phone 353-7225 or 353-5312.

Late September

Depot Days - Sparkman Park, Hartselle - The central Morgan County town of Hartselle celebrates its transportation heritage with Depot Days. Inspired by the depot on Railroad Street, the celebration features Indian folk arts, sidewalk sales, a car show and craft displays. Phone 773-6537.

Third weekend of November

Southern Wildlife Festival - Calhoun Community College - Duck decoy carvers, painters, wildfowl photographers and other artists from many states compete for ribbons in the most important such event in the Deep South. Crowd-pleasers include the working decoy competition held at a tank of water and a duck calling exhibition. It was begun in 1982. The college is north of Decatur on U.S. 31. Phone 350-2028 or 353-7243.

Late December

Holiday Tour and Christmas decorations - Historic houses in two historic neighbor-hoods are open for evening tours the second or third Saturday in December. For dates, phone 1-800-524-6181.

The Old Decatur historic district between Lee Street and the river glows with hundreds of thousands of tiny white lights covering houses and yards across 26 blocks. To see the best lights, drive along Ferry, Line and Oak streets.

Another display is in a modest neighborhood near the Beltline where half a dozen families try to out-gaudy each other with plywood snowmen, nativity scenes and Santas. Colored lights wrap trees, houses, fences and garages. From the McDonald's on Hwy. 67, turn north on Danville Road, then right at AmSouth Bank and then the first right on Cleveland Avenue. You'll see the glow ahead in the 2300 block.

Rubin Williams started the neighborhood tradition at 2323 Cleveland with his 24,000-light display. The house is dark at Christmas now. A heavy smoker, Williams died of cancer in 1990 and his wife, also a smoker, contracted cancer and sold the lights to pay bills.

COTTON PICKING TIME

If you're under 45, chances are you've never picked cotton. But it's not too late. A farmer just off the interstate between Decatur and Huntsville invites you to wade into his fields in September and pick a few bolls for souvenirs.

Merge from I-65 onto I-565 and take exit 2, turning to the northeast corner of the intersection. You'll see Roberts Catfish restaurant. Park in the restaurant's parking lot and walk into the field to pick some cotton to take home.

Cotton is usually fully open by the second full week in September when harvesters are rushed into the field to begin picking, often working into the night to remain ahead of the rain which degrades the quality of the cotton. For the best scenes of snow-white fields in late September, follow Hwy. 20 between Tuscumbia, Decatur and Huntsville.

Hurry, because cotton doesn't stay long in the field. The Tennessee Valley plants about 60 percent of the state's 430,000 acres. Growers need a bale and a half per acre (700-750 pounds) to remain profitable. The first killing frost which stops any remaining unopened bolls from opening is usually around Oct. 20.

Motorcoach groups can contact the convention and visitors bureau in the area to arrange a tour of a cotton gin during harvest.

FLORENCE-TUSCUMBIA

- **Claims to fame:** University of North Alabama, great fishing
- **Don't miss:** Helen Keller birthplace, Alabama Music Hall of Fame
- **Nickname:** The Shoals
- **Populations:** Florence, 36,426; Tuscumbia, 8,413; Sheffield, 10,380; Muscle Shoals, 9,611
- **Tourist information north of the river:** Virginia Gilluly, Tourist Director; Chamber of Commerce of the Shoals, 104 S. Pine St., Florence, 35630. Fax 766-9017. Phone 764-4661.
- **Tourist information south of the river:** Glenda Butler, Executive Director; Colbert County Tourism and Convention Bureau, P.O. Box 440, Tuscumbia, 35674. Fax 383-2080. Phone 383-0783.

Florence is one of the Tennessee Valley's three college towns and, like Huntsville and Athens, dates from the earliest portion of the 19th century. It is the largest of the cities in the Shoals area and maximizes its position along the north bank of the Tennessee River. Although it was an early trading post along the **Natchez Trace** and home to various Indian tribes, it owes its name to an Italian surveyor who laid out the town.

Florence was established in 1818 by a group of prominent land developers, including Gen. John Coffee, surveyor general of the territory, and James Jackson, a wealthy planter and prominent horse breeder whose Forks of Cypress mansion dominated the landscape. **Andrew Jackson** was one of the first to buy a lot in the new town. The town was popular with settlers heading west because it was on a major military road.

The rivertown overlooked the dangerous shoals which was impassable by barge traffic. The influential citizens of Florence convinced President James Monroe and the federal government to build a canal around the obstacles. It was completed in 1836, but became inoperable within a year. With the coming of the railroad, transportation ceased to be a major problem, however, it would not be until many years later that river hazards were overcome.

One of the most tragic chapters in American history touched the Shoals in the late 1830s when Andrew Jackson's policy of moving Native Americans off their homeland went into effect. Some 18,000 Indian men, women and children - many of whom died - were forced to march through what became nine states. Tuscumbia Landing and Waterloo were among the key points along this tragic **Trail of Tears**.

Florence escaped the devastation of the Civil War which befell such towns as nearby Decatur and entered the 20th century as a center of power generation, regional trade and education.

Today, it is home to 5,000 students attending the **University of North Alabama** at the north end of Court Street, as well as many industries utilizing hydroelectric power generated nearby. Likewise, many residents maintain summer homes on Wheeler, Wilson and Pickwick lakes to take advantage of fishing opportunities on the impounded river.

South of the river are the Colbert County cities of Tuscumbia, Sheffield and Muscle Shoals, each with unique attractions and histories.

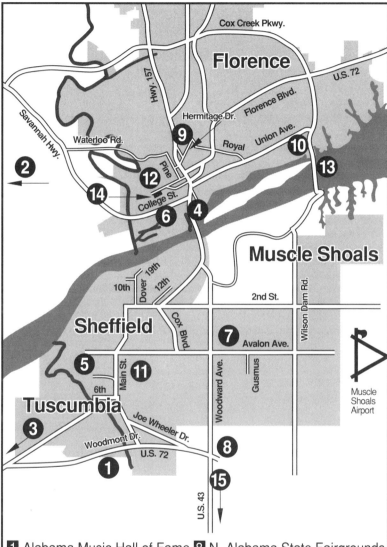

1 Alabama Music Hall of Fame
2 Colbert Ferry
3 Coon Dog Cemetery
4 Indian Mound & Museum
5 Ivy Green
6 McFarland Park
7 Muscle Shoals Music
8 N. Alabama State Fairgrounds
9 Pope's Tavern & Museum
10 Renaissance Tower
11 Tuscumbia Commons
12 W.C. Handy Home & Museum
13 Wilson Dam & Lock
14 Rosenbaum House
15 Bellmont Mansion

STEVE ANTLEY/Florence TimesDaily

Tuscumbia, the oldest town in the Shoals, was named for a Chickasaw Indian chief whose village was destroyed in 1787. The antebellum **Colbert County Courthouse**, broad streets and well maintained homes provide a sense of time and place. **Ivy Green**, the home of Helen Keller, and the **Alabama Music Hall of Fame** are the two top attractions south of the river.

In 1917, after various schemes failed to control the rapids in the river, the Army Corps of Engineers began construction of the **Wilson Lock and Dam** as a War Department project to supply power for World War I munitions plants. Eight years later Wilson Dam was completed, successfully submerging the treacherous "mussel shoals."

An interesting struggle evolved over the operation of this mighty source of power. Auto manufacturer Henry Ford became interested in the Shoals when Congress cut appropriations in 1921 for completing the dam and hundreds of construction workers were laid off. He envisioned building a new manufacturing center powered by Wilson Dam.

Ford knew that steel was manufactured in the area long before it was in Birmingham. Convinced that a 60-mile-long industrial corridor like the one paralleling the Ruhr River in Germany was possible, Ford visited the dam and the two plants in 1921 with inventor Thomas Edison, a long-time friend. He offered to buy the dam and nitrate plants for $5 million and lease the dam for 100 years if the government would spend the $28 million needed to complete construction.

Land speculators flocked to the area and began buying and developing property. Streets and sewers were installed. Fire hydrants and sidewalks blossomed along what is now Wilson Dam Road.

Naturally, residents were delighted at the prospects of having a giant auto manufacturing plant and other industries locate here. Ford's plans were reviewed by the Senate's military affairs committee and the issue became a political hot potato because many thought Ford was getting the nitrate and power plants at bargain basement prices. Congress invited other offers for the property and the debate dragged on for three years until Ford gave up and withdrew his offer in 1924.

During the height of the Depression, U.S. Sen. Frank Norris of Nebraska advocated using the mighty dam to produce power to help lift the Mid South from the grips of poverty. Legislation authorizing the creation of the **Tennessee Valley Authority** passed in 1933 and Wilson Dam became the first in a series of hydroelectric power plants to develop the resources of the river. Later TVA projects included **Wheeler Dam** and **Pickwick Landing Dam** downstream in Tennessee.

The 650-mile navigation channel and the generating capacity of the dams provide economic potential for the Muscle Shoals area and the Tennessee River Valley. Industries include the TVA's National Fertilizer and Energy Research Center and the adjacent International Fertilizer Development Center. Both have free lobby displays and offer tours. Across Wheeler Dam is **Joe Wheeler State Park Resort**.

A major recording industry was born when Sheffield disc jockey Quin Ivy set up a studio in 1965. Percy Sledge, an orderly at Colbert County Hospital, came by and recorded a song entitled "When a Man Loves a Woman," which became the first gold record released by Atlantic Records. The **Muscle Shoals Sound** was born.

For almost three decades, a number of major artists were attracted to as many as eight studios because of the high quality session players. They could record cheaper in the Shoals than in Nashville or New York, and they liked the small town atmosphere.

The area gained the reputation as "Hit Recording Capital of the World."

Rick Hall, who created Fame Studios, recorded Aretha Franklin singing "I Never Loved a Man the Way That I Love You" and "(You Make Me Feel) Like A Natural Woman," Wilson Pickett's "Hey Jude," Clarence Carter's "Patches," and other soul artists. One of Hall's most famous session guitarists was Duane Allman, who went on with his brother, Greg, to form the Allman Brothers Band.

Four of Hall's session musicians broke away in 1969 and formed Muscle Shoals Sound Studio in Sheffield. David Hood, Roger Hawkins, Jimmy Johnson and Barry Beckett became known as the Muscle Shoals Rhythm Section and attracted a spectacular range of artists to their studio. Among them were Bob Dylan ("Slow Train Coming"), Paul Simon ("Kodachrome," "Loves Me Like a Rock," and "Still Crazy After All These Years"), the Rolling Stones ("Brown Sugar"), the Staple Singers ("Respect Yourself," "I'll Take You There" and "Come Go With Me") and Bob Segar ("Old Time Rock and Roll," "Night Moves," and "Main Street"). Studio owner David Johnson, who now directs the Alabama Music Hall of Fame, recorded Clarence Carter's "Strokin'" and early material on the Outlaws and Lynyrd Skynyrd.

Other chart busters recorded here are "When You're in Love With a Beautiful Woman" (Dr. Hook), "Smoke from A Distance Fire" (Sanford and Townsend), "Go Away Little Girl" (Donnie Osmond), "Having My Baby" (Paul Anka), "Torn Between Two Lovers" (Mary MacGregor), "If Loving You is Wrong" (Luther Ingram), "Baby Don't Get Hooked on Me" (Mac Davis) and "Tonight's the Night" (Rod Stewart).

Although many of the studios have closed their doors, Muscle Shoals Sound and Fame remain significant forces in the recording and publishing industries. Fame now emphasizes country music and generates hits for artists like the Forester Sisters, T.G. Sheppard and Shenandoah while the Muscle Shoals Sound is the home to recordings by John Hiatt, Etta James, Shenandoah, Bobby "Blue" Bland, Denise LaSalle, and the Jackson Southernaires.

The Alabama Music Hall of Fame honors many of these contributions.

ATTRACTIONS NORTH OF THE RIVER

ROSENBAUM HOUSE is an architectural landmark designed by Frank Lloyd Wright that is open to the public after being a private residence for a half century. Owner Mildred Rosenbaum takes visitors through the brick and wood house Wright designed and built in 1939-40 for her and husband, Stanley.

Wright had just completed a prototype of an "affordable" house in Wisconsin when the newlyweds commissioned him to design a $7,500 house in Florence. He incorporated radical features, at least radical for 1940. For example, the flat, linear house was one of the first to have an attached carport, walls of glass and radiant heating under the floor. The house just a stone's throw from one of TVA's largest electric plants is now heated by gas. Mrs. Rosenbaum says they conceived their first child on the first night they lived in the house. When the family grew to include four boys, Wright added a wing in 1948 and turned the L-shaped house into a T-shape totalling 2,800 square feet.

Other than beds and chairs, there is very little furniture. Wright designed built-in closets, cabinets and even tables in this experimental house. Some experiments didn't work, such as the chairs supported by a fin on the back and only one leg in the front, causing children to lose their balance.

The Rosenbaum House is the oldest Wright house in the U.S. occupied by the original owner and the only building he designed in Alabama. Rosenbaum, a Harvard graduate who managed the local movie theaters and later taught English at UNA, amassed an immense library which fills the shelves lining nearly every wall and hallway in the house. He died in 1983. The house now belongs to a family-controlled foundation and $5 admission is charged to help maintain the house.

Mrs. Rosenbaum conducts daily tours only by appointment from 10-5. Phone 764-5274.

Getting there: 601 Riverview Dr. Turn west off Court Street at the Comfort Inn to Dr. Hicks Boulevard and go 4 blocks. Turn left at Riverview and follow the sign to the Board of Education. The house is next door.

KENNEDY-DOUGLASS CENTER FOR THE ARTS contains galleries set in two landmark houses, the 1917 Kennedy-Douglass and the 1914 Wright-Douglass. Open Mon.-Fri., 9-4. Phone 760-6379.

Getting there: 217 E. Tuscaloosa St.

INDIAN MOUND AND MUSEUM, a ceremonial Indian mound whose museum displays fluted points and pottery dating from between 1200 and 1500, is the largest domiciliary north of Moundville. The Wawmanona mound, either a chief's house or ceremonial temple, was surrounded by villages and cultivated fields. Relics found nearby indicate they were skilled farmers, although still in the Stone Age.

The natives belonged to a sophisticated culture with religious teachings and a political structure. The mound builders populated a vast region from the Gulf of Mexico throughout most of the Mississippi Valley and the Southeast.

The base measures 310 by 230 feet, height measures 42 feet and the summit is approximately 145 by 94 feet. It once was enclosed by an earthen wall which began on the downstream end of the mound, encircling it to a point on the river's upstream side. Steps on the east side originally reached the summit. Open Tues.-Sat. 10-4. Closed major holidays. Adults $2, children $.50.

Getting there: Go south on Court Street and follow the signs. One block from the river near the highway bridge. Phone 760-6427.

POPE'S TAVERN is a restored stagecoach inn operated as a house museum by the city. The one and a half-story white brick building with a long, wide porch was built about 1830 for Huntsville developers LeRoy Pope and Thomas Bibb, the second governor of Alabama. Construction is attributed to Christopher Cheatham, a Scottish immigrant who traveled through Virginia to Alabama to build houses. It served periodically as a hospital for Confederate and Union soldiers during the Civil War. Members of the Lambeth family lived here from 1874 until it was sold to the city in 1965.

Park in the rear garden and enter the small foyer. To the left is a large tavern room furnished with antiques of the period, as are the formal rooms opposite. Framed engravings reflect the area's close connection with Andrew Jackson, a contemporary of the town's founders, including the horse breeder who built the Forks of Cypress, a hilltop mansion which burned several decades ago. Step out onto the wide veranda supported by poplar columns and try to envision what the road in front might have been like when it was the Military Road, the most direct route from Nashville to New Orleans. (A revised history of the tavern indicates that the long-held construction date of 1811 was probably inaccurate, although evidence exists of an earlier structure on the same site where Andrew Jackson stopped in 1814 en route to battle the British at New Orleans.) Climb the interior stairs to a low ceilinged room and a display of military items.

The City of Florence restored and operates the museum. Allow 30 minutes. Open Tues.-Sat., 10-4. Closed major holidays. Adults $2, children $.50.

Getting there: Follow Seminary north past the Post Office, Wilson Park and the AmSouth Bank housed in a replica of the Forks of Cypress. The tavern faces Hermitage. Continue straight on Seminary and park behind the building. Phone 760-6439 .

RENAISSANCE TOWER is a 300-foot-tall observation tower and restaurant at TVA's Wilson Dam that overlooks the heavily wooded Shoals region. It cost $5.5 million, weighs 10,000 tons, contains 500 tons of steel and 3,500 cubic feet of concrete and can withstand winds of 110 mph.

The top structure is 95 feet in diameter and seven stories high housing a restaurant and an observation deck. On cold, clear days, you can see up to 30 miles. The view is best enjoyed over dinner. Arrive shortly before sunset and ask for a table on the lower level overlooking the dam. By the time dinner is completed, the lushly wooded countryside will have faded into the night with lights illuminating Wilson Dam 415 feet below.

Some residents scoffed when promoter Bob Martin advocated erecting a tower, and then suddenly, it was financed with a state bond issue and built. When donations and the restaurant's rent failed to pay the debt, the state had to oversee operations.

Getting there: The tower is on the north bank of the river on Hwy. 133. Follow signs to Wilson Dam. From downtown Florence, turn east on Spring just north of the river bridge and go about 2.5 miles. Phone 764-5900.

W.C. HANDY HOME & MUSEUM includes the simple log cabin where the great blues composer was born in 1873 and grew to early manhood. The son and grandson of ministers who wanted him to follow their footsteps, he wanted instead to play music. As a child he saved his pennies to buy a guitar, only to be told by his father he must trade it in for something useful, like a dictionary. He left home at age 19 and eventually formed his own band. Almost penniless, the band arrived at the Chicago World's Fair only to find it had been postponed for a year.

He overcame many problems to pursue his dream. He taught at Alabama A&M in Huntsville and, at age 38, wrote a political campaign song in Memphis which, with new lyrics, became the classic "Memphis Blues," the first written song to include a jazz break, as the wildly filled-in pauses were named. The song is regarded as the birth of the blues. He lived his later years in New York state.

When the City of Florence was constructing a housing project 5 blocks north of here in the 1950's, the city dismantled and stored the log house for reassembly. Handy advised on the restoration, but died in 1958 before it began. In addition to the log cabin, there is an adjoining museum filled with personal items contributed by Handy's family.

The piano on which he wrote his most famous song, "Saint Louis Blues," and his trumpet are displayed, along with original sheet music, Braille scores he composed after losing his sight, letters and photographs from presidents and entertainment figures and honors testifying to his contributions to American music. A third log house containing a library is to the rear. Handy's life and works are spotlighted during a week-long celebration each August. Allow 30 minutes. Open Tues.-Sat., 9-noon and 1-4. Closed major holidays. Adults $2, children $.50.

Getting there: Turn west off Court to College and go 5 blocks to Marengo Street. Phone 760-6434.

WHEELER DAM, between Decatur and Wilson Dam, measures 72 feet high and stretches 6,342 feet across the Tennessee River. The dam creates a 74-mile long lake that provides good recreation and fishing opportunities in the vicinity of Athens, Decatur and Huntsville.

(JOE) WHEELER STATE PARK covers 3,400 wooded acres surrounding Wheeler Dam and offers an abundance of outdoor recreational opportunities. The centerpiece is the Resort Lodge near Rogersville. The imposing three-story lodge features 75 over-sized guest rooms facing north across Wheeler Lake. Each room has a private balcony, television, phone and individually controlled heating and air conditioning units. Suites have kitchenettes.

The main entrance on the third floor opens into a spacious lobby. Restaurant and convention meeting rooms are on the second floor. A two-level parking arrangement allows guests to park and enter directly onto the second or third floor of the building without using stairs. The main dining room seats 125 and overlooks the lake and outdoor pool area. Casual dress is encouraged. The outdoor pool is open seasonally and is accessible via redwood walkways from guest rooms. The resort is a popular headquarters for fishing tournaments, family reunions and business retreats. Planning a weekend at Joe Wheeler? Phone as early as possible in advance so as not to be disappointed. Rates are comparable to medium-priced motels in the area.

The relative isolation of the lodge means that only the occasional sounds of fishing boats and crickets break the stillness of Joe Wheeler Lodge. Up the hill behind the lodge are four lighted tennis courts and a golf course with pro shop. One of the river's most modern marinas is in front of the lodge. Some 134 slips are available for lease or open for transient boaters and served by a gasoline island and store. Rental boats are available seasonally. The park has 25 cottages, 116 improved campsites and full facilities. A group pavilion and store serve the cottages and campground. Open year round.

Getting there: The lodge is 25 miles east of Florence and 5 miles west of Rogersville. Watch carefully for the directional sign on U.S. 72, turn south and wind 4 miles through the park to reach the lodge. Phone 247-5461. Secure a reservation with Visa or Master Card. **Phone 1-800-ALA-PARK.**

WILSON DAM, the granddaddy of TVA, is worth a special effort if you've never toured a huge dam. Wilson Dam straddles the Tennessee River at the foot of a 37-mile stretch of rocky rapids known as the "mussel shoals" which blocked navigation downstream for more than a century. During periods of heavy rains, the area flooded, and during drought, boats often ran aground on the shallow shoals.

The power plant, at 629,840 kilowatts, with the biggest generating capacity of any dam on the Tennessee, stands on a high bluff at the south end of the dam. The dam is 137 feet high. Tours visit the turbine rooms and tunnels deep beneath the dam. The powerhouse lobby and lockmaster control building are open daily. Most people, however, skip that tour unless they're fascinated by engineering.

Drive over the 4,541-foot-long dam, turn left and down to the Corps of Engineers lock. You can walk on top of one of the world's highest single-lift navigation locks. Look down 100 feet as commercial tows and pleasure boats are gradually raised that far in a single operation. It takes about 30 to 45 minutes for enough water to flow into the 600-foot enclosure for a "lock through." The lock is literally jammed with pleasure boats on summer holiday weekends, especially on the Fourth of July. Wilson Lake created by the empoundment stretches 15 miles upriver to Wheeler Dam. The dramatic spillways on the lower (western) side of the dam are used only to reduce dangerously high water levels. Water is normally directed through the powerhouse to generate electricity.

Getting there: Hwy. 133 is a north-south road parallel to and east of U.S. 72 which bisects the cities south of the river. Approaching from the southeast, travel Hwy. 20 to 133 and go north 7 miles to the river. You'll pass several blocks of sidewalks and fire hydrants with no houses nearby. This was to be Henry Ford's mega-city. From the north, exit U.S. 72 onto 133 and head south. Phone 386-2442.

ATTRACTIONS SOUTH OF THE RIVER

ALABAMA MUSIC HALL OF FAME celebrates the contributions of the state's musicians to every form of music, from blues to country to jazz. Bronze stars in the lobby identify many inducted during biennial ceremonies since 1985. The large museum displays memorabilia from the careers of such musicians as Tammy Wynette, Emmy Lou Harris, the Commodores, Hank Williams Sr., Hank Williams Jr., Jimmy Buffet, Lionel Richie, Erskine Hawkins and, of course, Fort Payne's favorite sons, the group Alabama. At last count, the contributions of 1,000 musicians, vocalists, songwriters, and behind the scenes talents are acknowledged.

A lifelike Nat King Cole at the piano greets you inside the door. Born Nathaniel Coles in Montgomery in 1919, he grew up in Chicago and scored his first hit, "Mona Lisa," in 1949. In 1956, he became the first black entertainer to headline a syndicated TV series. Cole recorded "Rambling Rose" in 1962 and died three years later.

Music by a variety of artists plays over speakers in walk-through guitars and a giant 1940s style jukebox. Look for the original 1955 contract where Sam Phillips of Sun Records sold Elvis Presley's "performance agreement" to RCA for $35,000, the highest amount paid to that date for an artist's contract. Elvis, Col. Tom Parker and Vernon Presley signed the agreement.

One of the most intriguing experiences is boarding and walking through the *Southern Star*, the plush bus in which the Alabama Band used to tour. It gives a glimpse of what life is like on the road for the more successful artists.

Many artists have given costumes and musical instruments that played key roles in their star development. For example, Jim Nabors' "Gomer Pyle" uniform and Tony Tennille's fancy jeans - emblazened with the words to "Love Will Keep Us Together" - are displayed, as are the Commodores' white military-style suits and Hank Jr.'s trademark sunglasses.

A room devoted to rhythm and blues showcases Percy Sledge, W.C. Handy, Dinah Washington and others. The final section salutes the musicians and producers of the Muscle Shoals studios which claimed the title of "hit recording capital of the world" because of the volume of chartbusters recorded in Muscle Shoals. Visitors can get into the act as well. If you've ever wanted to step into a sound booth and record over a track, you can.

A cotton field was transformed into the Hall of Fame, thanks to a state bond issue. Future plans include an audio visual theater and a library of Southern music. Allow an hour. Open daily. Adults, $6; ages 13-18, $5; ages 6-12, $3; over 55, $5. Phone 381-4417 or 1-800-239-2643. Write P.O. Box 709, Tuscumbia, 35674.

Getting there: Located on U.S. 72, 2 miles west of the U.S. 43 intersection. Since you are only about 4 miles from the Helen Keller Birthplace, visit there, as well.

BELLE MONT MANSION is one of Alabama's first great plantation houses and one of the South's most outstanding examples of the Palladian style which influenced Thomas Jefferson.

Jefferson placed an emphasis on high-quality brickwork, with contrasting wood trim and a preference for hilltop building sites.

Although the architect is unknown, it was built about 1830 for Dr. Alexander Mitchell, a Virginian physician and planter. It dominated the hilltop overlooking Mitchell's 1,680-acre plantation of cotton, corn, clover and grass. It was surrounded by a kitchen and "all necessary out houses" as well as an orchard of fruit trees brought from a Long Island nursery.

Isaac Winston, related to Dolly Madison and Patrick Henry, and with ties to Thomas Jefferson, bought the estate in 1833. He and his wife, Catherine, maintained Belle Mont as a showplace until his death in 1863. She died in 1884, and it remained in the family until 1941 when it was sold. It was last occupied in 1969 and later fell into disrepair. In 1983, the house and 35 surrounding acres were donated to the Alabama Historical Commission by members of the prominent Fennel family. Restoration began in 1986.

Counterclockwise from the entrance salon are the corner parlor and two bedrooms on the west side. On the opposite side of a courtyard with U-shaped gallery were two more bedrooms. At the east entry which gave exterior access to the corner dining room are double doors with oval-shaped windows such as those Jefferson used at the University of Virginia. A staircase which hangs to the east wall of the front entry leads to the second floor salon which was used as a music room. The roof of this two-story section was originally crowned by a balustrated deck reached by ladder-like steps.

You can see rooms restored to their original glory and visualize the work yet to come on the U-shaped rear courtyard which is framed by extended wings. Open Sun., 1-4 p.m. and by appointment. Closed. Jan.-March. Phone 381-5385 or 381-5052.

Getting there: From the intersection of U.S. 72, go south on U.S. 43 about 3/10 mile and turn right on Cook's Lane.

COON DOG CEMETERY is the final resting place for scores of beloved and faithful coon dogs. Key Underwood began the tradition when he buried his trusty 15-year-old dog "Troop" on Sept. 4, 1937, on the site of his last hunt. Scores of other hunters have followed suit over the years. It is isolated and unattended except on Labor Day when a celebration and picnic are held. Burials cost $50 and only hunting dogs are accepted. Although it is thought of as the Arlington Cemetery of coon dogs and a romantic subject for journalists, it is far off the beaten path and could leave you wondering if the pilgrimage was really worth it.

Getting there: Go west 7 miles on U.S. 72 and turn south on Hwy. 247. Go 12 miles and turn right, following signs.

HELEN KELLER BIRTHPLACE (IVY GREEN) is the childhood home of the famous writer and lecturer and scene of the events chronicled in the inspiring play *The Miracle Worker*.

The daughter of a prominent Alabama family, Helen was a ordinary child from birth in 1880 until an attack of scarlet fever at age 19 months left her deaf, mute and blind. She lived in a dark and confusing world until the latest in a series of teachers was able to establish a form of communication when she was seven.

Her difficult education at the hands of teacher Anne Sullivan eventually permitted her to excel in college. Later, Helen, as a widely recognized humanitarian, toured the world as an unofficial ambassador for the handicapped.

Many of the family's original furnishings are displayed in the white frame house her grandfather built in 1820. Just a few steps away is the small cottage with a bay window where she was born and which served as home and classroom for Helen and Anne. The simple pump behind the house is where the frustrated teacher first tapped out a series of five alphabet codes as the water flowed over the child's hand and Helen learned the sign language meaning of "w-a-t-e-r." Before the end of that breakthrough day, she had learned 30 words.

As an adult, she became an internationally famous author. Her books included *The Story of My Life* (1902), *The World I Live In* (1908), *Out of the Dark* (1913), and *Let Us have Faith* (1940). Miss Keller, who died in 1968, and Mrs. Anne Sullivan Macy, who died in 1936, are buried at the National Cathedral in Washington.

The international appeal of the Helen Keller story is demonstrated by the gifts from various nations in a garden west of the house.

What was intended as a gift in the 1970s nearly became a major disaster. Sears was having the house painted for a TV paint commercial when an accidental fire severely damaged the house and many original mementoes. The house was repaired and the commercial aired, giving the house museum some appreciated national exposure.

Although small, this is a house museum where you should take your time. The Keller family's 19th-century furniture alone would make this a worthwhile place to visit, but the many personal items bring the story of this remarkable woman to life. Hundreds of mementoes, photos, Braille books, gifts and a Braille typewriter on which Helen wrote her books are displayed in a room in the back of the house. The handicaps which this remarkable Alabamian overcame make this one of the state's most poignant shrines. It is worthy of its status as a National Historic Landmark.

The best time to visit is on a weekend in the summer when *The Miracle Worker* is performed in the simple outdoor theater behind the house. For the home only, allow 30-45 minutes. Some 30,000 people visit a year. Open Mon.-Sat., 8:30-4; Sun., 1-4. Last tour at 4. Adults, $3; ages 6-11, $1; groups of 10+, $2.50. Phone 383-4066.

Getting there: The birthplace is 2 blocks west of Tuscumbia's Main Street on Keller Lane. From the intersection of U.S. 72 and U.S. 43, go west on 72 about a mile and turn north on Main Street. Follow the signs to Keller Lane. If coming from Florence, go south on 72 and watch on the right for the small signs that direct you to the shortcut to Ivy Green.

NATCHEZ TRACE - A tranquil, limited access two-lane highway stretches from Nashville through the northwest corner of Alabama and down to Natchez. The parkway generally follows the route of the old pioneer road to the Mississippi River, an important 500-mile long wilderness pathway in the late 1700s and early 1800s.

Because trucks and buses are prohibited, the parkway provides a leisurely drive through forest and rural landscapes. You can visit Indian mounds and sites, historical landmarks, natural trails and recreation areas. Picnic areas and outdoor recreation areas maintained by the National Park Service provide opportunities to stretch your legs on a journey free of traffic lights, fast food places and Kmarts. At mile marker 320.3, stop for an exhibit shelter and audio station which tells the story of Levi Colbert, a Chickasaw chief who operated an inn near here in the early 1800s.

Getting there: Exit to the trace on U.S. 72 at mile marker 6 near the Mississippi state line.

WHERE TO STAY NORTH OF THE RIVER

Comfort Inn-Florence, 400 S. Court St., is a high-rise budget motel on the west side of U.S. 72 just north of the river. It features executive king suites, standard kings and double rooms. Free continental breakfast, free local calls. **Phone 760-8888** or 1-800-221-2222.

Best Western Executive Inn, 504 Court St., was originally a Holiday Inn. Pool, restaurant, lounge. **Phone 766-2331** or 1-800-538-1234.

Ho Jo, 1241 Florence Blvd., was formerly the Regency Inn. Phone 764-5421.

Tourway Inn, 1915 Florence Blvd., has all rooms on the ground level. Pool, complimentary coffee and paper. Free local calls. **Phone 766-2620** or 1-800-633-3131.

WHERE TO STAY SOUTH OF THE RIVER

Holiday Inn-Sheffield, 4900 Hatch Blvd., just a mile south of the Tennessee River on U.S. 72, is a three-story motel with 206 rooms and has been ranked among the top 100 Holiday Inns. It has a three-story atrium lobby, indoor Jacuzzi, outdoor pool and courtyard. The restaurant provides room service. Lounge. Rooms have cable TV. Free airport transportation. Double rate: $65-$72 plus tax, weekends $52-$65. **Phone 381-4710**.

Ramada Convention Center-Sheffield, 4205 Hatch Blvd., has 150 guest rooms with coffee makers and offers free use of Gold's Gym during the stay. A 2.6 mile walking and jogging trail is nearby. An on-site restaurant offers breakfast and lunch buffets Mon.-Fri. A full dinner menu and room service are available. Fax 381-2838. Double rate: $53-$55 plus tax, weekends $40. **Phone 381-3743** or 1-800-228-2828.

The **Key West Inn-Tuscumbia** on U.S. 72 west of U.S. 43 has 41 rooms with two double beds each. Cable TV includes HBO. Free local telephone calls. Deluxe rooms have microwaves and refrigerators. Guest laundry on premises. RV and bus parking. Complimentary power hookups for boats and RV's. Free continental breakfast. Fax 383-3191. Double rate: $43-$46 plus tax. Special welcome/departure packages are available for motorcoach or church groups. **Phone 383-0700** or 1-800-833-0555.

WHERE TO EAT IN THE SHOALS

**Court Street Cafe, a block east of Court at Mobile and Seminary, serves buffalo wings, appetizers, fancy burgers, soups and fish at reasonable prices. Its success led owners Rick Elliott and Jake Jacobs to open a restaurant in Decatur. Open Sun.-Sat. Phone 767-4300.

Dale's, 1001 Mitchell Blvd. at the north end of the O'Neal Bridge, serves great charcoal steaks and seafood. It is the survivor of the legendary chain of restaurants once operated out of Birmingham. Open Mon.-Sat. for dinner. Phone 766-4961.

George's Steak Pit, 1206 Jackson Hwy. in Sheffield, is a second-generation, chef-owned steak restaurant well known for its fish, 12-ounce ribeyes and 8-ounce filet mignons that are grilled over smoldering hickory logs. These and other entrees like lobster tails and shrimp are served with tossed salad, garlic bread and a choice of baked potato, wild rice, a vegetable or fries. Another house specialty is the Greek salad seasoned with Greek olives, anchovies and feta cheese and dressed with oil and vinegar or homemade Roquefort. A large selection of wines is available to enhance the pleasure of dining at George's. Frank Vafinis owns and manages the restaurant his father opened in 1966. Checks range from $11-$23 and the average is $17. Open Tues.-Sat., 4:30-10:30 p.m. except major holidays. Phone 381-1531.

*Fisherman's Resort, just south of Wheeler Dam on Hwy. 101, has excellent fried catfish and deviled crab, both available when the seafood buffet is on the steam table after 5 p.m. Thurs.-Sat., after noon Sun. You drive through a trailer park of fishing cabins to get here. Open Sun.-Thurs., 10-9; Fri.-Sat., until 10. Phone 685-2094 in Town Creek.

Painted Lady, 1104 N. Main St., Tuscumbia, is a delightful Victorian restaurant in a restored building filled with antiques and set against a hunter green color scheme. Even the bar dates from 1900. Selections range from large salads with grilled chicken ($5.50) to $13 ribeye. Open Mon.-Thurs., 11-10; Fri.-Sat., until 11 and Sun. until 4 p.m. A Victorian gift shop is upstairs. Phone 389-8256.

Princeton's, east end of Regency Square Mall, specializes in fancy finger platters of baby back ribs and chicken tenders while serving prime rib, Caribbean ribeye and chicken tender salads at reasonable prices. The average lunch check is $7 and dinner, $10. The large restaurant, with a handsome brick exterior and brick and brass interior, has an intimate atmosphere which is popular with dating couples and older adults. Open Mon.-Thur., 11 a.m.-10 p.m.; Fri.-Sat., 11-11; Sun., 11-9. Closed Thanksgiving and Dec. 24-25. Phone 766-7163.

ANNUAL EVENTS IN THE SHOALS

Fourth weekend in April
Arts Alive! - Wilson Park, Florence - Regional art exhibition presents craftspeople and their pottery, sculpture, fiber arts and other media. Phone 760-6379.

First weekend in May
Florence Heritage Tour - The tour features private homes and other structures which range from the simplicity of the log home where composer W.C. Handy was born to the elegance of Courtview, the antebellum mansion at the north end of Court Street. Phone 764-4661.

Third weekend in May
Recall LaGrange - LaGrange College Site, Leighton - A Methodist college chartered in

1830, LaGrange was one of the antebellum era's most prominent educational institutions. Its handsome brick campus dominated a mountaintop. Prominent Tennessee Valley planters built a village of summer homes nearby in the 1840s and 1850s. The college was burned April 28, 1863, by Union horsemen under Col. Florence N. Cornyn. During the annual festival sponsored by the LaGrange Living Historical Association, artisans and craftspeople honor the resourcefulness of the pioneers by demonstrating basketmaking, sheep shearing, cooking and other skills which recall the rugged mountain culture. Phone 446-9324.

Last weekend of June

Helen Keller Festival - Ivy Green and other locations - The accomplishments of Helen Keller are celebrated during this festival on the weekend near her birth anniversary of June 27, 1880. Music, drama, tours and the achievements of today's handicapped citizens create a unique event. Activities on Friday are held on the courthouse lawn on Main Street. Musical acts perform at Spring Park, site of an arts festival. Tickets to a weekend historic homes tour are available at Ivy Green. Sports and food events are also scheduled. The season premiere of *The Miracle Worker* usually coincides with the festival. Phone 383-4066 or 383-0783.

Late June thru late July

The Miracle Worker - Performances of William Gibson's inspiring story of the blind and deaf mute child being taught to communicate through the sense of touch has been staged outdoors on weekends since 1962. Local actors, many of whom have performed for several years, portray members of the Keller family and the teacher Anne Sullivan. A typical season runs 12 performances.

Actress Patty Duke portrayed Helen Keller in the Broadway version at age 13 and won an Oscar for the 1962 movie version. Tours of the Keller home at 7 p.m. precede the performances Fri.-Sat. at 8:15. Chairs and bleachers provide seating for 450 persons. Since reserved seats sell out, phone well ahead or write Tickets, 300 W. Commons, Tuscumbia, 35674. Bleacher seating is usually available up to showtime. Eat before arriving because only snacks are sold on the grounds. Phone 383-4066.

Fourth of July

Spirit of Freedom Festival - McFarland Park - Tens of thousands of people converge on the popular riverfront park below the O'Neal Bridge to be entertained by musical acts, cheer patriotic remarks and watch a massive show of fireworks. In what may be unique for such a celebration, politicians are not invited to speak. Bands perform on the elevated stage for much of the day. Picnicking and sunbathing go on all day and families stroll among food and merchandising booths knowing they can cool off in the river. After the peak of the afternoon heat, the crowd begins to pack the park for entertainment and fireworks. Many other people watch from boats in the river and adjacent canal. After the fireworks end late, there's always a lengthy traffic delay exiting the park.

Early August

Alabama Music Hall of Fame Anniversary Celebration - Entertainers with Alabama roots celebrate the anniversary of the opening of the Hall of Fame in Tuscumbia. Live performances are scheduled throughout the day. Phone 381-4417 or 1-800-239-2643.

First full week in August
W.C. Handy Festival - Scores of people holding festively decorated parasols strut around the Wilson Park fountain to the beat of Handy's blues music as the people of Florence salute the native son whose talent created an entire form of popular music. Spirituals, jazz and contemporary music share the program with the blues. The annual celebration comes alive with outdoor food events, riverside concerts, antique car and truck show, jam sessions and lots more. Most of the events are free.

Handy would be amazed at the attention generated by the event started in 1984. Check *The Times-Daily* newspaper for schedules. Phone 764-4661 or 760-6434.

Saturday during cotton harvest
Lawrence County Cotton Festival - Town Creek - The Tennessee Valley leads the state in cotton production, with Lawrence County consistantly among the top two or three producers. Fifth- and sixth-generations of the families who migrated from Virginia's Albemarle County in the early 1800s to settle North Alabama still own the 39,000 acres planted in cotton. Date varies from late September to early October. Phone 974-2464.

Fourth weekend of October
Renaissance Faire - Wilson Park - Florence celebrates its link with Florence, Italy, during a weekend of visitors playing medieval games, costumed knights engaging in swordplay and damsels being rescued from distress. Music, crafts and food highlight the activities which seek to recall the period from the 12th through the 16th centuries. Corner of Tuscaloosa Street and Wood Avenue. Phone 764-4661.

Second Saturday in December
NCAA Division II Football Championship - Braly Stadium on UNA campus - The top teams in Division II college football meet in the finals for the national title. Phone 383-4704.

FORT PAYNE

- **Claim to fame:** Hometown of Alabama, the popular band
- **Don't miss:** Alabama Band Museum, DeSoto Falls
- **Best souvenir:** Anything with Alabama Band's logo
- **Nickname:** Sock Capital of the World
- **Population:** 11,838
- **Tourist information:** Contact the DeKalb County Tourist Association, P.O. Box 1165, Fort Payne, 35967. Phone 845-3957.

Fans of country music's **Alabama Band** who pull off I-59 to drive through the hometown of the popular country music group don't have to wait until the annual music festival to feel close to the boys. They can tour a museum of personal memorabilia and purchase souvenirs of all descriptions any time of the year.

Whether or not you buy Alabama's records, you may be wearing another of Fort Payne's products - socks. Some 6,000 local people work in scores of hosiery mills to turn out 23 percent of the nation's socks. The $300 million industry began when W.B. Davis came from Nashville in 1907 and started the first mill. Things have continued to spin since.

The knitting machines weave an open-toed tube that falls off the bottom of a cylinder when completed and the machine starts again at the top of the cylinder. In addition to the large mills, some people even set up machines in their garages and leave them running unattended while going off to real jobs. Tubes are taken to the mills where they are sewn up and dyed.

The area has a rich Native American heritage. The **Cherokee Nation** thrived from Northeast Alabama to North Carolina. The sophisticated Cherokees devised their own alphabet and educational system, published a newspaper, and raised corn, cotton, cattle and hogs. But in 1838, 7,000 U.S. soldiers corralled thousands of Cherokees and forced them to walk to Oklahoma. The town sprang up in the late 19th century around the stockade named Fort Payne which was built to corral the Indians.

Fueled by New England businessmen hoping to create a mining and manufacturing center, the town boomed in 1889. Investors erected the dazzling DeKalb Hotel in the center of town. The **Fort Payne Opera House** was built to showcase some of the nation's first theatrical talents. The art deco **DeKalb Theater**, built in 1935, now seats 500 to 600 and is being renovated as a performing arts center.

Fort Payne is best known for being the hometown of country music's most beloved group, **Alabama**. The foursome write and sing about hard working people, true love and the South. Lead singer Randy Owen and guitarist Teddy Gentry are first cousins and fiddler-guitarist Jeff Cook is a distant cousin. Drummer Mark Herndon is the son of a Marine pilot who was stationed in several states.

They got their start playing in Carolina clubs and began recording in 1980. Since then, their hand-clapping, toe-tapping songs have sold nearly 50 million albums. More than 25 songs have made it to the top of the charts. The Academy of Country Music selected the band as Entertainer of the Year for a record three times and in 1989 honored them as Entertainer of the Decade. Individually and as a group, they lend their considerable influence to support worthy charities and work for the betterment of the state. Their anthem, *My Home's in Alabama,* was almost named the state's official song by the Alabama Legislature.

Thousands of local people help "the boys" stage their annual **June Jam** fundraiser which supports local schools and other worthy projects.

Fort Payne is in the valley below **Lookout Mountain** and close to a number of the state's most interesting natural attractions.

ATTRACTIONS

ALABAMA FAN CLUB and MUSEUM pays homage to the popular country music band and their love affair with their fans. You can watch a short video about the group and see the many personal items which belong to the band members. A gift shop offers a variety of merchandise featuring the band's logo. Admission. Open Mon.-Sat., 8-5; Sun., noon-5. Phone 845-1646.

Getting there: 201 Glenn Ave. S. is easily reached from I-59 exit 222. Follow U.S. 11 into town and watch for the fan club on the north side of the street.

DeSOTO STATE PARK spreads over 5,000 acres along the ridge of Lookout Mountain which begins in Chattanooga and embraces some of the state's most dazzling natural wonders. The park is best known for **DeSoto Falls** and the pristine **Little River** which carved a deep canyon along the top of the mountain. Hiking and nature trails lead to ridge tops and the canyon floor.

Overnight accommodations at DeSoto State Park are more rustic than those of Lake Guntersville. Guests may choose from a variety of accommodations. There are 25 guest rooms in the lodge, each with double beds, a television, telephone and a porch. The lodge serves three meals a day and has a pair of meeting rooms which can accommodate up to 40 each.

Twenty-two chalets and rustic cabins accommodate up to eight people. Depression-era CCC workers used hand-hewn logs and local stone to build the cabins. They made some furniture by hand, too. Several A-frame cabins have fireplaces and kitchenettes.

In addition to the park's natural beauty, guests enjoy an Olympic pool, tennis courts, picnic shelters and a playground. Room rates are higher on weekends and March-Nov. Visa and MasterCard accepted to hold reservations. Write Rt. 1, Box 205, Fort Payne, 35967. Fax 845-3224. Phone 845-5380.

Getting there: DeSoto is 8 miles northeast of Fort Payne. Exit I-59 at Hwy. 35. On top of Lookout Mountain turn on County 89 and follow the signs along the ridge road.

FORT PAYNE DEPOT served as a passenger station, 1891-1970, and is a museum with historical displays. Phone 845-5714.

Getting there: 105 Fifth St. NE.

FORT PAYNE OPERA HOUSE was built in 1889 to showcase some of the nation's first theatrical talents. It was converted into a movie house in 1918 and remodeled in 1932. It closed in 1935 and was used for storage until community leaders formed Landmarks of DeKalb County and restored it during the state's 150th birthday. The state's oldest theater, it reopened in 1970 and now is the scene of cultural events and pre-arranged tours. Phone 845-2741.

Getting there: 512 Gault Ave. N.

LITTLE RIVER CANYON - The Little River begins as a natural spring which appears on top of the mountain and wanders southwesterly before plunging 100 feet over **DeSoto Falls**. It continues south, flows under the bridge at Hwy. 35 and drops another 60 feet over **Little River Falls** to begin **Little River Canyon**. It is the only river in the Western Hemisphere known to begin and end on the top of a mountain. The 16 miles of heavily wooded, steep walls form the second deepest canyon east of the Rockies. The gorge has an average depth of 400 feet and is 600 feet at its deepest point. To see the canyon, follow the scenic parkway which follows the west rim for 22 miles and stop at marked overlooks.

The river, which provides a habitat for some species of animal and plant life found nowhere else, is among the purest on Earth. Fish swimming in water several feet deep can easily be seen.

Sportsmen hunt, hike, rappel, kayak and canoe the length of the river before its tumultuous journey ends at **Canyon Mouth Park**.

Because of its natural beauty, Little River Canyon is the core for a 15,000-acre national preserve encompassing DeSoto State Park and the adjacent state wildlife management area. Some nearby landowners opposed the congressional action to put the area under protection of the National Park Service because of concern that adjacent property might be seized under the right of eminent domain. Others favored the legislation, believing that more development would occur in the area if the government didn't create the preserve. To see what all the fuss was about, visit the area as part of a day trip to Mentone and Fort Payne.

Getting there: Exit I-59 on Hwy. 35 at Fort Payne and go east about 10 miles to Little River Falls. For the scenic route to the canyon, take I-59 exit 188 in Gadsden at Noccalula Falls and follow signs up the hill. Go north on Lookout Mountain Parkway to the Dogtown community. Turn right on Hwy. 176 and go 4 miles to the canyon rim.

MENTONE - See separate listing.

SEQUOYAH CAVERNS, in extreme northeastern Alabama and a stone's throw from I-59, is a relatively compact series of "rooms" with still pools of flowing mineral water offering crisp, mirror-like reflections of natural formations.

The limestone cavern stretches about a quarter-mile inside the base of Sand Mountain. The highest point straight up inside is about 120 feet. Temperature remains a constant 60 degrees and the pure mineral water flowing throughout stays at 58. The crisp, clear water, fed via underground streams, is responsible for several illusions. At one point in the tour, your attention is directed to a spray of water which appears to be flowing upward. In reality, you are looking at a reflection in the pool of water flowing down.

A column rising about 20 feet bears the date 1830 and the name of Sam Houston, the frontiersman who married Sequoyah's daughter. Sut from fires made by Cherokees tarnished the ceiling in only two places, suggesting that the tribes spent little time inside. The cavern is named for the legendary Indian chief who lived in the area and devised the Cherokee alphabet, although there is no direct evidence linking him with the caverns. The melodic sounding name of Sequoyah in Cherokee actually means "pig foot," a reference to the club foot caused by childhood polio.

In the 1960's, Clark Byers was the first contemporary man to explore the cave extensively. Lights were installed and the attraction was opened to the public in 1964. Byers, who painted "See Rock City" on Southern barns for decades, sold the attraction to the owners of Rock City who sold it to Trenton, Ga., accountant Ben Hill. An estimated 24,000 people tour a year.

Expect to be inside for an hour or less. Picnicking, camping and hiking are permitted. Open 8:30-5 from Mar. 1 - Dec. 1. Weekends only, Dec.-Feb. Adults, $6; ages 6 -12, $4.

Getting there: Follow signs off I-59 to U.S. 11, then 1.5 miles. It is 10 minutes from the interstate exits. Phone 635-6423.

WHERE TO STAY

Best Western, 1828 Gault Ave. N., has a scenic view of the mountains and is close to the Alabama Fan Club and Museum and other sites. The 68 guest rooms have cable TV with HBO and ESPN. A full-service restaurant offers a lunch buffet Sun.-Fri. Fax 845-6251. Double rate: $44-$50. **Phone 845-0481** or 1-800-528-1234.

FORT PAYNE'S ANNUAL EVENTS

Second week of June

Alabama June Jam - The band members sponsor one of the music industry's largest annual charity concerts.

Speakers are set up several hundred yards from the giant stage so that people spread out over the 47-acre field can hear. Most shows have drawn from 30,000 to 67,000 fans, and have generated more than almost $3 million for charities since 1982.

Alabama Band members attract country music's biggest names, including Dolly Parton, Ricky Van Shelton, the Gatlin Brothers, Travis Tritt, Garth Brooks, Doug Stone, Glen Campbell and Charlie Daniels by agreeing to perform in charity events supported by other acts. The Jam also showcases promising talent. Toward the end of the show, fireworks shower the skies overhead.

The Jam culminates a 10-day festival centered around Fort Payne, with athletic events including soccer, horseshoes and tennis. **Randy Owen** headlines a celebrity golf tournament and **Jeff Cook** hosts a celebrity bass tournament. **Teddy Gentry** and **Mark Herndon** are involved in the VIP softball game and other activities.

A parade and street dance, plus talent search finals, classic car show, barbecue and gospel singing, add to the festivities. In addition, bus tours past the band members' homes, sponsored by the **DeKalb County Tourist Association**, depart Wed.-Fri. from the Fan Club headquarters on Glenn Avenue. Phone 845-3957 for homes tour reservations.

Order tickets by mail prior to late May (P.O. Box 529, Fort Payne, 35967) or phone 845-9300 and charge with Visa/MasterCard.

Many fans camp out near the gate in order to get a good seat close to the stage. Gates open at 7 a.m. and music starts before noon, but don't expect to get to the site without a lengthy traffic delay. The Jam usually occurs on a hot, sunny Saturday, so bring a broad-brimed hat, folding chairs and plenty of sunscreen, but no alcohol; DeKalb County is dry. The grand finale comes late in the night when the band Alabama takes the stage. It is staged by hundreds of volunteers loyal to the band members who have stayed close to their DeKalb County roots. The date is pegged to the conclusion of Nashville's Fan Fair, so it may vary from year to year. Phone 845-9300 or 845-2741.

Second Sunday in October

Sacred Harp All-Day Singing - Chestnut Grove Baptist Church, Ider - Singers read shaped-note hymnals to sing gospel harmonies a capella with gusto. Each of the four musical notes is shown with a different shape - circle, diamond, rectangle and triangle - for easier reading of the music. "Fasola" singings were common in the South during the 19th and early 20th century and began to fade as congregations became more sophisticated. Ider's all-day singing, listed in church records as early as 1927, is among the most traditional of styles. Equally Southern is a meal of turnip greens, chicken and fried okra. Ida is on Hwy. 117 some 11 miles north of the I-59 Hammondville exit.

GADSDEN

- **Claim to fame:** Goodyear tires, Noccalula Falls
- **Nickname:** All-America City
- **Population:** 42,523
- **Tourism information:** Lloyd Wagnon, Director; Gadsden-Etowah Tourism Board, 1500 Noccalula Rd., P.O. Box 8267, Gadsden, 35902. Fax 549-0352. Phone 549-0351.

Gadsden lies at the southern end of Lookout Mountain which begins in Chattanooga and is best known for an impressive natural waterfall, Goodyear tires, colorful Indian celebrations and a large antique car show.

The boundary between the Creek and Cherokee nations had been defined through the area when John Riley built a log cabin near the Coosa River in 1825 and other settlers followed as Indians were forced from their homeland. Riley's house served as a stagecoach station and later as the first post office.

Immigrants flowed into the area about 1834 in advance of the removal of the Indians. The town's original name of Double Springs was changed in 1845 to honor Gen. James Gadsden of South Carolina who negotiated the purchase of land from Mexico for what became the states of New Mexico and Arizona.

The Civil War interrupted Gadsden's development and an act of bravery by a young girl created one of the war's enduring legends. In 1863, Confederate calvarymen chasing Yankee raiders were aided by a young heroine, Emma Sansom. At the same time, contract mail carrier John Wisdom made a 67-mile night ride from Gadsden to Rome, Ga., with word of approaching Federal troops.

In hopes of enticing investors into the Coosa River area, William P. Lay started building what became the nation's first hydroelectric plant in 1899. He directed scores of workers who struggled for four years to fashion a 200-foot-wide dam across the surging force of a drop along Big Wills Creek near presentday U.S. 431. Four years later, Lay ran wires 5 miles to a pole in a parking lot across from Walker Drug Store in Attalla and - to the amazement of onlookers - illuminated a single light bulb.

The firm Lay formed to build the dam was the **Alabama Power Co.**, which today supplies electric power to all but 16 of the state's 67 counties. Alabama Power still honors Lay's initial contract with the Town of Attalla and provides free power to light its municipal buildings and schools.

Manufacturing thrived for the next half century as Gadsden became one of the Deep South's major industrial cities.

Goodyear opened the first rubber plant in the South here in 1929. It was later expanded for radial tires and became the largest tire and tube manufacturing plant in the world. Other employers like Gulf States Steel, Mid-South Industries and Health-Tex Clothing produce steel, fabricated metal, electrical equipment and electronic devices, although recent plant reductions have reduced the population and the economic luster of the city.

Civic leaders have put an increased emphasis on the performing arts. The Cultural Arts Center, the Gadsden Convention Hall and Wallace Hall are sites for exhibitions, concerts and performances throughout the year. A book titled "The Best Towns in America" recognized the quality of life in the Queen City of the Coosa by featuring the city among its selections. Gadsden was named an **All-America City** in 1991 in recognition of its high degree of community involvement.

Gadsden, just east of I-59, is linked via the east-west I-759, which parallels a portion of U.S. 431 between Huntsville and Anniston. To reach the main downtown businesses on Broad Street from 431 (Meighan Blvd.), go west 2 blocks on Third Street North. **Amtrak** service between Birmingham and Chattanooga stops west of Gadsden at Attalla.

GADSDEN ATTRACTIONS

EMMA SANSOM MONUMENT - Facing downtown from the center of Broad Street is a statue honoring the 16-year-old girl who defied enemy bullets and bravely led Confederate Gen. **Nathan Bedford Forrest** across a swollen creek.

For three days Confederate troops had pursued 1,500 Federal raiders commanded by Col. Abel Streight across 120 miles to prevent them from burning railroad bridges leading to Rome, Ga. On May 2, 1863, with Confederates in hot pursuit, the Yankees crossed a wooden bridge over rain-swollen Black Creek and set it afire. When Forrest stopped at the home of the Widow Sansom in hopes of getting directions to another crossing, the daughter quickly volunteered to lead them to a spot where the family's cows crossed.

She swung up behind Forrest on his horse and they rode toward the ford and into Union fire. When a bullet from a musket pierced her skirt, she waved her bonnet in defiance and shouted, "They have only wounded my dress." The enemy soldiers cheered and stopped firing until she reached safety. The Southerners pursued and captured many of the raiders the next day and prevented the attack on Rome. The night of his victory Forrest sent "his highest regards to Emma Sansom for her gallant conduct" and asked for a lock of her hair as a keepsake.

In honor of her heroism, the Confederate Congress expressed its thanks and the Legislature voted her a gold medal and a parcel of land, neither of which she ever received. She married a Confederate private in 1864 and they moved to Texas in 1876 where they raised five sons and two daughters. Although she died in 1900 at the age of 54, she remains a determined girl of 16 in the annals of Southern patriotism.

In 1907, the United Daughters of the Confederacy erected the monument which depicts the young Emma clutching a bonnet and pointing the way to the shortcut. On the base is a bas relief of her on horseback with the legendary general.

Getting there: It is in the center of Broad at the corner of First Street near the Coosa River. The blue building near the statue is City Hall.

CENTER FOR CULTURAL ARTS draws people downtown to enjoy arts, entertainment and cultural activities in a dramatic setting which formerly housed a Belk Hudson department store. Community leaders and the Gadsden Arts Council identified the need for a community arts center in 1984 and reviewed several options, including the old Belk's at 501 Broad St. Gadsden native and architect Preston Phillips, associated with a New York firm, designed the soaring building with a high atrium and bold barrel-shaped profile. The center includes exhibition halls, meeting rooms, two concert halls, an auditorium for school and civic club dances, studios for art classes, and dining facilities. The **Imagination Place** is a high-tech romper room for bright youngsters. A separate admission applies.

A permanent exhibit is a 72-foot railroad and building scale model of Gadsden as it looked in the 1940's. Open daily except major holidays. A restaurant is open Sun.-Fri. Admission. Phone 546-7435 or 543-2787.

Getting there: Exit I-59 to U.S. 431. Turn right on Fifth and right on Broad.

NOCCALULA FALLS PARK - One of the South's natural wonders is the waterfall created as water from Black Creek plummets 90 feet from a limestone ledge into a heavily wooded gorge below.

The falls are named for Noccalula or Alivilda, the legendary daughter of a Cherokee chief who leapt to her death rather than marry a Creek chief chosen by her father, who had banished the brave she truly loved. The spot from which she supposedly jumped is marked by a 9-foot statue of a grief-stricken Princess Noccalula.

Having run along the summit of the southern spur of Lookout Mountain, Black Creek flows underneath Noccalula Road near the park entrance and then spills over the falls, continuing westward through a heavily wooded gorge which separates the main park from a large campground and empties into the Coosa River.

Although you can walk to the statue and waterfall without paying admission to the park, you would be missing the even more dramatic view from beneath the falls. Just beyond the ticket booth, turn right and carefully descend the 71 steps into the cool gorge and follow a marked footpath about 100 yards to the underside of the falls. Photographs made in mid-afternoon with a wide-angle lens can be rewarding.

The amount of water flowing into the ravine ranges from a trickle to a torrent depending on recent rainfall. The falls are most impressive right after a heavy rainfall.

The swirling waters of Black Creek have smoothed and shaped a number of rock formations which have been given the names of mystery fort, pyramid rock, mushroom rock and fat man's squeeze. Among the rare plant species found in the gorge are the endangered carnivous mountain pitcher plant and the rare flimsey fern. Wear appropriate athletic shoes to explore the damp gorge. (Because at least five people have drowned in the gorge, it may be closed by the time you visit.)

Flanking the gorge is a large wooded park with banks of azaleas and many beds of daylilies set among the bald rock outcroppings.

A collection of homestead and farm buildings has been assembled in a setting of pine trees and landscaped with blooming shrubbery. Walk past the grocery store and grist mill to reach the covered bridge, which serves as the entrance to the old homestead. Beyond the small lake is a log house built in Tennessee in 1777, with authentic out buildings for cooking food, curing meats and washing clothes. A blacksmith shop, tool shed and privy are nearby. A large barn, chicken house, hog pen and corn crib have been assembled from nearby farms to complete the story of a typical farmstead. You can't enter most of the unattended buildings because iron bars are in the doorways, but you can look inside.

You can walk through a log house that was used for meetings and school classes and sit on the split-log benches as people did four or five generations ago. Jesse and Frank James stayed overnight in the Arledge Cabin after reputedly robbing an Army payroll master in 1881.

Ride the miniature train called the *Kiwanis Special* on a 1-mile loop past the bridge and around the pioneer buildings. A snack bar and picnic tables are available. Covered pavilions for group picnics may be reserved by phoning 543-7412. To reserve space at the 250-site campground with pool, bath house, washeteria and store, phone 543-7412.

Maintained by the city's parks department, Noccalula Falls Park is supported by many civic groups and individuals who work to enhance the natural beauty of the falls and surrounding area.

Visit in April when thousands of colorful azaleas bloom. Open daily 9-sunset. Adults, $1.50; ages 11 and under, and senior citizens, $1. Phone 549-4663.

Getting there: Take I-59 exit 188 to U.S. 431 and go west to Hwy. 211 (Noccalula Road), turn north and go almost 2 miles to the park entrance. It's about nine minutes from the interstate. A handsome dome-shaped war memorial honoring the county's 457 military casualties fronts Hwy. 211.

OHATCHEE CREEK RANCH is a 200-acre wildlife park of open fields, swamps and lakes between Anniston and Gadsden which is home to more than 50 species of animals. Only the large cats are caged. This naturalistic arrangement sets the Ohatchee Creek Ranch apart from zoos which usually segregate animals by region or habitat.

Being fed plenty of food prevents the animals from looking upon each other as a potential next meal.

You have the option of driving through the ranch or walking along the elevated walkway to observe the animals from North and South America, Europe, Austria, Asia and Africa, which alone is represented with 20 types of animals. From the dark continent have come zebra, tigers, giraffe, springbuck, antelope and gazelle. The admission allows you to drive through several times, which you should do because the animals move around a bit, creating a changing panorama of wildlife scenes as they wander across pastureland and distant hillsides and pause for a drink at watering holes.

Bring a camera with a long lens to photograph the animals. Bring a picnic lunch to enjoy outside the park. This is a great companion trip with the **Anniston Museum of Natural History**. Open Fri.-Sun. from 10-5. Groups of 20 or more receive discounts by reservation. Phone 442-1453.

Getting there: From Gadsden, go south on Hwy. 77 and turn east at the Boys Ranch sign near U.S. 431 mile marker 97 and go 8 miles. From Anniston, watch for the turn after the Hwy. 204 turn to Jacksonville.

SPECIAL FOR CHILDREN

IMAGINATION PLACE is a hands-on activity center for children within the downtown cultural arts center. Exhibits encourage youngsters to try out careers such as delivering the mail, hosting a radio show or even driving a patient to the hospital. Children are challenged by basics of science as they "float" in mid-air with the anti-gravity mirror or light up bulbs as they bicycle their way to generate electricity. It opens onto a sculpture garden with a unique trait: all sculpture must be climbable. Admission. Phone 546-7435 or 543-2787.

Getting there: Exit I-59 to U.S. 431. Turn right on Fifth and right on Broad.

SIDE TRIP NORTH TO COLLINSVILLE

If it's Saturday, go about 16 miles north of Gadsden on U.S. 11 to the sprawling **Collinsville Trade Day** to see hundreds of vendors selling everything from wrench sets to apples and furniture to old magazines. It is open from about 5 a.m. to 2:30 p.m. Phone 524-2536.

WHERE TO STAY

Days Inn, 1600 Rainbow Dr. near I-759 exit 4A, has 103 rooms overlooking the Coosa River. The Days Inn has cable TV, movies, pool. Restaurant next door. Double rate: $48-$56 plus tax. **Phone 543-1105.**

Holiday Inn, I-59 exit 183, has 143 rooms on two floors with cable TV and Showtime. The motel has a swimming pool, wading pool, full-service restaurant, lounge and free coffee. Free airport transportation. Fax 538-1010. Double rate: $42-$56 plus tax. **Phone 538-7861.**

WHERE TO SHOP

If you enjoy handmade crafts, visit **Corn Crib Corner** in an old cattle barn north of **Noccalula Falls**. You'll be intrigued with the quantity and quality of the quilts, pillows, signs, dolls and potholders that members of the W.R. "Russ" Elliott family make and sell.

Elliott's daughters used an old corn crib to store their crafts between shows and eventually ran out of space. They and other relatives spent two years of their spare time restoring the old barn to display their handiwork and love to talk to visitors about their crafts. They'll even take special orders if you're in no hurry.

Go 6 miles north of the Falls on Tabor Road and turn left on Elliott Road. Open Mon.-Sat., 9 a.m.-5 p.m.; Sun., 1-5 p.m. Phone 546-2040.

ANNUAL EVENTS IN GADSDEN

Third weekend in July

Antique Automobile Show - Noccalula Falls - Antique automobile restorers from throughout the South display hundreds of classic cars beneath the pine trees of the park and campground. A flea market, fashion show and awards presentation are included in the show which has been sponsored by the Gadsden Antique Automobile Club since 1965. It is among the largest car shows in the state. Phone 549-0351.

Mid-August weekend

450-Mile Outdoor Sale - Lookout Mountain Parkway - Residents along a stretch of highway through northeast Alabama, Tennessee and Kentucky put up roadside booths to sell anything from canned goods to collectibles to junk. The event, begun in 1987 to promote travel along the rural road, has grown each year. Merchandise is sold Thurs.-Sun. Phone 549-0351.

Getting there: Take the parkway from Noccalula Falls to Chattanaooga and then U.S. 127 to Cincinnati.

GUNTERSVILLE

- **Claim to fame:** Bass Fishing on Lake Guntersville
- **Don't miss:** Aeroplane museum, state park
- **Unique accommodation:** State park lodge
- **Special event:** Eagle Awareness in January
- **Population:** 7,038
- **Tourist information:** Lisa Socha, Executive Director; Marshall County Tourism Commission, P.O. Box 711, Guntersville, 35976. Phone 582-7015.

Fishermen from across North America wet their hooks in the sprawling Lake Guntersville in search of championship bass and crappie. With 962 miles of shoreline, it has become one of America's premier fishing destinations. The 69,700-acre lake was created when the Tennessee Valley Authority completed **Guntersville Dam** in 1939 and its reservoir made Guntersville a peninsula city.

The river has always played a major role in shaping the destiny of the community. John Gunter, a Welshman from South Carolina who lived with the Cherokee Indians as a trader, opened a trading post on the southern bank of the river in 1785 and founded the town of Guntersville. He married a Cherokee woman and their great-grandson, Will Rogers, became one of America's most famous and beloved humorists.

The town which grew up around John Gunter's trading post thrived as a commercial center prior to outdoor recreation becoming a major economic factor.

Lake Guntersville State Park, which offers the combination of both lakes and mountains, has an excellent lodge for family retreats in the spring, summer and fall. In the winter, the park has the unusual added attraction of the state's largest concentration of eagles.

WELCOME CENTER

The **Marshall County Tourism Commission** is located in the Lake Guntersville Chamber of Commerce building. Brochures are inside the front door of the large Victorian-style building on the right just after you cross the bridge on U.S. 431 from Huntsville.

ATTRACTIONS

AERO REPLICA FIGHTER MUSEUM displays more than two dozen military aircraft, including a number of vintage and replicated World War I bi-planes. The five-building complex, financed by Arab industrialist Frank Ryder, includes a Sopwith Camel, a Caudron 277, Nieuports, a British SE.5a with squarish lines, an Albatros DVa, four Fokker D-VII triplanes and a Dehavilland DH5. Among aircraft used in the filming of the movie "The Blue Max" is a Pfalz D-111 flown by actor George Peppard. Authentic ground-based vehicles such as a WWI ambulance and a 1914 Ford Model T delivery wagon in mint condition add period interest to the displays.

In addition to the full-size planes, the 30,000-square-foot museum houses scale models and displays of military art and wartime memorabilia. The museum doesn't make patriotic judgments: American and enemy planes are given equal treatment.

The self-guided museum is the toy of a local industrialist whose 300 patents include the Delco battery "green eye" used in all General Motors cars. Ryder began collecting replica WWI aircraft in 1987 and opened the museum five years later.

A pilot with several ratings, he staged an international Aerodrome air show which attracted vintage planes from around the nation on the 75th anniversary of WWI. An aviation historical hall of fame honors aircraft builders, writers and other enthusiasts who promote preservation of military aircraft. Open daily. Adults, $5; ages 6-15, $2.50. For group rates, write P.O. Box 366, Guntersville, 35976 or phone 582-4309.

Getting there: Located at the Guntersville Airport near mile marker 308 on U.S. 431, 2 miles north of the big bridge.

BUCK'S POCKET - The isolated state park around a box canyon is ideal for camping, swimming and fishing. The canyon was formed as South Sauty Creek cut a deep natural pocket at the southern end of the Appalachian chain. It is subject to flooding during heavy rainfall with no way out for unsuspecting picnickers and campers.

Several miles to the west, the hills which come to the water's edge at Morgan Cove are especially enjoyable in mid-October when the hardwoods' leaves turn yellow and orange. Another place of interest is Point Rock overlook.

The park spreads for 2,000 acres over the common point where DeKalb, Marshall and Jackson counties touch 10 miles north of Geraldine. According to legend, the name stems from a cornered buck deer which jumped to its death from a ledge in the canyon rather than be captured by Cherokee hunters. Although few people go there, it has a reputation for a totally different reason. **Big Jim Folsom** started the tounge-in-cheek tradition of defeated politicians retreating to Buck's Pocket to ponder their losses.

Getting there: From Guntersville, take Hwy. 227 past the big state park and follow the signs to Buck's Pocket. From Gadsden, take 227 to Grove Oak. Phone 659-2000.

CATHEDRAL CAVERNS, notable for its record 128-foot-wide opening, contains two wide chambers, an impressive stalagmite "forest" and a massive 60-foot-tall column with a girth of 200 feet. Fossils of sea life estimated to be 220 million years old dot the walls.

Amateur spelunker Jay Gurley first explored the caverns in 1952. He hocked his personal belongings for a $400 down payment to buy the 160 acres of Gunter Mountain above it. He dynamited an access into the largest chamber, moved boulders, carved trails, installed 40 miles of lights and opened it as a tourist attraction in 1955. A round trip inside covered about 1.5 miles. A second owner went bankrupt in 1974 and it was closed.

The state bought it in 1987 with plans to improve the paths and operate it as a state park when funds became available. It hasn't happened yet. Gurley, meanwhile, continues his four-decade obsession with the caverns and is the leading advocate to re-open it to the public. When it re-opens, turn off U.S. 72 between Huntsville and Scottsboro onto County 5 and go 3 miles and turn east. (Closed.)

GUNTERSVILLE DAM stretches 3,979 feet across the main channel of the Tennessee River to create a 76-mile-long lake which backs up to where the states of Tennessee, Alabama and Georgia meet. The dam impounds 69,000 acres of water for flood regulation and some of the best fishing in America.

Guntersville Dam was completed by TVA in 1939 and has the distinction of being the southernmost dam in the TVA chain of lakes. Water spills through the dam to form the tailrace which is one of the many popular places to fish for large bass around

Guntersville. Wheeler Lake begins below the dam. You can visit the dam and picnic on the grounds.

Getting there: Watch for the TVA sign to Guntersville Dam Access Road off U.S. 431 about 24 miles south of Huntsville. Drive 4 miles to the dam. The road is County 27. To reach the dam from the south, leave Hwy. 69 at Scant City on County 27 and go 5 miles.

WHERE TO STAY IN GUNTERSVILLE

The **Holiday Inn**, 2140 Gunter Ave., is the nicest place to stay directly on the lake. The 100 rooms have cable TV and Showtime and 20 have kitchenettes and views of the lake. It has a restaurant and lounge. Double rate: $49-$69 plus tax, weekends $53-$73. Lakeside rooms are slightly higher than streetside. Fax 582-2059. Romance packages include a lakeside king room and champagne. **Phone 582-2220** or 1-800-465-4329.

Lake Guntersville State Park Lodge is the centerpiece of the 6,000-acre park. The large wooden and rock lodge and convention center faces the lake from atop a tree-covered bluff 500 feet high. The main building contains two restaurants and is flanked by west and east wings with a total of 94 rooms and six suites.

The rooms are much larger than in the average motel. Balconies of the bluffside rooms have breathtaking views of the lake below. For the absolutely best view, ask if room 309 is available. Sunsets are marginally better from the west wing. Expect to pay a few dollars more for the bluffside rooms than those with a view of the parking lot.

The coffee shop serves breakfast and lunch daily. The ****Chandelier** dining room is an impressive place to eat. With its huge metal chandeliers, it seems less like a state park restaurant and more like a baronial hall awaiting shields and armor. Dominating the center of the room is a lifelike pine tree with a stuffed bald eagle nesting at the top. The buffet, an excellent value, is offered nightly and each Sunday in summer; weekends only, the rest of the year. Several kinds of meats, vegetables and desserts are served.

An outdoor swimming pool with the same spectacular view of the lake and a kiddie pool are on the main terrace near the meeting rooms. A gift shop is just off the dark lobby. A pine-lined, 18-hole golf course and tennis courts are close by. In addition to the lodge, there are 19 chalets, 16 cottages, and 322 campsites. No pets. Visa and MasterCard accepted. The lodge is 9 miles northeast of Guntersville. Take Hwy. 227 off U.S. 431 in Guntersville and follow the signs. Fax 571-5459. **Phone 571-5440** or 1-800-548-4553.

The **Overlook Mountain Lodge** has balconies offering a paroramic view of the lake. Some kitchenettes. The budget motel is on top of the hill overlooking the Holiday Inn on U.S. 431 South. **Phone 582-3256.**

WHERE TO EAT

*The **Northtown Cookery** on North Gunter Avenue near Hammer's discount row serves lunch and dinner in the summer, dinner only, in off-season. It's popular with residents and visitors. Phone 582-5498.

*The **Catfish Cabin** on U.S. 431 in Albertville specializes in catfish fillets and serves broiled and fried fish. The kitchen-made cole slaw is as good as you'll find. It is one of a string of catfish restaurants owned out of York, Ala. Phone 878-8170.

The **State Lodge Restaurant is worth the drive for the evening buffet, even if you're not staying overnight. Phone 582-3666.

*Reid's Restaurant** on U.S. 431 overlooks Lake Guntersville at the foot of a mountain and has been popular since Homer and Juanita Reid opened in 1962. Locals and guests enjoy the casual family atmosphere as well as the catfish and chicken fingers. Owner Van Reid also serves a vegetable lunch every day. The menu is very reasonably priced, and most chicken and seafood dishes are fried. The restaurant accommodates large groups. Open Sun.-Thurs., 5:30 a.m.-10 p.m.; Fri.-Sat., until 11. Phone 582-3162.

WHERE TO SHOP

Looking for antiques? Browse **Mervin McCormick Antiques** at 372 North Gunter across from Hammers. He's been there 20-plus years. Open Mon., Wed., Fri. and Sat. afternoon. Phone 582-3762.

The name **Hammer's** has meant bargain shopping on Sand Mountain since 1942. Stores are located in several large stores in downtowns and feature huge quantities of discount merchandise, especially fabrics. The one at 355 Gunter Ave., between the river bridge and the courthouse, also has a large selection of dolls, ranging from Madame Alexander to Norman Rockwell and Boots Tyner to Zook. Open Mon.-Sat. Closed Thanksgiving and Dec. 25. Phone 582-1977. Fax 582-1977.

ANNUAL EVENTS

Weekends in January

Eagle Awareness - Guntersville State Park - Birdwatchers flock to the state park to learn about the habitat of the nation's symbol and watch for bald eagles circling overhead.

Educational programs include seminars, a field trip at 5:30 a.m. and a 4 p.m. "return to roost" watch. Make reservations for a room at the lodge a couple of months in advance. However, if you don't have reservations and want to come on short notice, do so, because anybody can drive to the roosting sites and watch the eagles. Nobody will mind if you sit in on the lectures either. Shorter programs are held midweek.

You can see the eagles any day of the month. They leave their roosts at dawn and return before sunset after a day of fishing. The best place to see them is from the guardrail on Hwy. 227 between Lake Guntersville and Bucks Pocket State Park.

It is a scenic, 10-mile drive from the lodge. Go down the mountain and turn left at the park entrance back onto 227 and go about 6 miles. At the intersection of the four-lane road, keep on 227 to the right and go up a long hill. When you reach the powerlines crossing the road about mile marker 41, pull over and watch for eagles circling overhead about 3:30-4 p.m. Go on up the road another 1.5 miles to where the road widens for a passing lane and look on your right for the guardrail. Make a U-turn and park on the other side of the road and walk over.

Chances are other people will be there. With luck, you may see several dozen eagles circling for a landing. If you get there too late, ask someone to point them out. You must have a very powerful telescope to see the birds roosting in the trees.

Fifteen years ago, with the population decimated by DDT, only a dozen bald eagles were known to be around Lake Guntersville. Thanks to bans on certain types of pesticides and the reintroductions of 35 eagles since 1985, the numbers have grown to about 100. The hatching of the first eaglet in the state in 30 years occurred in 1990. The watch programs have grown dramatically in popularity since they began in 1987.

Eagles have been spotted as early as October and as late as February. Phone 571-5440 or 1-800-548-4553.

Second weekend of August

Summerfest - Civitan Park - Music and food are abundant at the edge of Lake Guntersville in the annual late-summer event staged by the Jaycees and the Mountain Valley Arts Council. Festivities begin with bands on Friday night and continue all day Saturday and on Sunday afternoon. Phone 582-3612 or 582-1454.

Labor Day Saturday

St. William's Seafood Festival - Carlisle Park Middle School on Sunset Drive - Parishioners boil, bake and fry fresh seafood to the delight of hundreds who line up for a meal. You can eat at the school or get a to-go dinner of Gulf Coast shrimp, gumbo, oysters on the half shell, boiled and deviled crab, flounder and, naturally, hush puppies. The church brings in 5,000 pounds of fresh gulf seafood - half of it shrimp - and cooks 400 gallons of seafood gumbo, equal to 6,400 half-pint servings. If you don't like shell fish, there's a 600-pound pile of barbecue chicken. Hours are 11-6. Phone 582-4245 or 582-7015.

HALEYVILLE

On July 4, 1861, Haleyville residents put down their tools, took up weapons and decided to fight against the South. Refusing to shoot at the flag of their fathers but willing to enter the Civil War, town and Winston County inhabitants joined the fray on the side of the Union. More than 2,000 men enlisted in the army of the proposed state Nickajack after Confederate recruiters resorted to burning homes and jailing or shooting resisters. The First Alabama Cavalry of the Federal force fought in the Carolinas, Georgia, Mississippi and Alabama. Their story is told in "Looney's Tavern" outdoor drama.

Today, Haleyville enjoys a placid, rural atmosphere as residents have returned to farming, mining and lumbering this mountainous region. Five miles east is **Bankhead National Forest**, the state's last virgin hardwood forest, covering 181,237 acres. (See Moulton listing.)

ATTRACTIONS

The DISMALS is a cluster of geological formations believed caused by an earthquake which heaved boulders and rocks into unusual angles. A remarkable number of plants, waterfalls, rock formations and other natural wonders, including "glowing" worms, are found within the "gardens." There is a small museum and gift shop.

Interesting tales are associated with the Dismals. After killing Alexander Hamilton in a duel, Aaron Burr reportedly took refuge here before being captured near Mobile. Artifacts suggest that prehistoric men lived in the canyon thousands of years ago.

The Dismals Canyon is a pleasant destination when combined with a trip to **Natural Bridge** near the intersection of U.S. 278 and Hwy. 5. Open daily. Closed in the winter. Phone 993-4559.

Getting there: It is most easily reached from Hamilton on U.S. 278. Go north on U.S. 43 through Hackleburg to Hwy. 8 and follow the signs.

NATURAL BRIDGE, a sandstone arch spanning 148 feet and 60 feet high, is reputedly the longest natural bridge east of the Rockies. The area abounds with blooming native plants from spring into fall. Although it is no rival to Virginia's Natural Bridge, the nature trails, picnic areas and a concession area offer a nice picnic and hiking outing for the family. Admission. Open daily, 8-sunset. Phone 486-5330.

Getting there: From Cullman, travel west on U.S. 278. It is about a mile west of the intersection off U.S. 278 and Hwy. 5.

CRAFTS

Jerry Brown, one of the South's best known traditional potters, spins clay which has been worked in his mule-driven mill and fires pots and other utilitarian stoneware in a kiln heated by burning oak and dry pine.

Brown is a 9th-generation potter who makes churns, plates, mixing bowls, milk pitchers, bird baths, glazed jugs and jars. He mixes wood ash or lime to produce a distinctive green glaze. He learned the craft working with his father and brother as a youngster and returned to it in 1982 after spending many years in the logging industry. His wife, Sandra, and stepson, Jeff Wilburn, are also potters.

The clay is dug 6 miles from the Browns' home and hauled by truck. His mule named Blue walks in circles to process up to 6,000 pounds of clay a day. Working at a fast pace, the trio can produce up to 200 pieces a day. Ugly "face jars" once made for storing toxins are highly desirable decoratives and sell for around $75.

Folk curator Hank Willett's film *Unbroken Tradition* chronicles the work of Brown, who was one of 13 American folk artists recognized last year by the National Endowment of the Arts. Prices range from about $7 to $80. Write Rt. 4, Box 66, Hamilton, 35570 or phone 921-9483.

Getting there: Hamilton, west of Haleyville, is located on U.S. 43 between Florence and Tuscaloosa. It can also be reached via U.S. 278 from Cullman. Follow signs along Hwy. 17 and U.S. 78 to Brown's studio.

ANNUAL EVENTS

Fourth Saturday in September

Winfield Mule Day - Teams of mules pull wagons in a parade and are judged for prizes. Winfield's Mule Day began in 1975 after Curt Estes suggested to the Chamber of Commerce that the town honor the vanishing farm animal which had meant so much to the South. Estes led the first parade with his own "Old Kate." Now, some 150 mules brought from Tennessee, other parts of Alabama and other southern states are paraded and judged individually and in pairs by physical makeup. Plow mules are judged on strength and straightness of their back line, while smaller "wagon"mules are also judged on alertness and cuteness. As a part of the festival, children can ride mules. A flea market and antique car show are part of the day-long event which honors the lowly farm animals. Mules are hybrid offsprings of a horse and a donkey and are now raised mostly as pets, although some are still used for logging in rough terrain. Phone 487-3271 or 487-4277.

HUNTSVILLE

- **Claim to fame:** Rockets that took astronauts to the Moon
- **Don't miss:** U.S. Space & Rocket Center, Alabama's Constitution Village
- **Best souvenir:** Astronaut ice cream
- **Eat at:** Eunice's, Village Inn, Green Bottle Grill
- **Shop at:** Harrison Brothers, Lawren's
- **Nickname:** America's Space Capital, Rocket City
- **Population:** 159,789
- **Tourist information:** Judy Ryals, Executive Director; Huntsville/Madison County Convention & Visitors Bureau, 700 Monroe St., Huntsville, 35801. Fax 551-2324. Phone 533-5723 or 1-800-SPACE 4 U.

Approaching Huntsville from the west on Interstate 565, you see a towering rocket at the **U.S. Space & Rocket Center** which symbolizes Huntsville's unique leadership in space exploration.

While the Saturn I rocket is impressive, it's dwarfed by the giant 363-foot Saturn V "moon rocket" or even the full-size Space Shuttle Pathfinder.

The space hardware and other exhibits displayed within the space museum - Alabama's top tourist attraction - are among the legacies of the rocket team led by **Dr. Wernher von Braun**, who came to Huntsville in 1950 to work for the U.S. Army.

The von Braun team developed the Army's Redstone, America's first rocket, which gave the nation the capability to launch an artificial satellite as early as 1954. However, it was not until the Soviets launched a basketball-sized *Sputnik* in 1959, and the U.S. Navy failed in several attempts to launch a satellite, that the Eisenhower administration gave von Braun the green light. Huntsville engineers worked virtually around the clock, test firing and perfecting engines in a test stand now on the National Register of Historic Places.

Shortly after midnight on Jan. 31, 1959, the flash of a brilliant white flame underneath a Redstone rocket lit up the launch pad at Cape Canaveral as the rocket roared into the dark Florida sky. Tense moments passed before confirmation came that the Redstone had successfully put the Explorer I satellite into proper orbit around the Earth. The Huntsville team had established America's prestige as a technology leader and demonstrated only the first in a series of scientific "firsts" to come in the decades ahead.

Less than three years later, the reliable rocket launched astronaut Alan B. Shepard, Jr. on a 15-minute sub-orbital trip. Congress preferred that space exploration be

Just days after Alan B. Shepard became the first American in space in 1961, President John F. Kennedy announced the goal of puttting astronauts on the Moon before 1970. Kennedy then came to Huntsville to see the boosters being developed by Dr. Wernher von Braun's rocket team.

When the young president asked if a Moon landing by his ambitious timetable were possible, von Braun said that it was. Asked what would be required to achieve the goal, the Huntsville scientist replied simply "The will to do it."

conducted by a civilian team rather than military and established the National Aeronautics and Space Administration. Von Braun's team members switched badges and his buildings' numbers at the arsenal were changed from green to blue. His team was the nucleus of NASA's new **Marshall Space Flight Center**. Test pilot John Glenn orbited the Earth in 1962 and the von Braun team was hard at work to meet President John Kennedy's goal of putting men on the Moon before 1970.

The space program's "glory days" of the 1960s brought together one of the world's greatest pools of scientific talent working on a single project as the town's population exploded by 50,000 in four years. So many engineers arrived in the Rocket City from other parts of the country that fewer than half of the workforce were native to the state.

For the Apollo moon program, the Huntsville team of NASA and its contractors developed the series of Saturn rockets, including the massive Saturn V, the world's most powerful rocket. The successful launch on July 15, 1969, propelled three astronauts toward the Moon and Neil Armstrong stepped onto the surface five days later. The rockets worked flawlessly for the seven Apollo missions, but the public euphoria waned and Congress cut back funding for NASA.

Many of the Germans retired and von Braun transferred to Washington. The new Marshall management developed the Skylab space station which housed three crews of astronauts in the mid-1970s, collecting a wealth of scientific data still being analyzed today.

Despite a major effort in the post-Apollo era to reduce reliance on federal government programs for the city's economic base, fully a quarter of all non-farm jobs are with the U.S. Army or NASA.

Although NASA centers at Houston and Cape Canaveral are much better known to the public, the NASA center in Huntsville receives a larger share of the agency's budget (24 percent) for the space shuttle and other programs. An estimated 3,500 NASA employees. on an annual payroll in excess of $158 million, manage the shuttle's main engines, external tank and solid rocket boosters, as well as other non-shuttle projects.

In addition, several thousand contractor employees are designing major components of the space station *Freedom* as a result of Boeing being selected prime contractor over another contractor, which would have based work in New Orleans.

The **U.S. Army**, however, remains the largest employer in Huntsville. The Army Missiles, Armaments and Chemical Command, Strategic Defense Command and Army Materiel Command - among others - employ 9,000 civilians and almost 2,000 military specialists with an annual payroll of nearly $380 million on programs ranging from Patriot and Avenger missiles to "star wars" research. The Pentagon's national base closing program will bring thousands of new jobs to Huntsville in the next several years.

Although the average person can't drive around **Redstone Arsenal**, you can drive by the SDI or the "star wars" headquarters in the red brick building where about 1,400 military and civilian employees work. It is at 106 Wynn Dr., north of the space museum across I-565.

To the north of I-565 exit 14 lies **Cummings Research Park**, a research and development campus with 16,000 high-tech employees, many of whom are under contract to the Army and NASA. Only Silicon Valley and the Raleigh-Durham Research Triangle have more high-tech engineers.

Huntsville is home to two of Alabama's four Fortune 500 companies. Intergraph and SCI each are homegrown, computer-related giants employing more than 4,000 persons locally with annual revenues exceeding $1 billion. Each was started by a man who left government work to form private companies.

Some 12,000 engineers are in the city's total workforce of about 133,000 and more than 700 residents have doctoral degrees in non-medical professions.

The population has increased tenfold since the first rocket scientist arrived in town four decades ago and transformed the small cotton town into America's space capital. Growth has not been confined to the city limits. The neighboring city of Madison was a sleepy town of 4,000 in 1980, but soared to 14,904 in only a decade.

Huntsville and Atlanta share the top two spots for the highest average incomes in the South.

The influx of educated, high-tech workers has contributed to a strong sense of support for education and the arts, and protecting the environment, in particular, limiting residential development on the slopes of mountains overlooking the city.

Kiplinger's Personal Finance Magazine lists Huntsville among the nation's best 15 smaller and medium-sized cities in which to live, citing lifestyle, economics and environment. It is also featured in a retirement manual of the nation's 50 best places to live and retire.

Long before rocket scientists came to Huntsville for a base to explore "the last frontier" of space, it was a highly desirable area in the new nation's westward movement. Settling the land of "the great bend" of the Tennessee River had been a goal of American westward expansion since the close of the American Revolution. Claimed alike by Chickasaws, Creeks and Cherokees, as well as the State of Georgia, this fertile piedmont became the object of many illegal land-sale schemes.

In 1796, President George Washington appointed an agent to secure "the great bend" through payments and treaties. Between 1802 and 1806, the land was legally annexed as American territory.

A major problem in the new territory was the presence of 5,000 illegal squatters, including John Hunt, a Tennessee pioneer, who had moved his family into a log cabin near a gushing limestone spring 10 miles north of the Tennessee River. Like many others, Hunt had no legal claim to the land, and when the Federal Land Office opened in 1809 in Nashville, **LeRoy Pope** of Petersburg, Ga., purchased the choice 160 acres surrounding the spring, the site of Hunt's cabin.

Pope and other wealthy Georgians wanted to develop a town by the spring to serve as a seat for the newly designated Madison County which the governor of the Mississippi Territory created on Dec. 13, 1808, on the eve of land sales. From his purchase, Pope deeded 60 acres around the spring for a town to be named **Twickenham** in honor of the country home of the English poet, Alexander Pope. The name was never popular and by 1811 the citizens changed the name to **Huntsville** to honor the original pioneer.

Huntsville's growth was rapid from 1810 to 1819 because the land office was in Huntsville and because of a new westward surge into the Mississippi Territory. A visitor to the town in 1817 marveled at the two-story courthouse and market on the public square surrounded by stores and craft shops. The town contained more than 260 brick houses as well as a weekly newspaper, a bank, a library, a Masonic lodge, a school and numerous cultural organizations. Anne Royall wrote, "You will hear a great deal of this city in the future."

On March 2, 1819, Congresss passed the Enabling Act authorizing the people of the Alabama Territory to adopt a constitution prior to becoming a state. While a capital city was under construction at Cahawba near Selma, the **Constitutional Convention** was held here during the summer and fall of 1819. Therefore, Huntsville has the distinction of hosting the writing of the state's first constitution, the inauguration of the first governor and the sessions of the first legislature for the new state.

Because the fertile land was ideal for cotton, plantations north of the Tennessee River flourished.

The Bell Cotton Factory was established in 1832 as the first mill in the state to convert raw cotton into sheeting, shirting, denims and yarn. Cotton milling would play a role in the town's economy for the next 150 years. Huntsville was the cotton trading center of the region during the 1840s and '50s when merchants, attorneys and bankers built impressive town homes in the neighborhood now known as Twickenham.

Throughout the antebellum period, Huntsville furnished political leadership to the state and nation. It also remained a commercial, social and cultural center in the heart of a rich agricultural hinterland. River transportation, stagecoach lines and the railroad between Memphis and Charleston all contributed to the town's prominence in the valley.

After Abraham Lincoln's election as president in 1860, many Southerners advocated secession from the nation. North Alabama was divided on the issue. After secession, support in Huntsville for secession solidified and native son Leroy Pope Walker served Jefferson Davis as the first secretary of war. Walker issued the telegram order from Montgomery for Southern troops to fire on Fort Sumter, in effect, beginning the Civil War.

In order to control troop movement on the Memphis & Charleston Railroad, Federal troops occupied Huntsville from April-September, 1862, and July, 1863-April, 1865. Numerous homes were requisitioned for use as Union officers' quarters and troops were stationed in schools and churches. As a result, the town was spared the wholesale destruction by occupying forces as occurred in nearby Decatur. Only a few structures were destroyed, and those by accidental fires. The legendary Greene Academy, however, was deliberately destroyed.

The defeat of the Confederacy left many people in Huntsville economically destitute and recovery became a slow and tedious process for the next 20 years.

Eventually, the town's business leaders encouraged Northern and Western capitalists to join them in textile and real estate projects which improved the economic base of the area. Tourism was encouraged through the development of **Monte Sano Mountain** as a vacation and health resort. The development of nurseries and fruit orchards also added new dimensions to agricultural pursuits.

The World War I period and the decade which followed were prosperous years for the people of the area. By 1930 the city could point with pride to its downtown expansion, which added three tall structures to its skyline. But the years of the Great Depression caused a major decline in its industries and commercial enterprises.

Life in the cotton mill town changed when the **U.S. Army** needed a place to manufacture chemical weapons at the beginning of World War II. The Army wanted a large tract of government land located inland and not within the enemy's bombing reach. Local businessmen convinced John Sparkman that it would bring jobs to the district and the congressman campaigned successfully to locate the chemical plant here.

Some 39,000 acres of cotton fields became **Redstone Arsenal** and workers built thousands of chemical weapons and other ammunition during the war. At war's end, however, the arsenal struggled to remain open.

The salvation turned out to be missiles and rockets when the Army decided to consolidate its missiles and rocket research. Sparkman again played a key role in convincing the Army to bring **Dr. von Braun** and his 117 German rocket scientists to Redstone. The era of high-technology was about to begin, ironically in a mill town of 16,437 people.

TRANSPORTATION

You can fly into **Huntsville International Airport** on most major carriers, connecting in Atlanta for Delta, Nashville or Dallas for American, Memphis for Northwest and Chicago for United.

More than 1 million passengers a year board from the newly renovated boarding areas and high-tech terminal. The airport has 80 daily jet departures, give or take a few, plus service on commuters. A handsome mural hanging over the lobby showcases the city's role in space exploration, past, present and future.

A number of major rental cars companies have counters opposite baggage claim. Several others operate from off-site.

Most hotels offer free shuttle van service on request. Taxi fare to downtown is about $20 while the Execution Connection van operation near baggage claim charges $15 for the first person, $1 additional for the second.

The airport is located at I-565 exit 7.

TOURIST INFORMATION CENTERS

You can get a wealth of information on attractions and special events at a pair of tourist information centers operated by the **Huntsville/Madison County Convention & Visitors Bureau**. The main information center is in the **Von Braun Civic Center** on Monroe Street. It is staffed Mon.-Sat. 9 a.m.-5 p.m. and Sun. afternoons. The center on the second level of the airport is also staffed every day. The visitors bureau is also the office to call if you are planning a group tour or convention. Phone 533-5723 or 1-800-SPACE 4 U.

HUNTSVILLE ATTRACTIONS

U.S. SPACE & ROCKET CENTER is America's largest hands-on showcase of the space program. The earth's largest space museum complex of three buildings contains the actual Apollo 16 spacecraft returned from the Moon, a moon rock, spacesuits and rare training equipment astronauts used while preparing for missions in space. This is Alabama's most popular tourist attraction and draws more than 500,000 visitors a year, some 70 percent of them from out of state.

It is also home to the internationally acclaimed **U.S. Space Camp** which draws thousands of youngsters and adults from around the globe for realistic training in space and aviation simulators.

Space museum: In the largest exhibit hall, the real spacecraft, satellites and mockups are suspended overhead. See the actual Apollo 16 command module which took astronauts to the Moon on the next to last mission. Other important exhibits are the trainers used by Mercury, Gemini and Apollo crews. You can walk inside the model of the Skylab where astronauts trained before being launched into space to live aboard America's first space station.

What distinguishes Huntsville from NASA centers in Florida and Texas are the number of "hands-on" astronaut-training devices which visitors enjoy. The technology has been simplified so that people of all ages are comfortable trying their hand at being an astronaut. For example, you can fire a rocket engine, handle materials robotically, guide yourself through space and view the Hubble Space Telescope (also a Huntsville project) - all without leaving the ground.

The most exciting addition to the space center in a decade is the spectacular "Journey to Jupiter" experience which zooms visitors on a breathtaking trip through the solar system. After a pre-flight briefing sets the right mood, you board the futuristic ship which then dashes and darts around orbiting stations and colonies to tour the largest planet in the universe. You cruise by moons and stars before passing through the gaseous rings of Jupiter. The dynamic motion of the "spacecraft" leaves you feeling you've *really* been in hyperspace.

When you're ready for more astronaut training, you choose from several simulators. Strap yourself in the spinning Centrifuge and feel the tug of gravity which astronauts feel during launch. Walk aboard the Spaceliner for a brief "flight" aboard the space shuttle. Allow 60-90 minutes to tour the museum.

The young people dressed in smart blue flightsuits you are likely to see are attending one of a myriad of programs under the umbrella name of **U.S. Space Camp**, a high-tech education program which has mushroomed to include training centers in Florida, Japan and Belgium.

What began in 1982 for a few children a week has expanded into a score of educational programs. They range from astronaut training for 10-year-olds to the advanced **Aviation Challenge** jet pilot instruction for kids, teachers and other adults. You can watch Space Camp participants train in realistic shuttle simulators and "mission controls" in the Training Center of the main building.

However, the Space Camp Habitat and the Aviation Challenge training center for future "top guns" are open only to family members during registration and after graduation.

Behind the museum is the world's largest collection of rockets which were developed in Huntsville to put astronauts and satellites into orbit. Huntsville scientists and engineers developed the rockets to launch the first satellite (Explorer I atop a Redstone), put the first astronaut (Alan B. Shepard atop a modified Redstone) into space and took the first men to the Moon riding a Saturn V rocket.

Just over a small rise from Rocket Park is *Pathfinder*, the world's only full-size space shuttle equipped with main engines actually used on launches. The dull orange external fuel tank was originally used by NASA in developing the shuttle's propulsion system.

Spacedome Theater: The giant-screen **Omnimax** gets rave reviews from virtually everyone who sees a feature here. While seated inside a 67-foot planetarium dome screen, your entire field of vision is swept by scenes of Earth hundreds of miles below. As the continents and oceans glide by, you feel suspended in space. Being seated comfortably inside the Huntsville theater gives you the feeling of being in space without actually going.

The 70-millimeter projection system provides incredibly realistic trips. It puts you at the launch pad when the shuttle thunders into the sky. It flies you over volcanoes, earthquakes and typhoons. It can transport you into the future. In essence, it takes you places you never thought you'd see.

The films, such as "Blue Planet" and "The Dream is Alive," are made possible because astronauts carry specially-built cameras aboard the shuttle to give viewers a first-hand impression of what *they* see in space. In fact, this theater is the one where those astronauts are trained to use Omnimax cameras. Although Imax theaters with *flat* screens are located at the Kennedy Space Center and the Smithsonian in Washington, the domed screen in Huntsville is the favorite of the astronauts.

Films are shown throughout the day. If you need help climbing steps, an elevator can lift you into the theater.

NASA Bus Tour: To see where scientists and engineers develop rockets and plan future missions, take the NASA tour to see inside NASA's **Marshall Space Flight Center**, the nation's top propulsion research center. Huntsville scientists and engineers developed the giant Saturn rockets that took men to the moon, as well as the boosters which launch the space shuttles. Marshall developed the Skylab space station in the 1970s and is currently designing the space station *Freedom*. Other responsibilities include management of Spacelab missions flown aboard the shuttle.

Von Braun's team was the nucleus of the Marshall center, which has grown to become NASA's largest research center. It is located within **Redstone Arsenal**, the 38,000-acre military post which is also home to several of the U.S. Army's most important programs. The Strategic Defense Command, for example, is responsible for research, development, production and worldwide support of missiles, rockets and related programs.

The U.S. Space & Rocket Center is open every day except Dec. 25. Hours are 8 a.m.-7 p.m. in the summer and 9-6 the rest of the year. You can purchase a ticket which provides admission to the museum, Spacedome and NASA tour. Phone 837-3400.

Getting there: The U.S. Space & Rocket Center is located at I-565 exit 15.

ALABAMA'S CONSTITUTION VILLAGE - To commemorate the 150th anniversary of Alabama's statehood, an extraordinary effort was undertaken to recreate the historic neighborhood associated with the dramatic events of the summer of 1819 in Huntsville. Years of painstaking research and archaeological excavations were required to verify the plans of the structures. When the completed village opened to the public in 1982, the buildings were so authentic that some older residents who had played as children in some of the original buildings were unable to tell that the structures were new.

After purchasing tickets at the **Confectionery Shop** on Gates Avenue, begin your tour inside **Constitution Hall**, the two-story wooden building on the corner of Franklin and Gates. The simplicity of Walker Allen's carpenter shop belies its historic significance. It was inside that eight delegates from Huntsville and 36 from other parts of the state met from July 5 to Aug. 2 to write a constitution for the future state. Several delegates had gained significant experience in governments in the states from which they migrated. This group included three former congressmen and a pair of Supreme Court judges from North Carolina.

Chief among these delegates was **William Wyatt Bibb** of Georgia. He had resigned from the U.S. Senate due to public anger after he voted himself a pay raise and moved to the new frontier in Alabama. U.S. Secretary of the Treasury William Crawford, a native Georgian who handled political appointments for the territory, named his friend as the territorial governor. Bibb chaired two sessions of the Territorial Legislature which met north of Mobile at the now abandoned town of St. Stephens in 1818.

John Williams Walker, one of the founders of Huntsville and son-in-law of LeRoy Pope, chaired the convention, and John Campbell, another Huntsville attorney, was secretary. Clement Clay, still another Huntsville attorney, chaired the committee that drafted the Constitution. Indian fighter Andrew Jackson, who owned land near Florence and had close ties to Huntsville businessmen, visited the convention in Walker Allen's carpenter shop during the deliberations. Four years earlier, Jackson and his men had camped in Huntsville on their way home to Tennessee after defeating the Creek Indian Nation at the Battle of Horseshoe Bend.

Because of the caliber of educated delegates, most of whom were prominent community leaders mindful of the wishes of the more numerous small farmers and poorer residents, Alabama's 1819 Constitution was one of the nation's few original state instruments to last without major changes until the Civil War began.

The first General Assembly returned to the carpenter's shop in October and elected William Bibb as governor. They also named John W. Walker, one of the founders of Huntsville, and William Rufus King, founder of Selma, to represent the northern and southern parts of the state in the U.S. Senate. Alabama officially became a state on Dec. 9, 1819. In the years to follow, the 44 who served as delegates would provide the new state with six governors, six U.S. senators and six state Supreme Court justices.

Political importance aside, the scene inside the cabinet shop today primarily focuses on the craft of the carpenter, Walker Allen. A master cabinetmaker demonstrates woodworking tools, lathes and marquetry. You are invited to turn the great wheel lathe and watch a knife shape the design of a table leg.

You approach the **Stephen Neal House** from the rear by passing the Neal stables, barn and detached kitchen. Inside the small kitchen, a domestic skills interpreter is usually busy cooking meats and vegetables over an open fire. She prepares bread, cheese, sausage and sweets from 19th-century "receipts," depending on the ingredients available. Children are usually intrigued by the "ugly" jar which was used to store toxic ingredients.

Enter the **Neal House** through the back door to peek in the formal dining room with period antiques. The large number of chairs suggests this was also Neal's office. Among other responsibilities, he was the first sheriff of the county. Across the hall, inspect a barn loom used for making fabric and two spinning wheels in the formal family room used for turning wool or cotton into thread to be used to weave cloth. Young girls prepared cotton for spinning by lamplight while adults might have played cards or other parlor games.

While the buildings provide a realistic setting to recall the 1819 convention, the village becomes far more than an architectural tour because of the manner in which the "townspeople" perform routine chores. In some instances, you can participate.

An early 19th-century calendar is used. In the spring, interpreters quilt and weave baskets, craft furniture, churn butter, make lye soap, create a bee skep from straw and prepare sheep's fleece for spinning and weaving. In the summer, the men and women also weed and hoe the garden and pick vegetables to "put up" preserves. They make beer and wine in August in their spare time. In the fall, they pick cotton from the small patch and use colors from vegetables and other natural sources to dye textiles. They also pickle and preserve food for the winter. During the colder months, they dip candles, smoke meats, grind sausage and prepare the garden for spring.

Across the garden is the **John Boardman Complex** where you enter from the rear to see slaves' and servants' quarters, the newspaper shop where the first Constitution was printed, and a library. Boardman was editor of a weekly paper, *The Alabama Republican*. An historic interpretor uses the Ramage press, ink stand and type stand to demonstrate how newspapers of the period were printed. It was here that Boardman printed the official *Journal of the Constitutional Convention* and the first Consitution itself. Within the Boardman complex is a small law office with a separate entrance from the street which housed the state's first incorporated library. Library subscribers were allowed to check out books twice a week during the attorney's dinner hour.

Pre-scheduled classes of elementary children may visit the "discovery house," a learning center designed to instill a positive sense of history at a young age. It is upstairs in the 1848 **Humphrey-Rodgers House**, a brick Georgian Revival townhouse. It wasn't always here. The 330-ton house was moved from its original location on the corner of Clinton and Monroe near the Von Braun Civic Center. The ground floor is available for group tours and receptions.

The museum complex houses traveling exhibits from such institutions as the Smithsonian and also stages a variety of seasonal special events which attract out-of-towners, as well as locals.

Before you leave, take a few minutes to visit the two-story Federal brick **Clement Clay Law Office** which housed Clay's law practice. It was in this small building that Clay, who had served in the state's Territorial Legislature, drafted portions of the Constitution. After Alabama became a state, he would be the first chief justice of the Alabama Supreme Court at age 30. He later was elected governor and eventually resigned to serve in the U.S. Senate. He rented the upstairs to the federal land surveyor who platted and sold land throughout the Tennessee Valley, and the downstairs was used as the local post office. You can see the types of chain links used to mark off and divide land.

School groups come in large numbers on weekday mornings in April and May, so families and senior groups should visit in the afternoons.

Plan 90 minutes for a complete guided tour, but you are free to more from building to building at your convenience. Save enough time afterwards to walk around the Twickenham historic district. (The village is close to the building where city court is held. If you park in a metered space on the street, be forewarned that police patrol regularly and unfortunately do give parking tickets.) Open Mar. 1-Dec. 23. Open Mon.-Sat., 9-5; last tour begins at 4. Closed each Sun., Easter and Thanksgiving Day. Admission. Phone 535-6565.

Getting there: It is just a block south of the courthouse square, right behind the Harrison Brothers Hardware Store. From I-565, take exit 19 C (Washington), turn right and go 4 blocks on Jefferson/Madison. Or from Governors Drive, turn on Madison near Huntsville Hospital and drive to Gates Avenue.

ALISTAIR VINEYARDS grows and bottles varieties of wine grapes in picturesque Hurricane Valley near New Market. The vineyards started in 1981 when Dr. Donald "Mac" and Noel McCalistair planted grapevines in their backyard as a hobby to make a little wine. It has grown into a small, successful farm winery, with their first commercial vintage coming in 1988. Now, four of their 45 acres are planted in grapes and one with cherries. The totally self-contained operation begins with grapes on the vine and ends with neatly labeled and sealed bottles ready to be sold.

You may sample wines in the tasting room, watch a video explaining the whole process and tour the winery each Sat. from May-Dec.

Getting there: The vineyard is 15 miles north of Huntsville. Go north on Memorial Parkway to Winchester Road, turn right and go 8.1 miles to County Lake Road and turn right. Go 2.9 miles to Hurricane Road. Turn left and go one more mile. It is located at 2978 Hurricane. Phone 379-3527.

BIG SPRING PARK begins near the site of John Hunt's cabin which marks the town's founding in 1805. Water from the spring formed the Indian Creek Canal, which was used for decades prior to the Civil War to float bales of cotton from the cotton warehouses on the square 10 miles to the river.

The large volume of fresh water comes from beneath the rocky bluff dominated by the 1835 First Alabama Bank and flows into a lagoon surrounded by a handsomely landscaped park. A bright red Oriental "friendship" bridge, donated by a Japanese major general formerly stationed at Redstone Arsenal, provides an attractive walkway over a narrow portion of the lake. At the edge of the park facing the Hilton is a patriotic monument topped by an"eternal" flame first lit by President Richard Nixon on Washington's Birthday in 1974.

The lake is home to waterfowl which paddle along, watchful of picnickers who might toss some bread their way. It is a beautiful park with 50 cherry trees lining the water's edge. Walking on the grass is permitted.

Getting there: It is immediately west of the Courthouse Square toward the Von Braun Civic Center.

BOTANICAL GARDEN is a maturing public gardens near the Space & Rocket Center with plans to reflect the city's aerospace legacy. In addition to a variety of handsome gardens already in place, an enclosed biosphere for plants is on the drawing boards.

You can see rare plants native to North Alabama, walk around the aromatic herb garden and stroll the dogwood trail where annual plants like the shasta daisy are mixed with blue forget-me-nots. In summer, daylily beds are alive with dozens of varities. The most photographed residents are Australian black swans who paddle the lake near the rose garden.

The entrance on Bob Wallace Avenue is marked by three fluted stone columns from the 1914 Madison County Courthouse razed in 1964. The city/county garden opened in 1988 on land which was originally the northeast corner of Redstone Arsenal.

The best time to visit is during Cornocopia on the first Saturday in October for a plant sale, an art show and sale, hayrides, Halloween ghost stories and food. Other special events include a spring plant sale, moonlight stroll, fall flower show and Christmas greenery sale. Admission. Open Mon.-Sat., 9-5; Sun., 1-5. Closed Dec. 25. Phone 830-4447.

Getting there: A block west of the intersection with Jordan Lane. To reach the garden from the U.S. Space & Rocket Center, stay on the access road past the Marriott and continue east on Bob Wallace.

BURRITT MUSEUM AND PARK is notable for its architecture and surroundings, as well as the contents of the house museum. Completed in 1938 for a prominent physician and inventor, the 11-room house is in the shape of a capital 'H,' with the curved front overlooking Huntsville from the top of Monte Sano Mountain. The ground floor rooms are brightly lighted by numerous windows with sweeping mountain vistas. Interesting interior details of wood and plaster give the house a truly unique character. The interior walls are filled with 2,200 bales of wheat straw insulation to help cool the house.

Antiques fill the large parlor and family sterling silver is displayed in the dining room. The other rooms are given over to an interesting amalgam of exhibitry. As a museum, it follows in the tradition of a large house becoming the repository of often unrelated collections to become a city museum. Such was the case when the owner died childless and gave his home to the city in 1955, along with 167 mountain acres now laced with trails open to the public.

Encased exhibits range from mineral chunks and Indian pottery fragments to 19th-century surgical instruments and relics of the "first public water system west of the Appalachians." Most curious of all are tiny oil paintings on cobwebs achieved 50 years ago by a local artist. Other curiousities are tiny scenes which were scratched onto oak leaves a half century ago.

Behind the house is a collection of pioneer buildings, including the Balch House, cabins, smokehouse, blacksmith shop, barn and 19th-century frame church. Also on the estate are nature trails marked for the handicapped.

Special events include Earth Day in April, Earth Camp, a summer Folklife Festival, an Indian heritage event in October and candlelight Christmas. A Christmas gift shop opens in early November. Burritt's luminaries prior to Christmas are a Huntsville tradition.

The museum grounds, which offer the best view of downtown Huntsville, are open free year round. The house museum is open daily, except Mon., from Mar. 1 to late-Dec. Allow an hour. Free except for special events. Phone 536-2882.

Getting there: Travel east on U.S. 231 (Governors Drive) up Monte Sano and turn left at the crest of the mountain on Monte Sano Boulevard.

CHURCH OF THE NATIVITY is a beautiful Episcopal church a block from the courthouse square. It is one of the most pristine examples of Ecclesiological Gothic architecture in the South and, as a result, is a National Historic Landmark. A 151-foot metal spire tops the brick sanctuary completed in 1859. The dark interior has a narrow nave flanked by clerestory windows with stained glass designs of Christian symbols (keys, dove, anchor, lamps, grapes, etc.). It seats 250 worshippers.

The famed New York team of Frank Wills and Henry Dudley, who designed St. John's in Montgomery and Trinity in Mobile several years earlier, were the architects. Of the 17 existing churches they designed, it is among the least altered.

It was the only church not confiscated by Union soldiers who occupied the town during the Civil War. Soldiers had been ordered to use it as a stable for their horses, but did not. The church's name is appropriate because the congregation was organized in December of 1843.

Go through the front courtyard into a small hallway and enter the first door on the left. The best time to visit is in the morning when the sunlight shines through tall stained glass windows of Jesus flanked by the Apostles. Notice the rich colors, particularly the reds and greens in Jesus's robe, and the dark blue starry field surrounding His head.

Getting there: It is a block east of Harrison Brothers, 212 Eustis at Green.

HARRISON BROTHERS Hardware Store has operated on the town square for nearly a century and retains an atmosphere of a true original. Two brothers opened the business in 1879 as a wholesale tobacco operation and moved to the present location in 1897 and added hardware, furniture and crockery. Following a fire in 1901, they enlarged the store. When the last of second-generation owners died in 1983 and the store was closed, members of the non-profit Historic Huntsville Foundation didn't want the city to lose a piece of living history. They bought the building and inventory and reopened the following year.

Enter past wooden screen doors into a narrow, dark building literally jammed with old merchandise on the upper shelves not for sale and new houseware gadgets on lower shelves to buy and take home. For a relatively dark place - complete with ancient safe, cash register and squeaky wooden floors, it is cheery and full of discovery. Homemade jams and jellies, crockery and other gifts are available. If you've searched in vain for black iron skillets or fine wooden rockers, this is the place. Dozens of volunteers take turns staffing the store. Open Mon.-Fr., 9-5; Sat., 10-2. Free. Phone 536-3631.

Getting there: It is at 124 South Side on the courthouse square just off Franklin.

RIDE THE TROLLEY

For a truly memorable way to see the exteriors of Huntsville's historic attractions, ride the bright red Huntsville Trolley.

It shuttles throughout the day along a regular route of the downtown attractions. The trolley conductor narrates the historic sites along the way. You pay $1 and can step off at any of the museums to tour and board the next trolley which stops by a half hour later.

After leaving the depot, you pass the Von Braun Civic Center housing the Huntsville Museum of Art and the Tourist Information Center. You ride through the Twickenham historic district and pass the 1819 Weeden House Museum and Alabama's Constitution Village. The trolley passes the historic Harrison Brothers store on the courthouse square and through Big Spring Park en route back to the depot. For exact departure times, phone 539-1860.

HUNTSVILLE DEPOT MUSEUM is one of the nation's oldest railroad passenger depots, built in 1860, and now adapted as a lively transportation museum. The three-story brick building was designed to serve as the local passenger house and corporate offices for the Eastern Division headquarters of the Memphis & Charleston Railroad.

When confiscated by Union forces during the Civil War, it functioned as a prison for captured Confederate militia, a billet for Union troops en route to major battles and a hospital for the wounded.

The M&C used the depot until Southern Railway bought the line in 1898. Southern operated passenger service until its Memphis-to-New York streamliner *Tennessean* made its final run in 1968.

The building is well preserved and appears much as it did in 1860. Although the brick was originally unpainted, the current color scheme of gold painted brick and dark green shutters reflects the corporate colors of Southern Railway.

Among the famous personalities who passed through the depot are Confederates Robert E. Lee and Jefferson Davis; social activists Helen Keller, Susan B. Anthony and Carrie Nation; bank robbers Frank and Jesse James; entertainers P.T. Barnum, Buffalo Bill Cody and Calamity Jane; and politicians William McKinley, Theodore Roosevelt and James A. Garfield. The German rocket team also arrived in town at the depot.

Your guided tour begins with a narrated slide program on the history of Huntsville and explains the depot's role in the city's development. Three Disney-type animated characters depict a typical crew of telegrapher, engineer and mechanic who explain their jobs. Afterwards, a guide leads you upstairs to see exhibits of early commerce, including a scale diorama of the depot during the Civil War. You can see examples of names, comments and other graffiti written on the walls of the upper story by Civil War soldiers and prisoners.

Visit the gift shop behind the depot for t-shirts, post cards and reproduction railway memorabilia. Open March-Dec. on Tues.-Sun. for tours on the hour. Closed Mon. and each winter.

Getting there: The depot is at 320 Church St. at the I-565 exit 19 ramp. Phone 539-1860.

MAPLE HILL CEMETERY is the city's oldest burial ground, dating from 1818. Five Alabama governors, Confederate Secretary of War Leroy Pope Walker, Studebaker president Russel Erskine and local poet Maria Howard Weeden are among the thousands buried in the beautiful walled cemetery. Huge cedar trees and dogwoods shade the statuary of angels, lambs and simple stones marking final resting places. The ideal times to visit are spring when the pink and white dogwoods bloom and October when the sugar maple leaves turn golden. Open during daylight hours.

Getting there: Go east on Governors Drive past the hospitals, turn left on California and drive until you see the cemetery on the right. Drive inside and park. Phone 532-7439.

MONTE SANO STATE PARK covers 2,140 acres on top of 1,800-foot Monte Sano Mountain and affords a recreation area, picnic spots and scenic overlooks. Well marked nature trails range over beautiful hills overlooking the city. An attractive Japanese teahouse in a garden stands in a small clearing by a wandering creek. A variety of native and Japanese plants and demarcated trails are nearby. The trail to the garden begins at the country store across from the ranger headquarters. A number of the German rocket scientists, who built homes on Monte Sano because it reminded them of their native Bavaria, still live nearby.

Getting there: Go east on Governors Drive (U.S. 431) up the mountain and follow the signs. Phone 534-3757.

MUSEUM OF ART contains a collection of 1,800 works, including paintings, sculpture and historical and contemporary prints by such artists as Audubon, Currier and Ives, Warhol and Estes. The museum has a small, but excellent collection of furniture, paintings, watercolors, crafts and other media by artists with Alabama connections. These are shown on a rotating basis in the first gallery on your right from the foyer and in the Partnership Gallery.

Major traveling exhibitions of period and contemporary art are presented regularly. Of the annual attendance of about 70,000 visitors a year, more than 10,000 are school students on field trips and another 5,000 adults participate in family education programs. Allow a half hour. Open Tues., 10-9; Wed.-Fri., 10-5; Sat., 9-5; Sun., 1-5. Closed Mon. and major holidays. Free.

Getting there: The museum is in the east wing of the Von Braun Civic Center. It is scheduled to move to a new building on the opposite end of Big Spring Park in 1996. Phone 535-4350.

TALLULAH BANKHEAD BIRTHPLACE is a three-story building on the southeast corner of the courthouse square. She was born in a second-story apartment on Jan. 31, 1902, where her parents were staying. Her mother died soon after her birth and was buried in Maple Hill Cemetery.

Her father and uncle became two of America's most powerful congressmen while Tallulah carved a reputation as one of the most colorful actresses either side of the Atlantic. Her off-stage behavior - such as turning cartwheels sans undergarments - often eclipsed her talent. The trademark of the 5' 3" Southern aristocrat was calling everyone "Dah-ling" because she couldn't remember people's names.

Tallulah left the family home in Jasper for New York at age 15. She took the English stage and society by storm at age 21 and remained abroad for eight years. Her most memorable roles in the U.S. were as Regina Giddens in *The Little Foxes* and Sabina in *The Skin of Our Teeth*. Her movies were mostly forgettable, with the exception of Alfred Hitchcock's 1943 *Lifeboat*.

The 1845 Schiffman Building was altered in 1895 in the Romanesque Revival style. The Bankheads' apartment has since been carved into offices. There is no marker identifying the building's historical connection. Private.

Getting there: Corner of 231 East Side Square at Eustis.

TWICKENHAM HISTORIC DISTRICT contains the homes built by the early physicians and merchants of the town. Many were built as part of working plantations located outside the city limits. As Huntsville grew, the land between the plantations was sold and housing became more dense. It is one of the most concentrated neighborhoods of antebellum homes in the South.

Although the 1819 Weeden House Museum is the only one open to the public, you should walk around the neighborhood to admire the architecture. Since Huntsville was the first town to be settled by whites on land obtained by treaty from the Indians, the early homes reflect the scale and design of houses in Virginia and the Carolinas. The neighborhood is a showcase of the talents of Virginia native George Steele (1798-1855), a self-taught architect who moved here in 1818. For the town's planters, he designed Federal and Greek Revival homes between 1824 and 1849, including eight remaining in Twickenham. In addition, Steele designed the bank on the square which was begun in 1835. Other early houses were designed by architects Thomas and William Brandous, whose contributions are just beginning to be recognized.

Union soldiers occupied Huntsville periodically from 1862 to 1865. There was never any major battle here to endanger the houses and citizens, therefore, the town survived the war with limited destruction. The town grew slowly during Reconstruction and the Victorian period, therefore, many of the houses' facades were never modernized.

Although these homes were considered bargains in the 1960s, real estate values have escalated and the area between Franklin and Randolph streets is the most socially desirable in town.

TWICKENHAM HISTORIC DISTRICT WALKING TOUR

The handsome homes of Twickenham are too beautiful to absorb simply by driving through, so the following 45-minute tour only works on foot. Park in the metered parking lot in front of the **Episcopal Church of the Nativity** a block east of the courthouse at the corner of Eustis and Green. Walk to the historic **Harrison Brothers** hardware store on the square and face the courthouse to get your bearings. To your left is the 1835 **First Alabama Bank**. To your right on the corner is the 1845 Schiffman Building where actress Tallulah Bankhead was born.

*At **Village Inn**, turn right down Franklin Street.*
***Alabama's Constitution Village**. Enter from Gates Street.*
After touring Constitution Village, return to Franklin Street.
403 - Victorian residence houses office of U.S. Rep. Bud Cramer
405 - 1821 Bradley house is now lawyers' office

At Williams, detour a half-block to 1818 Public Inn and return
501 - 1902 Classical Revival house has stained glass *Iliad* scene
515 - 1819 home of Dr. Alexander Erskine, partner to Fearn
517 - 1820 home of Dr. Tom Fearn, attended Confederate Congress
516 - 1819 Mastin home with original siding and chimneys
527 - 1818 Erskine home has blue panes thought to "promote health"
558 - 1825 home with 1857 facade, birthplace of John Hunt Morgan, Confederate hero
601 - 1835 Hollowell porticoed cottage had basement dining room
600 - 1818 home to fifth generation of Dr. John Bassett family

Turn on Cruse Alley for 2 blocks, right on Adams Street
600 - 1825 Cruse house altered in 1920s
604 - 1871 John Weeden House rebuilt in 1913 as Classical Revival
702 - 1858 Episcopal rectory "haunted" by rector Banister
704 - 1853 antebellum split-level home of UA president Carlos Smith

Cross the street and go back up Adams
619 - 1875 house later home of Sen. John Sparkman who was instrumental in bringing German rocket scientists to town. Sparkman was the Democratic nominee for vice president in 1952.
603 - Moore-Rhett House, distinguished by the tall 1920 portico on the house. A small house built about 1826, it was expanded about 1860 with a three-story Italianate Revival facade. In 1892, the home was painted yellow for a formal ball honoring Samuel Moore's award-winning Jersey cow. Lily Flagg, the Chicago world's fair champion butterfat producer, stood on a platform of honor on the patio and was toasted by hundreds of guests. Civic leader Harry Rhett, a Moore descendant, has lived here since 1964.
528 - 1825 Yeatman home designed by Steele, expanded 1853
517 - 1848 McDowell house built backwards while owner was abroad
518 - 1835 Powell-Fackler house scene of antebellum socials
511 - 1835 cottage of George Lane, appointed U.S. judge by Lincoln

Detour right to 416 McClung to see galleried 1838 McClung house.
Look across the intersection to see:
403 Echols St. The Pope Mansion, circa 1814, the oldest brick house in the state. It was built atop the highest hill in town for **LeRoy Pope** (1765-1844), considered to be the founder of Huntsville because of his leadership in the civic and cultural development of the town. In 1814, he hosted a dinner on the lawn for Andrew Jackson and his troops returning in triumph over Creek Indians in the Battle of Horseshoe Bend. George Steele later added the majestic Classical Revival portico. It is privately owned. It does not front a street and is easily bypassed.

Turn right on Lincoln Street
409 - 1917 Masonic Hall houses the oldest order in the state
401 - 1815 home of Mississippi territorial legislator Peter Perkins
311 - Known as the Spite House because Joshua Cox built it in 1825 with very tall ceilings to block the view of his enemy LeRoy Pope
312 - First Presbyterian Church, 1860 Gothic Revival

Retrace steps to Willliams Street
310 - 1823 house of Francis Mastin, military aide to Andrew Jackson
300 - 1836 house built by Gov. Thomas Bibb, home to 9th generation Bibb

Turn right on Green to Gates Street
300 - **1819 Weeden House Museum**. See description.

Continue on Green to Eustis Avenue
212 - **Episcopal Church of the Navtivity**. See description.

HISTORIC DISTRICT WALKING TOUR MAP

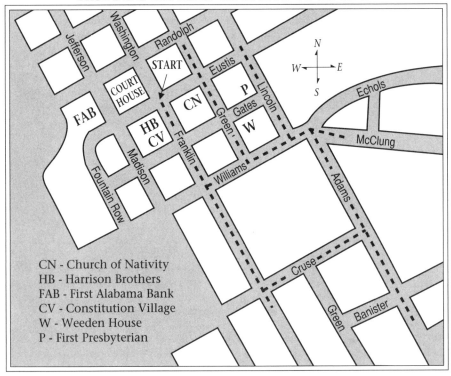

CN - Church of Nativity
HB - Harrison Brothers
FAB - First Alabama Bank
CV - Constitution Village
W - Weeden House
P - First Presbyterian

VON BRAUN CIVIC CENTER, 700 Monroe St., houses an entertainment and sports arena, concert and exhibit halls, playhouse, separate rehearsal hall for the Huntsville Symphony Orchestra, the **Huntsville/Madison County Convention and Visitors Bureau** tourist information center and Huntsville Museum of Art. Phone 533-1953.

HUNTSVILLE, ALABAMA

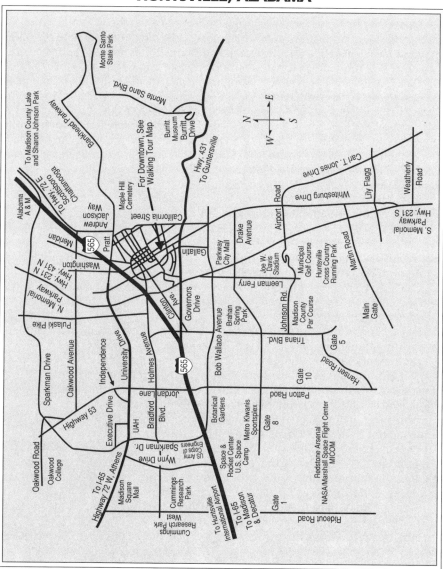

WEEDEN HOUSE MUSEUM preserves furniture and architecture of the Federal period. The birthplace of artist-poet Maria Howard Weeden, the 1819 house features hand-carved mantels and a leaded-glass fanlight over the entrance. Miss Weeden's watercolors of former slaves who were friends of hers and other works are displayed during tours. Allow 30 minutes. Open Tues.-Sun., 1-4 p.m. Closed Jan.-Feb. Admission. Phone 536-7718.

Getting there: 300 Gates Ave. at Green, a block east of Constitution Village.

SUGGESTED ITINERARIES

Three-day/two-night tour: Past and future

Most visits to "America's space capital" begin at the Space Center, the state's number one tourist attraction. Afterwards, move to the historic area around the state's first courthouse square and tour the museums and attractions there. Wrap up your stay at the mansion-museum on top of Monte Sano Mountain which overlooks the city.

Day 1: Arrive in Huntsville at mid-morning via I-65 and I-565, taking exit 15 to the **U.S. Space & Rocket Center**. View a program in the spectacular Spacedome Theater to get an understanding about the Space Shuttle and how it works. Tour the museum's exhibits and walk around the giant rockets outside. Have **lunch in the cafeteria**. Afterwards, step aboard the NASA Bus for a guided tour of the **Marshall Space Flight Center** where you see the giant neutral buoyancy tank where astronauts train for weightlessness and the Space Station *Freedom* under development. Plan to spend at least a half day to take in everything.

Afterwards, turn right past the Marriott onto Bob Wallace Avenue and go about a mile to tour the beautiful **Botanical Garden**.

If your budget allows, check in at the **Huntsville Marriott** or **Huntsville Hilton**. If you bring several children and need two bedrooms, stay at the **Radisson Suite Hotel**, the **Executive Lodge Suite Hotel** or **Amberley**. There are several economy motels near the airport (I-565 exit 7) and on University Drive (U.S. 72 West.).

Celebrate your successful "mission" into space with **dinner at the Green Bottle Grill** just off South Memorial Parkway on Airport Road, the street which led to the old airport no longer in service.

Day 2: Stop by the tourist information center in the **Von Braun Civic Center** to have any questions answered about special events or attractions.

Drive around the lake at **Big Spring Park** to Gates Street. Park a half-block south of the **Madison County Courthouse** square. Step back into the year 1819 at **Alabama's Constitution Village**. Costumed interpreters demonstrate seasonal chores of rural and city life. Lunch and two significant stops are within a block.

Walk up Franklin Street to South Side Square and turn left. Just past the **Village Inn** restaurant is the 1879 **Harrison Brothers Hardware**.

The Greek Revival building on the corner toward the civic center is the 1835 **First Alabama Bank** designed by local architect George Steele. It is the oldest bank building in use in the state and one of the most beautiful. Facing it across the square is the **Schiffman Building** where Tallulah Bankhead was born.

Lunch at the **Village Inn** for Jello-type salads or sandwiches. Below the square is a festive wings and nachos place named **Bubba's**.

A block off the Village Inn corner on Eustis Street is the **Episcopal Church of the Nativity**. Walk down Green to tour the 1819 **Weeden House** which was standing when the first legislature met a block away.

Drive north on Franklin 5 blocks (the name changes to Washington) and recall the excitement of rail travel at the **1860 Huntsville Depot Museum**. Allow an hour for the tour. The three-story **Railroad Station Antique Mall** across the street is one of the best in the state.

Get back on I-565 behind the depot via Washington and go west to exit 15 to Governors Drive (Hwy. 20 East). Continue past the hospitals and up **Monte Sano Mountain**. Turn left to **Burritt Museum and Park** where you encounter a spectacular view of Huntsville.

For dinner, drive out I-565 to exit 3 and go north 2 miles to the **Greenbrier Restaurant** and order barbecue, catfish or seafood. Everything is good, but the hushpuppies are the best in the state.

Day 3: It is worth staying another night in Huntsville to eat breakfast at **Eunice's Country Kitchen**. Take I-565 to Oakwood and turn right on Andrew Jackson Way. You'll see Eunice's ahead on the left.

WHERE TO STAY

Near the Space Center

Amberley Suite Hotel, University near Madison Square Mall, has 170 suites with full kitchenettes and parlor, free coffee, *USA Today* paper, pool and health room. Breakfast and lunch buffet available. Write 4880 University, Huntsville, 35816. Double rate: $71-$77 plus tax, weekend $50-$60. **Phone 1-800-456-1578** or 837-4070.

Executive Lodge Suite Hotel, on Sparkman just north of University Dr./U.S. 72, is more like an apartment house than a motel. Many of the 313 rooms are suites with separate living rooms/kitchens. Two pools, local calls, continental breakfast, cable TV with movies, airport shuttle, nearby health club privileges. Honeymoon and Space and Rocket Center packages available. Double rate: $50-$90 plus tax. Fax 830-8899. Write 1535 Sparkman Dr., Huntsville, 35816. **Phone 1-800-248-4722** or 830-8600.

Hampton Inn, University at Wynn Drive, is convenient to Cummings Research Park and Huntsville's "restaurant row" on University. The 128-room motel offers continental breakfast, free local calls, cable TV with HBO, outdoor pool, Jacuzzi, passes to a local health club, and non-smoking rooms are available. Double rate: $52-$54, plus tax, weekends $44-$54. **Phone 830-9400** or 1-800-426-7866.

Huntsville Marriott, I-565 exit 15, is the city's largest full-service hotel and is in the shadow of the rockets at the U.S. Space and Rocket Center. Rooms on the west side of the seven-story, 290-room hotel overlook the Space Camp Habitat next door and the full-size space shuttle. Those on the east face the mountains which rise up at the edge of downtown. A two-story cabana wing faces the landscaped courtyard and indoor-outdoor pool.

The Marriott is a popular headquarters for parents of youngsters attending Space Camp. Youngsters enjoy the indoor-outdoor pool while parents may prefer the sauna and weight room. A fifth-floor concierge level offers a continental breakfast and honor bar. ****Seasons** is the family restaurant open seven days and nights. The grilled chicken caesar salad ($6) is very good. *****Cortlands, A Southern Bistro**, offers many gourmet interpretations of Southern ingredients, such as smoked Alabama quail ($18), Chicken Oscar ($18) and free range chicken ($14). A special delight is the self-serve wine bar. Courtlands is open Mon.-Sat., 5-10 p.m. Room service, lounge. Write 5 Tranquility Base, Huntsville, 35805. Double rate: $111-$120 plus tax, weekends $69-$79. A "two for breakfast" package includes a deluxe room and buffet breakfast. **Phone 830-2222** or 1-800-228-9290.

Staying downtown

Huntsville Hilton, across from the Von Braun Civic Center and Big Spring Park, is within walking distance of the downtown square, historic districts and city museums.

The remodeled hotel has 277 rooms with coffee makers, clock radios, remote TVs with cable and Showtime and *USA Today* newspaper. It is a great weekend getaway headquarters for touring historic Huntsville. **Lofton's** restaurant serves three meals daily and offers room service. Outdoor pool and sauna. Golf package available. Write 401 Williams Ave., Huntsville, 35801. Fax 533-1400. Double rate: $79-$95 plus tax, weekend $69. **Phone 1-800-534-8877** or 533-1400. Out of state: 1-800-544-3761.

Redstone Arsenal area lodging
Radisson Suite Hotel, 6000 S. Memorial Parkway, is convenient to South Huntsville and the arsenal's Gate One. Each of the 150 guest rooms has a separate living room, wet bar, refrigerator, desk and coffee maker. The lobby area of the two-story, lowrise hotel features a small, informal lounge bar and the ***Plantation** restaurant. (Don't miss the spectacular dark chocolate praline dessert.) Room service. A year round pool is just off the lobby. Write 6000 Memorial Parkway S., Huntsville, 35802. Fax 882-9684. Double rate: $63-$85 plus tax, weekends $59-$85. **Phone 882-9400** or 1-800-333-3333.

Hotels near Huntsville Airport
Days Inn Airport, near I-565 exit 8, offers 143 rooms on two floors, with in-room coffee, continental breakfast in lobby. Pool, cable TV. Free airport shuttle. Kmart and restaurants are nearby. Fax 772-9550, ext. 278. Double rate: $41-$45 plus tax. **Phone 772-9550.**

Federal Square Suites, located near I-565 exit 8, offers 72 suites with kitchens and laundries and 48 studios with microwaves, refrigerators and coffee makers. Guests receive continental breakfast, *USA Today*, local calls and cable TV with HBO. Fast-food restaurants nearby. Fax 772-0620. Double rate: $45-$75 plus tax, weekends $34-$66. **Phone 1-800-458-1639** or 772-8470.

Holiday Inn-West, located at I-565 exit 8, is convenient to the airport and across the intersection from Intergraph corporate headquarters. Because this was built by businessman Woody Anderson as an independent hotel, the 168 rooms are larger than you might expect for a Holiday Inn. Rooms offer cable TV with HBO, in-room coffee, all king beds, Jacuzzi, pool, newspaper, local calls, airport shuttle and health club passes. Car rental companies are nearby. The **Port of Madison** restaurant serves three meals daily. The seafood platter ($17) and Bourbon Street steak ($16) are very good. Write 9035 Hwy. 20 W., Madison, 35758. Fax 464-0762. Double rate: $65 plus tax, weekends $48. **Phone 1-800-826-9563** or 772-7170.

Howard Johnson Park Square Inn, 8721 Hwy. 20 W., is a brick courtyard hotel surrounding an outdoor pool and sauna. The 140 rooms include parlor suites and some rooms have microwaves and refrigerators. Guests in the executive section receive morning coffee and *USA Today*. TVs have cable with HBO. A restaurant serves three meals daily. This was the prototype of Howard Johnson's upscale inns. Fax 464-0783. Double rate: $64-$95 plus tax, weekends $39-$75. **Phone 1-800-882-3067** or 772-8855.

Sheraton Inn, located within the Huntsville International Airport terminal, is uniquely convenient for arriving or departing air travelers. It is the state's only hotel within an airport and the registration desk is just a few steps from the gates. If you stay in one of the 146 newly renovated rooms, you are close to a sauna, outdoor pool, lighted tennis courts and exercise room. An upgraded 18-hole golf course is on the grounds. The **Veranda Room** offers casual dining and the Celestial Bar & Grill is located in the Launchpad lounge. Write Box 20068, Huntsville, 35824. Fax 464-9116. Double rate: $69-$99 plus tax, weekends $49-$99. "Space golf," Jacuzzi suite retreat packages. **Phone 772-9661** or 1-800-241-7873.

WHERE TO EAT

Because of the high average incomes in Huntsville, people eat out frequently. As a result, there are many restaurants, including most franchises (TGI Fridays, Ruby Tuesday, Sizzler). The number of locally-owned restaurants has grown in recent years, making dining out more adventuresome.

If you are staying in a hotel without a restaurant and want the convenience of room service, phone the **Restaurant Connection** at 882-2020 to place an order from more than 30 restaurants. The Connection will pick up and deliver your order for a small additional charge.

Downtown

Because Huntsville mushroomed in the 1960s and growth was primarily urban sprawl, the downtown area remains tiny compared with the overall city. But several places are available to enjoy lunch while walking visiting the historic attractions around the courthouse square.

Bubba's - *Snack on ribs in the downtown courtyard*
109 Washington just off Clinton Ave. Phone 534-3133
Mon.-Thurs., 11 a.m.-9:30 p.m.; Fri.-Sat., until 10:30
Bubba's serves up good ribs, juicy burgers and salads to the courthouse crowd by day and singles at night. It's a friendly downtown sports bar with seating at tables or in the bar area. A nice option is eating at the wrought iron tables on the patio when the weather is favorable. There's a bit of a New Orleans feel to the enclosed courtyard.

Eunice's Country Kitchen - *Best for breakfast*
Andrew Jackson Way just off I-565. Phone 534-9550
Mon.-Sat., 4 a.m.-noon
Eunice Merrill's place is legendary for biscuits, country ham and big hugs. When NBC's Jane Pauley selected Huntsville for a "Real Life" feature on Southern "civility," she noted how politicians and civic leaders can be seen going from table to table with the coffee pot pouring refills without distinction to race or status. Newspaper columnist Lewis Grizzard says Eunice's serves "the best country ham and homemade biscuits on earth" and Willard Scott still raves about her cookin' from the morning he walked in and said, "I'll have one of everything."

This is not the place to eat if you worry about cholesterol. Eunice Merrill, who opened the small restaurant in the mill section of town in 1952, loves to hug her customers, new and old.

The Village Inn - *Great lunch spot*
South Side Square and Franklin. Phone 533-9123
Mon.-Sat., breakfast, lunch and dinner; Sun. brunch.

If you are visiting the historic spots around the courthouse square, the Village Inn on the Square is convenient and quick for a lunch break. The soups, salads and sandwiches are tasty and don't threaten your diet. It has a tearoom atmosphere, but the plate lunches are manly enough to attract busy attorneys from the courthouse. It's next door to Harrison Brothers hardware.

Restaurants on the Parkway
***Cafe Berlin - *Authentic European dishes*
Westbury Square on Airport Road. Phone 880-9920
Sun.-Thurs., 11 a.m.-9 p.m.; Fri.-Sat., 11-10

The food and atmosphere of Cafe Berlin are reminiscent of the cosmopolitan cafes of the capitals of Europe. Leave room for their excellent selection of French, Austrian and German cakes and tortes and cordials. It is operated by Dieter Schrader, whose **Ol' Heidelberg Cafe** has been a fixture for 20 years for Huntsville's German community and anyone else who likes real Bavarian food. Ol' Heidelberg's sausages, knackwurst and sauerkraut are wunderbar. It is in the HQ shopping center on U.S. 72, west of Rideout Road. Phone 922-0556. A fine Italian restaurant, **Tortellini**, near the Radisson, is under the same ownership.

****Green Bottle Grill - *North Alabama's finest*
505 Airport Road. Phone 882-0459
Tues.- Fri., 11 a.m.-2 p.m.; Mon.-Sat., 6-10 p.m.

The Green Bottle Grill specializes in Southern dishes prepared with a continental flair and served in a sophisticated atmosphere of mirrors and photos of France. The culinary talents of former caterer Anne Pollard and chef Michael Tucker (in the checkered pants) of Highlands fame blend well with the wine knowledge of partner Rick Paler (in the sweater) to deliver an excellent dining experience. Luncheon entrees of fish, chicken and veal average $6-$7. The caesar salad with parmesan cheese and croutons is excellent. Tucker transforms black-eyed peas, sweet potatoes and grits into surprisingly interesting sidedishes. For dessert, try the dacquoise meringe with chocolate cream or the praline pecan pound cake. Green Bottle operates a bakery next door where you can take home desserts, muffins, croissants and cookies.

Don't be bothered by the fact that the Green Bottle is in a shopping center. Weekend dinner reservations recommended.

Sample **Green Bottle Grill** *menu*

Before supper

Sweet potato cake with sherry vinaigrette & thyme $4.25

Duck & pistachio pate with homemade mustard $6.50

Stone crab claws from the Keys with Saffron sauce $8.25

South Carolina quail stuffed with sausage $7

Smoked salmon salad, spinach & tomato caper relish $8.25

Double yoke eggs scrambled with herbs & truffles $9.50

Wilted slaw with apple smoked bacon, cheese & walnuts $5

For supper

Sauteed Tennessee rainbow trout with wine, almonds $16

Grilled Canadian salmon with spaghetti squash $17.25

Farm leg of lamb with white bean ragout & ratatouille $17

Sauteed scallops with blood oranges, wine & potatoes $17

Pan roasted New Zealand venison with dates, walnuts $17
Grilled beef tenderloin with cognac-peppercorn butter $17.25

**Michael's - *Good food at the Ramada*
3502 Memorial Parkway SW. Phone 881-6120
Seven days.
   Located in the Ramada near the baseball stadium, Michael's serves a good plate lunch and offers evening specials. Choices include braised tips of beef, breaded veal cutlet and fried fillet of flounder. The roast leg of lamb with gravy and mint jelly is a favorite.

Dining on University Drive
***The Fogcutter - *Steaks in a dark clublike setting*
3805 University Dr. Phone 539-2121
Tues.-Sun.
   The Fogcutter has been the city's mainstay for steaks and good seafood for decades. Restaurants come and go in this city where everybody eats out, but fortunately, the Fogcutter remains a top place for business lunches. The decor is very dark with red leather booths or plush chairs on casters. Waitresses dress in blouses and short skirts unchanged since the 1960s. Popular for lunch and dinner.

**Mill Bakery and Eatery - *Good food without the fat*
2003 Whitesburg Dr. Phone 534-4455
311 Jordan Lane. Phone 837-8555
   The Mill offers the opposite of Eunice's fat food. The menus of healthy deli sandwiches and salads list grams of calories, fat and sodium for each item and note which selections earn American Heart Association approval. Don't be discouraged if there is a long line when you enter at lunch. Cheerful and speedy college-age employees ensure that the cafeteria line for custom orders moves quickly. The spartan decor in the buildings of exposed rafters is a blend of collegiate chic and country clean. Bakery cases of fresh muffins, cookies and cakes at the cash register offer multiple options for wrecking your diet.
   The Mill near I-565 has a neat patio covered with wisteria vines that smell distinctly Southern when blooming in spring.
   The Mill at Governors and Whitesburg near Huntsville Hospital has live entertainment on some nights in the rear dining room. They serve their private label Rocket City draft beer.

HUNTSVILLE ENTERTAINMENT
   Several downtown restaurants offer live entertainment. The **Kaffeeklatsch Bar** at Clinton and Jefferson is a popular blues and jazz spot where the local band, Microwave Dave and the Nukes, plays on occasion. **Judge Crater's Tavern** is a basement bar and restaurant on the courthouse square. **Bubba's** features live bands on the patio on summer weekends.
   Touring bands perform at the **Vapors** at 2407 S. Memorial Parkway. The **Carousel Club** at 3000 University Dr. has been a popular country dance spot for years. **The Comedy Club** at 1407 N. Parkway has been open since 1987. For acts playing in town, check Mike Kaylor's column in the Leisure section of *The Huntsville Times* each Thurs.

HOW LYNCHBURG LEMONADE CAME TO BE

Local nightclub owner/troubadour Tony Mason was nursing a cold in 1980 when he ran out of medicine and mixed several concoctions with alcohol. A blend of triplesec, 7Up, sweet and sour mix and Jack Daniel's turned out to be quite tasty so he started serving "Lynchburg Lemonade" in Mason jars in his University Drive club.

Lo and behold, the folks up U.S. 231 at Lynchburg, Tenn. (pop. 361), started distributing Lynchburg Lemonade posters and point-of-sale items. Tony sued and the Brown-Foreman corporate guys testified in state court that Jack Daniel's had no intention of selling the cocktail, and was merely promoting the liquor itself. Tony won a court-ordered $1 judgment in the case, but today he no longer operates the club where he made Lynchburg Lemonade famous.

Today you can buy Jack Daniel's Lynchburg Lemonade cordial in most liquor stores.

SPORTS

Huntsville is home to a AA baseball team affiliated with the Oakland A's. The **Huntsville Stars** play in Joe Davis Stadium, one of the finest minor league ballparks in the nation. Average annual attendance of more than 235,000 ranks the Stars among the Southern League leaders. A record of 300,810 watched the Stars capture the league championship in the 1985 inaugural season. The Stars made the playoffs four of the next five years. Former Stars players Jose Canseco, Mark McGwire and Walt Weiss played key roles in three American League titles for Oakland. Phone 882-2562.

For golfers, the statewide **Robert Trent Jones Golf Trail** begins in a mountain-ringed valley outside Huntsville and stretches south to Mobile. **Hampton Cove** has two championship 18-hole courses and an 18-hole short course designed by the legendary golf architect which provide some of the finest public fee golf in the state. Phone 551-1818 or 1-800-949-4444 for tee times at any course on the trail.

Ice skaters enjoy skating on the NHL regulation surfaces at the **Iceplex** on Leeman Ferry Road off South Parkway. Phone 883-3774.

WHERE TO SHOP

North Alabama's largest mall is **Madison Square**, with 200 stores on U.S. 72 (University Drive) at Rideout Road. Anchor stores are **McRae's, Parisian, JC Penney, Castner Knott** and **Sears**.

The **Parkway City Mall** on South Memorial Parkway features **McRae's, Parisian** and **Montgomery Ward**. The **Huntsville Art League** operates a high quality, non-profit co-op gallery inside Parkway City to showcase about 80 local artists. The media include pottery, watercolor, acrylic, pastels, oil, photography, sculpture, jewelry and handmade baskets.

Each artist spends several hours a month on duty at the **HAL Gallery** to keep overhead costs low. Open Mon.-Sat., 10-7; Sun., 12:30-6.

Lawren's is the city's finest gift shop for housewares, kitchen items, china and silver. A Lawren's sticker on a gift box is Huntsville's top label of good taste. 809

Madison St. near the hospitals. Phone 539-3812.

Wild Birds Unlimited is a unique shop for gardeners and birdwatchers. The shop sells bird feeders, bird houses, garden ornaments, fountains, windchimes, recordings of birds and huge bags of bird seed. It is open every day at 901 Monroe St. behind the Huntsville Hilton. Phone 536-9128.

Railroad Station Antique Mall covers 23,500 square feet of display space in the three-story Lombardo Building. At last count 8: dealers stocked clocks, silver, flatware, china, Victorian dining room suites, upholstered chairs, old books and beds. Quality is higher than in most antique malls. Open Mon.-Sat., 10-6; Sun., 1-6. On I-565, take exit 19 C and it's right there, across from the exit ramp. Park behind the antique mall (to avoid feeding parking meters on weekdays).

CULTURAL ACTIVITIES

The city's oldest performing organization, the **Huntsville Community Chorus**, was formed in 1946. With the arrival of German rocket scientists, as well as engineers from throughout the U.S. in the early 1950s, Huntsville experienced rapid growth in population and the arts. A symphony orchestra was founded in 1956, the **Huntsville Art League** in 1957, the **Huntsville Museum of Art** in 1973 and the **Huntsville Opera Theater** in 1976. Locals perform in productions staged by **Huntsville Little Theater**, **Twickenham Repertory Company** and **Fantasy Playhouse**. The **Broadway Theater League** brings national touring companies to the city.

On a regular basis, new exhibits open at the **Huntsville Museum of Art** in a wing of the **Von Braun Civic Center**. The **Huntsville Symphony Orchestra** provides regular programs of orchestral music to Huntsville and the surrounding area. The season consists of a four-show season and a pops concert in the concert hall of the Von Braun Civic Center

Consult the entertainment pages of the two daily newspapers for current productions and exhibitions.

ANNUAL EVENTS IN HUNTSVILLE

Third weekend in March

NEACA Craft Show - Von Braun Civic Center - About 150 members of the **Northeast Alabama Craftsmen's Association** fill the exhibit hall of the Von Braun Civic Center with ceramics, baskets, pottery and other handmade items on the third weekends of March and September and the second weekend in December.

Late April weekend

Huntsville Pilgrimage - Twickenham and Old Town historic districts - Selected 19th-century homes are open to the public for either of two days. Architectural styles include Tudor, Prairie School, Georgian, Federal, Victorian, Italianate and especially Greek Revival. Related pilgrimage activities occur citywide, including special tours of Constitution Village, the Weeden House museum and Harrison Brothers hardware store. An antiques show and sale is sometimes held. Funds raised are used to restore historic areas of Maple Hill Cemetery. Phone 551-2230.

Second Friday and Saturday in May

Poke Salat Festival - Arab - If you've never seen the large, leafy purple-stalked poke plant growing wild, then you might not understand the fuss over "the poor man's greens" celebrated on Brindlee Mountain. A cooking contest has drawn entries of poke salat meatballs, poke salat pie and poke salat corn muffins. The crowning of the king and queen, plus a street dance, are prelude to the serving of special dishes of poke salat (salad) at L'Rancho Cafe for lunch both days. Date varies.

Second weekend of May
Panoply - Big Spring Park - Performing and visual arts fill the schedule with quality artists from the Huntsville area, as well as guest artists such as African-American dance ensembles, jazz dance groups and a variety of artists representing the visual arts. Singers, dancers, musicians and actors entertain thousands who gather at stages under tents scattered around the lagoon at Big Spring Park.

The outdoor festival draws big crowds to see art exhibits, watch craft demonstrations and applaud dancers and singers competing on stage. Many booths encourage children to express themselves artistically. Children in the Discovery Area decorate shiny balloons and draw chalk pictures on the sidewalk while kids at the Art Museum's Designamation create decorative designs.

To make the event appeal to the entire family, a Discovery area encourages children to make kites or wind socks, or help build such articles as a train or tunnel. Panoply recognizes new talent as well with competitions in musical composition, dance and acting. Finalists perform during the festival.

Panoply opens to the public on Friday night. A full schedule of stage events and exhibits runs through the weekend, concluding with colorful fireworks. Park on a side street and walk to Big Spring Park. Even though the temperature is likely to be comfortable, you may want to use sunscreen and wear a cap and sunglasses.

Some 4,000 volunteers help the **Huntsville Arts Council** stage Panoply. (The word means "a splendid array.") It has been held in Big Spring Park each May since 1982. Phone 535-6565.

Fourth of July
Fireworks Celebration - Milton Frank Stadium - An evening fireworks program celebrating Independence Day includes bands, singers and other entertainment in the high school football stadium off Bob Wallace Avenue. Donations benefit the Exchange Club of Greater Huntsville.

Labor Day
Hurricane Valley Harvest Festival - New Market - Taste North Alabama-grown wine, stomp ripe grapes, listen to music, eat food and play games at the free grape harvest festivities at Alistair Vineyards. Phone 379-3527.

Labor Day Week
Northeast Alabama State Fair - Jaycee Fairgrounds - Scores of midway rides, shooting games and entertainment shows highlight the area's largest fair. Traditionally begins the weekend prior to Labor Day and runs through the following Saturday. Off Airport Road. Check local newspapers for schedules. Phone 881-1412.

Saturday after Labor Day
Old Fashioned Trade Day - Courthouse Square - Downtown Huntsville takes on the appearance of the square 50 years ago when people came to town to trade. Scores of

booths selling crafts, antiques, food and general merchandise line the streets which are closed to cars. The program, staged by the Historic Huntsville Foundation, benefits preservation activities. The non-profit group operates Harrison Brothers Hardware. Phone 883-9446 or 536-3631.

A Saturday in the fall
Fall Train Excursion - Climb aboard a train pulled by a steam engine and head through the mountains of North Alabama for a ride into the past. The North Alabama Railroad Museum, with the cooperation of Norfolk-Southern Railroad, has sponsored steam excursions to various destinations since 1971. When Chattanooga is the destination, the train departs the depot at 8:30 a.m. and passes the Chase Depot museum and the Stevenson Depot museum. The train has a lengthy stopover at the Choo Choo before returning home by 8 p.m. Write the museum at P.O. Box 4163, Huntsville, 35815. Phone 851-6276.

Third weekend of September
State Fiddling and Bluegrass Convention - Pulaski Pike at Winchester Road - Pickers and fiddlers from across the state compete for thousands of dollars in prizes at the Cahaba Shrine Temple's annual convention held since 1978. Categories range from junior harmonica to bluegrass mandolin to novelty and buckdancing. Dealers sell leather and metal crafts, as well as hats and crafts. Food is sold and camping is available. Proceeds benefit Cahaba Shrine Temple charities. In case of rain, the event is moved inside a nearby building. Check dates. Phone 859-4471.

Third Sunday of September
Mountain Dulcimer Festival - Burritt Museum - The sweet and steady strumming of the dulcimer attracts players from Southern and Midwestern states who perform ballads of mountain people, Irish and Scottish songs and some classical selections. The dulcimer, which means "sweet sound" in Latin, was white America's first native instrument, originating in 18th-century Appalachia, and made of locally found wood. Bring a blanket or lawn chairs and picnic lunch. In case of rain, the festival is held in the old church on the museum grounds. Phone 536-2882.

Late Saturday in September
Madison Street Festival - Madison -Upwards of 15,000 residents of this high-tech suburb to Huntsville gather downtown to celebrate the town's heritage. Crafts booths, a road run, parade, a street dance and music are highlights in the festival sponsored by the Optimist Club. Schedule appears in *The Madison Record*. Take I-565 exit 8 and go north on Wall-Triana Road.

First Saturday in October
Cornocopia - Botanical Garden - The festival includes a plant sale, an art show and sale, hayrides, Halloween ghost stories and locally prepared food. Phone 830-4447.

Third Saturday in October
Indian Heritage Festival - Burritt Museum and Park - Members of the Five Civilized Tribes return to the mountaintop Burritt estate to demonstrate crafts and dances. The all-day festival explores the history, culture, traditions and skills of Alabama's Indian

people. At camps of various tribes, visitors see demonstrations of skills, such as cooking, pottery, basketry, crafts and period clothing. Children can make a traditional Indian souvenir to take home. Park your car at Huntsville High School and ride the free shuttle bus. Phone 536-2882.

Second Saturday of December
Rocket City Marathon - As many as 1,200 runners dash to cover the 26.2-mile course through the streets of Huntsville. The race, sponsored by the Huntsville Track Club, begins in front of the Hilton, then winds through downtown and South Huntsville to Green Cove Road for the return trip north. Phone 881-9077.

Second Saturday in December
Museums Christmas Open House - Historic district - Public and private museums which usually charge admission open their doors to display Christmas decorations. Phone 551-2230.

Second Saturday night in December
Parade of Lights - Ditto Landing on the Tennessee River - Boats festooned with Christmas lights drift by Ditto Landing 10 miles south of downtown on U.S. 231 around dusk. Boats circle Hobbs Island and sail or motor to Whitesburg bridge before returning to the dock. Phone 882-1057.

Third Saturday in December
Holiday Homes Tour - Twickenham Historic District - Owners of historic homes open their doors for the Twickenham Historic Preservation District Association's Christmas tour. Luminaries line the streets for visitors who tour the several homes and the 1819 Weeden House Museum after dark. Tickets are sold at the Weeden House. Phone 534-0429.

Mid-December weekend
The Nutcracker - Von Braun Civic Center concert hall - More than 100 local dancers perform in the Huntsville Civic Ballet's production, a local tradition which dates to 1969. Tickets available at Parisian or by calling the VBCC box office at 533-1954 or Fastix.

Late December
Weeden House Christmas - 300 Gates Ave. - Boxwood wreaths, pine boughs, fir trees, holly, and nandina berries tied with garlands create a 19th-century Christmas. The decorations recreate the mood when the Weeden family occupied the house in 1845. The Huntsville Garden Club - the state's oldest - continues the decorating tradition which dates to the year the home was first opened as a museum. Open Tues.-Sun., 1-5. Phone 536-7718.

MENTONE

- **Claim to fame:** Snow skiing, DeSoto Falls
- **Eat at:** Log Cabi Deli
- **Unique accommodation:** Mentone Inn
- **Population:** 474
- **Tourist information:** Contact the DeKalb County Tourist Association, P.O. Box 1165, Fort Payne, 35967. Phone 845-3957.

Lookout Mountain stretches 83 miles from Chattanooga to Gadsden like a long narrow rock box covered with boulders and trees. The mountaintop gradually widens to a span of 8 miles just north of Fort Payne. Perched on its western rim 1,000 feet above the valley floor is the isolated community of Mentone which has provided a summer retreat for five generations. Numerous religious and outdoor recreational camps for young boys and girls from Alabama, Georgia and Tennessee were scattered across the mountain early in this century. A dozen remain, constituting the town's major source of income.

In recent years, Mentone residents have staked out a new identity by hosting seasonal crafts festivals which attract admirers from as near as Fort Payne to collectors from Birmingham, Chattanooga and Rome, Ga.

The unusual is almost the norm here: Nowhere else in the state can you snow ski or be a ranch "dude" for a weekend or hike to such a spectacular waterfall or overlook a broad canyon carved by a river that begins and ends on the same mountain. You can even shop for dolls fashioned from gourds.

The development and promotion as a health resort date from 1872 with the arrivals of the John Mason family from Iowa and Dr. Frank Caldwell from Pennsylvania who wanted to be near the healthful spring waters.

Dr. Caldwell boarded with the Mason family while building a 57-room hotel in 1884 and asked for suggestions for a name. One of the Mason daughters who had read of Queen Victoria's visit to the French town of Mentone noted that the name meant "a musical mountain spring."

Guests enjoyed "taking the mineral springs," nature walks to Eagle's Nest lookout point and DeSoto Falls, as well as seeing the brilliantly colored foilage in autumn. Recreational activities included lawn tennis, croquet, bowling, dancing and other sports. The season ran from the first of June through September.

In the past century, at least 20 owners have held title to the hotel. A Coca-Cola executive from Atlanta and his wife spent weekends and summers in the 1980's upgrading the landmark. When he was unexpectedly transferred to Europe, they put it on the market for $220,000.

Mentone is a place that time has almost forgotten, but the 476 residents aren't about to let that happen. They formed a non-profit preservation association in 1982 to encourage restoration of the weathered resort town and revive the social fabric of mountain life through events focusing on music and handicrafts. While the success of the crafts festivals has been impressive, the town still has a distance to go in terms of tourist amenities and conveniences.

Even on sunny weekends when nothing special is going on, a drive up to Mentone for a stroll around the falls and a look at the local crafts is a pleasant diversion. Winters, however, are foggy and much colder than in the valley below.

It is not as remote as you may think. It is only 6 miles from I-59. Take the interstate north past Fort Payne to exit 231 and go east to the caution light at the U.S. 11 intersection. Turn right on 11 and proceed to the next caution light. Turn right on Hwy. 117 and follow it through Valley Head. Go up Lookout Mountain for 3 miles to the caution light at the intersection with County Road 89, also known as the Lookout Mountain Parkway. The empty hotel, Log Cabin restaurant and several shops are within walking distance.

The corner **Hitching Post**, built in 1898, is the source of good information about what is happening on a given day, especially if owner Beatrice Crowe is on duty. It houses the Crow's Nest Antique Shop, Village Boutique, Country Corner and Gourdie Shop. It functions as a shop and tourist welcome center.

The **Mentone Area Preservation Association** is the sponsor of special events and publishes a monthly newsletter, *The Groundhog*. Write P.O. Box 50, Mentone, 35984. Pick up a copy at the Hitching Post.

ATTRACTIONS

CLOUDMONT SKI AND GOLF RESORT - Since North Alabama usually gets only one or two light snowfalls a year, it might be the last place you'd expect to find a successful ski resort. But, here it is, albeit small with artificial powder.

Less than 2 miles down an obscure, unpaved road sits Cloudmont Resort. When overnight temperatures dip to 28 degrees, a series of machines spout artificial poly snow down a pair of 1,000-foot slopes which have a vertical drop of 150 feet. Skiiers from Alabama and Georgia come to learn and practice prior to taking trips to slopes further north where Mother Nature provides the snow.

Purchase lift tickets at the small snack building in the parking area at the end of the road. After putting on your skis at the base of the slope, grab the rope tow up the slope. Balance yourself with the poles at the top of the hill, lean forward and push. Depending on skill and slalom ability, each downhill run takes about 30-45 seconds.

Don't own skis and can't ski, anyway? All the equipment you need (skies, boots and poles) can be rented for an afternoon packaged with beginner lesson and lift tickets for as little as $17. On weekends and holidays, the full-day rate is around $25. Ski at night under the lights for $20. Skiing begins daily at 9 a.m. and continues at night if it's cold. Phone for an update on snow-making conditions.

Play nine holes of golf from 18 tees. The first tee is atop an unusual rock formation. You can also rent a chalet which overlooks the slope. Phone 634-4344.

Getting there: Cloudmont is north of Fort Payne on County Road 89. At the sign marked to Saddle Rock girls' camp, turn down the unpaved road and go 1.5 miles. The golf course adjoins the camp and the ski slopes are at the oppposite end. Cloudmont is 3 miles from DeSoto Falls.

DeSOTO STATE PARK/FALLS- See listing under Fort Payne.

SHADY GROVE RANCH is the state's only dude ranch. Like nearby Cloudmont, it's a product of the Jack Jones family.

Motorists who have lost their way outside of Fort Payne and happen to see the red "Pioneer City Stage" making a mail run can be forgiven if they feel like they've been transported to the Old West, but it is all part of the frontier scene at Shady Grove Lodge dude and guest ranch. You can ride horses over 100 miles of trails through 3,000 acres near Little River Canyon for a small hourly rate or take a wagon ride.

Breakfast rides are popular with guests staying at the nearby state park. You can arrange for a longer ride and a meal cooked on the trail. Special evening rides are available by arrangement for a minimum of 10 people. Your group can enjoy horseback riding and a steak dinner cooked outdoors. After-dinner entertainment consists of square dancing and Jack Jones telling spooky tales around the campfire.

It is truly the place to get away from it all. There are no TV's or phones.

The Round House Lodge has stone fireplaces, a kitchen and two guest rooms. Bring your own linens and stay the night in a bunkhouse that sleeps 10 or make reservations for the farmhouse which has four private entrances and accommodates 18 in the five bedrooms. Serious about roughing it and want to sack out in your sleeping bag? That's okay, too. Overnight guests have access to the outdoor kitchen. The farmhouse kitchen is equipped with a microwave, coffee maker, refrigerator and pots and pans. It even has a washer and dryer in case you fall off your horse. Bring your own linens. Open year round. Phone 634-3841.

Getting there: On top of Lookout Mountain next to Cloudmont Ski Resort off Hwy. 117.

WHERE TO STAY

DeSoto State Park Lodge - The lodge has 25 guest rooms which have double beds, TVs, telephones and porches. Twenty-two chalets and rustic cabins accommodate four-eight people each. The cabins are furnished with furniture made on site. Several A-frame cabins have fireplaces and kitchenettes.

The lodge has an Olympic pool, tennis courts, picnic shelters and a playground. Room rates are higher on weekends and March through November. Visa and MasterCard accepted. Fax 845-3224. On top of Lookout Mountain, turn on County 89 and follow the signs along the ridge road. **Phone 845-5380.**

The **Mentone Inn** across from the old hotel is a seasonal bed and breakfast in a mountain retreat built in 1927 and restored a decade ago. The main lodge offers 12 rooms with private baths and a separate cottage with three bedrooms. A patio and porch allow guests to gather and talk and play card games. If you are planning to visit during one of the major festivals, make reservations with owner Amelia Kirk well in advance. It is only open May through October because it has no heat. Write Box 284, Mentone, 35984. **Phone 634-4836.**

WHERE TO EAT

*****Log Cabin Deli** restaurant is a center of activity in Mentone. The inside seating is rather cramped and dark. Ask to sit out back on the screened-in porch. The Log Cabin serves inexpensive salads, sandwiches and desserts. Owner Collette Forester prides herself on the wide range of drinks served out of Mason jars: lemon soother tea, cabin cooler, apple juice, coffee and - in season - hot chocolate with marshmallows. Phone 634-4560.

*****DeSoto State Park Lodge** - The lodge serves three meals a day.

******The **Cragsmere Manna** restaurant serves fine country dinners on Friday and Saturday nights in a rustic, rambling 19th-century home on the brow of Lookout Mountain. The restaurant enjoys a colorful history dating from 1898 when a former slave and his wife built the cabin and served Sunday picnics for blacks and whites together. Ronnie and Bonnie Barnett of Fort Payne bought it in 1988.

If you're visiting the mountain on a weekend, stop by from 5-9 p.m. to enjoy fried mushrooms as an appetizer and filet mignon ($15), prime rib ($13) or cordon bleu chicken ($10). Dinners are served with soup or garden salad and side dishes such as rice pilaf, baked potato or Texas fries. The average dinner check is $12.

Cragsmere Manna is located on the DeSoto Parkway midway between Mentone and DeSoto State Park. Phone 634-4677.

ANNUAL EVENTS

Third weekend in May

Rhododendron Festival - The rich red blossoms of the wild rhododendrons color the mountainside and provide a setting for the semi-annual art show in this resurrecting mountain resort not far from Fort Payne. The rhododendron sale and quilt raffle are usually sellouts. Clog dancing, food and a parade add to the good times. Phone 845-3957.

Third weekend in October

Fall Colorfest in the square coincides with the peak time of "leaves turning" on Lookout Mountain. Expect music, clogging, a parade, crafts and food. The event begins Friday night with ghost stories and a marshmallow roast around a bonfire. Lace up your sneakers on Saturday morning for the Groundhog Classic Run along 4.2 miles of Lookout Mountain Parkway. Phone 845-3957.

MOULTON

ATTRACTION

ANIMAL HOUSE ZOOLOGICAL PARK, operated by Thomas and Carolyn Atchison, is the fifth largest breeder of exotic animals for zoos. The animals cover 40 of the 100 acres on the farm. You can see African lions, camels, goats, ostriches, rare monkeys, Bengal tigers, European brown bears, pythons and other animals living in areas separated by chain-length fences. Many of the animals are rented to producers of movies and television programs. The new-borns live with the Atchisons in their rambling 20-room, 7,000-square-foot house.

Atchison, a Birmingham native who earned medical and psychiatry degrees in Chile and Bolivia, met and married Carolyn Gillespie, a Moulton native who was already raising cats. Tours take one to two hours. Open seven days from mid-March to Labor Day. Gifts and food are available. Admission. Phone 974-8634.

Getting there: Located off a remote dirt road 5 miles from Hatton.

BANKHEAD NATIONAL FOREST - For the picnicker, hiker, camper and canoeist, **Bankhead** offers a wide range of recreational opportunities. Alabama's largest national forest with nearly 180,000 acres, Bankhead takes up more than half of Lawrence County and a large portion of neighboring Winston County. The forest offers its more than 400,000 annual visitors an opportunity to enjoy nature in a setting unparalleled in North Alabama. It also holds the remains of Indians who lived here long before Columbus sailed to America, plus the graves of two men who fought in the Revolutionary War.

In recent years, local descendants of native tribes have protested the clear cutting of the forest's hardwood on symbolic as well as ecological grounds. Two areas of special meaning include Kinlock Shelter, a large outcropping of rock in southern Lawerence County, and Indian Tomb Hollow, about 15 miles to the east. About 1774, a fierce battle between Cherokees and Creeks left about 60 warriors dead.

The northern or **Black Warrior** district has scattered facilities, including camping sites and picnic tables at Brushy Creek and tables and barbecue pits on the Sipsey River while the southern district's recreation is concentrated in sites around Smith Lake.

The **Corinth** area, 8 miles east of Double Springs, and **Houston**, 10 miles east of Corinth, charge for camping and day use. Both offer boat launches, beaches, bathhouse, camping and picnicking on a first-come basis. Horseback riding is another popular pasttime in the forest. The campground at the Corinth area is being improved to accommodate large RVs with each site having water, electricity and sewage hookups.

Campers can use the **Clear Creek** recreation area 12 miles north of Jasper while Corinth is being upgraded. Phone 489-5111.

The **Sipsey Fork** of the Black Warrior River starts from small tributaries in Bankhead just north of the 26,000-acre **Sipsey Wilderness**. It winds 61 miles through the wilderness and eventually flows into **Smith Lake** near Double Springs. Sipsey Fork is the only river in Alabama designated and protected by Congress as "wild and scenic" and is likely to have future use restrictions placed on it by the forest service, such as limiting open camping currently allowed in the wilderness. One endangered species on the Sipsey is the flattened musk turtle.

Access the water at Big Bridge on Hwy. 33 and Sipsey Bridge on U.S. 278 south of Double Springs.

MUSCLE SHOALS

See Florence-Tuscumbia

SCOTTSBORO

- **Claim to fame:** First Monday Trade Day
- **Don't miss:** Bargains at Unclaimed Baggage
- **Unique accommodation:** Goose Pond Colony
- **Eat at:** Paine's
- **Population:** 13,786
- **Tourist information:** Rick Roden, Chamber of Commerce, 407 E. Willow St., P.O. Box 973, Scottsboro, 35768. Phone 259-5500.

Scottsboro's downtown may have the appearance of many small towns arranged around a courthouse, but a transformation takes place each month that sets it apart. It is called **First Monday**, a trade day unique in the state.

On the first Monday and preceding Sunday of each month, scores of antique and junk dealers arrive to unload pickup trucks and vans and take up positions around the square to display their wares. Throughout the day, people scan the booths and browse through boxes of old household items, guns, silverplate, polished rocks, magazines and almost anything else collectible.

Many vendors have been in the exact same parking spot for decades. The most desirable ones are those on the courthouse grounds. Relative newcomers have to seek out locations within walking distance of the courthouse, although they get less traffic.

While it may have the appearance of common flea markets, First Monday is a tradition that has continued unbroken for more than a century. It began as a market for locals to trade crops for goods after Scottsboro became the county seat in 1868. Court opened on the "first Monday" of March and September, drawing crowds who, among other things, traded horses. The Monday event eventually backed up to Sunday as traders began arriving during the weekend to get the best parking spots.

Over the years, the local business community and the vendors have been at odds over the practice of tying up parking places in front of the courthouse by out-of-town traders. Parking meters were even installed for a time. And it was only a few years ago that local officials, citing health regulations, outlawed the sale or bartering of 'coon dogs, horses and other animals.

Today, however, the town recognizes that local businesses benefit and promotes First Monday as a tourist attraction. A newer event called **Art Sunday** is held at nearby Caldwell Park.

Because of the number of booths and the large amount of merchandise available, prices are usually reasonable. You can make your best deals late on Monday afternoon when dealers would rather sell below the marked price rather than haul the goods to the next swap meet. The event is held every month of the year, but the Labor Day weekend draws the largest number of dealers and as many as 25,000 shoppers. Phone 259-5500.

Getting there: Take Hwy. 35 off U.S. 72 into downtown Scottsboro and look for the courthouse dome. Park and walk to the square.

SCOTTSBORO ATTRACTION

GOOSE POND COLONY is an excellent municipal recreation resort on a 360-acre peninsula surrounded by Lake Guntersville. It is an ideal retreat for a weekend of golf, fishing, camping, family reunions or just wandering nature trails through the woods along the Tennessee River. You can even see Canada geese year round.

Two-bedroom vacation cottages facing the lake can accommodate up to eight people and have televisions, a fully-equipped kitchen, two baths, dining and living areas (queen sofa sleeper) and porches with lounge chairs. Use the fully-equipped, fully-stocked kitchen and cook on the charcoal grill in the yard. Bring your own food, of course. Rates are $100 a day from November through February and $125 from March through October.

If you'd rather camp, select from the 115 paved campsites with water and power hookups, including some with sewage connections. Each has a picnic table and is close to the two bath houses and playgrounds. A camp store, boat launch ramp, fishing piers and dump station are convenient. Phone 259-1808.

A full-service marina on the south end of the causeway is the place to begin a day of fishing for largemouth bass, bream and catfish. It has a tackle shop and restrooms, launching ramp and fuel, docks and wet and dry storage. It is at river mile marker 378. Phone 259-3027.

Goose Pond has a highly regarded 18-hole championship golf course with bent grass greens which extend over the peninsula. Green fees for 18 holes are $14 during the week and $18 on weekends and holidays. Between practicing on the putting green and driving range, you can visit the snack bar and pro shop where PGA professionals on staff offer lessons. Three-day, two-night golf packages including cabin, green fees and cart rentals are about $155 per person, quad occupancy. Phone 574-5353.

During the summer, you can swim in the Olympic-sized pool and use the playground and picnic area for a fee. Concerts are held at a 1,500-seat amphitheater and community events take place in a 900-seat civic center or smaller clubhouse. For further information, write Rt. 9, Box 440, Scottsboro, 35768. Fax 259-3127. **Phone 259-2884**.

Getting there: Goose Pond is 5 miles south of Scottsboro on Hwy. 79 toward Guntersville.

SIDE TRIP NORTH

Drive east on U.S. 72 to Hwy. 117 to downtown Stevenson to see the **Stevenson Railroad Depot Museum**. Artifacts related to railway heritage and the town's history are displayed. For hours, phone 437-3012. Closer to the Tennessee line, near Bridgeport, is the **Russell Cave National Monument**, one of North America's earliest documented shelters for prehistoric man. Phone 495-2672.

WHERE TO EAT

*Payne's, 101 E. Laurel St., is an attractive sandwich shop with roots dating from the opening of W.H. Payne Drugs Co. in 1869. The pharmacy moved from the original location near the railroad to the square in 1891 and a soda fountain was installed. When the last pharmacist retired a couple of years ago, Ann Kennamer bought the building and kept the name Payne's and the recipe for their famous red slaw for hot dogs. Waitresses wear poodle skirts and cheerful staff members pull sodas and scoop ice cream at the old-fashioned fountain. Phone 574-2140.

DID THE AIRLINE MISPLACE YOUR BAGS?

If you've ever lost your checked luggage while traveling by air, it probably landed at Unclaimed Baggage Center at 509 W. Willow St. Under contract to the airlines, Doyle Owens' firm receives unopened bags by the truckloads and sorts through the merchandise. Everything from overcoats, dresses and half-empty tubes of toothpaste, to radios, books and cameras is for sale at a fraction of their original purchase prices.

Manufacturers' labels remain intact and clothing is warehoused until the right season. Clothing is cleaned and sorted by sizes before being placed on racks. Some examples: a $40 Polo shirt sells for $15 and a $400 Burberry raincoat might sell for $65. If you'd rather travel with slightly scarred luggage which costs you just a few dollars instead of new luggage costing hundreds, pick from Unclaimed Baggage's large selection of hard cases and hanging bags.

Because there is too much for one location, stock is shipped to smaller sister stores in Decatur, Boaz and Albertville. Phone 259-5753 or 259-1525.

SHEFFIELD

See Florence-Tuscumbia

CENTRAL ALABAMA

*"Martha White," a 500-pound polar bear, who lives at the **Birmingham Zoo**, poses for a photo. The bear is enticed to perform the trick each morning when a zoo employee waves an apple before pitching it to her. (Author photo)*

ALEXANDER CITY

- **Claim to fame:** Russell Mills, Lake Martin
- **Don't miss:** Horseshoe Bend Park
- **Eat at:** Cecil's
- **Unique accommodations:** Still Waters
- **Population:** 14,917
- **Tourist information:** Alex City Chamber of Commerce, P.O. Box 926, Alex City, 35010. Phone 234-3461.

If you're thinking about retiring to a lakeside home in a friendly town with a moderate climate or if you're just looking for a place to get away for the weekend, you'll find Alex City a good choice.

For most people, mention of Alex City brings to mind athletic clothing and boating on the beautiful 40,000-acre Lake Martin. The connotation of being "a company town" is worn proudly here at one of the nation's most successful textile corporations. The home-grown **Russell Mills** employs 16,000 persons, including many local residents, who make Jerzees activewear and athletic uniforms worn by most pro football and baseball players, as well as numerous other amateur, collegiate and professional sportsmen. Russell is also a major supplier to Disney theme parks. Overall, Russell employs about as many people as the population of Alex City.

The company bucked the national trend and survived the flood of third-world textiles by delivering superior products at competitive prices. Today it makes apparel, active wear, athletic uniforms, knit shirts and woven fabrics. The company is involved in all aspects of production from spinning yarn to marketing its products worldwide.

As for the town's appeal to retirees, no less an authority than the *Kiplinger's Personal Financial Magazine* picked Alex City as one of the top 10 retirement spots in the nation. The researchers cite low cost of living, average house price of $47,900, low crime and high number of physicians and hospital beds, 1.4 golf holes per 1,000 residents and 800 miles of lake shoreline. Alex City scored 98 out of a possible 100. Many moving into Alex City are leaving Florida in search of a mild climate, but which still retains four distinct seasons.

ATTRACTIONS

HORSESHOE BEND MILITARY PARK commemorates **Andrew Jackson**'s decisive victory over the Creek Indian Nation on March 27, 1814. His volunteer militia campaign crushed Indian resistance, ended the Creek War of 1813-14, and forced the loss of 60 percent of Indian territory, including three-fifths of the present state of Alabama and one-fifth of Georgia.

The war grew out of a tribal feud between Upper (or Red Stick) and Lower factions of the Creek Nation over cooperation with the white man. The Lower Creeks preferred peaceful co-existance with the whites while the Upper Creeks were hostile to further white encroachment on their lands. Because of a growing mistrust between whites and Red Sticks, the conflict grew beyond the boundaries of a tribal feud.

On July 27, 1813, Creek half-bloods and frontier militia ambushed a Red Stick ammunition supply train at **Burnt Corn Creek** in South Alabama. In retaliation a month later, Upper Creeks attacked and burned **Fort Mims**, killing more than 500 men, women and children. It was a massacre of unprecedented proportions, which outraged the nation.

Starting from Huntsville on Oct. 10, Jackson's forces moved south. After five months of wilderness fighting, he took an army of 3,300 volunteers, infantry and Indian allies to within 6 miles of a peninsula on the Tallapoosa River where the Red Sticks were encamped.

The Indians, meanwhile, believed their prophets' stories that they could not be defeated. Jackson's fighters attacked **Chief Menawa**'s Red Stick band of 1,000 Creeks.

At the beginning of the attack, Jackson's two cannons pounded the barricade some 80 to 300 yards away for two hours with little effect. The soldiers of the 39th Regiment charged the barricade and eventually got to the other side at a costly loss of life to engage in fierce hand-to-hand combat. A number of prominent officers were killed and a young **Sam Houston** (later a Texas hero) was wounded three times. Walk up the hill to the cannon and see the monument.

Cherokees friendly to the whites had been stationed across the river at the opposite end of the peninsula to prevent the Red Sticks from retreating to safety. However, the Cherokees became excited by the sounds of battle and swam across the river where they stole the Red Sticks' canoes. They burned the village and drove their enemies up from the bank of the river to the breastworks as the 39th Regiment attacked.

After five bloody hours, the battle left 557 warriors dead on the battlefield, another 250 dead in the river and beyond, with about 300 women and children taken prisoner. Jackson lost only 26 of his men and 23 Indian allies. Menawa escaped in a canoe and went into hiding. Indian leader William Weatherford, "destroyer of Fort Mims," surrendered the next day.

Jackson was so touched by the sight of an Indian child clinging to his dead mother that he sent the child temporarily to Huntsville and eventually to his home in Tennessee to be raised as his son, Lincoyer.

For Jackson, the victory was the first step to the White House. The defeat of the Red Sticks deprived the British of a powerful ally in the Indian territory. The treaty with the Upper Creeks opened the heart of the future cotton kingdom to white settlers. Nine months later, on Jan. 8, 1815, he defeated the British at the **Battle of New Orleans**, ending the War of 1812.

Jackson became president in 1829. A year later, he signed the Indian Removal Bill requiring all tribes east of the Mississippi River to migrate to new western lands. The "old Indian fighter" achieved final victory over his enemies and former allies when thousands were forced to march west in the 1830s.

In 1956, some 2,040 acres of Horseshoe Bend were declared a National Military Park.

Visit the National Park Service museum at the entrance to see the scale map which explains the movement of Jackson's troops and the Indians' defense. A short video gives an overview of the park and the significance of the battle.

Outside, notice the unusual color of the cannon carriage: light blue! The color matched the uniforms of the soldiers. The soldiers of the period wore colors on the battlefield which could easily be seen by their commanders. It was not until later that this philosophy was changed in favor of soldiers blending in with their surroundings.

Driving tour: A counter-clockwise, 3-mile loop tour of the battlefield with several stops provides an excellent interpretation of the sequence of events. It takes about 45 minutes.

Skip the overlook unless you especially enjoy a steep climb to see an open field and trees. The 15-acre island seen across the narrow river to the right was occupied by Tennessee milita to block a possible escape route. A line of poles stretching across a clearing indicates the sophisticated log breastworks behind which the warriors awaited the attack. The line enclosed the "neck" of the peninsula at its narrowest point of 400 yards. It was intended to keep out the whites, when, in fact, it ultimately boxed in the defending warriors.

Relic hunting at Horseshoe Bend is illegal. No food is sold. Allow an hour. Open daily 8 a.m.-4:30 p.m. Closed Dec. 25 and Jan. 1. The loop road is open 8-6 in summer, 8-4:30 the rest of year. Free. Phone 234-7111.

Getting there: The park is best reached via U.S. 280 through Dadeville. Turn north on Hwy. 49 and go 12 miles. If coming through Alex City, travel to New Site and go south on Hwy. 49. It is 18 miles from Alex City. Write Rt. 1, Box 103, Daviston, 36256.

KOWALIGA is a legendary Indian which **Hank Williams** commemorated in a song. The father of country music was visiting Lake Martin, so the story goes, and wrote "Kaw-liga" after hearing the story of a wooden Indian who fell in love with an Indian maid. His love was in vain since he was, after all, wooden, and "never got a kiss."

The statue with the right hand upraised in salute out front of **Cecil's on the Lake** is neither wooden (it's plastic) nor the one Williams saw 40 years ago. Wood rots, after all, but it's still a good story. The Indian is at the restaurant on Hwy. 63 South.

LAKE MARTIN is one of the state's most popular recreational destinations. Until a decade or so ago, people who built weekend homes along the 750 miles of shoreline were fairly isolated, but now, most desirable undeveloped lakefront lots are gone. Those that remain are listed at prices that make oldtimers shake their heads in disbelief.

There are no reliable counts of how many Birmingham and Montgomery families have "lake houses" on this huge Alabama Power-regulated lake. But during periods of drought when the lake level is dropped to generate power, it affects so many boaters, fishermen and skiers that the protests frequently reach the front pages of *The Birmingham News* and *The Alex City Outlook*. For an update on lake levels, phone the power company's hot line at 1-800-LAKES11.

STILL WATERS is a major residential resort covering 2,300 acres of deer and turkey woodland with 5 miles of lake shoreline. Guests enjoy fresh water fishing, waterskiing, sailing, tennis, horseback riding, hiking, hunting and an 18-hole championship golf course designed by George Cobb. A sauna, pool and exercise rooms are available to guests staying in the 41 two-bedroom condos. The Harbor restaurant and 19th Hole lounge overlook Mariner Cove. Write 1000 Still Water Dr., Dadeville, 36853. Fax 825-4273. Two-bedroom condo rate: $134-$166 plus tax. A golf package of $109 per person, quad occupancy, includes green fee for 18 holes of golf and cart plus dinner, buffet and lodging. A guided hunting package is also available. **Phone 1-800-633-4954** or 825-7021.

Getting there: Close to Hwy. 49 outside Dadeville.

WIND CREEK STATE PARK occupies a prime stretch of the shoreline of Lake Martin and boasts one of the largest and finest camping complexes in the state.

The 1,445-acre park's major attraction is access to Lake Martin, the 40,000-acre, manmade lake stretching over a large portion of East Alabama and managed by

Alabama Power for hydroelectric power. The lake has ideal conditions for sport fishing for white bass, hybrid bass, largemouth bass, salt water striped bass, catfish, bluegill and crappie.

A 320-acre campground on the water allows campers occupying the 669 campsites to dock their boats at many of the campsites. A marina and a store with more than the usual bait and ice merchandise round out Wind Creek as a top choice for Central Alabama camping.

Wind Creek's summer interpretive programs offer special activities for all ages. Hiking, arts and crafts shows, square dancing and bluegrass music are among the highlights offered regularly from May through September. Self-guided trails through the woods near the edge of the water are well marked, as well as being included on maps available at the store. A 3-mile hiking trail passes wildflowers and dogwoods, as well as sites where white-tail deer feed. The trail winds over hardwood ridges and through tall pines down the shoreline where you see great sunset views of the lake.

Because the large picnic pavilions are ideal for family reunions, church groups and other outings in the summer, you should try to reserve one week in advance. For camping, write earlier if you want Lot 70, the prettiest on the lake. Write Route 2, Box 145, Alexander City 35010. Phone 329-0845.

Getting there: The park is 7 miles southeast of Alex City on Hwy. 128.

WHERE TO STAY

Horseshoe Bend Motel, U.S. 280 at Hwy. 22, has 90 rooms with cable TV. Free local phone calls. Swimming pool. It is 20 miles to Horseshoe Bend, 7 miles to Wind Creek State Park and 10 miles to Willow Point golf. A 24-hour deli, service station, lounge and package store are adjacent. Fax 234-6311. Double rate: $45-$50 plus tax. **Phone 234-5394.**

Kowaliga Beach Cottages offers one-and two-bedroom cabins with linens to accommodate up to eight people and furnished kitchens with cooking utensils. Rental pontoon boats are available. A restaurant, food store, marina, boat ramp and interdenominational church are on site. Located on Hwy. 63 at the bridge. **Phone 857-2162.**

BED AND BREAKFAST

Hill-Ware-Dowdell Mansion in adjacent Chambers County is an impressive Greek Revival mansion which has been home to some of Lafayette's finest families for a century and a half. Col. Waid Hill, who erected the five-bedroom frame house about 1840, sold it in 1868 to Judge Jonathon Ware, who willed it in 1888 to a daughter, Ella, the wife of attorney James Render Dowdell. Dowdell was a judge of the Fifth Judicial District and in 1898 became an Alabama Supreme Court justice.

At the turn of the century, the Dowdells added a second-story balcony, and matching doorways and windows.

A quarter-century ago, the house was extensively restored and a wing with kitchen, den and dining area attached to the rear was added, giving the house a total of 4,700 square feet. An elegant staircase leads to the four guest rooms, the largest of which has a king bed. The house also hosts weddings and receptions.

Nick and Althea Mendaloff, who lived in an 1819 stone house in Gettysburg, Pa., saw an ad for the house in *Colonial Homes* magazine and bought it after a trip. Its future as a bed and breakfast became in doubt because of Nick's pending transfer with a federal agency which prompted the owners to put the house on the market. From Alex City, take U.S. 280 to Camp Hill and Hwy. 50 to Lafayette. For information, write 203 Second Ave. SW, Lafayette, 36826. **Phone 864-7861.**

WHERE TO EAT

Cecil's Public House, just off the square at 405 Green St., serves delicious steaks and fish dishes, salads and sandwiches in a historical home setting enhanced by antiques. A daily luncheon special is offered. Dinner is served Mon.-Sat. after 5 p.m., plus you can eat in the large lounge. A second location, **Cecil's on the Lake, is home to the South's most famous wooden Indian. Phone 329-0732.

*Pineywoods Restaurant is convenient whether you're traveling by boat or car. Enjoy fried catfish and hamburgers in a family atmosphere. Located on Hwy. 128 a mile east of Wind Creek State Park. Open Fri.-Sat. nights. Phone 234-5688.

**Red's Catfish Cabin sits above a pair of lakes in remote Clay County between Newsite and Lineville and serves broiled, fried and filleted catfish as good as you'll find anywhere. The rustic dining room and porch overlooking a forested landscape seats approximately 260. On the day of a recent blueberry festival in Lineville, they served nearly 1,100 customers in a day. Plates comes with cole slaw, fries and hushpuppies. To reach Red's, take Hwy. 22 to Newsite and turn left. Take Hwy. 49 to between milemarkers 48/49 and turn left at the portable sign. If you miss the turn and get as far as Hwy. 77, double back 3 miles. Open for dinner Thurs. and Fri. and also afternoons on weekends. Reservations suggested on Sat. night. Phone 354-7705.

WHERE TO SHOP IN ALEX CITY

The **Russell Mills Retail Store** is a large attractive showcase of the nation's premier athletic sportswear. Much of the merchandise is first quality at one-third savings. Seconds are half off retail. It's worth a visit if you're passing through while winding up a weekend of boating or fishing on Lake Martin. Open Mon.-Sat., 9-6. Located on U.S. 280 bypass near the Horseshoe Bend Motel. Phone 329-4464 or 329-4414.

Visit the **Queen's Attic Antiques** on the square at 104 Calhoun St. for imported English mantles, armoires, pub tables, stained glass, silver and china. Open Mon.-Tues. and Thurs.-Sat. from 10-4. Phone 329-0653.

ANNUAL EVENTS

Weekend in June

Wind Creek Rock Swap - Wind Creek State Park - One of Central Alabama's oldest and largest rock swaps is set along the shoreline of Wind Creek at the silo parking lot area and grounds. Vendors set up tents or sell from vehicles. You can shop for geodes, pan for Alabama gold or Arkansas quartz and see stones cut and faceted. Fried pork skins and lemonade are sold. Phone 234-3150 or 234-8446.

ANNISTON

- **Claim to fame:** Fort McClellan Army base
- **Don't miss:** Anniston Museum of Natural History
- **Unique accommodation:** The Victoria Inn, Noble B&B
- **Nickname:** The Model City
- **Population:** 26,623
- **Tourist information:** Cindy Bailey, Executive Director; Calhoun County Convention & Visitors Bureau, 700 Quintard Ave., P.O. Box 1081, Anniston, 36202. Phone 237-3536. Tallacoosa Highland Lakes, P.O. Box 1787, Anniston, 36202.

In the late 19th century, Pennsylvania naturalist William Werner began collecting and mounting endangered birds which eventually would be shipped to Alabama and become the nucleus of the **Anniston Museum of Natural History**. Soon his collection included 1,800 specimens, and he painted dioramas and mounted scores of birds, eggs and nests in encased natural habitat groupings.

H. Severn Regar acquired and displayed the collection in Norristown, Pa., from 1915-29. When Regar moved to Anniston, he offered the collection to the city in exchange for shipping and exhibition costs. A wing was added to the Carnegie Library and it housed the Regar Museum from 1930-65 when the collection was moved to a temporary home.

Board chairman John B. Lagarde, a collector of mounted African animals, offered to donate his extensive collection if funds for a larger building were found. The city secured 185 acres of surplus land from Fort McClellan and joined with civic leaders in 1976 in funding construction of the Museum of Natural History. You can see the Werner-Regar bird exhibits in their ornate Victorian cases as well as the Lagarde animals in authentic settings. The collections impress visitors from around the globe.

The natural history museum is not the only significant cultural institution created in this small, but active city. The townspeople started the internationally recognized **Alabama Shakespeare Festival**, even though it outgrew facilities here. It continues to draw rave reviews in its home in Montgomery.

Such civic involvement might be considered rare for a city where the U.S. Army is a major employer; however, this town has never been conventional. Even its origin is unique.

The entire town was laid out by Northern industrialists more than a century ago. Samuel Noble and Daniel Tyler established textile mills and blast furnaces here in 1872 to help the South recover industrially from the devastation of Union raids during the Civil War.

In 1879 the owners hired noted architect Stanford White and landscape architect N.F. Barret among others to build a modern company town. The founders laid out the streets, water supply, sewer lines, schools, churches and other utilities before it was opened to the public in 1883. Originally known as Woodstock, the name was changed to Anniston, a contraction of "Annie's Town," in honor of Mrs. Annie Tyler, wife of the industrialist.

Numerous churches and homes of the era remain, including the **Victoria Inn**, and the nickname **the Model City**. Quintard Avenue, with a broad median filled with century-old trees, slices through town as sort of a grand main street, although the character has evolved from residential to largely commercial. The beauty of the city is enough reason to visit. Noble and Tyler would be proud of the care with which residents have handled their legacy.

The Army's **Fort McClellan**, established 5 miles north in 1917 as a military reservation, employs about 4,100 civilians. The Army Chemical Corps has almost 24,000 troops, all of whom have been through the base school. Even though it is the only base which provides live-agent chemical warfare training, McClellan narrowly escaped a closure attempt by the Pentagon in 1991. It is also the former home of the Women's Army Corps.

ATTRACTIONS

ANNISTON MUSEUM OF NATURAL HISTORY began as a private collection and evolved into an impressive municipal institution enviable to larger cities. Building on several collections, the museum's creative staff has developed remarkable exhibits and mounted a variety of specimens to give Anniston a world-class natural history museum.

A replica of a pteranodon, a prehistoric flying reptile, hangs from the ceiling with its 30-foot wing-span dominating the room.

Filling the Lagarde African Hall's jungles and deserts are more than 100 life-like animals, including a leopard, giraffe, monkeys and a menacing elephant. Because plants and towering trees form tropical rain forests and marshlands, the animals seem comfortably at home. In the chilly replica of an Alabama cave, stalactites hang from the drippy ceiling and shelter cave-dwelling creatures.

Near the end of your tour, stop to study the pair of mummified "working class" Egyptians who died in the 3rd century before Christ. Reading from the head to toe, decorations on the coverings appeal for eternal life (Re), protection of heaven (Nut), a permanently mummified body (Osiris) and protection of the corpse (Anubis) to provide a home of the soul (Ba). Their "Anubis," threatened by deterioration since before Regar bought them in 1926, received modern preservation treatment from experts in 1978. The faces on the head masks do not represent the likenesses of the man and woman since they were commoners.

Before you leave, visit the gift shop. The merchandise is not only educational, it's fun, too.

Outside, a nature trail winds through four acres of wilderness where you might spot deer and opossum tracks, not to mention birds and lizards.

Although the serious naturalist student could spend a full day here, even the most casual visitor should allow at least an hour. The best time to visit is Thurs. from noon-5 p.m. when admission is free. Phone 237-6766. Open Tues.-Fri., 9-5; Sat., 10-5; Sun., 1-5. Closed Mon. and holidays. Adults, $3; ages 4-14, $2; ages 60+, $2.50. Phone 237-6766.

Getting there: The museum is 2 miles north of town on McClellan Boulevard. Follow the signs to Lagarde Park off the intersection of Hwy. 21 and U.S. 431.

CHEAHA STATE PARK, a mountainous park showcasing broad vistas from the highest point in the state, lies 25 miles south on the Clay Cleburne county line. The area south of I-20 contains a large expanse of the **Talladega National Forest**. A drive down U.S. 431 and onto some steep, winding paved roads will lure you higher into the elevated peak of the state and to the relaxed and restful Cheaha, spreading over 2,500 acres of eastern Alabama.

Daytrippers can swim at the base of the mountain in a lake with a bathhouse developed by the CCC in the 1930s, or go up to where the views are. Climb the rustic rock tower to get the official view of the state's highest point (2,407 feet above sea level). Unlike Rock City, you'll see only one state, but you'll feel like you see a lot of Alabama, which you can on a clear day. Other peaks within the park are Hernandez at 2,344 feet, Bald Rock at 2,326 feet and Pulpit Rock, 2,080 feet.

Next, follow the signs to the trails. If you're wearing sure-footed treads, try the half-mile Bald Rock Trail or the Pulpit Rock Trail. The hardy might attempt the steep mile-long Lake Trail.

Try to have lunch in the restaurant which serves three meals a day. It isn't famous for the food, but your table will face tall windows and a sweeping eastern view of rolling mountains and trees like nowhere else in Alabama. You'll notice car tags from several states and meet other people who wanted to get away, but didn't want to go too far to get there.

For families or groups who want a true retreat for picnicking or overnighting in a cabin without a TV set, this is it. Cheaha isn't one of the state's most comfortably appointed parks like Lakepoint or Joe Wheeler. It's an old-fashioned state park that doesn't give you the feeling that Holiday Inn arrived ahead of you.

In addition to primitive and improved campsites, there is a reasonably priced 30-unit motel with swimming pool. Cabins for four or eight persons are available, as are chalets which sleep six. If you have a lot of friends, the Bald Rock Group Lodge sleeps 50. Most overnight lodgings are booked well in advance in the fall.

Check-in is at 4 p.m, with check-out at 11 a.m. No pets are allowed in the rooms. A store carries t-shirts, tanning lotion and other items travelers forget to pack. The park closes at dusk. Cheaha (an Indian word for "high") makes you appreciate the fact that the state has many natural beauty spots, with this being one of the very special places. The leaves are at their most colorful in mid to late October, the time of an annual arts and crafts fair. Reservations may be secured with Visa or MasterCard. **Phone 1-800-ALA-PARK** or 488-5115 or 488-5111.

FORT McCLELLAN added to the town's fortunes when established in 1912 and became an important World War II training center. Today it is a major training center of the U.S. Army and the headquarters of the Chemical Corps Training Command.

Although the military facilities are not open to the public tours, several related museums on post are open free Mon.-Fri., 8 a.m.-4 p.m.

Chemical Corps Museum in Building 2299 traces the development and use of chemicals in war. Gas masks, chemical detection and identification kits and other chemical warfare-related equipment are displayed. Phone 848-4449.

Military Police Corps Regimental Museum surveys the history of this U.S. Army branch since its inception during World War II. Displays include police uniforms and weapons, a war criminal exhibit, and Military Police vehicles. Phone 848-3050.

Women's Army Corps Museum in Building 1077 exhibits uniforms and other items used by women in the Army from the founding in 1942 to decommission in 1978. It chronicles the service of past and present women in the Army. Individuals who contributed to military service are honored, including Confederate spy Belle Boyd and Yankee spy Harriet Tubman, who also ran the "underground railroad" for runaway slaves. Phone 848-3512.

Getting there: Go north of town 3 miles on Hwy. 21. Follow signs to enter at Galloway Gate.

OLDE MILL ANTIQUE MALL is an interstate highway landmark that offers two floors of great antiques browsing, with an abundance of glass, kitchen items, 1950's collectibles and paper items. Because it is a century-old mill with huge open spaces, there's no air conditioning or heavy-duty heating system. Open daily 10-5, except Sun. 1-5.
Getting there: On I-20, take exit 185 and follow the signs.

ST. MICHAEL AND ALL ANGELS EPISCOPAL CHURCH was designed by New York architect William Halsey Wood for Anniston founder John Ward Noble, who is buried near the entrance. The simple Norman-inspired church was completed in 1890 by masons from Noble's native Cornwall.

The simple exterior contrasts with the elaborate chancel dominated by a 12-foot altar of white Carrara marble shipped from Italy. The archangels Raphael and Gabriel flank Michael behind the altar cross. A pipe organ installed in 1889 was expanded to 2,715 pipes. A dozen bells, weighing 17,715 pounds, ring from the 95-foot tower, noting each passing quarter hour. The church ceiling is the traditional replica of a ship's framework carved by Bavarian craftsmen.

The church's real masterpieces are the 15 windows of Jesus and the Holy Family signed by the J.& R. Lamb Co. of New York and others. Notice the Tiffany "Madonna and Child" and the Rose window above the south entry.

The Noble name is virtually everywhere, from the windows to the inscriptions on the bells. The church derives its name because the benefactor was born on Sept. 29, St. Michael's Day. Allow 30 minutes. Open daily 9-4. Phone 237-4011.

Getting there: From Quintard, turn west on 18th Street and go 12 blocks to Cobb Avenue. Drive around the church to park near the flagpole on the east side and enter under the clock tower.

TOUR ITINERARIES
Two-day/one-night tour: Shopping and Charm

Day 1: Arrive in Anniston by midday and eat **lunch at Betty's Barbecue or Morrison's cafeteria.** Drive to the **Church of St. Michael's and All Angels** to see the fine stonework and stained glass windows. Visit the impressive **Anniston Museum of Natural History** or the **Olde Mill Antique Mall.** Then, **dine** at the restored **Victoria Inn** and stay there overnight.

Day 2: Head for the **Boaz outlet stores.** Eat lunch at **Mrs. Tupper's,** owned by Morrison's. If you still have time, continue to Gadsden to see the beautiful waterfall and pioneer village at **Noccalula Falls Park.** Depart for home.

Two-day/one-night family tour

Day 1: Begin near Childerburg with a morning stop at **DeSoto Caverns Park**, an Indian mini-theme park designed for children around an impressively illuminated caverns tour. **Eat lunch** here before driving to Talladega via Hwy. 21 to see the world's finest racing cars at the **International Motorsports Hall of Fame** off I-20. Go east to the Anniston-Oxford exit and check-in for the night at the **Holiday Inn** or the **Victoria Inn.** Drive south on U.S. 431 to Hwy. 49 South to **Cheaha State Park for dinner** and watch the sunset from the state's highest mountains.

Day 2: Check-out after **breakfast** and drive to the **Anniston Museum of Natural History**. (Closed Sun. a.m. and Mon.) Head toward Gadsden on U.S. 431 N. to see the exotic animals at **Ohatchee Creek Ranch** (open weekends) by car or elevated walkway. Or continue to Gadsden and **Noccalula Falls Park**. Then depart for home.

WHERE TO STAY IN ANNISTON

The **Hampton Inn**, 1600 Hwy. 21 S., Oxford, is next to the Olde Mill antique mall at I-20 exit 185. The motel has 129 rooms and offers continental breakfast, local phone calls and in-room movies. The Quintard Mall is just across the interstate. Double rate: $42-$48 plus tax. **Phone 835-1496** or 1-800-426-7866.

Holiday Inn at Oxford exit 185 of I-20 is the largest in the area with 237 units on two stories. Amenities include in-room coffeemakers and Showtime on cable TV. Also, several Jacuzzi suites and courtesy airport transportation are available. Breakfast, lunch and dinner are served. Room service. The Holiday Inn is convenient to most attractions. A large shopping mall is across the street and the state's largest antiques mall is 1/2 mile. Fax 831-9560. Double rate: $47-$53 plus tax. Honeymoon, golf, family reunion and romantic retreat packages are available. **Phone 831-3410.**

Noble-McCaa-Butler House B&B, 1025 Fairmont, is a regal Queen Anne house which was home to Anniston's finest families for a century. Completed in 1886 by the brother of the town founder, it has been carefully restored by Robert and Prudence Johnson with period reproduction fabrics and a great deal of hard work to showcase the antique furnishings. The house sparkles, from the front door imported from Britain, to the shiny floors in the upstairs hallway. The owners have truly earned their accolades received from the American Bed & Breakfast Association. Five guest rooms are available, including a honeymoon suite with a private side entrance. To pass the time, stroll the grounds being restored by Robert or take a bit of afternoon sun from the second-story balcony. Double rate: $90-$115. Credit cards accepted. **Phone 236-1791.**

The **Victoria Inn**, 1604 Quintard, is a picturesque Queen Anne mansion which John McKleroy completed in 1888. Tucked away on a hillside shrouded with ancient trees and shrubbery, it hides from traffic on the city's busy main street. Climb the stairs near the tiny registration desk to view the three large, comfy bedrooms with antique furnishings and private baths.

If neither of the three is available, you will still be comfortable in the rear wing of 44 rooms furnished in reproduction antiques. In addition to a free daily newspaper, you'll appreciate the nightly turndown service which includes an imported chocolate left on your pillow.

A series of covered walkways connect to the main house and encloses a swimming pool and attractive courtyard. The handsomely landscaped house is an ideal getaway for a romantic weekend or a delightful alternative to standard motels. Dining is downstairs in the main house. Fax 236-1138. Double rate: $64-$140 plus tax. **Phone 236-0503.**

WHERE TO EAT

**The Annistonian, 1709 Noble St., has a large menu selection which includes steaks, seafood and German weiner schnitzel. Period photos, plants and a warm decor combine with the good food to make it a pleasant place to dine. Closed Sun. Phone 236-5156.

Betty's Bar-B-Q, 401 S. Quintard, has developed a loyal following for pork ribs, catfish and chicken cooked over hickory wood. A daily special offers a choice of meats and vegetables served with cornbread, onion and tomato for $5 or a vegetable plate for $4.25. A "beans and greens" plate with the same extras is just $2.75. Popular pies are lemon ice box, chocolate fudge and peanut butter. The 198-seat restaurant Betty and Clayton Walker opened in 1989 is decorated with business cards and antique furnishings given by customers. Open Mon.-Thurs., 10:30 a.m.-8:30 p.m.; Fri.-Sat., until 9. Closed Sun., Fourth of July week, Thanksgiving, Dec. 24-25 and Jan. 1. Phone 237-1411.

***The Victoria Inn**, 1604 Quintard Ave. The restored house provides an elegant backdrop for good food. The McWhorters can seat up to 97 inside several rooms at the front and on the glass-enclosed porch of their charming 1888 landmark inn. The menu changes nightly, with grilled tuna, swordfish, gulf shrimp, chicken breasts and scallops garnished by a changing variety of ingredients. Filet mignon, pasta alfredo and Kansas City strip are usually offered. Every Wednesday, the Victoria serves its crab cakes that have been featured by *Southern Living*. Fresh seafood, pork terrine and chicken with pecan sauce are other favorites. All meals are served daily except Sun., breakfast only. Average meal costs: breakfast, $4-$8; lunch, $5-$10; dinner, $13-$22. Fax 236-1138. Reservations recommended. Closed major holidays. Phone 236-0503.

WHERE TO SHOP

For routine shopping, **Quintard Mall** is on Quintard in Oxford. If you're looking for gifts, visit the **Wren's Nest** next to the Victoria Inn at 1604 Quintard. Phone 238-0710.

ANNUAL EVENT

Third Saturday in August

Museum Day - Anniston Museum of Natural History - Children are the main party people for the birthday celebration held since 1990 when the museum turned 60. Activities focus on those of earlier generations. Youngsters may ride ponies, throw safe tomahawks and watch archery and blowgun demonstrations. They also enjoy magic shows, clowns, dancing and music. Phone 237-6766.

BIRMINGHAM

- **Claims to fame:** Civil rights, medical center, football
- **Don't miss:** Galleria, civil rights and art museums, race course
- **Eat at:** Highlands, Bottega, John's, Mauby's
- **Unique accommodations:** Pickwick, Twin Pines
- **Nickname:** The Magic City
- **Population:** 950,000 (metro); 265,968 in city
- **Tourist Information:** Ed Hall, President; Greater Birmingham Convention & Visitors Bureau, 2200 Ninth Ave. N., Birmingham, 35203-1100. Fax 254-1649. Phone 252-9825 or 1-800-962-6453.

Birmingham, the state's largest city, perches atop numerous wood-covered mountains and hills that rise at the end of the Appalachian chain. Its towering skyscapers and network of looping interstates are all the more dramatic when you consider that a scant 120 years ago it existed only as a developer's dream.

It is in the center of a mineral-rich region known as Jones Valley, with rich red iron outcroppings so pronounced that one of the tallest mountains is simply called Red Mountain. The area was first settled about 1813, with several small villages scattered over the area during the next half century. The largest, named for a government land surveyor, was Elyton.

The valley's rare abundance of the three major minerals for steel production was known as early as the 1850s, and small furnaces were erected in the surrounding area during the Civil War to produce munitions for the Confederate Army. However, the absence of rail lines to move iron and steel products prevented any significant attempts at industrial development.

As in many settlements, the area grew at the spot where two railroads intersected. The east-west Alabama & Chattanooga Railroad crossed the South & North RR in 1870 in a valley where land developers knew major concentrations of coal, limestone and iron ore could be easily mined. Capitalists from around the nation poured in to exploit the resources. So certain were the railroad owners and Northern industrialists of the area's potential that they named it Birmingham after the industrial city in England.

Within several years, the number of smelters and other steel-related processes soared - along with the population - giving rise to the nickname **the Magic City**. Within five years of the first furnace, Birmingham boasted some 50 blast furnaces - including **Sloss Furnaces** - and a number of rolling mills. For two generations, Birmingham was truly the **Pittsburgh of the South** and **U.S. Steel** employed tens of thousands. It became the South's largest steel production center and remained a worldwide manufacturing power for decades.

Although the magic faded during the great Depression as thousands were put out of work, the industry was somewhat revived again during World War II. Eventually, cheaper and higher quality iron ore from Japan combined with dwindling steel orders to shut several factories, resulting in widespread unemployment.

More than a quarter million people - a majority black - live inside the city which is surrounded by scores of other towns. Another 100,000 people live in four middle-class suburbs "over the mountain." Taken by themselves, several would rank among the state's top 20 cities. The newest and southernmost suburb, Hoover, with 39,788

BIRMINGHAM, ALABAMA

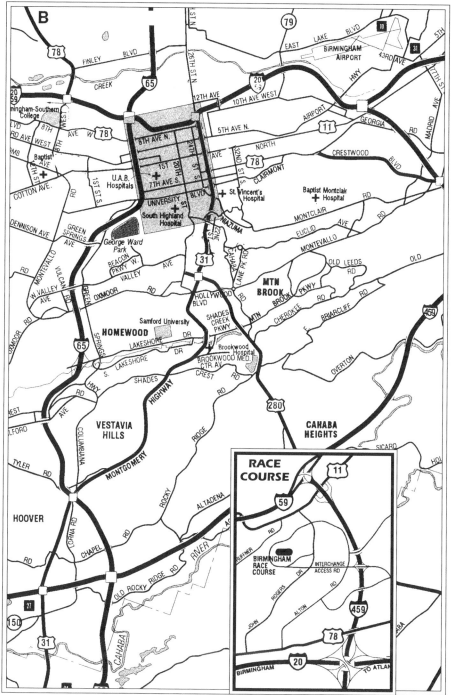

people, is the state's 9th largest. Other suburbs' populations and statewide rank are Homewood, 22,922, 17th; Mountain Brook 19,810, 20th; Vestavia, 19,749, 21st.

The southward middle-class sprawl has continued at such a pace that Shelby County, just across the **Cahaba River** below the Jefferson County line, mushroomed in a decade by 50 percent to 99,358 people. Columbiana, the county seat, still has the character of a sleepy little town seemingly unaware of the giant creeping toward it.

In the 1960s when major department stores and upscale retail establishments were still downtown, the owners lived over the mountain, primarily in Mountain Brook, Homewood and Vestavia. A radio announcer of the day would remark about sundown that the merchants "are closing the cash registers and taking the gold over the mountain." As shopping centers sprang up on the edge of town, the "gold" no longer even made it to downtown. Instead, shopping was done in Homewood and elsewhere closer to where the people lived. Downtown became primarily an office, finance and government district.

Alabama's largest and most dynamic city is also among its youngest. In little more than 100 years, Birmingham has transformed itself from empty farmland to steel boomtown to major commercial, medical and service center. Another part of Birmingham's special magic is its nearly perfect blending of cosmopolitan style with smalltown charm. The traditional Southern hospitality shown by Birmingham's people proves that this is still the heart of Dixie.

In the 1960s, a cloud formed over the city when the racial unrest that had been building across the South finally erupted. Civil rights leaders who selected Birmingham as a target for confrontation over integrating public facilities found the perfect foil in Police Commissioner Eugene "Bull" Connor. He ordered the fire department to turn hoses on black children who attempted to march to City Hall. Other acts of violence, such as whites attacking a busload of "freedom riders" and the bombing of the **Sixteenth Street Baptist Church**, shocked and saddened both blacks and whites. The international media attention embarrassed the entire state and created an image that the city must still deal with three decades later.

Yet, good did come out of the conflict, as Birminghamians rallied around the common goal of peaceful resolution. The spirit of cooperation revitalized the community and inspired a commitment toward growth and development that characterizes the city today.

If you haven't visited Birmingham in the last 20 years, you haven't seen Birmingham. Gone are the pollution-billowing stacks of the heavy manufacturers; the city's renovated central business district boasts a smog-free skyline. Racial tensions have likewise dissipated. By 1971 the nine-member city council included four minority members. In 1979, **Dr. Richard Arrington** became Birmingham's first black mayor, later winning repeated re-election campaigns with support from both races.

Newsweek magazine heralded the city's renaissance as "one of America's hot cities" and the National Conference of Mayors proclaimed Birmingham as the nation's "most liveable city."

An indication of Birmingham's livability is **Birmingham Green**, a parkline streetscape which runs along 20th Street from **Linn Park** in the heart of downtown toward Five Points South. Begun a generation ago as a beautification project to stem the flow of retail stores to the suburbs, it failed at its primary mission, instead, it created a lush pedestrian environment for the financial district.

Having experienced the pitfalls of a single-industry economy, Birmingham has diversified to include medicine, engineering, education, finance and high-technology among its top resources. The largest single employer is the **University of Alabama at Birmingham**, with fully one-tenth of the work force involved in health care.

In 1970, the metro area had 270,000 workers, including 75,000 in manufacturing and 38,000 in service jobs. Now, with an increase to 437,000 jobs, the emphasis is on service-oriented jobs, at more than 100,000. Manufacturing has slipped to 55,000. Birmingham is the dominant force in retail sales in the state, with registers ringing up $7 billion annually.

The city's position as a national leader in scientific research and medical treatment is supported by the **Southern Research Institute**, a private facility serving industry and government in the Southeast, and the **University of Alabama in Birmingham Medical Center** which specializes in open-heart surgery and diabetes treatment. UAB is also one of only seven AIDS research centers established nationwide by the federal government.

An international leader in sports medicine, Birmingham regularly hosts champion athletes from all sports who seek treatment or rehabilitation at **Health South Sports Medicine**. Health South is the SEC's treatment and rehab center.

Business matters aside, life in Birmingham is certainly not all work and no play. An extensive system of public parks provides opportunities for recreation, relaxation and just plain fun.

VISITOR INFORMATION CENTERS

If you follow the directional signs with the giant question mark, you'll wind up at the visitor information center operated by the **Greater Birmingham Convention & Visitors Bureau**. It offers a full range of brochures and information on attractions and other places of interest in Birmingham and the surrounding area. Maps and soft drinks are free of charge. Open Mon.-Sat. 9-6, Sun. 1-5.

It is located at University Boulevard (Eighth Avenue) and 12th Street South. Take the University exit off I-65. The visitor center is located at the western edge of the UAB campus. Phone 930-0212.

The main offices of the convention and visitors bureau are located at the **Birmingham-Jefferson Civic Center**.

A tourist information center inside the **Birmingham Airport** is open for extended hours seven days a week.

For events and lodging information, phone 252-9825 or 1-800-962-6453. After hours, call 868-0660.

DRIVING IN TOWN

Birmingham is fairly easy to navigate even for a newcomer because the optimistic founders laid out the town with wide streets in an orderly grid pattern. The downtown area is bounded by I-20/59 to the north, I-65 to the west and U.S 280/31 to the east. North-south thoroughfares are streets, while east-west routes are avenues. Both streets and avenues are numbered, although a few also have names, such as University Blvd. (Eighth Avenue) and Birmingham Green (20th Street).

You should know that there are two of each avenues. There are First Avenue North and First Avenue South, separated by the railroad tracks which run east-west, and each set of avenue numbers goes progressively higher the farther from the railroad tracks.

To reach the Highland Avenue area, go south on 20th Street and turn left.

Homewood and Mountain Brook are linked to downtown via U.S. 280. Locals call it the Red Mountain Expressway, but the signs say Elton B. Stephens. To get to the Galleria, take I-65 to the Hoover Holiday Inn and exit south on U.S. 31.

If you arrive at the **Birmingham Airport**, take a moment to survey the artwork while you wait for your luggage. (You'll wonder why that chair is suspended in the air.) A $94 million facelift has created a beautiful and functional facility serving two million passenger a year. The visitors information center has a helpful staff with plenty of answers and directions.

BIRMINGHAM ATTRACTIONS

ALABAMA SPORTS HALL OF FAME showcases dozens of exhibits and mementoes related to 161 of the state's best athletes. While browsing through the three levels, you can see autographed footballs and baseballs from important games, photos of legendary games, players and coaches. Check out priceless trophies and watch video clips from sports' most memorable moments in the 75-seat auditorium. Play electronic games, listen to tapes of the voices of inductees and get tips on how to prepare for different sports.

Dioramas with lifelike figures highlight the achievements of Olympic track legend Jesse Owens, football's Bart Starr and Bear Bryant and baseball's Hank Aaron.

Regardless of your alma mater, you can't help but be impressed with the football exploits of Shug Jordan, Joe Namath, Kenny Stabler, Tucker Frederickson, Travis Tidwell, Joe Cribbs and Heisman Trophy winners Pat Sullivan and Bo Jackson. The hall also honors baseball's Willie Mays, Willie McCovey, Early Wynn, Joe Sewell; boxing heavyweight champ Joe Louis, and harness racing's Sanders Russell. The first class was inducted in 1969. The induction of a new class draws important sports figures to Birmingham each winter.

Check out the interesting gift shop. A unique souvenir is the audiotape you can purchase of yourself calling a baseball play while seated next to Yankee announcer Mel Allen!

The museum, which opened in 1981, was recognized as the finest state hall of fame in the country even before it gained greater visibility with a move to the $8 million, 30,000-square-foot home in the BJCC. Adults, $5; students, $3; ages 60+, $4. Phone 323-6665.

The Southeastern Conference Headquarters is diagonally across the street with gallery space for sports art and displays from the member schools. The SEC has been headquartered in town since 1947. The city spent $2 million for the new building to keep the staff of 23 from leaving town.

Getting there: Civic Center Boulevard (Tenth Avenue North) at 22nd Street.

ALABAMA THEATER - The mark of a truly major city in the 1920s was the opening of at least one opulent movie house. Atlanta's was the Fox; Birmingham had the Alabama. It was designed in 1925 as a "silent movie" house. Talkies were invented during construction and it opened on Christmas Day, 1927 with the silent feature "Spotlight." It became a grand home for films with sound and reigned like a dowager over the finest movies for more than a half century.

When the major downtown department stores and their customers fled over the mountain, the owner filed bankruptcy and the gilded doors closed. The faithful few of the Alabama Theater Organ Society, cherishing the rumbling majesty of the mighty

Wurlitzer pipe organ with the sound capacity of a 70-piece orchestra, rallied to save the building from certain destruction. Because *nouveaux* Birmingham's eye has always been on the future instead of the past, it had already lost the monumental Southern Railway terminal and the Temple of Vestia to "progress" and citizens decided that enough was enough.

The vertical sign out front does not adequately prepare you for this Spanish palace with motifs of many periods. Heavy Moorish details with spiraling terra cotta columns greet you at the face of the theater. The hall of mirrors, just inside the ticket lobby, is a two-story marble room hung with heavy mirrors. The hexagon-detailed lobby ceiling is still finished in the original gold leaf and is highlighted by a nine-foot chandelier which weighs 1,300 pounds.

Inside the 3,000-seat auditorium, rich stained glass arches and gilded plaster ornaments grace the walls.

Watch the newspapers' entertainment sections for frequent showings of classic movies or other special events, but go primarily to see this architectural jewel. Take the time to climb the stairs and walk through the various seating tiers. The place is honeycombed with the kind of architectural details you rarely see anymore. While here, say a silent "thank you" to organist Cecil Whitmire who rallied the troops to save this masterpiece.

The theater screens classic movies on summer weekends, showing such films as "Gone With the Wind," "Casablanca" and "Key Largo." In a recent year, some 360,000 people attended 265 events performances at the Alabama. Each admission paid helps preserve this rare jewel because the annual maintenance bill is in the neighborhood of $750,000. Secure parking is reached via the parking deck entrance on Second Avenue. Phone 251-0418.

Getting there: The Alabama reigns at 1817 Third Ave. N. Enter the Second Avenue parking deck around back.

ARLINGTON is a grand Greek Revival mansion dating from the 1840s and is open as a house museum.

Judge William Mudd, who settled in Elyton about 1830, purchased the property at auction in 1842 and erected the house known as "the Grove" during the next few years. He served several terms in the Legislature and served for over 25 years as a circuit judge. He died in 1884 and the property changed hands several times. Businessman Robert S. Munger purchased the property in 1902 and added closets, bathrooms, electricity and central heat. He also replaced a small balcony with the second-story gallery which extends the width of the north-facing house. A daughter acquired Arlington in 1924 and sold it to a civic group in 1953 for use as a house museum.

The house's brush with history came when it was commandered in the closing days of the Civil War by Maj. Gen. James H. Wilson. His Union troops marched from Florence through Elyton to destroy the Confederacy's furnaces at Tannehill and Selma. It was from Arlington that Wilson dispatched part of his forces under Gen. John T. Croxton to burn the University of Alabama in Tuscaloosa where Confederate officers were being trained.

As a house museum, it is furnished with a superb collection of period antiques. The large double parlor on the west side and the dining room and music room on the opposite side of the hall contain exquisite furnishings and the finest mirrors in Alabama. Upstairs, the master bedroom contains a Renaissance Revival bedroom suite.

The furnishings in the southeast bedroom include a Louis XV bed with rosewood graining. The collection of decorative arts includes an array of drapery and bed linens.

Giant boxwoods on the west side form a garden. Seasonal displays of azaleas, roses, magnolia blossoms and other plants complete the atmosphere of sophisticated taste and wealth.

An attractive iron fence separates Arlington esthetically and physically from the surrounding neighborhood of housing projects and rundown apartments.

For visitors passing through the state, and wishing to visit a splendid antebellum house museum close to an interstate highway, Arlington is unsurpassed in Alabama. The best time to visit is the first December weekend when Arlington is tastefully decked in Victorian Christmas trimmings. Adults, $3; ages 6-18, $2; groups 10+, $1. Open Tue.-Sat., 10-4; Sun., 1-4. Last tour at 3:30 p.m. Purchase tickets at least 30 minutes prior to closing. 331 Cotton Ave. S.W. Phone 780-5656.

Getting there: Arlington is 1.5 miles west of downtown. From I-65 South, take the Sixth Avenue North exit; from I-65 North, take the Third Ave. North exit. Then follow the green and white directional signs. Or from downtown, travel west on First Avenue North, which becomes Cotton Avenue.

BIRMINGHAM BOTANICAL GARDENS, with thousands of shrubs, trees, flowers and more than 230 species of birds, offers a delightful respite from the pressures of city life. The gardens were begun in 1955 when Mayor Jimmy Morgan established the gardens and zoo to symbolize the city's emergence as a major force. The 67-acre site had been used to quarry rock during the Depression and yielded materials for Vulcan's original pedestal on Red Mountain.

Morgan built a conservatory with a floral clock as the centerpiece. Succeeding city administrations have transformed the space into a series of tranquil gardens.

Start at the orientation center in the stylish structure it shares with an upscale restaurant and gift shop. Wander through the formal rose gardens to the South's largest climate-controlled conservatory housing hundreds of varieties of rare plants. The humid greenhouse shelters changing seasonal displays of flowers. At its north end is the camellia house which salutes the state flower with a display of more than 100 varieties which bloom in the early spring. On the opposite end is the desert house where many unusual and arid plants are displayed. Visit the fern glade, formal garden, wildflower garden and *Southern Living*'s lovely traditional Southern garden.

Pay particular attention to the Japanese Garden, with its tea house built for a New York World's Fair. The Japanese garden, with a new cultural center, is designed with narrow walkways to slow your pace and separate you from the rush of the outside world.

Blooming schedule: January- azaleas, camellias, cyclamen, cineraira; February-Japanese Garden flowering apricot, camellias, crocus, azaleas; March- azaleas, daffodils, dogwoods, herb garden, ferns; April- cherry trees, peak wildflowers, dogwoods, rhododendrons, magnolias, Easter lilies; May- peak roses, iris, ferns, cherry trees, magnolias, hydrangeas; June- annuals, crepe myrtle, magnolias, roses, iris, hydrangeas; July, same as June with peak daylilies; August- same as June with dahlias; September- same as June with peak dahlias, chrysanthemums; October- roses, vegetables, mums; November- herb garden, vegetables, mums; December- herbs, vegetables, japonica and poinsettias. Always on show are bonsai, orchids, cacti, bromeliads and begonias.

The gatehouse gift shop is open afternoons except Monday. While visiting the gardens, plan a sidetrip to the zoo across the street. Open daily dawn to dusk. Free. 2612 Lane Park Rd. Phone 879-1227.

Getting there: Exit the Red Mountain Expressway on U.S. 280 and follow the signs to the zoo. The entrance on Lane Park is across the street on your right. Park on the roadside and walk to the entrance.

BIRMINGHAM BREWING CO., is a microbrewery on Southside which offers private tours to show how its Red Mountain Beer is hand-crafted and bottled. The 20-minute tour shows how barley malt, fresh hops, water and yeast are steam-brewed in stainless steel vessels before being bottled or kegged. Afterwards, you can sample what you've just seen made. Try the copper-colored red ale, the golden ale or the premium golden lager. Attorney Ben Hogan owns this, the first brewery in Birmingham in 80 years.

Beer is delivered to grocery stores and restaurants within hours of being made. Look for the label with the yellow oval surrounding the statue of Vulcan or ask for it by name in local nightspots.

To make arrangements to visit, leave a message on the answering machine that you're calling regarding a tour. The ideal size for a group is 5-15. Phone 326-6677.

Getting there: It is at 3118 Third Ave. S. Take Third Avenue South exit from U.S. 280 Expressway. Then take Second Avenue to 32nd and make two quick right turns.

BIRMINGHAM CIVIL RIGHTS INSTITUTE is an emotionally charged museum and research center which depicts the events leading to the city's racial conflicts of 1963 and the impact of the Civil Rights Movement on the city since then.

With its theme of Walking to Freedom, the 58,000-square-foot institute is a reminder of the past and a teacher for the future.

A gallery of black and white photographs leads to an introductory film about the segregated, ethnic diversity of Birmingham. The screen lifts and you walk into sets representing schools, churches, homes and theaters. Galleries contain giant photos, videos and audio presentations.

You see "white" and "colored" drinking fountains, and a 1950s lunch counter which symbolizes segregation in public places. A "whites only" taxicab represents segregated transportation.

You hear the voices of neighbors talking about the arrest of **Rosa Parks** which led to the bus boycott in Montgomery before you arrive at a striking tableau at the end of the hallway. The life-size figures of Mrs. Parks, the bus driver who ordered her to leave her seat, and a white passenger waiting to be seated are frozen in time.

One of the most jarring exhibits is the charred remains of a Greyhound bus representing the violence against **Freedom Riders** in Anniston and Birmingham in 1961. A six-minute film chronicles the episode.

The struggle of blacks trying to register to vote in Selma is told in a 10-minute film climaxing with the 1965 **Selma-to-Montgomery March**.

While you stand in front of the jail cell where Martin Luther King wrote his famous 1963 essay *Letter from Birmingham Jail* when in custody for civil disobedience, you hear him say, "One day the South will know that when these disinherited children of God sat down at the lunch counters, they were in reality standing up for what is best in the American dream."

The familiar pictures of Birmingham police using firehoses and dogs on marchers are contained in a riveting film titled *The World is Watching*.

The exhibit program culminates with a gallery on human rights that shows the impact the movement in Birmingham had on quests for freedom in other parts of the world. Waist-high plaques mark Birmingham's racial advancements, such as the repeal of segregation laws and the election of the first black public officials.

Adults of both races are likely to be touched by the struggles depicted in the superb historical exhibition. If it has a shortcoming, it is that the exhibits do not sufficiently explain that the marches and violent confrontations were in the shadow of the building. The 1963 church bombing is underplayed so that visitors will learn that story next door at the church.

The institute is a dramatic example of Birmingham's self examination and coming to terms with its past and the continuing process of racial healing. *The New York Times*, which had criticized the city's racial attitudes in the 1960s, headlined a story on the opening of institute: "Facing Up To Racial Pains of the Past, Birmingham Moves On."

The $11 million institute, funded by corporations and local government, is the interpretive portion of the **Civil Rights District** which includes the adjacent **Sixteenth Street Baptist Church** and **Kelly-Ingram Park** where the marches were formed. The **Fourth Avenue Business District** and the **Alabama Jazz Hall of Fame** are other components of the historic district.

This is Birmingham's world-class attraction. If you have time for only one stop in Birmingham, don't miss it! Open Mon.-Sat., 9-5; Sun., 1-5. Admission. Phone 328-9696.

Getting there: 16th Street and Sixth Avenue North.

BIRMINGHAM-JEFFERSON CIVIC CENTER is Alabama's largest venue for exhibits and conventions. The BJCC complex features a 19,000-seat arena, a 1,070-seat theater, a 3,000-seat concert hall, the 30,000-square-foot Sports Hall of Fame and two wings which offer 240,000 total square feet of exhibit space, 29,000 square feet of meeting-room space and 50,000 square feet of pre-function space. For large parties, a ballroom seats 1,200.

In recognition of Birmingham's preeminence in the health-care field, a unique **Medical Forum** provides 364,000 square feet of meeting space for health-care professionals. Along with space for medical manufacturers and pharmaceutical companies to display their wares, the mart houses continuing education venues with satellite links and wireless interactive response pads for attendee votes to judge the success level of a particular lecture or demonstration, video projectors, wireless-translation headsets for three languages and a television studio. Some 30 "wet labs" or work stations can be used to try out the latest in healthcare techniques and technology. The 10-story trade mart fills between the peaks and valleys of convention business.

The adjacent 771-room **Sheraton Civic Center Hotel** towers 16 floors above the civic center. It offers two presidential and two vice presidential suites and several hospitality suites. Three restaurants, a sports bar giving UAB, Auburn and Alabama equal billing and a deli provide food and drink. The **Greater Birmingham Convention & Visitors Bureau** has offices and an information center visible from the interstate.

Getting there: Take either Civic Center exit off I-20.

BIRMINGHAM MUSEUM OF ART near the civic center is the finest and largest city-supported art museum in the Southeast, thanks to a new wing which displays a $50 million French collection.

The 166,000-square-foot museum houses a permanent collection of more than 13,500 objects, including fine examples of Western European Renaissance art in the **Kress Collection**, an exhaustive Wedgwood collection, and world-class acquisitions of French art from the 1700s in the new Hitt Galleries.

The majority of Western European and American art in the permanent collection is displayed in the first-floor galleries. On this level, see the Kress Collection, which is strong in 17th-century Dutch and Flemish, 18th-century English and 19th-century French paintings. Northern European art, 19th- and 20th-century American works and a photo gallery are also on this floor.

Along with the west lobby and a large gallery showcasing temporary exhibits, you will find the museum gift shop and its interesting collection of books, pottery, toys, jewelry and other gifts.

The second floor has 1,400 objects in the **Dwight and Lucille Beeson Wedgwood Collection**. It is generally regarded as the largest and finest collection outside of Great Britain. Also, see 19th-century decorative arts, Native Indian artifacts and a fine collection of Pre-Columbian art. African art and Oriental galleries are also here, along with temporary exhibits.

The glory days of the museum under director John Schloder are just beginning. Galleries in the $19 million, 50,000-square-foot wing were built to showcase the collection donated by **Mrs. Eugenia Woodward Hitt**, heiress to the Woodward coal fortune. Her collection of 600 French objects from the 18th century includes splendid Louis XV furnishings and court paintings.

As well as a 350-seat auditorium, the wing includes a spectacular sculpture garden with a massive waterfall in textured granite. Some 6,500 numbered bricks, representing financial support, surround a pair of elegant pools inlaid with colorful tiles.

When you arrive, go to the gift shop and purchase a copy of the Wedgwood Collection guide book by decorative-arts curator Elizabeth Bryding Adams. Open Tues.-Sat. and Sun. afternoons. Free. 2000 Eighth Ave. N. Phone 254-2565.

Getting there: Corner of 21st Street and Eighth Avenue North.

BIRMINGHAM RACE COURSE - Sitting on the eastern edge of Birmingham is the Taj Mahal of dog racing where you can sit in comparative luxury to watch trim greyhounds speed around a small oval or watch powerful horses gallop around a larger course.

Dogs and horses are arch-enemies every other place in the nation, but the lion laid down with the lamb in Birmingham in a compromise that could only be made in politics. Saddled with losses totaling $43 million, the race course and creditors were rescued by **Milton E. McGregor** who won approval for dog racing in 1992. He made a fortune operating VictoryLand near Tuskegee and brought back horse racing in 1992 as part of the deal to be allowed to race greyhounds here. He pays out 4.5 percent of the profit to charities.

The near-immediate failure in 1986 of the $84 million track occured because the inexperienced developers were short on cash, yet mortgaged everything to build a state-of-the-art grandstand on glossy market projections of $1.1 million in bets a day. But wagers by the area's novice horseplayers averaged only $313,000. It lost $100,000 a day and quickly was in trouble with creditors.

The Montgomery businessman spent $30 million while gaining control and retrofitting the track into America's largest and grandest home for dog racing. The first greyhound race was won Oct. 28, 1992, when Epitome clocked 31.56 seconds over the 5/16-mile course before a crowd of 12,048 people.

Another milestone came the following April 28 when McGregor's track became the first in the nation where live thoroughbred racing, thoroughbred simulcasting, live quarter-horse racing and live greyhound racing happened at the same track.

Dogs run 3/8- and 5/16-mile races on the smaller oval which is on the inside of the horse track in front of the homestretch of the grandstand building.

With the infusion of McGregor's dogs and marketing genius, the track is expected to handle $150-$200 million a year, one of the highest totals in the country. You don't have to understand pari-mutuel betting to enjoy the festivities. Even a novice will probably be swept up by the enthusiastic crowd to place a small wager.

The running of the **Alabama Derby** on July the Fourth is a highlight of the spring and early summer thoroughbred season.

The grandstand is organized into five seating levels in the general admission grandstand, clubhouse and private club levels. In the 1,300-seat clubhouse, most dining tables have a small color TV so you can watch the races on a closed-circuit screen. Reservations are required for the dining area of the clubhouse, but not for the other area. In the sports bar, none of the 475 seats has a view of the track, but races are shown on closed-circuit TV.

A wide variety of food and drink is available, starting with a beer and chips at the concession stands. McGregor has high dining standards in the seafood and oysters bar named Breakers. Upscale dining is delivered in Winners, the fine-dining restaurant where food is prepared under the supervision of track chef Wiley Poundstone, formerly chef at Commander's Palace in New Orleans.

Racing is nightly, Mon.-Sat., with matinees several days a week. Check sports pages in *The Birmingham News* and *Post-Herald* for times.

For reservations in the clubhouse and sports bar, phone 838-7444 or 1-800-998-UBET. Dining reservations are recommended for weekends.

Getting there: Take exit 132 off I-20. The track, beyond Irondale, can be reached via I-59, I-459, U.S. 78 and U.S. 11.

BIRMINGHAM ZOO is the perfect place to spend a leisurely afternoon with or without kids. Even on a sunny summer day there are plenty of shade trees scattered about as you visit the more than 1,000 exotic animals from every continent of the globe. A stroll allows you to see Siberian tigers, white rhinos, polar bears, gorillas and orangutans, as well as rare birds and reptiles.

The zoo evolved around four 1930s Works Progress Administration ponds that were once the state fish hatcheries. The first exhibit of what was originally known as the Jimmy Morgan Zoo was the monkey island, built by volunteers in 1955.

It is already the South's largest municipal zoo and the world's first to use life-style themes rather than species or geographic areas to exhibit animals. The social-animals building is home to 13 families of animals that depend on social behavior for their survival in the wild, such as gorillas, wolves and mandrill baboons. Another unusual collection of animals is located in the predator building. Cheetahs are the newest residents of the zoo.

A highlight of a visit to the zoo is watching a pair of retired Ringling Brothers circus elephants, Mona and Susan, exercise each afternoon. A trainer started the "stair climbing" and stretch routines to help them lose weight.

To see the 70-acre zoo without a great deal of walking, climb aboard the miniature train, the *Magic City Express*. More than half of the zoo's 500,000 annual visitors do. Open daily, 9:30 a.m.-5 p.m. Adults, $4; ages 2-17 and senior citizens, $1.50. 2630 Cahaba Rd. Phone 879-0408.

Getting there: It's easy to find near Mountain Brook on Cahaba Road off U.S. 280. It's across the street from the Botanical Gardens.

CAHABA RIVER is the most ecologically diverse river in North America and shelters 131 species of flora and fauna.

It forms near Trussville and winds 165 miles through densely populated Birmingham and a half dozen counties until it empties into the Alabama River below Selma at Cahawba.

Birmingham has been pumping drinking water from the Cahaba since 1895. In the past few years, however, the Cahaba has come under serious threat of pollution and "urban runoff" by the intense construction and development within its watershed. The sprawling growth of Birmingham is most intense near the river as it separates Jefferson and Shelby counties.

The recreational value of the Cahaba is enormous because 60 percent of Alabama's residents live within 100 miles of the river and a million are within a 30-minute drive.

Because of development pressures, environmentalists list it as one of the nation's 15 most endangered rivers. The Cahaba shiner is an endangered fish believed found nowhere else. The rare Cahaba lily or *Hymenocallis coronaria*, which resembles a white exploding star, is another symbol of the beauty and frailty of the stream. The plant grows only in rock crevices in shoals where the water is clean and swift.

An environmental organization formed to "save the Cahaba" has several thousand members. It stages canoe trips on the river several times a year, with those in July and August being the most popular. Contact the **Cahaba River Society** at 2717 Seventh Ave. S. or phone 322-5326.

Although access points are not abundant, you can wade in the headwaters in Trussville. Take Parkway Drive to U.S. 11 to reach Civitan Park where a pedestrian bridge crosses the shallow stream. Further downstream, between Lake Purdy and I-459, is where the river is most seriously threatened by developers wanting to build housing subdivisions and office parks within a stone's throw of the fragile stream. Grants Mill Road is a popular place to camp and put in canoes. Because there are no roads which parallel the river's route, it is best explored by canoe, as it is by many weekend canoers, although its lack of depth at times requires that boats be carried for short distances.

Some of the most beautiful stretches of the river are found on the Lower Cahaba below Centreville. Canoers find beautiful sand and gravel bars, large islands ideal for picnicking and camping, wide sweeping bends, lush forests along the banks and more birds and wildlife than are found in almost any other section of the river.

For about $25, you can rent a canoe to explore the river:

• Take a 10-mile float on the Cahaba from Lorna Road in Hoover down to **Alabama Small Boats**. It takes from four to six hours. Take exit 6 of I-459 to Hwy. 52 and go south 6 miles to Alabama Small Boats for canoe and kayak rental and shuttle service. Open Mon.-Sat. Phone 424-3634.

• **Bulldog Bend Canoeing Park** is on Little Cahaba up in Bibb County. Rent canoes or tubes to float down the river and get a shuttle ride back to your car. It is 3 miles from Hwy. 25 on Jct. 65 at the end of the bridge. Phone 926-7382.

COBB LANE is a quaint cluster of restaurants and specialty shops grouped around a cobblestone alley just above Five Points South. Cobb Lane evolved from Prairie-Craftsman style luxury apartments and carriage houses built in 1909. Antiques shops and the **Cobb Lane Restaurant** are constants in the varying lineup of businesses. Others include gift and art shops, as well as dress shops and interior design firms.

Getting there: Cobb Lane fronts 20th Street South between Highland and 14th avenues. Shops flank the alley between 19th and 20th streets and 13th and 14th avenues.

CULTURAL DISTRICT is the umbrella designation the city is giving to the downtown attractions in the civic center area and beyond. Its two parts include the black heritage area on the west, encompassing the Sixteenth Street Baptist Church, Birmingham Civil Rights Institute, Alabama Jazz Hall of Fame; and the Fourth Avenue business district, a cluster of black-owned businesses that city officials hope will be revitalized by the cultural emphasis and the tourism the district attracts. The eastern half of the district includes the BJCC, Birmingham Museum of Art, Boutwell Auditorium, SEC Headquarters, Alabama School of Fine Arts at 8th Avenue North and 18th Street, Alabama Sports Hall of Fame, Southern History Library, Linn Park, Lyric Theater, Alabama Theater and so forth. Colorful street banners define the boundaries.

Getting there: It extends from Fifth to 12th Avenue N. and 15th to 26th street.

DISCOVERY 2000, the merger of Red Mountain Museum and Discovery Place, educates and entertains youngsters through "see and touch" experiences. **Discovery Place** encourages kids to explore various aspects of the human body, dress up as fireman or construction workers, watch baby animals, experiment with magnets and guess sounds of animals. Children under 12 need a grownup with them. A proud volunteer corps augments the staff.

Open Tues.-Fri., 9-3; Sat., 10-4; Sun., 1-4. Closed Mon., holidays and the month of September. School groups should make reservations. Admission. Phone 939-1176.

The **Red Mountain Museum** overlooks and explains the gigantic geological "cut" in Red Mountain created for the bisecting expressway. After visiting the small educational center which explains the earth's geological history, take the path along the face of the cut. Some 150 millions years of geological history are exposed. The round-trip takes about 20 minutes and covers about a half mile. Small signs explain the various layers of rocks and minerals along the sheer walls about 200 feet above the expressway between downtown Birmingham and Homewood.

The museum is a favorite of kids on school field trips. The hands-on exhibits explain topics ranging from earthquakes to land mass plates. Open Tues.-Sat. 10-4:30, Sun. 1-4:30. Admission. 1425 22nd St. S. Phone 933-4104 for recorded information.

By 1995, the combined Discovery 2000 science center is moving to the old **Loveman's** (1935-80) department store at 19th Street and Third Avenue North. Loveman's and Pizitz stores anchored downtown shopping until the 1960's.

Getting there: Discovery 2000 is located in a residential district off Highland Avenue. At the Highland curve at the police department on the Arlington Avenue intersection, go under the Red Mountain Expressway and follow signs directing to the right. Go up the steep hill and park on the right between Discovery Place and the Red Mountain Museum.

FIVE POINTS SOUTH - Initially one of Birmingham's first streetcar suburbs, the town of Highland was incorporated in 1887 and became a part of the city in 1893. The heart of the town was Five Points Circle, now the business district with a charming collection of restaurants and boutiques distinguished by Spanish Revival and modern architecture. Following a major sports victory in town, celebratory fans congregate around (and sometimes in) the fountain. The spot is routinely popular on Saturday nights. The backdrop of the fountain is **Highlands United Methodist Church**, a beautiful example of Spanish architecture with dome, towers and buff brick exterior designed by architect P. Thornton Marie. The church bears a resemblence to the now-demolished Terminal Station (1909-69), also designed by Marie. Within a block are several excellent shops, an alternative bookstore, upscale gift shops and places for casual food and drink.

Five Points is the heart of Southside, Birmingham's mountainside home to singles, professionals, gays, and other affluents, many of whose homes and apartments have spectacular views overlooking the lights of downtown and beyond. Southside is roughly the area between the Medical District and Red Mountain.

Formed by the 20th Street intersection of 11th Avenue South, with Magnolia Avenue radiating outward, Five Points is transformed after dark into the center of city dining and nightlife. Several of the state's best restaurants are nearby, including Highlands and Bottega. The large Barber's Dairy clock facing downtown has been a landmark for decades. The intersection with 20th Street is the beginning of Highland, the beautiful boulevard laced with azaleas and dogwoods that winds past three parks and ends at Highland Park golf course.

Two sculptures bridge fantasy and reality. The statue of the kneeling minister in the shadow of The Mill restaurant is of Rev. James Alexander Bryan. Known simply as **Brother Bryan**, he was an inspirational minister to the poor and hungry from his arrival in 1889 to his death in 1941. Birmingham sculptor Georges Bridges created the white marble statue in 1934. It stood underneath Vulcan from 1966 until it was returned in 1982 to Five Points, the center of his ministry.

On the opposite end of the artistic spectrum is Frank Fleming's grouping of **The Storyteller** presiding over a peaceful kingdom in front of the church. The main statue is a six-foot clothed figure with the head and legs of a ram and the body of a man. Clutching a staff with an owl perched on it, he reads to an attentive lion, a turtle with a rabbit on its back and a dog with a small fawn on its back. Five frogs surrounding the storyteller spray water toward his feet. Fleming was inspired by the Br'er Rabbit stories.

On special occasions, you can enjoy the neighborhood during a romantic carriage ride. Several companies charge about $20 a couple for a trip of about 18 blocks.

Getting there: Travel 20th Street south from downtown or exit U.S. 280 at Highland Avenue.

JAZZ HALL OF FAME is located in the Carver Theater, an art deco movie theater in the black Fourth Avenue North business district at 17th Street. It has exhibits on famous local jazz musicians and regular performances by the **Birmingham Heritage Band** in the 550-seat theater.

KELLY-INGRAM PARK was the gathering site for many historic civil rights marches in 1963 which attempted to cover the four blocks along Sixth Avenue and 19th Street to City Hall. It was along this route that police used firehoses and police dogs to halt and arrest children and adults during the stormy days of confrontation.

The one-block park has been transformed by a series of dramatic sculptures by Texan James Drake to give visitors the uncomfortable feeling of participating in the pivotal events. If you follow the circular Freedom Walk, you will face bronze fire hoses and leaping, snarling dogs. One of the more evocative images is that of a crouched figure symbolically trying to withstand the brutal pressure of firehoses. A "victory stand" commemorating the children's marches has a pair of youngsters atop steps marked with the words: "I ain't scared of your jail."

Traditional statues have Rev. Martin Luther King facing the Sixteenth Street Baptist Church and a limestone sculpture of three ministers kneeling at the corner of Fifth Avenue North and 17th Street. A statue of Rev. Fred Shuttlesworth faces the park from the front of the Civil Rights Institute.

Getting there: The park is bordered by 16th and 17th streets and Fifth and Sixth avenues North.

KIRKLIN CLINIC is the medical "superclinic" housed in the five-story structure designed by internationally renowned architect **I. M. Pei**. The $103 million clinic pulled all of University Medical Center's scattered clinics under a single roof to centralize ambulatory patient care and improve health-care quality. The **University of Alabama Health Services Foundation** anticipates that the 430,000-square feet Kirklin will eventually rival Mayo Clinic in Minnesota and Ochsner Clinic in New Orleans for ranges of service and quality.

The initial white and glass building houses more than 660 physicians affiliated with the university. Some 32 clinics are housed in the facility from the departments of Medicine, Surgery, OB/GYN and specialty clinics. Pei's master plan calls for a second building across Sixth Avenue South that is a mirror image of the first and connected by pedestrian bridges. The name honors Dr. John Kirklin, the Birmingham pioneering heart surgeon who inspired its development.

Getting there: It is on 20th Street with entry fountains facing Sixth Avenue South. Park across 21st Street in one of the 1,450 spaces in the parking deck.

LEGION FIELD - The stadium earned for Birmingham the nickname of "the Football Capitol of the South" during the 1960s when Alabama and Auburn played many games here each fall. With the SEC championship, the grand old stadium remains one of the titans of the sport.

Legion Field became the third largest stadium in the South with 83,000 seats, including a 220-person press box and 15 skybox suites with sitting area and kitchen which accommodate a total of 1,000 people. One of the largest suites even holds 300 fans. The expansion and facelift figured prominently in the SEC's decision to award Birmingham the conference's football championship game.

Food: Plan to snack on hot dogs and Cokes at the stadium or tailgate it from your car. There are no restaurants nearby.

Transportation: Because parking in the neighborhood is limited, ride a Max shuttle bus. For information on departure points, check Max ads in the local papers or phone 521-0101.

Vans: For a fee, you can park your motorhome overnight on the grounds and party until it is time to walk into the stadium.

Getting there: If you must drive, travel I-59 to the Arkadelphia Road exit, go south and turn left on either Eighth or Graymont. Legion Field's parking lot accommodates about 2,700 cars.

LINN PARK is a neat urban park that literally is the heart of downtown Birmingham. The park, surrounded by government buildings, is a serene oasis for passing a peaceful lunch hour. The centerpiece is a grand fountain flanked by a water flume that flows down the slope from the middle of the park to Eighth Avenue North. Linn Park vibrates with excitement during the annual City Stages musical weekend.

Getting there: Linn Park is sandwiched between Boutwell Auditorium, City Hall and the library at the north end of 20th Street.

MOUNTAIN BROOK is the wealthiest of the suburbs and has the highest per capita income in the state. Mountain Brook was carefully carved from the woods along Shades Creek in a real estate development by Robert Jemison intended to reflect the charm of the estates and countryside of England. He succeeded. Boston landscape architect Warren Manning developed the plan during 1926-29, with many residential lots six times the size of regular lots, and a village shopping center included. Linear parks along Mountain Brook Parkway and Overbrook Road offer delightful scenery during afternoon drives.

Getting there: Follow U.S. 280 E. through Homewood and take the "zoo" exit. Or follow Montevallo Road from Irondale.

OAK MOUNTAIN AMPHITHEATER is a truly remarkable setting for an evening concert of the Alabama Symphony Orchestra or the latest rock group and is adjacent to the **Oak Mountain State Park**. The amphitheater has 5,000 permanent seats, with additional grounds seating for 3,000. Musical performances are staged regularly.

Getting there: Take exit 246 off I-65 S. and follow the traffic. Phone 985-9797.

OAK MOUNTAIN STATE PARK allows city residents to get away to the woods and lakes without having to go far at all. The state park in North Shelby County covers 9,940 acres of rolling hills and stream-filled valleys. It is handy that the state's largest state park is within a few minutes of the state's largest city. Some 500,000 visits a year make it among the most heavily-used parks in the state.

There is a lot to do. You can fish or ride a rented paddleboat in four beautiful lakes, ride bikes, hike along a choice of five trails which cover 35 miles, play golf on an 18-hole course and play tennis. You have a choice of overnight options: tent camping, RV camping and 10 lakeside cabins for rent.

You can also see and do things at Oak Mountain that you don't normally expect at a state park, like seeing sheep being sheared at the demonstration farm or the chance to walk along a tree-top nature trail at the **Alabama Wildlife Center**. The unusual nature trail is an elevated boardwalk winding 300 feet into a hardwood valley and gives you a closeup view of hawks, owls and other birds of prey. The birds are housed in three large elevated treetop enclosures.

The **Oak Mountain Nature Center**, set atop the foothill mountains, has a variety of live and preserved wildlife species, diorama nature exhibits and aquariums.

In addition to the nature exhibits, the staff at Oak Mountain also offers numerous programs dealing with recreation and the environment to groups by reservation. Other events include orientation meets, water ski tournaments, triathalons, bike motor-cross races and an annual bowhunters convention. Phone 663-6783. Phone 663-6771 for cabin rental and 663-3061 for RV reservations. Another phone is 664-0854.

Getting there: Take exit 246 off I-65 S. and follow the signs.

RED MOUNTAIN MUSEUM - see Discovery 2000

The RIVERCHASE GALLERIA is Birmingham's spectacular enclosed shopping mall and topped by the world's largest enclosed atrium and longest skylight, which is made of 110,000 square feet of glass. About 200 specialty shops and stores are here. Open Mon.-Sat., 10-9; Sun., 1-6.

Getting there: Take exit 13 off I-459.

RUFFNER MOUNTAIN NATURE CENTER - City people can escape from city life in only a few minutes. The nature center exhibits the natural features of the last undeveloped ridge of Ruffner Mountain. Nature trails and a wildflower garden are located within the 538 acres. Open Tues.-Sat., 9-5; Sun., 1-5. Free. Phone 833-8112.

Getting there: It is north of Irondale at 1214 S. 81st St.

SIXTEENTH STREET BAPTIST CHURCH - One of the city's most painful experiences puncutuated months of racial unrest on Sept. 15, 1963, when a bomb exploded outside the leading black Baptist church and killed four girls attending Sunday School.

Because of the church's prominence in the black community, it had served for four months as headquarters for mass meetings and rallies which created emotional confrontations with police, but had not lessened segregation.

The bomb exploded at the rear stairs to the church at 10:22 a.m. and killed the girls, age 11-14, who had crossed the basement to go to the bathroom.

The deaths horrified people around the world and focused attention on the state's racial polarization. The national response to the tragedy was a major turning point in the civil rights movement. A longtime Klan member was eventually convicted of murder and died in prison in 1985.

An outpouring of sympathy and financial contributions permitted the congregation to repair the damage and re-open the church. The most visible memorial gift was a contemporary blue and purple stained-glass window of the image of a black crucified Christ which was given by the people of Wales.

The Romanesque style church with twin towers and pointed domes is accented with a cupola over the sanctuary. Wallace Rayfield, Alabama's only black architect at the time, designed the church which was built by a contractor-congregation member. It was completed in 1911.

If you expect a roadside historic marker detailing the bombing, you won't see one. The subtly told story is within. If the sanctuary is locked, go to the adjacent office annex to the right of the church and ask to be allowed inside. If you enter through the basement, look for the memorial room at the back of the assembly area. It has photographs of demonstrations, confrontations with police and scenes of the bomb damage.

A rear steel door to the basement was put in after the bombing and the concrete stairs were not replaced.

The sanctuary is painted a peaceful light blue. Two windows depict traditional Christus figures. Classroom pictures of the girls and a plaque are just to the left of the pulpit. An unexpected archtectural feature is an overhead stained-glass window under the cupola. The Wales window designed by John Petts dominates the rear center area of the balcony. Look carefully at the bottom of the window to read the words: "You do it to me."

A restoration prompted by the opening of the **Civil Rights Institute** across the street refurbished the baptistry and pews and restored the Pilcher pipe organ. Prior to the restoration, cracks in the plaster walls and a general weary look re-enforced the fact that, while the building is an important shrine, the reality is that this is not an affluent congregation. A memorial observance is held each year on the Sunday closest to Sept. 15. A reception follows in the basement auditorium. The address is 1530 Sixth Ave. N. Phone 251-9402.

Getting there: Corner of Sixth Avenue North at 16th Street. A statue of Martin Luther King watches from across the street in **Kelly-Ingram Park**. The church faces the **Civil Rights Institute** across the street.

SLOSS FURNACES NATIONAL HISTORIC LANDMARK - While Vulcan may symbolize the spirit of the iron and steel industry of the city, Sloss is the real thing. Towering over the eastern approach to downtown, the two giant blast furnaces produced pig iron that fed Birmingham's foundaries for much of a century.

James Withers Sloss (1820-1890) was an important North Alabama industrialist when he completed the final gap in the railroad between Decatur and Birmingham which became the L&N Railroad. He organized the Sloss Furnace Co. and began producing "Sloss" brand pig iron in 1882. For the next nine decades, Sloss produced much of the iron that fueled America's growth as an industrial nation.

The Jones Valley is among a few places in the world where deposits of coal, iron and limestone - the three ingredients necessary for steel - are found. But the first steel furnace in Birmingham in 1887 was not the "birthplace of the Birmingham steel industry." The Tannehill furnaces on the other side of Bessemer preceded Birmingham's first by four decades.

Gradually lower Japanese steel prices crippled the American steel industry. Environmental awareness turned the orange smokestack plumes which were once a symbol of prosperity into an embarrassment. After the Jim Walter Corp. bought out Sloss-Sheffield, the last to produce iron in 1971, the plant was abandoned. Former employees supported a $3 million bond issue to rescue the landmark from rusting away and Sloss became a museum of the city in 1977.

Sloss is not only a National Historic Landmark, it is a popular tourism attraction as the only example of 20th-century iron-making technology preserved in the world. During the past few years the city has transformed the rusting hulk of Sloss into a remarkable 32-acre industrial museum of international stature.

Begin your visit with a 10-minute audio visual presentation on Birmingham iron and the people who made it. A guided tour follows, often given by retired furnace workers, permitting access through the yard to view close up the massive 1920s furnaces, blowers, stoves, trestles, ladles and boilers - all the equipment needed to produce iron.

Despite being short of gothic mansions, Birmingham is not without its hauntings. According to local lore, the spirit of Theopholus Calvin Jowers, a former foundryman who died a gristly death, roams Sloss.

Although the furnaces no longer rumble, a variety of other sounds do fill the grounds through the year. Its amphitheater is a popular venue for parties and various types of evening social events. Deep bass tunes from rock concerts echo under the casting shed. Ghost stories are whispered around Halloween and hammers and anvils clang out during an annual blacksmith festival. The Kudzu Festival draws large crowds in the heat of August.

Director James Burnham is restoring Sloss in stages, with ambitious plans to make it a major facility in the metal arts. Open Tues.-Sat., 10-4; Sun., noon-4. Guided tours at 1 p.m., 2 and 3 on weekends. Closed Thanksgiving, Dec. 25 and Jan. 1. Free. Allow 30 minutes. Phone 324-1911.

Getting there: Located on First Avenue N. at 32nd Street. Take First Avenue N. to 34th Street, then left on Second.

SOUTHERN MUSEUM OF FLIGHT near the Birmingham airport houses more than a dozen planes related to Alabama's air history under its four wings. An F-4 Phantom displayed on a 12-foot platform on the front lawn marks the location. Inside, walk around and under aircraft dating from 1910 to the Vietnam era. The oldest is the 1910 Curtis "Pusher," the second powered airplane after the Wright Brothers' historic flight. Exhibits range from artifacts related to Germany's Red Baron and the Flying Tigers of World War II to a 1925 Delta Air Lines crop duster and several home-builts and ultra-lites. The Alabama Aviation Hall of Fame has enshrined Birmingham astronaut Hank Hartsfield, Tuskegee aviator Gen. Ben Davis and William Quick, inventor of the first airplane built and flown in Alabama about 1910. His original plane hangs inside the U.S. Space & Rocket Center in Huntsville. Open Tues.-Sat., 9:30-5; Sun., 1-5. Adults, $2; students, $1; seniors, $1.50. 4343 73rd St. N., Birmingham, 35206. Phone 833-8226.

Getting there: Located 2 blocks east of the Birmingham Airport. Turn right off I-59 exit 131 to 73rd Street North and 43rd Avenue.

TEMPLE OF SIBYL, a classical gazebo which marks the north entrance to Vestavia Hills on U.S. 31, is all that remains of the temple residence of former Mayor **George Ward**. The small dome supported by columns was part of a replica of the ancient Temple of Vesta which Ward built in the 1920s to overlook Birmingham from the crest of Shades Mountain. The civic leader had been inspired by the original during a visit to Rome in 1907. His name for his temple-shaped home of "Vesta Via" (literally "home by the road") provided the name of the city which grew up around it. A Baptist congregation bought and later demolished the temple-home. The gazebo was moved to the Homewood side of Vestavia Hills in 1975. On the Hoover side of Vestavia (U.S. 31 at I-65) stands an out-of-proportion contemporary colonnade inspired by the gazebo.

Getting there: U.S. 31 South at Shades Crest Road.

TUXEDO JUNCTION was a popular black entertainment area in Ensley that inspired Birmingham native **Erskine Hawkins's** famous 1939 hit "Tuxedo Junction." The second-story dance hall built in 1922 was at the social hub of the city's black community in the Tuxedo Park neighborhood where the No.7 streetcar to Wylam crossed the No. 5 to Fairfield. A larger dance hall in the Thornton building across 20th was razed in the late '50's. The historical marker on the Nixon building, owned by a prominent black dentist, identifies the junction. A sign on the second story where jazz once reigned now promises only "same day dentures."

Getting there: Leave I-59 at exit 120 for Hwy. 269 and go 2 blocks north to 1728 20th St.

VULCAN - The city's best known attraction is a 56-foot high iron statue patterned after the mythical Roman god of fire and the forge. It is the largest iron figure ever cast. Vulcan was the city's entry in the 1904 Louisiana Purchase Exposition, better known as the St. Louis world's fair. The Commercial Club commissioned Italian sculptor **Guiseppe Moretti** who cast him from Birmingham iron on First Avenue North (near the old Sears building).

Moretti first built an eight-foot model in his New York studio, then structured a full-size clay model in sections to build a negative mold. A positive mold was then made and shipped to Birmingham to be cast.

Because of the immense weight - 120,000 pounds - it was cast using separate molds for the head, arms, legs and torso. The $15,000 project took only seven months and it was rushed unfinished to the exposition's Palace of Mines and assembled after the fair started. Vulcan won the grand prize. Because of competing liquor and prohibition interests back in Birmingham, Vulcan was christened not with champagne, but with a bottle of clear water from the Cahaba River.

Unfortunately, Vulcan fared poorly upon returning home. People complained that he was ugly and that his chest was too short. Between the years that he returned home to rest unassembled beside railroad tracks and his eventual perch atop Red Mountain, he suffered a series of indignities; his right hand and uplifted arm were on backwards for 21 years, bees built hives in a cavity when his thumb fell off and he held aloft a variety of products - including pickles - when he guarded the entrance to the state fairgrounds.

Since his arrival in 1939 to overlook the city from a spectacular vantage point atop Red Mountain, the years have been marginally better to him, but he is still working. Thanks to the safety-minded Jaycees, his torch burns red if a traffic fatality has occurred in the past 24 hours, green if not. A renovation a generation ago put Vulcan on a 124-foot pedestal. The observation deck is underneath his platform, giving visitors not a closeup view of the statute, but a great view of the city and surrounding countryside.

But Vulcan's future is not burning green. Concrete, filled up to his armpits to keep him from blowing off the mountain, has been expanding and pushing against the cast iron shell, causing serious cracks. A hole in his head a yard wide allowed rainwater to well up inside and form rust. And, if that weren't bad enough, park officials say cast iron only has a life of about 90 years, an age reached in 1994.

Vulcan Park is open daily until 10 p.m. The gift shop sells small Vulcan statues and post cards.

Getting there: Travel 20th Street S. to Valley Avenue in Homewood and follow signs to the park. Drive slowly up the steep hill. Phone 254-2699.

SIDE TRIPS NORTH

Springville is a small town 25 miles north off I-59 with a reputation for quality antiques, crafts and fine arts. **Homestead Hollow** has several craft and food events annually worth attending, particularly during Spring Fest, the first weekend in June. The **House of Quilts** has been selling homemade quilts and antiques for 20 years since being opened by M.S. and Diana Sullivan. Nearby are other shops, including S.S.

Junior's Antiques, Charlotte's Web, the Emporium and Diane's Antiques. **Blackwood Gallery** at 296 Main Street showcases regional wood, clay and fiber artists. Phone 467-7197. Springville is located just west of I-59 exit 154.

Braswell's Winery produces and sells farm wines near Dora between Birmingham and Jasper. Wayne Braswell started production in 1984 and produces more than a dozen varities from locally grown berries, fruits and grapes. The colorful label appears on scuppernong, peach, pear, elderberry, blackberry and white grape wines. Head northwest on U.S. 78 West. About 20 miles from Birmingham, you'll cross the Little Warrior River bridge at mile marker 83. After about 500 yards, bear to the right onto old Bankhead Hwy. Go about a mile. The winery at 7556 Bankhead will be on your left.

SIDE TRIP TO TANNEHILL

Tannehill State Historical Park preserves the remains of a pioneering ironworks which operated from 1829 until it was destroyed by Union troops at the end of the Civil War. The old works lay in ruins for a century until the Alabama Legislature established a park in 1969 to restore the area. Now the restored ironworks is the nation's only Civil War-era furnace put back in blast after being shut down for more than a century. A growing collection of 19th-century buildings has been assembled in clusters along Mill Creek and throughout the wooded park to provide a unique setting for many special events.

Hillman's Forge, a crude forge erected on Roupes Creek, laid the foundation of the future massive stone furnaces which followed. South Carolinians Moses Stroup, William Sanders and John Alexander used the area's abundant iron ore and limestone, as well as sandstone to build the furnaces in 1830. Trees were used to make charcoal to fire the furnaces. Cotton planter Ninion Tannehill bought the forge in 1832 and over several decades expanded the iron plantation to produce plows, skillets, kettles, irons and other cast-iron goods for farmers.

The first 30-foot furnace with charging bridge and cast shed was built circa 1859. Workers standing on a bridge near the top of the stone tower dropped as many as five tons of ore and charcoal a day into the furnace.

During the Civil War, the Confederate government added a pair of furnaces. With a legion of workers, including 600 slaves, the furnaces were soon turning out 20 tons of molten pig iron a day. The Tannehill works, along with a handful of smaller Alabama furnaces, produced 70 percent of the Confederate iron. Most of Tannehill's production was sent south by rail to Selma where cannon balls, gun barrels, battleship armor and other items were forged.

Three companies of the Eighth Iowa Calvary stormed the mill camp on March 31, 1865, just nine days before Robert E. Lee surrendered at Appomattox, and rendered the ironworks useless by burning trestles, tramways, casting houses and foundries. In fact, everything except the three furnace towers themselves was burned. Within days, 14,000 Union raiders under the command of Maj. Gen. James Wilson moved west and destroyed most of Selma and much of the University of Alabama at Tuscaloosa before heading on to capture Montgomery.

Fortunately, the industry rose from its ashes several decades later and moved northeast to become Birmingham's huge iron and steel industry.

Tannehill today is a fascinating 1,500-acre historical complex of more than 40 buildings, many of them log cabins dating from pioneer times and relocated from around the state. They range from homestead cabins, a blacksmith shop and an 1822 dairy barn to an 1858 cotton gin house with the original gin used to separate the seeds from the cotton and the machinery which powered it. Some cabins are studios for craftsmen such as potters, quilters, weavers, broommakers and candlemakers who demonstrate their crafts on weekends from March through November and sell samples.

When you arrive from the interstate, look for the two-story frame house flanked by chimneys. It dates from 1879 and was recently moved 43 miles from Trussville and restored as the visitors information center. You'll get a map here to plan your day. Be sure to walk to the furnaces and the 1867 John Wesley Hall grist mill where you can buy a two-pound bag of "unbolted-water ground corn meal." (Recipes for buttermilk corn bread and Southern spoon bread are right on the back of the bag.)

Save time to visit the **Alabama Iron and Steel Museum** which contains the South's largest collection of ironworks artifacts. It offers a fascinating look at the evolution of the steel industry which was responsible for the rapid growth of Birmingham.

With all of the crafts to see and outdoor trails to explore, it is easy to overlook the historical importance of the birthplace of the steel industry. Wear comfortable shoes to cover the wooded paths to see the towers. You'll find that it's hard to see the furnaces and all of the restored buildings scattered through the woods on your first visit.

More than 350,000 people a year visit Tannehill, making it one of the most popular tourist attractions in the state. Because of a very small admission charge, it is also one of the state's best family travel values.

The best time to visit is on a Trade Day - usually the third weekend of the month from March through November - or during other special events. There are many special events to choose from: the folklore festival in April, dulcimer festival in May, gem and mineral show in June, Civil War re-enactment in November, Frontier Days in October and Tannehill Village Christmas. To enhance future visits, buy a copy of director Jim Bennett's history, "Old Tannehill." Open daily from 7 a.m. to sunset. Adults, $1; ages 6-17, $.50. Write 12632 Confederate Parkway, McCalla, 35111. Phone 477-5711.

Getting there: It is an easy drive 20 miles from Birmingham. Take the interstate past Bessemer. Leave I-59/I-20 at exit 100. Drive east on Tannehill Pwy. 2 miles to the park. From Tuscaloosa, it's about 25 minutes.

Bessemer is an industrial city southwest of Birmingham. It was developed by leading industrialist Henry DeBardeleben and named to honor the British engineer who perfected steel-making processes.

Three of Jefferson County's oldest landmarks are pioneer homes located along Eastern Valley Road parallel to the lower end of I-459. The **Sadler Home** began as a modest structure in 1818 and was expanded to a two-story frame house with a dog trot about 1830. The **Owens Home** was erected as a small house in 1833. A two-story addition with a long covered porch was later added to the front. The **McAdory House**, a dog-trot cabin built of hand hewn logs and wooden pegs in 1840, was the birthplace of Bessemer's first mayor.

Grounds of the houses are open daily. Take exit 10 off I-459, go 3 miles and turn left on Eastern Valley Rd. To arrange for tours of the interiors, phone 425-3253.

To learn more about the city's history, head downtown to the old Southern Railway Depot built in 1916. See historic photographs, Indian artifacts and exhibits illustrating the history of Bessemer within the **Bessemer Hall of History.** The depot museum at the corner of Alabama Avenue and 19th Street is accessible from I-59/20 exit 112. Open Tues.-Sat. Phone 426-1633.

The **Bessemer Flea Market** is open weekends at 1013 8th Ave. N. Some booths are indoors. It is open Fri.-Sun., 8-5. Take I-59 exit 112 or 108. Phone 425-8510.

SUGGESTED BIRMINGHAM ITINERARIES

Two-day/one-night tour: Family magic

Day 1: Arrive in mid-morning and follow U.S. 280 to the **Birmingham Zoo** where you can ride a miniature train to get a glimpse of the habitats you want to visit on foot. Make sure the kids see the elephants and polar bears. Eat a hot dog or hamburger at a snack bar for **lunch.** Next, walk across Cahaba Road to tour the **Botanical Gardens.** Drive through Homewood on U.S. 31 up Red Mountain to visit **Vulcan.** Take the elevator or walk up the tower to see the view of Birmingham he sees. Admission to all three is less than $5 per adult.

Birmingham has a number of family-oriented motels from which to choose. Phone the convention bureau in advance for a list and ask about specials where kids stay free. For example, at the I-65/U.S. 31 intersection at Hoover is the **Holiday Inn-Galleria** with a lake. Across the highway is a plantation-style **Days Inn** where Bo Jackson's mother used to work. A couple of blocks away on 31 is a **Hampton Inn.** For dinner, go to **Milo's Hamburgers** near the Hampton and enjoy their famous hamburgers, tea sweetened with molasses and the city's best French fries.

Day 2: In the morning after checking out of the hotel, go on a field trip to **Tannehill State Historical Park** with lunch at the **Bright Star** in Bessemer or visit **Ruffner Mountain.** A third choice is **Discovery 2000,** the hands-on children's science museum.

Two-day/one-night romantic tour

Day 1: For an anniversary or birthday getaway, disappear into the romantic side of Birmingham. Go to the **Birmingham Zoo** and hold hands even when other people are looking. Kiss in front of the monkeys just to get a reaction - from the monkeys. Make reservations in advance to treat yourself to a nice room at the **Pickwick Hotel** in charming **Five Points South** just down from Vulcan. The most difficult decision is where to have dinner. (Hopefully, this was settled days or weeks ago with reservations expeditiously made.) Excellent choices would be **Highlands, Bottega** or **Bombay.** (More than 30 restaurants deliver to the Pickwick.) If it's not too late after a nightcap, take a walk around the fountain at Five Points.

An option for a romantic evening is to stay at the restored **Redmont-Holiday Inn,** the city's oldest hotel, and attend a play at the civic center. If you're into nostalgia and it's a summer weekend, drive to Second Avenue North to see a classic movie on the huge screen at the **Alabama Theater.** Notice how impressive the craftsmanship of the Moorish architecture is and how *big* the silver-screen stars were. Return to the Redmont and order room service.

Day 2: Have breakfast in the hotel, check out and head south on U.S. 31 to the spectacular **Galleria,** the South's most beautiful and successful shopping mall. The glass atrium is the largest in the country.

Return to downtown and go west on First Avenue North to share a midday meal at the **Rib-It-Up** barbecue place. Afterwards, drive a mile out Cotton Avenue to tour

Arlington, Birmingham's antebellum mansion. Return home at your leisure.

Two-day/one-night father and son retreat

Day 1: Arrive in mid-morning and exit I-20 at the Civic Center. Park nearby and stop in at the **Convention & Visitors Bureau** office facing Ninth Avenue North to ask about tickets remaining for any sports events going on. Walk past the **SEC Conference** headquarters to tour the **Alabama Sports Hall of Fame**. Walk over to **Pete's Famous Hot Dogs** at 19th and Second North for lunch. Drive out I-20 to walk through the massive **Sloss Furnaces National Historic Landmark** which symbolizes the power that made Birmingham the steel capital of the South. Or, to see how steel was originally made, go west on I-20/59 beyond Bessemer to **Tannehill State Historical Park**.

Drive east on I-20 to Irondale and eat at **Golden Rule Barbecue**, the state's oldest barbecue restaurant, just a couple of miles from the **Birmingham Race Course**. Cheer your favorite horses or dogs to victory throughout the evening. Thoroughbreds run in summer and greyhounds circle the track throughout the year. Children under 19 not allowed. As an alternative to barbecue, consider the many dining options at the race course, including fine cuisine prepared by the former chef at Commander's Palace. A convenient place to overnight is **Motel Birmingham** at Eastwood Mall where all rooms are on the ground floor or the **Rime Garden Suites** just off I-20 at exit 133.

Day 2: After check-out in the morning, go west on I-20 to U.S. 280 East and take the Eighth Avenue South exit. Go east a couple of blocks on Clairmont to **Bogue's** restaurant for a big breakfast. Next, head south on I-65 for **Oak Mountain State Park** where you can canoe, fish, bike, hike or just wander in the woods.

An option for the morning is to tour **Tannehill State Historical Park** and see what was left of the 19th-century furnaces after the Yankees burned them. For lunch, head for the **Bright Star** in Bessemer, one of the region's most enduring restaurants.

One-day tour: Black achievements

Few cities in the nation have played such a pivotal role in the advancement of civil rights as Birmingham. Targeted by the Southern Christian Leadership Conference to desegregate public facilities and jobs in 1963, downtown stores felt an economic boycott while blacks of all ages attempted to march 4 blocks from Kelly-Ingram Park toward City Hall.

The violent clashes set up by the resistance of Police Commissioner Bull Connor generated the national media coverage sought by the group and the unexpected bombing of a black church. The death of four Sunday School girls triggered a national outcry and caused an ugly mark against Birmingham which to this day, despite decades of racial cooperation and the long tenure of a black mayor, has not been completely erased. Without any attempt to condone the actions of previous generations, tourism officials encourage visitors to examine all phases of the black experience in the city. A tour of black heritage landmarks also encompasses the joys and triumphs of blacks who are finally receiving the attention they deserve.

Start at **Kelly-Ingram Park** where marchers assembled to organize and pray at the height of the movement. A bronze statue of Martin Luther King Jr. was erected in 1986 to face the **Sixteenth Street Baptist Church**. The statue of King appears to look toward the side of the church where the bomb exploded. Inspect the newer monuments. After touring the church, walk across Sixth to tour the **Birmingham Civil Rights Institute** which depicts historical events from the 1920s through the racial progress of today.

The **Fourth Avenue North Business District**, between 16th and 18th streets, comprised the the the heart of the black business district. The 550-seat **Carver Theater**, an art deco movie theater on 17th Street, houses the Jazz Hall of Fame and hosts live performances.

Drive a few blocks to the **Alabama Sports Hall of Fame** where such black Alabama natives as Jesse Owens, Joe Louis and Willie Mays are enshrined.

Go west on I-59 to exit 120 to reach the suburb of Ensley and the **Tuxedo Junction** trolley crossing which Birmingham native Erskine Hawkins memorialized in the jazz tune "Tuxedo Junction." The only remaining building housing a former jazz club is now a dentist office, so there's nothing to tour, but you can read the historical marker to remember that you've heeded the musical invitation to "come on down to the Junction."

WHERE TO STAY: MODERATE PRICES

Courtyard by Marriott - 500 Shades Creek Parkway near Brookwood Mall off U.S.31 - The 140 rooms with king or double beds have in-room coffeemakers, remote control TVs with cable and in-room movies, shower massage, oversize desks and reach anywhere phones. A swimming pool, whirlpool and exercise room are available. A restaurant is open for breakfast and lunch. A lounge is open six nights a week. Fax 879-6324. Double rate: $72-$82, weekends $59. A breakfast for two package is available. **Phone 879-0400** or 1-800-321-2211.

Days Inn - 5101 Airport Hwy. - A location convenient to the airport has 143 rooms with amenities including free continental breakfast, free local phone calls and cable TV. Guests can enjoy a swimming pool and shuttle service to the airport. Fax 591-5623. Double rate: $47-$90 plus tax. **Phone 592-6110** or 1-800-325-2525.

Fairfield Inn - 155 Vulcan Rd., Homewood - The motel overlooking I-65 exit 256 (Oxmoor Road) has 132 rooms with remote control TV and HBO. Swimming pool. Fax ext. 709. It is next door to Bennigan's and Fifth Quarter restaurants. Double rate: $44-$49 plus tax. **Phone 945-9600** or 1-800-228-2800.

Hampton Inn South, U.S. 280 in Mountain Brook, has 133 rooms with free breakfast, local phone calls, in-room movies, outdoor pool. Next door is Rossi's Italian restaurant. Write 2731 U.S. 280, Birmingham, 35223. Fax 871-7610. Double rate: $47-$52 plus tax. **Phone 822-2224**.

Holiday Inn Airport, located at exit 129 of I-20/59, has 224 rooms on nine stories. Amenities include an outdoor pool, exercise room, restaurant with nightly specials and live entertainment in the lounge. Room service. Free airport shuttle. The Holiday Inn is very close to the airport and convenient to the Birmingham Race Course, Eastwood Mall and Century Plaza. Fax 591-2093. Write 5000 10th Ave. N., Birmingham 35212. Double rate: $61-$71, weekends $39-$59 plus tax. Romance and bed and breakfast packages available. **Phone 591-6900** or 1-800-465-4329.

Holiday Inn East, a short distance from Eastwood Mall, Birmingham Race Track and Century Plaza, has 204 rooms with full-service restaurant, room service, a lounge, swimming pool and airport transportation. More than 50 fast-food and full-service restaurants are nearby. Fax 956-1234. Write 7941 Crestwood Blvd., Birmingham, 35210. Double rate: $48-$55 plus tax. **Phone 956-8211** or 1-800-465-4329.

Holiday Inn Homewood, convenient to I-65 exit 256, has coffeemakers in the 194 guest rooms and complimentary passes to Sportlife health club. A restaurant serves three meals daily. Room service. Lounge has DJ with recorded music. Fax 290-9309. Write 260 Oxmoor Rd., Birmingham, 35209. Double rate: $59-$67, weekends $40-$57 plus tax. Golf and romantic packages available. **Phone 942-2041.**

Motel Birmingham, nestled alongside Eastwood Mall, has been a landmark on U.S. 78 since 1952. All 242 units, including a dozen suites, are located on the ground floor and offer a private balcony or patio. Rooms include breakfast and a daily newspaper and cable TV with HBO. A large outdoor swimming pool and children's playground are on the grounds. Although there is no on-site restaurant, the motel is surrounded by plenty of places to eat. It is easy to reach, off I-20 exit 132. Fax 956-3011. Write 7905 Crestwood Blvd., Birmingham, 35210. Double rate: $45-$55 plus tax. Honeymoon and Birmingham Race Track packages are available. **Phone 1-800-338-9275** or 956-4440.

Mountain Brook Inn, 2800 Hwy. 280, has 161 rooms, bi-level suites with circular staircase in suites, and an outdoor pool. A restaurant and lounge are available. The Inn is very close to the botanical gardens and the zoo. Fax 870-3100, ext. 3828. Double rate: $79-$89, weekends $61-$71 plus tax. Packages are available for golf, race course and weekend getaways. **Phone 1-800-523-7771** or 870-3100.

Redmont-Holiday Inn, Fifth Avenue North at 21st Street, is the oldest survivor of the city's hotels built during the boom years of the Magic City era. The Thomas Jefferson, Tutwiler and Molton are consigned to memories, but the Redmont has been reborn by inkeeper Julian MacQueen. Small by most standards, it has a European feeling with only 112 rooms and suites and is an alternative for convention delegates who don't mind walking the 5 blocks to the BJCC. Each room has a refrigerator and cable TV with HBO. Guests have access to a health club and complimentary airport transportation. In addition to a piano bar in the lobby, you can eat in Julian's or enjoy the sidewalk cafe view from a balcony overlooking Fifth Ave. Fax 324-2101 ext. 652. Double rate: $79, deluxe rooms with garden tub and wet bar $89 plus tax. **Phone 324-2101.**

Riverchase Inn, on U.S. 31 at Hwy. 150, has free local phone calls, continental breakfast, pool and cable TV with Showtime. The 138-room Riverchase is within walking distance of the **Galleria**. Fax 733-8122. Write 1800 Riverchase Dr., Birmingham, 35244. Double rate: $53-$56 plus tax. **Phone 985-7500** or 1-800-239-2401.

Twin Pines Resort, 30 minutes south of Birmingham, is a 200-acre wooded resort and conference center with 50 lakeside rooms. After business people meet during the week, its facilities are enjoyed on weekends by families and couples looking for a relaxing getaway that's close to home. Dress is strictly casual.

You can walk out of any room onto a deck and find rocking chairs with a view overlooking a 46-acre lake. Each of the deluxe rooms and suites has a charcoal grill and the suites come with a kitchen, sitting area, fireplace and double beds. The deluxe rooms have refrigerators, coffeemakers, hair dryers, clock radios and remote-controlled color televisions.

Resort getaway packages include three meals served in the Owl's Nest. A Southern country breakfast includes eggs, pancakes, country ham and grits cooked by Geraldine and her crew who make their own breads and brownies. Later in the day, enjoy fried catfish, chicken and dumplings, and pork roast with cornbread dressing.

To work off a large meal, go fishing. The lake is 35-40 feet deep in places and well stocked with bass, catfish, bream and crappie. It's one of the few public places in Alabama where you don't need a license to fish. Twin Pines' package encourages parents to bring their children. If they are under 6, there is no charge for their lodging or meals. If older, the parents pay for just their meals. Youngsters may paddle around in their own smaller lake. Paddleboats are included.

Afterwards, enjoy a haywagon ride, hike, play tennis, softball, shuffleboard, volleyball and horseshoes.

The lake is home to a thatched-roof boat where you can enjoy a libation without having to leave the comfort of your canoe.

Twin Pines, originally a retreat for the Saunders trucking family, is only 12 miles from U.S. 280. From 280, turn left onto County 43 to Hwy. 45, then to Twin Pines Road. The address is 1200 Twin Pines Rd., Sterrett, 35147. Fax 672-7575. The business office is 868-6506 with a fax at 868-6557. Double rates: $72-$95 plus tax.

The getaway package for two is one of Alabama's best bargains. It includes dinner on arrival, Southern breakfast and lunch the next day for $98 plus tax. The $40 plus tax "room-only" rate for Easter, Mother's Day, Thanksgiving and December is also a great deal. Visa and MasterCard accepted. **Phone 672-7575.**

UAB University Inn, at the center of the 64-block campus, has 169 rooms with coffeemakers. Pool. Airport shuttle. The seven-story motel is within a half-block of Five Points and the Medical District. Fax 930-0192. Write 951 18th St. S., Birmingham, 35205. Double rate: $45-$60 plus tax. Golf and couples packages. **Phone 933-7700** or 1-800-888-5673.

LUXURY ACCOMMODATIONS

Crown Sterling Suites Hotel, just off the Red Mountain Expressway in Homewood, is a beautiful hotel which was constructed as an Embassy Suites hotel. The major architectural feature is the lushly landscaped tropical atrium with polished marble flooring which is a delightful place to relax over drinks or coffee. The 243 guest rooms are two-room suites with king-size beds and kitchenettes and have color TVs with in-room movies. An executive floor has additional amenities.

Guests enjoy a full cooked-to-order breakfast each morning in the atrium and receive free cocktails for two hours each evening. Ruth's Chris' steak house is the new restaurant. Guests have access to an indoor swimming pool, tennis and racquetball and sauna/steamroom. Double rates: $110, weekends $79 plus tax. Write 2300 Woodcrest Place, Birmingham, 35209. **Phone 879-7400** or 1-800-433-4600.

Pickwick Hotel, at **Five Points South**, is a delightful small art deco hotel which was originally a medical arts building. The eight-floor building was renovated in 1986 into 63 rooms and named for a local ballroom that was popular in the '40's. Rooms are furnished with deco reproductions, have cable TV and suites have kitchenettes. Fresh coffee is on each floor in the morning and you can go downstairs for a free continental breakfast. An afternoon tea with pastries is served in the lobby parlor, followed by wine and cheese.

The hotel shares a colonnade with interesting shops and restaurants. It is only a block from the heart of Five Points which is one of the state's best dining and entertainment districts. Don't feel like dressing for dinner? You can choose from menus of 30 nearby restaurants which provide "room service." A lounge serves drinks until midnight. Free airport shuttle is offered. Fax 933-6918. Write 1023 20th St. S., Birmingham 35205. Double rate $105-$119 plus tax, weekends $59-$69. **Phone 933-9555.**

Sheraton Civic Center Hotel has 771 rooms, 68 suites, plus banquet rooms and restaurants and is the largest hotel in Alabama. It has a dramatic curved glass and concrete facade and is connected to the civic center via a skywalk. The 16-story atrium overlooks the public spaces. The hotel has a health club, an indoor pool and more than 15,000 square feet of meeting space. The hotel is connected to the civic center's Medical Forum and its exhibition hall. Amenities include a sports bar which seats 250, a 154-seat, canopied Atrium Cafe. **Phone 324-5000** or 1-800-325-3535.

Sheraton Perimeter Park Hotel - just off I-459 and U.S. 280 - is a first-class corporate hotel which serves many businesses on the southern edge of the city. It overlooks the **Colonnade** shopping center and several office buildings as well as a TGIF restaurant. Each of the 209 guest rooms has coffeemakers, *USA Today*, color TV with remote and in-room movies. The hotel has a swimming pool, two lounges and a large dining room which offers room service until midnight. Gift shop. Pets allowed. Free airport shuttle. Fax 972-8603. Write 8 Perimeter Dr., Birmingham, 35243. Double rates $85-$95, weekends $57-$67 plus tax. Shoppers weekend package includes transportation to Galleria. **Phone 967-2700** or 1-800-325-3535.

Tutwiler Hotel is the best of both worlds, an intimate, first-class hotel in a classic landmark, crowned with a name which has been synonymous with quality accommodations since 1913. As the only National Historic Landmark in Alabama with overnight accommodations, its petigree is beyond question. It was built as the Ridgely Apartments by Maj. Edward Magruder Tutwiler and developer Robert Jemison Jr. the same year they constructed the original Tutwiler Hotel 3 blocks away. The Ridgely served the city's in-town gentry until 1986 and the major's great-grandson championed the movement to reconfigure the stately eight-story building into a hotel at a cost of $15 million. It was rechristened the Tutwiler in honor of the hotel at Fifth Avenue and 20th which had been demolished in 1975 to make way for First Alabama Bank.

Venetian-style terra cotta arches accent the exterior. The elegant lobby of polished marble and glistening brass welcomes guests who prefer the European intimacy of a smaller hotel to the city's larger accommodations.

Guests stopping in the richly paneled Tutwiler Bar may look across the street to Linn Park, the visual focus of downtown Birmingham. Temple Tutwiler III, the same descendant involved in the hotel's metamorphosis, also led the movement which transformed Woodrow Wilson Park between City Hall and the courthouse into the urban park which hosts the City Stages music festival. Those dining in the comfort of ***Christian's** enjoy the ambiance of a gentleman's private club.

With 147 rooms, including 43 suites with working fireplaces, the staff provides amenities, such as flowers in each room and complimentary shoeshines, found only in the finest hotels.

To taste the high life, move up to the concierge floors on the sixth and seventh, the latter being the club level where complimentary food is provided, along with monogrammed towels and terrycloth robes. Six suites with balconies overlook the courtyard area. The Presidential Suite has two bedrooms joined by a living room and comes by its name honestly. George Bush stayed in number 723 for several hours during a visit to Birmingham. Fax 325-1183.

The Tutwiler is at Sixth Avenue and 21st Street North. **Phone 322-2100.**

Wynfrey Hotel at the **Riverchase Galleria** balances quality with quantity. The hotel is on U.S. 31 just off I-459 exit 13. Although it has 329 rooms and 12 suites, the staff offers a high level of personal service. Guests have access to the on-site health club, gift shop and cable TV movies, as well as valet services and laundry. The Chancellor's Club offers a complimentary continental breakfast, a fulltime hostess and a private lounge. For diversion, the state's largest shopping mall is just a few steps down the hallway.

For fine cuisine, ***Winston's** is an excellent white-tablecloth restaurant. If you prefer more casual dining, the Chicory Grille cafe is open all day. Fax 988-4597. Write 1000 Riverchase Galleria, Birmingham, 35244. Double rates $120-$165, weekends $89-$165 plus tax. Specials packages are available related to shopping, honeymoons, special occasions, gourmet getaways and the Best of the Wynfrey. **Phone 987-1600** or 1-800-476-7006.

WHERE TO EAT IN BIRMINGHAM

**Baby Doe's Matchless Mine - *Good food, stunning view*
2033 Golden Crest Drive off Valley Avenue. Phone 324-1501
Open Sun. 10:30 a.m.-3 p.m., Mon.-Sat. 4-11 p.m.

Watch the sunset from high atop Red Mountain and see the lights of downtown twinkle after twilight. The menu offers a wide selection of seafood, salads and steaks, but don't order anything that requires you to concentrate on the plate and miss the view.

It's the same view that members of The Club have farther along the ridge, but without the high cost of membership. Baby Doe's accommodates large groups easily.

*Bogue's - *Country breakfast on Southside*
3028 Clairmont Ave. Phone 254-9780
Open Mon.-Fri., breakfast 6-11 a.m., lunch 11 a.m.-2 p.m.; Sat.-Sun., breakfast 6-11:45 a.m.

People who aren't from the South and looking for traditional Southern cookin' should look no further than this unpretenious daytime eatery on Southside. For nearly 50 years, regulars have enjoyed eggs, bacon and grits at breakfast ($2.40), and meat and vegetable plates ($4-$5) at midday. Waitresses wear shirts that promote "Greg's eggs" and call regulars by name. It's good food quick and relatively cheap just a couple of blocks from the U.S. 280 Expressway out the Eighth Avenue South exit. Although the menu carries a disclaimer that prices are subject to change, the current menu is four years old. The Strayners are the owners.

***Bombay Cafe** - *Excellent seafood in white tablecloth atmosphere*
29th Street and 7th Avenue S. Phone 322-1930
Open Mon.-Thurs. for dinner 6-9:30 p.m., Fri.-Sat. till 10:30 p.m.

Owner-manager Wayne Neugett has established a reliable, upscale white-table-cloth restaurant which serves Chef Darryl Borden's exotic appetizers: peppered quail or stuffed artichoke bottoms; and splendid entrees like broiled basil wrapped filet of Hawaiian moonfish with jumbo crab covered in a pair of sauces. If you don't have an immediate special occasion that requires a trip to Bombay, make up one. There's a small bar in case you arrive before the rest of your party. Bombay is a bit pricey, but worth every penny.

*Sample Menu - **Bombay***
Appetizers
Broiled stuffed artichoke bottoms with lump crabmeat and herbs $5.50
Pan fried softshell Louisiana crawfish with garlic beurre blanc $8
Tempura softshell crab with cilantro linguini and roasted nuts $6.75
Salads
Tossed green salad with Mandarin almond vinaigrette $4
Southwestern Caesar salad with grilled fajita shrimp and feta $5
Soup
Cup of shrimp, scallop and lobster bisque $2.75
Entrees
Chargrilled peppered ribeye with white wine bercy butter $17
Mixed seafood grill with tile fish and marlin topped with crab $20
Pan-fried dill salmon filet with crawfish tails and dijonnaise $20
Peppercorn cobia steak with coconut shrimp and pineapple aioli $20
Glazed tuna with curried bay shrimp and pablano pepper fritters $19
Grilled filet with lobster, mushrooms and peppercorn bordelaise $22
Baked snapper with bay scallops, spinach and mozzarella cheese $20
Desserts and After Dinner Drinks
Raspberry sorbet and peach schnapps frozen yogurt $3.50
Plantation pecan pie $3.50
Fresh summer berries with whipped cream $3.50
Grand Marnier and Tia Maria blended with Creme de Cocoa $5
150th Year Anniversary Grand Marnier $22.50

****Bottega** - *Great Italian food in a landmark building*
2240 Highland Ave. Phone 939-1000
Dinner Mon.-Thurs., 6-10 p.m.; Fri.-Sat.,until 11 p.m. The adjoining cafe is open for lunch and dinner 11 a.m.-11 p.m.

Bottega features Northern Italian creations by the executive chef in a stunning stone Mediterranean building. By all standards of food, service and atmosphere, Bottega ranks comfortably among the top five restaurants in Alabama. A well stocked bar, rich mahogany paneling and terra cotta tile flooring set the stage for a delightful evening.

Dine inside for white tablecloth service, or, depending on the weather, dine under the stars at wrought iron tables in the courtyard in front of the building. The menu changes several times a year, but there's always fresh grilled fish, veal, pasta and scallopini. A meal here is always memorable and usually expensive. The restaurant, by the way, got its name from the words "Bottega Favorita" etched above the entrance to the building.

Bright Star - *Landmark restaurant has a Greek accent*
304 19th St. N., Bessemer. Phone 424-9444
Mon.-Sat., 11 a.m.-10 p.m.; Sun., 11-9 except major holidays

Downtown Bessemer near the old railroad station may seem like an unusual place for a Greek-influenced restaurant which is probably the oldest in the state, but it has been putting out fine dishes since 1907 and in this location since 1915. The murals painted by transient European talent which set the mood date from the opening and lend a romantic - if somewhat dated - atmosphere. And the people of Bessemer wouldn't have it any other way. Niky and Jim Koikos serve classical Southern food enhanced by traditional Greek flavorings. The house special is beef tenderloin Greek style marinated with garlic, olive oil and oregano. Lobster and crab au gratin are seafood favorites. The pies are homemade. Lunches average $4-$7 and dinners are $11-$17.

Browdy's - *Kosher food with a tradition*
2713 Culver Rd., Mountain Brook. Phone 879-8585
11 a.m.-9 p.m. The deli is open daily, 8:30 a.m.-9 p.m.

For more than a half century, Birminghamians have known you don't have to be Jewish to eat at Browdy's. All it takes is a taste for great deli food. If you're shopping in Mountain Brook, stop in for the roast beef sandwich with cole slaw and Russian dressing served on a Kaiser roll. Take home some lox and bagels or smoked whitefish.

Cobb Lane Restaurant - *Hideaway for she-crab soup*
One Cobb Lane. Phone 933-0462
Mon.-Fri., 11 a.m.-2:30 p.m.; Sat., till 3 p.m. Evenings also in spring and fall.

Cobb Lane serves continental cuisine and specialty Southern meals in delightful cafe settings indoors or outside under the arbor of cherry laurel trees.

In 1948, the widowed Virginia Cobb dug out the basement in a luxury apartment building on 20th Street between Highland and 14th avenues and opened a highly successful tea room. Even when the management changed, the quality didn't. Owner Mikki Bond maintains the Cobb Lane spirit and her she-crab soup specialty. The delicately seasoned creamy lump blue crab soup is served as an appetizer or with a tomato salad covered with cucumber dressing as an entree. The grilled tuna fillet with sweet peppers, potatoes and olive relish is delicious. The chicken supreme, a baked chicken breast in a mushroom sauce with rice pilaf is a delightful Southern dinner. Homemade rolls are served with each entree. If you prefer, Cobb Lane offers a good selection of healthy salad entrees.

Save room for the legendary swirled chocolate roulage or cream caramel. Not only is the food legendary, three waitresses have a combined tenure of more than 60 years. Luncheon checks range from $5.50-$10. Dinner, which is served in spring and fall, costs from $8.50-$16. You can pick up a pint of she-crab soup for $10.25 plus tax and a whole roulage cake for $27.50.

Connie Kanakis Cafe - *A master of great steaks in a new home*
3423 Colonnade Parkway off I-475. Phone 967-5775
Lunch Mon.-Fri., 11 a.m.-2:30 p.m.; dinner Mon.-Sat., 5-10.

Greek restauranteur Connie Kanakis became associated with Michael's Sirloin Room, the city's first fine-dining restaurant, in 1962 and later opened the first Rossi's. He left Southside not long ago for the suburbs to follow his corporate clientel with the same quality steaks and salads for which he has been noted. Connie's hospitality has earned him the nickname "Mr. Birmingham."

***Dexter's on Hollywood - *Popular with BMW-to-bes*
354 Hollywood Blvd. at U.S. 280. Phone 870-5297
Mon.-Thurs., 11 a.m.-10 p.m.; Fri.-Sat., 11-11.

Dexter's has a varied menu of seafood and steak in a grey bistro setting with white tablecloth service. Try the excellent signature dish chicken pecan frangelico. Both Sat.-Sun. feature an outstanding champagne brunch, with specials that change weekly. Unique seafood appetizers are a trademark at Dexter's.

**Dugan's - *Eat great sandwiches in the glow of stained glass*
2011 Highland Ave. Phone 933-9020
Mon.-Tues., 11 a.m.-10 p.m.; Wed.-Thurs., until 11 p.m.; Fri.-Sat., until midnight.

Dugan's is one of the oldest nightspots in the Five Points South area. The eight-ounce gourmet burgers, specialty hot or cold sandwiches, and salads are served amidst rich stained-glass shades and dark panelled walls. It has the authentic surroundings to which TGI Fridays aspire. Old Birmingham photos, especially some of Vulcan under construction, give the impression Dugan's has been around a lot longer than 17 years. Stop in after work or on a Saturday afternoon to see local professionals at ease.

**Hamburger Heaven - *Burgers and corn balls*
1729 Crestwood Blvd. Phone 951-3570
Mon.-Thurs., 10 a.m.-8 p.m.; Fri.-Sat., till 8:30

The delicious hamburgers taste like Mama used to make, with fresh lettuce and onions. They're the best burgers in town, even if the antiseptic atmosphere reminds you of the school lunchroom. Get a side order of their unusual corn balls. It's cream corn rolled in batter and deep fried. The average meal is about $5.

****Highlands Bar and Grill - *State's finest restaurant*
2011 11th Ave. S. - Phone 939-1400
Lunch Tues.-Sat., 11 a.m.-2 p.m; dinner 6-10 p.m.

Owned by Frank and Frances Stitt, Highlands is located in a Spanish Revival commercial building erected by the Munger family in the late 1920s and is part of the Five Points South historic district. The main dining room adjoins a comfortable, informal bar which is often populated with some of the city's most influential people. It sets the Southside standard for food and drink (especially martinis of Bombay gin or Absolut vodka).

Southern ingredients presented in a classic French style, the beef, poultry, pasta and veal selections are wide ranging and imaginative. The seasoning and spices form a broad flavor pallate. Appetizers and entrees blossom under crawfish relish, saffron aioli, eggplant tomato gratin, soy-ginger dipping sauce, basil relish and Alabama goat cheese.

Stitt's restaurant, attitude and success gave the city a long-awaited reason to be written about in major dining magazines. Dress is slightly more formal than for Bombay and Bottega.

*Sample **Highlands** Menu*
Appetizers
Soup: Creamed corn with crabmeat, basil and roast pepper $6
A half dozen Apalachicolan oysters on the half shell with sauces $6.75
Soft shell crab with tarragon mayonnaise and roast vegetables $8.75
Oysters with duck sausage crepinette and glass of Domaine Grassa $10.75
Fried banana pepper with cornbread, crawfish and tomato relish $8
Homemade tamale with ancho chili sauce and green tomato salsa $7.75
Stone ground baked grits with wild mushrooms, ham and thyme $6.75
Grilled duck sausage with rosemary-potato gratin and bitter lettuces $7.75
Local melons with prosciutto di Parma and lime $7.25
Salads
Organic lettuce with tomato vinaigrette and Parmesan cheese $5.76
Spinach salad with Feta cheese and olive-oregano vinaigrette $5.75
Main Courses
Grilled dolphin, sweet peppers, grilled onions and caper butter $17.50
Crab with shrimp, mussels and clams in tomato corn broth $18.25
Tenderloin with beans, potato gratin and red onion butter $19.50
Pork chop with corn pudding, blackeyed peas and pepper coulis $16.50
Duck breast with port wine, mushrooms, roast shallots $18.25
Marinated lamb with arugula, baked goat cheese and caponata $17.50
Grilled salmon with vegetable salad and basil mayonaise $18. 25
Apalachicola gigged flounder with basil meunier and grits $16.25

***Jake's Grill** - *The son of Dale's has food, music*
2627 Seventh Ave. S. Phone 328-5253.
Lunch Tues.-Fri., 11 a.m.-3:30 p.m.; dinner Tues.-Sat., 5-11 p.m.

Jake's offers an interesting combination of dining opportunities that makes it a one-stop place for a night on the town. You are entertained by a bartender/magician as you wait for your table, dine in a white-tablecloth supper club or sit in the casual room and listen to a jazz band over diner. A private room upstairs offers intimacy for small parties. To top off the evening, go for a carriage ride around Southside.

Jake's was on Lake Martin before Larry Levine moved into the location down the street from Bombay. The name honors his father who started the **Dale's Cellar** restaurants and created the steak sauce. Jake's uses many of the old Dale's recipes, but the specialties go far beyond steaks.

In addition to chicken, pork ribs and beef - all cooked over hickory wood in a pit, Chef Dave Schatz prepares stuffed grilled lobster at a reasonable price. Jake's bakes their own bread daily and prepares fresh flavored butter for each table. A good wine list and moderately proportioned mixed drinks top off a great lunch or evening. The specialty dessert is fried apple pie covered with butter sauce.

Irondale Cafe - *It inspired "Fried Green Tomatoes"*
1906 First Ave. N., Irondale. Phone 956-5301
Mon.-Fri., 10:45 a.m.-4:30 p.m.; Sun., 10:45-2:30

Every true Southerner should make a pilgrimage to the restaurant which inspired Fannie Flagg's best selling book *Fried Green Tomatoes at the Whistle Stop Cafe* and the movie. Bess Fortenberry opened the cafe in 1932 and Fannie's aunt owned it when

Fannie was a child. The aunt's stories and a shoebox of a woman's meager possessions - the sum total of her life - inspired Birmingham's funny woman to write the novel. Fannie's screenplay for *Fried Green Tomatoes* was nominated for an Oscar.

The success of the movie triggered an upsurge in the cafe's business. One midafternoon the owner, working behind the buffet line, grumbled to herself that "these 'Fried Green Tomatoes' are killing me." Suddenly realizing a customer had walked in, she looked up into the smiling face of actor Robert Wagner!

A meat-and-three-vegetables plate with iced tea costs around $5.50. Dinner runs a little higher. The fried chicken, country fried steak and turkey and dressing are all made from scratch. Vegetables include green beans, turnip greens, squash, corn, and macaroni and cheese. You may want to phone to see if they are serving fried green tomatoes. Or go sometime for breakfast and enjoy the old-fashioned thick country bacon and grits.

The business district of Irondale is just north of Eastwood Mall. From U.S. 78, the highway to Atlanta which parallels I-20, turn up into Irondale on 16th Street S. just east of Goldbro and go until you approach the railroad tracks. Turn right on First Avenue S. and look for the cafe in the middle of the block across the tracks.

**John's - *Downtown's finest restaurant*
112 21st St. N. Phone 322-6014
Lunch Mon.-Sat., 11-2; dinner 5-10 p.m.

From the time Joy Young's left for the suburbs, John's has remained one of the downtown stalwarts for businessmen's lunches. Bankers, lawyers and insurance executives head for John's at noon. You rarely have to wait long for a table because the relatively small exterior belies the capacity for seating and cooking within. Likewise, the quality of the food far surpasses what you might expect from the plain decor. Seafood and steaks are specialties.

John Collas opened John's in 1944. His nephews immigrated from Greece and eventually bought him out. George Hontzas is the current owner. Pick up a bottle of John's delicious Greek Salad Dressing or the orangish Slaw and Salad Dressing to take home.

**Lloyd's - *Vegetables and huge tea glasses*
U.S. 280 4 miles south of I-459. Phone 991-5530
Daily, 11 a.m.-9 p.m. except major holidays

Lloyd's often comes to mind when travelers and locals alike are hungry for good regional food and lots of it. Since 1937, Lloyd's has served heaping portions of meat and vegetables and the giant 32-ounce glass of tea. Lloyd Chesser originally operated the restaurant along the winding portion of the road toward Sylacauga known as the "narrows."

Relocated a couple of decades ago, it is convenient to the urban sprawl down 280. Eli Stevens continues the tradition of large portions of Southern cooking, with hamburger steaks, catfish, chicken, barbecue and home-made pies among the favorites. One of the state's largest restaurants, Lloyd's can seat 500. Inexpensive, but bring cash. The average check is $6. (After eating, drive across the highway and ride around Meadow Brook Corporate Park, one of the state's most beautiful places to work. Fountains and lakes abound. Located near mile marker 11.)

***Mauby's** - *Sophisticated fare for the Dockers crowd*
121 Oak St., Mountain Brook. Phone 870-7115
Mon.-Thurs., 11-2, 5-10; Fri.-Sat., 11-2, 5-11; Sun., brunch 11-3, dinner, 3-9 p.m..

Mawby's, tucked away on a side street behind the City Hall, serves excellent seafood in an art-filled environment and a patio when the weather is favorable. College students home from Rollins and Vanderbilt mingle with downtown professionals over grilled or blackened fish.

Start with a cup of the excellent oyster and artichoke soup ($3). The cajun fried softshell crab ($6) is a reliable appetizer to be followed by a Greek salad ($5) and a choice of tuna ($17), grouper served over salmon mousseline ($18), mahi mahi with a saute of mushrooms, artichoke hearts ($17) or broiled lemon sole with Meditteranean spices ($17).

****Meadowlark** - *Excellent food in a pastoral setting*
534 Industrial Rd., Alabaster. Phone 663-3141
Thurs.-Sat., 5:30-10:30 p.m. Reservations recommended.

A restaurant outside of Alabaster, Meadowlark is a closely held secret dining experience. The restaurant Raphael Carins started in a house in 1978 serves only a few meals a week and is often overlooked because of its isolation. The dining rooms, with a view of rolling farm meadows, can accommodate 110 diners. The Meadowlark menu is changed regularly, reflecting the season's freshest foods and the chef's current interests. An evening's menu might include such entrees as grilled lamb chop with mint basil and pesto sauce ($24.75), chicken coq au vin with burgundy, mushrooms, garlic, tomatoes and bacon ($21.50), chateaubriand surrounded with garden vegetables ($49.75) and the chef's special veal presentation ($25.24). A popular appetizer is coquilles St. Jacques sauteed scallops on a bed of duchess potatoes ($7.50) and a recommended dessert is the Amaretto ice cream ($5.75). A large selection of domestic and European wine is offered.

Meadowlark is a bit pricey, therefore, it is not surprising that most of the guests are corporate clients or anniversary celebrants.

Michael's Restaurant - *Where the steer butt was first cut*
431 20th St. S. Phone 322-0419
Mon.-Thurs., 11-10; Fri.-Sat., 11-11.

Michael Matsos opened Michael's in 1958 and it became the focus of a dining and entertainment strip on 20th Street South. The steer butt cut ($20), which was originated here, has become a staple in steak houses everywhere. Even with different owners, Michael's has maintained its high quality ribeyes ($17) and Greek style red snapper ($15), along with beef kabob ($13) and sports memorabilia which make it an oasis for sports fans. Don't miss the homemade sweet rolls.

The Mill - *Healthy food and a view*
1035 20th St. S. at Five Points South. Phone 939-3001
Mon.-Thurs., 7 a.m.- midnight; Fri.-Sat., until 2 a.m.

While sightseeing around Five Points, walk in for a light lunch or just a muffin and relax under a canopy of baskets which cover the ceiling. A large bakery case inside to the left of the entrance contains temptations of all descriptions. Although donuts and croissants are sold, the muffins are baked throughout each day to insure freshness. The blueberry sour cream ($1.25) is the best.

If you prefer a healthy sandwich or soup, have a seat for table service. A grilled chicken breast is served atop a fresh garden salad ($6) and the chicken salad is served with greens and tomatoes ($5).

Sit by the window or outside under the trees near the statue of Brother Bryan. You can watch interesting people stroll by and enjoy the surrounding architecture.

The Mill lists the calories, fat and sodium content of each salad or entree directly on the menu. Owned by doctors, it is an offspring of several locations in Huntsville.

Milo's Hamburgers - *Take home jugs of sweet tea*
Various locations citywide
Mon.-Sat., 10 a.m.-9:30 p.m.; Sun., 10:30 a.m.-9 p.m.

Looking for a quick meal without the franchise monotony? Pull into a Milo's and go in for a double hamburger, fries and iced tea. The square patties are heavily spiced and covered with a brown sauce. The thick golden fries are the best in town when dipped in the burger sauce. Purchase a jug of Milo's sweet tea to take home to the refrigerator. Molasses gives it a distinctive punch.

*Pete's Famous Hot Dogs** - *Hot dogs with sauce and heritage*
1925 Second Ave. N. Phone 252-2905
Open daily, 10:30 a.m.-7 p.m.

Theo Gulas took a tiny 7- by 20-foot space between two buildings in 1915 and opened a hot dog stand. Pete Koutroulakis bought it in 1939 and his nephew, Gus, has operated it since 1954. You can stand inside and enjoy one of Birmingham's oldest and cheapest traditions: hot dogs with Pete's famous sauce for under $1. Splurge on cheese beef dogs or cheeseburgers for $1.30. Look for the colorful wedge-shaped neon sign in front of the city's smallest building.

Barbecue
Demetri's - *Great sandwiches, great sauce*
1901 28th Ave. S. in Homewood. Phone 871-1581

Demetri's serves a variety of barbecue sandwiches and pork and chicken plates with baked beans and potato salad or cole slaw. The dark brown tomato-based sauce with chili sauce, vinegar and Worchestershire is outstanding. Buy a bottle to take home.

***Golden Rule Barbecue** - *Alabama's oldest barbecue place*
I-20 exit 132 on U.S. 78. Phone 956-2678

Golden Rule dates from 1891 and is the state's oldest barbecue spot. The pork is crunchy, outside meat served on a bun with pickle. The tomato-based sauce is very good. Golden Rule's old location on the south side of the highway in Irondale was wiped out by the interstate to Atlanta and the restaurant moved in the current building in 1976.

It is especially convenient to patrons headed to the Birmingham Race Course. An attempt to franchise Golden Rule outside Birmingham failed because local people always think *their* barbecue is best.

***Jim 'n Nick's Barbecue** - *Barbecue that is hard to beat*
744 Clairmont on Southside. Phone 323-7082

Compared to Ollie's and Golden Rule, Jim 'n Nicks may be a relative newcomer to the barbecue scene, but for a four-star barbecue meal, you need go no farther than the large pork sandwich and a large plate of the state's best crispy onion rings. The barbecue sauce is heavy tomatoey and the pork is chopped into big chunks. The restaurant owned by brothers Jim and Nick Pihakis occupies their old Lakeview restaurant location just off University. A Riverchase location is at U.S. 31 and Hwy. 150. Phone 733-1300.

Ollie's - *Supreme Court ruled he had to serve blacks*
515 University Blvd. just west of I-65. Phone 324-9485

Open since 1928, it's the only barbecue place in the nation which had a lawsuit go all the way to the U.S. Supreme Court. Ollie McClung unsuccessfully challenged the constitutionality of the public accommodations section of the 1964 Civil Rights Law, arguing that he was not involved in interstate commerce. The court ruled that he was and that he had to serve blacks inside. Good barbecue. The ketchup-based sauce is for sale at the counter next to the t-shirts and free religious tracts. Closed Sunday. No beer is served at Ollie's.

Pat James Full Moon Barbeque - *It's worth the wait*
525 25th Street at Fifth Avenue South. Phone 324-1007
Mon.-Sat., 10:30 a.m.-5:30 p.m.

Legendary University of Alabama sports figure Pat James has mastered the art of great barbecue at this small Southside hidden treasure. Almost impossibly crowded at lunch, a wait in the drive-thru window is worth it for the tender sliced pork sandwich, adorned with a unique onion-based relish. Smoked turkey is another unusual, and outstanding offering.

FOOD

Birmingham is a city that loves to eat. And eat well. Among the food traditions are birthday cakes from **Marsh Bake Shop** on Third Avenue West, marinated meat from **Vincent's Market** at Brookwood, 32-ounce tea glasses at **Lloyd's**, **John's** Famous slaw dressing, **Cobb Lane's** roulage dessert and **Red Diamond** coffee.

One of the largest food plants is **Bama Foods** at 3900 Vanderbilt Rd., owned by Borden's. The plant manufacturers jellies, jams, preserves, peanut butter, mayonaise, salad dressing, ReaLemon, aspectic juices and Bennett's sauces.

While the city is also the home of **Barber's** ice cream, **Golden Flake** potato chips, **Mrs. Stratton's Salads** and **Greg's** cookies, it has numerous upscale restaurants and enough of the best barbecue in the South to warrant arguments over whose is really best.

The **Bruno's** grocery store chain based in Birmingham is the state's largest. The son of Italian immigrants, Joe Bruno started a corner grocery in 1932. The Bruno family business has grown into a $2.6 billion empire with more than 250 stores in six states.

Buffalo Rock, a strong golden ginger ale with origins a century old, is bottled by the Lee family, but they make most of their money as one of the nation's leading bottlers of Pepsi.

MARINATE IT IN DALE'S

A statewide best-seller is Dale's Steak Seasoning, a dark, salty, soy sauce marinade made since 1946 from a Filipino recipe. Herein lies an interesting family tale.

Jake Levine and a buddy came home from World War II with a tasty soy-based sauce and opened Dale's Cellar restaurant across from Woodrow Wilson Park in 1946. Within a few years, they were operating a string of restaurants serving marinated steaks. Because of requests from customers, they began to bottle the sauce by hand and sell it in the restaurants.

However, a dispute prompted Jake to sell his share of the restaurants to his brother and he kept the sauce operation. The strain of looking after a mushrooming business took its toll. Several years later, at age 42, Jake died while fishing one Sunday with his 11-year-old son, Larry.

While all of the restaurants closed except one, demand for the sauce has continued to grow and it is sold in grocery stores throughout the Southeast. The Dale's Steak Seasoning bottling operation in Irondale long ago quit bottling by hand and the automated plant has a capacity of 500 cases a day. Huge tankers deliver shipments of soy sauce to the plant, which is the largest customer of soy sauce in the Southeast.

Larry, now 40, owns the sauce business with his mother and brother and is using many of his father's original recipes in his Southside restaurant, Jake's. (For a copy of Dale's Cookbook, send $3 to P.O. Box 130684, Birmingham, 35213.)

Incidentally, there never was a Dale. The name is derived from the first two letters of the partners' last names.

WHERE TO SHOP IN BIRMINGHAM

Riverchase Galleria rises like the Land of Oz in Hoover. A visitor standing under the world's largest glass skylight and surrounded by a double-deck concourse stretching a quarter mile could be forgiven for thinking, "I'm not in Alabama anymore." The $300 million Galleria encompasses some 200 specialty and department stores, most notably **Parisian**, **Macy's**, **Rich's** and **McRae's**. Even **Brooks Brothers** is here. A central food court with 12 choices is a popular meeting place, (possibly because **Godiva** chocolates are nearby). With furs to toys and shoes to cars spreading over 3.3 million square feet, it is Alabama's largest concentration of retail shopping. On a square foot basis, it is the South's most successful shopping center. The upscale **Wynfrey Hotel** adjoins.

To get there, travel I-65 and exit on U.S. 31 south in Hoover. Go south and under the I-459 interchange and you can't miss it. Approaching from either Tuscaloosa or Atlanta, exit I-459 at 31.

On the east side of Birmingham off I-20 are **Century Plaza**, **Eastwood** and **Eastwood Festival Centre**, with a multi-plex theater. Over the mountain, **Brookwood Village** (**Rich's** and upscale **Vincent's Market**) on Lakeshore Drive at U.S. 31 is convenient to Homewood, Vestavia and Mountain Brook. Brookwood has been handsomely remodeled to compete with the Galleria.

Century Plaza is a million-square-foot mall anchored by **Rich's, Sears, JCPenney** and **McRae's**. The mall, with about 120 stores, has been among the state's largest since opening in 1976. It received a major facelift in 1990. The focal point is an atrium surrounded by towering white columns around a 16,000-gallon pool with a fountain spray rising 20 feet in the air. It's a good place to gather during shopping breaks. A food court is near **Penney's**. Located near Irondale between I-20 and Crestwood Boulevard.

Alabama's first mall, **Eastwood**, opened in 1960 across the street and has gone through several transformations to compete with the newcomers. Following a major renovation in 1990, it now features the largest **Parisian** in Birmingham, second largest in the chain only to one in Ohio. It has an airy interior with palms and skylights (and more white columns). Located at Oporto-Madrid Boulevard and Montclair Road.

Parisian is a Birmingham-based clothing retailer with a reputation for quality and service that inspires a fierce loyalty. The cheerful staff corrects any problem and accepts virtually any return with a no-excuses policy. The company began in downtown Birmingham in 1887 and opened its first store outside its home base in 1963 in Decatur. Parisian has expanded to more than 20 stores throughout the South with revenues of $360 million. *Forbes* magazine has listed Parisian as one of the 200 best small companies in the nation. Customers breathed a sigh of relief when the Hess family, which had sold out to an Australian holding company that ran into cash flow problems, bought it back. Parisian has expanded to Atlanta, Orlando, Dayton and Nashville.

Wonder where your Parisian clothing returns wind up? In the back room of the **Parisian Clearance Center**, where discounts range up to 75 percent. End-of-season leftovers from more than 22 stores wind up here. Several shipments weekly keep the merchandise stock ever changing. The clearance center shares Wildwood Centre at I-65 exit 255 and Lakeshore Drive with a **Sam's** and a clearance center for **Yeilding's**. Open Mon.-Fri., 10-8; Sat., 10-6; Sun., 1-5:30.

WHERE TO BUY ANTIQUES

Antique shopping is easy in Birmingham. Large malls are located on major thoroughfares. The largest is the 100,000-square feet **Carriage Antique Village** in the old Sam's Wholesale location on Green Springs Highway at Valley Avenue. Booths display silver, furniture, books, clocks, glass and vintage clothing. An auction area and an area for collectibles are also included. You can even eat here. Phone 942-8131. **Riverchase Antique Mall**, in a former Hoover skating rink, covers 36,000 square feet. It has a huge floor of stock, plus a balcony. Merchandise ranges from collectibles to baroque dining room suits, with brass beds, old books, dolls, bird cages and lamps in between. Hours are 10-6, except Sun. 1-6. It's 10 miles south of town, just north of the Galleria at the intersection of I-459 and Lorna Road. From U.S. 31, turn just above the City Hall and drive several blocks and you'll find it. Phone 823-6433.

Hannah Antique Mall at 2424 Seventh Ave. S. has an above-average quality of merchandise on two floors. Silver and jewelry are near the entrance. A large room at the rear carries wardrobes and beds. Open Mon.-Sat., 10-5; Sun., 1-5. Phone 323-6036.

Homewood Antique Mall at 2921 18th St. S., up the hill in Homewood, occupies an old grocery building with a reliable selection of silver, jewelry, small furniture and collectibles. A large selection of Staffordshire figures is usually available. Open Mon.-Sat., 10-5:30; Sun., 1-5. Phone 870-7106.

Down and around the corner at 1820 29th St. S. is **Martin Antiques**, which carries some of the finest English, French and Oriental selections in the state. Huge chandeliers costing five figures and imported marble mantles are common here. This is a place for serious Gold Card shopping. Open Mon.-Sat. Phone 879-0049. Several other high quality antiques shops are across the street.

SPECIALTY STORES WORTH A VISIT

Alabama Outdoor - 3054 U.S. 31 in Homewood. This store sells clothing and equipment for backpacking, skiing, canoeing, climbing. Topographical maps of Alabama for outdoor enthusiasts are available, along with the latest information on efforts to save the Cahaba River from over-development. Phone 870-1919.

The Arbor - 3401 Fifth Ave. S. - Scores of handcrafted statuary and working fountains for sale are displayed within a Mediterranean courtyard on Southside. Large urns, unglazed gardenware and outdoor furniture will enhance any Southern home. The merchandise isn't cheap. The best deals come during their sales in January, on Memorial Day and Labor Day. Phone 251-0203.

Bromberg's, founded in Alabama in 1836, is one of America's oldest family-owned jewelry stores. The stores carry gifts by Tiffany, Wedgwood, Lenox and Waterford. In addition to the main store downtown, locations are in Mountain Brook and the Galleria.

Dee's ABC Store - 2398 Green Springs Hwy. - You can buy liquor and beer 24 hours a day (except for Sunday morning) at this convenience store just above the Goodwill Store. You can find premium brands not found in normal beverage stores. Of course, you pay a bit extra for the convenience. Phone 322-3333.

The Peanut Depot - 2016 Morris Ave. near the railroad tracks downtown. The aroma of freshly roasted peanuts wafting from the old warehouse is hard to resist. The Peanut Depot, roasting peanuts on Morris Avenue since 1907, ships the peanuts trucked in from Virginia and North Carolina to grocery stores throughout the Southeast. Phone 251-3314.

Vincent's Market - Brookwood Village shopping center. What may appear to be another **Bruno's** grocery is, in reality, 45,000 square feet of gourmet heaven. In addition to usual grocery products, Vincent's offers exotic vegetables, handmade salads and desserts and a mouth-watering selection of marinated meats ready for the grill. Don't want to cook? Select whole cooked fowl straight from the rotisserie or let Executive Chef Brian Coates's staff prepare a picnic basket. Adrian Drapkin will suggest the perfect wine. It is one of the few grocery stores in the state with an ATM inside and they even take American Express. Phone 871-2800.

SPORTS

The city's minor-league baseball team, the **Birmingham Barons**, plays in the modern Hoover Met Stadium off I-459. It has seen players go directly to the New York Yankees and Chicago White Sox in recent years. Professional baseball came to Birmingham in 1885 when the Coal Barons first played. Rickwood Field, home to the Barons 1910-75 and 1980-87, is the nation's oldest professional park. The Barons moved to the $14 million Met in 1988 and won the Southern League pennant the next year. Phone 988-3200.

The **Birmingham Bulls** play 64 regular season games in the East Coast Hockey League and play homes games in the BJCC. Exposing a bit of Southern demeanor, Coach Bruce Garber's club slogan is "kick ice." For tickets, phone 458-TUFF.

If you play golf, take the challenge of the **Robert Trent Jones Golf Trail** at **Oxmoor Valley**. The mountaineous terrain of the Homewood courses challenges pro and weekend duffer alike. A handsome clubhouse offers a retreat worthy of any country club. Two 18-hole courses are of championship lengths. while the third, a par three, also has 18 holes.

CULTURE

Major cultural institutions enrich the quality of community life. The **State of Alabama Ballet** has several major performances in the city and tours the state and region. The company consists of about 20 professional dancers and apprentices. Phone 252-2475.

The **Birmingham Children's Theater**, established in 1959, is a professional company of adults who stage approximately five productions a year, performing for some 200,000 school children. Phone 324-0470. The consolidation of two companies led in 1987 to the **Birmingham Opera Theater** which maintains a strong commitment to community outreach and education. Phone 322-6737. The largest municipal art museum in the South is the expanded **Birmingham Museum of Art**, with annual attendance of more than 165,000.

Samford University theater performs at Harrison Theater. Phone 870-2853. **Birmingham-Southern College** theater. Phone 226-4780. **Town and Gown Theater** is supported by UAB and usually stages five plays and musicals from October through May. Performances are held in the Clark Memorial Theater just off Highland Avenue at 1116 26th St. S. Gary Robertson is the director who succeeded founder/director James Hatcher, after 41 years. For schedules, phone 934-3489.

Summerfest is a series of three musicals and plays staged July through August at the Boutwell Auditorium. The series is an outgrowth of UAB's Town and Gown. Phone 934-3489.

Birmingham Festival Theater stages plays from September through August. BFT is located at 1901 1/2 11th Ave. S. Phone 322-5259.

Birmingham Broadway Series offers an annual subscription series of professional touring plays, with "Cats" and "Buddy" visiting Samford's Wright Center the inaugural season.

The **Comedy Club** at 430 Green Springs Hwy. features nationally known comedians, such as Marsha Warfield and Sinbad, and lesser lights in the stand-up field. Phone 942-0008.

WHAT'S HAPPENING TODAY

Birmingham is blessed with two daily newspapers which give aggressive coverage to local happenings. In addition to daily entertainment news, the morning *Post-Herald* inserts the occasionally irreverant *Kudzu* tabloid on Fridays which points out special events and concerts worth attending. The larger afternoon *Birmingham News* features entertainment, arts and travel on Sundays, plus *Marquee* on Fridays. Both are full of details, times, prices and "what's playing where."

The city has an excellent upscale monthly magazine produced by the Chamber of Commerce. Appropriately named *Birmingham*, it profiles leaders, characters, readers' choice polls, memories, restaurants, events, local sports and business trends.

Want to know what bands and singers are performing in town this month? Pick up a free copy of *Fun & Stuff*, available at most popular restaurants and nightclubs. The tabloid lists restaurant hours by sections of the city. *Black & White* promotes alternative entertainment.

BIRMINGHAM'S ANNUAL EVENTS

First full weekend each month

Birmingham Flea Market - State Fairgrounds - The state's largest flea market is held the first weekend of most months in a large building off Third Avenue West. Jewelry, collectibles, coins, magazines, books and assorted junk are sold. The buildings are not air conditioned, so it gets stuffy during summer. Open Fri., 3-9; Sat.-Sun., 7-6. Phone 785-FAIR. Dates vary, especially in winter and prior to holidays.

Third Monday in January

King Memorial Events - The Unity Day breakfast at the BJCC is open to the public, as are other events, including the march from Linn Park to the Sixteenth Street Baptist Church.

Third or fourth Saturday in February

Alabama Sports Hall of Fame Induction Banquet - Civic Center - Banquet and reception honor the athletes of the Sports Hall of Fame enshrined in the civic center. Outstanding Alabama athletes honored during the past two decades include such legends as football's Bear Bryant, auto racing's Red Farmer and basketball's Wimp Sanderson. Date may vary. Phone 323-6665.

Second Thursday thru Sunday in March

Birmingham Home and Garden Show - Civic Center - Exhibits on gardening, home improvement projects and fashion shows attract large crowds throughout the annual four-day event. Phone 681-4795.

Palm Sunday

Churches Tour - Downtown - A walking tour of five historic churches built between 1885 and 1916 is led each Palm Sunday by members of the Birmingham Historical Society. The tour begins at St. Paul's Cathedral at 2120 Third Ave. N. and continues to First Presbyterian, Cathedral Church of the Advent, First United Methodist and Sixteenth Street Baptist.

Late weekend in March

Spring Railroad Excursion - Train lovers enjoy the thrill of rail travel as steam engines pull vintage passenger cars along the tracks through the beautiful countryside of North Alabama. Trains leave the site of the razed Terminal Station on 26th Street for a round-trip excursion and a romantic memory. While destinations and departure dates change yearly, previous trips have carried train lovers via Norfolk-Southern Railway tracks to such places as Chattanooga and Columbus, Miss. The "where" is not as important as the "how" of travel, since few steam and diesel locomotives have survived to offer these nostalgic adventures. Advance ticket reservations are required since the trips sell out.

Passengers are encouraged to bring a sack lunch. Profits from the excursions benefit the Heart of Dixie Railroad Museum in Calera. (Rail cars belonging to the club, including L&N's handsome "Alabama Club" tavern lounge car in service in the 1930's, are parked at 18th Street and Powell Avenue in Birmingham) A fall trip occurs the second or third weekend of November. To charge tickets with Visa or MasterCard, phone 252-2716.

Early April weekend
Indian Dance & Craft Festival - DeSoto Caverns Park, Childersburg - Tribal Native Americans hold ceremonial dances, display and sell native craftwork and cook traditional foods. The park management adds a few gunfights, funnel cakes and polish sausage stands to add to the carnival spirit. It is about 45 minutes from Birmingham. Phone 378-7252.

Third Friday thru Sunday in April
Spring Fling- Horse Pens 40 - Steele - A primitive rock mountaintop is the backdrop for seasonal craft fairs. Bring comfortable shoes for hiking the Chandler Mountain trails to view a collection of homemade crafts and knicknacks. Funnel cakes, barbecue and boiled peanuts are washed down with Cokes if the day is warm. More impressive than the wares are the strange rock formations which encourage inspection by the nimble-footed. The name? The 40 acres of giant boulders formed a natural horse corral during the Civil War. Warren Musgrove opened the rustic park to visitors on Labor Day weekend in 1961. Because of health problems, he recently put the park up for sale. Go 40 miles north of Birmingham on I-59 to Ashville-Oneonta exit. Follow signs for 5 miles. Phone 538-5159.

Late April through early May
International Festival of Arts - Eighth Avenue civic areas - The nation's oldest arts festival honors a different country each year, with a centerpiece expo at the Birmingham-Jefferson Civic Center, exhibition at the Birmingham Museum of Art and musical programs throughout the city. The expo at the BJCC exhibition hall features native dancing, demonstrations and gift and food shops with merchandise from the honored country. Some 20,000 people attend the weekend expo. Switzerland, Spain, Egypt, France, Great Britain, Australia and China have been saluted. Check Birmingham newspapers for schedules. Phone 323-5461, ext. 52 or 53.

Late April
Vestavia Dogwood Festival - When spring blossoms near their peak, Vestavia residents mark the dogwood trails, a group of walking tours highlighting exceptional flora and landscaping. Information at City Hall on U.S. 31.

First Sunday in May
Southern Appalachian Dulcimer Festival - Tannehill Historical State Park - This uniquely Southern event provides the opportunity to view craftsmen creating and playing the dulcimer, one of the most beautiful of the primitive native instruments. Phone 477-5711.

Second week in May

Gala - BJCC - International women of distinction are honored in ceremonies every other year. Since 1973, proceeds from the event have been used to provide scholarships for students in the fine and performing arts at Birmingham-Southern College. Previous honorees have included Bette Davis, Betty Ford, Nancy Lopez, Marylou Vanderbilt Whitney, Nancy Reagan and Donna Mills. Phone 226-4921 or 1-800-523-5793.

Third Saturday in May

Do-Dah-Day Parade - Highland Avenue - Every major city has at least one zany event without a reason for being, other than to have an excuse to party and parade. Birmingham's is Do-Dah-Day, a combination dog parade, costume party and charity fundraiser. Activities start early in the a.m. with parade registration at Highland Golf Course. The parade starts at Highland Golf Course at 11:01 a.m. sharp and winds past Independent Prestyterian Church to Caldwell Park for entertainment and the Ugliest Dog competition. Phone 251-5166.

Third weekend in May

Alabama Folk Fair - Old Railroad Depot, Bessemer - Residents display household items to showcase earlier lifestyles at the Bessemer Hall of History. Exhibitors sell food and craft items and perform musical instruments.

Saturday in early June

The Ball of Roses - Birmingham Country Club - Debutantes are presented in one of the most select social events of the season. Presentees wear pastel dresses and carry bouquets of fresh flowers. The ball has been sponsored by the Ballet Guild of Birmingham since 1961 and benefits the State of Alabama Ballet.

First Friday thru Sunday of June

Summerfest in the Country - Homestead Hollow, Springville - Set among stands of hardwood trees on a rural road, a pioneer homestead provides a special environment for a homespun food and crafts fair. Local craftsmen sell cloth dolls, wooden toys and baskets. Cooks serve corn boiled in husks and warm peanuts straight out of the roaster. Others offer barbecue and hamburgers. Costumed hostesses in log houses explain how garden vegetables were dried or stored for winter meals before refrigeration became commonplace. The food is hearty and fairly priced. Springville is located near exit 154 of I-59 north of Birmingham. Follow Hwy. 174 about 2 miles past Springville to a dirt road entrance to Homestead Hollow. Phone 467-6072.

Third Friday thru Sunday in June

City Stages - Linn Park - Birmingham's musical street festival celebrates jazz, gospel, blues, reggae, country and pop music with tens of thousands of fans sandwiched between multiple stages in the park between city hall and the courthouse.

You can spread blankets on the grass, watch people, drink beer, play in the usually off-limits fountains and party, giving credence to the city motto "Birmingham feels like a celebration."

The carnival-like atmosphere appeals especially to those *twentysomething* as a post-college music and beer fest, although babes in arms and grandmothers are attracted and entertained as well. City Stages is decidedly urban, a happening you might associate with a city much larger than Birmingham.

The boundaries defining the festival site stretch from the Museum of Art on the north to AmSouth-Harbert Center on the south and Kelly-Ingram Park on the west. Even the city's architectural firms are showcased by creating dramatic entrances to the park.

Scores of headliners and future superstars perform on as many as a dozen outdoor stages. The day's biggest act usually plays last each evening, followed by a laser light show on city hall.

Some 38,000 people cheered the first festival in 1989 when a three-day pass to see Chuck Berry and the Temptations was only $5. The second year Bo Diddley and the Commodores drew more than 100,000.

Even organizers were overwhelmed with the 150,000 who saw B.B. King, Jerry Lee Lewis and Emmylou Harris in 1991. Beer lines were long and the venue was too small for the crowds. By 1992, the number of stages spread over 12 blocks had grown to 10 so that the 235,000 total who watched 150 acts - including James Brown, Al Green and the Four Tops - were comfortably accommodated. The festival perimeter for 1993 was designed to accommodate 350,000.

All of this comes for a modest admission fee which makes City Stages one of the city's true bargains. The locals buy advance weekend passes because there's enough variety to fill the weekend.

The enthusiasm which has been created at and by City Stages ripples throughout the community, further affirming the quality of life in the state's largest city. Civic booster George McMillan is the driving force. Watch for details in the local media, particularly in *The Birmingham News* and *The Post-Herald's Kudzu* tabloid on Friday.

Wear comfortable shoes, cotton shorts and a t-shirt in case an afternoon shower cools things off and bring a blanket to stake out your territory for the major entertainment.

Check the Convention & Visitors Bureau for a brochure outlining weekend hotel packages. You can buy tickets at the gate. Advance passes are available by mail through Fastix at 939-FAST or 1-800-277-1700. Children under six are admitted free.

Third or fourth Saturday of June

Miss Alabama Pageant - Samford University - Scores of young women compete for scholarships at the 2,700-seat Wright Center concert hall and the chance to represent Alabama in the Miss America Pageant in September. Contestants are judged in interview, swimsuit, talent and evening wear competitions.

Each year the director picks a theme that best suits the personality of the outgoing Miss Alabama, with the music also complementing the reigning woman. Although nearly all of the performers are amateurs, the pageant puts on a Broadway style show each year, including performances by the contestants.

The Alabama contest founded by *The Birmingham News* in 1921 is the oldest state preliminary in the Miss America program. Tickets are available at Parisian stores. Phone 871-6276.

Mid-July to early August

Summerfest - Boutwell Auditorium- Broadway-style entertainment arrives in the form of three musicals which run for a week each, including a Sunday matinee. Among past favorites have been *The Music Man, Camelot* and *Me and My Girl*. Local director-icon James Hatcher launched the series in 1979 to showcase community actors and encourage young theatrical talent.

Non-Equity singers and dancers who appear in all three productions provide the core of the company. Nationally known stage and screen actors, directors and choreographers participate. Phone 939-FAST.

Third or fourth Saturday in July

Function at Tuxedo Junction - Ensley - The nightspot that inspired Birmingham native Erskine Hawkins's famous tune *Tuxedo Junction* is gone now, but the music lingers, due in part to the annual birthday party for the trumpeter/composer. Held since 1985, the event showcases the city's jazz heritage. Phone 583-4776.

First weekend in August

Black Heritage Festival - State Fairgrounds - A three-day festival which salutes and showcases African-American culture includes scores of black entertainers, ethnic foods, folk art, fashion shows and much more. Vendors sell African and African-American prints, sculptures and clothing. The first event drew 18,000 people. Many parents bring their children so that they can learn about black culture from a black point of view. Phone 324-3333.

Week in late August

Bruno's Memorial Classic - Greystone Golf Club - Golf's best players over age 50 participate in the annual 54-hole tournament. With the purse above $700,000, it is one of the richest in the 40-plus Senior PGA Tour. Greystone is located off U.S. 280 and Hwy. 119. To purchase tickets and see players of the caliber of Gary Player, Chi Chi Rodriguez, Miller Barber and Raymond Floyd, visit a Bruno's store or phone 939-GOLF.

Last Saturday in August

Great Southern Kudzu Festival & Run - Sloss Furnances - Beat the dog days of August with off-beat sweatless fun. The day begins with a 5K (3.1 mile) family run from the Vulcan overlook down 20th Street to First Avenue North to Sloss and continues with off-beat fun events. See how far you can spit a watermelon seed. Stand in the circle of cooling fans. Walk or run through ice cubes. Try your hand at creating a maypole structure out of kudzu. Kids can draw on the sidewalks. Who's got the ugliest dog? Like to play games? Tournaments are held for darts, volleyball, horseshoes, checkers and so forth. The fun turns to music, with traditional sounds during the day, followed by an evening concert under the stars. Pack a picnic supper for the concert.

Sandy Amman, editor of Kudzu, *The Post-Herald*'s popular Friday morning entertainment section, started the festival in 1984 as a way to promote Sloss Furnaces. The run has become one of the largest 5K runs in the state. Funds benefit Camp Smile-A-Mile, a camp for children with cancer. Phone the paper at 325-2108 or Sloss at 324-1911.

Third weekend in September

Oktoberfest - Civic Center - Authentic bands from Bavaria join local German bands to perform waltzes and polkas in the exhibition hall. Bring a healthy appetite for such authentic German fare as bratwurst, knackworst, sauerkraut, German mustard and a variety of imported and domestic beers. A shop offers Alpine gifts for sale. The event started in 1977 as a small street fair. Dates vary. Phone 252-9825.

Third or fourth Saturday in September
Arlington Country Fair - 331 Cotton Ave. NW - Grounds of the city's antebellum house museum are transformed into a country fair for a day. Young ladies stroll the gardens in hoopskirts. Out on the sweeping front lawn, cloggers tap to country rhythms as spectators feast on box lunches and homemade desserts. Quality plants are offered for sale in the garden shop. Part of the country fair is a flea market.

Some 130 Southern craftsmen and antiques dealers fill booths with colorful works. The fair, sponsored by the Arlington Historical Association as the only fund-raising project to support the house, is a local tradition dating from the 1950's. Phone 780-5656 or 252-9825

Late September weekend
Fall Home Show - BJCC - Stroll down the aisles of the exhibit hall to visit literally dozens of home-improvement company booths selling everything from Jenn-Airs to Jacuzzis and burglar alarms to tulip bulbs. The three-day show attracts 20,000 and vendors get sales leads from the show for months. An adjacent food hall is a succession of booths sponsored by a grocery stores offering samples and coupons for a variety of products. Admission. Phone 591-6712.

September weekend
Birmingham Jam - Sloss Furnaces Amphitheater - An outdoor celebration of Southern music, food and culture headlines major jazz, blues and gospel performers. The Alabama Jazz Hall of Fame's induction ceremony to recognize contributions that Alabama natives have made to jazz history opens the weekend. Children's rides and crafts and food booths add to the wholesome carnival atmosphere. The Birmingham Heritage Band, Count Basie Orchestra, Gatemouth Brown, Dr. John, Erskine Hawkins, Huntsville's Microwave Dave and the Nukes and the late Johnny Shines of Tuscaloosa have performed.

The jam is staged with the support of corporate sponsors and Lakeview businesses and draws upwards of 20,000 during the two days. Date varies to October. To find Sloss Furnaces, take U.S. 31 off I-65 in downtown Birmingham and look for the First Avenue North exit. Phone 323-0569 for information or 939-FAST for advance weekend passes.

First Saturday of October
Bluff Park Art Show - Bluff Park Community Center - Birmingham's most prestigeous art show brings together knowledgable craftspeople and art collectors. Up to 20,000 people gather in a small, wooded area near the crest of Shades Mountain to meet about 120 invited Southern artists and purchase their pottery, stained glass, sculptures, watercolors, paintings, jewelry and weavings. Artists like the show because of the sophistication of those who shop.

Held since 1964, the show features musical entertainment, hands-on art fun for youngsters and food, ranging from barbecue to Alabama peanuts and soft drinks. Judges award more than $5,000 in purchase prizes and visitors can vote on their show favorites.

Proceeds from the show, sponsored by the non-profit Bluff Park Art Association, support a variety of cultural organizations. Parking isn't permitted at the show. Instead, drive to Bluff Park United Methodist Church, Shades Mountain Independent Church or Shades Mountain Plaza Shopping Center to catch a shuttle bus to the art show.

Easiest directions from I-65: exit at Alford Avenue and go west, then right on Tyler Road, left on Valley Street to the Methodist church for the shuttle. Hours are 9-5. In case of rain, it is held Sunday. Free. Phone 822-7961 or 979-1336.

First Sunday of October

A Day in Old Birmingham - Downtown - An event celebrating the preservation and renovation of Birmingham's architectural heritage. Walking tours of restored commercial buildings showcase the architectural diversity of the city. Food, music, photo exhibitions and lectures expand the calendar.

The event brings hundreds of local people into the inner city for an afternoon of special activities to celebrate the architectural heritage of the Magic City. It is co-sponsored by the Birmingham Historical Society, the local chapter of the American Institute of Architects and the City of Birmingham. Emphasis varies by years. Phone 251-1880.

Second half of October

Alabama State Fair - Fairgrounds off Third Avenue West - A midway of thrill rides vies with livestock shows and live entertainment for fair-goers' attention. Special attraction venues are the arena, midway stage, family fun center, exposition stage, entertainment tent, ice building, exhibition building, poultry and rabbit building and south grandstand. The 11-day fair has special discounted days for school kids, government employees, senior citizens and "midnight madness" nights when rides run until 2 a.m.

The fair traces its roots to 1872. Annual attendance ranges from 350,000-400,000. Specific daily calendars are listed in newpapers. During the warmer months of the year, you can enjoy the thrill rides at the fair's Family Fun Center amusement park. Phone 939-FAST or 1-800-277-1700 for discount advance passes. Dates vary.

Late fall weekend

Magic City Classic - Legion Field - The annual football game between Alabama State in Montgomery and Alabama A&M in Huntsville is the state's largest social event for blacks and attracts upwards of 40,000 fans. The game started in 1924 and moved to Birmingham in 1940 and became known as the Magic City Classic. A pep rally and other social events add to the festivities.

Second or third weekend in November

Fall Railroad Excursion - The annual fall railroad outing sponsored by the Heart of Dixie Railroad Museum and Norfolk-Southern Railroad operates round-trip excursions to a nearby city such as Chattanooga. The train leaves from the site of the Terminal Station on 26th Street North on Sat.-Sun. at 7 a.m. and passes through valleys in the Appalachian foothills between Sand Mountain and Lookout Mountain.

After a stopover in Chattanooga from noon to 3 p.m., the train returns to Birmingham by 8 p.m. Coach tickets are about $65. Proceeds benefit the group's museum in Calera. To charge tickets with Visa or MasterCard, phone 252-2716.

November 11
National Veterans Day Parade - Downtown - The nation's oldest Veterans Day parade attracts top military leaders from Washington. Birmingham celebrated its first Veterans Day program in 1947, although Armistice Day did not become Veterans Day until 1953. In addition to being the oldest annual observance to honor the veterans of all wars, the number of events and participants make it the largest such observance.

The two-hour parade begins in front of a reviewing stand at City Hall and features active and reserve units of the military, high school bands, ROTC units and floats. The night before the parade, a dinner at Boutwell Auditorium usually attracts some 1,500 dignitaries of all branches of the services and veterans' organizations. Prior to the parade, a World Peace luncheon is held. Phone 252-9825.

November weekend
Civil War Living History Exposition - Tannehill State Park - More than 600 Civil War re-enactors gather at this important military site for authentic instruction in artillery, cavalry and infantry subjects, with studies ranging from individual classroom seminars to full-scale battalion drills. The public is invited to observe activities, with the primary re-enactment Sunday at 2 p.m. Phone 477-5711.

Weekend before Thanksgiving
Vulcan Run - Major road races of 10K and a marathon attract many of the nation's leading distance runners. The 10K run on Saturday morning is preceded on Friday by a fitness expo at Boutwell Auditorium. A later 2-mile fun run attracts local beginners. Although half of those who participate in Sunday's grueling 26.2-mile race are first-time marathoners, some serious competitiors use it to qualify for the Boston Marathon. Cash prizes are given in men's and women's divisions and masters (over age 40). Sponsored by *The Birmingham News* and the Birmingham Track Club. Phone 640-6509.

Thanksgiving weekend
Alabama-Auburn Football Game - The annual season ender for the Crimson Tide and the Tigers is the biggest game and social event of the year for both teams' fans. Weddings, reunions, and even funerals have to be worked around the game. Those in Alabama who don't attend the game almost certainly watch it on television.

After being held at the neutral site of Birmingham's Legion Field for four decades, Auburn moved the 1989 game home to its newly-enlarged stadium on *odd* years. It is being played in Birmingham on *even* years.

Newspapers' sports sections and television sportscasters cover every aspect of the game heavily for at least two weeks prior. Game date may be moved to accommodate television schedules. Avoid driving and parking by taking a shuttle bus. Phone 844-1151.

First week of December
Festival of Trees - BJCC - Scores of exoticly decorated Christmas trees are the focus for a holiday fundraiser for the Children's Hospital of Alabama. Volunteers use everything from handmade needlepoint ornaments to toys to decorate the trees which are pre-bought by corporations for $750-$2,500 and often donated to charities. You can enjoy music and children's performances, shop in holiday boutiques and visit with Santa. Phone 252-9825.

First weekend of December
Christmas at Arlington - 331 Cotton Ave. SW - Hostesses in Victorian gowns conduct tours of the antebellum mansion decorated with greenery and fruit by local floral designers. A children's tree is decorated with antique toys and ornaments and Santa takes up residence in the country kitchen. A living nativity graces the gardens during a portion of the weekend. Refreshments are served. The restored house museum is located at the west end of First Avenue North. Phone 780-5656 or 252-9825.

First Saturday in December
SEC Football Championship Game - Legion Field - Winners of the East and West divisions of the Southeastern Conference meet in a championship game to pick the host team for the Sugar Bowl. Because Alabama and Auburn are both in the West, they can't meet in the contest. Arkansas, LSU, Ole Miss and Mississippi State are also in the West. Eastern teams are Tennessee, Vanderbilt, Florida, Georgia, Kentucky and South Carolina. Unique in college football, teams go into "sudden death" if the score is tied at the end of the fourth quarter.

Birmingham folded its All-American Bowl begun in 1977 as the Hall of Fame Bowl in order to successfully compete against Atlanta, Memphis, Tampa and Orlando for the championship game. The Crimson Tide defeated Florida in the first title game after the league expanded to 12 teams in 1992. Legion Field is home to the title game at least through 1996.

Because the SEC's "take" is about $6 million, it's the most expensive sporting event in the state, with some seats as much as $780 in the "champions' suites." Many tickets available to the general public start at $105, which includes a mandatory $75 donation, albeit tax deductible. End zone seats at only $30 are available through Fastix at 1-800-277-1700. For ticket information, write the Birmingham Football Foundation at P.O. Box 11304, Birmingham, 35202. If you decide at the last minute to go and don't have tickets, chances are you can get them cheap just before kickoff.

Second weekend of December
Christmas at the Alabama - Alabama Theater - The annual musical production features the traditional Christmas story performed in song and verse and Santa's village and workshop come to life. Local dance corps and choirs celebrate the season by participating in the event started in 1987. The grand theater is lavishly decorated with garlands, wreaths and Christmas trees. The Alabama's Mighty Wurlitzer organ is featured. Evening performances are Friday and Saturday with a matinee Sunday. Phone 939-FAST.

Second weekend of December
Holiday House Tour - Several of the city's more elegant homes are decorated with fresh greenery, fruit and towering Christmas trees in the annual tour of homes sponsored since 1950 by the Independent Presbyterian Church Woman's Organization. The tour benefits their children's fresh air farm and other missions. For tickets, visit the church at 3100 Highland Ave. or phone 933-1830.

Mid-December
The Nutcracker - BJCC - The concert hall is transformed into a fantasy of pagentry, music and dance with the traditional holiday performance presented by the State of

Alabama Ballet. The ballet showcases the talents of more than 250 dancers in five performances. Tickets are available through Fastix at 939-FAST.

Mid December
Christmas decorations - The images of Christmas trees 23 stories tall cover the sides of the AmSouth/Sonat building. To achieve the effect, red, green and white sleeves are slipped over the 2,484 fluroescent tubes nearest the windows on each side of the building.

Weekend before Christmas
Redstone Ball - Birmingham Country Club - The daughters of Birmingham's social elite are presented to society during the holidays in a ritual dating from 1908. By invitation.

CHILDERSBURG

Long before Childersburg was founded by frontier settlers in the early 19th century, the site served as a prosperous and sacred Indian capital known as Coosa, which was discovered by **Hernando De Soto** on July 16, 1540. For 35 days, the Spanish explorers rested here and visited the Indian cave which now bears the leader's name before continuing to the southwest across present-day Alabama.

De Soto came to the New World to explore and claim territory for Spain. Instead, he turned the mission into a march of conquest, looking for gold and other treasures, using his weapons, dogs and horses to control the Indians. In the wake of his passage were left disease and the deaths of thousands of natives.

In the 20th century, the town has evolved into a lumber and farm community. The major industry is paper manufacturing. The mill is located on the Coosa River on the western edge of the town.

ATTRACTIONS

DeSOTO CAVERNS PARK encompasses 80 acres surrounding the historic onyx marble caverns. The caves were occupied from about 1000 B.C. by the Eastern Woodland Indians. The Creeks, who arrived from the west in the late 16th century, considered the caves to be a hallowed place from which their forefathers emerged to form the Creek Nation. Confederates mined saltpeter from bat droppings to make gunpowder. Today, the caverns are owned by the fourth generation of the Mathews family who make it one of Alabama's most heavily promoted tourist attractions.

Hour-long guided tours include a sound, water and laser light show in a large onyx chamber. The entrance to the caverns is through the side of a hill. A flight of 70 steps takes you down to the "great cathedral room," a name justified when a guide illuminates the room which is higher than a 12-story building. The ceiling shimmers with thousands of stalactites in moist colors of yellow, orange and red. One of the first things you see is the oldest example of graffiti in an American cave. A fateful "1723" was carved near the entrance by a fur trader named I.W. Wright, who was subsequently carved up by the locals for desecrating their burial ground.

A few feet away is a 2,000-year-old burial site. Because federal law prohibits *insitu* skeletal displays, the bones have been reburied and replaced by reproductions in a glass case. One of the jawbones was from a man estimated to have stood seven feet tall.

Onyx formations - some dozens of feet long - have been given imaginative names, such as the draperies, charging rhino, frozen waterfall and giant's foot. Guides enjoy striking some formations with a rubber mallet to produce delightfully resonating tones. At the end of the tour the lights are turned off in the great onyx cathedral room and up shoot the lasers and dancing water fountains for a spectacular finale.

Back outside is a 3/4-acre maze of wooden poles which children delight in dashing through against a clock. The management suggests, with tongue-in-cheek, that the maze was inspired by the Spanish explorer's circuitous expedition trail, although the extra fee for the maze might be a more credible explanation.

The park offers numerous special events throughout the year, with several focusing on native traditions and crafts, as well as camping and picnic tables. Even panning for gems and gold is available. DeSoto Caverns Park is among the best family attractions in the state. Open Mon.-Sat., 9-5:30; Sun., 12:30-5:30. Closed Dec. 25. Adults, $8.50; ages 4-11, $5. Phone 378-7252 or 1-800-933-CAVE.

Getting there: Despite the impression given by numerous signs, arriving at DeSoto Caverns requires attention by the family navigator. The nearby town of Childersburg is between Birmingham and Sylacauga on U.S. 280. Turn onto Hwy. 76 and follow the signs.

KYMULGA GRIST MILL PARK includes an 1864 water-powered mill, which makes stone ground meal, and a country store fronted by Talladega Creek which flows beneath a covered bridge. Nature trails. Picnic shelters. Pay at the store. Open Mon.-Sat. 9-5, Sun. 1-5.

Getting there: Three miles from DeSoto Caverns Park, leave Hwy. 76 East on Forest Hill Rd., then take the first right. Go 4 miles.

SELWOOD FARM is a good source for mail-order smoked food products and shelters the 800-acre Selwood Hunting Preserve. You can have turkey, ham and other farm-raised products shipped anywhere in the U.S. To request a catalog, phone 1-800-522-0403.

WHERE TO EAT

*Mister J's, on U.S. 280 south of town, has a breakfast buffet and huge lunch food bar. Phone 378-5561.

CLANTON

To travelers, Clanton is the halfway point between Birmingham and Montgomery, and is the geographical center of the state. To people who know their produce, Clanton is the Peach Capital of Alabama.

Stop at I-65 exit 205 at either **Durbin's** opposite Burger King on the west side or **Peach Park** to the east to purchase fresh produce. The **Chamber of Commerce** office is in a railroad caboose at **Peach Park** near the Shed restaurant. Look for the world's largest peach about six feet across. A mini-museum housed in an 1828 log house, peach orchard, flower garden and a small stream flowing through Peach Park add charm to the visitor center. An 1840s smoke house is behind the visitor center.

You can expect to find Chilton County peaches all summer. Junegold is available in late May. Dixiered is a popular variety for pickling in late June. Loring is a favorite for freezing and ready in July. Also expect to find plums, nectarines, peanuts and vine-ripened watermelons. The markets have expanded to include yogurt, soft drinks and other fast food for travelers. Even after peaches go out of season, vegetables are sold as long as they are available.

Although orchards are found as far north as Limestone County, 75 percent of all Alabama peaches are grown near Clanton. Sixty percent of the state's 8,000 acres of peach trees are in Chilton County. Alabama's 117 growers harvest between 15 and 24 million pounds, depending on the weather, good enough to rank among the top 10 in the nation.

Weekend boaters on Lake Mitchell need not miss Sunday worship services. They can tie up their pontoons and ski boats at Higgins Ferry Landing to attend early morning services at the **River Church** without even leaving their boats. The come-as-you-are church, established about 1965 by the First United Methodist Church, draws the largest number of worshippers during summer holidays. The theme? "We Shall Gather at the River."

A retirement home for Confederate veterans, which peaked at 104 veterans and their wives around World War I, is now **Confederate Memorial Park**, an 80-acre cemetery and park near Mountain Creek where the birthdays of Confederate heroes are celebrated.

North of Clanton is **Thorsby** where sweet potatoes are grown and used in ice cream!

The biggest event of the year is the **Chilton County Peach Festival** held the third weekend each June. Events feature local contestants competing for the title of peach festival queen, a recipe contest and tasting event, golf tournament, art show and parade.

Clanton Jaycees give prizes to the person who can eat a peach and spit the peach pit the farthest distance. One of the most intriguing events is the auction at Jack Hayes Park where growers enter their peaches to be judged. The top five bring cash awards and the baskets are auctioned. A basket once brought $2,000. This event dates from 1947 when Thorsby banker Archie Ogburn suggested having an event to spotlight the hard work of the county's peach growers.

WELCOME CENTER

Visit the **Chamber of Commerce** office in a railroad caboose at **Peach Park** near the Shed restaurant on the east side of I-65 exit 205. Phone 755-2400.

WHERE TO STAY IN CLANTON

Key West Inn, on U.S. 31 near I-65, has 43 rooms on two floors. Complimentary beverages are in the lobby and several fast-food restaurants and Durbin's produce market are within walking distance. Write 2045 Seventh St. S., Clanton, 35045. Fax 280-0044. Double rate: $43-46 plus tax, higher during Peach Festival. **Phone 755-8500** or 1-800-833-0555.

Holiday Inn, U.S. 31 at I-65, is a two-story motel of 100 rooms with cable TV, and a restaurant overlooking the outdoor pool. Non-smoking rooms and lounge are available. The motel has received awards from Holiday Inn for a number of years. Write 2000 Holiday Inn Dr., Clanton, 35045. Double rate: $45-$50 plus tax. Ask about Great Rate reservations. **Phone 755-0510.**

Shoney's Inn, I-65 exit 208, has 74 rooms on two levels, with recliners in king rooms and some connecting doubles. Cable TV. Shoney's restaurant on site. A large parking lot accommodates RV's, trucks and boats. Write 946 Lake Mitchell Rd., Clanton, 35045. Fax 280-0306. Double rate: $42-46 plus tax. Packages are available for seniors, school groups and business travelers. **Phone 280-0306.**

WHERE TO EAT IN CLANTON

**The Shed is a restaurant that Buddy Chambliss built with architectural antiques and a Southern Railway Pullman car just off I-65 to replace the landmark Shed which burned in 1989. You can request to eat in the *Tombigbee* car from the railroad's New York-to-New Orleans run or in three other dining areas shaped with wood and old brick and enhanced by stained and leaded glass. The Shed has a wide variety of food, from fried chicken ($9) to smoked prime rib ($11) and fried shrimp ($11). Chilton County peaches are used in the peach fuzzy navel pie. It is located on U.S. 31 off I-65. Open daily from 11 a.m. Phone 755-6497.

EUTAW

Eutaw is a small, antebellum town with a number of restored landmarks, a grand mansion operated as a bed and breakfast and a major greyhound racing park.

Just 3 miles from the bustling traffic of I-59, the antebellum town laid out by Asa White in 1838 seems content to remain in the past century, proud of the 25 architecturally significant buildings listed on the National Register of Historic Places. The centerpiece of the town is the stuccoed 1868 **Greene County Courthouse** on Main Street which replaced a nearly identical one built in 1839 and burned during Reconstruction to destroy accusations "brought against citizens for their roles in the Southern rebellion." The two-story building was originally erected with outer brick walls 19 inches thick and interior walls measuring 15 inches. When it was rebuilt, workers razed the damaged building to the first-story windowsill level and reused original materials in the rebuilding.

Two other county government buildings predate the Civil War. The **Probate Office** was built in 1856 on the northwest corner of the square. Originally a one-story structure, a second story was later added. The marble square flooring and solid iron doorways and window shutters are original. The office holds records dating from 1818 and newspapers from 1830. A small two-story brick structure on the northeast corner is even older. The **Grand Jury Building/Sheriff's Office** was erected in 1842, and houses the circuit clerk and board of registrar offices.

The entire town square was named to the National Register of Historic Places in 1979. Several commercial buildings are noteworthy. John B. Clark built four row shops about 1855 in the 200 block of Main. The **Banks & Company Building** was built in the 1880's at the southeast corner of Morrow and Boligee streets.

Drive west on Main to Wilson Avenue where the white frame **First Presbyterian Church** built in 1851 is topped by a square bell tower and octagonal spire. Within its shadow is the 1841 **Vaughn-Morrow House** moved to 310 Main St. and restored by the **Greene County Historical Society**. It is their headquarters and tourist welcome center.

Across at 309 Main is the Alexander-Webb House erected in 1836 as a stagecoach inn in Erie. Dr. A. F. Alexander moved the two-story house to Eutaw several years after the town on the Black Warrior River ceased to be the county seat.

Unlike in most towns, Main Street does not extend to the western edge of town. Mesopotamia, a block north of and parallel to West Main, is the western access and site of several prominent houses. Two early houses are the Asa White-McGiffert House, c. 1838, 314 Mesopotamia, distinguished by a two-tiered covered gallery across the front of the house with six doorways to the interior, and the Archibald-Tuck House, early 1840s, 507 Mesopotamia.

Eutaw boasts four handsome mansions distinguished by Greek Revival facades. The Coleman-Banks House, 430 Springfield Ave., is north of the courthouse. Four massive round columns crowned with Ionic capitols support the impressive portico of the late 1840s house. The Reese-Mancini House, 244 Wilson Street, is south of Main. Successful carriagemaker Edwin Reese, who built a modest house at 236 Wilson about 1842, commissioned this two-story mansion which is said to have taken three years to build around 1858. Across the street at 241 Wilson is the Catlin Wilson House, circa 1844.

WELCOME CENTER

The **Greene County Historical Society** welcome center at 310 Main St. is open weekdays. Their 30-page guide to more than 75 structures around Eutaw is worth buying. Phone 372-2871.

EUTAW ATTRACTIONS

The most popular draw in Eutaw has nothing to do with historic buildings. It is **Greenetrack**, one of the nation's most successful greyhound dog tracks. The season is year round except for a Christmas break. Races are run nightly at 8 except Sun. Matinees are held Wed., Fri., Sat. and major holidays. The Kennel Club restaurant provides air-conditioned comfort and closed-circuit television coverage of the races outside. Minimum age is 18.

The schools in the black-majority county have been the big winners from Greenetrack's success, although the amount wagered has dropped by 45 percent since dog racing began 70 miles away in Birmingham. Paul Bryant Jr. owns Greenetrack and others in Texas, Idaho, Kansas and Iowa.

Getting there: It's near Eutaw just off I-59 exit 45. Phone 758-2709.

Thirteen miles south on U.S. 43 is Forkland. Turn right on County Rd. 4 to **St. John's Episcopal Church**, a pure example of religious rural Gothic architecture. Originally constructed in 1860 on the east side of the Black Warrior, the board and batten church was dismantled and rebuilt on the present site in 1878. To see **St. Andrew's Episcopal Church**, another Gothic church inspired by architect Richard Upjohn, drive south to Demopolis and go west on U.S. 80 and follow signs to the Gallion post office. St. Andrew's is also known as the Prairieville church.

WHERE TO STAY

Kirkwood bed and breakfast, which is also open for daily tours, is one of the Black Belt's most romantic showplaces. Eight fluted Ionic columns frame the south and west sides and create a veranda where guests may enjoy an afternoon breeze.

Its construction was nearly complete when the Civil War broke out and blockades prevented the delivery of an iron grille for the second-story balcony, crystal chandeliers and other decorative elements which he had ordered.

Descendants, most recently Dr. H. A. Kirksey, lived in the house with many of the original furnishings into the 1960s. At some point, the stately cupola had been dramatically reduced in height. By the early 1970s, Kirkwood stood vacant and in serious need of maintenance. Virginia attorney Roy Swayze and wife, Mary, bought the house soon after touring it while visiting friends in Eutaw. They devoted years to meticulous restoration, including raising the cupola to its original 17-foot height. The National Trust for Historic Preservation presented the couple with an honor award in 1982.

After Roy died, Mary decided to open her house to overnight guests where she lives with her daughter and granddaughter.

When you approach the house, you can see the details of the Ionic columns which support the massive portico. A seasonal theme is established in the multi-colored Bohemian glass framing the front doors: amber for spring, emerald for summer, ruby for fall and cobalt for winter. After you take your luggage upstairs, Mary gives a detailed tour of the house. An Iowan by birth, Mary has become something of an authority on the Civil War and illustrates her tour with stories of the war's impact on Kirkwood and the surrounding countryside.

A central hall on the ground floor leads to a breath-taking, sun-drenched double parlor. Ornately carved marble fireplaces adorned with the goddesses of the seasons, and massive Waterford crystal chandeliers which hang from enormous plaster medallions in each room, set the tone of the elegance of the mansion. French windows are raised in warmer months so that guests may walk out on the veranda to watch the sunset from a wicker rocking chair.

Two bedrooms are available for guests. A plantation bed from nearby Rosemount and Empire furniture furnish one room while twin Sheraton beds and a secretary, chairs and tables original to the house fill the other. Guests share what must be among the largest bathrooms in the state. A former bedroom converted to a bath has a marble mantle and a clawfoot tub which sits beneath a 12-foot gilt-frame mirror.

The $75 double rate plus lodgings tax includes a plantation breakfast, including Mary's special recipe of bran muffins. Take I-59 exit 40 to Hwy. 14. Drive east for 2 miles and turn left to 111 Kirkwood Dr. **Phone 372-9009.**

WHERE TO EAT

**The Cotton Patch is a West Alabama tradition dating from 1937 when Elizabeth Ward opened the Patch. The present building erected in 1977 is a large log building in a pine forest clearing. The eight open fireplaces and wooden chairs and tables in the dining rooms are illuminated by candles stuck in bottles. Bradley Brown Jr.'s restaurant serves large steaks with sauteed mushrooms ($15) and overflowing portions of country cooking like drop biscuits and chicken gizzards served with fluffy, steamed rice. Draft beer is served in Mason jars. Your first serving of the pickled watermelon rind appetizer is on the house. After dinner, search for Joe Namath's signature on the log walls. Checks average $10-$11. Open for dinner Sun., Tues.-Thurs., 5:30-9:30; until 10 on Fri.-Sat. Closed Thanksgiving Day and a week each at July the Fourth and Christmas. Take I-59 exit 45 and go north 100 yards and look for the turn on the right.

ANNUAL EVENTS

First weekend in April
Market Day - The Chamber of Commerce-sponsored festival promotes antebellum and Victorian homes on the market, as well as the quality of life and historic preservation in a small-town atmosphere. Phone 372-2871.

Last Thursday in July
Plantation Tour and Panola Barbecue - Grand houses in rural areas are featured in this mid-summer tour. For reservations, phone 372-2871 or 372-9480.

Fourth weekend in August
Black Belt Folk Roots Festival - Courthouse square - Native forms of crafts and music are celebrated throughout the town. People from various cities in West Alabama and East Mississippi travel to Greene County for the event. Phone 372-2871.

Fourth weekend in October
Eutaw Pilgrimage - Enjoy a boxed lunch while taking guided tours of homes and churches and watching a living-history encampment. A period dress ball is a highlight, along with an organized stroll around the courthouse square. Phone 372-2871.

MONTEVALLO

The town of Montevallo houses the attractive campus of the **University of Montevallo**, a co-ed college founded in 1895 as **Alabama College**, a woman's college. Several period campus buildings and the circa 1823 King House add to the school's charm.

Brierfield Iron Works Park is a primitive park located just off Hwy. 25 between Montevallo and Centreville. It is built around the ruins of the Bibb Furnaces destroyed by Yankee troops near the end of the Civl War.

Begun by wealthy Black Belt planters to profit from the Civil War, the works were taken over by the Confederate government in 1863. Two brick furnaces were built here and destroyed by a Federal calvary raid on March 31, 1865. Rebuilt, they were in operation occasionally and finally closed on Dec. 24, 1894.

Although the ruins are fenced off, you can camp, swim, picnic and see a variety of musical festivals on a nearby stage. A Civil War re-enactment in March is followed by a bluegrass festival in May, gospel music in September and Heritage Days in October. Free. Open daily. Phone 665-7982.

Contact the **Chamber of Commerce** at P.O. Box 45, Montevallo, 35225 or phone 665-5124.

ONEONTA

Blount County is home to four of Alabama's 12 remaining covered bridges and claims the title of Covered Bridge Capital of the state. **Horton Mill Bridge** is the highest covered bridge over water in the country. It measures 220 feet long and is 5 miles north of town on Hwy. 75. Easley Bridge, 95 feet long, is 1.5 miles northwest of U.S. 231, 3 miles northwest of town. Nectar Bridge, whose 385-foot length spans the Locust Fork of the Warrior River, is a mile east of Nectar off Hwy. 160. Swann Bridge, at 324 feet, is 1.5 miles west of Cleveland, a mile off Hwy. 79. Contact the **Chamber of Commerce** at 274-2153.

COVERED BRIDGE TOUR

A special type of structure built to span rivers and creeks is rarely seen by today's travelers, but several excellent examples of covered bridges are nearby.

Early in this century, families living in the mountains of north central Alabama were isolated by deep ravines carved by tributaries rushing to form the Black Warrior River northwest of Birmingham.

To avoid arduous journeys around the canyons, road builders erected spans of bridges on stilt-like piers across the ravines. These engineering marvels were built of heart pine and covered to protect the bridge planks and substructure from the weather and to keep them from rotting. For cross ventilation, boards on the sides were nailed in an open lattice work pattern.

Four of the state's 11 remaining bridges stand in Blount County north of Birmingham and can be toured on a 25-mile route which combines history with rugged and beautful scenery. You'll understand why Blount County lays claim to the title of **Covered Bridge Capital of Alabama.** All four are within a mile of good surface roads. The scenic route covers backroads along mountainous plateaus which permit views of great distances on a clear day. In the woods surrounding the bridges, wildflowers and dogwoods abound in the spring and oakleaf hydrangeas dot the shaded landscape each summer.

Directions: Gas up the family car, pack a picnic and take plenty of film for the camera. The tour begins on U.S. 231 several miles south of Blountsville. (From Birmingham, take Hwy. 79 through Tarrant and Locust Fork.) At mile marker 37, turn east off 231 and go about a mile to **Swann Bridge.** It spans 324 feet and is the second longest in the state.

Continue beyond the bridge on the same road and go 2 miles and take the first left onto County 37. Next, turn left onto Hwy. 160 in Nectar and go a half-mile before turning right at a church and cemetery. A half-mile beyond is the **Nectar Bridge.** Four sections supported by piers of rocks span 385 feet, making it the longest in Alabama and fourth longest in the nation. Drive across and park along the roadside.

There is a steep walk down a sandy slope to the Black Warrior. Canoers use the spot for taking out their boats and floats. If you walk into the center of the bridge and look straight down on the upriver side, you'll see an old pole barge submerged in shallow water (and possibly some of the biggest sturgeon fish in the state). Make a u-turn and go back to the cemetery.

Turn right back onto Hwy. 160 and go 3.5 miles to the intersection with Hwy. 79 where it may be time for a rest stop at either of the service stations. Across the highway is **Hickory Pit Barbecue** (take-out only).

Go straight across 79 and pick up U.S. 231 East for 5 miles and turn right at mile marker 258 to Pine Grove Baptist Church. The **Old Easley Bridge** is about a mile beyond. Only 96 feet long, the one-span bridge completed in 1928 is a bit out of plumb. Notice the interesting rock formations carved by the narrow Dub Branch.

Make a u-turn and turn right onto 231 and then left shortly at the highway sign to **Palisades Park** and head up the mountain. Three miles up the mountain is a county park with large picnic shelters, museum pioneer village, picnic shelters and rest rooms. From atop the narrow 80-foot bluff you can look down on a new golf course and see mountains far into the distance. However, the view of the bluff from underneath is even more interesting and offers a chance to stretch your legs.

To return to the route of the covered bridges, descend the mountain road to the stone directional marker and turn right. Follow this road for about 3 miles to reach the fourth bridge and drive across. (You will be just a few yards off Hwy. 75.)

Horton Mill Covered Bridge, the highest covered bridge above water in the nation, soars 70 feet over the Calvert Prong of the Black Warrior River. Follow the trail down to the water to appreciate this 220-foot bridge built in 1934-35 supported by a single concrete pier. If people are walking overhead inside the bridge, you can probably hear the loud creaking caused by their footsteps. In fact, a car driving across makes less noise.

The scenery of the gorge matches the beauty of the bridge. Walk carefully around an angular rock the size of a garage and other boulders near the edge of the stream. Unfortunately, because this bridge and gorge are so accessible to the picnicking public, it is littered with fast-food wrappers, motor oil cans and old tires.

Horton Mill bridge can be easily reached independent of the tour. From U.S. 231 in Oneonta, go north on Hwy. 75 about 5 miles to near mile marker 34. A metal sign points toward the bridge. If you are traveling through Oneonta, it is worth the short detour to view one of the South's most picturesque covered bridges.

WHERE TO STAY

A pair of bed and breakfast inns northeast of Birmingham are convenient headquarters if you're interested in a driving tour of Blount County's covered bridges.

Beeson House: Curtis Grubb Beeson built an imposing two-story frame plantation house in the shadow of Chandler Mountain in 1840. Now, his fourth great-grand-daughter, Katie Rich, and husband, Jerry, operate the house as a rural bed and breakfast for people looking for a retreat from city life.

The Beeson House stands against a backdrop of magnolias and other trees on 117 acres. A portico covers a second-story balcony over the front door and galleries run the depth of the house on the first and second stories, giving guests both privacy and access to the outdoors. The galleries offer a relaxing place to watch the sunsets. In the fall, you can watch the trees on Chandler Mountain turn to shades of red and orange.

Enjoy a mint julip or milk and walk out to the springs where watercress and fresh mint grow in abundance. You may even fish in the pond. In case you decide not to drive 11 miles into Oneonta for dinner, you are welcome at the Rich dinner table.

Old family portraits, including one of the builder whose picture is on the wall in the library, and period wallpaper designs complete the authentic restoration. Rooms are furnished in Early American and eclectic collections. A continental breakfast is served in the dining room. If you are agreeable to being photographed, your picture will be added to the photo gallery of previous guests.

Katie and Jerry invite guests from the previous year to attend a Christmas party to mix and mingle with others. A drawing determines who gets a free weekend at Beeson House.

Write Katie and Jerry at Rt. 1, Box 521, Steele, 35987. Phone 594-7878.

Roses and Lace Country Inn: In Ashville, Confederate Army veteran Elias James Robinson and wife Susan constructed a large Queen Anne house a few blocks from the courthouse square about 1890. He had become an attorney at age 20 and was elected probate judge when he was 25. After a second term, Robinson sold the house to James P. and Clara Inzer Montgomery and moved out of town.

After the house passed through several ownerships, the Tony Sparks family bought it in 1987 and spent two years restoring it as a family project. Today, Mark and Shirley Sparks operate the Robinson-Montgomery House and live in an apartment on the third floor.

A deep veranda where you can view Shirley's rose garden frames the ground floor public rooms and Victorian elements accent the upper floor. The dusty rose color and stained glass windows lend a romantic air to the house which attracts many newly-weds. The three upstairs bedrooms gleam from elbow grease and brightly polished hardwood floors. The theme of the inn has been carried out in each guest room, from lace-curtained windows to lace tablecloths, from hand-crocheted bed coverlets to rise print wallpaper and paintings of roses in antique frames.

Members of the Sparks family, who found pine floors in good condition beneath layers of paint, are now landscaping portions of the 11 acres of pecan trees behind the house for walking trails and sculptured gardens.

The kitchen, where Shirley Sparks cooks a full Southern breakfast, is connected to the main house via a breezeway which has been enclosed. Rates include breakfast and range from $55 for a room with shared bath to the downstairs honeymoon suite for $75. Dinner can be provided at an additional cost with reservations.

Go 2 blocks south of the courthouse square on U.S. 231. Write P. O. Box 852, Ashville, 35953. Phone 594-4366.

SYLACAUGA

Sylacauga is built upon a foundation of solid marble which has been quarried since 1840. The marble seam is estimated to be about 400 feet deep, 32 miles long and more than a mile wide. In places it is within 12 feet of the surface. The clean white stone was used to build a number of government structures such as the U.S. Supreme Court, the Washington Monument, the General Motors Building in Detroit and the Archives and History Building in Montgomery. Peak activity was reached in the 1920s prior to a declining demand for marble in monumental architecture.

Sylacauga's quarries no longer chisel large chunks for buildings, but furnish crushed and ground marble for products as diverse as paint and toothpaste.

The town holds the bizarre distinction of having a resident actually hit by a meteorite. Mrs. Hewlett Hodges was listening to the radio at home in 1954 when an 11-pound meteorite ripped through the roof, bounced off a table and struck her hip, leaving a serious bruise. She was the first person struck by a meteorite since a monk was killed in Italy in 1650. The **Hodges Meteorite** is in the Natural History Museum in Tuscaloosa.

The headquarters of **Avondale Mills** is located in town. Sylacauga is also known as the hometown of actor/singer **Jim Nabors**, whose downhome "Gomer Pyle" character was a favorite in the *Andy Griffith* family.

ATTRACTION

ISABEL COMER MUSEUM displays local artifacts, archaeological relics and works by native artists, as well as several sculptures by Vulcan creator Giuseppe Moretti, who often used local marble for his works. The museum founded in 1982 by Mrs. Comer and supported by Avondale Mills, other businesses and individuals is housed in the old library building. Open Tues.-Fri., 10-4. Closed major holidays. Phone 245-4016.
Getting there: 711 Broadway Ave. N.

WHERE TO EAT

**J. Oliver's, halfway between Sylacauga and Childersburg on U.S. 280, serves grilled seafod and steaks and is especially noted for homemade desserts. Open Tues.-Sat. Phone 249-3633.

TALLADEGA

- **Claim to fame:** NASCAR stockcar races
- **Don't miss:** International Motorsports Hall of Fame
- **Best souvenir:** Racing caps, Purefoy Hotel Cook Book
- **Population:** 18,175
- **Tourist information:** Chamber of Commerce, 210 East St. S., P.O. Drawer A, Talladega, 35160. Phone 362-9075.

Talladega is home to the **Talladega Superspeedway**, the world's fastest NASCAR track, which hosts some of the most exciting events on the Winston Cup circuit.

The **Winston 500** is on the first Sunday in May, and the **DieHard 500** runs on the last Sunday in July. Qualifying and other events bring many fans to town the week prior to the major races.

You can tour the track most days of the year. Be sure to visit the **International Motorsports Hall of Fame** next door.

The Hueytown Allison family of Bobby, Donnie and Davey accounted for nine of the first 21 Winston 500 victories. Dale Earnhardt became the first driver to log five career victories at Talladega, surpassing Bobby Allison, Darrell Waltrip and Buddy Baker as the track's all-time winner.

The two race weeks have the largest economic impact of any sports events in the state, estimated at $65 million. Hotels from Birmingham to Atlanta are booked solid for the weekends. If you can't get a room, you can camp in the infield on Saturday night, with a 2-day ticket including admission to the race on Sunday afternoon.

The excitement of racing is the latest chapter in the history of the town which began as an Indian settlement and later became home to institutions which educate deaf and blind children.

The most dramatic moments of the Indian era occurred when **Andrew Jackson** led his Tennessee Volunteers to aid besieged pioneers inside Lashley's Fort on Nov. 9,

1813. In the **Battle of Talladega**, Jackson's forces defeated a large number of Creeks from the nearby village of Talatiga ("border town") which Jackson then burned. A contemporary pavilion a few blocks from the present courthouse square on Battle Street covers markers which detail the battle.

Founded in the Appalachian foothills in 1834, Talladega is one of the oldest towns in East Alabama. It remained a principal trading center into the middle of this century, with family-owned stores thriving around the historic 1836 **Talladega County Courthouse**. The brick detailing has Egyptian influences which symbolize wheat.

Several landmarks are near the courthouse, which is the oldest in the state in continuous service. A Greek Revival building erected in 1912 at the northwest corner served as the **U.S. Post Office** for many years and now houses the city water and sewer board. Standard Furniture, at the southwest corner, was built in the 1880s as the Chambers Opera House. The brick walls of the **First Presbyterian Church** at 130 North St. E. were erected in 1861, but the Civil War delayed completion until 1868.

Talladega was famous for the family-style dining at the **Purefoy Hotel** at 120 North St. E. Food critic Duncan Hines praised the Purefoy in his 1955 book of the nation's best restaurants, as did *Life* magazine and *Ford Times*. Although the hotel was closed in 1961 and demolished to make way for a bank, Eva Purefoy's 1941 cookbook remains a prized possession of local people. (Buy a $9 reprint at Elaine's Newstand at 122 E. Court Square or send $11 to Higginbotham Printing Co., Box 1408, Anniston, 36202.)

TALLADEGA ATTRACTIONS

BRYANT VINEYARDS is open for tasting wines just a grapeshot from where the Coosa River gets backed up as Logan Martin Lake. Kelly Bryant, a fireman, planted five acres of muscadines in the early 1980s and began commercial production of wine in 1985. Other grapes were planted. The first case of Bryant wine went on sale a couple of years later. The Villard Blanc, a dry white wine made from a French hybrid grape, is the Bryant favorite at Vincent's Market in Birmingham. You may taste and purchase wine Mon.-Sat. 10-5. Phone 268-2638.

Getting there: Take I-65 exit 165 to County 207 south and turn right at the Baptist church to County 191 and follow the signs to 1454 Griffin Bend Road.

INTERNATIONAL MOTORSPORTS HALL OF FAME is a five-building complex next to the Talladega Superspeedway which showcases a $12 million collection of more than 100 of the most famous racing cars ever to blur past a checkered flag. It was founded to preserve this history of motorsports on a worldwide basis, and to enshrine the people who have been responsible for the sport's growth.

Still sporting their giant numbers and gaudy product logos, they are parked quietly in enormous showrooms. The Daytona room houses the legendary "Bluebird," which set the world's land speed record of 335 mph at Daytona Beach in 1935. Richard Petty's trustworthy Dodge Charger, Bobby Allison's No. 22 Buick and a limited edition Ford Talladega Torino which Hueytown's Donnie Allison piloted to many victories are also here.

Bill Elliott set a world average speed record for 500-mile stock car races in 1985 in the bright red Ford Thunderbird spotlighted here. Because of mechanical restrictions on today's race cars, the 186.3-mph record may stand for many more years.

Go into the UNOCAL 76 building, largest in the complex, to see the the bullet-shaped Budweiser rocket car capable of blasting from standstill to 140 mph in a single second. It measures 39 feet long and is only 20 inches wide. The bullet car once broke the speed of sound on a California desert at nearly 740 mph. A wide variety of brightly polished vehicles, exhibits and even a race car simulator are under the wide-span roof.

A couple of cars in the International room remind racing fans that the stock car sport isn't all beer commercials, speed and trophies. The crumbled remains of the car in which Phil Parsons survived an 11-car crackup during a 1983 race and a halved Pontiac which Michael Waltrip luckily walked away from in 1990 are scary symbols of the real danger of racing at 200 mph. In addition to stock cars, the Hall displays Indy cars and even a Don Garlits drag racer that hit over 240 mph on a 1/4-mile track. You can also see memorabilia of the great drivers, inventors and races.

The Motorsports Hall of Fame includes three-time Indy 500 winner Bobby Unser, Parnelli Jones, Stirling Moss, Barney Oldfield, Eddie Rickenbacker, Louis Chevrolet, Junior Johnson, promoter Bill France, and designer Carroll Shelby, as well as other "who's who's" of racing. The UNOCAL-sponsored, televised black-tie induction banquet is held in Birmingham and the enshrinement is in Talladega. Each honoree receives a specially cast medallion and display in the hall of fame. Racers retired for five years are voted upon by more than 150 writers who cover motorsports.

The best time to tour the museum is during race week in May or July when the addition of race crowds fuels the excitement of the sport.

Researchers have access to the 14,000-volume McCaig-Wellborn International Motorsports Library.

Tickets for races and other events are available in the main routunda where a fully stocked gift shop is also located. Plan to spend at least an hour. Open daily 9-5 with hours extended on race weeks. Closed Easter morning, Thanksgiving Day, Dec. 25 and Jan. 1. Adults, $5; ages 7-17, $4. Phone 362-5002

Getting there: From Birmingham, take exit 173 on I-20, turn south and go 2.5 miles to Speedway Boulevard. From Atlanta, take exit 168.

JEMISON-CARNEGIE HERITAGE HALL housed in the former 1908 library contains exhibits on the De Soto expedition, the Creek Indian Nation routed by Andy Jackson and the Civil War. It is one of four surviving Carnegie library buildings in Alabama. Open Tues.-Sat., 1-4; Sun., 2-5. Located 2 blocks from the square at 200 South St. E.

LOGAN-MARTIN DAM across the Coosa River west of Talladega creates a 15,000-acre reservoir more than 48 miles long with banks dotted with weekend and permanent homes. An earthen dike which stretches 5,464 feet across the river is one of seven dams built by Alabama Power to generate electricity. To tour the dam, phone 672-2332.

Getting there: Take I-20 exit 158 and go south on U.S. 231. Turn on County 054.

SILK STOCKING HISTORIC DISTRICT is south of the square. Talladega's residential section retains much of its 19th-century appearance, especially homes in the district off East South Street. Governmental and institutional buildings, including those of the predominately black Talladega College and the Alabama Institute for the Deaf and Blind established in 1858 are of interest. Take time to drive around behind the AIDB campus to see a surprising collection of stately 19th-century homes.

From the square, go south on East Street past the old L&N Depot (Chamber of Commerce offices) and take the next left on South Street. Drive five blocks to enjoy one of the loveliest streets in the state. Double back and go left on Cherry, right on Margaret and right on East Street.

TALLADEGA COLLEGE, founded by two ex-slaves in 1867 as the first college in the state open to all races, is a well-known predominantly black college. The 1854 Swayne Hall predates the founding and is the last surviving original structure. The imposing building with columns supporting a portico dominates the central campus and is a National Historic Landmark for its association with black education. Facing Swayne Hall is the library named for founder William Savery. Inside, three frescoes recall an incident in 1839 when Joseph Cinque led a revolt aboard the Cuban schooner *Amistad*, to liberate a shipload of his fellow Africans. Georgia-born artist Hale Woodruff painted the lifesize figures in 1939. To see the murals, phone 362-0206 or 1-800-762-2468 in Alabama. A chapel with a belltower honors Dr. Henry Swift DeForest, the first president.

Getting there: The college is 6 blocks west of the square on Battle Street. Park at the chapel to see if it is open. Then, drive around and up the hill to Swayne and Savery.

TALLADEGA SUPERSPEEDWAY, the world's fastest speedway, is home to major NASCAR stockcar events. The two main races are the largest sporting events in the state, with attendances of 100,000-135,000. It is a year round testing facitility used by Harley-Davidson Motorcycles Co., tire manufacturers and automakers. Bus tours of the speedway begin at the Motorsports Hall of Fame each day except when races are held or equipment is tested. NASCAR founder Bill French opened the track in 1969 on a 2,000-acre site 40 miles east of Birmingham. Write P.O. Box 777, Talladega, 35160. Phone 362-2261.

Getting there: From Birmingham, take exit 173 on I-20, turn south and go 2 1/2 mi. to the Speedway Blvd. From Atlanta, take exit 168.

WALDO COVERED BRIDGE, 6 miles from town on Hwy. 77 toward Ashland, is 115 feet long, adjacent to Riddle's grist mill and a log cabin. A harvest festival is held in the fall.

WHERE TO STAY

Colony House Motel has 100 rooms, a pool, a restaurant and a lounge. It made the supermarket tabloids when Tammy Faye Bakker stayed here while PTL preacher Jim Bakker was jailed at the federal prison a few miles away off County Rd. 203. Colony House is south of the speedway, between the Hwy. 77 and 275 intersection and town. **Phone 362-0900.**

Oakwood B&B is a Federal style frame house with four large bedrooms just east of the courthouse square. Oakwood features a portico over a small second-story balcony. It was built in 1847 for Alexander Bowie, who became the first mayor of Talladega. Owners Al and Naomi Kline restored the two-story house to host business and leisure travelers in Talladega. Turn east off Hwy. 77 at the northeast corner of the square and go about a mile to 715 E. North St. **Phone 362-0662.**

WHERE TO SHOP

Palm Beach Mill Outlet is an excellent place to buy first-quality Gant and Palm Beach suits, jackets and shirts at substantial savings. From I-20, take exit 168 to Hwy. 77 and go south for 9 miles. At the Colony House Motel, turn opposite the entrance to **Shocco Springs Baptist Assembly** and follow the signs to the store at the Palm Beach factory. Open Mon.-Sat., 9-5:30; Fri., until 8:30; Sun., 1-5:30. Phone 362-8401.

ANNUAL EVENTS

Second weekend of April

April in Talladega - The Silk Stocking district is the focus of the tour which includes churches and other antebellum and Victorian homes such as the circa 1830s log cabin at Boxwood. Antiques, art exhibits and tea room luncheons enhance a visit to this quiet town. Phone 362-6184 or 362-9075.

First Sunday of May

Winston 500 NASCAR Race - Talladega Superspeedway - Competitors in the world's fastest stock car race circle the 2.66-mile track about every 51 seconds at speeds up to 200 mph. National television coverage of the race on the trioval, high-banked track with its pair of 33 degree turns testifies to the importance of its outcome in NASCAR standing. A stock car of the '90's may look like a family sedan, but beneath the sponsors' decals hums a $20,000 custom engine in a $100,000 speedster.

The Winston 500 is the second of NASCAR's Big Four - along with the Daytona 500, the Coca-Cola 600 at Charlotte on Memorial Day weekend and the Southern 500 at Darlington on Labor Day weekend. A driver winning three of the four earns the Winston $1 million bonus from series sponsor R.J. Reynolds. Because the Talladega race is the second each year, attention is usually focused on the winner of the Daytona race to see if he can repeat the victory lap here. The first bonus winner was Bill Elliott in the 1985 inaugral bonus season.

Upwards of 130,000 people wheel off I-20 for this event held annually since 1970. You can either sit in the grandstand and watch the race as you would a football game or join the rowdy infield crowd and participate by walking around in the sun with a beer in your hand. It has been described as a huge party where a race happens to be going on, sort of a redneck Woodstock. The infield crowd can even pay to set up camp and spend the night within the track instead of camping on the grounds nearby.

Attendees like to park close to the stands for occasional trips to the car or van because beer is not sold on the track grounds. Attending? Wear a broad-brimed cap, carry extra sun block and be prepared for a long traffic line to get away. Not attending? Stay clear of the traffic jam on I-20 between 3 and 5 p.m.

For information and tickets, write the superspeedway, P.O. Box 777, Talladega, 35160. Phone 362-9064.

Fourth Sunday in July

DieHard 500 - Talladega Superspeedway - The final major NASCAR Winston Cup stock car race of the season draws about 100,000 fans to the world's fastest speedway off I-20. It has the reputation of producing the most surprising wins of any race on the NASCAR Winston Cup circuit. Suggestions are the same as for the race in May: bring sunscreen if attending; if not, avoid I-20 because of the heavy traffic. Tickets go on sale weeks in advance. Phone 362-9064.

Mid December
IMHOF Induction Ceremony - Inductees of the Motorsports Hall of Fame are presented at a banquet in connection with the Checkered Flag weekend.

TUSCALOOSA

- **Claim to fame:** Crimson Tide football
- **Don't miss:** Bryant Museum, Moundville
- **Where to eat:** Cypress Inn, Dreamland
- **Where to shop:** Kentuck Museum
- **Best events:** Heritage Week, Kentuck Festival
- **Population:** 77,759
- **Tourist information:** Leon Maisel, Executive Director; Tuscaloosa Convention & Visitors Bureau, P.O. Box 032167, Tuscaloosa, 35403. Fax 391-2125. Phone 1-800-538-8696 or 391-9200.

"Mama called" in 1958 and **Paul "Bear" Bryant** answered to come home to Tuscaloosa and become head coach of the **Crimson Tide** at the **University of Alabama**. Neither the man nor the school nor the city would ever be the same again.

After coaching at Maryland, Kentucky and Texas A&M, he returned to his alma mater to establish a 25-year dynasty, with his teams winning 72 of 74 games played at home and six national championships, not to mention Bryant being voted the greatest coach in football history for his total of 323 victories.

His fans believed he could walk on water. His bass growl of a voice spoke volumes to his players and their opponents. He was the most influential man in Alabama.

So overpowering was Bryant's persona that players called to his office for conferences used to swear that the legs on the sofa they had been sitting on were cut off because the man behind the desk seemed to tower above them. In a museum built to honor the man and the coach, you can "visit" his re-created office. The desk is here and so is the sofa, with its legs intact.

Even though the Bear has been gone for more than a decade, his legend continues to grow. His name is on the stadium, the football museum, the players' dorm and the second longest street on campus. Even **Coach Gene Stallings** said after winning a national championship in only his third season at Tuscaloosa that he owes much of his success to the man he served as an assistant coach.

While you can stroll the campus which football made famous and spend hours lingering over football memorabilia at the **Paul Bryant Museum**, you should remember that Tuscaloosa offers a wealth of other historical and cultural distractions which have nothing to do with sports.

Prior to the arrival of whites, **Taskalusa** was a major Native American village. In the Choctaw language, tusko means "warrior" and loosa means "black." The name honors the great chef who in 1540 was taken prisoner by Spanish explorer Hernando De Soto.

The present city is one of the state's oldest, and even housed the state government for two decades in the 19th century. With permission of the U.S. Government, Creek Indians established the town in 1809. Four years later it was burned after a revolt. Davy

Crockett, a scout for the American troops, was certain the town had been "wiped from the face of the earth forever." However, settlers from South Carolina rebuilt Tuscaloosa into a significant settlement by the time Alabama became a state in 1819. Just two days after statehood, the Legislature authorized that the first state road be built from Huntsville to Tuscaloosa. Today the south end is University Boulevard.

In 1826 it became the state capital. Four years later, the old Indian fighter **Andrew Jackson** had become president and influenced Congress to pass legislation to clear the Indians from their ancestral lands. When Jackson sent federal troops to forcibly remove the remaining natives, Gov. John Gayle denounced the action, and federal mediator Francis Scott Key traveled to Tuscaloosa to negotiate a settlement with Gayle.

Just before the forced migration, the great Chief Eufaula asked to address legislators at the Capitol. He told them, "I come, brothers, to see the great house of Alabama and to say farewell to the wise men who make the laws. I leave the graves of my fathers. The Indian fires are going out."

Inspired by the tireless efforts of **Julia Tutwiler**, the **University of Alabama** was opened in 1831, giving the city two of the state's major institutions for nearly two decades. It was during this period that many of the city's handsome homes were built near Queen City Avenue and today comprise the **Druid City** district. Though Tuscaloosa suffered a devastating blow when the state government was transferred to Montgomery in 1847, its economic recovery became certain by the late 19th century when the federal government installed locks to improve navigation along the Black Warrior River.

Later developed by the U.S. Corps of Engineers into the Tenn-Tom Waterway, the project now permits the easy movement of more than nine million tons of freight annually between Birmingham and Mobile. In addition to its tremendous power-generating capabilities, nearby **Holt Lock and Dam** creates one of the state's cleanest lakes which offers many water sports.

More than 100 antebellum homes are scattered throughout the county, which led Marvin Harper and others to establish the state's first county historic preservation society in 1965. The society has preserved a number of important buildings and generated widespread community support for preserving the area's colorful heritage.

The best time of the year to visit is **Heritage Week** when doors to some of the most elegantly restored mansions are opened for tours and the century-old azaleas and dogwoods are in bloom.

WELCOME CENTER

Visit the **Tuscaloosa Convention & Visitors Bureau** in the Jemison House at 1305 Greensboro Ave. at 13th Street. Phone 391-9200.

Contact the **Tuscaloosa County Preservation Society** at P.O. Box 1665, Tuscaloosa, 35043. Phone 758-2238. Read the feature pages of *The Tuscaloosa News* for special happenings in the area.

OFF-CAMPUS ATTRACTIONS

BATTLE-FRIEDMAN HOUSE, one of Tuscaloosa's impressive house museums, was begun about 1835 by Alfred Battle, a prosperous merchant from North Carolina. Six paneled square columns support a portico across the broad width of the house and frame the double front doors topped by a fanlight. Plaster stucco scored and painted to look like pink marble distinguishes the facade. In 1875 the mansion was purchased

TUSCALOOSA, ALABAMA

by Bernard Friedman, a merchant who added the two-story brick wing at the rear and imported from his homeland the Hungarian chandeliers that grace the parlors. Other furnishings date from the early 19th century.

The Battle-Friedman House is surrounded by towering trees and a half-block of large azalea bushes and other shrubbery. Open Tues.-Sat., 10-noon and 1-4; Sun., 1-4. Adults, $3; students, $.50; seniors, $2.50. Phone 758-6138.

Getting there: It is set back from the west side of Greensboro Avenue between Bryant Drive and 11th Street.

GULF STATES ART COLLECTION includes historical Americana, classical and modern paintings at the headquarters of the paper company. Sculptures include Southern Pacific primitives and African examples. The Warner Family which founded Gulf States is without peer in Tuscaloosa for their civic-mindedness and support of the arts and historic preservation. The corporation built the NorthRiver Yacht Club and filled it with American masterpieces.

Once, during a split with family members and stockholders over what was perceived as excessive spending on art, Jack Warner told *The New York Times*, "It's about time somebody did something for the rich." You can see what Warner did. Guided tours Mon.-Fri., 5-7 p.m.; Sat. and holidays, 10-7; Sun., 1-7 p.m. Free. Phone 553-6200.

Getting there: A mile east of U.S. 82 on 1400 River Rd.

JEMISON HOUSE is a striking two-story Italianate residence in the heart of Tuscaloosa which will serve as the city's tourism welcome center when a major restoration is complete. It had been neglected before being rescued by the Tuscaloosa County Preservation Society and the Heritage Commission of Tuscaloosa County. It was constructed circa 1860 for politician Robert Jemison Jr. and later became the home of physicist Robert Jemison Van de Graaf. It served as the Friedman Memorial Library for a number of years.

Getting there: 1305 Greensboro Ave. at 13th Street. It is just down the street from the Battle-Friedman House museum.

MILDRED WARNER HOUSE is a Georgian residence noted for its architecture and impressive art collection assembled with Gulf States money. Authentic furnishings dating between 1730 and 1860 include many pieces acquired from Carter Hall near Williamsburg, Va. Of particular note is a fine collection of American art, featuring such renowned artists as William Aiken Walker and James Whistler. The house began as a two-room cabin in 1822 and a brick addition was built circa 1835 for David Scott. The house was restored in 1977 for the David Warner Foundation. It was called the Janus Place early in this century by owner Dr. George Little because the north and south entrances were nearly identical. Open Sat., 10-6; Sun., 1-6. Free.

Getting there: The Scott-Moody-Warner House is at 1925 Eighth St. and 20th Avenue. Phone 345-4062.

NORTHRIVER YACHT CLUB is a exclusive resort developed by paper baron Jack Warner on 1,200 wooded acres on Lake Tuscaloosa northeast of town. The main lodge offers 56 private bedrooms and the Apothecary Lounge. Overlooking the tree-lined, 71-par golf course designed by Gary Player and Ron Kirby are 25 guest villas. The best way to visit is to attend a meeting or conference held at NorthRiver. Phone 345-0202 or 1-800-622-2029.

Getting there: Go north on U.S. 82 across the Black Warrior, turn right on Rice Mine Road and then right on Watermelon Road.

The OLD TAVERN dates from 1827 when William Dunton erected it as one of several public houses where members of the Alabama Legislature boarded. The kitchen was located in a basement and food was served on both upper floors. An overhanging covered balcony on the second story suggests French architectural influences. William Dunton built the tavern at 2512 Broad St.

Preservationists cleaned the stucco off the brick building in 1966 when it was moved to the western end of University Boulevard and restored near the ruins of the old 1826 **State Capitol**.

The museum is furnished with period antiques and artifacts from Tuscaloosa's capital period. Open Tues.-Sat., 10-noon, 1-4; Sun., 1-4. Admission. Phone 758-8163.

After the seat of government was moved to Montgomery, the Grecian-style Capitol was used by the Alabama Central Female College. It burned in 1923. The county preservation society is recreating the ruins of the Capitol with its Doric columns. The 1820 **McGuire-Strickland House**, the city's oldest frame building, is a raised cottage next to the ruins. Free. Phone 758-2238 or 752-2575.

Getting there: Capitol Park is at 28th Avenue and University Boulevard.

TOURING THE UNIVERSITY

The University has a long and impressive academic history that parallels the growth of the state. A year after being named as the state capital of Alabama, Tuscaloosa was selected from among 13 towns as the site of the state university as well. State Architect William Nichols was selected to design a campus about a mile from the town.

The handsome Rotunda was still under construction when classes began on April 17, 1831, with a faculty of five and an enrollment of 52 students. The main building's dome room contained the library and the natural history collection. Additional structures were built during the next three decades.

In 1855, the school installed military training to discipline the students, and a decade later, the presence of this military unit was the reason the campus was destroyed.

After hearing rumors of impending Yankee raids, University President Landon Cabell Garland received word early on the morning of April 4, 1865, that Union troops were crossing the river from Northport to invade Tuscaloosa. He rushed to the small guard house and ordered the drum corps to muster the school's 300 student cadets to repel the attackers. After the first clash with 1,500 seasoned troops under Brig. Gen. John Croxton, Garland ordered a retreat to save the cadets' lives.

Union troops set fire to the school's beautiful Rotunda, dormitories and class-rooms. When the president's wife, Mrs. Louise Frances Garland, heard that the campus was being destroyed, she rushed to the mansion and found 300 soldiers looting her property. A fire had been set on a sofa. Mrs. Garland was so forceful in her attempt to save the house that the soldiers helped put out the fire and left.

A woman living near the Observatory was able to persuade soldiers not to burn it since it had not contributed to the spirit of rebellion. Although they spared the building, they destroyed the valuable scientific instruments which had been imported from London. By the end of the day, only a few faculty houses, the ruined Observatory, the President's Mansion and minor outbuildings remained.

The University reopened in 1870, with most campus and academic life centered at Woods Hall. During the postbellum period, a collection of Gothic buildings (flanking the sides and rear of the present Gorgas Library built on the site of the Rotunda) characterized the architecture of the campus. Later would come the Beaux Arts and Classical Revival buildings as the campus expanded. Enrollment grew from 400 in 1912 to 4,000 some 25 years later, the period Dr. George Denny served as president. Denny gave rise to the nickname the **Capstone** when he wrote in 1913 that the University was "the capstone of the public school system of the state."

Racial strife hit the campus in 1956 when a 26-year-old black woman enrolled. Autherine Lucy attended classes for three days before a violent demonstration moved the trustees to expel her. Seven years later, Gov. George Wallace stood in the doorway of **Foster Auditorium** on June 11, 1963, in an unsuccessful attempt to prevent Vivan Malone and James Hood from integrating the school.

Today the University covers 850 acres and has an enrollment of some 20,000 students. Some 850 faculty members teach in 17 colleges, divisions and schools with more than 120 academic departments and more than 270 accredited undergraduate and graduate degree programs. The administration building is named for Frank Rose, longtime 20th-century president.

Guided tours from Rose room 151 begin each weekday at 10 a.m. and 2 p.m. and Sat. at 2 p.m. Phone the Office of Admission Services at 348-5666.

CRIMSON TIDE TRADITIONS

The Alabama Crimson Tide has been the dominant football team in the South during its 100-year history, winning more national championships than any other SEC team (12) and the most bowl games of any team in the country (29 of 45).

A student named W.G. Little formed the first squad in 1892 to begin the football tradition. Wallace Wade coached the first great era from 1923-30 with a record of 61-13-3, including trips to the Rose Bowl and national championships in 1925, 1926 and 1930. Frank Thomas coached the second great era of Tide football from 1931-46 with a record of 115-24-7 and national championships in 1934 and 1941.

Paul "Bear" Bryant, a former Tide player who was an assistant coach under Frank Thomas, was head coach at Maryland, Kentucky and Texas A&M for 13 years. During his tenure at Alabama, his teams captured national titles in 1961, 1964, 1965, 1973, 1978 and 1979 and he was Coach of the Year three times. Bryant was voted the greatest coach in football history by a poll of experts for ESPN in 1990.

The record-setting victory number 315 came over Auburn in a 28-17 win in 1981. Bryant retired in 1982 after winning 323 games, the most for a major college football coach. Beyond touchdowns and victories, Bryant became a charismatic figure which drew fans to the Tide in numbers far greater than Bama alumni. His stature and movitation of players pervade the museum. Sportswriters deemed him a legend long before his career ended. When he died 37 days after retirement, hundreds of thousands of people viewed the procession from Tuscaloosa to the burial in Birmingham.

Gene Stallings, who played and coached under Bryant for 12 years, returned as head coach in 1990 and beat **Pat Dye**'s Auburn teams three games straight. In just his third season, he won Football Coach of the Year as the Tide went undefeated in 13 games. Alabama stunned top-ranked Miami 34-13 in the Sugar Bowl to win the university's 12th national championship during a century of college football.

Colorful traditions have been linked with football for a century. The earliest teams wore white uniforms and crimson stockings, although the term Crimson Tide was first used by a Birmingham writer to describe a muddy clash with Auburn in 1907. Since 1919, the nickname Crimson Tide has stayed with Alabama sports. Military cadets had worn crimson and white since 1885.

University accounts differ on the origin of the elephant mascot. Key chains supplied by Birmingham Trunk to players on the 1926 Rose Bowl team featured the company's elephant logo. The athletic department says the mascot originated with an Atlanta Journal sportswriter referring to members of the 1930 team as being as big as elephants. The 1930 team went 10-0, beat Washington State in the Rose Bowl and was declared national champs. The costumed-student elephant mascot received the name **Big Al** during a campus referendum in 1978.

CAMPUS LANDMARKS

Begin your tour at the **Gorgas House**, the oldest building on campus, where you'll learn about the antebellum history of the University. Walk by the elegant President's Mansion. Even though it isn't open to the public, you'll still enjoy seeing the exterior up close. Visit the **Museum of Natural History** as much for the impressive interior as the Victorian and contemporary exhibits. Wind up at the **Bryant Museum** for a real shot of Crimson Tide spirit.

BRYANT-DENNY STADIUM is the home stadium of the Crimson Tide. The west side of the stadium was built in 1929 with a capacity of 12,072. When Bryant arrived as coach in 1958, the capacity was 31,000. During Bryant's tenure, the stadium "bowl" was completed, with flat rather than round ends, to keep the endzone seats closer to the playing field, bringing the capacity to 56,000. The most recent 10,000 seats were added in 1988, bringing capacity to 70,123, some 12 years after Bryant's name went on the stadium.

(PAUL) BRYANT MUSEUM showcases a century of Alabama football with memorabilia displayed chronologically throughout the quiet and cool 7,000-square-foot museum.

Visitors are greeted in the lobby by a picture of the famous goal line stand against Penn State which won the 1979 Sugar Bowl and the national championship. Right away, you know this is the heart of college football country. The museum is relatively small and can be covered in a short time, although there are plenty of exhibits and videos to engross even the most casual fan.

Beginning with 1892, exhibits cover early years of coaches **Wallace Wade** (three national titles and Rose Bowl appearances in the 1920's) and Frank Thomas.

Men who became legends on the field are well represented, too. Jerseys worn by Joe Namath, Bobby Humphrey and Scott Hunter are here, along with Cornelius Bennett's Lombard trophy and the Butkus Award won by Derrick Thomas. Coaches after Bryant aren't forgotten. Exhibits touch on the careers of Ray Perkins, Bill Curry and Gene Stallings, with special attention on his 1992 national champions.

Highlights of the biggest victories and bowl games are featured, along with such items as Bryant's practice jacket and shoes, his last houndstooth hat and game notes on which plays to run in various situations.

A bronze bust sculpted by the artist who creates busts for the Pro Football Hall of Fame occupies a prominent space. A Waterford crystal replica of the famous houndstooth hat also gets a lot of attention. Van Tiffin's shoe, tee and the football kicked for the winning field goal against Auburn in 1985, jerseys from the 1940s, an 1893 football sweater worn as a uniform on cold days, and a 1938 Rose Bowl blanket are other popular exhibits.

The successes of Stallings' teams are gaining an increasing amount of attention in the museum, especially the 1992 national championship team which crushed the reigning champion.

You can listen to radio broadcasts from some of the biggest Tide victories. Video highlights of exciting games are shown, including the 1963 Orange Bowl, the thrilling win over Penn State in the 1979 Sugar Bowl and George Teague's famous "steal" against Miami in the 1993 Sugar Bowl.

The best (or worst) time to visit is the day of any home game, simply because of the former players you might spot there; but be forewarned, it can attract up to 3,500 on game days. Because it is a museum for reflection and remembering, you might be wiser to visit on a weekday when the average attendance is closer to 300. Open Mon.-Sat., 9-4. Admission. Phone 348-4668.

Getting there: 323 Bryant Dr., opposite the entrance to Coleman Coliseum and near the stadium. This can be difficult to find if you're not familiar with the campus. From U.S. 82 (McFarland Boulevard), take the University Boulevard exit and go west to Bryant Drive. It is a block south of University between the Sheraton and the Bryant Conference Center.

DENNY CHIMES is the tower which was constructed in 1929 to honor the retired university president. The original carillon was replaced in 1945 with an electric system. For 20 years after 1966, a set of 305 bells on the first floor was heard via loudspeakers in the tower. Then 25 bells, weighing 60 to 1,411 pounds, were installed and today chime across the Capstone on the quarter hour. Look for the **Walk of Fame** where foot and hand prints of Tide football captains are preserved in cement.

Student legend has it that bricks will fall from the tower when a virgin walks nearby, a legend not to be confused with the Civil War Lathe on the Auburn campus which is expected to turn again for the same reason. Denny is located on the north side of University Boulevard between Colonial Drive and Sixth Avenue.

The GORGAS HOUSE is an 1829 house museum in the middle of the campus which is identified with several of 19th-century Alabama's most important personalities.

Built in 1829 as a dining room and steward's residence, it was the only building of the original master plan that soldiers did not burn in 1865. Once known as the Pratt House for the professor who lived there, it became the residence of Josiah B. Gorgas when he retired as president in 1879. The former chief of ordnance for the Confederacy was married to Amelia Gayle, daughter of the sixth governor.

Their son, Brig. Gen. William Crawford Gorgas, was a pioneer in the prevention of yellow fever. As chief Army medical officer, he eradicated disease-carrying mosquitoes from Panama during the construction of the Panama Canal. He also stamped out yellow fever in Cuba, South America and Africa. Dr. Gorgas received the highest medals from several European nations and was knighted by King George V of England. He was surgeon general of the U.S. during World War I. When he died in London in 1920, he was given a royal State funeral in St. Paul's Cathedral and was returned to Washington for burial at Arlington Cemetery.

Mrs. Amelia Gayle Gorgas served as University matron of the infirmary and postmistress, serving both jobs in the house. After the death of her husband in 1883, she assumed the position of librarian and lived here until her death in 1913. The last of the Gorgas daughters lived here until 1953 and the house became a museum the following year.

Social guests arriving at the raised cottage in the 19th century ascended the sweeping curved stairs from the ground to the upper story where the Gorgas family entertained. Today's tourists, however, enter the door under the dual stairs and walk through the study, dining room and kitchen, where two Yankee cannon balls found in 1863 are displayed. Two of the most memorable items upstairs are paintings with optical illusions. A portait of an elderly Amelia Gorgas over the parlor mantle appears to turn towards you, regardless of from which of the two entrances you view the painting. A painting in the rear bedroom has a "wooden" frame painted on the canvas.

A front garden outlined in old bricks is framed by azaleas, dogwoods and magnolias. The exterior curved iron railing, a feature copied for many buildings on campus, embraces old boxwood and ivy plants. Open Mon.-Sat., 10-noon, 2-5; Sun., 3-5. Free. Phone 348-5906.

Getting there: Drive up Hackberry Lane north of University and turn left behind the Geological Survey of Alabama. Turn right at Smith Hall (Museum of Natural History) onto Colonial and drive to the end of the long parking lot.

MUSEUM OF NATURAL HISTORY has a collection of millions of specimens representing the state's natural heritage, including dinosaur-age and ice-age fossils. Minerals are displayed with dioramas of geologic periods. The museum began with a collection of fossils assembled the year before the university opened, although most of the original exhibits were destroyed in 1865.

The major oddity is the **Hodges Meteorite**, the only one known in modern times to have struck a person. It fell to earth at 1 p.m. on Nov. 30, 1954 and crashed through the roof of a rental house in the Oak Grove community northwest of Sylacauga. It bounced off a cabinet radio and bruised the thigh of Elizabeth Ann Hodges, who was lying on a sofa. Several miles away the next day, a local farmer found a second meteorite when his horse shied away from an object on a road. Mrs. Hodges gained legal possession of the one which hit her and gave it to the museum. The smooth, black, 8.5-pound meteorite, about the size of a child's head, is protected under glass. The farmer's rock is in the Smithsonian in Washington.

In 1910, state architect Frank Lockwood designed the museum hall which is more interesting than the exhibits. The barrel-vaulted glass roof illuminates a beautifully proportioned interior which is surrounded by a colonnade of Corinthian columns.

Dr. Doug Phillips produces the excellent TV series *Discovering Alabama* and the Alabama Natural History Society publishes the slick quarterly *NatureSouth*. Open Mon.-Fri., 8-4:30. Closed weekends and major holidays. Free. Phone 348-2040.

Getting there: Smith Hall is the cream-colored building behind the Geological Survey of Alabama Building at the corner of Sixth Avenue and Capstone Drive.

PRESIDENT'S MANSION is the stately, two-story white house across University Boulevard from Denny Chimes. The raised cottage Greek Revival mansion built in 1841 features elaborate interior frescoes and medallions created by slaves. It survived the burning of the University in 1865 when the wife of the president intervened.

The school spent more than a decade restoring the house before the current president moved in on the house's 150th anniversary. **Dr. and Mrs. Roger Sayers** live on the third floor. The rest of the house, including a reception room with antique hardwood flooring and gold-leafed cornices, is used for campus socials and community events.

It is open to the public only on special occasions, but the front grounds are worth a look, especially in the spring when hundreds of tulips fill beds with brilliant color.

WOODS HALL, a three-story Tudor Gothic dorm known initially as the "barracks," was completed in 1868. Workmen used bricks salvaged from the original campus to complete what was expected to be only the northern half. It was designed to house 180 students and feed 500 in the first-floor dining room, but few showed up the first year. The south half was never built. It was later named Woods Hall in honor of the first president. A plan to demolish Woods in the mid-1970's led instead to an alumni push for its restoration. Woods is the open-sided building facing the three Victorian stone buildings behind the library.

SIDE TRIP: THE MYSTERY OF MOUNDVILLE

Moundville Archaeological Park is North America's best preserved group of prehistoric mounds and was the largest and most sophisticated city in the Southeast for centuries.

Its farming culture developed about 900 A.D. and peaked about 1300 when an estimated 3,000 nobles, traders, farmers, warriors and artisans lived here. Another 10,000 were scattered in villages nearby.

The city, whose name is unknown, grew into one of the most advanced civilizations north of Mexico. In fact, *National Geographic* magazine called the settlement "the Big Apple of the 14th century."

It was the civic and cultural center of a 50-mile stretch of the river valley from the falls at Tuscaloosa to the swamps just north of Demopolis. Leaders selected this site in the flood plain because squash, corn and other crops grew well in the sandy loam soil replenished by the annual floods. The fall line provided rich seasonal harvests of deer and turkey.

The mounds were not used for burials, but were the foundations on which workers built temples and wooden houses for the royal chiefs.

The highly skilled Indians took their crafts of shell-tempered pottery, copper working and stone carving to new levels of refinement. Their stylized artwork demonstrated a complex cult faith and belief in things both natural and supernatural.

As in other chiefdoms, the ranks of residents were determined by the genealogical distances from the highest ranked member of the society. Contact among residents was determined by protocol. Chiefs were paid the tributes of food, wives, and assistants. Tightly structured public rituals accompanied a chief's birth, marriage and death.

To develop the flat-topped mounds for temples, council houses and leaders' houses, generations of workers carried millions of basketloads of soil to the top. The mounds weren't constructed to their full height in a step. Instead they were the result over time of the cult ritual where the dwelling was cleared when the resident died and another layer of dirt was added and another structure was erected on the new top.

What happened to these prehistoric people remains unknown, but the complex political system which created the need for a "capital city" was probably its undoing. As the population grew and became more far flung, it gradually fragmented into several petty chiefdoms and the capital's importance waned. It would be hundreds of years before any other city in the Southeast approached the city at its zenith. It was probably abandoned by the time DeSoto passed through the state in 1540.

By 1820, settlers had built a stagecoach inn and hostelry near the mounds. A cotton gin, warehouse, grist mill and several saloons followed and the town was organized and named Carthage. It was renamed Moundville in 1897.

Philadelphia explorer **Clarence B. Moore** learned of the mounds from an 1848 book and financed the first excavation in 1905. He wrote that Moundville was "an important religious center and the great mounds within the circle were connected with the cults held sacred at that place." The artifacts he collected eventually became part of the Heye Museum in New York which was acquired by the Smithsonian Institute. They will be displayed in the Museum of the American Indian scheduled for completion on The Mall in Washington in several years.

Moore's writings attracted looters and potfinders to the site. When the mounds began to be disturbed by crop and cattle farming in the 1920s, Tuscaloosa archaeologist Walter Jones began a campaign to save the mounds, even mortgaging his own house to raise funds. During excavations which followed in the 1930s, workers sifted through 500,000 cubic feet of ground. They found a remarkable 3,000 burials, 75 house sites and more than a million fragments of pottery, religious and artistic objects.

The 300-acre archaeological park is on a plateau 60 feet above the river which flows along its northwestern boundary. A 2-mile interior loop road passes the 20 flat grass-covered mounds which range from 3 to 60 feet tall, although most are about 14 feet high. The large plaza in the center was originally the scene of markets, ceremonies and games.

Tour: When you arrive at the park, follow the drive to the right and stop where other cars are parked at the base of a large mound. To get a good view of surrounding mounds and see inside a typical timber dwelling, climb the 82 steps to the top. Inside the walls made of woven limbs dabbed with mud are lifesize figures which depict an Indian ceremony and the lives of the inhabitants.

The modern museum farther down the road was built on top of two excavations that uncovered 57 skeletons which were displayed for decades just as they had been unearthed. The natives were buried with pottery, ornaments and other objects. For decades, visitors looked down on the skeletons of men, women and children, which were the most interesting features of the museum. But because of changing sensitivities about skeletal displays, the remains were taken to the Museum of Natural History in 1989 for storage. The museum features metal, shell, stone and pottery illustrating the moundbuilders' culture.

A short distance away, you can walk through an enclosed village, with each aboriginal house scene illustrating a different facet of Indian life. Picnic facilities, nature trails and camp sites are available. Allow at least an hour. Many of the 35,000 who visit annually are Alabama and Mississippi students on field trips. A sunrise pageant is held in the park each Easter. An annual four-week field expedition attracts scores of adults and high school students each June. Open daily 9-5. Closed major holidays. Adults, $4; under age 12, $2. Phone 371-2572.

Getting there: Take I-59 exit 71 to Hwy. 69 and go 13 miles. The 317-acre park is operated by the Alabama State Museum of Natural History, University of Alabama.

SIDE TRIP NORTH

Drive north of Tuscaloosa for an hour to **Fayette**, which has produced several of the state's best known folk artists.

Jimmie Lee Suddeth uses mud and wild plants as sources of color for his paintings. The poke plant, for example, makes a green color while the berries make red. He says there are 15 different colors of mud in Alabama, including blue. The elderly artist uses tools, as well as paint brushes, to work the mud onto Masonite and other surfaces. While he is best known for his works of buildings, attempts at recognizable portraits are less successful.

Prices start at about $50 and go to $300 and up for larger works. If he is in good health when you visit, he may give an impromptu recital on harmonica whether you buy anything or not.

He and the late Rev. Benjamin Perkins, who lived in nearby Bankston and was known for painting religious messages on gourds and other objects, are featured in the documentary *Outside Artists*. Phone 932-5060.

From U.S. 82 in Northport, go 41 miles via Hwy. 171 or U.S. 43 to Fayette. Look for First Street between the railroad track and the courthouse and go north to the 800 block of First Street NE. Beyond the housing project is a vocational school. Suddeth's house is ahead on the left as you go up the second hill past the school. It is a ramshackled white house with a green roof.

SIDE TRIPS WEST

A bizarre place called **Ma'Cille's Museum of Miscellanea** near Gordo is an extremely dusty and oddball collection of everyday items and stuffed animals which line the shelves of several attached buildings. "Mama Lucille" House began collecting bottles, dolls, shells, pots, canned goods, ink wells and other items 30 years ago at flea markets so that her children could learn from their own museum.

It's 25 miles west of Tuscaloosa off U.S. 82. At Gordo, turn left on Hwy. 86 toward Carrollton. Go 3.5 miles and look for a sign directing you to turn left. Go a mile and watch for the place on the left.

While you are in this part of the country looking at oddities, continue west to Carrollton to see the **Face in the Window**. While a lot of towns have ghost stories, few can actually boast of having theirs on display. Such is the case at the **Pickens County Courthouse**.

A fire burned an earlier courthouse in 1876. A freed slave named Henry Wells was arrested Jan. 29, 1878, and taken to the attic of the new Italianate courthouse during a severe storm as a lynch mob gathered outside.

As the frightened Wells peered out the window at the mob, a huge bolt of lightning flashed nearby, freezing the image of his face in the window pane like a glass negative. Or so the story goes. The face can't be seen from inside the attic and attempts to wash off the image have been unsuccessful. From the street in front of the courthouse, however, a cloudy white pumpkin face can be seen. A metal sign points at the lower right pane in case you aren't sure where to look. Phone 367-8132.

If you've made it to Carrollton, continue on U.S. 82 for 10 more miles to Pickensville to tour the **Tom Bevill Resource Management Center** housed in a $3 million reproduction antebellum mansion. The Corps of Engineers exhibits explain the lifestyle of the cotton plantations and their reliance on river traffic prior to the Civil War. The Tenn-Tom Waterway is adjacent. Architects copied elements from Selma's Sturdivant Hall and Eutaw's Kirkwood. Quite likely, it will be the last Southern mansion built with three million federal dollars. Open daily except major holidays. Free. Phone 373-8705.

WHERE TO STAY IN TUSCALOOSA

Holiday Inn, McFarland Boulevard at I-59 exit 73, is a convenient two-story motel with 166 rooms which have cable TV. A pool, restaurant and lounge are on the grounds. Double rate: $67-$72 plus tax. **Phone 553-1550.**

La Quinta, McFarland at I-59 exit 73, has 122 rooms and free continental breakfast. It's near McFarland Mall. Fax 758-0440. Write 4122 McFarland, Tuscaloosa, 35405-3833. Double rate: $43-$60 plus tax. **Phone 349-3270** or 1-800-531-5900.

Sheraton Capstone Hotel, located on Bryant Drive next to the **Bryant Museum**, has 152 handsomely appointed rooms with cable TV. The hotel has a full-service restaurant and lounge and is a part of the high-tech Bryant Conference Center which hosts meetings for the University and other organizations. It's the nicest place to stay in Tuscaloosa. Fax 759-9314. Write 320 Bryant Dr., Tuscaloosa, 35401. Double rate: $89-$99 plus tax. **Phone 752-3200.**

Sleep Inn, I-59 exit 76, has 73 rooms, including 20 suites, with cable TV, in-room coffee, refrigerators, continental breakfast, pool, fitness center. 4300 Skyland Blvd., Tuscaloosa, 35045. Double rate: $42-$75 plus tax. **Phone 556-5696.**

Quality Inn, I-59 exit 73 on U.S. 82, has 120 rooms, with cable TV and Showtime, large pool, wading pool. Restaurant, lounge. Double rate: $46-$56 plus tax. **Phone 556-9690.**

WHERE TO EAT IN TUSCALOOSA

*Archibald's in Northport is a tiny barbecue restaurant that does a lot more take-out business than eat-in. Archibald's has only five stools. George Archibald has cooked pork with a mild red sauce over a waist-high pit rack for three decades for those who can find the place. For directions, phone 345-6861.

*Capstone Grill, University Mall. Students who order steaks or sandwiches pass the time waiting for their food by doodling on large sheets of brown paper provided by the management. The restaurant walls are covered with the signatures of customers. Phone 553-3985.

*City Cafe, Main Avenue in Northport, is where bankers and students alike go for breakfast or a cheap blue-plate lunch of meat and vegetables. Closes mid-afternoon and weekends. From downtown, take U.S. 43 across the river and exit to Main. Phone 758-9171.

***Cypress Inn, 501 Rice Mill Road, Northport. Drew Henson built this rambling wooden restaurant literally on top of the north bank of the Black Warrior River.

It offers one unnerving feature: it is in danger of being flooded when the river rises over its banks, as it often does. A series of signs nailed to a small tree chronicles the dates and levels of previous floods. The highest sign, marking the 1900 flood, is level with the waists of guests in the main room. Although the building sits on a framework of support to keep it above harm's way, high water has threatened twice: once while the building was under construction in 1984 and another time when all the patio furniture floated silently away during the night.

From its carefully landscaped parking lot to the big front porch and the huge dining rooms overlooking the river, the restaurant creates the atmosphere of being in someone's home for dinner. Nevertheless, it seats 300.

Try the excellent smoked chicken breast served with white barbecue sauce as an appetizer ($5) or entree ($11). Other specialties are broiled red snapper and sauteed gulf shrimp with mushrooms over angel hair pasta, topped with cheese ($13). The Cypress makes delicious bran muffins and cole slaw. Side vegetables include mustard greens and hoppin' john.

White cloths cover the tables and the college-age servers are friendly. This being a college town, dress is casual and jeans are fine. To avoid waiting for a table, eat in the Sandbar lounge where the main difference is that the music is faster and louder. You can also eat on the patio down by the river.

From downtown, take U.S. 43 across the river into Northport and take the first right. Go 2 miles and look for the sign. Lunch is served 11-2 except Sat. For dinner, Mon.-Thurs., 5:30-9:30; Fri.-Sat., until 10, Sun., until 9. Closed major holidays. Phone 345-6963.

***Dreamland** is the best known restaurant in Alabama and it doesn't even have a menu. Operated by the John Bishop family since 1958, the barbecue rib place ranks high on atmosphere and higher on taste.

The decor is vintage barbecue-joint. When you enter, a long counter with a backdrop of Golden Flake potato chip products and fronted by 10 stools is to the left. Against the wall to the right are four booths. In between are four Formica tables. Framed photos of Tide players and coaches are intermingled with beer signs, national championship posters and old personalized car tags like "Bamalady" and "Roltide."

The reason for no menu is simple: you get a plate of about 20 sweet, meaty ribs dripping in sauce that have been simmering over a pit for 30-45 minutes "depending on the fire." Ribs are served with white bread on a paper plate and covered with sauce. Golden Flake potato chips are extra. A lunch option is a rib sandwich: three meaty ribs dripping in sauce served on white bread. In case you decide that the secret is in the spicy tomato-based sauce and ask what-all's in it; the staff won't tell you.

If you go on a weekend, expect a wait of an hour or more. The line parallels the bar, so beer is nearby. On average, Dreamland prepares about 1,000 pounds of ribs a night. If you walk in after they've reached the limit, someone behind the counter will simply yell, "We sold out." The place is as full of character as it is characters.

To try duplicating Dreamland ribs at home, buy a jar of the sauce and order ribs from Southeastern Meats like Dreamland does - pork ribs cut in 3.5-pound slabs. Dreamland gained widespread attention during the years that Keith Jackson covered Bear Bryant's teams on ABC-TV. A second Dreamland is in Birmingham.

From I-59, take exit 72 to U.S. 82 South. Just past McDonald's, turn left onto Jug Factory Road. Go almost a mile to the fifth right turn. Closed Sun. and Mon. Phone 758-8135.

*****Kozy's**, across from the VA Hospital, serves good steaks and seafood in a former residence with a sophisticated black and white decor offset by a colorful jukebox. Turn off U.S. 82 at University Mall and go 5 miles. Phone 556-0665.

*****Waysider** Restaurant, 1512 Greensboro Ave. at 15th St., is where Tuscaloosa eats breakfast. If you're lucky enough to find one of the 16 tables free, order the homemade, mouth-watering biscuits with a full egg and bacon breakfast. You won't be disappointed. Phone 345-8239.

****Wings & Things**, 1011 University Blvd. Phillip Weaver has specialized in spicy Buffalo wings since he opened at the edge of the campus in 1980. You can have them regular, extra spicy, garlic or Southern-style barbecued. Order a basket of curly-cue fries on the side. A variety of burgers, sandwiches, salads and yogurt is on the menu. Bama memorabilia decorates the walls. Meals average $5-$6. Daily 11 a.m.-1 a.m. Phone 758-3318.

SPECIAL FOR CHILDREN

The *CHILDREN'S HANDS-ON MUSEUM*, known locally as CHOM, encourages children to give free rein to their imagination. The options in the storefront building allow children to become a nurse or doctor, be a make-believe TV newscaster, create pottery, weave fiber, ride in a dugout canoe and even explore an Indian village. Downtown on University Boulevard. Admission.

WHERE TO SHOP

Tuscaloosa's favorite shopping center is **University Mall**, at McFarland Boulevard and 15th Street. The mall is anchored by **JC Penney, Parisian, McRae's and Sears**.

When you make a purchase at a **Harco Drugs** store in any of the 120 stores in the Southeast, you're saluting a Tuscaloosa tradition. From a small drugstore in downtown, the Harco chain has grown to be the state's largest.

Tuscaloosa is home to **Zeigler's**, one of the South's major meat processing companies. Bear Bryant sold his interest in Ziegler's and sportsman Jimmy Hinton is sole owner.

Just across the river is **Northport**, population 17,366, virtually an extension of Tuscaloosa. Look beyond the heavily developed U.S. 82 bypass and find an historic community with its own identity and a well earned reputation as the crafts capital of Alabama.

Adams Antiques offers the best selection of quality and affordable English antiques in West Alabama. Carl Adams was a second-generation pharmacist in the late 1960's when he refinished furniture as a hobby and developed an appreciation for antiques. He eventually closed the drugstore and opened an antiques shop and an upscale garden shop on Main Avenue. Open Mon.-Fri.

Kentuck Museum is an outstanding small gallery which features changing exhibitions of contemporary art, traditional craft and folk art. The museum shop sells wood, glass, pottery and fiber arts items from the studios of Alabama craftsmen. It is also home to the **Alabama Craft Council**. Open Mon.-Fri. 9-5, Sat. 11:30 a.m.-4:30 p.m. Phone 333-1252.

It is next to the library inside the **Northport Civic Center** at the intersection of U.S. 82 and 35th Avenue.

The **Main Avenue Pottery and Gallery** is an excellent storefront collective and studio in downtown Northport with exhibitions of professional craft artists from throughout the South. In case you drop in, understand that they may be working on a deadline for a show and may not have a great deal of time to chat. The gallery is open Tues.-Thurs. from 10-5. Phone 758-5002. Several other studios and galleries are on Main.

TUSCALOOSA'S ANNUAL EVENTS

Third Monday in January

King Memorial Events - Stillman College, King Elementary School and Central High School West hold "unity" events to memorialize Martin Luther King on the holiday near his Jan. 15 birthdate. The most popular event is the "Realizing the Dream" Concert which has attracted such black entertainers as James Earl Jones, Della Reese and William Warfield.

First full week in April

Heritage Week - The rich architectural heritage which dates from the Capital period of 1826-46 is celebrated. Choose among four tours. Of special interest is the candlelight tour and the yacht club luncheon. Heritage Week has been held annually since 1970. Phone 758-2238 or 758-2256 or 1-800-538-8696.

Mid April

A-Day Football Game - The Quad and Bryant-Denny Stadium - The weekend includes campus musical entertainment and the scrimmage game which ends spring training. At the Walk of Fame ceremony at Denny Chimes, Tide football captains add their foot and hand prints in wet cement alongside those of Tide legends. Harry Gilmer and John Wozniak began the "prints" tradition in 1947. You can buy game tickets at the stadium until kick-off. For concert tickets, phone 939-FAST.

Easter Sunday

April 3, 1994; April 16, 1995; April 7, 1996; March 30, 1997; April 12, 1998.
Easter Sunrise Pageant - Moundville - Local actors chronicle the last week of Christ's life on Earth through a series of 18 narrated scenes accompanied by the First United Methodist Church and other local choirs. "The Road to Calvary" recounts Jesus Christ's last days, culminating in the Crucifixion. Other scenes include the Last Supper, His encounter with Pilate and finally, Christ in the garden of Joseph of Arimathea. The pagent is presented on three of the archaeological park's 20 mounds. Cast members hail from Moundville and many of them play the same role every year. Some former residents return to reprise their roles. However, only a Moundville church member may portray Christ. The pageant, held since 1948, starts before the sun comes up - at 4 a.m. - so that the dramatic Resurrection scene occurs at daybreak. Bring folding chairs or blankets. Phone 371-2227 or 371-2306.

Second or third Sunday in August

Fan Picture Day - Hank Crisp Indoor Facility - If you can't wait to put on the ole crimson t-shirt until football season starts, show up to have your picture made with Coach Stallings and get autographs of players. The event draws up to 10,000 fans for the hour or so that players and coaches are available.

Fourth weekend in August

Black Belt Folk Roots Festival - Eutaw Square - Native crafts such as quilting, basket-weaving and broom-making are demonstrated during one of the state's major folk events. Many items are available for sale. Also enjoy music and good food in the center of this historic antebellum town south of Tuscaloosa. Take I-59 exit 40 or 45 to Hwy. 14.

Mid-September

Alabama Catfish Festival - Lions Park and Rodeo Corral, Greensboro - Catfish farmers and townspeople gather to salute the growth of fresh-water catfish farming with catfish fingerling "races," an arts and crafts show, a trade show showcasing advances in technololgy, entertainment, an antique car show and a rodeo affiliated with the International Rodeo Association. You can tour catfish farms by bus on Saturday. Plan to eat a large plate of freshly fried catfish, cole slaw and baked beans. Bring your cooler to take away boxes of frozen catfish filets. Southern Pride, the state's largest catfish processer, is closely involved with the festival. Located on Hwy. 14 on the south side of Greensboro. Phone 624-4021.

First full week of October
Native American Festival - Moundville Archaeological Park - Skilled Indian artisans demonstrate native crafts, including beadwork, pottery, basket weaving, dress making, flintknapping of stone weapons and tools, music and hollowing reeds to make blowguns. Children can have their faces painted and grownups tour an archaeological excavation. You can eat native foods like dried pumpkin, fry bread and roasted corn. Among the highlights Saturday is when teams play the Indian game which led to lacrosse. Mon.-Sat. 9-5. Phone 371-2572.

October weekend
Cityfest - Downtown - Several stages set up on city streets are venues for dozens of musical groups ranging from jazz to rock and blues to zydeco. Famous name entertainment is featured. The festival began in 1985. Phone 391-9200.

Mid-October weekend
Homecoming - UA Campus - Festivities at the Capstone begin with entertainment on the Quad on Friday afternoon, with a pep rally, bonfire and fireworks after dark. Activities begin Saturday with the homecoming parade from downtown through University Boulevard to the Quad where tents showcase talents of various groups. The kids get a chance to meet "Big Al." You can tour the President's Mansion, Alumni Hall and see special exhibits at the Natural History Museum.

Third weekend of October
Kentuck Festival of the Arts - Kentuck Park, Northport - The South's best crafts event showcases the talents of more than 200 top artists in the shade of pine trees across the river from Tuscaloosa.

Kentuck selects only the best representatives in various media to exhibit. Craftspeople show children how to make dolls from cornhusks. Quilters give pointers on stitching and weavers turn vines into baskets. And surrounding it all are exhibitors receiving compliments on their art and selling pottery, stained glass, paintings and jewelry.

Of particular interest are the primitive artists whose simple shapes and natural media - such as grass and mud - make their work all the more extraordinary. Children can make puppets, play musical instruments like trumpets and tubas and try origami.

Kentuck, held since 1971, preserves traditional storytelling and music, with fiddlers, guitarists, singers and cloggers taking turns on stage. Food vendors do a brisk business. To handle the 25,000 people who attend, organizers operate a free bus service from the Northport Civic Center on U.S. 82 at 35th Avenue.

To have a chance at buying the very best artwork, you must come early the first day. Folk artist Rev. Benjamin Perkins once brought only 16 paintings and sold out in an hour. He was home before noon. Admission. Open Sat.-Sun. 9-5. Phone 333-1252.

Mid December
Tuscaloosa Christmas Afloat - Black Warrior - Local boat owners deck their decks with boughs of colored lights and parade along the riverbank to welcome the holiday season. Phone 391-9200.

SOUTH ALABAMA

*Youngsters gather around the **Civil Rights Memorial** to hear their adult leader explain the significance of the names and events etched on the granite table. The designer of the "Vietnam Wall" in Washington designed the Montgomery memorial. (Mark Bonner photo)*

ATMORE

Andrew Jackson's victory over the Upper Creeks at the Battle of Horseshoe Bend ended the influence of the Indians over much of what became East Alabama. A year after becoming president, he signed legislation requiring all Indians east of the Mississippi River to be moved to the West. Some in South Alabama who had fought with Jackson were allowed to remain and their descendants who congregated around Atmore are known as the Poarch Band.

Poarch means "head of the river," referring to the springs on the reservation that forms the head of the Perdido River, which flows into the Gulf of Mexico and separates Baldwin County, Ala., from the panhandle of Florida.

The Creek tribe has 1,850 enrolled members, most of whom live within 50 miles. An elected council oversees the tribal operations and a supreme court handles civil disagreements. Revenue from the Bingo Palace, matched by federal funds, is used to improve living conditions for those who live on the 229-acre reservation.

ENTERTAINMENT

The BINGO PALACE, operated by the Poarch Creek reservation, attracts hundreds each weekend night to play high stakes bingo. Up to 900 people pay $25 for admission and cards for 24 games of bingo in a huge metal building three-quarters the size of a football field. Prizes range from $100 to thousands of dollars per game. Television monitors broadcast MegaBingo games by satellite that allow players a slim chance to win staggering amounts a night. A huge lighted sign announcing "Indian Bingo" can easily be seen from the interstate highway at night.

The hall has been operated by the Poarch Band of Creek Indians for the past several years. In addition to bingo, the palace sells "pull tabs" and other gambling options, to generate about $500,000 a year to fund the reservation's police and fire protection. Casino gambling in nearby Biloxi, however, has slashed the take in recent months. Phone 368-8007 or 1-800-826-0493 in Alabama.

Getting there: The bingo hall is 55 miles north of Mobile. Take I-65 exit 57 and drive east past the Best Western motel until you see the large metal building off to the right.

PEACOCK VALLEY WINERY is Alabama's largest winery and one of the oldest. Except for a short period each winter when the bottling is done, this is primarily a wine sales outlet. Unless you know which varieties you wish to purchase, accept the invitation to sample the five or six types. The attendant will take bottles from the refrigerator and allow you to sample each. Located just off I-65 south of Atmore, it formerly was known as Perdido Bay Winery. Open Mon.-Sat., 9-6. Phone 937-5000.

Getting there: Take I-65 exit 45 and go east 1/4 mile and watch for the signs on the right.

WHERE TO STAY

Best Western, just off I-65, has 67 rooms on two levels. A swimming pool is outdoors. Next door is a restaurant with lounge and bakery. Double rate: $47-$50. **Phone 368-8182.**

WHERE TO EAT

*Creek Family Catfish Junction, located adjacent to the Best Western, is a full-service restaurant. Freshly baked breads and desserts are specialties. It is owned by Native Americans and is especially busy on bingo nights. Phone 368-4422.

ANNUAL EVENT

Thanksgiving Day
Poarch Band of Creek Indians Pow Wow -Tribal members return to visit friends and family on original Creek land and invite the public to observe the colorful festivities. The event draws colorfully costumed Indian dance teams from all over the country. Watch demonstrations on Indian culture, herbal medicine and drying food. Sample Indian dishes like fry bread, hominy and roast corn cooked over open pit grills. Handmade crafts, such as baskets, quilts, silverwork and beadwork are of special interest. To reach the Pow Wow grounds 8 miles from Atmore, exit I-65 to Jacksprings Road and go east. Phone 368-9136.

AUBURN

- **Claim to fame:** Tiger football
- **Don't miss:** Lemonade at Toomer's Drugs
- **Eat at:** Denaro's
- **Nickname:** Loveliest Village of the Plains
- **Population:** 33,830
- **Tourist information:** Pat Dakin, Executive Director; Auburn-Opelika Convention & Visitors Bureau, P.O. Box 2216, Auburn, 36831. Phone 887-8747.

Auburn, founded in 1836, is home to the state's largest university where students pride themselves with being big on spirit. Although **Auburn University** dominates the southwest section of town from **Toomer's Corner** almost to the interstate, the tree-lined streets east of College Street and north of Magnolia hint at the charm that remains from the turn of the century before the campus grew so large.

The town which was founded by Judge John J. Harper was named by his future daughter-in-law, Elizabeth Taylor, from a line in Oliver Goldsmith's poem *The Deserted Village*. The line reads, "Sweet Auburn, loveliest village of the Plains."

Founded as **East Alabama Male College** in 1856, the college opened in 1859 with 80 students and six faculty members. Two months later it came under the sponsorship of the Methodist church. Classes were suspended in 1861 because of the Civil War and resumed in 1866. The school became a state-supported, land-grant college in 1872 and the name was changed to Agricultural and Mechanical College. In recognition of the expanding academic program, the Legislature in 1899 renamed the college the Alabama Polytechnic Institute. However, students had always referred to it as "Auburn." It was officially named **Auburn University** in 1960. Enrollment is estimated at 21,800.

The institution's greatest growth has been since World War II. From a campus of 35 buildings at that time, the university's physical plant now includes 207 buildings on 1,871 acres, plus Auburn University at Montgomery.

Auburn has been ranked 12th among the nation's college and universities by *Money* magazine in its annual ratings of the best college buys in America.

The most enjoyable seasons are spring - when students respond to the warm weather and rediscover shorts, Frisbee throwing and bike riding - and football season, when tens of thousands of fans jam **Jordan-Hare Stadium** on Saturdays for the Auburn Tigers' home games.

The university gained a national reputation for something besides football when meat scientists Dale Huffman and Ross Egbert developed **AU Lean** ground beef, 91 percent fat-free and 23 percent fewer calories, and sold it to McDonald's as McLean. The secret ingredient? Seaweed!

AUBURN WALKING TOUR

Auburn is a great place to walk. Park somewhere downtown, get a lemonade at **Toomer's Drugstore**, walk a half-block south to **Johnston & Malone's** and cross South College. Then begin your campus tour at **Samford Hall** with a walk through the halls of the administration building. Further down College are the **Draughon Library** and the **Auburn University Hotel and Conference Center** across the street. Walk down Thach to the **Student Union** for a look at students engaged in leisure activities and continue down the hill to the stadium.

Unlike the University of Alabama which has a unified Georgian style of architecture, Auburn's campus buildings reflect the eras when they were built, with some designs standing the test of time more successfully than others.

Toomer's Drugstore, with a soda fountain which has served five generations of Auburn students, has been a landmark since 1897. A stroll around downtown should include a stop for the world's best hand-squeezed lemonade. Framed newspaper articles about Toomer's Corner line the upper walls of the drugstore. When the Tigers win a big football game, jubilant fans traditionally "roll" the trees at Toomer's Corner intersection with lots of toilet paper. The entrance gate for the university is diagonally across the street in front of Biggin Hall.

Although not actually on the campus, Toomer's is literally at the heart of Auburn. Corner of College Street (U.S. 29) and Magnolia. The intersection marks the dividing line of north-south and east-west addresses. Phone 887-3488.

The **Main Gate** flanking the campus entrance from Toomer's Corner was donated by the Class of 1917. The weathered eagles atop the gatepost were a gift of 1931 graduate W.C. "Red" Sugg.

Biggin Hall anchors the northeast corner of the campus behind the eagle gate. Built in 1951 to house the architecture school, it is named for the first dean of that school and now houses the art department.

Johnston-Malone Bookstore or J&M, is where students buy almost anything for class or anything else. Merchandise ranges from art supplies and used books to Auburn Tiger merchandise and Fiji caps. Business is especially brisk at the beginning of each quarter (for books) and on football game days (for anything orange and blue). The largest selection of officially licensed Auburn souvenirs, t-shirts, sweats, glasses, phones, etc. is found at J&M. Open Mon.-Sat. Phone 887-7007.

The focal point of the historic campus on College Street is the dark red brick **Samford Hall** which contains the president's and other administrative offices. Samford's four-sided clock tower with six-foot faces has been marking time for students since April 18, 1889 when the college was an "agricultural and mechanical" school.

Samford is on the site of the original Old Main which burned in 1887. It is named for Gov. William James Samford, who was a native of Lee County.

Anchoring the northeast corner of Samford is the landmark **Civil War Lathe** which turned out cannons in Selma for the Confederacy. According to student lore, the ancient lathe, now covered in many coats of gray paint, will begin to spin when a virgin walks by.

Towering trees and flowering shrubs in front of Samford create a parklike setting also shared by two other 19th century academic buildings, Langdon Hall auditorium and the "Music Building."

Landgon Hall is the porticoed Greek Revival auditorium next to Samford Hall where Auburn students watch movies in current release for free. It was built in 1846 as a wooden structure on the campus of the Masonic Female Seminary and moved to the campus in 1883 and bricked and remodeled. Charles Carter Langdon was a trustee during the last quarter of the 19th century.

Hargis Hall (Music Building) housed chemistry and pharmacy classes when completed in 1890. For decades, the sound of students singing and practicing musical instruments echoed from it while it was the Music Building. It was heavily damaged by fire in the late 1970s and renovated. It now houses the graduate school and cooperative education.

Ingram Hall, formerly Alumni Hall, was built in the mid-1920s as a men's dorm and was later used for women. It was renovated in 1988 to house administrative operations and renamed for former business manager and treasurer W. T. Ingram, who retired in 1973.

Smith Hall, a two-story building next to the chapel, was completed in 1908 as the college's first dormitory and now houses industrial design classes. O. D. Smith taught math and English.

The **Chapel** was built in 1850 as a Presbyterian church. It was used for classrooms in 1887 when the Old Main burned and as a YMCA Hut during World War I. From the late 1920s until 1972, the Auburn Players staged theatrical plays. It was restored in 1972 as the University Chapel. The Gothic Revival-style church functioned briefly as a hospital during the Civil War, and a soldier named Sydney who died haunts the building, or so the legend goes. Corner of South College and Thach.

Walk down Magnolia Avenue to the **Harbert Engineering Center**, a 1986 building funded by a $5 million gift from Birmingham developer John Harbert, one of the state's wealthiest men and a proud Auburn graduate. It is on the site of the demolished Broun ("brown") Hall.

Next is **Ramsey Hall**, home of the college of engineering. Erskine Ramsey, a coal company executive, helped fund the building completed in 1925. A high school in Birmingham bears his name.

Next to Ramsey is **Drake Infirmary**, the student health center which has been the butt of student jokes for generations. Students seeking excuses from class who complained of imaginery ailments were given orange and blue placeboes called "War Eagle pills." It was built in 1938 and expanded in 1976.

Next to a rose garden square behind Samford is the **Student Union** which is the hub of student activities. It houses organizations' offices and is the venue for free lectures, films and art galleries. To reach the information desk in the lobby, phone 844-4244.

Down the hill near the football stadium is **Haley Center**, the largest classroom building, which can accommodate 8,000 students. The two-tower building, completed in 1969, houses the colleges of liberal arts and education. The **University Bookstore** is on the first floor. Paul Haley was an Auburn trustee for 51 years.

Jordan-Hare Stadium, off Thach, is the home of the Auburn Tigers. Initially known as Auburn Stadium, it opened in 1939 with 7,500 seats. An expansion of 14,000 seats in 1949 came with a new name to honor former coach Cliff Hare. Coach Ralph "Shug" Jordan arrived two years later and produced the 1957 team which won the Associated Press national championship. The stadium, later renamed Jordan-Hare, was enlarged in 1955, 1960, 1970 and again in 1989 under Pat Dye.

It officially seats 85,214 fans. It is the second largest collegiate stadium in the South after the one at UT in Knoxville and the nation's seventh largest. The most memorable game played in the stadium was in 1989 when the Crimson Tide was lured reluctantly from Birmingham.

Auburn sells in excess of 55,000 season tickets annually. For ticket information phone 844-4750 or 844-4040.

WHAT TO DO GAME DAY

You can visit the real **War Eagle** mascot before each home game. The **Aviary** where the bird lives is directly east of Jordan-Hare across Duncan Drive. It is open from five hours to kickoff until one hour before. The Alpha Phi Omega trainers on duty explain the eagle's background, diet and personality. Phone 844-4978.

Another tradition before home games is the **Tiger Walk**, where cheering fans line the path between the athletic dorm and the stadium to exhort the team to victory.

TIGER TRIVIA

Auburn has been associated with college football for more than a century. Auburn played Georgia in its first game on Feb. 20, 1892, when they met at Piedmont Park in Atlanta. Auburn won 10-0 and began the oldest continuous rivalry in the South. Auburn first played Alabama that autumn in Birmingham.

The first great era of Auburn football began in 1904 under **Coach Mike Donahue**. He succeeded with a record of 99-35-5 through the 1922 season and was inducted into the National Football Foundation Hall of Fame.

During the next quarter century, Tiger football floundered. Only nine of the 27 teams led by a succession of eight head coaches posted winning seasons with an overall record of 108-132-23.

The second period of winning football began in 1951 with the arrival of **Ralph "Shug" Jordan**, a Southern gentleman with a rich Selma drawl. His tough 1957 Tigers, quarterbacked by Lloyd Nix and led on defense by Zeke Smith and Jackie Burkett, went 10-0 and won the Associated Press national championship.

Quarterback Pat Sullivan launched aerial displays to end Terry Beasley during the 1969-71 seasons and became the first player to win the Heisman Trophy at a school where John Heisman had coached (1895-99).

One of the most memorable games late in Jordan's career was against second-ranked Alabama in 1972. Trailing 16-3 in the fourth quarter, Bill Newton blocked two straight Tide punts and David Langer returned both for Tiger TDs and a 17-16 win in the legendary "Punt Bama Punt" game.

Jordan's 25 teams netted a record of 176-83-6, a dozen bowl game trips, 20 All-Americans and a national title. He retired in 1975 at age 64 and died of leukemia in 1980.

Following several forgettable years, the third great Auburn era dawned in 1981 with the arrival of **Pat Dye**, a Georgia player who had assisted under the Bear at Bama. In Dye's 12 seasons, he won more games than any other SEC coach in their first decade, and he matched Bryant with four SEC championships. Auburn went to nine consecutive bowl games. For four of those eight years, the Tigers had the fourth best winning percentage in the nation - 79%. The most successful teams in Tiger history were those of 1986-89 who compiled a spectacular record of 39-7-2 and defeated the Crimson Tide four years in a row.

Auburn's centennial year of 1992 had a disappointing record of 5-5-1 to leave Dye's Auburn record at 99-39-4. Dye resigned on the eve of the Alabama game amidst charges of player payments and was succeeded by Terry Bowden of Samford.

During Dye's tenure, the most important victories were the 1982 victory over the Crimson Tide to end a nine-year drought, the 13-7 defeat of Georgia that won Dye's first SEC title in 1983, the '83 team's Sugar Bowl win over Michigan and the biggest, the '89 Tigers stopping unbeaten and second-ranked Bama 30-20 in the first "Iron Bowl" played at Jordan-Hare.

Bo Jackson of Bessemer was the first Auburn player ever to rush for 4,000 yards. Bo became the most interesting athlete in modern times when he captured the Heisman Trophy in 1985 and went on to play pro baseball as well as pro football before being sidelined with an injury.

Auburn is the only SEC school with players to win the three major individual awards - Heisman Trophy (Pat Sullivan and Bo Jackson), Outland Trophy (Zeke Smith and Tracy Rocker) and Lombardi Award (Tracy Rocker).

WHERE TO STAY

AU Hotel and Conference Center is the "official" campus site for meetings and visiting guests. It is also the ideal location for seeing the campus. The 248-room hotel and conference center is a unique partnership between private industry and the university. The school owns the $20 million property and operates the south-wing conference center which consists of eight meeting rooms, two ballrooms, a 400-seat auditorium, a board room, a seminar room and a computer lab. A Denver-based management company manages the hotel and food service.

The architecture of the six-story hotel is an attractive blend of old and new Georgian, with terra cotta bricks reflecting the decorative touches of the original campus buildings.

The guest rooms, parlors and suites are handsomely furnished with antique reproductions. Guests have access to a fitness center, outdoor pool and nearby tennis and golf facilities. A 100-seat, full-service restaurant, lounge and deli are grouped on the ground floor near a small gift shop. Write 241 S. College St., Auburn, 36830. Double rate: $70-$85 plus tax, weekends $65-$85. A golf package includes green fees, cart, deluxe guest room and $5 food or beverage credit. **Phone 1-800-2-AUBURN** or 821-8200.

Auburn Conference Center and Motor Lodge near the interstate on U.S. 29 South is a bargain with rates in the $40-$60 range. The 122-room motel has cable TV, pool, cafe and gift shop. Write Box 1872, Auburn, 36831. Phone 821-7001.

Hampton Inn, I-85 exit 51 at U.S. 29, is the newest hotel in the area, with 75 rooms off interior halls on three floors. Amenities include pool, local phone calls, cable TV with movie channel and continental breakfast in the lobby. Write 2430 S. College St., Auburn, 36830. Fax 821-2146. Double rate: $48 plus tax. **Phone 821-4111** or 1-800-HAMPTON.

Heart of Auburn Motel, 333 S. College St. near the Alumni Center, is an older motel, but its 100 guest rooms, including eight suites with one or two bedrooms, have been remodeled. It has an outdoor pool. Double rate: $35-$40 plus tax for standard room; $74-$89 for suites. **Phone 1-800-843-5634** or 887-3462.

WHERE TO EAT

*****Auburn Grille** at 104 N. College has fed three generations of Auburn students since Lucas Gazes opened the grille in 1936. Framed photos of student athletes leave no doubt that this is a football town that supports (and feeds) its players. The decor has changed little over the decades. The brownish booths have the original round deco mirrors and metal hat racks. A breakfast of two eggs, smoked sausage, grits and a biscuit goes for around $3. A noon buffet is served. Recommended more for tradition and value than cuisine. Mon.-Sat., 7 a.m.-2 p.m. Phone 821-2702.

****Denaro's** is a popular Italian restaurant at 103 N. College across from Toomer's Drugs. Bob Fucci, who operated Sorrento's in the same block in the 1960's, opened Denaro's in 1983 and has expanded into a major entertainment venue. The restaurant upstairs seats about 150 and the ground-floor lounge another 150. The bar, which offers live entertainment some nights, is a good place to watch an Auburn football game on TV if you don't have tickets, provided, of course, that you're a Tiger fan. Veal marsala, chicken parmigiana, lasagna, fettuccini, steak and lobster are Denaro favorites. The restaurant is open Mon.-Sat. 5-10 p.m. Average dinner is $12. Phone 821-0349. Hungry on Sunday evening? Call 826-7773 for free delivery of salads, appetizers, Italian sandwiches, hogies, burgers and desserts.

****Behind the Glass Cafe**, 168 E. Magnolia, is a cross between a bookstore, dress shop, art gallery and deli. Owners Rod and Donna Popwell serve handsomely prepared salads, sandwiches and quiche dishes. A move to North College is planned. Open Mon.-Sat. 10-9. Phone 826-1133.

*****Sani-Freeze** at 109 E. Glenn Ave. is a walk-up pre-Dairy Queen-era hole in the wall for ice cream on a hot summer day. It has survived the influx of franchise fast-food joints in spite of its notorious nickname, the Sani-Flush.

****The **War Eagle Supper Club**, housed in a plain cinderblock building out South College Street near the interstate, has been the students' favorite place for excellent pizza and beer since "Mildred" oversaw the kitchen in the 1960's. A $5 bill makes you a member of the club. Phone 821-4455.

SIDE TRIP TO OPELIKA

If you are interested in outlet shopping, go west toward Opelika on I-85 to the U.S. 280/431 exit for the **USA Factory Stores**. Among the two dozen stores are Generra, Carolina Clock and Bugle Boy. Phone 749-0561.

Continue on U.S. 280 to see landmarks in downtown **Opelika**, especially the 1896 **Lee County Courthouse**, topped by a soaring clock tower. The **Museum of East Alabama**, 121 S. Ninth St., displays farm implements, vintage clothing and household goods no longer in use. The **First United Methodist Church**, completed in 1881, faces the 1915 **Federal Building**. The Chamber of Commerce is housed in a handsome Queen Anne building at Avenue A and 280.

SIDE TRIP FOR GOLF

Golfers have discovered that the **Robert Trent Jones Golf Trail** leads through Opelika. Beautiful lakes are woven through the **Grand National Golf Course**, a series of two 18-hole championship courses and an 18-hole par three course. It is one of the most beautiful settings for golf in the state.

ANNUAL EVENTS IN AUBURN

Last weekend in April

'A' Day Game - The annual intersquad football game between the blue and white teams at Jordan-Hare signals the end to spring practice.

Sunday in mid-August

Auburn Football Fan Day - Athletic Complex - Fans visit with coaches and members of the upcoming season's football squad to get autographs and take photos. Schedule cards, pens and posters are given away. The gates to the practice fields, located behind Eaves Memorial Coliseum off Biggio Drive, are opened in mid-afternoon.

Late October weekend

Syrup Soppin' Days - Loachapoka - Thousands cram into this small town of 259 people to observe traditional farming techniques and buy homemade crafts. You can watch syrup being made from freshly harvested sugar cane, snack on homemade cookies and funnel cakes, and tour a collection of historic buildings.

On the north side of the road, a mule trods in a counterclockwise circle to provide the pulling power to squeeze the juice from cane which volunteers boil over a hot fire to make syrup. Nearby, corn is ground in an old grist mill powered by a tractor.

Walk across the two-lane highway to the Lee County Historical Society Fair. For a fee, you can tour the two-story stucco museum which has exhibits representing a general store, barber shop, dentist's office and soda fountain. Period clothing, including a 1926 Ku Klux Klan robe, are upstairs. Outside are a century-old log house and blacksmith shop.

This is a great family event where children are exposed to vanishing farming techniques. The uneven terrain causes problems for baby strollers.

Try to arrive before noon and park in one of the designated lots. Parking along the shoulders of Hwy. 14 is a major problem because activities are located so close to the road. If arriving from Auburn 6 miles to the east, you should drive through the congestion and park on the west end. Phone 887-5560 or 887-8747.

Saturday in late October
Homecoming - AU campus - Tiger fans and grads gather on the Plains to celebrate Homecoming in a tradition dating from 1913. A pep rally Friday night at the Student Activity Center outdoor pavilion is followed by a concert at Eaves-Memorial Coliseum. Visit the Alumni Center on South College at Miller Avenue on Saturday morning for refreshments. The main event is the football game in the afternoon at Jordan-Hare Stadium. The first homecoming was held in 1911.

Thanksgiving weekend
Auburn-Alabama Football Game - The Tide visits Jordan-Hare on odd years. They play at Legion Field in Birmingham on even years when it is Bama's home game, although there has been speculation it may eventually move to Tuscaloosa.

BREWTON

The Escambia County seat just above the Florida line has thrived on timber milling and manufacturing, providing local timber barons to construct imposing residences on Belleville Avenue, many of which remain residences of descendants. St. Joseph Street, the main business street is U.S. 31 and bisected by a railroad line. A three-story dry goods store, the Robbins and McGowin Building, houses an antique mall and top-floor art studio at 102 St. Joseph. In recent years, the town has developed a thriving blueberry industry which employs some 200 persons each summer and is celebrated by a festival.

ATTRACTIONS

THOMAS E. McMILLAN MUSEUM showcases archeological artifacts and historical exhibits. Displays include prehistoric fossils, Indian and early American relics; other exhibits chronicle the Revolutionary, Civil and First World Wars. Open Mon.-Thurs. 8-3, Fri. 8-noon; closed first week of June and September and mid-to late December. Free. Phone 967-4832, ext. 68. It is located in the Jefferson Davis Junior College fine arts center.

BREWTON ANNUAL EVENT
Third Saturday of June
Alabama Blueberry Festival - Jefferson Davis Junior College - The harvest time for blueberries in South Alabama provides a reason to stage a communitywide festival which draws visitors from South Alabama and Northwest Florida to the shaded park within the Williamsburg-style campus. Hundreds of flats of berries, as well as potted plants, are sold. Blueberries are consumed in ice cream, gingerbread and cobbler. The festival, held annually since 1981, also features live entertainment, arts and crafts, kiddie rides, a recipe contest, a major antiques car show and the crowning of Little Miss Blueberry. You can even take a bus tour of a blueberry farm.

The success of the craft fair, however, tends to overwhelm the blueberries. Within the scores of crafts booths, the mighty watermelon is a more popular subject for t-shirts, decorative kitchen items and hats. (Watermelon festivals are held in Grand Bay, Greenville and Russellville.) This event has encouraged state residents to grow blueberries as a crop or in gardens as a specimen plant. Phone 867-3224

DEMOPOLIS

Demopolis is an attractive Black Belt town spreading from the carefully restored business district. A strong sense of pride is apparent from the well maintained 19th century homes, stores and churches. A leading trade center in West Alabama, it appears more prosperous than other Black Belt towns. Be certain to visit **Gaineswood**, a truly remarkable house which reflects years of invention by its owner, and **Bluff Hall**, if you have extra time.

Before cotton provided the wealth responsible for such houses, a number of exiled French families loyal to Napoleon labored in vain to carve a "vine and olive colony" from the wilderness a mile below the junction of the Black Warrior and Tombigbee rivers.

In 1818, the first of the 347 aristocratic families granted four townships of land by Congress arrived near the area known as White Bluff and established the town known as Demopolis, meaning "city of the people. " Ever loyal, they named the county Marengo for a city in Italy where Napoleon won victory over Austrians in 1800.

Because the noblemen were not used to farming and even had trouble clearing the land, they planted some vines and olive trees, but mostly raised vegetables. Once they were forced to move because they had settled the wrong townships. Within several years they abandoned hope and drifted off to Mobile and New Orleans or returned to France. Gradually, Americans took over their land and began to cultivate cotton.

Today, the historic marker on the eastern edge of town (west of the U.S. 80/43 intersection) and the place name are among the few legacies of the failed colony. In Montgomery, a highly romanticized wall mural of the "vine and olive colony" painted by an artist who obviously never visited Demopolis hangs upstairs in the **Archives and History Building**.

In 1919, an auction of roosters shipped by famous personalities was used to raise funds to build the U.S. 80 bridge over the Tombigbee. It was the final link in the Dixie Overland Highway between Savannah and San Diego and was officially known as the **Rooster Bridge**.

The area is sometimes referred to as the **Canebrake**, the fertile croplands of the Black Belt prairie which stretch from Demopolis to Uniontown and Dayton to Greensboro.

The white bluffs along the river become filled with people each December to watch the heralded parade of lights during **Christmas on the River**, one of the state's largest holiday celebrations. For good photos of the river any day of the year, follow signs to Bluff Hall and turn right on Capitol. Go between two nice Queen Anne houses 2 blocks to a deadend spot overlooking the "white cliffs" of the bend of the river.

WELCOME CENTER

The Chamber of Commerce at 213 N. Walnut St. is on the ground floor of a two-story building in the center of town. Phone 289-0270. Across the street is the three-story brick **Robertson Banking Co.**, an award-winning example of adaptive restoration of the former department store.

HOUSE MUSEUMS

BLUFF HALL exemplifies two major architectural trends in the antebellum South. The Federal townhouse was modified to the Greek Revival style in the 1850's by the

addition of the square columned portico, a large rear wing and white paint. Planter Allen Glover built the brick house in 1832 for his daughter and her husband, Francis Strother Lyon, who served in both the Confederate and the U.S. congresses. The restored house contains period clothing, Empire and Victorian furniture and a display about the French settlers and other local history. The house is derived from its position overlooking the Tombigbee River. Guided tours Tues.-Sat., 10-5; Sun., 2-5. Closed Thanksgiving, Dec. 25 and Jan. 1. Adults, $3; under 12, $1. Phone 289-1666.
    Getting there: From U.S. 80, follow signs to Bluff Hall at 405 Commissioners Ave.

GAINESWOOD is an important, architectural gem which is the result of 20 years of planning and construction.
    Originally a simple log house, it was transformed between 1842 and 1860 by the multi-talented Gen. Nathan Bryan Whitfield into a 20-room Greek Revival villa of great elegance. It features three orders of Greek architercture, with Ionic and Corinthian inside and Doric outside. The mansion also is noted for its domed ceilings, elaborate plaster friezes and medallions, galleried rooms and porticoes, huge drawing room mirrors, Italian marble mantels, wood graining and marbleized baseboards. *The Smithsonian Guide to Historic America* calls this National Historic Landmark "one of the three or four most interesting houses in America." However, only about 3,000 people tour it a year.
    What was once the center of a 1,400-acre estate is now boxed in by U.S. 43 and Demopolis High School, which occupies the site of the lake which graced the estate. Gaineswood follows none of the traditional designs of an antebellum mansion. In fact, it is even difficult to determine which is the front entrance. A double row of tree-shaped crepe myrtles suggests the approach to the west porte cochere. The house is symmetrical from the west, with the four-columned portico balanced by flanking colonnades. The north side has an entirely different character which is considerably less grand. Its large portico is softened by an adjacent, smaller, gently curving veranda.
    A small Greek garden pavilion, supported by eight columns which originally overlooked an artificial lake on the north side of the house, provides an attractive counterpoint to the delightfully asymetrical architectural wonder.
    Whitfield bought the property from Gen. George S. Gaines, the Federal government's agent whose negotiations created peace among the region's Choctaw Indians, and began remodeling the frame dwelling on it. The highly detailed masterpiece required years of careful construction by skilled artisans who followed classical pattern books. Whitfield insisted on the finest art glass, marble mantels and silver doorknobs for the house. Out of respect for Gaines, Whitfield named his mansion Gaineswood.
    When completed in 1861, it had 13 rooms on the ground floór and six on the second. During the years of construction, the owner built and removed several rooms to experiment with the architecture. The house escaped damage during the Civil War and the builder sold it to his son and died in 1868. The house was owned by family members until the 1920s when it fell vacant and into serious disrepair.
    Gaineswood was transferred from the Alabama Department of Conservation in 1971 to the **Alabama Historical Commission** and restored under the direction of Jackson Stell as a house museum. It is the most spectacular of the mansions owned by the state. Many pieces original to the house are on display, thanks to the generosity of family members who responded to a campaign by a great-grandson living in Kentucky.

To enter, follow the signs around the sandstone colored stuccoed house to the family entrance on the south side. In the small foyer, a host begins the fully guided tour by giving a history of the complex house. Of special interest is an inscription on a wood cap of an Ionic column dated Aug. 9, 1854, which was discovered during restoration by the historical commission.

The dining room in the right side of the hall features a domed ceiling with a cupola over the dining table. Against a wall of hand-blocked French wallpaper is a massive mahogany cabinet custom built to hold the silver epergne.

The general's talents are further displayed in the domed music room/library opposite the dining room. He invented a musical instrument called a flutina which creates the sounds of drums, flutes and bells using wooden cylinders. A painting the general executed of his 10-year-old daughter hangs in the room. It is with good reason that the evolution of Whitfield's house and his penchant for inventions draws similarities to Monticello and Thomas Jefferson.

In the room where the Whitfields' male guests retired after dinner is a portait of the Indian chief Pushmataha, who was a contemporary of the general. The bedrooms contain original family portaits. Mrs. Whitfield's bedroom is enlarged by a bay porch supported by columns overlooking the formal gardens and the lake site.

Gaineswood has the finest and most elaborate decorative plasterwork in the state. The 30- by 20-foot ballroom is a showplace of Corinthian columns and an elaborate plaster coffered ceiling. Reflecting French mirrors face each other across the room to make the flanking columns appear to march into infinity, greatly expanding the space. Understandably, the general called it "the most splendid room in Alabama."

Visit the first week in December during Christmas on the River. Allow at least an hour. Open Mon.-Sat., 9-5; Sun., 1-5. Closed state holidays. Adults, $3; students, $2; children under 13, $.50. Phone 289-4846.

Getting there: 805 Cedar St. (U.S. 43) at Whitfield Street across from the high school stadium just north of U.S. 80. Park in the small lot near the street and walk through the entrance gate up to the house.

SIDE TRIPS FOR GOTHIC CHURCHES

Within a few minutes from Demopolis are two Gothic churches - one active and one not - inspired by architect Richard Upjohn. Approaching Demopolis from Selma via U.S. 80, you'll see the bright red **St. Andrew's Episcopal Church** in the Gallion or Prairieville community on your right. Completed in 1854 as a clean example of religious rural Gothic architecture, it is a National Historic Landmark. Remarkably, the interior has never been painted, although the walls were reportedly "finished" with tobacco juice. The words "The Lord Is in His Holy Temple" are painted above the altar. The church is usually locked and the only signs of life may be a hive of bees swarming near the back door. Interested neighbors trim the grass around the church and cemetery. It is on a road just north of U.S. 80. Follow signs on Hwy. 69 to the Gallion Post Office.

Almost 2 miles south of the church on Hwy. 69 is Waldwic, an atypical antebellum plantation home. Turn in the second drive south of the railroad crossing for a look at the house that was transformed from an 1839 dwelling into a Gothic Revival masterpiece. It is private.

Twelve miles north of Demopolis on U.S. 43 is Forkland. Turn left on County Rd. 4 (Lloyd Chapel Road) for a block to **St. Andrew's Episcopal Church**. Originally constructed circa 1859 on the east side of the Black Warrior, the board and batten church was dismantled and rebuilt on the present site in 1878 where it still has an active congregation. Richly detailed stained glass windows illuminate the tiny interior. Check the bright red front door to see if it is unlocked for a quick look inside. An historic marker at the intersection directs visitors to the church.

WHERE TO STAY

Days Inn, 1005 U.S. 80 E., has 42 guest rooms with ceiling fans, cable TV with HBO. Executive king rooms have refrigerators and microwaves. The newest motel in Demopolis, the Days Inn has a pool, guest laundry and free continental breakfast. Double rate: $34-$50. Special rates for groups and family reunions. **Phone 289-2500.**

Econo Lodge, U.S. 43 North, has 25 rooms overlooking the Tenn-Tom waterway and marina. Parking is below rooms. Good for fishing trips. Double rate: $37 plus tax. **Phone 289-0690.**

WHERE TO EAT

*Red Barn serves good seafood and steaks in a rustic barn atmosphere. Evenings only. 901 Hwy. 80 E. Phone 289-0595.

ANNUAL EVENT

First Saturday in December

Christmas on the River Parade - More than 20 boats alive with colorful Christmas lights float down the dark Tombigbee River to the delight of tens of thousands watching from the riverbanks. Decorations range from elves the heighth of buildings to towering Christmas trees and huge stars.

The best viewing areas are just a few blocks from downtown. Bleacher seats go fast, but there are enough roadways lining the river that you won't have a problem seeing the spectacular light display floating on the water. The parade, which dates from 1972, and a week-long holiday schedule preceding it, draw upwards of 40,000 people. Expect traffic delays after the parade.

A crafts fair, barbecue cook-off, candlelight tours of lavishly decorated Bluff Hall ("Christmas in the Canebrake") and Gaineswood and an open house at the Robertson Banking Co. are among the preliminary events.

Because the few motels fill early, consider staying overnight 60 miles north in Tuscaloosa. Phone 289-0270.

DOTHAN

- **Claim to fame:** Peanut capital of the nation
- **Don't miss:** Landmark Park
- **Eat at:** Dobbs Barbecue, Garland House
- **Best souvenir:** Pecans from Troy Simms
- **Population:** 53,589
- **Tourist information:** Don Fabiani, Executive Director; **Dothan Area Convention & Visitors Bureau**, P.O. Box 638, Dothan, 36302. Fax 792-4683. Phone 794-6622.

When he was a young boy cleaning lamp chimneys at a hardware store in Troy, Edward Russell Porter wanted to own his own business. In 1889, at age 20, he and a friend named Joel Murphree rode a train down to the new town of Dothan and they decided it needed a good hardware store.

Tree stumps were being cleared to extend Main Street and they bought lots at 110 and 112 E. Main with money borrowed from Murphree's family and put up a store which opened Oct. 21, 1889.

They stocked merchandise in mahogany and glass showcases and even had an octagonal cabinet with enough drawers to hold 80 different types of bolts. They hammered nails into the wood floor five feet apart to measure rope, wire or chain. When customers asked for a pound or two of 10-penny nails, the merchandise was weighed on a set of iron scales. A sliding ladder was pushed along a track in front of the wall shelves to enable Porter and Murphree to reach stock up high near the 14-foot ceilings.

Incorporated as the town of Poplar Head just four years before the store opened, Dothan became a thriving timber shipping point when the railroad arrived. The turpentine and sawmill industries were important until timber was exhausted and Porter, who bought out his partner, shifted his inventory to respond to other farming needs. Meanwhile, Porter married and his children delighted in being pulled through the aisles of the store in little red wagons and tricycles.

Following the advent of modern farming techniques, the region abandoned cotton and became a major producer and cultivator of peanuts, livestock and vegetables.

Eventually, Porter's children continued the family tradition by working in **E.R. Porter Hardware**. During the Depression when times were hard, he kept the business open and customers remained loyal because of a tradition of integrity and a square deal. He invested well in real estate and served for years as president of the Dothan Bank and Trust (now First Alabama Bank). He also served on the City Council.

Although the store's founder died in 1944, he would probably be pleased to know that his great-grandchildren are involved in the store's operation. Also remarkable is the fact that a number of employees have remained with the store for more than 40 or 50 years.

Over time, the Dothan landmark has become the state's oldest continuously operated hardware and the only "old time" hardware owned by descendants of the founder.

Porter Hardware is an accurate reflection of Dothan and its remarkable growth. Despite being ringed with a bypass lined with franchise food and gas stations, Dothan remains an agricultural center at heart. In this era of increased mass competition and warehouse pricing, Porter's has expanded its merchandise to fit customers' needs and remains busy as a wholesaler and retailer because of the service it offers. Nevertheless, you can still see the nails in the old flooring spaced five feet apart, glance up at the ornate pressed tin ceilings and marvel at merchandise you didn't think anybody carried anymore.

Material from Porter's went into constructing many of the city's public buildings which are now architectural landmarks. The First National Bank (now SouthTrust) at Foster and Main was built in 1905. The Juvenile Services Building on Foster, and Foster Corner, now an architect's office, were constructed in 1907. The 1912 Municipal Electric and Water Building houses the **Wiregrass Museum of Art** at 126 N. College and the **Opera House** across the street was constructed in 1915. The Federal Building was erected in 1911.

Dothan is the **Peanut Capital of America** and stages the **National Peanut Festival** every fall to prove it. The two-week festival features national celebrities, parades, a carnival, a fair and a beauty pageant. Another major event is the delightful **Azalea-Dogwood Trail and Festival** each spring.

Dothan is the trade center for Southeast Alabama as well as nearby areas of Georgia and North Florida. Centrally located between Atlanta, Birmingham, Jacksonville and Mobile, Dothan is the region's fastest growing city. Its **Ross Clark Circle** perimeter road can be a real challenge, but it is the central focus for directions to nearly any place in town. To find downtown, find the east-west Main Street (U.S. 84) which slices through Ross Clark Circle.

Groups interested in touring a peanut farm during harvest in mid-August through September can make arrangements through the county extension agent and then return for the big peanut festival in November.

WELCOME CENTERS

Dothan promotes its location as being the short route to Florida. Travelers bound for the beaches are encouraged to travel I-65 through Alabama to Montgomery, turn off on U.S. 231 for Dothan and continue on to I-10. Arriving from Florida on 231? Stop at the **Alabama Welcome Center** 14 miles south of Dothan near Madrid for information on current special events.

The **Dothan Area Convention & Visitors Bureau** offers maps, brochures and plenty of friendly advice at 3311 Ross Clark Circle at the corner of Choctaw Street near Water World. Office open Mon.-Fri. 8 a.m.-5 p.m. Phone 794-6622 or 677-6363, the Dialing for Dothan 24-hour hotline for special events, attractions and entertainment.

ATTRACTIONS

DOTHAN OPERA HOUSE is a three-story neoclassic auditorium open for special events. Built in 1915 at a cost of $40,000, the opera house originally hosted traveling vaudeville and minstrel shows, but as talking pictures became popular, the opera house eventually became obsolete.

At one time, it housed city offices and was used for storage. It was not until the city decided to construct a civic center across the street that it also decided to refurbish the opera house for perfoming events.

The marble-appointed elegance was restored and the 590-seat auditorium was air-conditioned in 1979. Spacious parlors on both the first and second floors are used for receptions. Phone 793-0126.

FARLEY NUCLEAR VISITORS CENTER is an innovative, hands-on interpretive center at Southern Nuclear Power Plant that's even interesting to children. You can learn to play computer games and use muscle power to generate energy on a treadmill. Southern Nuclear has even duplicated the control room so you can see what the nerve center of a nuclear power plant looks like. Films trace the story of energy from prehistoric times to today's nuclear generators, such as those producing electricity at Farley. Never before has nuclear power seemed so downright friendly. Allow an hour. Free. Open Mon.-Fri., 9-4; Sun., 2-5. Closed holidays. Phone 899-5108 or 1-800-344-8295.

Getting there: Go east on U.S. 84 (outside the Ross Clark Circle) past Ashford toward Georgia. Turn north on Hwy. 95 and follow the signs. It's just a short hop from the Georgia line, and not far north of the Florida line.

HOUSTON CO. FARM CENTER hosts the **National Peanut Festival**. It is one of the busiest agribusiness centers in the state and holds sales and shows year round. Phone 792-5730.
Getting there: 1699 Ross Clark at Cottonwood Road (Hwy. 53).

LANDMARK PARK contains a unique living history Wiregrass farmstead with exhibits and demonstrations of tools and implements used by pioneering farmers. It also has a fine wildlife interpretive center and boardwalk.

A farm museum may not sound like great drama, but Landmark Park is well laid out and represents the agricultural importance of the region. It is quiet and peaceful, too. Unless you come on a weekend or for a special event, it is possible that you could spend an hour walking around and not see any other visitors.

A restored home appears in the natural country setting with gardens and crops as well as a windmill. The 1890's home with unpainted tongue and groove interior walls is the heart of the park. It is sparsely furnished as it would have been at the turn of the century. Walking through the hall of the house alone is a bit disquietening because the beds are unmade. It appears that the family which "lives" here is out tending to chores at the smokehouse or cane mill and might return any moment.

Don't be rushed. Look into the the 1908 wooden Headland Presbyterian Church, rest in the picturesque gazebo or photograph the wildflowers.

It is easy to get to the church and believe you've seen about all there is, but the wildlife area is ahead. Just down from the church, the interpretive center with a Starlab planetarium displays changing art and nature exhibits. The center has a major collection of fossils, rocks, insects and mammals. Walk past the interpretive center to the safe, elevated boardwalk through the woods to a reptile pavilion, a marsh exhibit, a woodland wildlife area and a bird exhibit. In addition to tourists and locals who attend special events, some 14,000 students visit on field trips.

Landmark Park stages two fall events. The **Pioneer Peanut Days** is a two-day event which highlights old-fashioned harvesting methods. At the **Fall Folklife Festival**, demonstrators make soap, grind cane, dip candles, and quilt. The 60-acre park is operated by Dothan Landmarks Foundation. Open Mon.-Sat., 9-5 year round; Sun., noon-5; until 6 from Apr.-Oct.. Closed Dec. 25 and Jan. 1. Adults, $1; children, $.50
Getting there: Go north of Ross Clark Circle almost 3 miles on U.S. 431, the highway toward Eufaula. Phone 794-3452.

WATER WORLD brings ocean waves to the Wiregrass. In addition to the area's only wave pool, Water World provides a fast and furious 400-foot waterslide, video arcade and a children's play area. Open Memorial Day weekend to the last weekend in August, Mon.-Fri., 10-6; Tues. and Thurs. until 9; Sat. 10-7; Sun., noon-7. Admission.
Getting there: A block north of Ross Clark Circle on Choctaw Street. Phone 793-0297.

WIREGRASS MUSEUM OF ART displays exhibitions of 19th and 20th century art and invites children to participate in a sensory exhibit hall in the restored 1912 Municipal Electric and Water Building. 126 N. College St. Phone 794-3871.

WHERE TO STAY

Best Western, 2325 Montgomery Hwy., is conveniently located between two major shopping malls. The 120 guest rooms have free local phone calls, hairdryers and some have recliners. Free coffee is in the lobby. A 24-hour restaurant is next door. Fax 793-7720. Double rates: $40-$45 plus tax. Commerical, AARP, government, military and group rates available. **Phone 793-4376.**

Comfort Inn, 3591 Ross Clark Circle, has 122 guest rooms on inside corridors with suites and rooms available with microwaves and refrigerators. A deluxe continental breakfast and an exercise room are available to guests. A Waffle House is next door. Double rates $43-$66, weekends $41-$66 plus tax. Fax 793-4367. **Phone 793-9090** or 1-800-221-2222.

Days Inn, 2841 Ross Clark Circle (231 Bypass), 121 rooms equipped with coffeemakers, cable TV and dataport hookups. Deluxe rooms are equipped with microwave-refrigerator units. Fax and copy services are available on request. Free coffee is in the lobby. 24-hour food and gas are available. A waste station for buses and RV's is on site. Fax 793-7962. Double rates $36-$45 plus tax. **Phone 793-2550.**

Hampton Inn, 3071 Ross Clark Circle, U.S. 231 at 84, has 112 rooms with cable TV and movies. Restaurant are nearby. Airport shuttle. Fax 794-6601. Double rate: $46-$52 plus tax. **Phone 671-3700.**

Holiday Inn South, formerly a Sheraton at 2195 Ross Clark Circle, has 144 rooms with cable TV and in-room movies. The Holiday Inn has a pool and a restaurant. Fax 671-3781. Double rate: $52-$54 plus tax, includes a breakfast buffet. Two-bedroom suites at $70 also include breakfast. Ask for lower Great Rate on weekends. The motel recently received a national Holiday Inn quality award. **Phone 794-8711.**

Holiday Inn West, 3053 Ross Clark Circle, has 102 rooms with cable TV and movies. It has a pool and restaurant. Free airport shuttle. Fax 794-6601. Double rate: $51-$53 plus tax. **Phone 794-6601.**

Howard Johnson Lodge, 2244 Ross Clark Circle, has 62 rooms with cable TV. Executive king rooms have desk, recliner, refrigerator and microwave. Rent VCR and movies in the lobby. Double rate: $37, weekend $34. Executive king: $45, weekend $41. **Phone 792-3339.**

Olympic Spa Golf Resort, Hwy. 231 South, is a good place to stay to play golf. The spa has 96 rooms with cable TV and movies. The restaurant is full service. Double rate in the $40's plus tax. Golf packages available. **Phone 677-3321.**

Ramada Inn, 3001 Ross Clark Circle, with 158 guest rooms, is a full-service, low-rise hotel spread over five acres with an on-site restaurant and a coffee shop. Other restaurants are nearby. The Ramada is 5 minutes from the Wiregrass Museum of Art, 10 minutes from Landmark Park and 15 minutes from the Army Aviation Museum at Fort Rucker. Fax 794-3134. Double rates: $54-$58 plus tax. Packages are offered for summer travelers, government and corporate. A "someone special" champagne romance package is available. **Phone 792-0031.**

WHERE TO EAT

Dobbs Famous Barbecue, U.S. 231 S., just south of Ross Clark Circle - Established in 1910, it may be the oldest restaurant in Alabama operated by the founder's family. Evell Lee Dobbs Sr. was about 21 when he opened a restaurant in Tallassee and moved here in 1948 where he continued the tradition of serving juicy pork barbecue with a tomato-base sauce. The modest restaurant has been a must-stop for people headed toward Panama City beaches for better than two generations.

Lee Jr. has been the owner for a number of years and has added dining room space onto the restaurant as demand warranted. That accounts for the rambling quality of the interior which is dominated by low ceilings and orange booths. In addition to the pork, beef and chicken barbecue, Dobbs serves freshly smoked honey ham and smoked turkey, good camp stew, hamburger steaks and shrimp. Save room for homemade strawberry shortcake. The average meal costs $6.

Lee Dobbs is happy to give a demonstration of his famous Hooie-Sooie Stick. It's a whirligig with two spinning propellers which he can make change directions by saying "hooie" or "sooie" at the stick. He sells a one-proppeller version about 14 inches long for $2. He claims to own and operate the only two-prop version. Open Tues.-Thurs., 9-9; Fri.-Sat., 9-10; Sun., 10-9. Closed Thanksgiving, Dec. 25 and Jan. 1. Phone 794-5195.

The Garland House, 200 North Bell St., is a restaurant in a renovated 1914 house 2 blocks from downtown with a reputation for outstanding homecooked luncheons. Chicken divan crepes, chicken salads, soups, eggs benedict and desserts are all made fresh daily, as they have been since Jo Garrett opened the Garland House in 1976 with Mary Alice Cleveland. For dessert, try Jo's bananas foster crepe. Average lunch is $5. Open Mon.-Fri., 11 a.m.-2 p.m. Closed major holidays. Private parties may be arranged at night. Phone 793-2043.

*Poplar Head Mule Co. Pub & Grill, 113 S. St. Andrews, is a delightfully nostalgic restaurant housed in an old mule buggy store where many of the original architectural elements remain and others have been installed. In addition to an atmosphere where it is easy to imagine the Dothan of a century ago, it serves good sandwiches as well as entrees of seafood, chicken and steak. A large, old fashioned bar sets the tone of the place. The grill is within walking distance of the opera house and civic center. Phone 794-7991.

The *Porch House Cafe up U.S. 431 in Headland at 8 Forrest St. is a Victorian cottage built in 1897 and converted into a restaurant. The Porch House serves a large buffet at lunch every day. Dinner is served Friday and Saturday nights. Headland is about 15-20 minutes from Dothan. Phone 693-2557.

WHERE TO SHOP IN DOTHAN

The **Ross Clark Circle** area off U.S. 231 has major shopping malls, Wiregrass Commons and Northside Mall. **Parisian, Gayfers** and **McRae's** have locations in Wiregrass Commons.

For fresh pecans, peanuts and other nuts, stop at any of several locations on the circle. The **Troy Simms Pecan Co.** is unique in welcoming visitors into the cracking room and the old fashion pecan market. During peak season from November through

December, you can watch as the growers bring their crops in to sell. Then you can watch the pecans being cracked and graded before being sold to the public. The nut outlet is a favorite tourist stop because of the large selections of jams, syrups, candies, baskets and nut products from around the world. When you stop you will receive a free peanut and pecan cookbook of favorite recipes. They will mail the cookbook if you send two postage stamps. Troy Simms is a block south of Ross Clark Circle on U.S. 231.

RECREATION
The **Highland Oaks Golf Course** on U.S. 84 some 2 miles east of Ross Clark Circle is one of the **Robert Trent Jones Trail** courses.

SIDE TRIP SOUTH
About 10 miles south on Hwy. 53 is the **Cottonwood Hot Springs Spa**. Nathaniel Bronner retired from his Atlanta hair-care products company to resurrect a family-oriented spa around the world's deepest mineral wells. The wells were discovered in 1927 when an oil well drill found the hot salt water instead.

Hot salt mineral water heated by the earth to 112 degrees surges to the surface to fill a pair of outdoor mineral pools and several inside. In addition to the 91-room motel, health food store and restaurant, the 700-acre resort offers bicycle trails, nature walks and a lake with fishing and paddle boats. You don't have to be an overnight guest to test the curative powers of the mineral water. Write P.O. Box 277, Cottonwood, 36320. Phone 691-4101 or 1-800-526-SPAS.

ANNUAL EVENTS
March-April
Azalea-Dogwood Trail - Various locations - The city showcases the beautiful gardens and homes with a marked route leading motorists. Phone 793-0191.

Second weekend in April
Indian Festival and Pow Wow - Omussee Creek State Park - Cherokees and other Native Americans gather near the Georgia state line for handmade crafts show and sale, dance competitions and other educational and entertaining events. It has been held near Columbia on Hwy. 95 since 1987. Phone 541-2505.

April
Kaleidoscope - Landmark Park - School students dance, sing, paint and participate in other lively arts near the old church at the rural park. Phone 794-3452.

July
Future Masters Golf Tournament - Rising young golfers compete in this closely watched tournament. Phone 792-6650.

Late October weekend
Pioneer Peanut Days - Landmark Park - The city celebrates the crop for which it is world famous, the peanut. Old fashioned harvesting techniques and agricultural demonstrations remind adults of how farm life used to be and give youngsters insights into how hard living on a rural farm could be. Antique farming equipment and implements are displayed. Demonstrators dip candles, churn butter and grind sugar

cane into syrup. Pioneer Peanut Days is a prelude to the National Peanut Festival. Phone 794-3452.

Late October-early November
National Peanut Festival - Various locations - Southeast Alabama honors the region's top cash crop with all the elements of a state fair, homecoming parade and farm celebration rolled into one.

A crowd of 200,000 gathers for the highlight of the Peanut Festival, the Saturday morning parade which stretches for 2.5 miles down Main St. and lasts two hours. It's the longest parade in the state.

Activities feature livestock, homemaking, youth exhibits, square dancing, recipes, greased pig and calf scramble, bowling, golf, tennis and karate tournaments, antique car show, 10K run, coloring contest and two beauty pageants. Prizes exceed $50,000.

The festival dates from 1938 when agricultural scientist Dr. George Washington Carver traveled from Tuskegee to be honored. Over the years, the event has grown in proportion to the importance the crop has in the Wiregrass. Except for a hiatus during World War II, the festival has been a major regional event. The carnival was added in 1954 and the peanut farmer of the year has been honored each year since 1956.

Fair exhibits were added in 1962 and big-name entertainment has been a highlight since 1983, with such stars as Chubby Checker, Hank Williams Jr. and Louise Mandrell.

Exhibits at the Houston County Farm Center explain the importance of peanuts to the Wiregrass region's economy. Peanuts generate approximately $150 million to the farmers in the 14 Alabama counties where they are harvested. An average acre yields around 30,000 peanuts, or about 55 of those 12-ounce jars of peanut butter. If you're an average peanut-lover, you consume 10.2 pounds of Dr. Carver's peanuts a year

The non-profit National Peanut Festival Association has donated proceeds from the festival to help build a cattle barn, enhance the midway and make other improvements at the fairgrounds. For Peanut Festival parade time and other schedules, phone 793-4323.

ENTERPRISE

Enterprise is best known for what is no longer there: the South's traditional cotton crops and boll weevils. This fact is dramatized by a monument that celebrates the area's decision to diversify following the arrival in 1915 of the feared Mexican boll weevil. The powerful insects destroyed the cotton crop that was the basis of the local economy.

Even though the farmers showered the enemy with insecticides, the tiny beetle succeeded in reducing the crop to a tiny fraction of its usual harvest. To survive, the local farmers planted a number of cash crops, notably peanuts, which flourished. The diversification of Wiregrass farming was so successful that Enterprise is credited with an important role in the region's agricultural revolution.

Crops introduced early in the century, especially peanuts, continue to support Enterprise's economy. Peanut butter plants are evident. The economy is also based on steel and aluminum fabrication, textile production and poultry processing.

The **Boll Weevil Monument** on the square is the country's only memorial to an insect. Erected in 1919, the statue of a woman holding a large bug above her head is a lot smaller than it looks in most photographs. It stands 4 feet tall on a 5-foot base. It pays tribute to the beetle responsible for reconstructing the South's economy by reducing reliance on cotton and forcing diversification into peanuts and other crops. The inscription reads, "In profound appreciation to the Boll Weevil and what it has done as the herald of prosperity." Pranksters have stolen and returned the beetle several times.

The statue even has its own gift shop. The Pea River historical society operates a gift shop and archives nearby. You can buy pins, postcards, paperweights and coffee cups with the statue on it.

ANNUAL EVENT

Piney Woods Arts Festival - Enterprise State Junior College - Artists and craftsmen gather at the campus to exhibit and sell their creations. Clogging and food sales are included. It began in 1974. Phone 347-5616.

EUFAULA

- **Claims to fame:** Fishing, Italianate mansions
- **Don't miss:** Shorter Mansion, Seth Lore district
- **Unique accommodations:** St. Mary's, Lakepoint Lodge
- **Population:** 13,220
- **Tourist information:** The **Eufaula/Barbour County Tourism Council**, Old Post Office, 240 E. Broad St. Phone 687-5283 or 1-800-524-PLAY.
  Eufaula/Barbour Co. Chamber of Commerce, 102 N. Orange Ave., Eufaula, 36072-0697. Phone 687-6664.
  Historic Chattahoochee Commission, Box 33, Eufaula. Phone 687-9755 or 687-6631.

Less than a mile south of where U.S. 82 flows into U.S. 431, the road curves slightly and narrows from four lanes to two. Towering oak trees flank the road and a tree-filled median appears as the pavement takes the shape of a small town residential street. Motorists who had been seeing the wide open countryside of rural Alabama are funneled along through the historic district of Eufaula, one of Alabama's most romantic towns.

Settled in 1823 as Irwinton, the postman kept getting mail confused with a Georgia town of the same name and the name was changed in 1842 to reflect the Creek heritage. Heavily bracketed houses rise like ornate wedding cakes, their fluted porch columns supporting second and third stories of gilded bric a brac. The architects of some mansions, it appears, did not know when to quit and added crowning cupolas where the masters could stand within a miniature version of the main floor and oversee the surrounding countryside.

Although the Italianate style, marked by overhanging eaves and verandahs, was also popular in Mobile and Montgomery, a greater concentration remains in this sleepy town. The **Seth Lore Historic District** contains scores of structures built between 1834 and 1915, which embody Greek Revival, Italianate and Victorian styles. Many can be seen on tours offered during Pilgrimage Week in April.

The grandeur of Eufaula's historic homes lures many regional meetings here, with the host committee frequently serving the legendary **Lake Eufaula Punch**.

LAKE EUFAULA PUNCH
Juice of a dozen lemons
A cup of honey
A fifth of gin

Although guests at Eufaula receptions who are served this eye-opening potent potion punch frequently ask for the recipe, it is not uncommon for them to fail to remember it the next day. Squeeze the lemons and put the rinds aside. Mix the juice thoroughly with the honey and add the gin. Pour the concoction in a large jar, add the rinds and put aside overnight. Prior to serving in a crystal punch bowl over finely crushed ice, squeeze the rinds and strain. Serve in punch cups or silver julep cups. The smooth drink has a reputation for sneaking up on the consumers. When serving, be a considerate host and suggest that there is a two-cup limit. Aspirin is optional.

The town hugs the west bank of the Chattahoochee River some 100 feet down a bluff. The Walter F. George Lock and Dam on the river forms **Lake Eufaula** which has periodically earned the title of "bass fishing capital of the world." Along the 640-mile shoreline are **Lakepoint State Resort** and the **Eufaula National Wildlife Refuge**.

VISITOR CENTERS
Because Eufaula is a cultural and recreational destination, information is readily available from several well-informed sources in addition to the tourism council. The **Shorter Mansion** at 340 N. Eufaula St. (U.S. 431), operated by the **Eufaula Heritage Association**, is open seven days a week and displays brochures just inside the front door.

Doug Purcell, executive director of the **Historic Chattahoochee Commission**, has headquarters 2 blocks south in the 1850 Hart House, 211 N. Eufaula. The commission promotes tourism on both sides of the Chattahoochee. Open Mon.-Fri., 8-5.

Buy a copy of *The Eufaula Tribune* at 514 E. Barbour near the Holiday Inn. Joel Smith's newspaper has been a leading advocate of preservation efforts for decades and carries news about landmarks and special events on the front page. Phone 687-3506.

WHAT TO SEE IN EUFAULA
The *SETH LORE AND IRWINTON HISTORIC DISTRICT* is among the largest in the state with more than 700 architectually or historically significant buildings. The National Register district includes homes built between 1834 and 1911. The town of Irwinton was settled in the 1820's, given the early Indian name of Eufaula in 1842 and incorporated in 1857. As a gesture of appreciation to Capt. Seth Lore for helping lay out the streets, the oldest were named with letters of his last name: Livingston, Orange, Randolph and Eufaula.

Today the major residential streets are North Eufaula Avenue (U.S. 431), as pretty as any street in Alabama, and North Randolph Avenue, a block east.

DRIVING TOUR

By using the following route, you can see many of the city's historic structures. Along the 4 boulevard blocks of Eufaula Avenue, the following tour is arranged with buildings listed in order on the right side of the street because of the median which makes looking at both sides of the street difficult, and because of the heavy U.S. 431 traffic. Broad is the main business street perpendicular to Eufaula and Randolph.

Note that building names in **bold** type are open to the public during business hours. Some phone numbers are listed in brackets so that you can call regarding hours they welcome guests. Dates, owners' family names, style and interesting archtectural features are listed.

To start the driving tour, begin just south of the U.S. 431/82 intersection.
North Eufaula Avenue
720 - 1863 Raney-Taylor, Greek Revival mansion
706 - 1896 Pitts-Gilbert, Queen Anne, gable
640 - 1848 Drewry-Moorer, Italianate, carved columns
420 - 1890s Foy-Beasley, Victorian, porch
340 - 1906 **Shorter Mansion** house museum and welcome center operated by Eufaula
       Heritage Association
214 - 1895 **Dogwood Inn** restaurant
100 - 1885 Bluff City Inn, three-story brick at Broad

Turn right onto West Broad
404 - 1886 Cope-Jones-French, Queen Anne
534 - Circa 1867 **Kendall Manor** house museum

Turn left on Rivers Avenue
206 - 1850 **St. Mary's B&B**, Italianate residence,

Turn left on West Barbour
917 W. - 1860 **Fendall Hall** house museum
823 W. - 1858 Lewis Cato House, large cupola repeats image of main floor; built by
       slaves of the noted secessionist
215 W. - 1907 Holleman-Foy, neoclassical, portico
Corner of Randolph - **First Baptist Church** (687-2045)
504 E.- 1837 Field-Sheppard Cottage

Turn right on Riverside Drive at Holiday Inn
*Follow signs to **Shorter Cemetery** where Gov. John Gill Shorter and family are buried.*
Return past Holiday Inn to
1 - 1882 brick Old City Jail houses accounting firm
105 - The Tavern, city's oldest remaining structure

Turn left on East Broad
630 - 1837 Wellborn House, moved in 1972, offices
340 - 1903 Reeves Peanuts, George Wallace's brother's law firm

World War I monument in Orange Avenue erected 1918
North side of 200 block
240 - 1913 **Post Office** houses Chamber, Tourism Council
218 - **Eufaula Bank & Trust** housed in contemporary French Colonial building;
      bank is major supporter of preservation efforts (687-3581)
206 - 1847 Lampley Building, pharmacy and law office

South side of 200 block
Farmers Market in replicated 1930s gasoline station
1872 Masonic Building, Skinners Furniture on ground
221 - 1866 Ross Carriage Factory houses Alfa office
215 - 1840 Jacob Ramser building, jewelers
205 - 1871 McNab-Pappas Building, gift shop
201 - 1850s bank with iron shutters, insurance office

MacMonnie's Fountain in Randolph Avenue was purchased by Eufaula in
1885 after Dayton, Ohio, officials, who had ordered it, rejected it as too small
South side of 100 block
141 - 1880s Bowden-Lampley, Magnolia Crow gift shop

North side of 100 block
140 - 1853 Hart-Spurlock building, florist

35-foot granite Confederate monument with soldier made of Italian marble
erected in Eufaula Avenue in 1904 in front of hotel
Turn right on North Eufaula
211 - **Hart House** with six fluted Doric columns built in 1843 for town founder
      John Hart, houses **Historic Chattahoochee Commission**, regional tourism
      agency (687-6631)
217 - 1904 **Carnegie Library**, bracketed eaves (687-2337)
301 - 1905 **St. James Episcopal Church**, bell tower (687-3619)
411 - 1850 Bray-Barron House with Doric columns
512 - Roberts Spurlock House, Queen Anne
525 - 1880s Roberts-Dean House, grand Queen Anne
621 - Pre-1870 Gaston-Gamble, Folk Victorian

Turn right on Browder Street
202 - 1870s Speake House, Folk Victorian

Turn right on North Randolph
725 - 1850s Milton-MacElvain, porch, square columns
641 - 1860s Scaife-McKee, Doric columns
633 - 1889 Rhodes-Purcell, Folk Victorian, cut frieze
606 - 1850 Macon-Thomas, Doric columns
539 - 1850 Dean-Page Hall with Gothic cupola is one of the state's finest,
      most elaborate Italianate residences
508 - 1870 Roberts-Archibald, three-bay porch
501- 1860's Pugh-Wilkinson, shed porch

422 - 1891 Skillman-Simms, nice porches
403 - 1870s Pruden-Acosta has Ionic columns
399 - Burch-Abraham House, 1816 log cabin remodeled in 1890s
315 - 1838 MacDonald-Comer, notable dormers
312 - 1845 Thornton-Rudderman, Colonial Revival
306 - 1890s irregular Queen Anne, dual porches
221 - 1855-60 Bray-Garrison, central gable
201 - 1869 **First Presbyterian Church**, gothic vaulted ceiling made of brick
    from Holland; fashioned after English parish churches (687-2523).

FENDALL HALL is an Italianate house with exceptional interior detailing which is being preserved as it appeared in the 1880s by the Alabama Historical Commission. Beyond the first floor entrance hall with original black and white marble floors, the house features unusual stenciled and painted walls in the hall, dining room and parlor. Edward Brown Young and his wife Ann Fendall Beall moved to Eufaula in 1837 and built the house between 1856-60. Young is credited for changing the town's name back from Irwinton to its original Lower Creek name of Eufaula.

    Fendall Hall is rare in that it is being *preserved* - not restored - to show the richness of the craftsmenship which might overwise be covered for the sake of "finishing" the house. Likewise, it is minimally furnished. Although owned by the state historical commission, tours are given by volunteers associated with the Fendall Hall House Committee. Open several days a week for guided tours. Adults, $3. Phone 687-6055.

    Getting there: From downtown, go west almost a mile to 917 W. Barbour St.

KENDALL MANOR is one of Alabama's most spectacular Italianate homes. Work was started on the foundation in 1859 and the narrow, three-story house, distinguished by a porch with many slender columns, was completed about 1867.

    The 15-foot-wide great hall stretches 44 feet, the depth of the original main portion of the house, and has a staircase with an unusual rail with octagonal and concave spindles.

    Front and back parlors are divided by a pair of original sliding doors with 24 panes of frosted and etched glass. Even the original porcelain keyhole covers are intact. The cornices in the front parlor are decorated with a lady's face which match the trim on the mirror over the mantle, as well as the wood trim on an upholstered sofa.

    Walk up 30 steps to the second story where another central hall divides four corner bedrooms with private baths. Ceiling fans cool the air in the rooms 17 feet high. Each bedroom has a marble mantle. The bedrooms have views of the surrounding landscape. To ask about tours, phone the Eufaula Heritage Association at 687-3793.

    Getting there: It is at 534 W. Broad St.

SHORTER MANSION is an outstanding example of neoclassical revival architecture and one of the state's most dramatic house museums. The two-story "wedding cake" exterior is festooned with elaborately detailed Corinthian columns which support an ornate entablature extending around three sides of the house. The plaster freize is decorated with acanthus leaves and scrolls.

    Eli Sims Shorter II, a wealthy cotton planter, and his wife, a Georgia-born heiress to the **SSS Tonic** estate, built the house in 1884. They enlarged the house in 1906 at a cost of $100,000. When the house was offered at auction from the builder's granddaughter, a group of preservationists purchased it in 1965 for $33,000 and organized the **Eufaula Heritage Association**. The following year they held Alabama's first pilgrimage which has grown into a major cultural event.

In addition to being furnished with period antiques, several second-story rooms house the Eufaula Historical Museum. The tour is self guided. When you step into the entry hall, the hostess will probably ask you to sign the guestbook. After doing so, turn and note the patterned glass in the double front doors. Also, observe the intricately patterned parquet floors and molded plaster cornices in the hallway. An angular staircase provides access to the second story.

The double parlors on the north side of the house have plaster walls with a gilded leaf design. Handsome mirrors over wooden mantels reflect the Waterford crystal and cut-glass chandeliers which hang over large Oriental rugs. The dining room contains a double pedestal Regency banquet table surrounded by 12 English Chippendale chairs flanked by a Regency sideboard. The silver epergne is Sheffield. A back porch gallery displays photos of other Eufaula landmarks. (Members of the Heritage Association are still talking about the great coverage of the town's houses in *Colonial Homes* magazine.)

Upstairs are period bedrooms, displays of period clothing, and several rooms honoring Barbour County notables, including six governors and **Adm. Thomas H. Moorer**, former chairman of the Joint Chiefs of Staff.

The spectacular Greek Revival style Shorter Mansion is one of Alabama's most spectacular house museums and serves as headquarters for the Eufaula Heritage Association which sponsors the pilgrimage. The best time to visit this "must see" mansion is during Alabama's top pilgrimage in April. Because the house faces east, the best time of day to photograph is mid-morning. Open Mon.-Sat. 10-4, Sun. 1-4; closed Thanksgiving and Dec. 24-25 and 31 and Jan. 1. Adults, $3; children, $.50. Phone 687-3793.

Getting there: It is at 340 N. Eufaula Ave. (U.S. 431), 3 blocks north of downtown.

THE TAVERN, which dates from 1837, was the first building constructed in Irwinton (Eufaula) and ranks among the most beautiful buildings in the South. It has served as a private home, a tavern, Confederate hospital, florist, photo studio and again as a private home. The L-shaped rear overlooks a brick patio and the Chattahoochee River. It is a block north of the bridge to Georgia. Turn north at the Holiday Inn. It is not open to the public, but you should drive by 105 Riverside Dr. to see it and the romantic riverbank setting.

SIDE TRIP TO LAKEPOINT

You can't visit Eufaula without paying your respects to the sportsman who hooked the world on fishing here for bass. **Tom Mann's Fish World Aquarium**, just north of town on U.S. 431, features a large collection of freshwater bass and other fish swimming comfortably in a huge 38,000-gallon tank measuring 40 by 20 by 8 feet. The highlight of the day occurs about 8 a.m. when the fish are fed. If you're here then, stay back or become fish bait. Ten 1,400-gallon aquariums contain species of fish native to Alabama. Tom's trophy display is upstairs.

Go outside to walk down steps and into a tunnel under part of a 10-acre lake stocked with fish from **Lake Eufaula**. The biggest resident is a 35-pound monster catfish. Mann built the attraction adjacent to his plant where his world-famous lures are made. While Tom might not be here the day of your visit, you can be assured that he's nearby perfecting another lure to entice more fish into the frying pan. Visit the pro shop next door to purchase Tom Mann's inventions and souvenirs.

Tom Mann has a special fish he credits with much of his success. His pet bass **Leroy Brown** was a finicky fish. If he nibbled on Tom's latest lure, it went into production; if he ignored it, Tom went back to the tying board. Leroy lived in the giant aquarium for seven years after Tom hooked him. When the fish died in 1981, the governor proclaimed a day of mourning and more than 1,000 people in town for a bass tournament attended the funeral.

To see the memorial to Eufaula's most famous fish, go beyond the aquarium and the tunnel entrance to the Oriental gate and look for the tombstone topped by a life-sized bass. J.J. Jackson carved the marker which reads, "Most bass are just fish, but Leroy Brown was something special." Open every day, 8-5 in summer, 9-4 other months. Aquarium admission: adults $2.25; $1 for children and senior citizens. It is not neccesary to pay to visit the lake tunnel and Leroy Brown's tomb. Four miles north on U.S. 431. Phone 687-3655.

Lakepoint State Resort is a recreation-filled state park which covers 1,220 acres at the edge of Lake Eufaula where overnight or daytrip guests can be passive or active. You can swim in the pool or lake, play golf on an 18-hole course at the water's edge, hike, picnic, go bike riding and play tennis under the lights. Of course, water is a major reason for visiting. You can water ski, sail and fish for champion bass in 45,200-acre Lake Eufaula. The full-service marina can provide current fishing information.

The state park's lakeside setting and modern resort facilities offer guests a variety of recreation and education programs. The Community Buiding in the campground is the site for naturalist activities including environmental slide shows, nature walks, guest speakers and bird-watching. A summer environmental camp provides youngsters with an introduction to conservation.

At other times of the year, the park has evening entertainment from gospel singers and bluegrass bands to bingo and square dancing.

Nearby on Hwy. 165 is the **Eufaula National Wildlife Refuge**, which offers an interpretive nature trail, a driving route and wildlife observation towers. The refuge attracts migratory birds, waterfowl, amphibians and reptiles, some of which are listed on endangered species lists. Sightseeing and nature observation are encouraged along trails, by car or boat and from the observation towers.

The refuge, managed by the U.S. Fish and Wildlife Service, is open every day of the year. From Eufaula, go north on U.S. 431 and follow the signs.

SIDE TRIP WEST OF EUFAULA

About 20 miles west of Eufaula on Hwy. 30 is Clayton, site of a pair of unusual attractions dating from about 1860. The **Octagon House** at 103 N. Midway St. was built 1859-61 for furniture merchant Benjamin Franklin Petty from a design published in 1854. The Town of Clayton purchased and restored the house. To arrange a tour, phone 775-3254.

On the same street stands the Clayton Baptist Church cemetery with a bizarre marker, the **Whiskey Bottle Tombstone**. The bottle-shaped head stone, matched by a smaller foot stone, identifies the grave of bookkeeper William T. Mullen. His reputation as a heavy drinker so rankled his wife, Mary, that she vowed to mark his grave with a whiskey bottle if he died of drink. He did, in 1863, at age 29, and she made good on her threat.

WHERE TO STAY

Lakepoint State Park Resort, 7 miles north on U.S. 431, is a recreation-filled state park which covers 1,220 acres at the edge of Lake Eufaula. A two-story lodge has 101 large, modern rooms, including six suites. You choose from 15 two-bedroom cabins, seven duplexes and a 190-site campground. Just off the main lobby are a highly recommended restaurant, coffee shop, a gift shop and a lounge for watching sporting events on television. Lakepoint is one of Alabama's most popular state park destinations. For weekend reservations from spring through fall, inquire several months in advance. **Phone 687-6676.**

The **Holiday Inn**, overlooking the Chattahoochee River at U.S. 82, is a comfortable place to stay if you more interested in a good night's sleep than recreation. The two-story, U-shaped layout features a pool in the courtyard and a restaurant where even local people eat. It is just east of downtown at the river bridge which crosses into Georgia. Take a stroll in late afternoon along Riverside Drive to the **Shorter Cemetery** a couple of blocks south and to the north where you'll pass three 19th-century landmarks: the Old City Jail, the beautiful Tavern and the Wellborn House. Double rate: $40-$47. A golf package with the Country Club of Alabama includes 18 holes of golf with cart, lodging, breakfast and dinner. **Phone 687-2021** or 1-800-465-43291.

St. Mary's Bed and Breakfast, just a couple of blocks from Kendall Manor, is a charming two-story Italianate home operated by Bob and Malinda Ross. Although the trim on the wraparound veranda could be considered Gothic, the former residence was used for decades as a retreat by the Holy Redeemer Catholic Church beginning in 1940. The house has several large bedrooms and informal public rooms. Guests are invited to walk around the neighborhood or peddle around town on a tandem bicycle. Doubles are $60 plus tax. Children under 12 are free and pets are welcomed. Smoking is permitted on the veranda. Visa and MasterCard are accepted.

St. Mary's is at 206 Rivers Ave., just off West Barbour past Fendall Hall house museum. **Phone 687-7195.**

WHERE TO EAT IN EUFAULA

Billy and Anna Nelson bake and sell about 80 dozen jelly- and creme-filled donuts a day from their small corner ***Donut Shop**, 3 blocks south of Broad at the corner of U.S. 431 and East Washington. The large, delicious donuts and other pastries are a real bargain. Locals still refer to it by the previous owner's name, Spivey's, who was at the location for two decades. To-go orders only. Phone 687-4580.

For lunch, consider the popular buffet at the ****Holiday Inn**. If you go at 10 a.m., you'll encounter the "coffee club," an unofficial gathering of retirees which has been meeting for half a century. Phone 687-2021. For excellent Southern meats and vegetables, stop by ***Pierce's**, located in an old fast-food place across from Kmart on U.S. 431 S. The fried okra is a must. Phone 687-4674.

For dinner, drive to ****Lakepoint Resort Lodge** for the prime rib dinner (phone 687-8011) or go to the ****Dogwood Inn**, a charming fine-dining restaurant in a large Victorian house 2 blocks south of Shorter Mansion. You can enjoy a cocktail or wine with a meal (687-5629). Good options for catfish and fried seafood are the ***Airport** restaurant north of town or the ***Creek**, formerly Tom Mann's, south of town. South on the lake is the ***Magnolia**, formerly the White Oak. Barbecue lovers head for ***Ribs 'N Things** behind the IGA on U.S. 431.

WHERE TO SHOP

Several attractive gift shops on the main business street of Broad offer distinctive gifts. If you enjoy handmade candies, turn off Broad at the Old Post Office onto Orange and go a block to 303-317 Britt Street to **Superior Pecans**. It's an old shelling plant where candies are made by hand, and retired ladies carefully pack shelled pecans for sale. Renee Ellis opens the shop September through March. Mail orders are handled year round. Phone 687-2031.

ANNUAL EVENTS

Late winter weekend

Watchable Wildlife - Lakepoint State Park - You can spend the weekend at the state park lodge and take part in field trips to view ducks, geese and other waterfowl wintering within the national wildlife refuge. Meet the other participants at an apple cider social Friday night and arise early Saturday for coffee and morning tours of the refuge. You are taken to sloughs and other points where waterfowl gather in the mornings. After lunch, a wildlife authority speaks about the migratory birds' life cycles. Another round of bird watching is followed by a banquet and program back at the lodge. On Sunday morning, participants go to other sites to watch ducks and geese in the wild. The lodging and meals are packaged. You can join in the lectures and tours without enrolling or paying a fee. The program was inspired by the success of the eagle-watching program at Lake Guntersville. For reservations, phone 687-8011.

First Friday thru Sunday in April

Eufaula Pilgrimage - Historic district -During Alabama's oldest and largest pilgrimage, costumed hostesses tell the stories of the former residents and the ornate Italianate and Greek Revival mansions scattered throughout the town. Some 90 National Register-listed structures comprise the rich collection of significant architecture in this charming, but relatively small Chattahoochee River town. About eight houses are shown during the day and several more on a candlelight tour. Both tours have been popular since the pilgrimage started in 1966.

Other activities include presentation of the pilgrimage court of prominent young women, an outdoor art show on North Randolph Avenue, antiques show and sale, concerts, free needlepoint exhibit at Eufaula Bank & Trust Co. and a Civil War re-enactment at Old Creek Town Park on Lake Drive.

Because some 6,000 people tour the homes, traffic is a problem, especially for those who just happen to be passing through town on U.S. 431 and get caught up in pilgrimage traffic. Frequently, however, the motorists simply park and buy tickets to see what the traffic jams are all about.

Tours are usually Fri.-Sat., 9 a.m.-5 p.m.; Sun. 1-5 p.m. Candlelight tours are 7-9:30 p.m. Phone 687-3793 or 687-6631.

Second weekend in October

Indian Summer Festival - North Randolph Avenue - The historic street a block east of U.S. 431 is transformed into a street fair of arts and crafts, live entertainment, clothes line art, food and children's games. The Chamber of Commerce sponsors the event. Open Sat. 9-5 and Sun. noon-5. Phone 687-6664.

GREENSBORO

This Black Belt town is the hub of Alabama's developing catfish farming industry and easily supports its claim as the **Catfish Capital of Alabama**. In addition to large ponds where catfish are raised, it is home to one of the largest catfish processing plants in the South.

Greensboro preseves scores of significant 19th-century structures in its downtown historic district, including commercial buildings, cottages and Greek Revival houses such as the temple-style Magnolia Hall. **Magnolia Grove** is the only house museum in this historic Black Belt town, but the town's architecture is worth going out of your way to survey.

A number of interesting structures are on Main Street. If you arrive from Tuscaloosa, turn left to see the 1907 neoclassical **Hale County Courthouse** with a later bell tower. While on this end of town, go 3 or 4 blocks east to tiny Otts Street and turn right into what appears to be a driveway and circle around to glance at Magnolia Hall, the grand Greek Revival house which David F. McCrary built about 1855. Now the Baines residence, it is hidden behind a lush growth of trees and shrubs. It is private.

To see other good examples of period houses, turn left at the courthouse on Centerville Street and then right on South Street. At the corner of Market is the Noel-Ramsey House. French settlers Thomas and Anne Hurtel Noel built it about 1821 after they left Demopolis. It served as the Catholic church for settlers of the Vine and Olive Colony.

Go right a block to Main Street and turn left. Four blocks west is the 1859 Presbyterian Church. Two blocks ahead on the left in an open field setting is the 1828 residence of Gov. John Gayle and the birthplace of his daughter, Amelia Gayle Gorgas, whose family contributed significantly to Alabama and American history. The two-story stuccoed brick house, known as the Gayle-Hobson-Tunstall-Sledge House, is marked by a small historical marker on the street.

Four blocks further on the left is the two-story Col. Sydenham Moore House distinguished by a wide Ionic portico. Moore reportedly incorporated materials from Gov. Israel Pickens' house, Greenwood, when building this house in 1855.

Just ahead where Main Street terminates is Magnolia Grove.

ATTRACTION

MAGNOLIA GROVE, the birthplace and boyhood home of Spanish-American War hero **Richard Pearson Hobson**, is an eight-room Greek Revival house now operated as a museum by the state.

Col. Isaac and Mrs. Sarah Croom built the house, detatched kitchen, slave cottage and office on a 16-acre estate about 1840. In 1867, Mrs. Croom invited her favorite niece and husband to live at Magnolia Grove. A son, Richard Pearson Hobson, was born to the niece three years later.

Hobson graduated from Annapolis in 1889. Nine years later during the Spanish-American War in Cuba, he sank the coal ship *Merrimac* in Santiago harbor in an attempt to bottle up the Spanish fleet. In 1907-15, he represented Central Alabama in Congress and led the Prohibitionist movement which culminated in the 18th Amendment to the Constitution. He received the Congressional Medal of Honor in 1933 for his wartime exploits and died in 1937.

The admiral's family gave the house and furnishings to the state in 1943 as a shrine. Opposite double parlors, a trophy room contains a portrait of the handsome admiral, military uniforms, naval text books and the nameplate of the ship, the *Merrimac*. Allow a half hour. Open Wed.-Sat., 10-4; Sun., 1-4. Adults, $3; students, $.50. Phone 624-8618.

Getting there: Magnolia Grove is at the western end of Main, at 1002 Hobson.

SIDE TRIP SOUTH

Eight miles south on Hwy. 61 is Newbern, with two early Greek Revival churches. The 1848 **Presbyterian Church** is a one-story frame with mortice and peg construction. Slaves sat on benches which flanked the pulpit. The 1849 **Baptist Church** is a two-story frame building with solid poplar Doric columns.

WHERE TO STAY

A retired airlines pilot, Thad May and his wife, Janet, operate his boyhood home as the **Blue Shadows Guest House**. Guests are invited to fish in the 10-acre pond or stroll the many marked nature trails within the 320-acre estate. Two guest double rooms in the main house share a bath. For privacy, stay in the separate guest house with a large living room/kitchen which overlooks the formal garden and main house. A balcony overlooks the woods and nature trails.

Restaurants within driving distance for dinner are the **Cotton Patch** near Eutaw and **Faunsdale Bar & Grill** near U.S. 80.

A continental breakfast is included for the $59 double rate. Children are welcome. No smoking. No credit cards. Located 3 miles northwest of Greensboro on Hwy. 14. For reservations, write Rt. 2, Box 432, Greensboro, 36744. Phone 624-3637.

GREENSBORO ANNUAL EVENT

Mid September

Alabama Catfish Festival - Lion Park - A catfish gala and children's carnival kickoff the annual celebration of the catfish industry. Exhibits, arts and crafts show, tours of local catfish farms, entertainment and a catfish industry trade show highlight the festival begun in 1988. Lion Park is off State Street behind the cemetery east of the Chevrolet dealership. Phone the Alabama Fish Farming Center at 624-4016.

MARION

Marion is a beautiful and historic college town with links to several of the state's most important educational and religious institutions. **Samford University** in Birmingham and **Alabama State University** in Montgomery began here, as did the **Southern Baptist Convention**.

Local Baptists founded the **Alabama Baptist State Convention** here in 1823 and **Judson College** in 1838. The *Alabama Baptist* paper began in 1843. The Alabama Resolutions, which inspired the Southern Baptist Convention, were passed at **Siloam Baptist Church** in 1844. The Home Mission Board was founded here the next year. The classical sanctuary erected in 1848 still stands at the corner of Early and Washington streets.

Today, young women from across the nation attend **Judson College** and prospective military leaders study at **Marion Military Institute.**
Marion is dotted with a remarkable number of antebellum houses for its size and is is one of the charming Black Belt towns where hospitality and grace have survived admirably. It is northwest of Selma and about 12 miles north of U.S. 80. In all, Perry County claims more than 100 structures dating before 1850. Because most houses do not display street numbers, it may be difficult to locate some.
The town's name honors Revolutionary War hero Francis Marion, who was nicknamed "the swamp fox." Most of the streets near the square honor Revoluntionary War heroes.
Dominating the small business district is a two-story temple-shaped courthouse built in 1856. A marker on the grounds honors Prussian music teacher and artist **Nicola Marschall**, who designed the Confederates' grey uniform and first Confederate flag (not the better known red Battle Flag) in the **Marion Female Seminary** building. The flag was presented to the Marion Light Infantry near the present site of Jewett Hall on the Judson campus. It was taken to Montgomery where it flew over the Capitol from March 4 through May while that city served as capital of the Confederacy.
Although several significant buildings are north and west of the square, most antebellum houses are south of the square and west of Washington Street (Hwy. 5). The non-institutional buildings are private residences.
Two blocks north of the courthouse is the 1886 **Marion Methodist Church.** Next, go west on Monroe to see the 1840 frame Scott-Harris-Moore House, the imposing 1856 brick **Marion Female Seminary** and the Gov. A.B. Moore House, a two-story frame house built in 1845 with a two-tiered central portico at 406 Washington St. (although house numbers aren't visible). Moore was governor during Alabama's secession from the Union and the formation of the Confederacy.
Sam Houston, who served as governor of Tennessee in 1827-29, married Margaret Lea in 1840 in her family's porticoed two-story house (Lea-Thatcher-Kramer) on West Green Street before his notable career in Texas later in the decade.
Driving south from the square on Washington, go a block and turn right to 110 Lafayette. The circa 1860 Reverie mansion is distinguished by four round columns supporting a massive portico. The Caffee-Lovelace Home, circa 1860, is also on Lafayette. Across Washington in the next block is the 1877 **Presbyterian Church** and the small 1835 *Alabama Baptist* newspaper office, most recently an insurance agent's office.
Turn east off Washington onto Early to see the main campus of **Judson College**, Alabama's only senior liberal arts college exclusively for women. Started by a group of Marion Baptists in 1838, it is one of America's oldest and most respected women's colleges. The main campus structure is **Jewett Hall**, the three-story brick administration building and dormitory. It is named for Milo P. Jewett, the first president.
About a mile south of **Marion Institute** on Washington (County 45) is the 1850's Lowrey-Ford House, a solid-looking frame house with sloping roof. A second-story gallery runs the width of the house. Six stucco-covered brick columns dominate the facade. It was damaged by a tornado in 1961 and fell into disrepair before the local preservation society started restoring it several years ago.

MARION POINTS OF INTEREST

JUDSON COLLEGE is Alabama's only senior liberal arts college exclusively for women. Started by a group of Baptists in 1838, it is one of America's oldest and most respected women's colleges. The main campus structure is **Jewett Hall**, a three-story brick administration building and dormitory. More than 40 of the state's outstanding women are honored in the Alabama Women's Hall of Fame. Bronze plaques displayed in Bowling Library honor such notables as Julia Tutwiler, Helen Keller and Amelia Gayle Gorgas. For information, phone 683-6161.

Getting there: From Washington, turn east on Lafayette Street 2 blocks and right on Bibb (Judson).

MARION INSTITUTE is a military prep school founded in 1842 as Howard College. It was reorganized and renamed in 1887 when Howard moved to Birmingham. The institute is a nationally recognized honor service academy preparatory school and junior college, with admirals and generals among its alumni. The 1857 **Chapel**, with its short clock tower, is the focal point of the campus. Cadets have carved their names in the soft brown bricks as high as a knife will reach. To see the interior, with its stained glass windows, check the front door. If locked, stop by the office of the Officer of the Day on Brown.

In the block behind the chapel is the library flanked by the old **City Hall**, a tiny structure with a bracketed roof built in 1832 which houses the **Alabama Military Hall of Honor.**

Getting there: A mile south of town, turn west on Brown Street.

WHERE TO SHOP

For antique shopping, visit **Camellia Place** at 1101 Washington. The handsome two-story home with slender columns built in 1849 houses **Antiques & Company**, a lovely antiques shop with room settings worth going out of your way to shop. Mr. and Mrs. Richard Avery operate the shop in the house which was in his family. Phone 683-4165.

MONROEVILLE

This picturesque town west of I-65 is the hometown of Pulitizer Prize-winning author **Harper Lee**, who used it as the model for the fictional town of Maycomb in her 1960 novel *To Kill A Mockingbird* .

Although the story was not based on any actual events, she used her father, Amasa Lee, as inspiration for attorney Atticus Finch. *To Kill A Mockingbird* received the 1961 Pulitzer Prize for fiction. In the 1962 movie version, Gregory Peck won an Oscar playing opposite two children from Birmingham. Although the movie was not filmed in the second-story courtroom, the 141-seat room inspired the movie set where blacks and Finch's children watch a trial from a railed balcony.

Author Truman Capote is represented in the story by Dill Harris, a young cousin who comes to visit Maycomb each summer. Capote was a childhood friend of Nelle Lee - as she is still known in Monroeville - and remained one of her few close friends until his death.

The novel has sold more than 30 million copies worldwide and is among the 10 most frequently assigned books in U.S. high schools.

Three decades after her literary triumph as a novice, Harper Lee has not published any other work. She wrote a novel based on an actual case of a black preacher accused of murder, but withdrew it shortly before publication. She remains a recluse, living in New York on substantial royalties from the book, and hasn't given an interview in 30 years. The townspeople are protective of Miss Lee's privacy and often frustrate nosey journalists who try to penetrate the town's shield. During the Christmas holidays, she returns home to visit her sister, an attorney.

Shoppers know Monroeville for **Vanity Fair Mills**, which has been making garments here since 1937. It has four plants and is the county's largest employer. Its VF Outlet began as a store for employees and introduced outlet shopping to the Monroeville area.

For more information on the past and present of Monroe County, phone Sandy Smith at the **Chamber of Commerce** at 743-2879 or write P.O. Box 214, Monroeville, 36461.

ATTRACTION

MONROEVILLE COURTHOUSE - Drive through the downtown square to see the old courthouse which inspired part of *To Kill A Mockingbird.*

The silver bullet-shaped clock tower of the three-story, neoclassical brick Monroe County Courthouse dominates the town square. The building, designed by Andrew Bryan of New Orleans, was built in 1903 and served as the seat of county government until a new courthouse was built adjacent in 1963. After years of fundraising and planning, restoration is under way, with the tower and clock getting first attention.

The courtroom is the venue for community events and stagings of plays based on Harper Lee's novel and Capote's Monroeville-based *A Christmas Memory.* Office space for the Chamber of Commerce and the historical society, as well as the county heritage museum, is in the building. It is open Mon.-Fri., 8-4. Phone 575-7433.

SIDE TRIP SOUTH TO FORT MIMS

The largest massacre in American pioneer history occurred on Aug. 30, 1813, at **Fort Mims** when Upper Creek Indians led by half-breed Chief Red Eagle stormed a stockaded settlement near the Alabama River and killed 514 people.

The Creeks, who strongly opposed cooperation with white men, attacked a small stockade built around the home of settler Samuel Mims. Despite warnings that an attack was imminent, sand had been allowed to build up against an open gate. Soliders and young women were dancing when the attack began at noon. An estimated 1,000 whites and Indians fought in hand-to-hand combat for five hours until the last of the pioneers was mortally wounded. In all, the Upper Creeks had killed 260 white settlers, children, slaves and soldiers in addition to 254 Indians friendly to the whites. Only 14 whites escaped into the woods and survived.

The victorious Indians scalped many of the dead and took the skins on poles to Pensacola where the British had promised $5 a scalp.

The rallying cry of "Remember Fort Mims" echoed throughout the frontier as a warning to other settlers to beware of Indians.

While less significant events in Alabama are lionized, the Fort Mims massacre has not been afforded even one of the familiar roadside markers to explain the site's importance. The only hint of what happened is given by a tombstone-type marker placed at the site by the DAR which lists an approximate number of whites (but not how many of their Indian allies) who were killed.

The Till family donated a four-acre site to the state in 1955 for development of a park. Owners of the land between the fort site and the river have resisted selling, thus stalling restoration efforts. Given its historical significance, it is amazing that the site remains so neglected.

The site is about 4 miles from Tensaw in North Baldwin County. Look for the simple highway directional marker on Hwy. 59 and turn off on County Road 80. Drive past several house trailers to a dead end to reach the site. To see Red Eagle's grave at Chief Red Eagle Park, go 10 miles north on Hwy. 59 and turn off on County Rd. 84. Follow the signs.

SIDE TRIP WEST

Go west on Hwy. 47, then 6 miles west on U.S. 84 to the old town of **Perdue Hill** where the two-story **Old Masonic Hall**, built about 1825, has been restored. Nearby is a charming two-room cottage built in the 1820s. It was the home of William Barrett Travis who practiced law in the rivertown of Claiborne before moving to Texas in 1831. He died while commanding the defenders of the Alamo in 1836. The Travis Cottage has been restored and moved near the Masonic Hall.

The area west of Monroeville, in Clarke County, is believed to contain the site of the legendary Indian village of **Mauvilla**, where 2,500 Indians were killed by the Spanish explorer **Hernando DeSoto** in 1540. Various expeditions, beginning with Tristan De Luna's group in 1560, have attempted to locate the site of the battle. Occasional finds of pottery shards encourage those seeking the battlefield to keep on digging.

SIDE TRIP EAST

Students of Alabama history know that the **Battle of Burnt Corn** was the first clash in the **Creek Indian War of 1814**. From Monroeville, go north on 21/47 and east on County 30 to Burnt Corn. Visit the 1908 **General Store** which also houses the post office. Masons and Methodists met on the second floor. Nearby is the circa 1820 **Watkins House** on the Old Federal Road.

WHERE TO STAY

When Mary Elizabeth Johnson was married in 1897, she was given a house built in 1840. Nearly a century later, the woman's namesake and greatniece, Mary Elizabeth Johnson Huff, returned to her childhood home with her husband, John, and operates the **Rutherford-Johnson House** as a B&B.

The parlor is furnished with period antiques, including a secretary original to the house. You may request the large bedroom downstairs with a large mahogany and walnut bed or one of the several rooms upstairs, also furnished with beds and washstands which have been in the Johnson family for generations.

A former books editor at the Birmingham company which owns *Southern Living*, Mary Elizabeth uses a large room downstairs to write books on quilts and other American crafts. Guests are invited to relax and read in wicker rockers on the front porch or wander around the house to the restored outbuildings where John - retired from the furniture business in Mobile - tends cows and chickens. Rosie Finklea cooks traditional Southern breakfasts with tomato gravy in the oldest part of the house and brings food to the dining room in the 1897 addition. Arrangements may be made for the evening meal. Rates for a couple are $75. Reservations are required. Children are welcome. No credit cards. Contact the Huffs at P.O. Box 202, Franklin, 36444. Phone 282-4423.

WHERE TO SHOP

VF Factory Outlet offers Vanity Fair, Jansen, Bassett-Walker and Lee clothing, as well as other lines. Open Mon.-Sat., 9-6; Sun., 12:30-5:30. Phone 575-2330.

Getting there: From the north, exit I-65 at the Evergreen-Monroeville interchange and take U.S. 84 to Hwy. 21 North. From the south, take the Atmore-Monroeville exit to Hwy. 21 to the 21 bypass and to Drewry Road.

ANNUAL EVENT

Last weekend of August

Re-enactment of the Fort Mims Massacre - Tensaw - Several hundred costumed re-enactors commemorate the massacre at the site where it occurred. "Settlers" and "Indians" arrive on Friday in period clothing and set up camp as if in 1813. Re-enactors sew beads, perform period folk music, dry meat and set up blacksmith operations. A narrator describes the circumstances leading to the massacre and chronicles the battle as Indians attack the settlers. A candlelight tour of the fort and camps is held Saturday night. On Sunday morning in the settlers' camp, a minister in period clothing delivers a sermon typical of the era.

The Poarch Band of Creek Indians from Atmore and the MOWA Choctaws from Washington County compete in costumed dancing. Tomahawk throwing is open to spectators. Authentic crafts are sold and the Tensaw Volunteer Fire Department sells barbecue. Phone 937-9464 or 937-1223.

Last Saturday of October

Pecan Harvest Festival - Monroeville Square - The courthouse is surrounded by a food and entertainment fair. Alabama pecan pies and other desserts are tasted and sold. Children's events are scheduled. Phone 743-2879.

MONTGOMERY

- **Claim to fame:** Confederate birthplace and civil rights
- **Don't miss:** Shakespeare Festival, Capitol
- **Eat at:** Young House, Bistro
- **Unique accommodations:** Riverfront Inn
- **Population:** 187,106
- **Tourist information:** Andy Britton, Vice President; **Montgomery Area Chamber of Comerce/Convention & Visitor Division**, P.O. Box 79, Montgomery, 36101. Phone 240-9455.

From its founding, Montgomery flourished as a cotton market and transportation center. Its commerce, central location in the state and the promise of a privately financed state Capitol atop Goat Hill triggered the transfer of the Alabama government from Tuscaloosa in 1846.

Following the election of Abraham Lincoln as president, Alabama left the union on Jan. 11, 1861 and joined the **Confederate States of America** on March 13 when it ratified the new CSA constitution. During the two intervening months, it was the **Republic of Alabama**.

For several months Montgomery served not only as the capital of Alabama, but as the capital of the new Confederacy as well.

South Carolinians suggested in January, 1861 that representatives of the six secessionist states meet in Montgomery to form a new government. Duly elected congressmen and senators boarded trains for Montgomery. They convened on Feb. 4 and adopted a Constitution four days later based on state's rights and slavery. The next day they elected two reluctant moderates to the highest offices: former Secretary of War **Jefferson Davis** of Mississippi as president and **Alexander Stephens** of Georgia as vice president.

The delegates chose Montgomery as the provisional capital until the government could be moved to Richmond, Va. Some delegates viewed Richmond - bearly 100 miles from Washington - as a risky location and thought the more isolated Montgomery as less vulnerable to invasion.

A delegation of officials traveled to Davis' plantation to notify him of his election. By the time he reached Montgomery on Feb. 16, he had given 25 speeches to well-wishers en route. After arriving in Montgomery, the fatigued and hoarse president-elect was taken to the Exchange Hotel at the foot of Dexter Avenue where he was introduced by firebrand sessionist William Lowndes Yancy of Alabama with the assertion that "the man and the hour have met." Davis addressed a cheering throng from a balcony: "Heaven will so prosper the Southern Confederacy and carry us safe from sea to the safe harbor of constitutional liberty. I will devote to the duties of the high office to which I have been called all I have of heart, of head and of hand."

At l p.m. on Feb. 18, an estimated 10,000 celebrants spread over the grounds in front of the Capitol portico for the inauguration when the new leader took the oath from Howell Cobb. Two weeks later, a granddaughter of former U.S. President Tyler raised the "Stars and Bars" flag of the Confederacy over the Capitol.

Davis initially used one of the parlors of the Exchange Hotel as his office and held cabinet meetings in his home only a couple of blocks behind the hotel.

Ten days later, the Confederate Congress authorized Davis to assume control of all military forces in every member state. On March 6, they gave Davis the authority to prepare for war and to issue a call to the states for volunteers.

The Southern Congress ordered all forts seized within the seceded states. Only Fort Sumter at Charleston and Fort Pickens at Pensacola were not immediately controlled. Despite attempts to persuade Lincoln and his secretary of war to surrender the forts, they refused.

A telegram sent from the Southern Telegram Co. office in the **Winter Building** to Confederate troops in Charleston to fire on Fort Sumter - if federal troops did not evacuate - began the Civil War on April 12.

As military action continued to be directed from Montgomery, the finest families of the city entertained visiting delegates from other states in grand fashion with balls, suppers and receptions. The brief period that the Confederacy was headquartered here was unequaled in terms of social activity.

In order to be nearer the military action in Virginia, sentiment swelled to shift the capital to Richmond. The Congress approved the action and Davis vetoed it. By the end of May, Congress had overridden the veto and suddenly the president and the department heads were gone.

During the next four years, the Tennessee Valley region of North Alabama would be the scene of occupation by Union forces and occasional raids would affect localized areas, but the capital city itself was spared military action until the very end. When news of the devastation of Selma on April 2, 1865, reached Montgomery, the city fathers knew what to do. The city council ordered the city's major asset - 88,000 bales of cotton stored in warehouses - burned by the city's volunteer black fire brigade.

When Major Gen. James Wilson's raiders reached Montgomery 10 days after their conquest of Selma, they were met by the mayor and aldermen who quickly surrendered the city. Apart from destroying five steamboats and the railroad machine shops, little damage was caused by the Yankees. One newspaper editor attributed their good behavior to the fact that the local supply of liquor had been carefully hidden.

Wilson set up headquarters in the **Teague House** at 468 S. Perry St. and vowed to maintain order. Ironically, the occupation came exactly four years to the day after the order had been sent from Montgomery to fire on Fort Sumter.

Montgomery suffered **Reconstruction** under carpetbagger and Black Republican rule, a period of stagnant existance.

But the city gradually recovered, thanks to its status as state capital, a position that attracted railroad lines in the 1880's. The grand Union Station and the impressive row of warehouses on Lower Commerce Street date from the turn of the century.

The **Civil Rights Movement** began just down the street from the birthplace of the Confederacy. In what has become the most famous two-block bus ride in history, black seamstress **Rosa Parks** boarded the Cleveland Avenue bus at the foot of Dexter after work on Dec. 1, 1955, and sat down in the only available seat. The bus rolled past the Alex Rice store and the Elite restaurant and pulled to a stop in front of the **Empire Theater**. When a white man boarded the bus and she refused driver Fred Blake's order to move to the back of the bus - as Montgomery ordinance required - Blake called police and Mrs. Parks was arrested.

Black leaders formed an organization the next day at the **Dexter Avenue Baptist Church** and elected **Rev. Martin Luther King** their president. To protest her arrest,

MONTGOMERY, ALABAMA

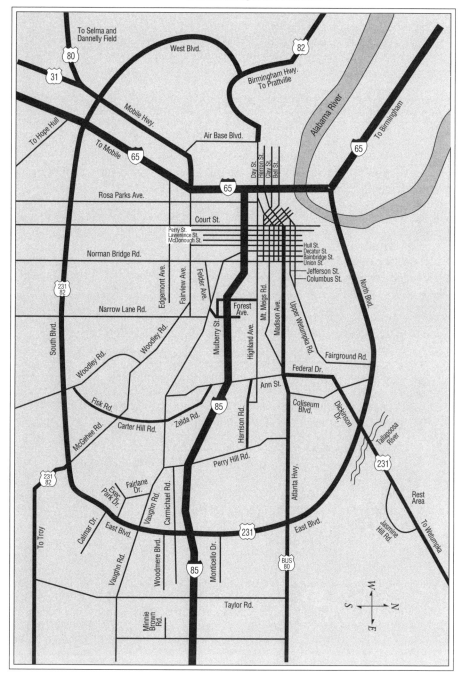

they nervously organized a bus boycott for Dec. 5, the day of her trial. (She was fined $10.)

Blacks walked to work and carpooled for the next 381 days and focused worldwide attention on Montgomery. Based on a suit stemming from the arrest, the U.S. Supreme Court ended legal segregation on public transportation. King, the symbolic leader of the movement, preached at Dexter Avenue Baptist Church until Jan. 31, 1960.

Montgomery became the center of international attention again in 1965 when organizers of a voter registration campaign in Selma dramatized their demands by marching to the State Capitol. After a few hundred protestors leaving Selma were attacked by police, they regrouped two weeks later to be joined by King, other black leaders and liberal entertainers. Their 54-mile journey ended four days later on March 25 as more than 25,000 gathered for a mass rally in front of the Capitol.

The city remains the commercial hub of South Alabama. State government and trade associations occupy most office space within walking distance of the Statehouse. The Retirement System of Alabama, directed by Dr. David Bronner, is the most prominent landlord. The contemporary green-roofed office buildings are owned by the RSA.

Getting around: Montgomery is linked via I-65 to Mobile and Birmingham. I-85 begins here and goes north to Atlanta. U.S. 231 North goes to Wetumpka and on to Huntsville. U.S. 231 South goes to Troy and Dothan. U.S. 80 West is the Selma Highway. U.S. 31 North parallels I-65 to Birmingham and Decatur, southbound to Mobile. A bypass encircles the city and traffic is bumper to bumper during the day with innumerable traffic signals pacing the traffic.

To reach Dannelly Field Airport, take I-65 exit 167 and follow the signs.

WELCOME CENTER

Stop by the **Thompson Mansion** at 401 Madison Ave. at Hull Street. It is the visitor information center for the **Convention & Visitors Division** and a remarkable attraction all its own. Pleasant guides offer brochures and directions. A video previews city attractions. Enter the parking lot off Madison. Open Mon.-Fri., 8:30-5; Sat., 9-4; Sun., 9-4. Phone 240-9455.

DOWNTOWN ATTRACTIONS

ALABAMA STATE CAPITOL has served as the seat of state government since 1851 and housed the initial Confederate government in 1861. The National Historic Landmark underwent extensive exterior and interior restoration between 1978 and 1992. The top constitutional officers of the state returned to the restored Capitol, but lawmakers didn't. Both Houses of the Legislature left the building for more spacious quarters in the **State House** building in the block behind the Capitol, where, for the first time in history, each legislator has a private office.

The historic Capitol is the second on the site. Montgomery civic leaders managed to entice the state government from Tuscaloosa in 1846 with the promise of a new Capitol at no cost to the state. So confident were the leaders of the city that they reserved the hilltop overlooking the main street as the future site of the capitol. (Goats grazed atop the hill, giving rise to the political nickname "Goat Hill" which remains to this day.)

The first Capitol, completed in 1847, was a Greek Revival building which architect **Stephen Decatur Button** designed to resemble the nation's capitol in Washington.

Unfortunately, Button's building burned Dec. 14, 1849, the 30th anniversary of statehood.

A panel headed by industrialist **Daniel Pratt** modified Button's design and hastily built the new Capitol in 1850-51 on some of the foundations of the original. Later additions include the rear wing in 1885, the south wing in 1906 and the north wing in 1912.

Although the Confederate government was only housed in Montgomery from early February until about May 21, the most important events related to the formation of the new nation and the beginning of the war took place here during that pivotal period.

Since being reopened to the public following a six-year, $30 million restoration by the **Alabama Historical Commission**, the building restoration has surprised many visitors. People used to the dull, off-white interior are amazed to see the ornate detailing that had been paneled, plastered and painted over through the decades. If you are a resident of Alabama, you should express appreciation to your legislators for funding this superb project which was executed by dedicated artisans working with commission liaisons Robert Gamble and Bill Woodsmall.

Due partly to the state's economic condition over the years, the building was enlarged several times rather than ever being replaced by a new building as was done in other states. The restoration reflects different phases of use: 1851, 1885, 1906, 1912 and 1992.

The building is now a combination working state office building and museum. The original 1851 center of the building functions chiefly as a museum attraction. The governor and other constitutional officers maintain suites in the three wings of the building.

Ground Floor

You can tour the Lobby and restored suites used by the Supreme Court, the Governor and the Secretary of State.

The pair of three-story spiral stairways which dominate the original **Entrance Hall** may have been built by Horace King, a former Georgia slave who had become a master carpenter and was subsequently freed by act of the Legislature in 1848. After the Civil War this same black man returned to the building for a significant reason: he had been elected to serve in the Legislature. (See listing for John Godwin's Grave in Phenix City.)

To reach the original **Supreme Court Chamber**, walk from the central hall past the elevators into the semi-circular room. The chamber housed the judicial branch of state government from 1851 to 1940 when the court moved to a separate building. After 1940, the space was divided into offices. The right column, capped by a "tower of the winds" capital and hidden in a later wall, was revealed during restoration, providing clues as to the room's original purpose. Two photos of Jefferson Davis lying in state in the room in 1889 aided in the room's identification and reconstruction.

Continue walking ahead into the east wing. By 1885, the **Supreme Court Library** had outgrown its original quarters in the 1851 south wing and this law library was built. The fluted cast-iron columns you see were eventually concealed by a double tier of bookcases. This room will house a museum telling the story of Alabama's statehouses from territorial days to the present.

Return to the Rotunda, turn right and look on your left for the **Original Governor's Suite** (1851-1912). Fragments of *trompe l'oeil* ("fool the eye") painting which date from the 1870s surround an old door opening on the right. The eye-popping 24 colors used on the walls and carpet in the reception room match those from a redecorating effort in 1869. The inner office, decorated in 18 muted and bright colors to resemble molded plaster, is furnished with handsome antiques from the 1870s. For decades, governors used a massive Wooten Desk, like one displayed, to hold state documents. The original mantle is made of Egyptian marble.

Across the hall, the outer office of the 1851 **Secretary of State's Suite** is another museum space furnished with antiques of the 1880s, as is the larger, inner office.

Down the hall on the left is the **1912 Governor's Suite**, which is the present governor's office and, therefore, not open for tours. If you have an appointment with the governor, you will see panels of dark Santo Domingo mahogany with handsome Regency antique and reproduction furniture and fixtures. This room has changed little since Emmett O'Neal of Florence moved into the office in 1912. Fifteen other governors have occupied this office.

One of the best tales about the building relates to a room not open to the public: the **State Treasurer's Office**, which is the first door on the right south of the lobby. Treasurer Ike Vinson, who campaigned as "Honest Ike," stole $230,000 in 1883 and skipped to Mexico. He was eventually traced to Texas in 1887, indicted on 39 counts, convicted and sentenced to 10 years in prison.

This is an active government office and not on the self-guided tour, but the walk-in safe on the right is worth describing. The original plaster-lined safe is intact. Tiny holes high up in the wall which lead into the vault were intended as air holes in case somebody was accidentally locked inside. To prevent thieves from using the holes to poke a wire through and steal state bonds stored here, the holes do not follow a straight line. Nothing of historical value is inside, other than some early wooden shelves.

As funding permits, organized tours enter through the rear addition for an orientation in the 260-seat auditorium. The state-of-the-art theater has video capabilities which allow groups to see and talk with a legislator on the floor while in session across the street in the State House. The gift shop opposite the auditorium features books and state souvenirs.

Second Floor

The second floor houses the Rotunda, flanked on the north by the Old Senate Chamber and on the south by the Old House Chamber, beyond which is the 1907 Archives and History Room.

The **Senate Chamber**: The most historic room in the building is interpreted to the day the delegates of the **Confederate Congress** planted the seeds for the Civil War. For five days, they deliberated on secession and state's rights. On Feb. 4, 1861, they adjourned, walked across the hall to the House Chamber and voted to secede from the United States of America and form the **Confederate States of America**. (Because of the expense of furnishing the room, visitors are not allowed on the Senate Chamber floor. Go to the viewing balcony on the third floor.)

The **House Chamber** across the rotunda is restored with decorative painting as it was at the end of the 19th century. It is used for special occasions, such as the opening of the legislative session and the governor's State of the State Address. It was in this chamber that Alabama delegates who had been elected to debate secession voted on Jan. 7, 1861, by a margin of 61 to 39, to secede from the Union. Their deliberation is portrayed in the Winston County outdoor drama, *Incident at Looney's Tavern*.

South of the House chamber is the large **Archives and History Chamber** dominated by an impressive skylight. The first state archives department in the nation was housed here from 1907 to 1940. The room is used for formal legislative receptions.

The majority of space in the 1906 south wing and the 1912 north wing is used by current officials and state employees.

Third Floor

Go to the **Senate Chamber Gallery** and look down into the small **Senate Chamber** to get a feeling of the intimacy which senators felt during debates and compromises for the nearly 150 years that lawmakers met here. A reproduction electrified oil-burning chandelier illuminates the senators' desks and chairs. The furniture was copied at a cost of $100,000 from originals which had been in the Tuscaloosa Capitol. The design of the gaudy carpet is authentic to the period. During the Civil War, the Legislature ordered the carpet in the building cut into small sections and sent to the battlefield where it could be used as blankets by Alabama soldiers.

The detailed restoration, even to the pictures hanging on the walls, is based on engravings published in newspapers at the time. The ornate ceiling fresco was replicated from a small fragment of the original that was discovered when a false ceiling was removed. The eight ornate wooden columns were carefully painted to look like bronze.

Notice the delicately carved cast-iron railing which is similar to the railing in the House Gallery and Rotunda.

The **Rotunda**: Under the ornate dome on the third floor are eight scenes Mobile architect Roderick MacKenzie painted in 1927 which romanticize moments in Alabama history. The first shows Frenchmen, backed by a priest and cooperative Indians, founding Mobile in 1711. The first governor and Legislature are shown drafting the Constitution in Huntsville in 1819, although the furnishings depicted are far more elaborate than they actually were. A gentleman and his lady on horseback represent the glory days of the cotton kingdom about 1850. Cheerful blacks load bales of cotton against a background of Birmingham steel mills in the tableau representing 20th-century agriculture, commerce and industry.

The dazzling color scheme of the Rotunda dome also dates from the 1927 renovation.

The Grounds

Sometime during your visit, remember to stand outside the giant front doors on the west portico and look down. A six-pointed bronze star marks the spot near where **Jefferson Davis** took the oath of office. According to tradition, each Alabama governor taking the oath of office has stood on the star. A wooden platform extending over the front steps actually put the Confederate president about 15 feet in front of the present star. Governors, however, are sworn in with the same bible Davis used.

A controversy over flying the Confederate Battle Flag overshadowed the reopening of the restored Capitol in 1992. In 1963, **Gov. George Wallace** ordered the flag flown in defiance of a visit by Atty. Gen. Bobby Kennedy in connection with the integration of the University of Alabama. Several black legislators had tried during the restoration to prevent the flag from returning and many business leaders agreed it was bad for the state's image. The blacks, who boycotted the ceremony, found an obscure 1897 law regulating flag displays which they cited in state court. A Montgomery circuit judge agreed and barred the governor from flying anything other than the state and national banners over the Capitol.

The majestic marble steps leading from the Capitol down to Dexter Avenue date from about 1950 when **Gov. Jim Folsom** had them constructed. Because the **Selma-to-Montgomery March** ended on the steps on March 25, 1965, the historical commision decided that event should be reflected in the restoration, too, and left them intact.

Many of the trees on the grounds were grown from acorns which were brought from battlefields where state regiments fought during the Civil War. A number of monuments are placed within the Capitol grounds. At the top of the Capitol steps is a nine-foot bronze statue of Jefferson Davis which was donated by the United Daughters of the Confederacy. Another bronze statute honors the now obscure Dr. Allen Wyeth, a Confederate surgeon who founded the New York Polyclinic Medical School.

The majestic **Confederate Monument** at the north entrance commemorates soldiers and sailors of the Confederacy. It is this monument which the governor can see from his office in the north wing. Davis returned to Montgomery to lay the cornerstone on April 26, 1886, 21 years after the Civil War ended.

Getting there: The Capitol dominates the downtown skyline from the top of Dexter Avenue. Follow the directional signs from the interstate or South Boulevard. Phone 242-3184.

ARCHIVES AND HISTORY MUSEUM documents the state's evolution through roughly a half-million items. Indian and pioneer artifacts, military history and domestic displays. Archaeological fragments, artifacts, uniforms, household goods and weapons from wars fought by Alabamians fill the stately 50-year-old museum.

Articles ranging from silver jewelry to bird points for hunting survey the evolution of the five Indian tribes which lived in Alabama before the arrival of white men. Examples of the crafts made by natives in Moundville, Russell Cave and Central Alabama are arranged chronologically.

Take a few moments to walk through the cultural exhibits on the second floor. Time will pass quicker than you realize. An exhibit on 19th-century life includes clothing, dolls, locally made silver, glass, weapons and even the Bible with which Jefferson Davis took the oath of office of Confederate president. One room has a wealth of papers from Selma's illustrious William Rufus King. He was the only Alabamian elected vice president of the U.S. The military room displays uniforms and weapons used in various wars, beginning with the Revolutionary War and Civil War.

Portraits of prominent Alabamians are grouped throughout the building by categories such as education, medicine and religion. Notables honored include humanitarian Julia Tutwiler, who also penned the state song; activist Dr. Martin Luther King; and Tuskegee peanut and sweet potato scientist Dr. George Washington Carver. Portions of a 19th-century French mural depicting the legendary Vine and Olive Colony of Demopolis dominate one room. Children especially enjoy an interactive, hands-on "attic" which permits them to role play with clothing and other articles.

Want to trace your family tree? Visit the first-floor reference library which also contains the official documents of state government, including papers of former governors and legislators. Military service records date to the American Revolution and include the Confederate era.

The museum, housed in a massive structure gleaming with polished brass and pristine Alabama marble, is especially popular with school children and teachers on field trips in the spring. Groups should phone 242-4363 for a reservation two weeks prior to a trip. Open Mon.-Fri., 8-5; Sat., 9-5. Closed Sun. and state holidays.

Getting there: The building erected in 1940 at 624 Washington is a block south of the Capitol. It is the massive building next door to the White House of the Confederacy.

CIVIL RIGHTS MEMORIAL is a starkly emotional monument to 40 people who died between 1955 and 1968 during the struggle for racial equality. The names and circumstances of their deaths are etched on a black circular granite table arranged like the hands on a clock.

Twenty-one landmark events are also chronicled. The list begins with the 1954 Supreme Court school desegregation decision (Brown vs. the Board of Education, Topeka, Kansas), includes the 1956 decision which banned segregated seating on Montgomery buses and ends with the death of Martin Luther King in 1968. The fact that there is blank space between the end of the inscriptions and the beginning indicates that the struggle had no definite beginning and eerily suggests there is room for more names, as well as more landmark events.

The circle of events and names is continually covered by a thin sheet of softly flowing water, magnifying the monument's powerful tactile dimension.

As a backdrop to the table is a 9-foot high black wall inscribed with the words: "...Until Justice rolls down like water, and Righteousness like a mighty stream." Martin Luther King quoted the verse in the Book of Amos at the start of the Montgomery bus boycott and eight years later at the Lincoln Monument at the Washington march.

The memorial completed in 1989 was created by sculptor **Maya Y. Lin**, best known for her design of the Vietnam War Memorial in Washington. Like the Washington memorial, this one invites people to touch the names and feel a connection with those who died in the social struggle. The table weighs 15 tons and measures 12 feet across. It is only 31 inches high so that it is easily accessible to children and adults who can trace their fingers along the names under the water.

People stop by for a few minutes at all times of day and night and reflect on what it represents. No one can touch the names under the flowing water and walk away unaffected.

As an unfortunate commentary on the times, it is attended day and night by a guard. On a positive note, the construction company which erected the memorial put up a temporary fence around the project to guard against any vandalism while it was being built. None occurred.

It is only a couple of blocks from the State Capitol which has ironic links with the civil rights movement. The Capitol served as the first seat of government of the Confederacy in 1861 and was the terminus of the Selma voting rights march a century later.

Getting there: Corner of 400 Washington Ave. at Hull Street. It sits in a small plaza in front of the Southern Poverty Law Center. Founder Morris Dees successfully prosecutes klansmen and other white supremists. You can park along Washington and approach the memorial easily from curbside. It is close to the First White House of the Confederacy, the State Capitol and Dexter Avenue Baptist Church. Phone 264-0286.

COMMERCE STREET HISTORIC DISTRICT contains one of the state's finest collections of intact Victorian commercial structures. Of special interest are the three lower blocks which face the Union Station and modern Montgomery Civic Center. Dates range from the 1880s to the turn of the century. Original uses ranged from wholesale grocery companies to a carriage factory to hardware stores. The eight-foot figure atop the law offices at 184 Commerce is Minerva, goddess of the hearth.

Getting there: Turn off Court St. to "Lower Commerce." The Chamber of Commerce is located in a restored 1916 building at 41 Commerce. Phone 834-5200.

COURT SQUARE FOUNTAIN, at the opposite end of Dexter Avenue from the Capitol, was erected during the boom of 1885 over an artesian basin. Hebe, the goddess of youth and cup bearer to the gods, faces Commerce and looks toward the river, both of which symbolize the city's role as a transportation and trade center. The fountain was restored by the city for its centennial.

Getting there: The fountain is at the intersection of Commerce and Dexter.

DEXTER AVENUE BAPTIST CHURCH can justly lay claim to being the spiritual birthplace of the civil rights movement. Rev. Vernon Johns had been using the pulpit of the modest brick church for years to call for racial equality before the congregation called **Dr. Martin Luther King, Jr.**, as pastor in 1954. The church served as the focal point for meetings of blacks who organized and carried out the bus boycott after the arrest of Rosa Parks.

Knock on the downstairs door and ask to see the folk art mural depicting King's work against racial segregation, beginning with Mrs. Parks's arrest. "The Beginning of a Dream, " inside to the left, shows blacks' struggles and triumphs as well as King's milestones from Montgomery to Memphis. On the back of a door, King is depicted in jail clothes after writing his famous "Letter from Birmingham Jail." You can buy a Civil Rights Tour Guide to Montgomery at the church. Next, you'll be taken upstairs to the sanctuary where King preached. The name was changed in 1979 to **Dexter Avenue King Memorial Baptist Church.** Open Mon.-Fri., 8:30-4:30; weekend by appointment. Donations accepted. Walk up the side street to Washington and turn right to view the **Civil Rights Memorial.**

The **Pastorium** at 309 S. Jackson St. where King lived is not open to the public, but a small plaque explains a dent in the porch caused by a bomb two months into the boycott. The home of black leader **Edgar Daniel Nixon**, Mrs. Parks's neighbor who conceived the idea of the boycott, is at 647 Clinton Ave. Other black history sites are the **Ben Moore Hotel**, corner of High and Jackson, where black and white leaders met at the roof garden restaurant during the boycott, and the birthplace of singer **Nat King Cole**, 1524 St. John St.

Getting there: The church at 454 Dexter Ave. is at the intersection of Decatur Street. It stands a block from the Capitol which served as the birthplace of the Confederacy. Phone 263-3970.

FIRST WHITE HOUSE OF THE CONFEDERACY was the home of Jefferson Davis and his family for the opening months of the Civil War while Montgomery was the Confederate capital.

The frame house was completed for merchant William Sayre in 1835 and changed in 1855 by John G. Winter to its Italianate style with large brackets beneath extended eaves. In 1861, it stood on the corner of Bibb and Lee streets. It was chosen for

Jefferson's residence because of the proximity to the Exchange, the finest hotel in Montgomery, where many members of the Confederate Congress and the cabinet stayed. The Confederacy leased the house for $5,000 a year from Col. Edmund S. Harrison of Prattville.

In addition to entertaining and living here with his wife and three children, Davis frequently held cabinet meetings here for privacy. The ground floor contained a double parlor, a spacious dining room, a library, reception halls and two bedrooms. Upstairs, a hall connected five rooms.

Davis was elected president by the Congress on Feb. 9 and arrived on Feb. 16. He was inaugurated two days later, but Mrs. Davis, a Natchez belle, missed the ceremony because she stayed behind in Mississippi to pack the family's possessions. She arrived on March 4, the same day a granddaughter of President John Tyler raised the Stars and Bars flag over the Capitol. She presided over many grand receptions until the government moved to Richmond in late May. She and the children followed in June.

The Ladies White House Association was founded in 1900 to purchase and restore the house, a feat which was not accomplished without a long struggle. The group finally acquired the house from the Tyson family and moved it to its present location in 1921. Jefferson's widow gave many of the family's belongings for display. The original iron fence was moved to the site in 1946.

When you go, notice the unusual cast-iron ventilator grills under the eaves. The "Liberty cap" design was a popular pre-war motiff.

The adjoining parlors on the first floor contain handsome period sofas and chairs. Climb the stairs and look into the bedrooms which are furnished as they were when occupied by the Davis family. A small Confederate museum with war relics and some of Davis' property is housed in an upstairs room on the northeast corner. Allow 30 minutes. Open Mon.-Fri. 8-4:30, Sat.-Sun. 9-4:30. Closed Easter, Thanksgiving and Dec. 25 and Jan. 1. Donations are accepted. The original site of the house across Bibb Street from the Montgomery Civic Center is now occupied by a Goodyear tire store.

Getting there: 644 Washington at Union. Phone 242-1861.

GOVERNOR'S MANSION is festooned with flags and fronted by a guard house, announcing that *this* handsome, white-pillared mansion on South Perry is the residence of Alabama's governor. Architect Weatherby Carter designed the home for Robert Ligon. It was built circa 1906 when Colonial Revival manors were the rage of the South.

The romantic and ornate exterior suggests a lavish interior, but such is not the case. The most striking feature is a central grand staircase leading from the family's private upper floor to the large foyer used for public receptions. Furnishings from various periods and portraits of past governors can be seen on prior arranged tours of the ground floor.

Legend has it that the niece of Gov. Jim Folsom pointed out the house to him one day and suggested that it was grand enough to be the governor's home, and that, by the way, she'd like to live in it. In 1950, it became the executive residence of Folsom and future governors. Incidentally, Folsom's niece became the second Mrs. George Wallace and she did live here for several years. With the exception of Fob James, all governors since Folsom have lived here. The guardhouse and fence were added by John Patterson during the racial strife of the 1960s. Open Mon.-Fri. 9-4 except holidays. Appointments are recommended. Phone 834-3022. Free.

Getting there: 1142 S. Perry St.

HANK WILLIAMS GRAVE - The father of country music is buried on a hilltop in the Oakwood Cemetery Annex just north of the state Capitol. En route to a show date in Canton, Ohio on Jan. 1, 1953, he died in West Virginia in the back seat of his Cadillac of a heart attack at age 29. Some 25,000 people tried to attend his funeral at the Montgomery City Auditorium. His well-maintained final resting place is often covered with fresh flowers left by fans who make the pilgrimage to Montgomery. His grave, and that of wife, Audrey, is covered with outdoor carpeting. A granite, 10-gallon hat is at the base of Williams' memorial. Cousins of Williams sponsor a musicial memorial service at his grave the Saturday closest to his Sept. 17 birth anniversary.

Getting to the cemetery: Go east on Madison to the State House Inn and turn north on Jackson Street for a block, then right on Upper Wetumpka Road for a half mile. Turn left into the cemetery at the Hank Williams sign.

MURPHY HOUSE, built in 1851 by cotton planter John H. Murphy, is an excellent example of Greek Revival architecture in the heart of downtown Montgomery. It housed Union troops during Reconstruction. Today, it houses city utility offices and visitors are welcome to visit the large drawing room. Allow 10 minutes. Open Mon.-Fri., 8-5. Free.

Getting there: 22 Bibb St. at Coosa St. It's 2 blocks below St. John's and the Madison Hotel.

OLD ALABAMA TOWN covers much of Central Alabama's rich history in an easily manageable walking tour of 3 blocks with 35 buildings restored by the non-profit **Landmarks Foundation of Montgomery**. Four blocks from the Capitol, the "town" depicts rural pioneer life, slave quarters, elegant in-town living by the town's gentry and a cross-section of professions and social activity. Many structures are furnished to illustrate various periods of the state's history and how people lived. More than a dozen are open, with some hosted by costumed interpreters demonstrating 19th-century skills and crafts. The **Ordeman-Shaw House** was built on this site about 1850. Charles Ordeman, a German-born architect and city surveyor, erected the town plantation, its original slave quarters and kitchens. A barn dates from the 1840s. Next door, Ordeman built the one-story Greek Revival cottage, the **Campbell-Holtzclaw House**, to raise capital. The complex is enhanced by gardens planted with trees, period shrubs and vegetables. The Ordeman-Shaw House was the first restoration to be opened by Landmarks in 1971 and served as anchor of the collection originally called the North Hull Street Historic District. Guided tours of Old Alabama Town begin with an audiovisual orientation at **Lucas Tavern** and encompass many of the historic buildings. An optional taped commentary read by Selma author Kathryn Tucker Windham weaves a fictional story linking the structures. Begin your tour in Montgomery's oldest building, the circa 1818 **Lucas Tavern** which previously stood on the old Federal Road at Waugh. The tavern was a landmark stopping place for thousands of Georgia settlers taking the road to the interior of Alabama. In 1825, the tavern hosted one of the first dignitaries on an official visit to the state. The aging **General du Motier LaFayette**, a hero of the American Revolution and a close friend of George Washington, stayed here April 3, 1825, during his week-long tour of the state, part of a nationwide journey which lasted for months. Walk out of the tavern and go east to the two-room country dogtrot home of statesman and orator **William Lowndes Yancey** built about 1850. Continuing east to the next building is the 1875

Grange Hall from Pintlala. Farmers and their families used the hall for town meetings and socials. The building just to the north is a carriage house where a prominent family kept their horse and buggy. Step inside the country doctor's office where period medical equipment and implements are displayed that were used to perform surgery and heal pioneer neighbors.

Walk over to Columbus Street and look around the neighborhood grocery stocked with period canned goods. Just south of the grocery is the shotgun house of Grant and Viney Fitzpatrick, a black family.

Black families such as the Fitzpatricks worshipped in the one-story clapboard **Cleveland Avenue Presbyterian Church** built in 1890. Visit the one-room **Adams Chapel School** used in Barber County from 1898-1948 to see how your grandparents or even great-grandparents might have been educated. Three houses facing Hull are used as private offices and not open for tours.

Cross Columbus to the Haigler House, now home to the **Alabama Center for Traditional Culture**. Visit the small gallery in the first room on the right which showcases state artists. Gallery hours are Mon.-Fri. 9-11 and 2-4. Directly behind is the **Rose-Morris House** where spinners, weavers and dulcimer makers demonstrate their talents weekdays until mid-afternoon.

In the center of the block is an intriguing **Drugstore** museum with pressed-tin ceiling and authentic pharmaceutical equipment. The Alabama Pharmaceutical Association developed the museum, with a 1924 soda fountain to reflect stores of the 1930s-50s. The wall fixtures from Price Drugs in Gordo date from 1903.

A replicated **Gin House** is equipped with an original cotton gin which reflects patents granted to industrialists Daniel Pratt and Robert Munger in the 1880s. It is one of the earliest examples of a plant which could clean, gin and bale cotton in a single operation.

Return to the **Lucas Tavern** gift shop which offers regional crafts, books, souvenirs and Landmarks guided tour tapes. Allow about an hour. Open Mon.-Sat., 9:30-3:30; Sun., 1:30-3:30. Closed Easter, Thanksgiving, Dec. 25 and Jan. 1. Adults, $5; ages 6-18, $2; groups 15+, $4. Write 310 N. Hull St., Montgomery, 36104. Phone 240-4500.

Getting there: Located off the intersection of Madison Avenue (U.S. 31) and Hull Street, 4 blocks from the Capitol.

ST. JOHN'S EPISCOPAL CHURCH is a striking cream-colored Gothic church with towering spire. Completed in 1855, it is Montgomery's oldest Episcopal church. Many political leaders worshiped here when Montgomery was the Confederate capital. Although Jefferson Davis of Mississippi was not an Episcopalian at the time he lived here, he rented a pew in St. John's for members of the family who were. It is 11th from the rear and marked by a well-worn plaque. The other pews in the church have been replaced. The beautiful blue stenciled wooden ceiling painted in 1869 has been preserved in its original glory. Notice the hundreds of needlepoint prayer stools placed throughout the church. Open Mon.-Fri., 8-4; weekends until noon. Free.

Getting there: Located at 113 Madison Ave. and Perry.

TEAGUE HOUSE stands amidst majestic magnolias on what was one of 19th-century Montgomery's finest residential streets. Built for Berry Owens in 1848, the Greek Revival home with Ionic columns was taken over briefly in 1865 by Union soldiers for their divisional headquarters after city officials surrendered Montgomery.

Standing on its porch on April 12, 1865, Wilson read the proclamation that declared the first Confederate capital to be under martial law. The war officially ended three days later, although Wilson's Raiders did not get the word until sometime afterwards.

The Teague family was the last to occupy it as a private residence in 1955. It houses the **Alabama Historical Commission**.

Getting there: Perry Street is one-way, from I-85 North toward downtown. It is on the left at 468 S. Perry St. Phone 242-3184.

THOMPSON MANSION serves as the city's tourist center. The two-story mansion, distinguished by a Corinthian portico, was erected in Tuskegee around 1850 by Judge Thomas S. Tate and was operated after the Civil War as the City Hotel. W.P. Thompson purchased the house in 1880 and once hosted President William McKinley who spoke from the balcony. The house gradually slipped into disuse in the middle of this century, succumbing to the ultimate indignity of a landmark: being vandalized to serve as a Jaycee "haunted house." It was dismantled in 1983 and taken to Georgia for reconstruction. When the owner was unable to complete his plans, he contacted the Montgomery Landmarks Foundation, which teamed with the Kiwanis Club and the City, to reassemble and restore the house at a cost of more than $1 million. The house features exceptional iron work, ornamental plaster, faux graining and marblizing.

Watch the brief tourism video and pick up brochures on the city. Open Mon.-Fri., 8:30-5; Sat.-Sun., 9-4. Closed Thanksgiving, Dec. 25 and Jan. 1. Write 401 Madison Ave., Montgomery, 36104. Phone 262-0013.

Getting there: Corner of Madison and Hull.

UNION STATION anchors the city's impressive collection of restored commercial buildings near the Alabama River. The sprawling Richardsonian terminal designed by B.B. Smith was the state's largest when completed in 1898. It continued to serve as the hub of L & N's Central Alabama travel when the railroads were the dominant mode of transportation into the first third of the 20th century. It was restored by Montgomery shopping mall kingpin Jim Wilson. The Baggage House to the right houses the SouthTrust Bank and the Railway Express Building on the left was restored by the Frazer Lanier Co. The train shed, a National Historic Landmark, is one of only a few long-span, trussed-roof sheds surviving in the U.S.

Montgomery boasts one of the truly unique passenger rail stations in America. The local **Amtrak station** is in a renovated grain silo complex on the north side of the tracks between Commerce and Coosa streets at Riverfront Park. A passenger can begin or continue a rail trip aboard the *Gulf Breeze*, hail a local taxi or step aboard a bus or trolley. The *Breeze* links Birmingham and Mobile and is an extension of the New Orleans to New York *Crescent* run.

Near SouthTrust bank, you'll see a tunnel entrance leading to the 2-acre **Riverfront Park**, an amphitheater which slopes down to the Alabama River, and features picnic areas and playground equipment.

Getting there: Turn onto Commerce and turn left onto Water.

DOWNTOWN WALKING TOUR

Most historic sites of interest to visitors radiate from the newly restored **Capitol**. While you're close, save enough time to walk across the street to get a glimpse of the human side of the South's political leaders at the **White House of the Confederacy**. Then go next door for a look at the military room on the second floor of the **Archives and History** building. All three buildings are free, but the women who maintain the Jefferson Davis home would appreciate a donation. Just a few steps away is the **Civil Rights Memorial** which chronicles landmark events in the movement.

Walk (or drive) down Dexter Avenue to the fountain and look to the right at the **Winter Building**, from which the telegram was sent to Charleston, S.C. to fire on Fort Sumter, starting the Civil War. Over on Monroe St. is the **Episcopal church** where Davis worshipped.

Now, fast forward a century to the beginning of civil rights. In an interesting bit of juxtaposition, **Rosa Parks's** famous bus ride started across the intersection from the building where the telegram was sent from which started the Civil War. No historic marker chronicles her arrest or the boycott. The civil rights struggle crystalized in the **Dexter Avenue Baptist Church** which you can visit. You still haven't spent a dime unless you made a donation at the Confederate White House.

DRIVING LANDMARKS TOUR

The best way to see the historic buildings is to follow the route recommended by the Landmarks Foundation, beginning near **Old Alabama Town**. Sites open to the public are listed in **bold**:

Turn right on Madison Avenue
401 - Tourist information center in **Thompson Mansion**
113 -**St. John's Episcopal Church** where Jefferson Davis worshipped
Follow Madison which angles slightly to become Bibb Street
22 - **Murphy House** used by Union military forces during Civil War

Turn right on Commerce
100, 200 block - Excellent restored Victorian commercial buildings
Montgomery Civic Center on the left hosts concerts, conventions
Riverfront Park where steamboats docked is amphitheater

Turn left on Water Street
300 - Union Station

Turn left on Molton, right on Bibb,
left on Catoma, left on Montgomery
234 - Empire Theater where Rosa Parks was arrested

Turn right on Dexter -
Intersection where Mrs. Parks boarded bus which led to arrest, leading to bus boycott
1 - 1856 bank building houses **State Council on Arts**
2 - Winter Building, site of telegraph office in 1861
300 - **Judicial Building**: new home for Supreme Court
422 - **Alabama Education Association** headquarters
454 - **Dexter Avenue Baptist** where boycott organized

Turn left on Bainbridge in front of State Capitol
State Capitol where Confederate States of America was formed

Go right on Monroe, after 3 blocks, right on Jackson
War Memorial honors Alabamians who have died in armed conflicts

Turn right on Washington Avenue
644 - **First White House of Confederacy** home to Jeff Davis
624 - **Archives and History Museum**
Alabama Center for Commerce - economic development agencies
400 - **Civil Rights Memorial** built by Southern Poverty Law Center

Left on Hull, right on Finley, right on Perry
1142 - 1906 mansion is **Governor's Mansion**
532 - 1850s house is "House of Mayors"
468 - **Teague House** used by Union Army in 1865
466 - Rice-Semple-Haardt House
419 - 1848 Knox Hall contains offices

ATTRACTIONS OUTSIDE DOWNTOWN

ALABAMA SHAKESPEARE FESTIVAL offers classical and contemporary theatrical productions each season. It is world class in every respect, from the superb facilities to its professional company and crew which number more than 200. On entering the grounds past the **Mongtomery Museum of Fine Arts**, you'll be impressed with the mood established by the rolling hills, trees and lakes. The grounds surrounding the theater and the nearby art museum were designed by a royal British landscape architect who recognized similarities between his native England and the Alabama setting, and emphasized those features.

Even before going inside the spectacular building, it is natural to assume that this is a product of taste and money. Construction magnate **Winton Blount** and his wife, **Carolyn**, were responsible. He amassed a fortune here and in the Middle East before he was named Postmaster General by President Richard Nixon. Carolyn Blount convinced her husband to build a $21 million home for the critically acclaimed Shakespeare Festival which had outgrown facilities in Anniston and faced serious financial problems.

The Blounts' gift was the largest single contribution to a theater in American history. Members of the family were involved in every step of the development. The Atlanta architectural firm of son Tom Blount and Perry Pittman was influenced by Shakespearean contemporary Andrea Palladio of Italy. The firm designed the theater on a curve to soften the impact of the massive brick building and to humanize the scale. The Blount family secured permission to replicate a massive sculpture of Shakespeare by John Quincy Adams Ward which stands in New York's Central Park. It is that twin which gazes over the grand lobby toward the entrance doors.

The **Carolyn Blount Theater** has two state-of-the-art theaters. The sharp angle of the seating levels in the 750-seat Festival stage offers a perfect view of the actors from any seat. The more intimate 225-seat **Octagon** showcases productions that can be performed in the round. It can also accommodate thrust stage and proscenium arch productions.

In addition to major guest artists, actors from the finest theatrical schools in America and England tread the boards in the classics and modern plays. They perform a variety of productions, from Shakespeare to Tennessee Williams and Chekhov to Moliere. Offerings have ranged from *Romeo and Juliet* to *Steel Magnolias* and *Julius Caesar* to *Inherit the Wind*.

One of five major Shakespeare companies in the nation, it is the only year-round professional classical repertory theater in the South. Some 400 performances and events a year make the Shakespeare Festival a cultural asset of wide-ranging proportions. Some 200,000-plus people visit annually.

You can charge tickets on Visa, MasterCard or Discover card any day from 10 a.m. to 6 p.m. (Open until 9 during performances.)

Shows are Tues.-Sun., with weekend matinees. Tickets are often available on short notice prior to a performance.

It isn't necessary to have a ticket to a performance to see inside. For information about availability of weekend walking tours of the theater (Sat., Sun., at 11 a.m.), phone by Thursday prior to the weekend you may be visiting. A $3 guide fee is charged. You can even watch open rehearsals for a fee.

The lobby and gift shop are open Tues.-Sun., 10-6. Phone the box office (10-6 or until 9 on performance nights) at 271-5353 or 1-800-841-4273. Major credit cards are accepted.

Getting there: Take I-85 exit 6 to East Boulevard. Go right. At second red light, take a left onto Woodmere and follow the signs..

MONTGOMERY MUSEUM OF FINE ARTS is an architectural companion to the Alabama Shakespeare Festival that is well worth a visit for its collection. A tree-lined drive leads to the imposing brick structure, flanked by a reflecting lake and massive seasonal flowering beds. The lake flows over a small dam to another lake which borders the nearby Shakespeare Festival.

A dome influenced by Thomas Jefferson's Monticello is the focus of the 45,000-square-foot museum. At the far end of the ground floor is the prized art donated by **Winton and Carolyn Blount**. Some 41 paintings and prints by 33 major artists are in the collection which surveys American art from colonial time to the present day. Works by John Singer Sargent, Thomas Sully, John Singleton Copley, Edwin Hooper, Georgia O'Keeffe, William Merritt Chase and Robert Henri are shown. Prints are by Whistler, Thomas Hart Benton and Rockwell Kent. You can rent audio-taped tours on the Blount collection at the gift shop.

Early American decorative arts, including glass, furniture and porcelain are also featured. Open Tues.-Sat., 10-5; Thurs., 10-9; Sun., noon-5. Closed holidays. Free.

Getting there: See directions to the Alabama Shakespeare Festival. Phone 244-5700.

MAXWELL AIR FORCE BASE is the site of the Air University, the Air Force's center of professional military education. **Orville and Wilbur Wright** established the world's first flying school on the site in 1910. Because the weather in Dayton, Ohio, was not suitable for flying, Wilbur came to Alabama that February to find a location for the school. Frank Kohn offered his flat plantation land and the first flight took place on March 26, 1910. For three months, the local people came out to watch student pilots aboard the Wright Flyer. During this time, the first night flight took place. During

World War I, the hangars built by local businessmen for the Wrights were used for repairs. Prior to World War II, Maxwell established **Gunter Air Force Base** for basic flying training for the air corps. Today Maxwell is home to the **Air University** and scores of advanced educational programs for officers. To tour, ask for a map at the Bell or Day street gates. Phone 293-2017.

Getting there: It is located at Day Street and Air Base Boulevard.

MONTGOMERY CIVIC CENTER hosts local events and conventions. The 182,000-square-foot multi-purpose building has a main exhibit hall measuring 200 by 300 feet with a 35-foot ceiling. The building has 20 meeting rooms and can accommodate a seated dinner for 4,000 people. Phone 241-2100.

Getting there: It is between Dexter Avenue and the Alabama River at 300 Bibb St.

MONTGOMERY ZOO is a study of contrasts of the old way to display animals - segregated by species behind chain-link fences - and the new - grouped together by native continent and allowed to graze together without barriers. It is like going from a petting zoo to actually seeing animals in the wild.

To fully appreciate the newer zoo, start with the old portion. At the ticket window, turn right and walk through the aviary for close inspection of a wide variety of birds. Golden eagles are segregated nearby. Children enjoy antics of monkeys and gorillas and get to pet sheep, turkeys and goats. The old zoo has little character and is marked by square fences and concrete sidewalks. Fortunately, it is marked for extinction.

Look toward the banners and soaring rooflines of what is obviously new construction. Walk past the little train station to reach the covered overlook where you can see waterfalls, lions and bison in the same glance. You can see animals roaming in the spacious "realms" of the various continents. Fences of inconspicuous poles separate the "continents," but there are no visual barriers between visitors and the residents. Sloping terrain near the balconies allows zoo guests to look down on the animals as they eat or sun themselves. Surrounding the overlook are Asian tigers, Australian animals, African lions and giraffes and North American sandhill cranes, swans, bison and others.

The best way to see most of the 800 animals is to hop aboard the miniature train named the *McMonty Express*. If visiting on a sunny day, wear a hat or cap because there aren't many trees. Picnic tables are provided and a snack bar serves a wide range of sandwiches and snacks. Allow an hour. Open every day Apr.-Sept., 10-5; Oct.-Mar., 10-4:30. Closed Dec. 25 and Jan. 1. Adults, $3.50; ages 4-12, $1.50; seniors, $2. Phone 240-4900.

Getting there: Follow signs from downtown to Lower Wetumpka Road or circle the city to the Northern Boulevard to exit onto Fairground Road and turn on Vandiver Boulevard. The entrance off the bypass is especially well marked.

F. SCOTT and ZELDA FITZGERALD MUSEUM is housed in a brown, two-story house on Felder Avenue in fashionable Cloverdale where the couple moved in 1931. Like no other couple, their names became synonomous with the jazz age. One of the apartments houses personal artifacts, copies of his Roaring Twenties novels, and letters they exchanged during their courtship and marriage. You can wander through the apartment and read copies of Zelda's letters and see her childhood furniture, family photos, cigarette holder, family photos, old typewriters and some of the paintings she created while Scott wrote.

Fitzgerald was an aspiring 20-year-old writer from Minnesota, and a recent graduate of Princeton, when he was stationed in Montgomery in 1918 at Camp Sheridan. While here, he met and courted Zelda Sayre, the high spirited 17-year-old daughter of an Alabama Supreme Court justice.

In one of her 1919 letters, she wrote, "Darling heart, our fairytale is almost ended, and we're going to marry and live happily every after." After their wedding in St. Patrick's Cathedral in New York on April 3, 1920, they traveled Europe extensively and came to personify the Roaring Twenties through their legendary parties and associations with Hemingway and other ex-patriots. He published a series of successful novels, such as *This Side of Paradise* (1920), *The Beautiful and the Damned* (1921), and *The Great Gatsby* (1925), often drawing on Zelda's personality and her letters for his heroines.

Fitzgerald spent six months in this Montgomery house with Zelda and daughter, Scottie, while he wrote *Tender Is the Night* (1934). He worked in Hollywood for several years as a screenwriter and died an alcoholic of a heart attack at age 44 in 1940. Zelda, diagnosed as a schizophrenic, died eight years later in a fire at a mental hospital in Asheville, N.C. She was 47.

Attorney Julian McPhillips, also a Princeton graduate, rescued the house from demolition when he purchased it in 1986.

The museum is operated by volunteers and supported by donations and membership fees. Open Wed.-Fri., 10-2; Sat.-Sun., 1-5. Allow 30 minutes.

Getting there: Travel Norman Bridge Road to Felder Avenue (just south of Carter Hill Road) and go to 919 Felder Apt. B, on the first floor. Phone 264-4222 during the above listed times to confirm opening hours. Other times, phone 262-1911.

SUGGESTED SIGHTSEEING ITINERARIES

One-day tour: Montgomery Hallmarks

Arrive in Montgomery at mid-morning and tour **Old Alabama Town** on your own. Eat lunch at the **Young House** restaurant. Go back to the Capitol and look for a parking space near the **First White House of the Confederacy**. After touring Jeff Davis' residence, walk next door to the **Archives and History** building and look at treasures of the Moundville Indians. Walk to the **Civil Rights Memorial** and depart in late afternoon.

One-day tour: Garden Scents

Arrive in mid-morning and spend an hour at the **Montgomery Zoo**. Drive up U.S. 231 to tour the large **Southern Homes & Gardens** garden shop. Continue north on 231 for **Jasmine Hill Gardens** and spread a **picnic lunch** on the grounds before touring the statuary-filled gardens. If you have time, go to the 165-acre **Fort Toulouse/Jackson Park**, scene of military garrisons built in 1717 and 1814. Depart in late afternoon.

Two-day/one-night tour: Capital Country

Day 1: Arrive in mid-morning and visit the antebellum **Thompson Mansion**, Montgomery's visitor information center on Madison Avenue. Spend at least an hour walking through the adjacent **Old Alabama Town** and eat lunch here at the **Young House**. Check in at the **Riverfront Inn** on Coosa Street. This afternoon, drive through downtown Montgomery and stop at **St. John's Episcopal Church** on Madison where Jeff Davis worshipped. Find a place to park and take a self-guided tour of the **State**

Capitol. Next, spend a couple of minutes viewing the **Civil Rights Memorial**. Have an early **dinner** in the Old Cloverdale neighborhood at the **Bistro, Kat & Harri's** or **Jubilee Seafood**. Drive out to the **Alabama Shakespeare Festival** to attend a performance on the Festival stage or Octagon theater. Return to the hotel for a comfortable night's sleep.

An evening option is driving out I-85 to exit 22 and enjoying **dinner** while watching **greyhound racing at VictoryLand**.

Day 2: After checking out of the hotel, consider a choice of plans for the rest of your stay:

• Have **breakfast at a Farmers Market Cafe** and follow signs to the **Montgomery Zoo**, stopping by the **Hank Williams' Grave** on Upper Wetumpka Road en route. Have lunch at **Country's Barbecue** on South Boulevard across from the Governors House motel. Afterwards, drive to Mulberry Street off I-85 to sample the many gift and antiques shops, making sure to find the **Unicorn Shop**.

• An alternative morning plan is a trip back to the Shakespeare grounds to tour the **Montgomery Museum of Fine Arts**. While you are in the neighborhood, stop in at the **Bookmonger** in the Waccamaw shopping center just off Woodmere and browse through their rare Alabama books section. Then go back into downtown to eat **lunch at the Sassafras Tea Room** near I-65. If you have time for only one antiques shop in Montgomery, browse the three floors of **antiques at Herron House**, 422 Herron St. between the interstate and downtown. Depart Alabama's Capital City in the afternoon.

SIDE TRIP EAST TO THE GREYHOUNDS

Just 20 minutes east on I-85 is **VictoryLand**, one of America's most successful greyhound tracks. You can dine at one of the state's busiest restaurants and bet on races six nights and several afternoons a week. Close by are **Tuskegee Institute** buildings operated by the National Park Service.

ATTRACTIONS NORTH OF MONTGOMERY

FORT TOULOUSE-JACKSON PARK is a strategic French, Indian and War of 1812 military site being excavated and reconstructed by the Alabama Historical Commission. The peninsula created by the confluence of the Tallapoosa and Coosa rivers was the site of two French forts and one built by American troops.

With the help of friendly Indians and to check British influence, the French built the original Fort Toulouse in 1717 to serve as a trading post on the eastern flank of their Louisiana territory. By 1749, riverbank erosion threatened its safety and a second fort was constructed 100 yards to the south. The 1763 treaty ending the French and Indian war transferred the fort to the British. In 1814, Andrew Jackson came to the site following his victory over the Creek Nation at the Battle of Horseshoe Bend and began a new fort at the site. The Treaty of Fort Jackson negotiated in the new fort ended the Indian threat and opened 20 million acres of land to American settlers.

Today the French fort's walls have been replicated and a portion of the larger American fort has been outlined. Re-enactors present a French colonial "living history" or War of 1812 program the third weekend of each month. Tasks include canoe building, tomahawk throwing and musket firing.

A Tidewater cottage built about 1825 functions as an interpretive center for this National Historic Landmark. Picnickers, history buffs and other nature lovers enjoy the isolation afforded by the open spaces, abundant plantlife and wildlife. Excellent RV campsites, shaded by spreading oaks and dripping with silvery Spanish moss, occupy the north end of the park. A boardwalk arboretum wanders through the forest and river bog where naturelovers can study the flora and fauna.

Below the fort, the Alabama River flows southwest through Montgomery and Selma toward its merger with the Tombigbee north of Mobile. Gate hours: Apr.-Oct., 6-9; Nov.-Mar., 8-5. Closed Dec. 25 and Jan. 1. Admission.

Getting there: From Montgomery, travel U.S. 231 north for 12 miles to the Wetumpka city limits and turn left opposite Wal-Mart. Go 3 miles. Phone 567-3002.

JASMINE HILL was conceived in the 1930s by Benjamin and Mary Fitzpatrick as a private garden on their 17-acre estate to showcase reproductions of famous Greek works of art collected abroad. During 20 visits over 23 summers, the couple imported some 40 pieces for their garden. The statues and fountains usually arrived at the Port of New Orleans and were transported by rail to nearby Wetumpka and pulled up the mountainside by horse and buggy. Now open to the public, a self-guided walking tour is especially appealing during the spring blooming season. The tour begins near the small parking lot and passes copies of such classics as Venus de Milo, Mourning Athena, the Lions of Delos and the Maiden of the Acropolis.

The dominant feature is an exact size copy of what remains of the Temple of Hera, from where the torch was lighted to begin the ancient Olympic games. A lily pond with fish occupies the center of the colonnade formed by the ruins here. A six-foot Winged Victory carved of Carrara marble presides over another reflecting pool. A reservoir the size of a large swimming pool provides water to the intricate series of fountains, pools and ponds.

Be certain to use the detailed map given at the gate to guide your footsteps or you will miss some objects. The map gives background on the original works. Most of the grounds are heavily shaded, so you can tour the gardens comfortably even in the summer. Women should wear flat shoes since there are a number of slight grade level changes. Flagstone walkways connect the various points of interest. Plan to spend about an hour. It is open to the public from the azalea-blooming month of March through September. Open Tues.-Sun. and Mon. holidays, 9-5. Admission.

Getting there: From downtown, go 4 miles north on U.S. 231, turn right on Jasmine Hill Road and follow signs 2 miles. Phone 567-6463 or 263-1440.

SOUTHERN HOMES AND GARDENS is a combination floral, home furnishings, gift, greenhouse, landscaping and nursery center, with a complete Japanese garden and pool. Outdoor lovers traveling U.S. 231 North can be forgiven if they slam on the brakes upon passing this impressive complex for the first time. In addition to a virtual indoor mall of home furnishings, the business offers the state's largest stock of gardening materials and plants and shrubs. Demonstrations, workshops and lectures are scheduled regularly. Seniors receive a special discount on Wednesdays. Open Mon.-Sat., 9-5; Sun., 1-5. Free, except for what you'll be compelled to buy.

Getting there: Exit I-65 at the Northern Bypass and then go north on U.S. 231. To receive the newsletter, phone 277-6746.

SIDE TRIP TO LOWNDESBORO

Lowndesboro is a once prosperous antebellum village which developed near a bend in the Alabama River so planters could ship cotton to market. Planters from Virginia and South Carolina settled here in 1819 to farm the rich land of the Alabama River valley and incorporated in 1832 in honor of William Lowndes. The wealthy farmers built stately homes and fashionable shops along the town's one main road. Dixon Hall Lewis, leader of the state's right wing of the Democratic party, lived here, and was appointed to the U.S. Senate in 1844. The 6-foot, 480-pound orator was so large that chairs had to be especially made for him in both the Legislature and Congress.

The cotton-based economy of the town did not recover after the Civil War. There are a number of churches and at least six significant pre-Civil War houses - three associated with Dixon Hall Lewis - which can be seen in a short drive into Lowndesboro and back. The descriptions are of buildings as they appear on the right side.

Turn off U.S. 80 and look for the **Lewis-Howard House** the politician built in 1840, eight years before his death. Ahead is the circa 1850 **Archibald Tyson-Randolph House**. It is arranged in the shape of an L for cross ventilation and has two major porticos, one with six Doric columns and one with four, prompting the name the Pillars. It is one of several credited to an itinerant English builder named Nunley. Ahead on the right is the **Lewis-Hall-James House**, a smaller dwelling Lewis built about 1835. Just beyond is the Gothic-styled **St. Paul's Episcopal Church** erected in 1857.

Next is the white monumental **Thomas-Meadows-Hagood House** with 13 Doric columns rising to support the bracketed roofline and forming a colonnade across the west and south sides. The Greek Revival house was built in 1853 for George Thomas by the same builder who three years earlier erected the "smaller" Tyson house. After the Civil War, owner Randolph Meadows named it Meadowlawn.

Drive past the aluminum-clad Methodist church to see the handsome 1856 **Presbyterian Church**, also built by Nunley, which features the familiar Doric portico with a square belfry and spire. The circa 1850 **Meadows-Powell House** just past the church is also known as Mockingbird Place.

The next religious landmark is in dire need of saving. The **Old Methodist Church**, built in 1833, features a simple portico crowned with an octagonal belfry. It is topped by the copper-plated dome salvaged from the first State House demolished that year at Cahawba. After the congregation built a larger church, this one was taken over by a black congregation. The CME district council has leased the dilapidated church to a local landmarks group which hopes to restore it.

Another frame church with square tower and steeple stands next to the **Oakview Cemetery** at 1.7 miles from the highway. Turn around and head back toward the highway. A Baptist church founded in 1888 has Victorian trim rarely seen on a religious building. A stately Federal style house built circa 1840 is **Boxwood**. It served as a female academy's president's home. It is distinguished by a double portico with detailed fanlights and sidelights flanking both doors. Down the road is the **Old Homestead**, the home of Francis Lewis, father of the future senator. Lewis built the house in the late 1820's, making it among the oldest residences in the Black Belt. The front was substantially altered late in the 19th century.

Getting there: 19 miles west of Montgomery. Turn north off U.S. 80 at Hwy. 97.

JUST FOR CHILDREN

The **Alabama Science Center** is a hands-on learning center for grades four through nine which uses 47 demonstrations and displays to boost interest in math and science. Youngsters learn about gravity, energy, motion, weather and other scientific principles at sit-down experiment stations. In the "classroom of the future," they use computers, a video wall and other interactive techniques to stimulate their interest. The science center funded by the **Alabama Power Co.** is in the power company's building a couple of blocks from the Capitol. To make an appointment to participate, phone 1-800-252-7753 or 223-5428.

WHERE TO STAY IN MONTGOMERY

Downtown hotels

The Madison Hotel, 120 Madison Ave., is a six-story skylit atrium hotel built in the 1960's as a Downtowner. It is across the street from City Hall and, because it is convenient to the major government offices, hosts a number of meetings. The 189 rooms and seven suites have phones with voice mail and computer dataports. Two restaurants, pool, airport shuttle. Fax 263-3179. Double rate: $58-$67 plus tax. **Phone 1-800-228-5586** or 264-2231.

Riverfront Inn, 200 Coosa St. Built in 1898 as a freight depot for the Western Railway, the U-shaped brick building was remodeled in 1980 as a Sheraton hotel. The loading docks were reconfigured into 130 guest rooms with windows so wide that the drapes don't close, but that's a small price to pay for character. Guest rooms have cable TV and some have kingsize beds. The front of the building, accented with original wooden floors which creak wonderfully when you walk, contains a reception desk, restaurant and meeting rooms. An outdoor pool is located at the opposite end of the courtyard from the lobby. The grill has a weekday buffet. The full service restaurant offers room service. Lounge is open daily. Fax 265-5500. Double rates: $57-$67 plus tax. Honeymoon, ghost and weekend packages are available. **Phone 834-4300.**

Red Bluff Cottage B&B, 551 Clay St. near I-65, is a two-story raised cottage which Anne Waldo and her retired Episcopal rector husband, Mark, have operated as a bed and breakfast since 1987. From a hilltop in the Cottage Hill historic district, the front porch affords an impressive view of the State Capitol and downtown Montgomery as well as the Alabama River.

They designed the house and integrated it so comfortably on the hilltop that it looks to have been here for a century.

The living room is filled with antique Oriental furnishings, accented by a handsome rug which has been in Anne's family for many years. Anne and Mark serve a full breakfast on china and sterling in the dining room each morning.

Guests park in a small courtyard at the rear and have a private ground-level entrance to the four guest rooms furnished with family antiques. Guests may select a queen-sized bed, twins, double or an antique three-quarter bed which belonged to Mark's great-great grandmother. All four rooms have private baths.

After dark, step up into the gazebo in the rear garden for a breathtaking view through the trees of the floodlit Capitol a mile away. Close to I-65 exit 172. Double rate: $55 double plus tax. Special arrangements for children under age 8 necessary. No pets and no smoking. No credit cards.

For reservations, write P.O. Box 1026, Montgomery, 36101. **Phone 263-1727.**

Bypass and interstate hotels

Courtyard by Marriott, 5555 Carmichael Rd., is accessible from I-85 at exit 6. It is a clean, no-frills, businessman's kind of place, with hot coffee in a thermos in the lobby in the morning. The Courtyard offers a restaurant and lounge, swimming pool, whirlpool and exercise room. 146 rooms on three floors. This is one of the few Courtyards which can claim a legitimate presidential suite: George Bush stayed in room 358 in 1992. Double rates $62-$79 plus tax. Fax 279-0853. Weekend packages available. **Phone 272-5533** or 1-800-321-2211.

Governors House, 2705 E. South Boulevard. Even though it is an "older" hotel by some standards, the guest rooms and public spaces of the Governors House are refurbished and kept in good condition for the frequent state conventions held here. A swimming pool in the central courtyard is in the shape of the state of Alabama. 192 guest rooms on three levels, seven parlors and a presidential suite. Amenities include cable TV with HBO and ESPN, room service. Executive section rooms have a king bed, Jacuzzi, refrigerator, in-room coffee maker, newspaper and free local calls. Some parlors have a large color TV, refrigerator and microwave. Fax 288-6472. **Phone 288-2800** or 1-800-334-8459.

Holiday Inn East-Holidome, 1185 East Blvd., convenient to I-85 exit 6, has a cover over the central courtyard and indoor swimming pool, giving it a humid, tropical feeling, which, in the winter, is an asset. The recreation area offers whirlpool spa, sauna, sundeck, game room, fitness center, billiards, Ping Pong and putting green. Savannah's Restaurant is open daily. Deacon Blues lounge has large screen TVs for watching sports. 213 rooms on two floors. Fax 270-0339. Double rate: $65-$73 plus tax. Packages offer golf, B&B, romantic night with champagne with gift basket. **Phone 272-0370.**

Holiday Inn South/Airport, just west of I-65 at 1100 W. South Blvd., is the nicest motel close to the airport and it's still convenient to other parts of Montgomery. The motel is 3 miles from downtown attractions and 3 miles from a mall. Guest rooms have TVs and in-room movies. The motel has a swimming pool, lounge and restaurant. 150 rooms on four floors. Double rate: $52-$58 plus tax. Honeymoon and Great Rate packages. **Phone 1-800-465-4329** or 281-1660.

Outlying lodgings

Colonel's Rest at East Folk Farm is a departure from traditional bed and breakfast concepts and evolved from the "empty nesting" experience of Jane and Jim Watson.

After they built a home a decade ago on a 80-acre farm east of Arrowhead Country Club, they attached four apartments near a screened-in pool to accommodate visits from their six grown children. When the apartments became underutilized, Jim suggested opening a bed and breakfast, which they did in 1986. So many travelers have enjoyed the friendly arrangement that the Watsons added three cabins just a few steps from the house.

The Watsons invite guests into their own large brick and wood combination kitchen and dining room for breakfast served beneath a brass chandelier. The retired colonel's culinary talents prompted them to transform a motor home garage into a place to cook for friends. The success mushroomed and required an expansion which has evolved into the Carriage House restaurant.

The $48 double rate for apartments with a private bath and kitchenette, includes fellowship with other guests, swimming, fishing and even use of the family media room.

East Fork Farm is a couple of miles from I-85 exit 11. Write 11091 Atlanta Hwy., Montgomery, 36117. **Phone 279-0380.**

Holiday Inn Prattville, I-65 exit 179, has 130 rooms on two levels off an attractive lobby. Guest rooms have cable TV and are near an outdoor pool. A restaurant serves three meals. Airport shuttle. Lounge. The motel is 7 miles from Montgomery. Double rate: $49 plus tax. Write Box A, Millbrook, 36054. **Phone 285-3420.**

WHERE TO EAT

A dining-entertainment area in Old Cloverdale at the intersection of Fairview and Woodley Road contains several of the best dining options in Montgomery as well as places to socialize and party. You can eat at **Kat & Harri's,** as well as at **The Bistro,** Montgomery's best restaurant, and the **Jubilee Seafood,** all owned by the original Harri, Harriet Crommelin. **Sinclair's** is nearby.

****The Bistro** - *Montgomery's finest restaurant*
1059 Woodley Road. Phone 269-1600
Open Mon.-Sat. 5:30-10 p.m.

The Bistro is a white-tablecloth, fine dining restaurant recommended for any special occasion. The sophisticated decor, accented by handsomely framed paintings lighted with sconces, signals that the expectations of the food and service should be high. Fortunately, the kitchen and wait staff deliver. Reservation recommended on weekends.

Owner Harriet Crommelin and the chef change the menus on a daily basis depending on the availability of fish and white meat. Attire is dressy casual.

Sample summer menu - **The Bistro**
Appetizers
Fish chowder $3.95
Terrine of rabbit with Cumberland sauce $5.25
Carpaccio of center cut sirloin with two sauces $7.25
Bistro smoked salmon with mustard sauce $7.95
Grilled marinated lamp chop with currant glaze and saffron orzo $6.50
Chilton County peaches with parma prosciutto $7.50
Salads
Caesar salad $3.50
Field salad with lemon/garlic vinaigrette and goat cheese $3.75
Fresh buffalo mozzarella with tomatoes and basil vinaigrette $5.25
Entrees
Grilled tuna with a ragout of kidney, azuki and white beans $16.50
Grilled king salmon with maple dijon glaze and pickled red onions $16
Roasted amberjack filet on a bed of oyster stew $16
Red-curried oysters, spinach and watercress cream $14
Sauteed blue prawns with cheese ravioli and tomato basil cream $15.50
Grilled center cut filet of beef with truffle butter $18

Braised lamb loin on white beans, tomatoes and rosemary sauce $16.50
Roasted tenderloin of pork with marsala and thyme $15
Bistro vegetarian sampler $9.50
Desserts
Key lime pie $4
Peanut butter cream cheese pie $4.25
Chocolate cheesecake $4.25
Sinful brownie fudge piece with The Works $3.75
Bread pudding souffle $4.25
New York style cheesecake $4.25

**Country's Barbecue - *Good Central Alabama barbecue*
Southern Bypass. Phone 284-1411
Mon.-Thurs., 11 a.m.-9 p.m.; Fri.-Sat., 11-10
　　Country's is a popular, brightly lit family-style restaurant with weathered barn siding decorated with old metal advertising signs. Excellent barbecue is served sliced or chopped with a choice of sauce hot, mild or medium. Sandwiches come with slaw. Ribs, turkey and chicken are other favorites. An amazing number of Southern side orders are available: Brunswick stew, baker sweet taters, field peas, cabbage, sliced tomatoes, butter beans and fried okra. Order to-go items just inside the front door. Larry Powell owns the Country's across from Krystal and the Governors House and two others in Montgomery, on Zelda Road and the Atlanta Highway. Phone 284-1411.

*Farmers Market Cafes - *Country cooking all over town*
Three locations. Phone 262-9163.
Breakfast and lunch
　　The Farmers Market Cafes are honest-to-goodness market/restaurants where Montgomery's political elite eat hearty breakfasts and cafeteria-style lunches side by side with average Joes. The good selection of meats and a wide variety of fresh vegetables at a low price make lunch a great value. Fried chicken, barbecue sandwiches, fried catfish and flounder are favorites. The average check is $2.50 for breakfast and $5 for lunch.
　　The business is a Norton family affair, with the parents and children looking after three locations. The 315 N. McDonough St. at Columbus location had been popular for a number of years when Phil and JoAnn Norton bought the location near the Garrett Coliseum from Cecil Tucker in 1985 and constructed a new building as part of the Department of Agriculture's new farmers market complex. They opened it as the State Market Cafe the next year. Several years later they expanded to the site of the old Beverly Restaurant at 1250 Air Base Boulevard. All three are open Mon.-Fri. with the Federal Drive cafe open weekends, too. No credit cards.

**The Great Wall - *Fine Chinese food*
3000A Zelda Road. Phone 244-8888
Mon.-Thurs., 11-2:30, 5-9:30; Fri.-Sat., until 10:30; Sun. until 8:30
　　The Great Wall serves very good Chinese food in an upscale shopping center. The food and service are matched by the authentic bright decor and atmosphere. Exit I-85 at Ann St., turn left on Zelda and go a mile.

**The Green Lantern - *Order steaks and the cheese biscuits*
Troy Highway (U.S. 231). Phone 288-9947
Open nightly except Sunday for dinner from 5-10 p.m.
        The Green Lantern has been a city fixture since 1933, and in this location since 1966. Dewey Davis's original Carter Hill roadhouse was so famous that the bank and post office built on the old site were named the Green Lantern branches. Current owner Paul Savelis's huge 32-ounce steaks for two and open biscuits with melting cheese are recommended. Dinners range from $7-$15. If you have trouble reading menus, bring your glasses because it's very dark inside. The waitresses have been here for years, so they'll help. It's 3 miles south of the Bypass.

**Jubilee Seafood - *Seafood in friendly surroundings*
1057 Woodley Road. Phone 262-6224
Tues.-Sat., 5-10 p.m.
        Jubilee serves such great shrimp, crab, oysters, snapper and other fish that you half expect to hear the waves breaking on the beach. Take your pick: boiled, fried, blackened and so forth. Regardless of what you order, it should be great. The atmosphere is collegiate casual. It is an excellent alternative if you can't get in The Bistro next door.

*Martha's Place - *Soul food without regard to color*
458 Sayre St. Phone 263-9135
Mon.-Fri.,11 a.m.-3 p.m.
        Martha Hawkins serves excellent traditional Southern cooking which attracts many whites and blacks to a black neighborhood near downtown. The hearty fare includes fried chicken, black-eyed peas, rice, sweet potato yams, steak and gravy and turnip greens cooked with ham. Naturally, she puts corn bread and ice tea with lunch, the only meal served. Phone 263-9135.

***Sahara - *A part of Montgomery's tradition*
Norman Bridge at 511 E. Edgemont. Phone 264-9178
Mon.-Sat., 11 a.m.-10 p.m.
        The Sahara has been a staple south of downtown for four decades while trendier restaurants have come and gone. The menu offers a broad selection from seafood and steaks to lamb. It is among the best places to lunch in Montgomery.

*Sassafras - *Tea room with a view*
532 Clay St. on Cottage Hill.
Phone 265-7277 for hours.
        Jim and Mary Wallace serve delightful luncheon meals in a meticulously restored Queen Anne house with views overlooking the Alabama River. A Michigan carpenter named Mills built the house about 1888. Enjoy a tour of the more formal rooms on the front and then ask to be seated in the back room with the rows of windows overlooking the river. The crunchy chicken salad, vegetable plate and quiche are recommended. The Wallaces live upstairs.

**Sinclair's - *Casual fare in Old Cloverdale*
1051 E. Fairview Ave. Phone 834-7462
Mon.-Thurs., 11 a.m.-midnight; Fri.-Sat., 11-2 a.m., Sun., 11-3 p.m.

Bill Flippo's latest restaurant serves char-grilled chicken salad, homemade soups, burgers and fresh seafood. Mama Nina's spaghetti pie is extra special. Lunches average $4.50-$8 and dinners $5-$17. The name? It's in a former service station just steps away from Kat 'n Harri's.

***Vintage Year** - *Great Italian food*
405 Cloverdale Road. Phone 264-8463
Open Tues.-Sat., 6- 9 p.m. or later
The Vintage Year is the right place if you are looking for an intimate, upscale restaurant to splurge. Fabric-covered walls which suggest a tent setting provide the right mood for good Italian food and unobtrusive service. You can eat in the dark bar or the main dining room. Appetizers include Sauteed eggplant baked with bacon, tomato and marinara sauce ($4.25) and entrees range from Mozzarella pizza with parmesan, provolone, sausages and spinach ($11) to grilled salmon in lemon butter or tomatoes, capers, garlic ($15) and beef tenderloin filet in Bearnaise butter or sundried tomato butter ($18).

Young House Restaurant - *A fine lunch place*
231 N. Hull St. in Old Alabama Town. Phone 262-0409
Mon.-Fri., 11 a.m.-2 p.m.
Young House is the ideal place to stop for lunch while touring downtown Montgomery. Set in a handsome, high-ceilinged Greek Revival cottage which dates from the 1820's, the Young House features true Southern cuisine. The luncheon specials, salads and desserts are prepared under the care of Chef Bo Judkins, who retired after 30 years at Montgomery Country Club. Other signature dishes are the bread pudding dessert smoothered in a whiskey-honey sauce, seafood gumbo and chicken pot pie.

The surroundings are a real bonus, especially if you've been going in and out of historic structures all morning. This is the one place where hospitality, antique furniture, architecture and Southern manners come together under one roof. If you've got a large group, reserve the room downstairs which overlooks the enclosed patio and fountain. Lunch only.

WHERE TO GATHER

Kat & Harri's, 1061 Woodley Road, hosts the bureaucrats, lobbyists, lawyers and, occasionally, legislators for the nightly exchange of government gossip. One prominent patron was such a regular that, as a 50th birthday gift, he was presented with his own bar stool, engraved plaque attached, and equipped with a seat belt! Be sure to try the wood oven baked pizza. Kat & Harri's is a suitable warmup prior to splurging next door at The Bistro. Seven days and nights, including Sunday champagne brunch. Phone 834-2500.

T.P. Crockmeier's, 5620 Calmar Dr., has a good bar, friendly staff, happy hours and entertainment on several nights. Closed Monday. Phone 277-1840.

WHERE TO SHOP

Eastdale Mall, at the intersection of U.S. 231 and U.S. 80 business route, offers a **Gayfers, Sears** and more than 90 other stores and restaurants. **Montgomery Mall**, at the intersection of U.S. 231 and U.S. 82 on South Boulevard, offers 100 stores including **Gayfers, Parisian,** and **JC Penney.**

Antiques: Herron House Antiques located at 422 Herron St., (inbound from I-65 toward downtown), has three floors of imported furniture, silver, crystal, accessories, rugs and paintings. Phone 265-2063.

Montgomery has a convenient "antiques district" on Mulberry Avenue across I-85 from Jackson Hospital. From downtown, go south on Decatur, left on Carter Hill Road and left to Mulberry. Coming into town on I-85, exit on Forrest, turn left at the school and right on Mulberry. **The Unicorn Shop** at 1926 Mulberry carries an excellent quality of merchandise at reasonable prices. Open Mon.-Fri. till 4:30 and Sat. till 1:30. Check out other affordable antiques and gift shops on the street.

The best steaks in Alabama are sold at **Penny Profit Store,** a small neighborhood grocery just south of I-85 which has been at 837 S. Hull St. for 55 years. Each hand-cut filet, sirloin strip and ribeye is covered with a secret recipe of a dry marinade refered to locally as charcoal. That seasoning is not available as a separate item, but "Mis' Rubins Seasoning" is available in White Magic and a spicy red cajun seasoning. Available in half-pint, pint and quart jars. Phone 264-0229.

Check out the **Montgomery Curb Market** in the 1000 block of Madison for produce fresh from the farm.

MONTGOMERY'S CULTURAL ACTIVITIES

A professional ballet company and a first-class symphony join with the **Montgomery Museum of Fine Arts** to offer a wide range of cultural events and venues to capital city residents and visitors. Established in the late 1950's, the **Montgomery Ballet** tours the state and region with a varied repertoire before some 20,000 adults and 15,000 students annually. The ballet is composed of professionals and apprentices. The **Montgomery Symphony** is a professionally managed and directed volunteer community orchestra with an annual attendance of more than 23,000 persons. The 60 musicians perform many concerts each season, including several in a subscription series.

The **Montgomery Art Guild,** with more than 250 members, promotes traditional, contemporary and abstract art through shows at the Montgomery Museum of Fine Arts, Auburn University at Montgomery, South Alabama State Fair and First Alabama Bank at 8 Commerce St.

Montgomery is home to the state's only art cinema house, the **Capri Theater** at 1045 Fairview Ave. Since 1983, a non-profit film society has shown foreign and sometimes controversial domestic films which are otherwise avoided by regular theaters. Phone 262-4858 for the current feature.

For information on current activities, pick up a copy of *Ticket,* an entertainment tabloid published each Friday in *The Montgomery Advertiser* or look for M.P. Wilkerson's byline in the daily newspapers. World traveler Starr Smith devotes a page each Sunday to domestic and international destinations.

Montgomery! magazine, published monthly, includes a detailed calendar in the center of each issue. It includes calendar items from the **Chamber of Commerce** (phone 240-9457), the **Arts Council** (phone 241-ARTS) and the magazine. The magazine also lists out-of-town events.

CRAFTS

Mose Tolliver, one of America's most highly regarded self-taught artists, is the state's most prolific folk artist. His bold, red watermelons and prehistoric animals have made the pop culture leap from plywood paintings to being reproduced on t-shirts sold by Parisian stores.

Because of a work-related injury and a period of depression which followed, he was encouraged to paint as a form of rehabilitation. Using left-over house paint, he depicted plants and birds on old furniture, Masonite and scraps of plywood. His work was brought to the attention of Smithsonian curators who included his paintings in an exhibition of folk artists in 1976. In 1982, his work was part of a folk art show at the Cocoran Gallery in Washington.

Working in his bedroom, Tolliver sits on the side of the bed next to a gas heater and often applies the same color of latex house paint to several paintings at a time. Because local people buy heavily at Christmas, he often paints past midnight to complete 20 a day.

Mose is usually glad to talk with visitors. Relatives sit and drink while he paints. They usually ignore the customers who walk around them to get a closer look at the paintings which hang by beer tabs on nails.

Subjects range from stick figures with round faces and long noses to strange animals and threatening birds. He spans an even broader spectrum, from a black Christ on the cross to women with legs spread apart giving birth.

Mose T's signature appears as MOSE T with a backwards "S". Paintings are priced by size. Because he uses scraps of often irregularly shaped plywood, sizes are far from standard. At the low end, 8-inch triangular watermelons or birds go for $30. Paintings measuring approximately 2 feet square are $150-$200. Depending on his mood, prices may be negotiable. From the Montgomery Civic Center, go up Catoma to Sayre. His two-story house past Martha's restaurant is at the far end of the 400 block.

Two Prattville families just off I-65 exit 186 practice their families' craft heritages. One family has been forming bowls from Alabama clay for eight generations while the great-grandson of a blacksmith uses that trade to produce graceful works of art.

As far back at least as 1831, Boggs family members have been creating utilitarian pots. Grandfather **Horatio Boggs** purchased an old brick kiln in 1961 because of a large supply of the good quality clay and moved his **Boggs Pottery** operation there.

Now son and grandson **Wayne Sr.** and **Wayne Jr.** produce a wide range of ornamental gardenware at the lowest prices in the state. The rows and rows of chalk white pots, planters, bunnies, lions, statues of the Four Seasons and a seemingly endless variety of unglazed gardenware are displayed in front of the kiln on U.S. 31. Three-foot-tall statues sell for as little as $25 while a 5-foot empress on a base is less than $200. Huge decorative planters sell for less than a fraction of garden shops' retail prices.

Leave I-65 at exit 186 (Prattville/Pine Level) and go west one mile up the hill past the Ramada to the intersection of County 85. It's on the right. This is where you turn to reach **Charlie Lucas**, the Tin Man. Drive straight for a mile and stop at the sign where 85 turns left, but continue straight on 82 for 1.4 miles and look for the Tin Man sign on the house on the right. Lucas's shop and menagerie are on the left.

When **Lucas** hurt his back in 1985 while doing construction work, he turned to blacksmithing - the trade of his great-grandfather.

He turns scrap metal into life-size horses, faces and three-dimensional paintings which critics say recall the art of West Africa. He has fabricated a collection of creatures you can see across the road from his home. For large objects, he uses lengths of flimsy, 2-inch-wide wrapping metal which is normally used in bands to secure wooden crates containing large cargo. Lucas literally wraps metal frames of objects in the dark strips. Although best known for recycling old tractor seats, bicycle wheels and farm tools into objects of abstract art for thousands of dollars, he also twists thin gauge wire into shapes of horses and other objects beginning at $400 a copy. His acrylic paintings also start at $400.

ANNUAL EVENTS

February or March
Zoo Weekend - A weekend of fun at the Montgomery Zoo on Vandiver Boulevard, held annually since 1976, features art, crafts, games and animals shows. Phone 240-4900.

Spring Break Week
Southeastern Livestock Exposition - Garrett Coliseum - Performances of the World Championship Professional Rodeo features the top cowboys and cowgirls in the nation. More than 500 contestants and 1,000 animals are entered. Other events include registered quarter horse shows, purebred cattle shows and sale, the 4H-FFA state steer show and the state rodeo queen contest. The annual event began in 1958. Phone 265-4011.

Second weekend of April – Fort Deposit
Calico Fort Arts and Crafts Fair - Calico Fort Compound - The outdoor event draws some 250 exhibitors from many states to display art in a variety of media. Held annually south of Montgomery and west of I-65 since 1972. Phone 227-44ll.

Memorial Day weekend
Jubilee - Civic Center and Riverfront - The event includes concerts, military displays, a boat regatta, parade and fireworks along Commerce Street.
    To get a special glimpse of rural life, attend the **Alabama Folklife Festival** at Old Alabama Town which gathers music, crafts, foods and stories for a celebration of Alabama folk tradition. Craftspeople demonstrate how music, oral and occupational traditions shaped life in Alabama's Piney Wood, Black Belt, Gulf Coast and Appalachian regions.
    Alabama's finest quilters, basket-weavers, potters, caners, wood-carvers and saddle-makers engage in their chosen crafts with a lot of love and expertise. The festival also offers an assortment of Southern food. Sample Poarch Indian roast corn, local barbecue, and Martha's restaurant's sweet potato pie. Phone 240-4500 or 242-4076.

Third or fourth weekend in September
Alabama Highland Games - Wynton Blount Cultural Park - Scottish culture comes alive with a tartan parade, pipe and drumming, border collie herding demonstration, Highland Fling dancing, athletics, food and crafts. Phone 272-2174 or 252-7548.

First Saturday of November
Pike Road Arts and Crafts Fair - Marks House, Pike Road - An 1825 house becomes the focal point of a country fair with many exhibitors selling hand-made wood carvings, quilts, stained glass, Christmas wreaths and gift items. Food, antiques, hay rides, children's games and a large flea market add a family flavor to this event. It began in 1967 when Geraldine Page starred in a TV movie of a Truman Capote story filmed at the house. Hours 10 a.m.-4 p.m. Go 12 miles south on U.S. 231 and turn left at the Pike Road sign. Phone 277-9989.

Christmas Day
Blue-Gray All-Star Classic - Cramton Bowl - A post-season collegiate football game sponsored by Kelly Tire and the **Montgomery Lions Club** pits all-stars from the North against those from the South. Famous players who have participated in this, one of the nation's oldest charity games, are Bart Starr, Fran Tarkenton, Terry Beasley, John Cain and Tommy Kramer. The Blue-Gray draws top pro scouts and a national television audience. The Lions Club donates the proceeds to assist children through sight conservation programs, an eye surgery center and camps for deserving youth. The 24,400-seat stadium on Madison Avenue behind the Capitol was built in 1922. Phone 265-1265.

OZARK

This Wiregrass region community is closely associated with **Fort Rucker**, home of the U.S. Army Aviation Center and School, the world's largest helicopter training center. Rucker spreads over 64,349 acres in two counties and provides training to pilots of other nations as well as the U.S. Air Force.

The area was settled around 1820 by Allen Cooley from South Carolina. Place names like Merricks and Woodshop were used before the name Ozark stuck. Some say a traveler likened the place to the foothill mountains of Arkansas, hence the name Ozark.

Cotton was the major crop in the 19th century. As in other South Alabama counties in the early 1900s, Dale County's crops were devastated by the Mexican boll weevil. Farmers abandoned cotton and discovered the soil would produce peanuts, corn, and timber, which provide the basis of present industries of textile production and peanut, timber and pulpwood processing.

Fort Rucker occupies land which the federal government initially set aside for a wildlife sanctuary in 1935. President Franklin Roosevelt promoted a Depression-era plan to buy unsuccessful farms operating on submarginal land and give farmers an opportunity to purchase better land upon which to resettle. Some 35,000 acres were voluntarily sold to the government in 1938 and, by 1940, farmers were resettled and their houses were torn down. When the threat of a major war in Europe surfaced, the property was selected for an army post which became a reality in 1942.

Fort Rucker straddles the Dale and Coffee county line and is sandwiched between several towns: Ozark to the east, Daleville to the south and Enterprise on the west.

When the Army consolidated all aviation flight training here in 1973, the post became the mecca for Army aviators. In addition, Air Force aviators have been trained as helicopter pilots here since 1971. The training spectrum from initial entry rotary wing courses to advanced courses in aviation safety is spanned. Servicemen from more than 60 countries have learned to fly helicopters in the skies over Ozark.

Fort Rucker supports a total daytime population of more than 20,000, including 8,000 military personnel, 7,000 civilian and contractor employees and thousands of military family members.

Tour the **Army Aviation Museum** to understand the contribution that Fort Rucker has made to the national defense. Then, take a few minutes to ride around and get the feel of a real Army post. A drive past the large motor pools and helicopter repair buildings reveals the magnitude of Rucker's activities.

WHERE TO STAY

Ozark Holiday Inn at the intersection of U.S. 231 and Hwy. 249 (to Fort Rucker) is an attractive, comfortable two-story motel with restaurant off the lobby and an attached lounge with a large bar and pool tables. A fenced outdoor pool is landscaped. The motel hosts many military personnel on temporary duty. Turn east here on Hwy. 105 to downtown or west on Hwy. 249 to Fort Rucker four miles away. The museum is 10 miles. 151 U.S. 231 N. **Phone 774-7300.**

The historic **Steagall House** is a bed and breakfast on E. Broad Street operated by Rod and Lynn Marchant.

ATTRACTIONS

ARMY AVIATION MUSEUM houses the largest helicopter exhibit in the world in its extensive collection of more than 100 Army aircraft. Thousands of American helicopter pilots learned to fly rotary-wing crafts over the pine forests of Fort Rucker.

Whether or not you are a pilot, you will enjoy walking among the more than 40 aircraft on display. The bright and airy aircraft gallery on the main floor of the 87,000-square foot museum showcases the best of the museum's massive aircraft collection. Helicopters are everywhere in various contexts: one medical copter with emergency personnel aboard to airlift a wounded Vietnam War pilot, a side-by-side scene recreating the use of the J-3 Cub in the 1941 Louisiana Maneuvers, and the AH-64 Apache in the Desert Storm of 1991. On display are aircraft ranging from the R-4, the Army's first helicopter, to the prototype of the current AH-64 Apache attack helicopter.

The presidential helicopter used by Dwight Eisenhower is also in the collection. Many of the aircraft are displayed on a changing basis. The museum has a replica of the first military plane purchased - the Wright Flyer B model. The first Army aviators were taught by the Wright Brothers.

The second floor contains exhibits which interpret the history of Army aviation, •which began with the Balloon Corps in the Civil War. Experimental aircraft used to develop the rotary wing flight are also located on the top floor. In addition, paintings and a chronology of uniforms worn by Army aviators from World War I to the present are displayed.

Exhibits upstairs encourage visitor interaction. Step over to the cockpit mockups against the walls. You can even slip inside one, but not the more famous, the Link trainer, the *Blue Canoe*.

The airy and spacious museum is the result of a 20-year campaign by the Army Aviation Museum Foundation to establish a suitable home for the world's largest helicopter collection. After raising $2.5 million, which was matched through the leadership of U.S. Rep. Bill Dickinson, the museum opened in 1990. Even though the museum owns more than 120 aircraft, it still can't display them all at once, which means you'll have to come back to see the balance: such as a TOW-equipped Huey, a XV-3 tilt roter and the Ryan vertiplane.

Annual attendance is more than 150,000. Allow an hour. Open seven days a week, 9-4. Closed Thanksgiving Day, Dec. 24 and 25, 31 and Jan. 1. Free. Phone 255-4443.

Getting there: Located west of Dothan near Daleville off U.S. 84, just east of Enterprise. From Montgomery, travel U.S. 231 to Ozark and turn right on 249 and go to Novosel. Follow the signs.

CLAYBANK CHURCH, a log church erected about 1852, is one of the oldest buildings in the area. It replaced one built in 1829 by pioneer preacher Rev. Dempsey Dowling. Even though Claybank is one of only a few log churches left in the state, it is not normally open to the public.

Getting there: It is on Hwy. 249 toward Fort Rucker, less than a mile southwest from U.S. 231. Turn west near the Holiday Inn and turn right at a farmers' market on Hwy. 249 toward Fort Rucker into the drive that leads into a cemetery. The church is at the end of the driveway.

ANNUAL EVENTS

Last September
Claybank Jamboree - Ozark Square and Maindale Plaza - The week-long festivities include an art and antique show, fiddlers convention and a 5K fun run. The celebration concludes with an arts and crafts sale the first Saturday in October. Phone 774-9321.

December
Ariton Christmas Lights - Tire dealer Max Hughes turns his hometown north of Ozark into a 2-mile Christmas City with scores of outdoor displays, animated carol scenes, holiday houses and more, outlined with more than 500,000 Christmas lights. It takes his family a couple of months to erect the decorations in time to be ready by Thanksgiving. An estimated 350,000 people drive through the town before the lights go off Jan. 1. From the Troy Hwy. (U.S. 231), go east on Hwy. 51 for 4 miles to reach Ariton. Follow the traffic.

PHENIX CITY

Phenix City has a long and eventful past which includes being a site for several forts during pioneer days. Northern soldiers burned the town of Girard on April 16, 1865, and it rose like the fable phenix. The town gained a reputation in the 1950s for gambling. Today, thanks to the Jaycees and the 8,600-seat Municipal Stadium, Phenix City is best known for hosting the **Amos Alonzo Stagg Bowl** each December to determine the NCAA Division III football championship.

Phenix City, just across the Chattahoochee River from Columbus, Ga., observes Eastern Time.

POINTS OF INTEREST

FORT MITCHELL was an important outpost for white men on the Chattahoochee River during the Creek Indian War of 1813-14. It was built by the Georgia militia on the main Indian trade route to the Tombigbee River, and abandoned in 1819. Another fort was erected about 1825. During the period of Indian removal in 1833, a census counted 8,065 Indians living along the river. U.S. trooops left in 1837. Now a National Historic Landmark, the Fort Mitchell area consists of the archaeological remains of the palisaded military forts, the Creek Indian Agency (1821-32), the Thomas Crowell Tavern (c. 1825), two historic cemeteries and the 1811 Federal Road.

In memory of the culture of these Upper Creeks, an outdoor museum is planned. It will consist of a symbolic spring emerging from the top of a large earthen platform. The site is near Hwy. 165 south of Phenix City.

JOHN GODWIN'S GRAVE - Ex-slave Horace King erected a 10-foot shaft and pedestal over the grave of his former master, a bridge builder. King placed the marker in "lasting remembrance of the love and gratitude felt for a lost friend and master." King, who is credited with building the State Capitol staircases, became an affulent businessman and provided a pension for his ex-master's widow. The cemetery is southwest of the intersection of U.S. 431 and 80.

ANNUAL EVENT

Labor Day

Seale Courthouse County Fair - Seale - Booths selling food and crafts attract thousands to generate funds to support the 1868 Old Seale Courthouse. The Greek Revival building with four Doric columns, which houses a room of Indian artifacts, is open other times by appointment. Phone 298-3639.

WHERE TO EAT

***Chicken Comer's Barbecue, 1222 10th Ave., serves perfect barbecue in the perfect barbecue setting. First, it isn't easy to find and caters primarily to locals; second, it is a joint in the sense that there's no pretention about decor; and third, they serve just great barbecue with white loaf bread on paper plates with plenty of napkins to wipe the yellow mustard sauce off your chin.

Many years ago, a black butcher named Anderson "Chicken" Comer decided to open a barbecue joint and called it Chicken Comer's. His niece, Mary Ann Screws, started working for him in the 10th grade. When Comer died, his cook took over, renamed it Cromwell's Barbecue and ran it until she retired in 1985. That's when Mary Ann decided to run it under her uncle's name.

Just like Dreamland's pre-eminence for ribs on the other side of the state, Chicken Comer's a real barbecue experience. You won't find a better barbecue-plate meal in Alabama.

Comer's is tucked back in a neighborhood of rental houses. Turn off 13th Street onto 10th. Closed Sun. Phone 297-9889.

SELMA

- **Claim to fame:** Antebellum houses, civil rights
- **Don't miss:** Sturdivant Hall, Live Oak Cemetery
- **Eat at:** Tally Ho, Major Grumbles, White-Force Cottage
- **Where to stay:** Best Western, Grace Hall B&B
- **Best events:** Spring pilgrimage, battle re-enactment
- **Tourist information:** Edie Morthland Jones, Executive Director; **Selma/Dallas County Chamber of Commerce**, 513 Lauderdale St., P.O. Drawer D, Selma, 36702. Fax 875-7241. Phone toll-free in-state 1-800-628-4291 or 875-7241.

A short time after Selma received a black eye over racial conflicts in 1965, civic leaders decided a bold effort was needed to restore its reputation for Southern hospitality. They planned an elaborate program to "kidnap" a family passing through town and shower them with good will and kindness.

When the day arrived, a selection committee watched traffic passing through on U.S. 80 and spotted a handsome couple in a nice car and pounced with an invitation to be the town's guests for a couple of days. Startled, they discussed the matter for a few minutes and then willingly agreed.

They were graciously wined and dined and given the red carpet treatment in the antebellum town. Merchants even waived the customary glance at identification when the couple decided to purchase more than a few items in local stores.

Soon, the couple happily resumed their trip and the townspeople basked in the glow of knowing they had changed at least one couple's impression of Selma. It wasn't long, however, before those checks started bouncing higher than the clock on the Presbyterian church.

A belated background check on Selma's waylaid guests revealed that not only was the couple not married, but the car was stolen and the man had just escaped from prison!

The red-faced committee vowed to return to conventional methods to revive the town's reputation. Although the name Selma is irrevokably linked to the trauma of civil rights, both white and black communities have forged an alliance to showcase the stories of Selma, pleasant and otherwise, to all who visit, whether highjacked or voluntary.

If you are interested in finding a city which has maintained the character, style and even accent of the Old South, look no further. Selma is the most feminine and romantic of Alabama's cotton-rich Black Belt towns. During its heyday of the 1850s, Dallas County ranked first in slave ownership and wealth among Alabama's counties. As founder **William Rufus King** hoped, it became the Queen City of the western Black Belt, that rich agricultural region stretching 300 miles across Central Alabama and into adjoining states. Residents constructed grand mansions which reflected their wealth and status.

Meanwhile, King was elected vice president of the United States in 1853. Unfortunately, ill health claimed his life shortly after he took the oath of office.

Following the election of Abraham Lincoln and the outbreak of the Civil War, Selma's location deep within the Confederacy and its river and rail connections made it ideal for operating a major supply depot to produce cannons and other munitions. It became second only to Richmond in importance to the South's war efforts. The

Selma Ordnance Works manufactured one of the most powerful muzzle-loading cannons ever built, as well as several ironclad ships. Late in the war, the destruction of Selma's foundry, powder mill and navy yard became a major strategic objective of the Union army.

Some 9,000 Union soldiers burned the University at Tuscaloosa, then blazed through Montevallo to target Selma. After torching furnaces at Tannehill near present-day Bessemer, Gen. James H. Wilson's men marched on Selma on April 2, 1865. They overpowered the vastly outnumbered Confederate forces under Lt. Gen. Nathan Bedford Forrest and marched on the munitions plants.

Wilson destroyed the 24-building arsenal, along with cannons, 60,000 rounds of artillery ammunition, a million rounds of small arms ammunition and three million feet of lumber. A five-building naval foundry, the iron works and 18-building nitre works, a railroad roundhouse and a score of box cars were among the other Confederate assets destroyed. Surprisingly, there were few casualties. Of the 4,000 soldiers in battle, no more than 20 Confederates were killed.

During the next two days, much of the town was destroyed as well. A Union prisoner set fire to a three-story brick building at the corner of Water and Broad where he had been held captive, touching off a wave of supposedly unauthorized looting and burning that left more than 100 homes and stores smoldering in ruins. When Wilson's forces marched on Montgomery 10 days later, they found no resistance and spared the city.

Selma fell and Richmond was evacuated on the same day, sealing the fate of the Confederate military. Robert E. Lee surrendered at Appomattox 13 days later.

The descendants of the region's slaves are now in the majority in Dallas and a number of nearby counties. The relative lack of an industrial base has kept the area one of the state's poorest.

Almost exactly a century after the first, another battle of Selma occurred, forever linking the city with the advance of civil rights. While the outcome of the Civil War freed the slaves, most blacks remained in the Black Belt during the succeeding generations. But their numbers did not translate into political power.

Early in 1965, Selma's blacks sought to protest the failure of the white politicians to allow blacks to vote and held a series of marches. During a nighttime march in Marion, 26-year-old marcher Jimmie Lee Jackson was fatally shot by a state trooper in a cafe while trying to protect his mother and 82-year-old grandfather from assault. His death galvanized the movement, inspired the historic march to Montgomery and eventually led to passage of the **Voting Rights Act of 1965**.

Emboldened by the strength of Selma's blacks, ministers Hosea Williams and John Lewis stepped from the pulpit of **Brown Chapel Church** on March 7, 1965, and led a group of 600 to begin a voter registration march to Montgomery 54 miles east.

As they crossed the **Edmund Pettus Bridge** over the Alabama River, they were attacked and beaten with billy clubs by Sheriff Jimmy Clark's mounted deputies and state troopers dispatched by Gov. George Wallace. Newspaper and television coverage of the "Bloody Sunday" attack shocked the world. Two weeks later, national entertainers and other black leaders led by Martin Luther King traveled to Selma to join the marchers. Under the watchful protection of National Guardsmen and Army troops, 3,200 marchers walked 12 miles a day and slept in fields at night. On the fourth day, their numbers swelled to more than 25,000 for a mass rally at the state capitol on March 25.

The demonstrations convinced President Lyndon Johnson to support the stalled Voting Rights Bill. Comprehensive legislation that addressed most of the injustices spotlighted by the Selma marches moved through Congress and was signed by Johnson on Aug. 6, 1965.

Those who dwell on Selma's more controversial incidents overlook other contributions the city's people have made to the state and nation. Native sons include **U.S. Sen. John Tyler Morgan**, who championed building a canal across Panama; and **Edmund Pettus** and **Sam Hobbs**, who also served in Congress. In the Reconstruction era of the 1860's, **Benjamin Sterling Turner** became the first black congressman from the state.

For nearly four decades, **Craig Air Force Base** was an integral part of the U.S. Air Force pilot training program. Thousands of pilots who fought in World War II, Korea or Vietnam honed their skills at the base. It closed in 1978, depleting a major source of income which attempts at industrial development have not replaced.

Selma is the capital of the Black Belt, with a display of wealth and charm that neither the Civil War nor the Depression could erase. Historic preservation and tourism have widespread support within Selma's diverse community. The town generates a remarkable number of brochures on special events and historic sites. Its annual pilgrimage and civil war re-enactments are among the highlights of the tourism calendar.

The five blocks of **Water Avenue** that survived the Civil War constitute one of the few antebellum riverfront business districts in the South. Scores of significant residential landmarks remain in the neighborhood between downtown and Sturdivant Hall. Selma is an excellent town for driving (or walking) to see the historic buildings.

Several important historic buildings are downtown. Built in 1837, the dilapidated **St. James Hotel** at the corner of Water and Washington is a rare example of an early riverfront hotel. Originally known as the Brantley, it was the Troupe when it housed Confederate officers and the arsenal and foundry personnel. It operated as the St. James from 1871 until competition from the new **Hotel Albert** on Broad prompted its closure in 1893.

While Selma has an impressive record for preservation, it suffered a major loss in 1969 when the dilapidated Hotel Albert was leveled to make way for the city hall complex. Inspired by the Palace of the Doges in Venice, construction began in 1860, but was not completed until 1892. The four-story hotel survives today only in photos and scenes from the Alan Arkin movie *The Heart is a Lonely Hunter.*

VISITOR CENTER

Maps and brochures of the Black Heritage Tour and cassette-tape tours of the **Old Town Historic District** can be picked up at the **Chamber of Commerce**, 513 Lauderdale St.

Selma has an unofficial second visitor information center that hosts more people than the Chamber. U.S. 80 is a major east-west artery north of downtown. Just off the intersection with Broad is the **Crossroads** information center. Cap and Elizabeth Swift operate the visitor center in a room on the end of their home for the 2,000 persons a month who sign the guestbook. Brochures, maps and posters of upcoming special events are available free. Open 8 a.m.-8 p.m. Phone 875-7485.

WHAT TO SEE IN SELMA

BROWN CHAPEL AME CHURCH was headquarters for the 1965 voting rights demonstrations and the starting point for the historic march to Montgomery. A bust of Rev. Martin Luther King is in front of the church. The black church was organized in 1866 and the present building was erected in 1908. Open by appointment. Phone 874-7897.

Getting there: From Edmund Pettus Bridge, turn east on Water Avenue and turn left on Martin Luther King Street. Go to 410.

EDMUND PETTUS BRIDGE has spanned the Alabama River for more than a half century, and was the scene of violence on March 7, 1965 during the historic Selma-to-Montgomery voting rights march. The 54-mile route from Brown Chapel to Montgomery is being considered for designation as a National Historic Trail by the National Park Service.

Getting there: Water Avenue at Broad Street (U.S. 80).

LIVE OAK CEMETERY was chartered in 1822 as West Selma Cemetery and contains the graves of many prominent Alabama officials and soldiers. Near the entrance, a state historic marker signifies the graves of U.S. Vice President William Rufus King and Senator John T. Morgan. It is estimated that 10,000 are buried in the cemetery, including Confederate soldiers killed in the Battle of Selma. Their mass grave is watched over by a granite soldier statue atop a draped column. Four Confederate generals, including Sens. Pettus and Morgan, are buried here. Confederate Capt. Catsby Roger ap Jones, who commanded the Selma ordnance works, and Benjamin Sterling Turner, the Reconstruction congressman, are among other prominent leaders interred.

The oldest graves are those between Selma and Dallas avenues and east of King Street, closest to town. The city added the area west of King in 1877 and planted the first of the live oaks, now draped with Spanish moss above the well maintained gravesites.

The best time to visit is during the re-enactment of the Battle of Selma each April when hundreds visit the Confederate graves marked by metal Confederate crosses. This is one of the few cemeteries in the South listed on the National Register of Historic Places. Phone the Selma Cemetery Department at 874-2160.

Getting there: Live Oak is 1.2 miles west of Broad Street via Dallas Avenue. Enter a half block past Pettus Street.

OLD DEPOT MUSEUM contains a wealth of Selma memorabilia. It displays a Victorian banking and investment's firm's mahogany cages, marble counters and typewriters, a wooden bicycle and buggy. Spinning wheels, quilts and farm implements are also shown. One room contains the silver and china William Rufus King used while serving as ambassador to France before he was elected vice president.

Civil War displays include shells and cannon balls produced for the Confederacy at Selma's important munitions works. The city's contributions to 20th century history are not overlooked. Rev. Martin Luther King is remembered for his contributions to Civil Rights while serving as pastor of a local black church. The Selma-Dallas County Museum of History and Archives operates the museum. Small admission charge. Open Mon.-Fri. and Sun. afternoon. Phone 875-9918.

Getting there: The depot museum is 6 blocks east of the Pettus Bridge at the intersection of Water Avenue and Martin Luther King Street.

OLD TOWN covers more than 1,200 structures in 58 city blocks, including the Ice House District and Riverview. Sturdivant Hall, the Morgan House, specialty shops and restaurants are included in a casette tape guided tour sponsored by Peoples Bank available at the Chamber of Commerce.

Getting there: The chamber's tourism division is at 513 Lauderdale St. Phone 874-2174 or toll-free in-state 1-800-628-4291.

PERFORMING ARTS CENTER is home to several performing and visual arts organizations. The handsome complex is anchored by the 260-seat Walton Theater, built in 1914 and renovated in 1985, and includes a contemporary art gallery and courtyard. Local industrialist Larry D. Striplin Jr. purchased the movie theater when it was dilapidated and gave it to the city for renovation as a performing arts facility. The restored and expanded complex bears his name. Gerald Ford dedicated the facility in 1985. Open Mon.-Fri., 9-5.

Getting there: 1000 Selma Ave. at Lauderdale Street. Phone 874-2146.

SMITHERMAN HISTORIC BUILDING was erected as a school at a cost of $15,000 in 1847 by the Selma Fraternal Lodge No. 27 of the Free and Accepted Masons. The three-story brick building later served as a Confederate hospital and became the Dallas County Courthouse from 1866 to the turn of the century. After a new courthouse was built, it again became a hospital in 1911. The city purchased the building in 1969 for use as a local museum and it houses the Art Lewis Civil War collection, furniture and displays of Selma's history.

Selma has a custom of naming historic buildings for people who were not associated with the history of the building, Sturdivant Hall, for example. The same is true for this building, named for longtime mayor Joe Smitherman who championed its public purchase. Open Mon.-Fri. 10-4. Closed major holidays. Free. Allow 30 minutes.

Getting there: Western end of Alabama Avenue. Phone 874-2174. Other interesting structures on Alabama are:

• 603 - 1852 cottage started by a Mrs. Philpot while her husband was in New York on business
• 627 - Early dwelling was the home of Rev. Leslie Devotie, a founder of SAE fraternity at Tuscaloosa, now an accounting office
• 816 - 1843 house of Louis Riggs, killed in Battle of Selma
• 1909 U.S. Courthouse and Federal Building, scene of civil rights cases

STURDIVANT HALL is the kind of antebellum mansion that deserves to dominate the countryside, like the fictional Tara. Instead, it was built in 1853-55 as the in-town residence of Edward T. Watts, a member of Selma's considerable gentry. Architect Thomas Helm Lee, cousin to the general, designed one of the South's greatest expressions of Greek Revival architecture for the Watts family.

Watts and his wife lived here until 1864 when banker John McGee Parkman bought it for $65,000. Parkman speculated in cotton with the bank's money - much of it government funds deposited by Union officers occupying the city - and brought ruin to his First National Bank. He was arrested and imprisoned at Castle Morgan at Cahawba. When he tried to escape, he drowned in the Cahaba River. Local merchant Emile Gillman bought the house for only $12,000 in 1870 and added the fresco work. It remained in the family until the city purchased it in 1957.

The house symbolizes Southern grandeur like few other buildings. A pilgrimage to Mabry Street is required for anyone seriously interested in seeing how the state's elite lived prior to the great conflict.

It would be unthinkable for such a mansion not to have at least one resident ghost, particularly in the hometown of **Kathryn Tucker Windham**, who raised the telling of ghost stories to a fine art. Sturdivant Hall is no exception. While touring the house you may be told that Parkman's ghost roams his upstairs rear bedroom or the grounds, or that some claim to have heard the laughter of his daughters playing in the front parlor. Mrs. Windham's book *13 Alabama Ghosts and Jeffrey* chronicles the tale of the restless spirit of the ruined banker.

The square two-story brick building, one of the South's most sophisticated Greek Revival houses, is stuccoed. Six fluted Corinthian columns rise 30 feet to support the portico roof. A second-story balcony runs the width of the house and is defined by laced iron grill work. A cupola, to which access is gained by a corkscrew stair between the attic and roof, crowns the flat slate roof.

The grand portico leads to a tiled hallway and elegant formal rooms used for entertaining the socially prominent and politically powerful. The parlors feature massive gold-leafed mirrors, oriental rugs and marble mantles. The bright color schemes are faithful to the period, enhancing the details of the elaborate friezes, milled woodwork and decorative plaster ceiling medallions. The upstairs contains bedrooms furnished with period pieces.

The detached kitchen and cook's quarters house an excellent museum gift shop and a large collection of antebellum utensils and other household items.

Formal gardens enhance the grounds, particularly beautiful during the spring citywide pilgrimage. The house is also used for weddings, receptions, parties and special tours.

The Sturdivant Museum Association was organized in 1957 to preserve the house following a $50,000 bequest from Robert Daniel Sturdivant to the city which paid $75,000 for the landmark. The Sturdivant estate also contributed many antique furnishings for the house museum. Garden clubs and local individuals presented the association with furnishings which have made the mansion truly a rare antebellum gem. Open Tues.-Sat., 9-4; Sun., 2-4. Closed major holidays. Photography inside is strictly prohibited. Adults, $5; students, $2; groups, $4.50. Phone 872-5626.

Getting there: 713 Mabry St. Turn west off Broad onto Jeff Davis. Go 2 blocks and turn left onto Mabry.

SELMA WALKING TOUR

Although Selma has several excellent museums, its Old Town historic district is filled with scores of dwellings that range from charming to impressive to stunning and should be viewed up close. Most are in excellent condition, thanks to tourism and restoration efforts that are supported by all segments of the community.

Because of management restructuring at some companies, several executives have been transferred and a number of significant houses are for sale. Given the quantity and quality of historic houses on the market, Northerners interested in retiring to an historic structure in a mild climate should seriously consider investing in a house in Selma.

A walking tour starting in the **Sturdivant Hall** block offers a sampling of the houses in this sprawling 58-block neighborhood.

From Broad, left to Jeff Davis and left onto Mabry
803 - 1850s Blake-Gantt cottage occupied by women preparing bandages
        when cannon hit roof in 1865
811 - **White-Force Cottage.**Tiny office was attorney's
Corner - **Sturdivant Hall**, important house museum

Turn right onto McLeod Avenue
Heritage Village on the left contains the McKinnon Riggs doctor's office, Calhoun law
office and Siegel's servants' quarters,
622 - 1830s Miss Minnie Sue's, hand-hewn timbers and pegs

Turn left onto Union Street
Fairoaks Square, award-winning neighborhood renovation project by Circle "S"
Industries of Selma, contains typical postbellum Southern homes. The 1853 Henderson
House on the corner is the corporate conference center for Circle "S", honored by the
National Trust for Historic Preservation for Fairoaks Square.
Turn left to Furniss, right to Mabry
431 - two-story frame, Electrolux store
430 - 1820s, Safford, stuccoed French Colonial
410 - 1840s Gamble, moved from Cahaba
329 - 1837 jeweler Samuel F. Hobbs hid silver in weatherboarding in 1865,
        Hobbs' son became congressman

Right on Parkman, right on Union
431 - 1861 Robbins-Mosely, Italian mantles
Left on Furniss, left on Lapsley
507 - Bow-front porch distinguishes residence
439 - 1856 Greek Revival home; in 1865, Washington Smith hid bank's gold in
        left column during Yankee raid
330 - Greek Revival, curved side porch

Turn left on Dallas
600 - George Baker home scene of Civil War skirmish, Union solider died
        under staircase
619 - 1866 Fellows, various architectural styles

If walking, return to car at Sturdivant Hall. Next, drive back to Dallas Avenue and
continue west to Live Oak Cemetery. See Live Oak listing.

Other notable addresses in neighborhood:
Dallas Avenue at Lauderdale Street - 1904 First Baptist Church is ornate Gothic style,
contains turrets, gargoyles and stained glass from earlier church
210 Lauderdale - 1875 St. Paul's Episcopal Church is English Gothic style with
        Norman bell tower adjacent to baptist church
1000 - Selma Performing Arts Center was the Walton Theater

Water Avenue historic district
1018 - *Selma Times-Journal* in 1870 storefront Victorian, paper published since 1828
Pettus Bridge built in 1940 was scene of Selma to Montgomery March in 1965

1200 - 1837 St. James Hotel, among the state's oldest hotels, empty
LaFayette Park contains a Confederate lathe, caboose
Marker indicates site of Confederate foundry where ironclad *Tennessee* was built, a
target of Federal raiders in 1865
Old Depot (L&N) Museum

Turn left on M.L. King,
Go 2 blocks to Selma Avenue
410 - 1906 Brown Chapel AME Church where Civil Rights demonstrations
         and marches began in 1963, King memorial
709 - First Baptist Church, financial hub of civil rights effort

Turn right on Washington
309 - 1869 Queen of Peace Catholic Church built with materials from ruins of the
         Naval Ordnance Works

Turn left onto Jeff Davis, continue to Broad and turn left
503 - 1900 Temple Mishkan Isreal contains beautiful stained glass windows
301 - 1893 First Presbyterian, features Seth Thomas clock in brick tower which is
         owned and maintained by the city.

SIDE TRIPS WEST

A circle tour around the western side of the Black Belt covers many of the Old
South's most charming communities. On the north side of Selma, take Hwy. 14 west
to Marion, Greensboro and Eutaw.

Traveling west from Selma on U.S. 80 leads to Demopolis and the house museums
of Gaineswood and Bluff Hall.

SIDE TRIPS SOUTH

The town of **Cahawba** downriver from Selma served as the capital city of Alabama
during 1820-25. Repeated flooding and political power struggles prompted the
Legislature to move the seat of government to Tuscaloosa in 1826.

Little remains of the town except for site markers, an active artesian well and brick
ruins. It is, however, an important archaeological site which is being purchased lot by
lot by the **Alabama Historical Commission** as funds become available.

Cahawba sat on a horseshoe-shaped peninsula soapstone bluff formed by the
Cahaba River before flowing into the Alabama. Because legislators could easily reach
the town by boat, they selected it as the state's first permanent capital. However, that
asset also proved to be its downfall and many merchants left town hastily to follow
lawmakers to the town on the Black Warrior.

Cahawba was devastated by the loss of the government and many of the
merchants, but the city rose again to become an important shipping port and
continued as the seat of Dallas County government. In 1859, the railroad arrived and
the town reached its peak of an estimated 3,000 residents by 1860. Most of the major
commercial buildings fronted Vine Street a block from the Alabama River.

With the outbreak of the Civil War, most men left to join the Cahaba Rifles, a unit
which served with distinction. The Confederacy seized a railroad cotton and corn
warehouse near the river and converted it into a military prison nicknamed Castle
Morgan. It became the second largest military prison in the South during 1862-65.

More flooding in 1865 caused residents to flee to higher ground once again and the county seat was moved to Selma a year later. The town declined over the decades. With little activity left by 1952, the town was unincorporated.

With the glory days long gone, the site today is a fishing camp with old trailers scattered about which fishermen use on weekends. Attention to the plight of the townsite is generated each May during a food and entertainment festival.

A marker on a large boulder in a small traffic circle indicates the site of the two-story brick State House that housed the state government. You can visit an artesian well at the site of the Perine House which once gushed 1,250 gallons a minute from a depth of 755 feet. It was drilled to support a planned factory, but the unfinished building was completed in 1857 as a residence. It still bubbles uninterrupted into a brick-line basin and flows into a stream.

At the south end of town are graves in the New Cemetery which was established in 1857 on part of the town commons.

From Selma, turn west off Broad Street to Dallas Avenue (Hwy. 22), go 8 miles to the Cahaba River bridge. About 3/4 mile past the river, at the top of the hill, turn left on the county road marked "To Cahawba." Go 3 1/2 miles to the dead end and turn left. Go 2 miles to the Cahawba welcome center. Quite likely, you'll be the only people visiting that day.

The **Freedom Quilting Bee** is a cooperative of black quilters formed in 1966, many of whom were Wilcox County civil rights advocates. The women of rural Possum Bend stitched such designs as Tulip Bulb, Bear's Paw and Joseph's Coat for themselves and their families before being organized by a white Episcopal minister to instill pride and generate income. Their colorful, patchwork quilts have been marketed locally and through such New York stores as Saks Fifth Avenue and Bloomingdale's. Write Rt. 1, Box 72, Alberta, 36720 or phone 573-2225. Open Mon.-Fri. 8-3. From Selma, go 35 miles south on Hwy. 5 and turn left on Wilcox Rd. 29 at Alberta.

Less than an hour south of Selma on Hwy. 41 is the antebellum town of **Camden** which was established in 1842. The county seat was moved here from Canton Bend the next year. Camden soon became a thriving political and social center. The 1859 **Wilcox County Courthouse** was the scene of voting rights demonstrations which were led by Dr. Martin Luther King and his associate, Dr. Ralph Abernathy, who was born in Camden.

Because it is somewhat isolated and small, the area is often overlooked by tourists interested in historic buildings, but outstanding antebellum structures are here in varying states of repair. The county boasts more antebellum structures than any other county between Mobile and Huntsville. The pride of the county historical society is the two-story brick **Wilcox Female Institute** built in 1849 on Broad Street (Hwy. 28) a short distance from the courthouse. Closer to the square, the **Masonic Lodge** also dates from the 1840s. The historical society stages tours of county landmarks in September, sometimes focusing on the communities of Snow Hill (Hwy. 21), Oak Hill, Possum Bend and Pine Apple (Hwy. 10). North of town is **Roland Cooper State Park**, widely known for excellent fishing at **Miller's Ferry**. Turkey and deer hunting is among the finest in the state. Contact the **Black Belt Tourism Council** at the Wilcox Development Council at Box 369, Camden, 36769. Phone 682-4929.

WHERE TO STAY IN SELMA

Best Western - The newest place to stay is the two-story motel on U.S. 80 with 51 guest rooms, including several kitchenettes. TV's have HBO and ESPN. Continental breakfast is offered in the lobby. Double rates: $42-$52. Fax 872-6635. Write 1915 W. Highland Ave., Selma, 36701. **Phone 872-1900** or 1-800-528-1234.

Holiday Inn - With 166 rooms, this older motel on U.S. 80 West with restaurant and pool has been well maintained. The lobby decor reflects its proximity to Cahawba, the first permanent capital of Alabama. **Phone 872-0461.**

Jameson Inn - The two-story motel at 2420 Broad St. has 41 rooms with cable TV and movie channel. Guests enjoy a pool, free local phone calls, continental breakfast and newspaper. Two- and three-bedroom suites have sofa sleepers and wet bars. Double rate: $44 plux tax. **Phone 874-8600.**

Grace Hall offers two B&B guest rooms in a handsome two-story frame house built in 1857 by Henry H. Ware. The preservation society purchased the house condemned in 1978 and sold it to Joey and Coy Dillion for restoration. The careful restoration certified by the Department of the Interior and furnishing of Grace Hall have made it one of Alabama's most successful B&B operations since 1986.

A brick walkway flanked by boxwoods leads to the symmetrical house influenced by neoclassical and Victorian designs. Ruby colored panes surround the front door which leads to the central hall. Large double parlors to the right of the hall contain period furnishings, marble mantles, elaborate draperies over French doors and oriental rugs covering restored hardwood floors. Guest rooms are likewise appropriately furnished.

If you visit Grace Hall, inquire politely about any recent sightings of the ghosts of former resident Eliza Jones, who helped operate a boarding house here after the Civil War, and her constant companion, Barney Doolittle, a black dog. Miz Eliza is said to be fond of leaving cups of coffee with lots of cream and sugar sitting about.

Children over 6 accepted, but no pets are allowed. Rates include refreshments upon arrival and a tour of Grace Hall. Coffee is served in the bedroom and a full breakfast is available in the formal dining room.

It is also open daily for tours 1-4 p.m. A small admission is charged. Dinner parties for 10 or more are also available. Credit cards accepted.

Getting there: Take Broad Street (Hwy. 22) to Dallas Avenue. Go west one block to Lauderdale, right 1 1/2 blocks to Grace Hall at 506 Lauderdale. **Phone 875-5744.**

WHERE TO EAT IN SELMA

**Faunsdale Bar and Grill is a popular restaurant and saloon, just off U.S. 80 between Selma and Demopolis, in a town of only 96 people. The rustic night spot that was formed by joining two mercantile stores has exposed brick and plaster walls. Customers sit in booths or in straight wooden chairs which scrape on worn wooden floors as overhead fans stir the air and an old pot-bellied stove still adds soot to the beaded ceiling. The cattle brands hanging on the wall correctly suggest that this is beef country, but the large steaks and baked potatoes which come out of owner Bill Mackey's kitchen affirm the reason for the grill's popularity.

During the spring crawfish season, hundreds of pounds of the boiled crustaceans are served a couple of nights a week. An annual balloon fiesta usually takes place the last weekend of May. For hours, phone 628-3240. It is easy to speed down U.S. 80 and miss the turn-off to Faunsdale. Watch carefully for Hwy. 25 intersection and go south a mile.

Major Grumbles offers an entertaining atmosphere and excellent steaks in a 19th century cotton warehouse off Water Avenue. Howard and Martha Strickland opened the restaurant in 1986 to provide downtown with an upscale dining experience and named it for a local character. Sit at the small bar for cocktails, imported beer or wine. Then, order a chicken sandwich ($6), marinated charcoal broiled chicken breasts ($14) or charcoal broiled prime rib ($13-$17). For dessert, try the homemade cheesecake ($3.75). A view of the Alabama River from a river walk is a bonus. Major Grumbles is 3 blocks up Water Avenue from the Pettus Bridge. Turn in the alley behind Warehouse Package Store. On the way in or out, notice the heavy black iron gates believed to be slave doors. Open Mon.-Sat., 11 a.m.-10 p.m. Closed federal holidays. Phone 875-1223.

***The **Tally Ho Restaurant** is West Alabama's finest restaurant. Owner Robert Kelley continues the tradition begun in the 1940's when Gene Thrash began serving steaks and fish dishes in a building which was originally a log cabin. Begin with oyster royale (oysters baked with garlic and herb butter and topped with cheese, sour cream and green onion) as an appetizer ($5) and select the chicken and shrimp saute served over seasoned rice ($11.50) or beef kabob ($13) or the daily special. The name Tally Ho is derived from the fox-hunting cry. Open Mon.-Sat., 5-10 p.m. From U.S. 80, turn north on Summerfield Road for 1/2 mile and then right at the Tally Ho billboard on Mangum Avenue. It is the third building on the left. Phone 872-1390.

White-Force Cottage is an outstanding food option for pre-scheduled groups visiting next door at Sturdivant Hall. Caterers James and Miriam Bearden offer a variety of lunches and teas, but their most popular is the Peach Basket Special which consists of Southern fried chicken breast or pimento cheese sandwich with fruit cup and extras delivered in a miniature peach basket for under $6. Guests may eat in the cottage or picnic on the grounds.

For an unforgettable treat, take the baskets to the moss-draped **Live Oak Cemetery**, sit near the life-sized statue on the grave of a former resident of White-Force Cottage and arrange for Kathryn Tucker Windham to tell stories, ghostly and otherwise. The quaint cottage was built in 1858 for Martha Todd White, half-sister to Abraham Lincoln's wife, Mary Todd. (Reservations a week in advance with a minimum of 10 lunches.) Write 811 Mabry St., Selma, 36701. Phone 875-1714 during office hours.

WHERE TO SHOP

Visit downtown for a pleasant walking tour of shops and stores. Broad Street near the river bridge offers a cafe, drugstore and clothing stores. The **Riverfront Mini Mall** on historic Water Avenue near the bridge offers sandwiches, antiques and collectibles.

Siegel Art Gallery displays local, regional and American art in several rooms of an 1840 Greek Revival cottage at 706 Broad St. Jerome E. Siegel opened the gallery in 1977 and has earned a reputation for representing quality artists. Open Mon.-Fri., 9-5. Phone 875-1138.

Mallory Alley is a group of specialty fashion shops around the block formed by Selma, Lapsley and Pettus. Of special note is Calico Cottage, built in 1912 and restored in 1981, at 412 Selma Ave. Baskets, candles, wreaths, silk flowers and party goods are sold. Visit the House Next Door at 213 Lapsley, built circa 1869 with ceilings stenciled later, for antiques and women's fashions. The Yard Chil' sells children's clothes.

Selma Mall, corner of Highland Avenue and Range Street, is anchored by JC Penney and has 31 other stores under one roof. It's on Hwy. 14 north of the historic district. Just across Hwy. 14 is the **Selma Marketplace Center** anchored by **Kmart**. The **Valley Creek** shopping center is on U.S. 80 West.

SELMA'S ANNUAL EVENTS

Fourth weekend in March

Historic Selma Pilgrimage - Citywide - One of the state's best collections of 19th-century buildings is on display. From Water Avenue to the magnificent Sturdivant Hall, the neighborhoods are usually ablaze with blooming azaleas and dogwoods. Descendants of original owners proudly take visitors through the homes passed down for generations and relate personal stories that make the tours more meaningful. Tour Grace Hall by candlelight. Admire the Tiffany stained glass windows in St. Paul's Episcopal Church and hear an organ concert in Temple Mishkan Israel. An antique show and a craft event are available on certain days, but can not compare with the architecture and ambiance of the Old South that Selma personifies. In addition to the house tour, tickets are sold to the antique show and the evening gala. An art show is free. Write the **Selma-Dallas County Historic Preservation Society** at P.O. Box 586, Selma, 36702. Call 875-7241 or 1-800-628-4291 in state.

Early Saturday in April

Selma Bridge Festival - Near Edmund Pettus Bridge - A celebration of arts and crafts, music and foods sponsored by the arts council. Phone 874-2177.

Third weekend in April

Battle of Selma - Bloch Park - Selma's Confederate Naval Ordnance Works and Army Arsenal were destroyed by Union forces on April 2, 1865. The event is celebrated annually with authentic encampments, nighttime artillery firing exhibitions and occasional riverboat tours. The battle re-enactment hosted by the 34th Alabama Infantry Regiment is the state's largest Civil War commemoration. The battlefield site near the Alabama River is covered with about 1,000 feet of breastworks, the low walls used as defense in battle. You can visit camp sites on Friday and Saturday. If you want to attend the ball at Sturdivant Hall on Saturday night, you *must* wear authentic period dress. The big battle Sunday at 2 p.m. attracts upwards of 2,000 re-enactors and 15,000 spectators. Expect traffic delays. The Smitherman Building is headquarters for the event sponsored by the **Kiwanis Club**. Phone 875-7241.

Second Saturday of May

Old Cahawba Festival – Cahaba

Protectors of the site of Alabama's first permanent state capital stage the annual arts and entertainment festival to generate support for an interpretive park. Events range from a greased pole contest to a flea market and crafts show and sale. "Save Cahawba" t-shirts are a popular fundraiser. Located 12 miles south of Selma. Follow Hwy. 22 for 9 miles and turn left on county road marked "To Cahaba." Go 3.5 miles and turn left at dead end. Phone 872-1026.

Second Friday-Saturday of October
Tale Tellin' Festival - National Guard Armory on West Dallas Avenue - Folklorists spin yarns nightly for hundreds gathered to hear tales of adventure, the improbable and ghostly goings-on. Visitors are invited to swap stories before the big names take their turns on stage Selma's own "ghost lady," **Kathryn Tucker Windham**, who helped create the first event in 1979, achieved a national reputation for her books about **Jeffrey**, her resident ghost.

During the day Saturday, downtown Water Avenue becomes a five-block street fair as scores of artists sell their wares during the annual **Riverfront Market Day**. Thousands gather in the closed-off streets to enjoy the food, music and festivities. Crafts include original artwork, books, handmade pottery, colorful quilts and dolls, among other crafts. The purpose of Riverfront Market Day is to draw attention to the restoration and preservation of historic Water Avenue. Funds raised have helped save several old warehouses and restore the bridgetender's house. Hours 9-5. Phone 875-7241.

TROY

A growing university is at the heart of community life. Troy State University has flourished over the past 20 years and even has campuses in Dothan and Montgomery. For information, **Pike County Chamber of Commerce** is located at 500 Elm St. Phone 566-2294.

WHERE TO STAY
Holiday Inn is a mile north of town on U.S. 231. **Phone 566-1150.**

TROY LANDMARKS
BYRD DRUGS is an old-fashioned drugstore with a soda fountain counter which is legendary for handmade milkshakes. Pharmacist Joe Watson, who began working at Byrd's while a student at Auburn and later bought the drugstore, maintains the traditional look and feel of Byrd's that local people have known for generations. Housed in a building more than a century old, it had been a pharmacy for years before Marvin Byrd bought the business in 1940. A lighted sign that features a "flying" bird has been a Troy landmark for more than a half century. Stop by and share a milkshake with someone special. Phone 566-0100.

Getting there: 81 N. Court Square.

PIKE PIONEER MUSEUM serves as an excellent introduction to the culture of the Wiregrass area. The 10-building compound of buildings moved from various parts of the county depicts a century of rural Southern life from 1830. Agricultural tools form the bulk of the museum's collection of artifacts, which are displayed in the main building formed around a courtyard as well as in several other structures. You can walk through the buildings to see period merchandise in the circa 1920 Adams General Store and artifacts in a split-log house and a tenant house.

The rural settlement is authentic, down to the original hitching rail with rings carefully spaced to accommodate horse-drawn buggies. Weaving, spinning and quilting demonstrations are given regularly. An amphitheater, windmill, picnic area and privy give the museum more of a community look than just a museum.

Curren Farmer began collecting old farming equipment in the 1960s and accepted other period items his Pike County neighbors no longer needed or wanted. From that modest beginning, the museum opened in a single building in 1971. Over the next two decades, the non-profit museum has received approximately 8,000 items from some 700 donors.

You can survey the various buildings in an hour. Open Mon.-Sat. 10-5, Sun. 1-5. Adults, $2, students, $.50. Phone 566-3597.

Getting there: If you're traveling south on U.S. 231 from Montgomery toward Troy, you can't miss it on the right. It's about three miles north of town.

TUSKEGEE

The accomplishments of blacks in the generations before the Civil Rights Movement are demonstrated nowhere in the nation better than in Tuskegee where educator **Booker T.Washington** and scientist **George Washington Carver** created the most respected black college in America.

A bill co-authored by a former slave and a former slave owner passed the Alabama Legislature to establish a black school in Macon County in 1881. In buildings on an abandoned farm and with an enrollment of 30 students, Washington began Tuskegee Institute as a model of higher education to train black teachers.

He advocated practical skills for rural blacks. As a result, students built most of the original campus themselves. He courted white politicians with his brand of conservative politics and attracted enough financial support from such Northern industrialists as Rockefeller and Carnegie to make Tuskegee the nation's best supported black school by the turn of the century.

At his death in 1915, he was the most influential black in America and Tuskegee was the best known black school. However, crop failures the next year prompted blacks to begin leaving the South in record numbers for jobs in Northern industries, and Washington's moderate racial philosophies waned.

Beginning in 1896, Carver headed the agricultural department and developed 300 extractions from peanuts and 175 byproducts from sweet potatoes.

The son of a former slave also succeeded in making paint from the clays common to the region and a synthetic marble from wood pulp. Carver's research proved to be crucial to the South's economy after the boll weevil wreaked havoc with the cotton crops about 1914. His study of peanuts and sweet potatoes opened new markets for Southern farmers.

An honorary membership to the British Royal Society of Arts in 1917 was among the many honors bestowed upon him. Thomas Edison repeatedly made Carver lucrative offers to become a consulting chemist for Edison Laboratories, but Carver chose to stay where he felt his services were best utilized.

During World War II, amid the rigid pattern of racial segregation of the armed forces, the federal government believed that blacks lacked the intelligence and perseverance necessary to become fighter pilots. For years, the Institute had attempted to add aviation to its curriculum and prove the military was wrong. Finally, through the efforts of Frederick Patterson, "Chief" Alfred Anderson and others, the **Tuskegee Army Air Field** was established for what would become known as the "Tuskegee Experiment."

Nearly 1,000 blacks were trained as military pilots for the war effort and 450 became combat aviators over Europe under command of **Lt. Col. B.O. Davis**, the first black officer to earn his wings. The 99th Pursuit Squadron was highly decorated and Davis became the Army's first black three-star general. The achievements of the Tuskegee pilots helped lead to the end of segregation in the military in the late 1940s.

School officials supported civil rights efforts during the 1960s. The name of the school was changed to Tuskegee University in 1985 and enrollment stands at about 3,700. The school that invented products derived from sweet potatoes is doing research for NASA on how to grow sweet potatoes without soil in conditions approximating outer space.

ATTRACTIONS

TUSKEGEE INSTITUTE NATIONAL HISTORIC SITE includes 27 landmarks associated with Washington and Carver. What began in a church and shanty in 1881 with a few students today is a sprawling campus which attracts more than 3,000 students from throughout the world. From its earliest days, Tuskegee Normal and Industrial Institute encouraged students to earn part or all of their education expenses. Students and professors built many of the institute's original buildings. Today the 1,500-acre campus consists of more than 165 buildings, 27 of them associated with Washington and Carver.

Drive to the campus. Follow signs and park in the lot by **The Oaks**, the Booker T. Washington house museum. Walk down the hill and look for the low brick building across the street housing the **Carver Museum**. After an orientation here in the building constructed in 1915 as a laundry, begin your walking tour.

CARVER MUSEUM traces Carver's research with various vegetables and forest products. As soon as you arrive, ask at the desk for the next available tour of the Oaks. A small National Park Service brochure contains a driving and walking tour of the historic area and bios on Washington and Carver.

If not pressed for time, begin the self-guided tour downstairs with a film on Carver and Washington. Vegetable specimens and samples of products derived from peanuts and sweet potatoes, Carver's two most important crops, are exhibited, along with paintings, biographical photographs and contemporary news accounts which help the present generation understand the importance of his career.

You can hear a recording of Carver reciting his favorite poem and see variations of house paint extracted from local clay, and woven materials from native plants. Especially interesting is a truck known as the "movable school" for community services. The museum was established in 1938. Plan an hour. Open daily 9-5. Closed Thanksgiving, Dec. 25 and Jan. 1. Phone 727-3200.

Depending on how much time is left before your tour of the Oaks, exit the museum and turn right and walk until you reach the inspiring 1922 **Booker T. Washington Monument**, where the educator symbolically lifts the cloak of ignorance from his race. Turn right and walk to the Chapel.

THE CHAPEL designed by Auburn architecture graduate **Paul Rudolph** is a contemporary 1969 successor to the original built by students in 1896 which burned in 1957. Walk in and look around to see the colorful windows. Washington and Carver are buried outside Rudolph's soaring brick chapel.

THE OAKS, an imposing 15-room Queen Anne residence, was built of locally manufactured materials by students in 1899. The architect was **Robert R. Taylor**, the first black graduate of MIT and a member of the Tuskegee faculty. Washington lived there until his death in 1915 and his widow remained a decade longer. One of the few surviving structures of this period designed and built by blacks, it was used as administrative offices for the school after 1950. Tours begin on the hour at 9, 10 and 11 a.m.; 2, 3 and 4 p.m.

Getting there: Take I-85 from Montgomery. Take exit 38 to Hwy. 81 South. Turn right at Hwy. 26 (Old Montgomery Rd.). Go to the second stoplight and turn right, then follow signs to the Oaks to park. (The regal 1857 mansion known as **Grey Columns** is the home of the president.) If you prefer a windshield tour, drive a block past the Oaks and turn right between the brick columns onto the campus. Turn right to the Carver Museum or drive past the statue and on to the Rudolph chapel.

VICTORYLAND is one of America's most successful greyhound tracks, yearly entertaining more than 1 million visitors who enjoy pari-mutuel wagering, top-notch food and beverage service and the thrill of 13 races every performance.

The track is Alabama's top traffic-generating, man-made attraction. Patrons' enthusiasm is evident in the healthy wagering handle (the total amount bet), which averages $185 million yearly, much of it from individual $2 wagers. Its $204 million handle in 1988 set a national record that stood for three years.

The $20 million facility with 1,320-foot oval track accommodates up to 12,500 patrons on three viewing levels: the glass-enclosed clubhouse, a second-floor sports lounge and a trackside grandstand, with ample seating indoor and out. More than 165 mutuel windows are located conveniently on all levels, so you can place your money quickly and with ease in the 10-minute break between each race. Selecting dogs is easy, with a computerized tote board to display odds. Assistance from personnel and a "how to bet" brochure make it easier for first-timers.

In addition to the thrill of watching the sleek greyhounds streak around the track at up to 40 miles per hour in pursuit of a stuffed bone, you can enjoy an impressive variety of food and beverage options. VictoryLand serves more meals than any single restaurant in the state. The clubhouse level offers tableside cocktail and dining service from full lunch and dinner menus. Entrees range from appetizers and hearty sandwiches to prime rib and the chef's specialties. Groups can enjoy a pre-planned menu or buffet service. The grandstand level offers cold beverages and snacks, from popcorn to chicken fingers. Valet parking is available and special unloading and parking areas are set aside for tour buses.

One of the biggest winners has been the tax man of Macon County. The track pays the county about $7 million a year, with half earmarked for the once destitute school system. Plus, state law requires that 75 percent of the track's 550 or so employees live within the county.

VictoryLand is open 50 weeks a year, Mon.-Sat., rain or shine. Doors open at 6 p.m. for evening races; open at 2 p.m. for matinees Mon., Wed. and Fri.; open at 11:30 a.m. for Sat. matinees. General admission for adults, $.50; $2 for clubhouse and sports lounge. Group reservations required. A group coordinator is available to assist in planning a trip. Clubhouse reservations are recommended. Minimum age is 19. Fax 727-0737. Write P.O. Box 128, Shorter, 36075. Phone 727-0540 or toll-free 1-800-688-2946.

Getting there: VictoryLand is located 20 miles east of Montgomery at I-85 exit 22.

GULF COAST

*The USS Alabama battleship is permanently displayed at **Battleship Memorial Park** near downtown Mobile. After being grey for most of the past 30 years, the 680-foot ship is now blue-grey as it was during World War II. A person painting the hull will use about 500 gallons and take about a month to complete the task. (Battleship Park photo)*

GULF SHORES-
ORANGE BEACH

- **Claim to fame:** The world's most beautiful beaches
- **Eat:** Fresh seafood in a number of great restaurants
- **Best special event:** National Shrimp Festival
- **Best places to stay:** Perdido Beach Resort, Gulf Shores Plantation
- **Tourist information:** Herb Malone, Executive Director; Alabama Gulf Coast Chamber of Commerce, P.O. Drawer 457, Gulf Shores, 36547. Phone 968-7511. Orange Beach Chamber of Commerce, P.O. Drawer 399, Orange Beach, 36561. Phone 981-8000.

First-time visitors to Alabama are often surprised to learn that the state has some of the finest, sugar white beaches in the nation. The 32 miles of beach stretching from Fort Morgan to Gulf Shores and Orange Beach easily rival Florida's better known vacation spots, such as Pensacola 30 minutes to the east.

The area is considerably less developed and congested, but still offers the necessary number of restaurants, leisure attractions, fishing charters and shops to make it not only a worthy contender, but an excellent destination year round.

Gulf Shores was essentially a summer retreat for residents of Alabama, Mississippi and Louisiana until the devastation of Hurricane Frederic in 1979 focused national television attention on the area. The big storm wiped out most of the small family cottages which dotted the 30,000-acre coastline and made way for a rapid development of condos and hotels which now line much of the beachfront.

With a year round population of about 8,000, the island maintains a small town charm where restaurant managers and shopkeepers frequently remember the names of repeat visitors. Locals are friendly and thrive on the reputation of being one of America's up and coming vacation destinations.

On the not-so-friendly side, the speed limit on Hwy. 59 is seriously enforced between I-10 and Gulf Shores. Be aware that the limit is as low as 35 mph in Foley and Loxley.

If you're arriving from the north, as most people do, you reach the center of beach activity at the southern end of Hwy. 59. To the west, you find some of the nicer resorts. Eventually, 22 miles from Gulf Shores, you reach Fort Morgan which anchors the western end of the island and guards the entrance to Mobile Bay.

East, past the Holiday Inn, Days Inn and the landmark Young's By the Sea, is the sprawling Gulf State Park Resort. At the eastern end, the Perdido Beach Resort is the showcase of Orange Beach, an old community with a strong identity of charter fishing. Still heading east, a soaring bridge over the Perdido Pass offers access to Ono, a private island of the area's toniest homes, and the Florida state line, straddled by the Flora-Bama, keeper of the flame of nightlife both in and out of season.

At the eastern end of the island, especially around and east of Orange Beach, you will see a growing number of condos between the road and the beach. The surge of growth that followed in Frederic's wake has added thousands of condo rental units to the lists kept by local real estate offices. Incidentally, the name Frederic has been "retired" by the meteorlogists who name these things. It's sort of like retiring a star baseball player's number.

Geologists and tourists agree that Alabama's sugar white sand beaches are among the most beautiful in the world in terms of softness and color. The coastline was formed about 80,000 years ago, with the main beachline about 3 miles inland of where it is now. The peninsula was formed a few thousand years ago as offshore spits, beaches, ridges and bars enclosed a series of lagoons.

Back in 1920, Alabama's coastline at the south end of Baldwin County was a barren marshy swamp held back from the crashing waves of the Gulf of Mexico by an isolated stretch of white beaches. A 42-year-old Minnesota developer, George Meyer, traveled the coastline of Florida looking for a location to develop a first-class family resort. He eventually came across the tip of Alabama and decided it was the location for him. He purchased 10,000 acres of land nobody else wanted and began trying to market the property. Eight years passed before he sold any lots, with the transactions followed closely by the 1929 stock market crash. Undaunted, he continued to lobby the state government for assistance. With so many pressing demands on the limited resources of the state, bridges and roads for an isolated wasteland was not high on Montgomery's list of priorities.

A major development occurred in 1933 when a canal was sliced across the bottom of Baldwin County to create a portion of the intracoastal waterway. One effect was to make the coastal area an actual island. While it connected the beach area to the rest of the world by water, it did nothing for vehicular travel. A barge powered by a hand-operated wench was established to connect the island with the mainland. Families trying to get to the beach by car would have to endure lengthy delays to cross via ferry, and later by swing-span bridge. Another 40 years would pass before a bridge over the waterway would allow quick and easy access to the island.

Meanwhile, the developers who foresaw the potential for resorts managed to find private backing, erected the Gulf Shores Hotel in the 1940s and built roads to make it accessible. Meyer not only gave Gulf Shores its name, he and his wife, Erie, gave land to the tiny community for a golf course, schools and civic buildings. He even gave beach frontage for the state park and other public beaches.

During a Lions Club meeting on July 4, 1949, with Gov. Jim Folsom on hand, Meyer proposed promoting the place as Pleasure Island. The name is still in use.

Serious interest in vacationing on Alabama's coastline did not materialize until the 1950s. Prominent families upstate began to construct cottages along the beach to retreat from the summer heat. Most Southerners, however, overlooked Alabama's little known beaches and headed for Panama City or Fort Walton because of more activities for families.

Some 120 persons called the beach home when residents voted in 1957 by a margin of 18 to 13 to incorporate 206 acres as the town of Gulf Shores. Six abstained.

In the late 1960s, Gulf Shores was becoming "discovered" by families who had tired of the tackiness of Panama City. They came to the simple motels and rental houses along the beach road. Those who liked what they sampled returned, many of them building modest frame cottages on pilings to be out of harms way should the tide rise too high. Some 1,500 people were living here year round as the end of the decade approached. A sure sign of status arrived in 1970 when a Holiday Inn opened. A bridge linking the island community to the rest of the state was completed in 1972. A bridge to the east at Alabama Point on the Florida line had recently made the area accessible from Florida.

Everything changed September 13, 1979, when **Hurricane Frederic** roared out of the warm waters of the gulf. The tide swelled to historic heights as devastating 110-mile-an-hour winds battered the coast and uprooted nearly everything in its path. When the terror passed, those residents who had evacuated inland with only the clothes on their backs returned to find their worst nightmares had been realized. Roads and highways had become sand dunes, houses were ripped apart and scattered, hotels and motels were battered and left in shreds.

After the flood water receded, damage was figured in excess of $2.3 billion.

Although no one thought it at the time, Frederic did Gulf Shores a big favor. It swept aside the scores of weathered little houses and cleared the land for a resurgence of first-class development. National media coverage announced to the rest of the nation that Alabama, in fact, had access to the Gulf of Mexico and the miles of sugar white beaches were on a par with Florida's, by the way. Investors arrived and serious development of condos and restaurants were soon under way. The census taken less than a year after the hurricane counted 2,000 residents. A decade later some 3,261 people lived here full time and more arrive monthly. Another 65,000 people in condos call Gulf Shores home for a part of the year.

During peak season, some 200,000 tourists are around and the amount of money they leave behind is substantial. In fact, half of the city's $6 million budget comes from sales, use and lodging taxes. "Snow birds" peak in January and February when at least 15,000 set up housekeeping along the coast. Projections for the year 2000 expect 5,000 permanent residents and 95,000 part-timers, with 300,000 at peak.

Immediately east toward the Florida line is the sister town of **Orange Beach** which had an estimated population of 750 in 1980 and some 2,253 in 1990.

The spurt in population has had a drastic impact on the price of land. In the early 1970's, 100-foot-wide residential lots fronting the Gulf could be bought for around $22,000. Right after the hurricane, the values doubled to $45,000. Today, the same lots are on the market for $165,000.

Even though the founder of Gulf Shores died in 1959, his family's interest remains strong. His widow remains active in the community. In fact, the family sold the land to build the Gulf Shores Planatation resort - with its many swimming pools and tennis courts - which made the kind of family resort that Meyer had in mind back in 1922.

Having been resurrected into a far better resort since Frederic's devastation, Gulf Shores and Orange Beach boast resort facilities and fine swimming and fishing. In fact, no less an authority than the people at *Southern Living* magazine have proclaimed Gulf Shores as the "finest" beach in the South, bar none.

All told, there are more than 8,000 guest rooms where you can spend the night.

In addition to the summer season, the best time to visit the beach is in October, long after most people have returned to their jobs or school. The reasons are obvious: the temperature remains in the upper 70's or low 80's and humidity drops from summer levels. The water temperature is still warm enough to enjoy a dip in the breaker waves. Or you may simply walk along the beach in shorts. Another compelling reason is that rates drop to off-season levels, a savings of perhaps 40 percent from spring and summer rates. For the absolute best value, come in December when the weather is mild and rates are rock bottom.

WELCOME CENTERS

The area has aggressive tourism organizations which are well informed as to events, restaurants, activities and accommodations at the score of beachfront hotels, countless condos and rental cottages. The **Alabama Gulf Coast Chamber of Commerce** in Gulf Shores is housed in the attractive welcome center at the foot of the intracoastal bridge on Hwy. 59. It has a large supply of printed material on all facets of interests related to vacationing or living at the beach. Open Mon.-Fri. till 5 and Sat. in season.

Visit the **Orange Beach Chamber of Commerce** right on the beach west of the Perdido Beach Resort on Hwy. 182.

Since property management, sales and rentals is a major industry, both can provide a complete listing of real estate firms. Pick up a copy of *Gulf Coast Lifestyles* for more information on real estate companies and their listings.

ATTRACTIONS

BEACHES stretch for 32 miles, from the western tip at Fort Morgan (Hwy. 180), and at the entrance to Little Lagoon (on Hwy. 182). Gulf Shores proper has 8 miles of beach frontage.

• Parking is most plentiful at the public beach in the center of Gulf Shores (Hwys. 182 and 59) and at Gulf State Park. Showers and restrooms are at each. Several beach accesses are maintained by the state Department of Conservation:

• The main Public Beach access is on Hwy. 182 about a mile east of the convention center and 6 miles west of Hwy. 59. A large pavilion includes restrooms and showers. A paved parking lot where a fee is charged to enter is open from 8 a.m. until sundown.

• The 4-acre Romar Beach on Hwy. 182 is 5 miles east of Hwy. 59. Parking is free.

• You can park free and swim at the Perdido Point beach on Hwy. 182 just east of the Perdido Pass Bridge. There is a 225-foot boardwalk.

• Parking is also free at the Cotton Bayou beach on Hwy. 182 across from the intersection of Hwy. 161.

You can drink beer from cans on the beaches if you are of legal age. But no glass containers, fires, grills, dogs or vehicles are allowed on the sand. If you swim, be alert for red flags flying on the beach to warn of rough surface conditions. Also, remember not to leave valuables in your car.

BON SECOUR NATIONAL WILDLIFE REFUGE west of Gulf Shores is 4,300 acres of the best of Alabama's last remaining coastal barrier habitat. It provides the last landfall for migratory birds on their way to the Yucatan Peninsula. You can walk through a 300-acre tract to nearly 4 miles of beachfront.

The dunelands, wetlands and pine-oak forests are dedicated to the protection of indigenous plant and animal life. Safe haven is provided for endangered species such as the Alabama beach mouse, huge loggerhead sea turtle and American alligators, some of which are between 6 and 12 feet in length. The refuge is also home to bobcats, cottontail rabbits, opossums, armadillos and squirrels.

More than 120 migrating species of birds, arriving in spring from Mexico, Central America and South America, can be spotted as they make landfall. Songbirds, blue herons, brown and white pelicans and osprey arrive in mid-April. Sea turtles begin digging nests in May for egg hatching which lasts through August.

Fall bird migration begins in August and peaks in mid-October when peregrines can be seen soaring overhead. October is also a good time to see hundreds of Monarch butterflies on the Pine Beach Trail as they draw nutrients from milkweed and other plants. Wildflowers bring color to fall from September to November, with goldenrod and red basil being particularly showy.

Getting there: The entrance to the beach access is 9 miles west on Hwy. 180. The refuge office on Hwy. 180, 6 miles west of 59, is staffed Mon.-Fri. except holidays.

FLORA-BAMA lounge started out as a hole-in-the wall straddling the stateline, and has evolved into a package store/oyster bar/nightclub steeped in colorful beach lore worthy of any novel. This den of loud beach music, longneck beer and Florida lotto tickets has an implied permission to over indulge and misbehave; the argument being: after all, you're *on vacation.*

Technically, the Flora-Bama is 4 inches inside Florida, but Alabama can lay some claim since the parking lot is in both states. Founded by the Tampary family in 1961, it has expanded over the years - exposed rafters and all - to encompass the main bar room with band stand, a pool room - with a portrait of Bear Bryant among the framed press clippings - a tiny oyster bar and large fenced party area out back. The apparent piecemeal, tacked-on appearance of enclosed rooms and open decks is prompted by zoning set-back laws intended to control beachfront developments. Current owners Joe Gilchrist and Pat McClellan book some of the region's hottest bands and promote new talent they like.

The deck bar overlooks beach volleyball, kite flying and the surf, not to mention great sunsets. The biggest crowds are on weekend nights, but parking spaces after about 8 p.m. may be hard to find.

The Flora-Bama figures in the beach's former reputation as the Redneck Riveria, a term coined by a writer for *The Washington Post* after visiting Kenny Stabler in his hangout in his NFL quarterback days before Frederic.

Getting there: Stateline on Hwy. 182. Phone 981-8555. The Florida number is 904-492-0611.

FORT MORGAN, at the western tip of the island, guarded the entrance to Mobile Bay during the Civil War. The clash between Confederate and Union naval forces on Aug. 5, 1864 for control of the harbor entrance was the most important sea battle during the war.

For three years, the Union navy had tried with varying degrees of success to blockade Mobile Bay, one of the most important Confederate ports. In the summer of 1864, with New Orleans fallen to Federal forces, Adm. David G. Farragut steamed toward Mobile Bay, the last Confederate stronghold along the Gulf of Mexico. If he could not actually take Mobile, he could at least run ships between Fort Gaines and Fort Morgan and occupy the port to neutralize Mobile's shipping. Confederate Adm. Franklin Buchanan had planted the 3-mile-wide channel into Mobile Bay with a device never used before, homemade anchored mines called torpedoes. The 209-foot ironclad ram *Tennessee*, the most powerful ship afloat, presented another formidable challenge.

At 6:30 a.m., the Federals' wooden sloops-of-war and four ironclad monitors pushed into the bay against heavy fire from Fort Morgan. The *Tecumseh* struck a "torpedo" and sank. Federal ships stopped. Farragut, in the flagship *Hartford*, scampered up the rigging to get a better view through a smoke screen and demanded to know why the column had stalled. According to legend, when told that more torpedoes were in the channel, he yelled, "Damn the torpedoes. Full speed ahead."

The Union's ship column continued moving through the channel toward the mines and the South's meager defense of four wooden ships. Fighting between the wooden ships was so close that sailors fought the enemy through portholes and decks ran red with blood.

By 10 a.m., the Selma-built *Tennessee* had been disabled by pounding fire and the wooden ships had been sunk. A wounded Adm. Buchanan and other Southerners were taken prisoner. Farragut secured victory and sealed off the bay, but the Union victory was costly: 145 killed and 174 wounded. On the other side, 12 Confederates were killed and 20 wounded. At Fort Morgan, only one died.

A ground troop assault, supported by Farragut's mighty cannons, bombarded Fort Morgan for 19 days before it fell on Aug. 23, the last major Confederate gulf fort at last in the hands of the Union.

In all, seven different flags have flown over forts on this site at Mobile Point. The massive pentagonal fort which you can tour was designed in 1817 by Simone Bernard, a French architect and former aide-de-camp to Napoleon. The pentagonal fort completed in 1834 was built on the site of two earlier forts - tiny Fort Serof, erected by early Luna colonists, and Fort Bowyer, which was seized from Spain by U.S. forces in 1813. British and Indians attacked the little wooden Fort Bowyer by land and sea in 1814. After three days of fierce assault, the British flagship *Hermes* was sunk and the British withdrew.

Though the significance of Fort Morgan waned after its critical role in the Civil War, it was revitalized and modernized as an active military base during the Spanish American War and World Wars I and II before being turned over to the state in 1977. The Alabama Historical Commission now interprets this important National Military Landmark. The history and physical remains at the fort tell the story not only of a specific battle, but also the story of America's constantly changing and modernizing military history.

Begin your tour at the museum which chronicles the fort's importance from early Spanish fortifications in the 1500s through World War II. Enter the fort, climb the steps and take a walk around the fortress that withstood the pounding from Union forces in 1864. Cannons still peer from gunports in the scarred walls and the graceful vaulted arches in the dark dungeon provide interesting photo possibilities. Except for the summer months, you might be the only person exploring the dusty corners of the fort. In the summer, ask if any guided tours are scheduled the day you visit.

Fort Morgan comes alive several times a year with authentic re-enactments and encampments. The largest commemorates the Battle of Mobile Bay. Plan at least an hour. Admission. Daily, 9-5. Closed Thanksgiving, Dec. 25 and Jan. 1. Phone 540-7125.

Getting there: Follow signs 21 miles out Fort Morgan Road (Hwy. 180) west from downtown Gulf Shores to Mobile Bay. Ferry service links the fort with Fort Gaines across the bay.

GULF STATE PARK RESORT is a sprawling 6,000-acre public resort operated by the Conservation Department's state parks division. There is literally something for everyone's beach vacation needs, as well as being able to accommodate a large crowd. As you might expect, it hosts a lot of family reunions and state association conventions.

The park includes a resort-convention center with 144 large rooms with cable TV and private balconies which overlook the gulf. The rooms are clustered in a dozen two-story buildings spaced out on either side of the main building. The restaurant has four large dining rooms which offer sweeping views of the beach. Adjacent is the Seamist lounge which has live entertainment several nights a week in season. The hall to the dining room and lounge are covered with original beach paintings for sale by local artists.

Outside is a nice swimming pool area that is the center of social life at the resort. A poolside luau is held twice a week.

On the opposite side of the highway is the huge Lake Shelby, which covers 500 acres, and is visible from Hwy. 135, the shortcut to the north. On the backside of the lake are 16 two-bedroom cabins and a single three-bedroom unit.

If you want to play golf, nearby is an 18-hole course with a pro shop offering a snack bar and equipment rental. The course has long tees, water hazards and well kept bunkers. A nice clubhouse overlooks the 9th and 18th greens and practice tees. There are tennis courts as well.

It is claimed that Shelby is the closest fresh-water lake to a large body of salt water in the world. In the summer, you can buy fishing licenses, snacks, bait and tackle at a store on Shelby where you can also rent a rowboat to explore the lake or row east through a small canal to check out a smaller lake.

On the north side of Middle Lake is a sprawling campground with 468 sites, each with water and electricity hookup, picnic tables and grill. Some have sewage hookups. To reach the golf course and the campground, look for County Rd. 2 about a half-mile east of the convention center.

Planning a family reunion or youth outing? A group lodge with 15 bedrooms and private baths can sleep up to 60 people. It is located on Hwy. 182 at the edge of Middle Lake and opposite the beach pavilion with the large parking lot. It has a fully equipped kitchen, meeting room and dining room. Groups have the convenience of the beach without the on-the-beach cost. It is about a mile east of the convention center.

The main attraction at Gulf State Park is the beautiful public beach. It stretches for 2.5 miles, uncluttered by condos or restaurants. There's plenty of room to unwind, and the sand is as squeaky and white as sand ever gets.

At the western end, an 825-foot fishing pier stands triumphantly on guard in the gulf and gives good access for salt water surf fishing. It is the longest pier on the Alabama coast. A fishing license is not required for state residents, but is for non-residents. A fee is required for admission, whether to fish or just enjoy the view. You can rent or buy tackle on the pier.

About 350 acres of park land have been set aside for nature trails along which visitors can explore the unspoiled flora and fauna of the coastal areas, marshes and wetlands.

Gulf State Park was established in the early 1930s. The first facilities were built by the Civilian Conservation Corps and the park was dedicated in 1939. The present facilities were authorized during the Wallace and Brewer administrations and built in the 1970s. Gulf and several other "superparks" were being operated by a major leisure contractor at a loss when the Department of Conservation took the parks back in 1988. Under the direction of Gary Leach, the parks are now 86 percent self-sufficient, the highest percentage in the nation. Gulf even makes a profit. The resort is a popular convention site and currently attracts some two million people a year. It usually ranks high by readers on *Family Circle* magazine's national poll of family resorts.

The state park is open year round. If you're planning to go during the summer, and, especially if your party will require several rooms, you should know that the park is heavily booked during peak season. The park's reservation office will take deposits up to 12 months in advance. **Phone 1-800-ALA-PARK.**

GOLF COURSES:
• Gulf Shores Golf Club, 18 holes. Public. Phone 968-7366.
• Gulf State Park Resort, 18 holes. Public. Phone 968-2366.
• Cotton Creek Club at Craft Farms, 18 holes. Phone 968-4622.
• Lakeview Golf Club, 18 holes. Phone 943-8000.

HORSEBACK BEACH RIDES along a half-mile stretch of beach near Fort Morgan are at a walking pace. The supervised rides normally last for about an hour. Reservations are required.
        Getting there: 12 miles west of Hwy. 59 on Hwy. 180 (Fort Morgan Road). Phone 1-800-824-2104 (in state) or 1-800-554-0344.

MOBILE BAY FERRY offers a coastal view of the gulf during a 30-minute trip across Mobile Bay. The ferry departure and arrival points are at Fort Morgan on the east and Fort Gaines on the west. The $12 (one-way) ferry trip can save about 80 miles of highway driving if you are headed from Gulf Shores to Dauphin Island. Departure times from Fort Morgan have been published as: 8:40 a.m., 10, 11:20, 12:40, 2 p.m., 3:20, 4:40, 6 and 7:20. Shorter hours in winter. For information, phone 973-2251 or 1-800-634-4027.

ONO ISLAND is a private island at the Florida line where the 450 houses are accessible only with permission of a guard at the bridge off Hwy. 182. The narrow strip of land 5 miles long was a peninsula attached to the mainland until a hurricane late in the last century enlarged the channel, creating the island. John Golightly paid $3,000 for the island in 1954 and made it his home. The western end was later sold to developers who built the guarded bridge and made it among the most desirable addresses on the gulf coast.
        Strictly controlled architectural requirements - and the high price of lots - ensure that the real estate values will continue to climb. Houses range from $250,000 to $650,000. The majority are built of wood and reflect a strong Caribbean influence. Many are raised to avoid high tides. About a third are primary residences while the balance are second homes. Since there is little to do on the island but sun and socialize, a favored pasttime is gossiping about the latest celebrity rumored to be considering buying a home here. Kenny Stabler and wife Rose have lived here since 1979; Tom Selleck does not. Realty information: 981-8500.

PERDIDO PASS Marina offers gift shopping, fishing supplies and a fine restaurant at the bottom of the soaring bridge near the Florida line. Phone 981-6481.
        Getting there: Go west on Hwy. 182 (the beach road) past the Perdido Beach Resort to Perdido Pass, 3 miles east of the state line.

PIRATES' ISLAND mini golf course is covered with tropical palms, waterfalls, lagoons and caves. Open daily in season.
        Getting there: Next door to the Alabama Gulf Coast Welcome Center on Hwy. 59, north of town. Phone 968-GOLF.

WATERVILLE USA is an attractive, well maintained 17-acre water park that gives youngsters who've tired of bobbing in the salt water of the gulf the opportunity to bob in a fresh-water wave pool and zoom down several water slides. The Raging River offers an 825-foot rafting ride while the more gentle Gulfstream tube ride circles a 1,300-foot route at a snail's pace. There are seven slides in all. Two 18-hole mini-golf courses challenge the entire family. Open weekends in the spring and every day from Memorial Day to Labor Day. Phone 968-2106.

Getting there: Located on the east side of Hwy. 59.

ZOOLAND ANIMAL PARK is a lushly landscaped, 16-acre park showcasing more than 200 exotic animals, from alligators and lemurs to zebras and camels. Emphasis is on endangered species, such as Siberian tigers and rare African monkeys. Other animals include lions, cougars, tigers and a 15-foot python which likes to be petted. A petting zoo and 18-hole, animal-themed mini-golf are also here. Open daily at 9 a.m. Admission. Phone 968-5731.

Getting there: Go north on Hwy. 59 1/2 mile above Waterville.

SIDE TRIP NORTH OF THE BEACH

Drive to the quaint port at the edge of Bon Secour River where the famed Bon Secour oysters are harvested. This French settlement whose name is roughly translated as "safe harbour" dates from the early 18th century. The main business is Bon Secour Fisheries, which employs a number of seafood processors and commercial fishermen.

A ruin known as the **Mystery Fort** has been dated between 1711 and 1750. It has a foundation known as "tabby," a mixture of sand, oyster shells and burned oyster shell mortar.

The origin is unknown, although it has variously been attributed to such visitors as Aztec Indians, Hernado de Soto and the legendary 12th-century Welsh explorer, **Prince Madoc Ab Owain Gwnedd**. Legends say that Madoc sailed a party of 10 ships from the west coast of Wales, wound up at Mobile Bay and established a settlement near here in 1170. Attacked by the hostile Mauvilian tribe, Madoc's party is believed to have sought refuge further up the Alabama River until they were able to form a colony of fortified camps in the region of Lookout Mountain near presentday Mentone. The Daughters of the American Revolution hung a plaque at Fort Morgan stating that Madoc "left behind with the Indians the Welsh language."

WHERE TO STAY

The peak season runs from early May through Labor Day. The best values are from early November to March. March and April and September through early November still offer good values.

Best Western, 337 E. Beach Blvd. (Hwy. 180), has 101 rooms, including large beachfront rooms with private balconies, some kitchenettes and two pools. A Denny's restaurant is located in the building. Rates vary by season. Write P.O. Box 398, Gulf Shores, 36547. Fax 948-6660. **Phone 1-800-788-4557** or 948-2711.

Days Inn, 26032 Hwy. 182 E., is near the Perdido Beach Resort in Orange Beach. Each of the 94 beachside guest rooms has free satellite TV movies, a microwave oven and refrigerator. The heated pool is indoors. A raised boardwalk leads to the sand where chaise lounges are available. The Days Inn is only 1/2 mile from fishing and shopping. In addition to a complimentary continental breakfast, a white-tablecloth restaurant is across the street. Write P.O. Box 1003, Orange Beach, 36561. Fax 981-9254. Rates vary widely by season, from $39 weeknight in November to $120 weekend in summer for a gulf front room with queen-sized bed. Rooms perpendicular to the beach are $10 less. A real bargain is the winter monthly rate as low as $475 for a side room. Golf, fishing and honeymoon packages are available. **Phone 981-9888** or 1-800-247-1982 for rates.

Holiday Inn at Hwy. 182, E. Beach Blvd., is a good family beachfront headquarters if you want to be near the center of Gulf Shores. The 118 rooms offer ocean views. Lighted tennis courts, outdoor pool, nearby facilities for windsurfing and sailing. The full-service restaurant serves breakfast, lunch and dinner. Kids eat free. Double rate: $51-$129 plus tax. Golf packages are available. **Phone 948-6191.**

Gulf Shores Plantation, located on the western end of the island, is the state's most complete private beach resort. With five gulfside pools and one indoors, and eight lighted tennis courts, (not to mention two health spas), there's plenty of activity available after you've walked the 4,000 feet of private beach. One, two and three-bedroom condo suites with kitchens offer variety for the size of parties gathering at the beach. Charter fishing can be arranged. Golfing is available through an arrangement with the Cotton Creek Club designed by Arnold Palmer. Fax 540-2291. Efficiency rate: $70-$95 plus tax. Write P.O. Box 1299, Gulf Shores, 36547. **Phone 1-800-554-0344.**

Island House Hotel, 26650 Perdido Beach Blvd. near Zeke's Marina, has 161 rooms on the beach facing the gulf and is the newest beach hotel. The Island Cafe serves three meals daily and offers food service. The lounge has a relaxed atmosphere for food and cocktails. Relax in the hotel swimming pool or rent watercraft on the beach. A golf course is nearby. Fax 981-6833. Executive king and penthouse suites are available. Double rate: $69-$119 plus tax, depending on season. Ask about golf, honeymoon and getaway packages. **Phone 1-800-264-2642** or 981-6100.

Perdido Beach Resort, 27200 Perdido Beach Blvd., Orange Beach, is the place to stay if you want the best and you're not on a budget. Superior service is matched only by amenities and beautifully appointed rooms. The twin, eight-story Mediterrean towers provide a bold, salmon-colored landmark for Orange Beach and the Perdido Bay area. Each room features a balcony with a panoramic view of the gulf. Most are either king or double/double bedded rooms. Ask for a corner room in the east tower for views of the sunrise on the bay and sunset over the gulf. The crunchy white sand beach just beyond the outdoor pool has been ranked in the top three in the nation, according to *The Washington Post*. Some 650 stretches of beach, from Maui to Maine, were judged on sand softness, number of sunny days, water and air temperature, litter and accessibility.
       Regardless of your eating or drinking pleasures, the Perdido offers plenty of options: The spacious lobby bar is good for socializing and watching sunbathers on the pooldeck. The hotel has a fine dining restaurant, Voyagers, which clearly deserves its AAA 4-diamond rating. The separate Cafe Palm Breeze has casual, all-day dining featuring seafood from local coastal waters. A poolside snack bar is open in season and a nightclub has dancing nightly.
       Thanks to a lower level beach entrance, you can reach the elevators in your wet suit and not have to go through the lobby. You can use the same route to the four

lighted tennis courts, whirlpool and saunas, full-service health club, five nearby golf courses and nine marinas.

It is the largest hotel on Alabama's Gulf Coast and attracts many conventions and meetings year round. It offers 30,000 square feet of meeting and pre-function space and a ballroom up to 8,384 square feet.

The hotel is on Hwy. 182, 8 miles east of Hwy. 59. Shuttle service to the Pensacola airport 40 minutes away is available upon reservation. Valet parking attendants and bellmen are part of the attentive staff.

It was a Hilton for many years, but the hotel became so succcessful that it didn't need the franchise reservation system. The hotel gained additional exposure as a location in the bestseller *The Firm*, (even though Tom Cruise didn't film any scenes here). Fax 981-5672. Double rate: $59-$150, depending on season. The Perdido Beach has a wide range of golf, weekly and three-night romance packages. Phone 981-9811 for package brochure. **Reservations 1-800-634-8001.**

Quality Inn Beachside, 931 W. Beach Blvd., is a six-story highrise with 158 units, including many suites and kitchenettes. Indoor pool and hot tub, outdoor pool and pool bar, health center, restaurant, lounge, room service. Double rate: $49-$129, depending on season. Pricebuster and B&B packages available. Fax 948-5232. **Phone 1-800-844-6913** or 948-6874.

CONDO OPTIONS

Great bargains are available in luxurious beachfront condominiums which are ideal for week-long stays at the beach. A sampling of realty companies which hold the keys to condos and beachhouses (all zip codes are Gulf Shores, 36547):

• **Brett/Robinson**, P.O. Box 1727. Phone 968-7363
• **Gold Coast Realty**, P.O. Drawer 1189. Phone 1-800-888-8591
• **Kaiser Realty**, P.O. Drawer 1018. Phone 968-6868
• **Meyer Real Estate**, P.O. Box 1359, phone 1-800-824-6331
• **Sugar Sands Realty**, Box 1647. Phone 981-6981
• **Young's Realty**, Box 2839. Phone 1-800-999-2313

WHERE TO EAT

Local cuisine is simply seafood. The nearby bays and gulf waters are prime beds for harvesting a large share of the nation's shrimp and oysters. You can visit retail seafood outlets to cook your own or select from more than 30 restaurants along the beach. Because of the stiff competition among seafood restaurants, those that aren't good don't last.

With some exceptions, most are along the Eastern Beach Boulevard (182), or near Hwy. 180 north of the beach.

*Kirk Kirkland's Hitching Post, on Hwy. 59 north of the intracoastal canal bridge, offers excellent hickory smoked baby back ribs and mesquite steaks which you can watch simmering on the grill. Relaxed rustic atmosphere. Phone 968-5041.

Two miles north of the beach, *Hazel's Nook at the southeast corner of Hwy. 59 and 180 is the place for breakfast. Regardless of what else you order, you must try the biscuits. They're best when covered with heavy sausage gravy. Phone 968-7065.

Just down 59 from Hazel's on the west side is Bayou Village, an attractive tropical shopping center housing the **Original Oyster House**, where freshly shucked oysters are just the beginning. Steaks and salads are big, too. Phone 968-2445.

Beginning from downtown (intersection of 183 and 59) and going east:

You can't miss the ***Pink Pony**. It's the brightly colored concrete beer box on the beach with a deck that's been overlooking the surf since 1956. One of the first questions regulars asked the day after Frederic hit was, "Did it get the Pony?" Nope, not even a hurricane could dislodge this last bar on the Gulf Shores beach. Try the sourdough cheeseburger. The Pony is recommended as a thirst quenching oasis after time spent in the sun.

A great view of the gulf comes with the food at ***Sea N Suds**, a restaurant and oyster bar on the pier at Young's By the Sea Motel just beyond the Holiday Inn. Phone 968-7893.

Across the street is ****Coconut Willie's**, with an extensive menu of local seafood served up broiled, fried or charbroiled. The gumbo is an award-winner. Frozen drinks are a specialty. Phone 968-7145.

*Nolan's across from the Lighthouse Motel is open evenings with seafood and steaks and dancing. Phone 968-2111.

The ****Sand Castle** restaurant at **Gulf State Park Resort Hotel** serves all-you-can-eat buffets for breakfast, lunch and dinner as well as menu service. Specialties are seafood and prime rib. The average dinner check is $8. Phone 948-4853.

Six miles east of downtown Gulf Shores is Romar Beach, with a Winn-Dixie grocery anchoring Gulf View Square across 182 from the beach. ***Hazel's Family Restaurant**, which has a Shoney's-like breakfast buffet, handles large crowds well.

**Perdido Pass is an excellent choice for drinks, view and dinner.

Highway 161 is perpendicular to the beach road (182) and links with the parallel 180. Turn left on 161, with Cotton Bayou on your right, where you'll find ****Cotton's**, with seafood, steaks and Maine lobster a specialty. Phone 981-9268.

**Hemingway's is off 161 on County Road 2 overlooking the Orange Beach Marina and serving up cajun cuisine created in the famous Prudhomme family tradition. Phone 981-9791.

Head out east on 180 toward the point of Perdido Bay where charter fishing boats depart and you'll discover other local favorites. ****Bear Point Marina** restaurant and lounge, 3.5 miles east of 161, serves award-winning cajun grouper and other local fish. Luxury yachts in the marina add to the scenery. Phone 981-6991.

****Voyagers at the Perdido Beach Resort sets the standard for fine dining at the beach. Chef Gerhard Brill features spectacular continental and creole cuisine. The hotel is 6.5 miles east of Hwy. 59. Phone 981-9811.

**Zeke's, with a marina, shop and lounge, is popular with the locals.

Near the Alabama Point bridge is the ****Oyster Bar** on Perdido Key, where locals mix easily with tourists.

***Perdido Pass Restaurant at the foot of Alabama Point Bridge is 8 miles from Hwy. 59. The Pass serves great seafood, mesquite grilled or cajun blackened angus beef for lunch and dinner. The restaurant overlooks the pass and the bay from the second story of the building. Phone 981-6312.

CLIMATE GUIDE

The average annual daily high temperature at the beach is 75 degrees. The monthly average high temperatures demonstrate why the beach is such a pleasant place to visit year round:

Month	Degrees	Month	Degrees
January	61	July	88
February	63	August	88
March	66	September	87
April	74	October	78
May	80	November	69
June	86	December	62

CIVIC CLUB DATES

In case you need to keep perfect attendance for a civic club while vacationing at the gulf, the following list is for your review:

• **Rotary** - Thurs. noon at Gulf State Park restaurant
• **Lions Club** - First and third Wed. noon at Gulf State Park
• **Lions Club** - First and third Tues. noon at Hazel's Family Restaurant, Orange Beach;
• **Optimists** - Tues. at 7 a.m. at Gulf Shores United Methodist
• **Kiwanis** - Tues. noon at Quality Inn, Gulf Shores
• **AARP**, Fourth Tues. at 1 p.m., G.S. Community Center. Phone 986-8424.

ANNUAL EVENTS AT THE BEACH

Late March to Easter Week

Spring Break - The beaches - High school and college students head to Gulf Shores and Orange Beach for sunning, socializing and beer drinking during the ritual Easter break. Alabama families rent condos for "AEA," what residents call the week when schools close and teachers attend the annual session of the Alabama Education Association. Between 100,000 and 125,000 young people and parents visit during spring break.

Last Saturdays in March and October

Elberta German Sausage Festival - Town Park - Volunteer firemen serve 6,500 pounds of their famous German sausage, not to mention sauerkraut, filled cabbage, hot potato salad, shrimp, crab, gumbo and goulash served over rice. The biannual German heritage celebration event features ethnic costumed dancers, cloggers and polka bands. More than 250 vendors sell baked goods, collectibles, local crafts and freshly squeezed sugar cane juice. A kiddie carnival is set up on the athletic field adjoining the tree-shaded park. Ale and soft drinks are sold to wash down the sausage. Upwards of 25,000 people come during the two-day event.

Park on the highway right-of-way and follow the crowds past the Uniroyal store. Bring lawn chairs to enjoy the entertainment in comfort, but go easy on the kraut on the sausage. The volunteer fire department and auxiliary began the festival in 1977 to benefit the fire department and other community projects. The festival is 8 a.m.-6 p.m. Town Park is bounded by State, Church, Pine and Main streets. Elberta is east of Foley on U.S. 98. Phone 986-5995.

Third or last weekend of April

Mullet Tossing Championship - Flora-Bama Lounge - The dubious world's championship of mullet tossing draws hundreds of competitors and thousands of spectators. The object is to see who can toss a dead fish the greatest distance across the stateline into Alabama. Qualifying starts Friday and continues into Sunday morning, with finals that afternoon. An entry fee gets you a t-shirt and a shot at the title. The record is more than 188 feet. Kenny Stabler usually tosses out the first mullet. Phone 981-8555.

Second or third weekend of May
Sea Oats Festival - Public Beach at Hwy. 59 - Sand sculpture contests vie with crafts displayed by invited Gulf Coast artists and musical concerts for the attention of beach lovers getting the jump on summer. Free. Phone 968-7511.

Second weekend of October
National Shrimp Festival - Public beach at Hwy. 59 - The biggest beach party of the year showcases Alabama shrimp served up in many delicious dishes: shrimp tempura, cajun shrimp, kabobs, jambalaya and shrimp that's simply boiled and peeled or fried golden brown. Want a seafood platter? Crab claws, blackened amberjack, grouper, mullet and even shark are available to sample.

The shrimp fest is more than just food; it's also one of the premier craft shows along the coast. The show of 250 exhibitors offers excellent crafts that range from photography, oil paintings and watercolors to jewelry and stained glass, with most art properly reflecting the gulf coast lifestyle. More than 25 booths, representing the finest restaurants in the Gulf Shores-Orange Beach area, showcase the talents of local chefs who display their most imaginative creations. The show features rows of crafts booths, as well as a special children's art village and continuous live music. There's even a sailboat regatta and skydiving.

Alabama ranks among the top five states in shrimping. It's shrimp festival, however, is in a class by itself. The event was started two decades ago as an event to attract people back to Gulf Shores in the fall. Obviously, it worked. The beach is jammed with 200,00 people and traffic on the beach road slows to a crab crawl. A tip for senior citizens and parents with children in strollers: come on Thursday when the crowd is the lightest. Make reservations for accommodations well in advance. Phone the Chamber of Commerce at 968-7511.

Fourth weekend in October
Re-enactment of the Battle of Mobile - Fort Morgan - The Confederate fort guarding the east entrance to Mobile Bay surrendered after being bombarded Aug. 5-23, 1864. The final day of the siege, more than 5,000 cannonballs struck the brick fort, forcing the Confederates to surrender.Watch costumed soldiers stage a mock battle outside on Saturday and then go inside the fort to watch demonstrations on the procedures for firing a cannon, ending with a thundering, resonnating boom that vibrates the enclosed fort. Tour the fort encampment by candlelight on Saturday night. Yankee re-enactors stage a final assault inside the fort on Sunday and win again, unfortunately. Bring a camera with an extra long lens to capture the best photos. Confirm the date. Phone 540-7125.

Mid-November weekend
Sea Harvest Festival - Perdido Pass - A sports festival which gives amateurs the chance to compete in windsurfing, beach volleyball, beach running and fishing also draws top national competitors and former Olympians. The sanctioned windsurfing competition is among the most unique and exciting to watch. Phone 981-8000.

FAIRHOPE

- **Claim to fame:** Relaxed resort atmosphere
- **Don't miss:** Punta Clara Kitchen, Grand Hotel
- **Unique accommodations:** B&Bs
- **Population:** 8,485
- **Tourist information:** Kolleen Crandall, **Eastern Shore Chamber of Commerce**, 327 Fairhope Ave., Fairhope, 36532. Phone 928-6387.

The attractive bayside town of Fairhope has a remarkable origin. A tiny band of dissidents from Des Moines, Iowa, supported economist Henry George's theory put forward in *Progress and Poverty* that people would be encouraged to profit if they were taxed only for the land on which they lived. They selected Mobile Bay over sites in western Tennessee and southwest Louisiana. Some 25 adults and children moved here in 1894 to form a single-tax colony.

Soap maker Joseph Fels provided funds to purchase a 132-acre tract for the experiment. Colonists built homes, roads and a wharf in exchange for script which could be used to pay their land lease or to purchase goods at the community store. They attracted innovative thinkers, artists and educators.

In 1904, the colony became the **Single Tax Corporation** and today remains the oldest and most successful single-tax operation in the nation. When the town incorporated in 1908, a quarter of the 4,000 acres where 500 people lived in 125 houses on colony leaseholds was owned by the corporation.

Marietta Johnson founded the Organic School with the belief that children should grow spiritually and physically as well as mentally. Her school gave no grades. The school site is now occupied by a junior college campus which most assuredly gives grades.

Colonists thought their effort had a "fair hope" of succeeding. Today the street names of Fairhope reflect some of the town's founders and such ideals as Liberty, Equity and Freedom.

What Fairhope's heritage means to visitors is that you pay no local sales tax. The legacy is also reflected in the town's cultural benefits, which include a respected art museum, equity theater, a major outdoor art show and beautification projects the year around.

On a bluff above Mobile Bay, Fairhope boasts 2 miles of beach along the water, the scene of local yachting competitions in the summer. Flounder, crab and shrimp can easily be caught during a **jubilee**, Mobile Bay's natural phenomenon in which bottom-dwelling marine life, delirious because of a sudden lack of oxygen in the water, migrate toward the shore. When word spreads, every available bucket, cooking pot and washbasin is enlisted to harvest this seafood bonanza. Some jubilees are highly localized, say, 50 yards in length, and other times they stretch 5 miles. Such events occur up to 10 times a year. The few other places in the world where such jubilees occur are off the coasts of Chile, Africa and Thailand.

Fairhope is the perfect place to escape for a leisurely B&B weekend. The usually balmy weather encourages strolls around town. The guest houses are within easy walking of the **Eastern Shore Art Center**, the 80 attractive downtown shops and restaurants, as well as the pier down the hill overlooking Mobile Bay. The main streets boast colorful displays of seasonal plantings. Red and white petunias or geraniums nod from planter boxes atop sidewalk trash cans. During the mild winter, poinsettias are planted in the ground!

The mild climate and a growing season of 318 days make Fairhope one of the nation's most attractive retirement communities. For reasons that are apparent on the first stroll around town, Fairhope is high on any national list of "quality of life" indexes and favorite retirement towns. As a result, the Chamber of Commerce gets about 300 inquiries a month and real estate values have skyrocketed. The best time to visit is during the arts and crafts festival the third weekend in March.

Fairhope is the major destination along Baldwin County's Eastern Shore. Bay Minette is the county seat to the north. Daphne, a bedroom community to Mobile with the largest population, is linked by Scenic Hwy. 98 to Fairhope, Spanish Fort, Point Clear, Magnolia Springs and Silverhill.

WELCOME CENTER

The **Eastern Shore Chamber of Commerce** displays a large selection of brochures on restaurants, shops, special events, accommodations and real estate in its streetfront building on the north side of Fairhope Avenue between Section and Church. Phone 928-6387.

The **Scenic Overlook** welcome center at I-10 and U.S. 98 at Daphne offers a great view of the bay, as well as brochures and directions.

ATTRACTIONS

EASTERN SHORE ART CENTER is a highly respected center for the visual arts. A handsome series of galleries showcase oils, watercolors, pottery, sculpture, fiber arts and photography by member and guest artists. Lectures and association classes are regular features of this, one of the state's most active arts centers. Free. Phone 928-2228.

Getting there: Located opposite city hall just north of the retail area at the corner of Section Avenue and Oak Street.

FAIRHOPE PIER extends 1,425 feet from the Eastern Shore into the shallow Mobile Bay, a reminder of the days when travel over to Mobile was by boat or a 60-mile trip via Jackson. The original wooden pier was an important recreational center with a casino and bathhouse. When it decayed, a concrete replacement was erected in 1969 to provide sportsmen with a suitable spot for fishing. It has also been discovered by retirees who know that two roundtrips equal a mile. Benches and telescopes are available for the less active. The ****Yardarm Restaurant**, opened in 1972 by Bob Pope, seats 58 and provides an additional reason to visit. The hundreds of roses planted around the fountain at the land end of the pier add that many more.

SEVEN GABLES is a private 1855 cottage which overlooks Mobile Bay in Montrose and open for group tours by reservation.

The two-story frame house was fired on by Federal ships after the Battle of Mobile Bay and fortunately the shells fell short. Northern soldiers poked bayonets in the front yard in an effort to locate family silver, but luckily, it had been hidden in the cornfield.

Now the home of Mr. and Mrs. William Buck Taylor Jr., Seven Gables is furnished in period antiques, including many pieces which have been in their respective families for generations. Write P.O. Box 415 Montrose, 36559. Phone 928-5454 or 928-9654.

Getting there: Follow Scenic 98 north to Montrose. The house is north of the post office on Main Street.

SIDE TRIPS

Inspiration Oak is a 500-year-old tree 65-feet tall with a shade which can cover half of a football field. It struggles to survive after someone girdled it with a chainsaw as the county was negotiating to buy it for a park.

After hearing news reports of the attack in October, 1990, Florida forester Stan Revis rushed to the site and grafted 200 pencil-sized twigs and 32 small trees across the gash to feed the branches. Volunteers trimmed excess branches off its 207-foot span and dug a 140-foot well to supply a sprinkler system. They erected an "intensive care" box around the tree in hopes the callous growth of the grafts would cover the circular wound. The tree is showered with about 100 gallons of water for 12 minutes every daylight hour. Children from around the world send "get well cards."

More than two years after the attack, the tree's condition remains critical. In 1992, it lost its new leaves just a couple of months after they sprouted. Meanwhile, the county condemned the tree and three acres for the park and filed charges against the former owner. Stop by for a tour of the Inspiration Oak. Many people do. Donations are appreciated, but not required. Write P.O. Box 475, Magnolia Springs, 36555. Phone 965-3556. The tree is south of the Fish River bridge in tiny Yupon where County 17 crosses U.S. 98.

The **Minamac Wildflower Bog** is a privately-owned, four-acre garden near Silverhill where more than 80 varieties of wildflowers - including some endangered - grow in unbelievable abundance in a marsh at the edge of a pond. Hooded pitcher plants, bladderworts, Venus fly traps and other carnivorous plants grow thickly with black-eyed Susans, blazing stars and native orchids. The bog was discovered on land owned by Mr. and Mrs. Webster MacCartee when they burned the brush around the pond over a three-year period and the wildflowers began to emerge.

After identifying and marking scores of plants, they built an 800-foot boardwalk and began giving tours by reservation. They rejuvenate the bog with a quick burning each February and plants gradually return. The best time to visit is during the peak blooming season in late August through September. For reservations and directions off Hwy. 104, phone 947-3044.

A drive to nearby **Daphne** takes you to a pair of unusual and lively places to hoist a few beverages. **Judge Roy Bean** is a tavern popular with collegiate party-goers because of the rustic atmosphere inside and the sports, socializing and entertainment in the courtyard outside. Owner Jack West also stages occasional concerts with big-name acts. Open nightly except Monday, it is most active on Sundays. Located on Old U.S. 98. Phone 626-9988.

A gas station built in 1920 is now **Manci's Antique Club**, a hangout with walls adorned with hundreds of old tools, Jim Beam bourbon bottles, jugs, cow bells and even a rickshaw in the corner. Inside the ladies' room is a lifesize mannequin of "Adam" whose fig leaf is rigged when lifted to sound an alarm throughout the club. Special times to visit are June 4 for the annual Corn and Tater Boil, and traditional holidays. Open seven days at the corner of Daphne and Bellrose avenues. Phone 626-9917.

The **Cock of the Walk** in Daphne is a popular restaurant.

North of **Spanish Fort** is **Historic Blakeley Park**, the 3,800-acre battlefield of the largest and most significant infantry action in the state during the Civil War. Some 32,500 Union soldiers fresh from victory at Fort Morgan and Spanish Fort defeated 4,500 Confederates. More than 1,000 were killed or wounded. The last major land battle of the war was fought April 12, 1865, just a few hours after Gen. Robert E. Lee surrendered to Gen. Ulysses S. Grant at Appomattox. Fighting did not actually end until May 8 when Confederate Gen. Richard Taylor gave up to Union forces near Citronelle.

A visit is recommended primarily for those who are serious about visiting every Civil War battlefield. A battle festival is staged in early April and the **Blakeley Cajun/ Bluegrass Festival** is held the first Saturday in October. Admission. Open daily, 9:30 a.m. to dusk.

Take I-65 exit 32 and follow the signs south on Hwy. 225 for 16 miles. At the sign, turn west 1.5 miles to reach the park. From I-10, go north of Spanish Fort on 225 for 4.5 miles. It is approximately 12 miles east of Mobile. Phone 626-0798.

WHERE TO STAY

Bay Breeze Guest Cottage at 742 South Mobile St. is decorated with a brass bed and family antiques surrounded by white pine paneling. The sofa bed in the living room expands accommodations of up to four people. Prepare snacks in the kitchenette or walk to nearby restaurants. Double rates are $75. No children, pets, smoking or credit cards. Phone Bill and Becky Jones at **928-8976**.

Doc and Dawn's is a Victorian cottage set within a garden flanked by a waterfall which splashes from an old tin bucket into a small rock pool below. The house began as a 222-square-foot board-and-batten workshop of retired dentist Sherold "Doc" Pope and his wife, Dawn. As a retirement project, they transformed the modest building into a one-room garden cottage with kitcken and bath.

Twin iron beds, lots of ruffles and gingerbread trim and framed poems and quotations provide more than a hint of Victorian decor. A little sprite named Victoria, who just might be a figment of the hosts' imagination, "shares" the cottage, although you'll probably never see her. A little girl's drop-waist dress and hat hang on the wall and a tiny nightgown hangs in the bathroom beneath a sign that invites guests to "Get a good night's sleep in another era."

A microwave and coffee pot (coffee included) are for guests' convenience. The nightly double rate without breakfast is $50; with breakfast, $75. Inn policy does not permit children, pets, smoking or alcohol. No credit cards accepted. Write 314 De Le Mare, Fairhope, 36532. **Phone 928-0253.**

The Guest House, an attractive bed and breakfast located a short walk from Fairhope Avenue, has three bedrooms, as well as a suite in the carriage house. Betty Bostrom restored the 1904 two-story frame house with broad wrap-around porch and land-scaped the courtyard to provide a serene retreat.

Each double guest room has a private bath. Bright, colorful prints and stripes in the bedrooms add a sense of resort crispness. The overnight rate of $75 includes a full breakfast, afternoon tea, and wine and cheese. A 10 percent discount is offered for senior citizens. No smoking. No pets. MasterCard and Visa accepted. Write 63 S. Church St., Fairhope, 36532. **Phone 928-6226.**

Marcella's B&B Inn, a two-story house toward the bay from Fairhope Avenue, was built in 1914 and enlarged in 1940. Marcella Gerhart drew on her interior design background to bring warmth and color to the house where six children were raised. In addition to upstairs bedrooms, a garden cottage with two bedrooms and a kitchen is available. **Phone 990-8520.**

Mershon Court was built at the turn of the century by Dr. C.L. Mershon, the town's first physician, and became a B&B in 1986. It is an attractive wooden house framed by a neat white fence which also encloses a gazebo and a private swimming pool for guests. Three bedrooms are upstairs with a fourth downstairs. One of the nicest bedrooms that overlooks the street is accessible to the deck above the front porch. Another has a deck overlooking the garden and the pool. A continental breakfast is served in the dining room. Rates of $59 to $69 for a double depend on whether a room has a private or shared bath.

Betty Jo and Rufus Bethea, who are teachers in Mobile, bought the B&B at the urging of their daughter-in-law. A previous operator who worked for Dolly Parton "found" the house at the suggestion of author Fannie Flagg. It is a two-block walk down to the famous Fairhope Pier which overlooks Mobile Bay and just 2 blocks from the center of the shopping district. No smoking, children or pets. Visa and MasterCard accepted. Write the Betheas at 203 Fairhope Ave., Fairhope, 36532. **Phone 928-7398.**

The Grand Hotel

"Point Clear remains the most attractive watering place of the South. The best people of the adjoining states flock there in summer to enjoy salt bathing right at their chamber door. The society, fishing, sailing and eating are unexcelled by any other summer resort in the United States."

Although the sentiments were written more than a century ago about a hotel built in 1847, the tradition of quality, romance, service and comfort are as relevant for today's guests who frequent the Grand Hotel on the same site.

For nearly 150 years, a luxury resort has anchored the sunswept point which juts into Mobile Bay, attracting travelers who face the gentle bay breezes by day and dance under the stars at night.

From the moment you turn into the driveway under a canopy of live oak trees flanked by a lagoon surrounded by azaleas, you know that the hotel will live up to the name.

The Grand sits on the point with wings of guest rooms spreading from the lobby to face the bay, the marina or the landscaped grounds. In addition to the 292 rooms and suites, there are 16 cottages tucked under the trees. The pine-paneled lobby, surrounding a tall brick chimney, reflects the casual air of a gentleman's lodge. The restaurants and lounge offer spectacular sunset views of the bay.

You have several choices of restaurants, beginning with the most upscale:
• The ***Grand Dining Room** is the largest restaurant, with seating on two levels which look across the bay toward Mobile. Its Sunday brunch draws people from miles around to feast on the crepes, eggs, roast beef, salads and desserts guaranteed to make you skip food for the rest of the day. Dress is casual, with jackets suggested for dinner.
• For the freshest seafood each evening, prepared to your specifications, enjoy the ***Bay View Room** which overlooks Mobile Bay. Appetizers range from crab cakes to smoked scallops. Entrees offered with soup, salad and vegetable are trout, swordfish, shark, salmon and grouper, to name a few. Come casually dressed.
• Golfers and others eat a casual lunch or dinner at the Lakewood Club Room overlooking the Azalea course fairway.
• Guests taking a break from swimming eat sandwiches, burgers and snacks at the poolside Pelican's Nest.
• The best place to enjoy a drink while admiring the sunset is the Birdcage lounge.

Perhaps Bucky Miller, who's been tending bar since 1941, will be on duty to serve you one of his legendary mint juleps.
- Make a date for afternoon tea at 4.
- If you need to stay sequestered, room service is available around the clock.

Far more than just a great hotel, the Grand is an outstanding resort by any standard. The gigantic swimming pool was made from the hull of a ship. Complimentary recreation also includes horseshoes, croquet, volleyball and fishing from the hotel pier. The hotel will even supply you with a pole and bait for fishing off the bay pier and the chef will cook your catch for dinner! For optional fees, the choices are almost unlimited. Play 36 holes of championship golf, with the 14th hole island green the signature hole. The hotel has 10 clay tennis courts, a scenic horse trail to ride, windsurfing, deep-sea fishing, Hobie Cats and 20 miles of trails for rented bicycles. At night, dancing under the stars out on Jubilee Point is about as romantic a setting as you could ask for.

If you'd rather be passive, dangle your feet in the lazy waters of Mobile Bay, relax under the moss-draped oaks by the lagoon or stroll the boardwalk past neighboring antebellum cottages facing the bay.

Those curious about how old the hotel is have reason to be a bit confused. It is the third on this site. F.H. Chamberlain built the first 40-room Point Clear Hotel in 1847. Its bar was called the Texas because it was set apart in a separate building, like the republic apart from the Union. It gained a reputation as "the queen of Southern resorts."

During the Civil War, a nearby building used for social events was hit by a shell after the Battle of Mobile Bay, and Alabama soldiers were encamped here while it was used as a hospital. Some 300 who died are buried in a small plot near the 18th tee of the Azalea course. Fire which started in the kitchen damaged the hotel in 1869. The first hotel to be called the Grand was built on the original foundation in 1875. The legendary Texas bar was swept away by the great hurricane of 1893, but the hotel survived.

The original heart pine flooring of the 1875 hotel was used in the main building when the present Grand was constructed in 1941, again on the site of the 1847 hotel.

Staff members and guests who had been coming for decades were nervous about the changes when the Marriott Corporation purchased the 550-acre resort in 1981 and doubled it to 306 rooms as a destination for conventions. The fears were not justified, for the management continued the high standards of service, even to having the same veteran housekeeping people clean the very same rooms every day. The staff was enlarged so that the ratio of employees to guests is one to one. Also in keeping with tradition, Chester Hunt continues to pilot special guests in the Grand's Cadillac limousine, just as he has done for decades. Bartender extraordinare Bucky Miller, who has greeted guests since 1941, is another Grand legend.

A glance around the parking lot verifies that what was true a century ago remains today, that "the best people of the adjoining states flock there in summer" to while away the days and nights in pampered comfort. The Grand is 23 miles southeast of Mobile. Exit I-10 onto U.S. 98 E. toward Fairhope and then Scenic 98 South through Fairhope. Turn left onto Scenic 98 and go 4 miles to Point Clear. Fax 928-1149. Write to Marriott's Grand Hotel, Point Clear, 36564. Double rate: $125-$175 plus tax. Open year round, with many inclusive holiday packages available. Phone 928-9201. **Reservations 1-800-544-9933.**

WHERE TO EAT

Fairhope is thriving with excellent places to eat. If you are in town for more than just a day, seek out some of the following: **Yucatan Cantina, Winslow's Cafe**, The **Vine Merchant, Santa Fe Grill, Andre's Deli** and **Maggie's Bistro**.

**Old Bay Steamer permits you to sit near the window and watch shoppers walk by or sit in seclusion beyond the bar or in the courtyard and enjoy steamed and grilled seafood. Be entertained by the framed quotes posted around the restaurant. It is on Fairhope Avenue just above Church. Phone 928-5714.

WHERE TO SHOP

The Punta Clara Kitchen is a "must stop" if you enjoy good candy. What began as a Brodbeck family hobby in 1952 has expanded into a second-generation mail order business offering hand-made pralines, English toffee and pecan treats. The business is in "Miss Colleen's House," a rambling Victorian house built in 1897. The firm's trademark black pot at the edge of the parking lot is a sign you are at the right place, but you might not be prepared for the feeling that Miss Colleen still lives within walls of dark beaded-ceiling. Several roped-off rooms down the hall are furnished in the cluttered look popular several generations ago and add a touch of interest - if not eeriness - to a visit. Watch candy being made by hand or browse through the gift shop/candy store. (The original Spanish name for Point Clear is "Punta Clara.") Open daily, 9-5; Sun., afternoon. It is a mile south of Grand Hotel on Scenic 98. Phone 928-8477.

Shops offering casual women's clothing with a distinctive upscale resort flair sit side by side with stores selling old books, antiques, craft supplies, beachware and excellent artwork by local artists. Because the pace in Fairhope is decidedly laid back, allow plenty of time to browse through such favorites as the **Obvious Place** (gifts and art) , **Moonstone** (gems and crystals) and **Sailor's Loft** (nautical). Fairhope has a good range of antiques from **Emporium**'s collectibles to **Crown & Colony's** pricey selection, with most shops along three blocks of Section flanking Fairhope. A couple of shops are down on Church.

Continue east to **Foley** for a shopping trip to numerous antique malls and South Alabama's best outlet mall, the **Rivera Centre**. It opened in 1988 on Hwy. 59 for the six million-plus visitors who each year go to Gulf Shores 15 minutes to the south. The "mall" is actually a circle flanked by a pair of stripmall wings. The 80-plus stores sell womenswear, menswear, children's clothes, shoes, handbags, electronics, housewares and other items at savings of 40 to 75 percent.

A partial list of stores: Aigner, Aileen, Arrow, American Tourister, Bass Shoe, Bugle Boy, Burlington Brands, Calvin Klein, Capezio, Coach, Corning, Dansk, Dexter Shoes, Duckhead, Evan Picone, Gitano, Guess, Hanes, Jerzees, Johnston & Murphy, Levi's, Liz Claiborne, Magnavox, Manhattan, Nautica, Oneida, OshKosh, Ralph Lauren, Reebok, Van Heusen, West Point Pepperell (anchor). A food court offers a variety of food. There's even a bank ATM, but stores accept bank credit cards. Open Mon.-Sat., 9-9 and Sun. 10-6.

To check seasonality of hours, phone 943-8888. Closed Easter, Thanksgiving, Dec. 25. From the north, exit I-65 at Hwy. 59 near Bay Minette and go 45 miles. Eastbound motorists on I-10 can take exit 35 to Fairhope and follow U.S. 98 East. Turn south on 59, go 2 miles. Westbound: take I-10 exit 44 at Hwy. 59 and go south 22 miles.

For antiques, visit the **Gas Works Antique Mall** on Hwy. 59. Formerly the offices for the local natural gas company, it houses two floors of dealer displays with lots of kitchen collectibles, books and silver. Open Tues.-Sat., 10-5; Sun., 1-5; Mon., in summer. Phone 943-5555.

The **Ole Crush Antique Mall** a couple of blocks south in a two-story, 1920 Orange Crush bottling plant sells furniture, silver, china and kitchen utensils. Open seven days until 5. Phone 943-8154.

The owners of the **Gift Horse** restaurant have added an antiques center next door at 215 W. Laurel and an antiques shop around the corner at 108 S. Alston. Phone 943-7776 and 943-7278.

Hope's All Natural Cheesecake is south of the outlet center on Hwy. 59. New York style cheesecakes containing Grand Marnier, chocolate Amaretto and various berry toppings are sold, along with gourmet coffee beans. Open Mon.-Sat., 9-6. Phone 943-5858.

Just north of Foley is the **Berry Barn** in Loxley. The combination farmers market and gift store sells fresh strawberries, blueberries, peaches, figs and vegetables in season. Loxley is best known for strawberries, usually sold from early April to mid-June when the Barnhills open their fields to permit self-picking. You can also pick blackberries in June. Open daily, 9-6. New pecans sold Nov.-Dec. shelled, in-shell or cracked. Light lunches are served year round. Located on Hwy. 59 a mile south of I-10. Phone 800-844-8573 or 964-6579.

Foley Fish Co., located at 321 S. McKenzie on Hwy. 59, packs fresh shrimp, crawfish and whatever else is in season for you to take home from the beach. It is a clean, unfishy-smelling store across the street from the art deco phone store. Eddie and Peggy Hesse are the owners of the business founded in 1921. It is open every day except Thanksgiving and Dec. 25. Phone 943-6461.

East of Foley, the **Baldwin Heritage Museum** preserves the rural heritage of Baldwin County in an 8,000-square foot building. Collections feature early farm and home implements and rare farm tractors in various states of restoration. The museum mirrors contributions from ethnic groups of Germans, Swiss, Poles and others in the late 19th century through 1950. It is located on land donated by retired banker John Haupt, whose father arrived in 1914. Open Fri.-Sat., 10-5; Sun., 1-5.

Go out of your way east of Foley to visit a neat cheese farm. Alyce Birchenough and husband, Doug Wolbert, personally do all the work related to dairying at **Sweet Home Farms**. They grow the feed, milk the purebred Guernsey cows, pasteurize the milk and pour it into vats where they separate and bag the curd. They age more than a dozen varieties at least 60 days before displaying the products in the refrigerated case in the tiny sales room.

Their creations include Elberta, a semi-soft cheese with a milky flavor, and Baldwin Swiss, a soft cheese with a nutty character selected for cheese trays and sandwiches. The garden vegetable is recommended for hors d'oeuvres while gouda is fine for cooking and appetizers.

Alyce and Doug match Alabama wine and cheese for gift baskets which are available by mail. Open Tues.-Sat., 10-5. Phone 986-5663. In Foley, turn east off Hwy. 59 to Hwy. 98 and go 2 miles past Elberta. Watch for the Sweet Home Farm sign and turn left. Go 1/2 mile.

When you get hungry shopping in Foley, there are several good places to eat. The ***Gift Horse Restaurant**, about a block west of the main highway at 209 Laurel Ave., is housed in a bright, airy building constructed in 1912. Since 1985, the mahogany buffet table has groaned under a large selection of well prepared salads, meats, vegetables and breads made from Jackie McLeod's recipes. The excellent seafood, steaks and fried biscuits attract regulars from Mobile and Gulf Shores at night. Open every day except Dec. 25. Phone 943-3663.

*Katy's Barbecue**, across Hwy. 59 from KFC, specializes in rib plates and SOB's (slaw, onion and barbecue on Texas toast). The pork and beef are cooked over South Alabama pecan wood and served with a choice of sauces: sweet, mild and hot.

Just 6 miles west of Foley, residents of the attractive waterfront town of **Magnolia Springs** receive their mail in a manner dating back 75 years - by boat. Episcopal Bishop C.M. Beckwith started the route along Fish River in 1916. Even though the area became accessible by road a decade ago, the mailman still travels by water. It's the most efficient way to reach 156 families on a circular route covering 22 miles. By land it would be 85 miles. Water delivery offers some unique problems. Carriers have trouble reaching the boxes in periods of low tide; in summer's high tide, they have trouble getting under the bridges. **Blanche's Restaurant** is widely known for its "fish-in-a-sack" specialty and the best fried eggplant around. The atmosphere is sparse and the service is slow, but the food is great and inexpensive. Be forewarned: no shorts allowed. Phone 965-7642.

ANNUAL EVENTS

Third Friday thru Sunday of March

Arts and Crafts Festival - Downtown - South Alabama's most important arts festival occurs along Section, Oak and Church streets, Fairhope Avenue and other locations. The festival includes entertainment and demonstrations in the streets. Throughout the festival area, artisans can be seen working with the area's native clays and metals and judges award thousands of dollars in prizes at this significant juried arts and crafts show.

Fairhope has earned a special niche among the South's crafts community, and it is most beautiful during the festival when dogwoods and azaleas are in bloom. Tulips and hanging baskets are in full color at every corner and storefront along downtown streets.

Artists consider an invitation to participate among the year's highlights. Some 250 invited craftsmen, artists and vendors make the event one of the state's largest cultural affairs. Some 35,000 visitors attend annually. The festival began in 1952 and the outdoor art show dates from 1972. Phone 928-6387 or 928-2228.

MOBILE

- **Claim to fame:** Live oaks, azaleas, Mardi Gras
- **Don't miss:** Bellingrath Gardens, USS Alabama
- **Eat oysters at:** Wintzell's, chili dogs at Dew Drop Inn
- **Stay at:** Admiral Semmes, Holiday Inn-Downtown
- **Population:** 196,278
- **Tourist information:** Eva Golson, Executive Director; **Department of Tourism**, 150 S. Royal St., P.O. Box 1827, Mobile, 36633. Fax 434-7659. Phone 434-7304 or 1-800-252-3862.

Mobile is Alabama's grand dame of charm, hospitality, civility and grace, shaded by ancient oaks dripping with Spanish moss. Settled nearly three centuries ago by the French and influenced by the Spanish and English, the Port City enjoys a spirit and lifestyle that is unique to America's older cities.

Whether visiting the museums around Fort Conde or sampling the local shrimp dipped in butter sauce in a favored restaurant, you easily come to appreciate the sense of history and tradition that Mobilians take for granted and willingly share with visitors.

King Louis XIV of France was at the height of his power when he directed the French in Quebec to establish a city on Mobile Bay under his patronage, the only city in the New World to be so deemed. He needed a French base along the Gulf Coast to achieve his grand plan to drive the English out of their Atlantic colonies.

When Mobile was founded in 1702 by **Jean Baptiste Le Moyne, Sieur de Bienville**, at a riverfront site north of the present city, a settlement of Maubilla Indians was already there. In less than a decade, the town at Twenty-Seven Mile Bluff consisted of several stores, a Catholic Jesuit church, a blacksmith shop and about 80 Creole cottages spread over a mile. The population consisted of about 300 French-Canadian men and a smaller number of women known as the Cassette Girls sent by the king to marry his loyal men. The women might have come from France, but the men often had to sail to nearby Spanish Pensacola for food and other necessities.

Because of continued flooding and an inadequate defense against intruders, the French moved 27 miles downriver to the west side of the Mobile Bay in 1711, and established the first permanent white settlement in Alabama. The location at present-day **Fort Conde** was strategic because control of the bay, 27 miles long and 8 miles wide at the mouth, could command the entrance to Alabama's major rivers.

For seven years Mobile was the capital of the French colonial empire. This vast interior region of North America claimed by the French in the early 18th century stretched from the Gulf to the Rocky Mountains and into Canada. Mobile seemed destined to become the Paris of the New World, however, in 1718, the capital was shifted 141 miles west to New Orleans. Mobile lost much of its royal luster, but remained an active fur trading center and important military garrison, for it would experience five changes of flags within the next century.

The French built Fort Conde in Mobile between 1724 and 1735 to protect their territorial claim from the Spanish who had established a fort to the east at Pensacola.

Mobile surrendered to the British on Oct. 22, 1763, and the grenadiers of the 22nd and 34th regiments took possession of Fort Conde and renamed it Fort Charlotte. The action ended the ambitious plan in which Bienville and Iberville LeMoyne had struggled to carve France an empire in the western world.

The British flag flew over Mobile for less than two decades. Spain declared war on England in 1779 and Spanish Gov. Bernard Galvez captured the British forts on the Mississippi River the same year. A small garrison of several hundred men in Mobile was no match for Galvez's forces and the city surrendered in March of 1780. The Province of West Florida remained under military law until it was ceded to the Spanish by the British two years later.

When the War of 1812 moved into the gulf, England received permission from Spain to use Mobile as a port of operation against New Orleans.

Under orders from President Madison, Gen. James Wilkinson marched from New Orleans with 600 troops and surrounded Mobile's Fort Charlotte, defended by only 60 men under Capt. Peres. Wilkinson seized Mobile for the United States on April 13, 1813, ending the city's rule by three European countries which spanned more than a century. A year later, Andrew Jackson set up headquarters here in the prelude to the Battle of New Orleans.

With Mobile finally firmly American, commerce increased, attracting successful businessmen and their families from the North and East. Society thrived. Churches and theaters multiplied.

Markets and transportation links were established with communities upriver. The city's economy soared in the 1850s because of the cotton production of the Black Belt plantations around Selma, Marion, Demopolis and other towns. Cotton brokers and shippers made substantial fortunes and built fine homes.

A footnote to slave trading occurred just prior to the Civil War. Even though Congress banned the African slave trade in 1807, illegal slave ships continued to slip into Southern ports with their human cargo. Timothy Meaher of Mobile completed the last known slave ship, the *Clotilde*, in 1859. It returned from its first voyage later that year with a cargo of natives kidnapped from the Guinea coast. Alerted to its arrival, federal patrols awaited the ship in the Mississippi Sound. But Capt. Bill Fowler managed to slip past them into the Mobile River, unload the people and burn the ship. With federal authorities all around the area, Meaher and Foster found it impossible to sell the intended slaves and eventually turned them loose. Many of the freed families banded together to form a community nearby in an area known as Plateau, now known as **AfricaTown**.

Although threatened numerous times during the Civil War, Mobile was the last major Southern city to be occupied by enemy troops. In 1864 the Union captured the CSS *Tennessee* in the Battle of Mobile Bay, but lost the monitor *Tecumseh*. The surrender of the two forts guarding the mouth of Mobile Bay, coupled with the siege of Fort Blakeley and Spanish Fort on the east side of the bay, led to the collapse of the defenders. Union forces finally occupied Mobile on April 12, 1865, just days before the end of the war.

After the war, the economy recovered in part due to shipbuilding, lumber and railroads. Mobile was Alabama's largest city until the end of the 19th century when it was overtaken by Birmingham.

Mobile's river channel has been expanded over the years to accommodate oceangoing ships. The discovery of a major natural gas deposit has also brought numerous drilling rigs to Mobile Bay. The Alabama State Docks was the first completely state-owned facility in the nation to handle the exchange of freight between land and water carriers. The docks has 33 berths to handle ships plying the 36-mile channel which has a 40-foot depth. The port handles exportation of grain, coal and industrial commodities.

During World War II hundreds of ships were built and repaired at Mobile, which remains the coast's largest shipbuilding center. Pulp and paper production, petroleum refining and chemical production are other important sources of jobs in the Port City. The **Tennessee-Tombigbee Waterway** which empties into the Mobile River has become a recent source of additional river traffic.

After the war, many of the shipbuilders, attracted by the area's jobs, stayed in Mobile to work at **Brookley Air Force Base** and adopted the lifestyle. Mobile suffered a severe blow in the 1960s with the phasing out of Brookley. Expansions in chemical manufacturing, construction and cargo handling at the State Docks provide a more optimistic outlook for Mobile's economy. Scott Paper Co. and International Paper Co. are the two largest employers, with more than 6,000 persons on payroll.

A new industry with a greater psychological boost than monetary is **Naval Station Mobile**. The "homeport" is base to a pair of Oliver Hazard Perry class frigates and two Knox class frigates.

Mobile's 1990 population of 196,278 was only slightly more than the 1960 figure of 194,856. The highest figure was 200,452 in 1980. Growth has been in the outlying areas, in Daphne to the east and Tillman's Corner to the west, as Mobile County's population has grown in 30 years from 314,301 to 378,643.

The city's reputation as **azalea capital of the world** dates from the 1930s when the city government planted azaleas along major streets and homeowners landscaped their yards with them. After a decline during the war years of the 1940s, interest was revived in the 1950s and led to an intense campaign of replanting throughout all areas of public property, including churches, schools and businesses. The **Mobile Azalea Trail** thrived and spread worldwide. A once painted pink curbside trail for motorists to follow for the best gardens has been neglected in recent decades, a casualty of shrinking city finances. Happily, homeowners have taken up some of the slack by maintaining streetside gardens and plantings along major streets.

Most of retail shopping has left downtown for shopping malls along major highways, leaving downtown primarily an office district. The $45 million **Mobile Convention Center** on Water Street is within walking distance of most of the historic attractions and is stimulating downtown economic growth. It has a large exhibition hall, meeting rooms and a skybridge across the street to the Riverview hotel.

Mobile has ambitious plans to attract more people to its historic downtown. In addition to a waterfront park and a hotel-office complex, the abandoned historic houses behind Fort Conde would be developed into a village of shops and bed and breakfast inns. An Omnimax theater like the one in Huntsville and a children's "discovery center" are proposed for the southwest corner of Government and Water Street.

A name which stands for Mobile food has spread throughout much of the Gulf Coast. The Mobile-based **Delchamps** operates more than 120 supermarkets in Louisiana, Mississippi, Alabama and the Florida panhandle. Annual sales approach $1 billion. The stores carry grocery items, as well as fresh cut flowers, fresh seafood and gourmet meats. A prominent local brand of coffee is **Hill & Brooks**, which owner Leroy Hill promotes with teams of Belgian horses.

The heritage, culture and lifestyle separate it from the rest of the state. Mobilians feel more of a kinship to New Orleans and Pensacola than to Montgomery and

Birmingham. Despite a sluggish economy in recent years, the city maintains its reputation for being a fun place to visit. Outstanding seafood restaurants, magnificent gardens, grand historic homes and the casual air of a coastal community infuse Mobile with a charm matched by few other cities in America.

Mobile knows how to throw a party. The pre-Lenten celebration now known as **Mardi Gras** has its origins in the French celebration of their patron saint on St. Louis' Day (Aug. 25). It was first held in the New World in 1703 at the early settlement of Twenty-Seven Mile Bluff, where Bienville first tried to establish what became Mobile. The annual fete of parades and parties survived both the French and Spanish occupations of Mobile and lasted with various changes until the mid 19th century.

A group called the Spanish Mystic Society was founded in 1793 to parade each Twelfth Night. The 12 days before Lent became known as "carnival," or "solace of the flesh," which permitted Catholics in Mobile and elsewhere in the world to indulge in worldly pleasures ending on Mardi Gras. The French phrase translates as "fat Tuesday," the day prior to 40 days of denial leading to Easter.

The more direct lineage of Mardi Gras dates from 1830 when 23-year-old **Michael Krafft** and friends began a New Year's Eve revelry which continued at La Tourette's cafe (corner of Water and Conti streets) and lasted to dawn. As they roamed about in the early morning hours, they chanced by Partridge's Hardware where clerks were hanging rakes, hoes and cowbells on the store front. Krafft and friends armed themselves with the implements and began making noisy New Year's Day house calls on the unsuspecting townspeople. They called themselves the Revellers and promised to celebrate New Year's the following year in similar fashion.

By the following year, they had renamed themselves the **Cowbellion de Rakin Society** and launched several years of celebrations, with horse-drawn wagons hauling masked celebrants through the streets. They staged the first parade in 1840, and later began the custom of elaborate masked balls. Krafft, meanwhile, had died of yellow fever in nearby Pascagoula, Miss., and the Cowbellions had his remains brought to Mobile, where today the emblems of the society he founded adorn his monument in Magnolia Cemetery.

Mobile's connection to New Orleans' festivities occurred during this period, although New Orleanians are not known for sharing the Mardi Gras' spotlight, they do acknowledge Mobile's head start. Two Cowbellions who had moved to the Crescent City found no comparable celebration and decided to organize a society called the Mistick Krewe of Comus. Today, it is among that city's most prestigeous carnival organizations and it traditionally staged the major New Orleans parade on Mardi Gras Day. Complaints by blacks over closing city streets for private, all-white parades have shaken festivities in New Orleans.

Mobile's New Year's festivities ceased during the Civil War. On Shrove Tuesday in 1866, town market clerk **Joe Cain** dressed up like a Chickasaw Indian and drove a charcoal wagon through the streets while singing. His merry portrayal of **Chief Slacabamorinico** was a political statement aimed at the occupying Union army since the Chickasaws had never been defeated in battle. Cain returned the following Shrove Tuesday with a band of off-key musicians, whose annual antics eventually caught the fancy of Mobile society which organized and refined the event. Cain died in 1904 and his epitaph in the Church Street Cemetery reads, "Here lies old Joe Cain, the heart and soul of Mardi Gras in Mobile."

By 1872, Carnival had its first monarch, **King Felix**, the emperor of Joy, whose empire "is so large and demanding of his time" that he can only spend two days in his capital city of Mobile. Purple and gold were selected as official colors.

The coronations were held in the Temperance Hall until the building was condemned in 1915. Festivities ceased in 1918-19 because of the war. Coronations were held on the windy waterfront for a quarter century until World War II when Mardi Gras was again suspended. Coronations took place in the Fort Whiting armory until the Civic Center was opened in 1964. After three decades, festivities honoring King Felix III and his queen moved to the new convention center.

Today, the two weeks of merriment climaxing on **Mardi Gras Day** follow time-honored traditions. Mystic societies hold elaborate, costumed balls and more than a dozen parades, often as many as three a day. At the balls, members wear themed satin costumes which change each year and their invited guests - an average of 3,000 - wear formal dress.

Although smaller and less decadent than New Orleans' version, it is a fun-filled celebration that draws huge crowds of parade-lovers who party and yell to those riding the brightly decorated floats for souvenirs.

The **Azalea Trail Festival** features cultural events involving music, theater and the arts. Don't expect azaleas though. While Mardi Gras often falls in the second half of February, the azaleas normally peak the second half of March.

A new emphasis placed on tourism within the city promises to return the trail to its former glory. Among the most popular Festival events are the Allied Arts Festival, which focuses on the city's fine and performing arts, and the homes tour.

As another example of Mobile's sensitivity to its heritage, the archaeological site of Old Mobile at **Twenty-Seven Mile Bluff** is being excavated. Partners in the project are the University of South Alabama and Laval University from Quebec, the home of Mobile's founders. Ultimately, supporters hope to reconstruct portions of the settlement.

DOWNTOWN ATTRACTIONS

FORT CONDE is the perfect place to begin your visit to Mobile. Exit the interstate via Water Street into downtown and head for the city's official welcome center. It's a special attraction in its own right. This one site vividly illustrates Mobile's rich history under a succession of flags from 1702 to 1813. Reconstructed and furnished to its 1735 appearance, Fort Conde features 18th-century artillery demonstrated by costumed guards.

Enter the gates and turn right into the welcome center. After you browse through the excellent selection of brochures on the greater Mobile area, head outside for a look at the ornate French fort and visit the various museum rooms. Remember to duck through a series of passages and storerooms opposite the visitor center to discover rooms of historical displays which tell fascinating stories of early Mardi Gras and other institutions of colorful Mobile. Artifacts uncovered from fort excavations are among the unique exhibits.

The original fort which stood on this site was administrative headquarters for the entire French Louisiana Territory in 1711 and served later as the seat of military rule of the Gulf Coast by France, then England and finally, Spain. The stockade consisted of 13-foot tall cedar stakes and was named for King Louis XIV who directed this city to be founded in 1702. The name Conde was attached in 1720 to honor a prominent French family.

The permanent brick and mortar fort now reconstructed was built within the stockade between 1724 and 1735. The English took possession in 1763 at the end of the Seven Years War and renamed it Charlotte in honor of the wife of the king. The Spanish, under the young governor of Louisiana, Bernardo de Galvez, seized the city on March 14, 1780, but did not own it until the Treaty of Paris was signed some three years later.

It is ironic that what is now Alabama's oldest city did not come under the American Stars and Stripes until nearly 40 years after the Declaration of Independence. Huntsville, for example, was already a thriving town in the territory given up by Indians while Mobile was still under Spanish rule. The Spanish occupied Mobile until American troops - under order of President James Madison - captured Mobile in 1813 and ended Spanish support of the British.

The original Fort Conde-Charlotte was razed in 1820. Its foundations were uncovered in the 1970s during construction of the nearby interstate interchange and the city of Mobile reconstructed Fort Conde as a major Bicentennial project. Open daily except Dec. 25 and Mardi Gras Day. Free. Phone 434-7304.

BIENVILLE SQUARE is a lovely downtown park with azaleas shaded by giant live oaks and honors the French founder of Mobile. When the site was purchased by the city in 1830, a municipal building was planned; however, none was erected. Mayor J.W.L. Childers planted the first oaks in 1847 and the park was dedicated in 1866 to the memory of Bienville. In 1890, a movement to take the oaks out of the square was fortunately defeated and the Mobile Water Works added the magnificent cast iron fountain to honor founder George Ketchum.

The spreading oaks of Bienville Square create a lovely respite from an afternoon of sightseeing, however, chances are you won't stay long. A French cannon from the original Fort Conde and a British cannon from Fort Charlotte guard the park, but don't deter the loitering vagrants. The resident squirrels, however, are chatty and aggressive. The squirrels will scamper over if you bring a bag of peanuts.

The square comes alive during the Christmas holidays with 15,000 white lights decorating small trees trimmed by volunteers. The fountain is lighted in the form of a giant Christmas tree and wreaths with bright red bows add to the seasonal spirit.

Getting there: Go east toward downtown on one-way Dauphin and it will be on the left, bounded also by St. Joseph, St. Francis and Conception streets.

CATHEDRAL OF THE IMMACULATE CONCEPTION was designed in 1833 by Claude Beroujon and begun in 1835 by the Rev. Michael Portier, first bishop of the Diocese of Mobile. Although still unfinished in 1850, the brick and stucco cathedral was consecrated for services. The east portico and twin towers supported by 10 fluted Doric columns were added in the 1890s.

Quebec's Catholic community sent a bishop to Mobile in 1702, the same year Mobile was founded, and established the archdiocese. It is the mother parish of Alabama.

The heavy iron fence with crosses flanking the central entrance was fabricated in New Orleans and erected in 1860 at a cost of $5,000. A marker under the portico notes that Pope John XXIII designated the cathedral as a minor basilica in 1962. When you enter, take time to study 12 of the finest stained glass windows in the South. They are rich in color, shading, detail and majesty. Walk along the left wall until you see the railed entrance to the crypt among the pews. Go down the marble steps to see the tombs of the bishops.

Getting there: It is located on the west side of Claiborne between Conti and Dauphin. Phone 434-1565.

CHURCH STREET CEMETERY - BOYINGTON OAK, behind the public library on Government, is the city's oldest existing "burying ground." It was established in 1819 for yellow fever victims and remained active until 1899. The section nearest the entrance is for Protestants, central section is for veterans and strangers, and the back third for Catholics.

Joe Cain, who revived the tradition of Mardi Gras following the Civil War, is buried here. Although he died in 1904, his remains were not moved here until 1966 and a Mardi Gras day honoring him was begun the following year.

Boyington Oak: Although many of the stone and iron markers are of interest, the most unusual burial and its aftermath is a story worthy of Ripley's "Believe It or Not." On May 10, 1834, Charles R.S. Boyington, a 23-year-old printer, went walking near the cemetery with a new friend and fellow New Englander, Nathaniel Frost, who had moved south because of the ravages of tuberculosis. Frost's bloody corpse was found the next morning and officials learned that Boyington had fled the city on a steamboat bound for Cahaba.

Convicted on overwhelming circumstantial evidence, he nonethless maintained his innocence during nine months of imprisonment and developed a literary reputation through his public writings. On the following Feb. 20, when asked on the scaffold if he had any last words, he read at length from a manuscript and cried, "I am innocent. When I am buried an oak tree with 100 roots will grow out of my grave to prove my innocence." After being hanged, he was placed in a shallow grave in the Potters Field section of the cemetery which, for whatever reason, is now outside the cemetery wall.

Much to the growing horror of the residents, a volunteer oak did soon take root and today a giant oak with *more* than 100 roots marks the spot where he was laid to rest, only about 60 yards from across Bayou Street where Frost's body was found. The unmarked oak remains one of Old Mobile's most enduring legends. Across Bayou is the Big Zion AME Church built in 1867. The strange case and his writings fill a book published in 1949.

Getting there: Park either behind the library or at the Arby's next door and walk west to the white entrance gate for the cemetery. To see the oak, walk back to Government and down Bayou Street. It is the first large oak against the cemetery wall.

CITY HALL is a handsome, two-story white building in the Renaissance Italianate style completed in 1857 to serve as a market and city hall. It was constructed as a U-shaped complex with two long frame rear wings behind the central building to accommodate the market stalls. Government offices were on the second floor. It served as a market well into this century.

The principal facade is made up of four projecting blocks connected by a continuous recessed arcade. Named a National Historic Landmark in 1974, it was heavily damaged by Hurricane Frederic in 1979 and handsomely restored by the city in 1982. With the completion of the government office building next to the Admiral Semmes Hotel, it will become a museum.

Architectural details include bracketed cornices, detailed cupola and curvilinear wrought iron in the windows along Royal and Water streets. The grilles and gates consist of interlacing wrought iron wires fastened by cast iron rosettes fabricated in New York.

Enter on Royal Street to see the impressive murals by John Augustus Walker chronicling the city's history in the small, but elegant lobby and climb the marble staircase to see the ornate, stage-like public chamber.

The murals installed in 1961 over the west entrance show the flags of five nations which have governed the city. The south wall depicts Bienville planning Fort Louis de la Mobile in 1702, pioneer Sam Dale fighting 12 Indians, plus a panel saluting Barton Academy. The east wall recognizes the role of steamboats, rail and trucking in stimulating trade. The final shipment of slaves to the U.S. in 1859 is shown on the north wall, along with building the Confederate submarine *Hunley* in 1863, and celebrating Mardi Gras in 1867. Open business hours Mon.-Fri.

Getting there: While visiting Fort Conde, walk the half-block on Royal to enter.

CITY OF MOBILE MUSEUM contains an excellent and comprehensive series of collections which trace the evolution of Mobile from the capital of a French wilderness empire through its Spanish and English periods and its strategic importance to the Confederate navy.

The highly ornate Italianate house was built in 1872 by Henry Bernstein, a wealthy boot dealer, for $15,250. In 1890, Maj. J. Curtis Bush purchased the house and it became a popular center of local society. The city bought it in 1972, restored the building and opened the museum in 1976. A pair of lions guards the entrance which is framed by a cast-iron porch topped by an elaborate cornice.

From the outside, you might get the impression that this is an ordinary house museum which you can breeze through in a few moments. The unobtrusive additions to this house allow for numerous displays which may overwhelm all but the most jaded museum-goer. If you only have time to see inside a single house in Mobile, this is the one. Allow an hour to do it justice. It is free.

The museum collection dates from Mobile's Bicentennial in 1902 and includes more than 125,000 objects. Famous Mobilians represented with artifacts include Confederate naval hero Admiral Raphael Semmes; the legendary stage actor Joe Jefferson, whose portrayal of "Rip Van Winkle," made him a major star; and 19th-century author Augusta Jane Evans Wilson, author of nine books including "St. Elmo," an 1866 best selling love story between its Byronic hero and the pious heroine, Edna Earl. The most contemporary figure commemorated is Vietnam POW hero and former U.S. Sen. Jeremiah Denton, a highly decorated native.

The Semmes presentation sword is one of the museum's finest treasures. It was crafted by London silversmiths and given by officers of the British Royal Navy to replace the one Semmes lost when the *CSS Alabama* sank. The only known portrait of Henri DeToni, who died of yellow fever in 1704 at the original site of Mobile, is considered a masterpiece. DeToni had been chief of staff to the French explorer LaSalle.

The most popular attraction at the museum is the Diamond Horseshoe, the mezzanine display which contains more than a dozen elaborate, glittering coronation costumes worn by Mardi Gras queens from the 1860s to the 1960s. The queens' handmade beaded gowns and trains are as regal (and expensive) as you are likely to find in any museum in the nation. A variety of recent Mardi Gras posters is displayed.

Don't overlook the interesting collection of weapons and carriages collected by

Dr. Charles Rutherford displayed in the rear building which also houses a small gift shop of unusual quality.

Room after room is packed with the finest articles of archival quality which demonstrate that Mobile's rich history of nearly 300 years sets it apart from the rest of Alabama. Original documents, letters, portraits, locally made silver, fashions and photographs make this a truly remarkable shrine to the fascinating tableau that is Mobile.

Open Tues.-Sat., 10-5; Sun., 1-5. Closed holidays, and three days leading up to Mardi Gras. Free. Phone 694-0069.

Getting there: 355 Government.

CONDE-CHARLOTTE HOUSE, dating from about 1822, is the city's oldest house museum. The Federal style house was the city's first jail between the south bastions of old Fort Conde and became a private residence in 1845. You can see the jail doors and a portion of the jail floor uncovered during restoration.

The Colonial Dames has furnished rooms in periods related to Mobile's history, ranging from the suite of French Empire furniture to a tufted-back Empire sofa dating from the Confederacy. A walled garden suggests Spanish influences. Allow 30 minutes. Open Tues.-Sat., 10-4. Closed holidays. Admission. Phone 432-4722.

Getting there: It's right behind Fort Conde at 104 Theatre.

GOVERNMENT STREET provides the focus to Mobile. This nationally recognized street is lined with live oaks which are the result of generations of planting. When the British occupied Mobile from 1736-1780, they named the street Government and planted many oaks.

Most of those planted by the British were chopped down by locals during the Civil War to erect fortifications and to prevent Union soliders from slipping into the city unseen. After the war, Mobilians began replanting trees in front of their homes to beautify the city and provide shade. In 1913, during a visit, President Woodrow Wilson congratulated Mobilians on their beautiful oaks.

The 135-year-old live oaks form an almost unbroken canopy of sweeping branches over the city's main east-west street between downtown and Ann. It's a grand scene not duplicated in any other city. Stan Tiner, editor of *The Mobile Register*, is a strong advocate of having the live oak designated as the city's official symbol. He wants every sixth-grade student each year to plant an oak as partial repayment to those who planted the trees a century ago.

Trying to drive down Government and get a look at the various landmarks isn't easy. The traffic lights can be lost in the trees and there are many buildings worthy of a driver's attention.

A guide to some of the more notable buildings, beginning downtown follows. Buildings open to the public are marked in **bold**. (Even numbered addresses are on the right.)

City Hall - Bracketed 1857 market building fronts Royal
150 - 1855 LaClede Hotel has 258-foot iron gallery
153 - Italianate doctor's office circa 1856
300 - 1836 **Presbyterian Church**, Greek Revival
355 - 1872 Bernstein House is **City Museum**
400 block **Spanish Plaza** commemorates 1780-1813

400 - 1860 Ketchum Mansion home to archbishop
504 - 1836 **Barton Academy**, state's first public school
701 - **Mobile Public Library** built 1928
802 - 1859 home of Confederate hero Semmes
806 - 1906 **First Baptist Church** has Doric columns
901 - **Methodist Church** remodeled as Spanish Baroque
907 - 1854 house remodeled is 1898 as Victorian

PHOENIX FIRE MUSEUM is housed in the home station of the Phoenix Steam Fire Co. No. 6, organized in 1838. Erected circa 1858, the small, two-story brick building topped by an octagonal cupola was restored for use as a house museum in 1964 and dedicated by Lady Bird Johnson.

The museum originally kept a horse in an authentic stall, but the authentic aroma prompted officials to replace the horse with a fire truck.

Several restored early fire wagons and trucks are displayed downstairs while the upstairs hall has cased displays of hats, firearms and other fire-fighting memorabilia. If you have time, plan about 15 minutes. Open Tues.-Sat., 10-5; Sun., and holidays 1-5. Free. Phone 434-7569.

Getting there: 203 S. Claiborne St. It is immediately east of the Civic Center.

RICHARDS-DAR HOUSE, built in 1860 by steamboat captain Charles G. Richards, is one of Mobile's best preserved and best known mid-19th century home museums. The handsome Italianate house features the city's most intricate use of iron-lace trim with exceptional designs, blending naturalistic patterns with neoclassical elements, including the allegorical detail of "the four seasons" which can be seen from the street.

When you go inside, note the etched panes of red Bohemian glass which surround the front entrance. The formal interiors contain a curved staircase and original Carrara marble mantels in the double parlors. Look for the Cornelius bronze and brass chandeliers designed with mythological figures holding etched and crenulated glass globes. In the hexagonal dining room, a massive crystal chandeliers hangs from a frescoed medallion and is reflected in a French mirror over the mantel. The DAR is responsible for the handsome Early Victorian and Empire furnishings which are pre-1870.

One of the best times to visit is the first weekend in December when the house is adorned in period holiday decorations by the six Mobile chapters of the DAR. Your mail can be stamped with the "Christmas at the Richards-DAR House" cancellation in the post office in the carriage house. Allow 30 minutes. Open Tues.-Sat., 10-4; Sun.. 1-4. Closed Dec. 25-Jan. 1 and other major holidays. Adults $3, children $1. Groups of adults $2. Phone 434-7320.

Getting there: Seven blocks north of Government, 256 N. Joachim St. is in the De Tonti Square historic district.

SAENGER THEATER, Mobile's splendid downtown theater, opened in 1927 during the heyday of grand movie houses and today is the venue for touring productions, local productions and special events. The French Renaissance interior features elaborate plaster ornamentations, a surprisingly bold original magenta color scheme and original carpeting in the balcony. The contractor was a black man named Canton who pushed so hard to finish the Saenger ahead of schedule that he became ill and died shortly after its completion.

For decades, it showcased America's major movies. The downtown theater fell on hard times in the 1960s and the owners gave the building to the University of South Alabama in 1971. Unfortunately, the building continued to suffer, as gold-leaf columns were covered with paint and inappropriate murals were hung in the lobby.

Getting there: Two blocks off Government on Joachim at Conti.

SPANISH PLAZA commemorates the Spanish period in Mobile between 1780 and 1813. It honors Mobile's sister city relationship with Malaga, Spain, and contains a statue of Queen Isabella which was featured in Spain's exhibit at the 1964-65 New York World's Fair.

Getting there: Corner of Government and Hamilton. The Malaga Inn and the civic Center are nearby.

MOBILE, ALABAMA

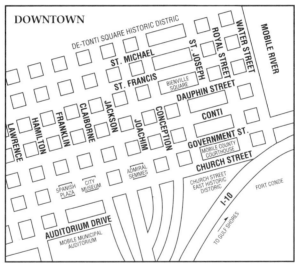

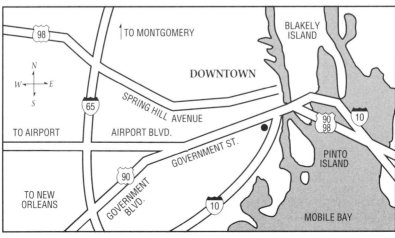

DOWNTOWN HISTORIC DISTRICTS

Oldest of the historic districts is the **Church Street East**, which encompasses most of the landmarks and museums between Fort Conde and the public library, including the 900 blocks of Conti, Government, Church, Monroe and over to the southern boundary, Canal, plus the side streets.

The **Municipal Archives**, dating to the 1700s, are among the nation's most complete. It is worth a visit to see the eight "Iron Ladies" statues made in Paris in 1800 for the Palace of Versailles. The records and statues are housed in the Eichold Archives Building at 457 Church.

The **Old Dauphin Way** Historic District north of Government and south of Spring Hill Avenue contains many frame cottages which originally housed steamboat captains, bar pilots and merchants and successful developers in the second half of the 19th century. The neighborhood suffered when Dauphin Way Baptist Church moved from 1255 Dauphin St. to the interstate, but its reuse as the **Alabama School for Science and Mathematics** has infused new life. The 1942 church is a modern, streamlined version of the Romanesque style with rounded arches and attached pilasters. The flanking buildings were added in 1949.

The giant **Duffee Oak** is thought to be the city's oldest "resident," having been planted long before American Independence. It boasts a 25-foot circumference, a crown spread of 120 feet and a total height of 50 feet. The *Quercus virginiana* oak was named in 1878 for Mayor George C. Duffee. A city ordinance protects the oak's low-reaching limbs from being disturbed. It is 2 blocks off Government at 1123 Caroline Ave. between Georgia and Hallett.

DOWNTOWN WALKING TOUR

To get to Fort Conde at 150 S. Royal St., take I-10 exit 26B and make a sharp left to Church Street. Park free in the large lot on Royal by entering in front of Rousso's restaurant.

After touring **Fort Conde**, enjoy the historic downtown by foot. The sidewalks are shaded by giant live oaks and the architecture is best seen in detail up close. Walk down **Theater and St. Emanuel streets**, encircled by the interstate, to see several residences that wear their aging charm with dignity despite being sorely in need of restoration.

Stop at 104 Theater for the **Conde-Charlotte** house museum. The 1845 Christ Episcopal Church at 114 **St. Emanuel** is the oldest Protestant Episcopal Church in the Diocese of Alabama. The steeple on the Greek Revival church was toppled by a hurricane in 1906 which fortunately spared the two Tiffany windows.

Walk down Church to Claiborne to discover the 1859 **Phoenix Fire Museum** and to 355 Government between Claiborne and Franklin to the **City Museum**, housed in a 1872 balconied townhouse with its stunning Mardi Gras ball gown collection. Return to your car via **Dauphin Street**, a block north of Government, and stop at **George's Candy Shop**, a block from Bienville Square, to buy a bag of sweets.

A sampling of houses in the neighborhood:
1017 Old Shell - 1859 cottage, carpenter John Bailiff
1120 Old Shell - 1865 Carpenter Gothic cottage was a school
1161 Old Shell - 1870 Carpenter Gothic cottage
1163-65 Old Shell - Twin Victorian cottages built 1880
1000 Dauphin - 1854, remodeled after 1884 fire
959 Dauphin - 1859 home of Mayor Gideon Parker
911 Dauphin - 1845 Protestant Children's Home
10 Common - Shotgun cottage with tall windows
8-10 Ann - Victorian structures built 1896 by Watsons
18 S. Julia - 1871, has Federal, Greek Revival elements
20 S. Lafayette - 1867 Catholic school in 1905
22-26 S. Lafayette - 1867 steamboat agency partners
1553 Monterey Place at Catherine - 1897 Queen Anne
1569 Dauphin - Carpenter Gothic, 1867 Macy
1570 Dauphin -1840 plaster-front Gulf Coast cottage
1664 Spring Hill - 1827 home of Michael Krafft

North of downtown is the **DeTonti Square** district developed during the 1850s by prominent cotton brokers, river pilots and maritine traders. Some of the early residents were descendants of ex-patriot Napolean loyalists who attempted to grow vines and olives at Demopolis a generation earlier. The name remembers Henri DeTonti, an Italian-born explorer from France who died of yellow fever at the original site of Mobile in 1704. Unlike the other districts, DeTonti has become less desirable and many endangered buildings are being moved and restored elsewhere in the city. The most remarkable residence is the **Richards-DAR House**, a lovely house museum at 256 N. Joachim St. The area is north of St. Louis between St. Joseph and Claiborne streets.

The **Oakleigh** garden district, bordered by Government, Georgia, Texas and Jefferson, boasts the unique house museum which gives the area its name.

OAKLEIGH MANSION is Mobile's most important antebellum house museum and centerpiece of the Oakleigh historic district. The raised-cottage style was taken to its ultimate execution by merchant **James Roper** when the South Carolina native designed and started his home about 1833.

Located on the high ground of the original 33-acre estate, it was constructed with slave labor with bricks fashioned from clay dug from the grounds. The architectural design affords a triple exposure to the prevailing breezes, ensuring maximum ventilation. The front exterior stairway winds gracefully to the second story entry from a brick landing. The sunken gardens surrounding the house occupy the original clay pits. The interior has Greek Revival influences and is noted for the unsupported, spiral wooden stairway from the main floor to the ground level.

When the City of Mobile restored the mansion in 1955 for use as a house museum, it was one of the earliest restorations by local government in Alabama and helped to pioneer the historic preservation movement in Alabama. The **Historic Mobile Preservation Society** has furnished it with antique furniture, silver, china and jewelry from the early Victorian and Empire periods.

Oakleigh boasts an important portrait collection, including the debutante portrait of Octavia Walton which Thomas Sully painted in his Philadelphia studio in 1833.

After marrying Dr. Henri LeVert, this granddaughter of a signer of the Declaration of Independence became **Madam LeVert**, the queen of Mobile society in the mid-1800s.

Begin your visit by purchasing your ticket at the 1850 **Cox-Deasy House**, a raised creole cottage designed and built as his personal residence by master builder George Cox. Because Mobile summers could be stiffling, the house was built with a central hall and French doors to encourage air circulation. In contrast to the grand style of Oakleigh's furnishings, the cottage is furnished with more modest items.

Between the historic buildings is the **Minnie Mitchell Archives** operated by the Historic Mobile Preservation Society. It contains a wealth of documents and local collections. Among the most important is a collection of glass photographic negatives which document Mobile between 1895 and 1908.

The best times to visit Oakleigh are in March when the azaleas are in bloom and prior to Christmas for the "Christmas at Oakleigh" decorations.

Allow 30 minutes minimum. Open Mon.-Sat., 10-4; Sun., 2-4; last tour at 3:30. Closed holidays and Christmas week. Admission. Phone 432-1281.

Getting there: Turn south off Government to Roper and go 3 blocks to the rear parking lot. Or turn on George and go right on Savannah.

After touring the historical Oakleigh complex, drive west down Augusta St. (off Palmetto) and park near the tree-filled **Washington Square** to stroll around and admire the excellent state of preservation of most of the houses. Toward the north of the fountain stands an old iron deer. During the Civil War, its twin and two cast-iron Negro boys were seized by Northern soldiers and flung into the river. At 906 Augusta is the 1859 home of **Joe Cain**. He is celebrated for resurrecting the tradition of Mardi Gras in 1866.

ATTRACTIONS NEAR DOWNTOWN

BRAGG-MITCHELL MANSION was built in 1855 by **Judge John Bragg** and remains one of the Gulf Coast's grandest antebellum mansions. The 20-room mansion framed by 16 slender fluted columns combines Greek Revival and Italianate elements. A spacious entrance hall which extends the length of the house ends with a sweeping curved staircase. The 15-foot ceilings on the ground floor allow for maximum ventilation by balmy coastal breezes.

The doors and wainscoting in the dining room are heart pine painted to resemble mahogany. Of special interest are the 19th century sterling silver tea service and Chippendale dining chairs. The marble mantels in the house are embellished with silver fenders. Damask draperies hang from gold leaf cornices. The mirrors in the double parlors are among a few treasures original to the house. Ironically, most of the furniture sent upriver for safekeeping during the Civil War was burned by Yankee raiders.

The second story has 13-foot ceilings. Among the 10 rooms being furnished are the master bedroom, the bride's bedroom, guest bedroom, upstairs parlor, nursery, the judge's law library and a large sun porch. The bride's room is in constant use due to the many wedding receptions at the mansion.

The original owner, John Bragg, moved here from North Carolina in 1835 to practice law. He was elected circuit judge in 1842 and elected to Congress in 1852. The house erected three years later was designed by the congressman's brother, prominent Alabama architect Alexander "Sandy" Bragg. A third brother was the controversial Confederate Gen. Braxton Bragg, commander of the Army of Tennessee and later military advisor to President Jefferson Davis. The general gave a speech from the second-story iron balcony during the Civil War.

Oaks surrounding the house were leveled during that period to give Confederate artillery a clear range in order to shell approaching Union troops. The trees which grace the lawn were planted from acorns saved by Judge Bragg and planted after the war.

The house was purchased in 1931 by Mr. and Mrs. A.S. Mitchell. The Mitchell Foundation later donated the mansion to a community board of directors. During restoration in 1986, elaborate Victorian stenciling and brightly colored moldings from the 1870s were discovered. The mansion was restored for $1.5 million.

Its romantic setting of towering live oaks is juxtaposed with the adjacent contemporary children's museum, the Exploreum. Both are managed by the same non-profit board. Open Mon.-Fri., 10-4; Sun., 1-4. Closed Sat. and holidays. Adults $4, children $2. Groups of 10 or more $3. Phone 471-6364.

Getting there: Take Springhill exit off I-65 north of Airport Boulevard and go east 2 miles to 1906 Springhill. The tree-canopied street is one of the city's loveliest.

CARLEN HOUSE is an attractive house museum on the grounds of Murphy High School free to the public. Broad galleries the width of the house are characteristic of the Creole cottage style unique to the Gulf Coast. Michael Carlen built the house in 1842. Period fashions in dress and home furnishings are displayed. Operated by the City of Mobile. Allow 30 minutes. Open Tues.-Sat., 10-5; Sun., 1-5. Closed holidays.

Getting there: Located off Dauphin between I-65 and downtown. Turn south on South and take the first left. Wilcox at Rickarby Street. Phone 470-7768.

The EXPLOREUM is a children's science center which encourages them to participate in hands-on exhibits that examine natural and scientific phenomena. Exhibits investigate regional flora and fauna, reptiles, gravity and the human body. Allow 30-60 minutes. Open Tues.-Fri., 9-5; Sat.-Sun., 1-5. Admission.

Getting there: 1906 Spring Hill Ave. adjacent to Bragg-Micthell Mansion.

MAGNOLIA CEMETERY was established in 1836 and contains the graves of a cross-section of the city's most notable figures. Even those not interested in history are certain to be impressed with the grand Victorian monuments to the departed throughout the 30 acres.

Magnolia is laid out in huge squares like city blocks. Some of the most elaborate tombs are near the center, close to the Virginia Street gate. Iron and cast markers and a variety of mausoleum styles are represented. The restored, 1860 Slatter Family Tomb surrounded by a fence has the finest ornamental cast iron in the cemetery. Some 1,100 Confederate casualties, including the crew of the CSS Hunley, the world's first submarine built on Mobile's waterfront; and CSA Gen. Braxton Bragg are buried near the statue marking the Confederate Rest at the end opposite Ann St.

John Gayle, who was Alabama governor during the Civil War, is buried at the southeast corner of square 6. The Bellingrath-Morse colonnade is on the northside of 22. Mardi Gras founder Michael Krafft's obelisk marker with symbols of the Cowbellion society is at the southeast corner of 6, near the picnic shelter, close to the George Street entrance on the northern boundary. Look for the crepe myrtle bush next to the pathway.

The cemetery has been restored and is being maintained by a non-profit group called the Friends of Magnolia Cemetery, Inc. A nearby 1880s building constructed for national cemeteries' offices is one of the few such to survive. It is used by the Friends.

Getting there: Travel Government and turn south on Ann. Go a mile to the entrance on your left.

OUTLYING POINTS OF INTEREST

ALABAMA CRUISES offers 90-minute harbor tours daily and longer evening dinner cruises which depart Feb.-Dec. from Battleship Park. Learn about the Civil War's pivotol Battle of Mobile Bay in 1865 and stories of Mobile's colorful history. The *Commander* enters the harbor - one of the coast's busiest - and ventures within sight of oil rigs, shipyards and dry docks. Schedules vary by season. Trips are most frequent in the summer. Pick up a copy of the colorful brochure available at most motels and tourist information spots. Adults $6.50, children 3-12 $3.50. Group rates $5.50 and $3. Reservations are not required for the daytime excursions. Phone 433-6101. Write Box 101, Mobile 36601.

Getting there: Follow signs to the Battleship and look for the Alabama Cruises dock.

BELLINGRATH GARDENS AND HOME is the Deep South's most beautiful gardens. The estate includes 65 acres of carefully landscaped gardens with a year-round spectacle of color highlighted by azaleas in spring. Some 200,000 people a year are drawn to the beauty of Bellingrath. While many arrive in cars, a large number arrive by motorcoach because Bellingrath is the state's number one destination for package tours. No wonder; its legendary reputation for beauty is richly deserved. Rarely has nature been improved upon with such spectacular results.

Coca-Cola bottling pioneer **Walter Bellingrath and wife Bessie** bought the first of 905 acres in 1918 for a fishing camp on the Isle-aux-Oies (Fowl) River. During their European travels, they gradually decided to transform the semi-tropical acreage into a garden paradise. They did. When the gates were first opened to the public in 1932, the garden attracted so much attention that police were called to control the flow.

In 1937, they built a home of old brick trimmed in antebellum wrought iron in the middle of the gardens and filled it with exquisite antique furniture, china and rare porcelian. After his wife died, the bottler gave his garden to a non-profit foundation in 1950 to maintain for the public's enjoyment. Following his death in 1955, the home was turned over to the foundation to manage, as well.

When you arrive at the gardens and enter the reception and ticket area, you'll receive a printed guide to the gardens. You may be tempted to pass up the home tour, thinking that you came only to see the gardens. It is well worth the additional time and money on your first visit to see the stunning collection of oriental rugs, china, silver and furniture that Bessie Bellingrath amassed during her trips in the U.S. and abroad. The sophistication of the gardens and home shows what her Coke-bottler-husband bought with his fortune. You won't find anything like this in Atlanta.

When you leave the reception area, follow the path which takes you over the bridge from which you can see the rose garden. Next, follow the signs off the main path to the left to the tranquil Oriental area, with tea houses and bright red bridges over a tranquil lake, home to numerous waterfowl.

The attractive bridal garden to the right of the path is pretty enough for weddings and often used for them.

Further down the walkway, flanked by seasonal bloomers, you'll reach the rockery which leads to the path to Mirror Lake. To reach the home and the surrounding gardens, you have the option of walking around Mirror Lake or continuing straight to the home. The vista across the lake is one of the gardens' most photographed spots. Regardless of season, there is always a display of blooming plants in the vicinity of the lake worthy of a roll of film.

On the far side of the lake, the prime haven for residential and migratory waterfowl, are another pond and bridge, as well as a summer house and an observation point overlooking the bayou. You may be tempted to bypass the walk to the other side of the lake, but go. It provides a completely different perspective and leads to the bayou for an idea of what the area was like before the Bellingraths began their magical transformation.

The reputation of the flowering plants overshadows the numerous fountains, reflecting pools and other water features which are carefully placed throughout the estate and most numerous near the house. The play of light off the water in the fountains provides almost as many opportunities for good photographs as do the flowers.

Arrive a few minutes before your tour of the home to enjoy another remarkable feature: the display of more than 200 Edward Boehm (pronounced BEE-mm) porcelain art pieces in the visitor lounge. The world's most complete public collection, it contains every bird, flower, soaring eagle or animal from Boehm that you've ever seen in magazine ads and couldn't afford to buy. Bellingrath has them all. Every single one.

The house contains 15 rooms, each containing one priceless antique after another. There are no fewer than three separate dining areas. The main dining room has an extended Chippendale dining table and chairs formerly owned by Sir Thomas Lipton, the English shipping magnate whose import company made tea a British tradition. The butler's pantry holds eight sets of fine china and nine sets of service plates, some that are 22-carat gold.

The bedrooms and other rooms are furnished with an equally impressive collection of antiques.

The upstairs galleries of wrought iron frame an interior patio with exotic plants and fountains. Windows on three sides open onto the gardens and overlook Fowl River and marshland, once the legendary home to the French pirate Jean La Fette.

The house is at the far end of a long loop. Most of the gardens are seen either before or near the house. The notable exceptions are a conservatory of exotic plants and the large rose garden you see from the bridge upon entering. The walking tour ends appropriately at the gift shop, with a small patio displaying plants for sale. An attractive souvenir book contains photos of plants in bloom throughout the year and serves as a reminder to revisit Bellingrath during other seasons.

A common question of "when are things in bloom?" does not apply here. Something is always is season, but there are two *best* times. Bellingrath is legendary for the 200 varities of 250,000 azaleas which normally bloom from early March into April. Dogwoods overlap the azalea blooming season, usually preceded by 90,000 daffodils, tulips and jonquils, hyacinths and other bulbs. Three thousand hybrid tea rose bushes fill the grounds with dazzling color from April to beyond Thanksgiving.

The lesser known but equally spectacular "second season" occurs in November when some 60,000 chrysanthemums of 12 varieties provide a blaze of color throughout the gardens. Yellow, white, bronze, red and pink mums cascade over the sides of bridges, walls and planters and from the balconies of the home. The sides of the rustic bridge over Mirror Lake overflow with six-foot drapes of mums. Again, the view looking back across the lake toward the house is the best perspective for large masses of color. The south terrace is ablaze with color while the border along the Great Lawn is wreathed in bright fall colors achieved by putting baskets of mums on poles to create a tree effect. Mums peak in mid-November.

Masses of poinsettias decorate the estate for Christmas, with the drawing room leading into the dining area especially decorated in seasonal displays. The formal dining room is set for Christmas dinner as when Mrs. Bellingrath entertained in the home. The traditional Bellingrath poinsettia tree is displayed in the gift shop.

Red and pink camellias cover the bushes during the winter. In fact, nowhere else in Alabama does the state flower appear in such abundance as at Bellingrath.

Plan to stay at least two to three hours, particularly if you plan to tour the home. Remember to bring your camera. You can buy film in the cafeteria-gift shop next door to the entrance. You can also rent an audio tape tour to increase your enjoyment of the gardens. Before you purchase your admission ticket, inquire about the small additional amount to make it a yearly pass. It will entitle you on future visits to free admission with a full paying guest or half price if you come alone or with another who has a pass. Adult admission to gardens and home tour, $14; children (6-11), $11; under 6, $8. Gardens only, $6.50; children (6-11), $3.25. Group rates available.

Best souvenir: the color souvenir book with the mums on the cover. Howard Barney's hardback book on the story of the Bellingraths also makes for interesting reading.

A good cafeteria adjoins the gift shop. Open daily from 7 a.m. until an hour before dusk. Guided tours of the house begin at 8.

Information: Phone 973-2217 or 973-2365 for an updated recording of what's currently in color.

Getting there: The spectacular beauty of Bellingrath is more than worth the side trip from Mobile to get there. Some 20 miles due south of Mobile, the gardens are near the town of Theodore. Leave I-10 at exit 15-A and follow signs to turn south on Bellingrath Road.

FINE ARTS MUSEUM OF THE SOUTH displays about 500 pieces of its permanent collection of 4,200 pieces which span more than 2,000 years of cultural history. The museum hosts several dozen exhibitions a year which attract more than 100,000 patrons. The museum's strengths are 19th century American and American art of the 1930's. Southern decorative arts including turned wooden bowls, contemporary ceramics, glass and furniture are also well represented.

A smaller location in the Turner Building at 300 Dauphin St. has galleries where people working downtown can stop in and see part of the FAMOS collection on display. The FAMOS-Downtown shares the building with the Mobile Arts Council and a studio shared by several artists. Allow 1 hour minimum. Tues.-Sun., 1-5. Closed Mardi Gras Day, July 4, Thanksgiving and Dec. 25. Free. Phone 342-2667.

Getting there: The museum is in a pine setting near a large lake. Go west on Springhill about 1.5 miles beyond I-65 and turn left on Pixie Drive. The museum is in Langan Park at 4850 Museum Dr.

GRAY LINE OF MOBILE offers sightseeing tours which depart from Fort Conde several times daily from Mon.-Sat. and Sunday afternoon. Gray Line also offers a variety of overnight packages ranging from one to three-night stays in a wide range of accommodations. Most packages include admission to Gardens and the USS Alabama Battleship Park. Specialized tours focus on history, architecture, black Americans and even ghosts. A three-night package during the second week in March coincides with the historic homes tour and includes admission to a dozen houses plus a river boat cruise. For reservations and information, phone 432-2229 or 1-800-338-5597.

MALBIS MEMORIAL CHURCH is a breathtakingly colorful Neo-Byzantine church built by the people of the Malbis Plantation at the request of their Greek immigrant leader, **Jason Malbis**. The former monk came here from Chicago in 1906 and bought several tracts of land, eventually establishing a plantation of 2,000 acres. He established a cannery, bakery, nursery, farm, ice house and power plant as the plantation became self-sufficient. Today, the estate's 5,000 acres encompass an industrial park and a portion of a residential golf community, TimberCreek.

Just before World War II, Malbis returned to Greece and was detained by occupying Germans. Shortly before his death in 1942, Malbis asked his co-workers in a letter to build a church to thank God for their successful Greek colony. The small group of immigrants began saving their money. With the design influenced by a famous church in Athens, they began construction in 1949 and completed work in 1964. The church cost more than $1 million.

The towers on either side of the west entrance rise to support open colonnades and domes, on which are surmounted large bronze crosses. The interior, in the shape of a cross, is remarkable for its brilliant icon paintings and mosaics consisting of hundreds of thousands of Byzantine tiles.

When you enter the main worship area, notice the high vaulted ceiling which is supported by red *faux* marble Corinthian columns. The vaulted ceiling represents the Greek Orthodox belief in continuity between Heaven and Earth and the unity of the divine and the human.

The 75-foot central dome, surrounded by a rich blue ceiling and covered with gold stars, is dominated by a mural of the Almighty. It was painted by three Greek iconographers laying on their backs for months on a scaffold two feet below the dome. Below, along the base of the dome between the windows are the Twelve Disciples. Below them are the major prophets of the Old Testament, and in the four corners are the Four Evangelists Matthew, Mark, Luke and John.

On almost every section of wall space are religious paintings. The building is vibrant with color. In all, there are about 150 paintings of religious leaders and scenes from Christ's life.

A 30-foot carved white marble screen, wooden pews to seat 250 people and altars fill the interior. The remains of Jason Malbis were returned from Greece and placed in a centoaph beneath a painting of Jesus before Pilate.

Visiting a Greek church east of Mobile Bay may not be high on your list if you are in Mobile to see azaleas or eat seafood, but its proximity to I-10 makes a visit not only memorable, but highly convenient. Free. Tours daily, 9-noon, and 2-5. Phone 626-3050, ext. 155.

Getting there: Take the I-10 Malbis exit and go south on U.S. 90 for 4 miles. Just past the Malbis Motor Inn (with the swimming pool shaped like the state of Alabama), turn right on County Road 27 and go a block.

MOBILE GREYHOUND PARK is the oldest greyhound track in the state and draws an estimated 600,000 patrons from Louisiana, Mississippi, Alabama and Florida. The traditional call of "Here comes Casey!" signals the start of another race where dogs can sustain speeds above 30 miles an hour around the track. You can sit in either the enclosed grandstand or trackside, or dine in the air-conditioned comfort of the clubhouse overlooking the track.

Due to the leadership of the late State Rep. Casey Downing of Mobile, the Legislature approved a 120-day racing schedule for the track which opened Aug. 5, 1973. The schedule was expanded to 180 days, then to 240 and now runs 300 days a year. In the first 17 years, the track generated $92 million for public agencies. The University of South Alabama is the recipient of the largest share of funds to local governments. Racing begins nightly Mon.-Sat. at 7:45, with matinees Mon., Wed., Sat. and major holidays at 1:15. Minimum age is 18. Phone 653-5000 or toll-free 1-800-272-5000.

Getting there: I-10 West at exit 13 (Theodore-Dawes).

USS ALABAMA BATTLESHIP, Mobile's top attraction, is berthed near the causeway in Mobile Bay alongside a submarine and other military exhibits.

Commissioned in 1942, the battleship assisted the British in protecting convoys through the North Sea against German warships and aircraft in occupied Norway. Several of the 680-foot battleship's nine battle stars were earned while serving as a strike force in the Pacific, most notably in Japan and Okinawa. The vessel's career was highlighted during the occupation of the Yokosuka-Tokyo area at the close of the war. It saw 37 months of active duty and was never damaged by enemy fire, earning the nickname "the Lucky A."

It was mothballed from 1947 to 1964 and painted gray. When the Navy announced it would be scrapped, Alabama school children led a fund drive with their dimes to berth the *Alabama* in Mobile Bay. It was towed 5,600 miles from Seattle in 1965 to become a memorial to state veterans of World War II and the Korean Conflict. It has been one of the state's most popular tourist attractions for nearly three decades.

Visitors returning to the park are surprised at its color scheme. Although initially painted in irregular shades of gray camouflage patterns, a horizontal blue band later covered most of the hull so it would blend with the sea. Its hull was recently repainted blue as it appeared in 1945.

A visit is self-guided. Start by seeing the eight-minute video where original crewmen describe its features. Use the printed guide which corresponds to numbered arrows on the ship where a crew of 2,500 lived. You tour the battleship decks, engine room, sick bay, radio room, messing and berthing compartments, captain's cabin, bridge and wardroom. Go into the 16" gun turrets and 5" gun mounts and see the 40mm and 20mm anti-aircraft batteries.

The submarine *USS Drum*, berthed alongside the battleship, became the hero of the western Pacific in 1942. Under the command of Robert Rice, she cruised down the coast from Tokyo to Nagoya on her inaugural patrol and sank the seaplane carrier Mizuho, at 9,000 tons, the largest naval vessel the Japanese lost in the war. Of all the subs in the Pacific, it had the highest total of enemy tonage sunk. Aboard the Drum, see how submarine crews lived, fired torpedoes and operated their ship as you walk through the historic torpedo rooms and crew quarters.

The park displays planes and weaponry from all branches of the military, most notably the world's fastest plane, an A-12 Blackbird spy plane, forerunner to the SR-71. The A-12 was capable of flying at three times the speed of sound at 95,000 feet. Blackbirds were shelved in favor of satellite surveilliance. Also on display are "Calamity Jane," a B-52 bomber, aircraft and other military exhibits.

A boardwalk and two-story observation deck allow you to watch many varieties of birds, mammals, reptiles and plants indigenous to Southern wetlands. The park is a memorial to all Alabamians who have defended the nation's honor in military conflicts.

Allow up to two hours. Open daily, 8-sunset. Closed Dec. 25. Ticket office closes 1 hour before sunset. Adults, $5; children 6-11, $2.50. Group rates $4.50 and $2.25. Parking fee charged. Fax 433-2777. Phone 433-2703 or 1-800-426-4929. Write P.O. Box 65, Mobile, 36601.

Getting there: Take I-10 about a mile east to Battleship exit on the causeway in Mobile Bay.

WILDLAND EXPEDITIONS offers a two-hour-plus guided tour of the Mobile-Tensaw Delta marshland and forest wetlands aboard Capt. Burrell's 22-passenger "Gator Bait."

The first part covers fresh water routes, followed by a rest break at the marina, with the second half into the tidal marshes. Length of tour depends on which of eight routes is selected by Burrell. After your first trip, you might decide to return at a different season since plants are in bloom at different times and half of the 350 species of birds is here in summer and the other half migrates here in winter.

The **Mobile-Tensaw Delta**, the largest inland delta in the country, is a 200,000-acre world of marsh, flooded timber and wetlands through which flows most of the river water of Alabama. Five rivers flowing through this region drain 43,000 square miles, which is why the delta is such a fertile fish and wildlife factory. There is a maze of rivers, creeks and backwater lakes in the north end of the delta, with cypress and moss-draped oaks lining the riverbanks. To the south and closer to the bay, the delta is treeless, with open water and bullrush and saltgrass marsh.

Burrell originally planned to operate only during the warmer months, but soon found that birdwatchers and other outdoor enthusiasts want to observe the wildlife during all seasons. Tours depart daily from Wed.-Sun. at 9 a.m. and 2 p.m. Reservations are strongly recommended to avoid being left at the dock. Call Burrell's answering service at 460-8206 and he'll return your call.

Getting there: Take I-65 exit 13 and turn east 2 miles to Hwy. 43. Go south 1/2 mile to the Chickasaw Creek Marina.

TRANSPORTATION AND TOURS

The **Mobile Municipal Airport** is a 20-minute drive from downtown. To reach Airport Boulevard, go west on I-10 to I-65 exit 3B. Alternate routes are westbound on Government or Dauphin.

Mobile is served by the east-west interstate highway I-10. Just west of downtown is the beginning of I-65 which goes to Birmingham and Nashville and ends in Chicago. A number of major U.S. highways link Mobile with other cities in the South: 31 north to Montgomery, Birmingham and Nashville; 98 west to Hattiesburg and east to Florida panhandle cities; 90 is parallel to I-10 westbound to New Orleans.

Amtrak's *Gulf Breeze* daily passenger service connects Mobile with Bay Minette, Atmore, Evergreen, Greenville, Montgomery, Birmingham, Atlanta and points beyond. The transcontinental *Sunset Limited* between Los Angeles and Miami stops in Mobile three times a week.

For those who had rather let someone else drive, **Gray Line Tours** offers tours of historic downtown Mobile year round. Patrons ride on open-air buses inspired by 19th-century horse-drawn trolleys. Purchase tickets at the Gray Line office at 607 Dauphin St. (next door to Wintzell's). Carol Peterson's tour company also plans and conducts unique special-interest themed tours for pre-arranged groups. Phone 432-2229.

Groups arriving in Mobile by motorcoach also enjoy step-on guide service arranged by Sue Lyons of **Mobile Tours**. Her tours range from a two-hour whirlwind tour to a day-long house and garden tour which includes a trip to Bellingrath Gardens. Meals could be a tea in an antebellum home or a full meal in a private club. Write P.O. Drawer M, Mobile, 36601. Phone 432-1146 or 1-800-411-1146.

WHERE TO SEE AZALEAS

Mobile is famous the world over for the lush shrubs which bloom each spring in a profusion of brilliant pinks, purples and whites. The first azaleas were brought here in 1754 by a French settler, Fifise Langlois. He brought pink, purplish-red and white from his grandparents' gardens in Toulouse, France. The organized planting of azaleas along city streets began in 1929 following a local horticulturist's visit to Charleston, S.C., The first "trail" began at Bienville Square and meandered 15 miles beneath the moss-draped oaks in the heart of the historic district. The idea of a festival materialized in 1950. One of the most popular varieties is "Pride of Mobile."

Young ladies dressed in brightly colored gowns with matching parasols are the trademark Azalea Trail Maids who are the festival's goodwill ambassadors.

It used to be easy to find the flowers. You could just drive around and look for the pink strip painted on the curb and follow it. Over the years, the paint has been allowed to fade and disappear, although small metal signs do help point the way.

The trail is actually two distinct and separate routes, the first in downtown and the other in the residential section west of I-65.

Downtown azalea trail: The route in the historic area is 12 miles and takes about 45 minutes to drive. Begin at Fort Conde, turn left on Government, right onto Catherine, left onto Monterey Place, right onto Monterey Street, right onto Old Shell Road, left onto Lafayette, left onto Spring Hill, left onto Tuscaloosa, right onto Old Shell, left onto Wisteria, left onto Dauphin, right onto Rickarby Place, left onto Wilcox, right onto South Carlen, left onto Hunter, left onto Houston, right onto Dauphin, right onto Ann, left onto Selma, left onto Oakleigh, right onto Savannah, left onto Chatham, right onto Palmetto, veer right onto Charleston, right onto Charles, right onto Augusta, right onto Chatham, right onto Government and back to Fort Conde.

West Mobile trail: The west portion covers 15 miles of largely residential areas and requires about 35 minutes to travel. Begin at Spring Hill Avenue and I-65. Then, turn left onto Avalon, left onto Batre Lane, right onto Old Shell, left onto College Lane, turn right onto the Avenues of Oaks. Turn right onto Old Shell, left onto Tuthill, left onto Spring Hill, left onto Pixie, right onto Museum Drive, left onto Gaillard, curve into University, left onto Old Shell, right onto Westminster, right onto Bit and Spur, left onto Wilkinson Way, turn right onto McGregor, right onto Pinebrook, go straight on Warwick, turn right on Wimbledon, take an immediate left on Hillwood, turn right on E. Hillwood, veer left on McGregor, go right on Spring Bank, left onto Edgefield, left onto Dauphin and return to I-65.

TOUR ITINERARIES

Two-day/one night-tour: History and Charm

Day 1: Arrive in Mobile before midday and eat **lunch at Rousso's** before going next door to **tour Fort Conde** or drive west on Government Street to see the collection of Mardi Gras costumes at the **City Museum of Mobile**.

Continue west on Government, then left on Roper to reach **Oakleigh Mansion**, one of the city's finest house museums. Afterwards, drive around the **Oakleigh historic district** to see some of the city's best restored homes surrounding Washington Square park.

Next, **check in at a hotel or motel** where you've made reservations and tonight **dine on seafood at All Seasons** or another of Mobile's outstanding restaurants.

Day 2: After breakfast, drive west on I-10 to spend the morning touring **Bellingrath Gardens and Home**. On your way back into Mobile, have **lunch at Kirk Kirkland's** restaurant in the Tillman's Corner area.

Consider several options featuring impressive architecture this afternoon. Tour the antebellum **Bragg-Mitchell Mansion**, see the period costumes at the **Conde-Charlotte House** or admire the furnishings of the **Richards-DAR House** before departing the city.

Three-day/two-night tour: History and Charm

Days 1 and 2: Follow the above tour and select another fine restaurant for tonight's dinner.

Day 3: After breakfast, check out of the hotel and go to the **Cathedral of the Immaculate Conception** to admire the stained glass windows. Drive east on I-10 across the bay to the spectacular **Malbis Memorial Church** which was built by followers of a successful Greek businessman. Drive through the charming bayside town of Fairhope and have **lunch** at the **Old Bay Steamer** restaurant or the legendary **Grand Hotel**. Take a candy break at the **Punta Clara Kitchen** before driving east on U.S. 98 to stop and hear the story of **Inspiration Oak**.

Two-day/one-night tour: Mobile and the Military

Day 1: The Port City played pivotal roles in military conflicts during the early 1700s, the Civil War and World War II. Get an overview of the city's role as capital of the French Empire at **Fort Conde**. Follow the signs to the Mobile Bay causeway to the **Battleship Park** where you should spend several hours touring the *USS Alabama* of World War II fame and other military exhibits. Continue driving east on I-10 to Daphne, then south on U.S. 98 to the **Nautilus restaurant for dinner** and watch the sun set over the battleship and Mobile. Check in at a motel west of the city such as the **Holiday Inn I-10** and take in dog races at the **Mobile Greyhound Park**.

Day 2: Getting an early start in the morning, drive south to see the Civil War-era **Fort Gaines** which protected the city prior to the **Battle of Mobile Bay**. Take the next **ferry across the bay** for a self-guided tour of **Fort Morgan**, which was devastated during the major naval battle of the Civil War. Drive north on Hwy. 59, west on I-10 and north on Hwy. 225 for an afternoon boat ride through the delta marshes with **Wildland Expeditions**.

One-day tour on a budget

You can see a great deal of history in a day and it will cost you practically nothing.

Begin your day tour at **Fort Conde** (30 minutes) to see artifacts related to the city's early military history. Drive to 355 Government and the **City Museum of Mobile** to see an impressive collection of Mobile's cultural and Civil War heritage (at least 60 minutes). Turn north to the **Cathedral of the Immaculate Conception**, park and go in to admire the stained-glass windows (20 minutes).

After a busy morning, it's time to spend money on lunch. Go to **Wintzell's Oyster House** or try to find the **Dew Drop Inn** on Old Shell Road.

In the afternoon, you can tour several other free city museums or browse the antique shops in the Loop area. For something totally different, drive out Government to look at all the Mardi Gras novelties available at **Accent Annex**. You really should relax your budget to take in the **USS Alabama** battleship or **Bellingrath Gardens** (two hours). Or choose from among **Oakleigh**, the **Bragg-Mitchell Mansion** or the **Richards-DAR House** to see at least one house museum.

WHERE TO STAY DOWNTOWN

Admiral Semmes (Radisson), 251 Government, is a handsome 12-story landmark hotel facing the new municipal office building and within walking distances of most downtown attractions. It was built in 1940 with marble floors, crystal chandeliers and a grand staircase. When renovated in 1985, the original 250 rooms were reconfigured into 170 larger rooms. This resulted in some junior suites which have a king-size bed, wingback chair, writing desk and wet bar in the same room. (This is any room number ending with 02.) All rooms have an armoire to house a TV set which carries personal messages across the screen. Fresh coffee and a copy of *USA Today* arrive after your wakeup call. In the evening, fresh cookies are left on the bed as part of the turndown service. An outdoor pool is heated and guests have access to the YMCA 4 blocks away.

**Oliver's restaurant offers weekday breakfast and lunch buffets and a Sunday brunch. Enjoy cocktails and hors d'oeuvres each afternoon in the Admiral's Corner bar. Fine dining specializing in seafood and beef is available each evening in Oliver's. Fax is 432-8000, ext. 7111. Double rates before tax begin at $69-79, weekends $49-59.

While the Admiral Semmes is ideal for Mardi Gras because it overlooks the parade route and the TV station which televises parades live, rooms aren't cheap. Rates are $130 a night the weekend before Fat Tuesday and climb to $150 on Monday and Tuesday nights, two-night minimum. Make reservations at least three months out. **Phone 432-8000** or 1-800-233-3333.

The **Church Street Inn**, 505 Church, may be the only bed and breakfast in Alabama which started out in Chicago. It is in a row of three Queen Anne houses which Jacob Pollock ordered prefabricated - wallpaper and all - and shipped to Mobile for reassembly as rental property in 1902. Inn owner-manager Linda Bennett restored the house, using New England inn colors, and planted gardens before opening in 1990.

Guests choose from the Mardi Gras suite, which features a sitting room, fireplace and private bath or the Azalea room, blushing with Mobile's favorite color, which also has a fireplace. The hostess nods to her Georgia roots with the name of the Dogwood room and her Oak View room has a view of the rear garden shaded by an ancient oak.

In the afternoon, Linda invites guests to relax with a glass of wine or sherry on the front porch or patio. In the morning, guests may opt for a thermos of coffee in the room or go downstairs for a Continental breakfast. No smoking. Rates range from $90-$125. Visa and MasterCard accepted. **Phone 438-3107.**

Holiday Inn Downtown, 301 Government, is a circular 17-story tower hotel with 210 rooms. Originally built as a Sheraton, it was extensively remodeled and reopened because of its proximity to the new convention center. An atrium lobby detailed with Mobile's famous wrought iron is a convenient place to meet friends or you can go to the Bayview Lounge on the 17th floor for a drink and a spectacular view of the harbor. **Lafayette's is the full-service restaurant on the lobby level and Garrow's is the 24-hour deli. Several small shops, including the Nut House and Gray Line Tours, are in the elegant lobby. An outdoor pool is on the third floor. Floors 10-15 have "view rooms" above the tree line which are well worth the slight increase in rates. Rooms have cable TVs with movie channels. The central location of the Holiday Inn makes it an excellent headquarters for Mardi Gras. Fax 594-0160. Write 301 Government St., Mobile, 36602. **Phone 694-0100.**

Malaga Inn, 357 Church St., is a small hotel constructed around twin Italianate houses which relatives built in 1862. Now it offers three suites and 37 large rooms with high ceilings and private baths. A lounge and restaurant are off the courtyard behind the inn. It is just a few steps from the Spanish Plaza and within walking distance of downtown attractions. **Phone 438-4701.**

Riverview Plaza (Stouffer's), 64 Water St., overlooks downtown Mobile, the river and the Mobile Convention Center. Some 375 rooms are arranged throughout the 28-story hotel, the state's tallest. The Riverview caters to conventions and large groups because of its variety of meeting rooms. Complimentary coffee and a copy of *The Mobile Press* are brought to your room at your wakeup call. Each floor from 5 to 10 has a parlor suite connecting two bedrooms. Twenty-eight luxury Club bedrooms are on levels 27 and 28 where hors d'oeuvres and a cash bar are available each afternoon. Two presidential suites are on 27 and 28. For the best view overlooking the bay at a standard rate, ask for the corner king room of 2102 or 2202.

A skywalk bridging Water Street connects the hotel's fourth floor parking deck with the Mobile Convention Center.

In addition to 24-hour room service, you can eat in the Oyster Bar or the fancier Julia's. The **Banana Dock offers three meals daily. For groups, a welcome reception is held in the lobby lounge and special menus are prepared for motorcoach groups. Fax 438-3718. Double rates: $117 (standard) to $137 (club) plus tax, weekends $81-$101. Several honeymoon and family weekend packages are available. **Phone 438-4000.**

ACCOMMODATIONS IN WEST MOBILE (I-65)

Holiday Inn I-65, 850 S. Beltline Hwy., is convenient to nightlife entertainment. Complimentary admission to the Mobile dog track and free airport shuttle offered. Located near Bel-Air Mall and Springdale Plaza. The 200 guest rooms have cable TV with Showtime and in-room movies. The motel has a restaurant with room service, lounge, swimming pool, kiddie pool and hot tub. Fax 342-8919. Double rates begin at $43. Package themes are golf, Battleship, Bellingrath Gardens, B&B and romantic weekend. **Phone 342-3220** or 1-800-HOLIDAY.

Howard Johnson, 3132 Government, has 159 units and a full-service restaurant. Amenities include a large, outdoor pool, heated Jacuzzi, lighted tennis court, jogging trail, free local calls and airport shuttle. Fax 471-9912. Double rate: $50-$65, weekend $39-$65. Phone 471-2402 or **1-800-535-8029.**

Ramada Inn Conference Center, 600 S. Beltline Hwy., has 236 rooms convenient to mall shopping and colleges. The upscale hotel has a heated indoor pool, outdoor pool with kiddie pool, whirlpool, exercise room, and a lighted tennis court. Casual dining is available in the restaurant. Lounge, room service. Fax 344-8055. Double rate: $59-$91 plus tax, weekends $39-$91. Golf package available. **Phone 1-800-752-0398** (Mon.-Fri., 8-5) or 344-8030.

Family Inns of America, 900 S. Beltline Hwy., is an economy motel with 83 rooms just off I-65. Amenities include continental breakfast, free newspaper, free local calls, non-smoking rooms and cable TV. No food service is available on-site, but many restaurants are nearby. Fax 342-4744. Double rate: $33-38, weekends $38-$40 plus tax. **Phone 344-5500** or 1-800-251-9752.

Bradbury Inn (Best Western), 180 S. Beltline Hwy. at I-65, has 102 rooms with free in-room movies, microwaves and refrigerators available at nomimal charge. Free hot breakfast buffet and afternoon cocktail receptions. Adjoins Weichman's All Seasons restaurant. Fax 342-5366. Double rate: $51-$58 plus tax. **Phone 343-9345** or 1-800-528-1234.

Drury Inn, 824 S. Beltline Hwy., has 110 rooms on four levels with cable TV. Some larger king rooms have recliners. Free continental breakfast. Pool. Double rate: $51-$57 plus tax. **Phone 344-7700.**

LODGINGS AT TILLMAN'S CORNER

Days Inn South, 1705 Dauphin Island Parkway, is convenient to downtown attractions and I-10. It has 148 rooms with corridor access. A pool is located in courtyard. Fax 471-6114. Double rate: $47-$52 plus tax. Motorcoach discounts available. **Phone 471-6114** or 1-800-325-2525.

Holiday Inn I-10, 6527 U.S. 90 W., located at I-20 exit 15 B, is the most convenient major hotel near Bellingrath Gardens. The five-story hotel is 5 minutes from the Mobile dog track, 10 minutes from downtown and 25 minutes from Bellingrath. For security, the 160 guest rooms are indoor accessible through the main lobby elevator. Children under 18 stay free in room with parent. Non-smoking and handicapped rooms available. Ask about availability on the upscale fifth floor. Complimentary airport shuttle. The hotel has an outdoor swimming pool with heated whirlpool. Complimentary coffee in the lobby most mornings. Fax 666-2773. Double rates $54-$70 plus tax. Packages include golf, dog track or Bellingrath Gardens. **Phone 666-5600.**

BEST HOTEL DEAL IN MOBILE

The Holiday Inn's Bellingrath Garden package. For only $50, you get two tickets to the gardens (house tour not included) and a room for much less than the published rate for the room alone. The rate drops to $42 plus tax for a second night. Advance reservation is required and based on availability.

FOOD

Mobile is home to **Morrison Inc.**, one of the Southeast's largest food operations. What began as a cafeteria chain now includes diversified specialty restaurants and contract food business divisions. When the company reported revenues in excess of $1 billion last year, the corporation operated 161 **Morrison's** cafeterias, 154 **Ruby Tuesday** restaurants, 40 **L&N Seafood Grills**, 15 **Silver Spoon Cafes**, and the Hospitality Group, an institutional contract food business. Groups planning tours through Alabama should consider the many convenient locations of Morrison's cafeterias.

WHERE TO EAT IN MOBILE

**Dew Drop Inn - *Mobile's best shrimp sandwiches*
1808 Old Shell Road. Phone 473-7872
Open Mon.-Sat., *11:30 a.m.-8:30 p.m.*
Dew Drop Inn features excellent hot dogs, crab omelets and shrimp sandwiches on a bun in a friendly neighborhood environment.

**Kirkland's Family Restaurant - *Excellent barbecue near I-10*
6500 U.S. 90 West. Phone 661-9303
Open Sun.-Thurs., *11 a.m.-9 p.m.; Fri.-Sat. until 10.*
Kirk Kirkland has served excellent seafood, chicken, baby back ribs and barbecue plates here since 1981. Service is prompt and friendly. Kirkland's is located in the Tillman's Corner area of U.S. 90 and accessible from I-10 via exits 15 and 17.

**Hemingway's - *Creole and cajun food in the Loop*
1850 Airport Blvd. Phone 479-3514
Open Mon.-Fri., *11 a.m.-9:30 p.m.; Sat., 4:30-9:30; Sun., 11 a.m.-2:30 p.m.*
Hemingway's offers creole and cajun food in a cafe setting in the Loop area just off Government. A second restaurant is equally successful in Gulf Shores.

**La Louisiana - *Continental cuisine*
2400 Airport Blvd. Phone 476-8130
Open six nights a week. Closed Sun.
La Louisiana serves Italian and Continental food in a fine dining atmosphere.

**Nautilus - *The great seafood is matched by the view*
U.S. 98 in Daphne. Phone 626-0783
Open Mon.-Thurs., *11 a.m.-9 p.m.; Fri.-Sat., till 10 p.m.*
The Nautilus offers a good view of Mobile Bay along with the seafood from its location in Daphne. It is on U.S. 98 just south of I-10. Ask for a table by the window to see the lights of Mobile from across the bay.

****The Pillars - *Continental food in a mansion*
1757 Government St. 478-6341
Open Mon.-Sat., 5-10 p.m.
The Pillars serves acclaimed continental dishes in 11 private dining rooms in a restored mansion on Government Street. Owner Filippo Milone, a graduate of Cordon Bleu, opened the Pillars in 1976. The framed certificates in the front parlor attest to the

accolades collected since, including five stars. Chef Ron Wilemon, acclaimed for his scamp saute pinot noir and snapper Pontchartrain, prepares daily dinner specials for pasta, lamb, beef, veal and seafood. Dinners start at $14 and full course Epicurean dinners begin at $22.50. The Pillars offers fine wines from a soundproof wine cellar. Pick up a copy of Milone's personal cookbook at the restaurant or Mobile bookstores for $15.

***Rousso's - *Good seafood in a nautical environment*
166 S. Royal St. Phone 433-3322
Open Mon.-Sat. 11 a.m.-10 p.m.; Sun. 11:30-9
   Rousso's is housed in a large, old warehouse next to the Fort Conde welcome center and is decorated with nets, buoys, mounted fish and other nautical gear. Rousso's offers a lengthy seafood menu based on ingredients fresh from Mobile Bay. The restaurant handles large groups quickly and even offers a tour of its gleaming stainless steel kitchen.

****Weichman's All Seasons - *A fine-dining tradition*
168 S. Beltline Hwy. off Airport Blvd. Phone 344-3961
Mon.-Fri., *11 a.m.-3 p.m., 5-10 p.m.; Sat., 5-10, Sun., 11-3, 5-9.*
   Weichman's is among Alabama's most honored fine-dining restaurants, repeatedly ranking among the nation's best in surveys by *Travel/Holiday* magazine. Owner-chef John Weichman upholds the family tradition of superior seafood dishes which began with the legendary Constantine's, founded by his father-in-law in 1934.
   While building a plant for Union Carbide in Italy in the 1970s, Weichman learned a great deal about Italian food and wines, and returned to Mobile where he co-founded the Vine & Cheese shop. Two years later he left the chemical company to manage Constantine's and opened All Seasons in 1982. He has been a leader in the state's restaurant and tourism industries for the better part of two decades.
   All Seasons seats 250 and is noted for its beautiful antique furnishings, solid mahogany wood decor, and large portions of great food at moderate prices. Head chef Leon Pettway's seafood gumbo, prime rib, filet, lamb chops, broiled calves liver, fettucini and seafood La Louisiana are favorites, followed by baked caramel custard or key lime pie for dessert. Lunch prices average $5-$7 while dinner runs $8-$15 and above. It is on the west service road off Airport Boulevard and I-65, visible from the interstate. Phone 344-3961.

*Abbreviated **All Seasons** dinner menu*
Appetizers
Baked select Gulf oysters, Bienville or Rockefeller, six for $7.50
Escargot in lemon herbed butter $6
Sauteed or fried crawfish tails $7
West Indies salad with marinated lump crabmeat $8.25
Soup
Crawfish bisque or Mobile's best seafood gumbo - cup $3.50, bowl $6.50
Salads
Mixed green salad: radish, cucumber and pecans $2
Spinach, egg, mushroom, bacon bits, parmesan $3.25
Seafood salad: marinated crabmeat, shrimp, scallops $3.50

Entrees
Baked snapper fillet, crabmeat (house specialty) $17
Fillet of gulf fish blackened in cast iron skillet $15
Shrimp Creole over rice, sweet peas $12
Prime rib served au jus - $14, $16
Blackened rib eye (Delmonico) $14
Broiled lambchops au jus, mint jelly $19
Veal and crabmeat in cream, brandy sauce $16
Chicken Oscar - crabmeat, asparagus, hollandaise $13
Fettuccini Alfredo: shrimp or crabmeat $12

***Wintzell's Oyster House** - *Oysters and seafood*
605 Dauphin St., Mobile 36602. Phone 433-1004
Open Mon.-Sat. 11 a.m.-9 p.m., Fri. till 9:45 p.m. Closed major holidays
The casual decor has basic tables and booths, but what you notice are the 10,000 (more or less) signs covering every available wall and post which quote witticisms and universal truths. Oliver Wintzell opened it as a six-stool oyster bar in 1938 and it has expanded greatly over the years to accommodate 250. The real star remains the simple oyster, served "fried, stewed and nude." Try the oyster bar where you can sit and eat oysters while watching the staff twist open fresh ones for customers.

Shell fish and other seafood are expertly prepared and served by friendly waitresses. Lunch checks range $5-15 while dinner costs $5-20. Tom Burke maintains the high standards of food and friendly service which Willard Scott plugs on the "Today" show when Mobile is in the weather news.

*Sample **Wintzell's** menu*
Oysters on the half shell: six for $3.75, dozen for $5.50
Baked stuffed oysters $10 and $13
Oyster stew $4
Seafood gumbo cup: $2.25, bowl $3.50
Crab claws: small $8.50, large $13
Peel and eat shrimp: small $4.25, large $6
Fried oysters or fried shrimp: small $8, large $10
West Indies salad: small $7, large $10
Large (oyster, shrimp or fish) loaf sandwich $4.25
Seafood special: carp, claws, oysters, shrimp, fish $13
Platter: crab claws, oysters, shrimp and fish $12
Catfish and hush puppies $10
Platter of two: shrimp, oysters, crab claws, fish $12
Crabmeat omelet $9
Soft shell crabs (two) $15
Mahi mahi, salmon, tuna, shrimp, shark $11-$13
Beer $2-2.75 or a pitcher of beer for $6

WHERE TO PARTY
Starting downtown and spreading east and west:
Grand Central is a blues bar owned by Crockmier's owner Bill Monahan. It's at 256 Dauphin St. near the Saenger.

G.T. Henry's attracts the college crowd and twenty-somethings for great regular bands and beer specials. When the weather's good, the band and the crowd party on an adjoining patio. 461 Dauphin St. Phone 432-0300.

The Lumber Yard Cafe caters to partying locals, with regular entertainment, homemade pizza, hamburgers and pasta with a creole touch. 2617 Dauphin at the railroad tracks. Phone 471-1241.

T. P. Crockmier's is a friendly, upscale neighborhood bar where regulars have been stopping by for a drink after work for more than a quarter century. 170 South Florida. Phone 476-1890.

WHERE TO SHOP

Mobile's largest shopping complex is the handsome 1.3 million square-foot **Bel-Air Mall** on Airport Boulevard, anchored by **Parisian, Dillard's, JC Penney** and **Sears**. An elaborate fountain, similar to the one in Bienville Square, is a focal point of the carpeted mall. Across Airport, closer to I-65, is **Springdale Plaza**, where **Gayfers, McRae's** and **Montgomery Ward** are anchors.

Airport Boulevard off I-65 is lined with shopping malls and retail stores, including the **Mobile Festival Centre** strip mall.

WHERE TO BUY ANTIQUES

Atchison Imports is the place for fine European antiques and imported garden furniture. Tony Atchison's landmark brick warehouse has three floors of merchandise. Open Mon.-Sat., 9-5, at 921 Dauphin.

Two malls are located off Government near where Airport Road veers off at the railroad tracks. **The Red Barn** is a packed, two-story collectibles destination at 418 Dauphin Island Parkway across from the Loop Post Office. The larger **Cotton City** at 2012 Airport Blvd. has more than 60 dealers and features lots of furniture, collectibles, advertising premiums, picture frames and so forth. Open daily.

The Gallery antique mall features more than 100 dealers and is located in a large, well lighted, two-story "butler building" between Mobile and Fairhope. It is next to the Chevrolet dealership on U.S. 98, about 5 miles south of the I-10 East exit at Spanish Fort. It's about 20 minutes from Fort Conde and worth the drive. Open every day.

Other dealers are located on Dauphin, Old Shell and Government.

Headed to Foley? Check out the **Gas Works** Antique Mall on Hwy. 59. Open Mon.-Sat., 10-5; Sun., 1-5.

TREATS UNIQUE TO MOBILE

George's Candy Shop is a block off Bienville Square at the corner of 226 Dauphin and Joachim. It has been a fixture in downtown Mobile since 1917 for its delicious candies still made by hand. If you walk by and see candy being made at the front window, you can't resist passing through the large front doors to sample the fudge, pralines and divinity made from scratch.

A soda fountain is at the rear of the store and an old-fashioned ice cream machine churns out varieties flavored with pralines and other candies and fresh strawberries when in season.

When founder George Pappas died, his widow, Euple, ran the shop and its mail order business. She recently sold it to an enterprising young couple named Scott and Siobhan Gonzalez, who renovated the landmark with a period storefront and black and white marble floors. She still works in the shop to make candy and teach the owners the old recipes. Under the supervision of George's brother, Scott uses the original molds and presses to make candycanes and other hard candies. Open Mon.-Sat., 9-5. Phone 433-6725.

George's products are among other Southern gourmet foods which Scott offers by mail-order via the **Pepper Mill** catalog. For a catalog phone 433-7919.

To buy the freshest baked goods loaded with pecans, visit **The Nuthouse** of the H.M. Thames Pecan Co. at 558 S. Broad and 273 S. McGregor. A small shop is inside the Holiday Inn on Government.

If you're ready to be put in the holiday mood or just enjoy shopping for gifts, Robert Moore's remarkable **Christmas Town and Village** is an excellent decoration destination. The staff displays more than 60 Christmas trees - up to 18 feet - throughout the year and stocks thousands of lights, animated Santas, wreaths, ornaments, creches, angels, wrapping and much more. Tired of Christmas? The staff does Easter, Valentine and even Mardi Gras arrangements.

Moore specializes in limited edition collectibles, from Hummels and Snow Village to Disney and Boehm. He handles orders by mail, too.

In addition to having the South's largest Christmas store, Moore has restored a unique village of quaint "shotgun" houses to sell candy, deli sandwiches, coffee and wine and cheese. A walled courtyard provides an ideal setting for motorcoach groups or families to sit down and consume their purchases. This "must stop" is in West Mobile near U.S. 90. Take I-10 exit 17B and turn right on Halls Mill Road and go 2.5 miles to 4213 Halls Mill. Open Mon.-Sat., 10-6; Sun., 1-6. Phone 661-3608.

WHERE TO SHOP FOR MARDI GRAS

Bienville Costumes at 1916 Government next to Krystal rents elaborate Mardi Gras costumes year round for parties. Sandra Oldham's shop, open since 1966, also makes original theme costumes for krewe members to wear to the balls and on floats. They also ship costumes via UPS all over the South. Open Mon.-Fri., 9-5; Sat., 9-noon. Phone 476-6542.

Accent Annex in the Skyland Shopping Plaza (Government Boulevard at Azalea Road west of I-65) is sort of the "Kmart of Mardi Gras." It sells beads and other throws, pins, masks, paper decorations, flags and even paper umbrellas. The New Orleans-based chain, which imports merchandise in huge quantities from Asia, uses green in its merchandise whereas Mobile's original Mardi Gras colors are purple and gold. Phone 661-9404. For a free catalog, phone 1-800-322-2368.

To buy a second-hand satin costume or gown for under $20, visit the **Unique Shop** at 213 Conti near the Saenger Theater. The shop has a lot of collectibles and antiques, as well.

Visit a **Delchamp's** grocery to buy the traditional Mardi Gras King's Cake. Each one contains a plastic baby. Whoever gets the slice with the baby is blessed with good luck.

CULTURAL ACTIVITIES

The **Port Symphony Orchestra** has an extensive seasonal schedule which draws more than 1,600 people to each performance. More than 15,000 students attend the youth concert series. The **Mobile Opera**, active since 1947, performs with the **Mobile Opera Orchestra**. The opera presents in-school workshops and performances for students and other groups, with its total annual audience exceeding 120,000.

The **Fine Arts Museum of the South**, better known as FAMOS, is west of I-65 in Langdon Park and has a small branch downtown in a building with the **Mobile Arts Council** which promotes the **Cathedral Arts District**, a designation of theaters and art-related activities north of Government.

Live entertainment is also provided at the **Saenger Theater** and the **Entertainer Dinner Theater** at 412 Holcombe Ave., and by such amateur companies as the **Joe Jefferson Players**, named for the famous Mobile actor, and the **Firehouse Theater**. Across the bay, the professional company of the **Jubilee Fish Theater** performs in the loft of the Lakewood Golf Club at the Grand Hotel.

For details on cultural events, check the columns by Gordon Tatum Jr. in the Sunday edition of *The Mobile Register* or contact the Mobile Arts Council, 300 Dauphin St., at 432-9796.

ANNUAL EVENTS

Third Saturday of January

Senior Bowl - Ladd Stadium - About 70 of the nation's most outstanding college football seniors square off on teams representing the AFC and NFC to impress pro scouts and improve their chances for the NFL draft. Over the past decade, 71 percent of the Senior Bowl participants have been selected in the first five rounds of the NFL draft. For example, Bo Jackson, Dan Marino, Joe Namath, Pat Sullivan, Frank Gifford, Walter Payton, Terry Bradshaw and Mean Joe Green have played in a Senior Bowl.

The Senior Bowl competes with the Hula Bowl for collegiate all-stars. It is the only collegiate all-star game associated with the pros. The practice and game week attracts between 400 to 500 coaches, general managers, scouts and front office personnel. Each year, two NFL teams bring their entire coaching squads to Mobile to coach the teams. Most NFL head coaches attend who are not involved in league championships games leading to the Super Bowl.

Almost 40,000 fans can be expected at Ladd Stadium where the game has been played since Finley McRae brought it here in 1950 from Jacksonville, Fla. Purchase tickets at various bank locations, the Bel Air Mall and Springdale Mall. The game televised on ESPN may be blacked out in Mobile unless the game is sold out 48 hours in advance. Phone 438-2276.

Late January Weekend

Mobile Camellia Show - The nation's top gardeners travel here with camellia blossoms for judging in outdoor and protected categories. Sponsored since 1940 by the Camellia Society of Mobile, the show is one of the oldest, consecutive annual shows in the camellia world.

At the encouragement of Mobilians, the camellia was named the state flower in 1959. Plan to purchase grafted specimens to take home for your garden. Phone 649-1426 or 666-0193.

February

AfricaTown Folk Festival - Tours of the Afro-American community, homecoming events, a re-enactment of the arrival of the *Clotide* slave ship and other events celebrate the unique community during Black History Month. Events are set at Mobile County Training School gym and cafeteria, and Pine Grove AME Zion Church.

Shrove Tuesday before Lent
Dates: Feb. 15, 1994; Feb. 28, 1995; Feb. 20, 1996; Feb. 11, 1997; Feb. 24, 1998; Feb. 16, 1999; March 7, 2000.
Mardi Gras Weekend - The two-week celebration of spectacular parades, gala mystic krewe balls and pre-Lenten family entertainment culminates the day before Ash Wednesday, 40 days prior to Easter. French Mobile celebrated the New World's first Mardi Gras in 1703.

Marchers in nearly 20 parades wind their way through Mobile. Revelers riding atop colorful floats toss baby-sized Moon Pies, beads, tin coins called doubloons, candy and other "throws." From babies in strollers to people using walking canes, crowds line the parade routes to watch elaborate showcases with ornate floats, marching bands and Mobile's elite dressed up as Mardi Gras royalty.

All in all, it's Alabama's biggest and longest party. During the two weeks, a different mystic society parades almost each evening, usually at 6:30 p.m. Check the schedules in the Mobile newspapers for excellent spreads and summaries of the floats themes the Sunday and the day prior to parades. Depending on the weather Tuesday, a crowd in excess of 200,000 may be on hand.

Each parade is led by a krewe's emblem float, which is an interpretation of its logo or graphic. For example, the Order of Myths features a costumed Folly chasing Death around the broken column of life, and the Knights of Revelry's leader, Folly, banishes tears and sorrow. A cat perched atop a bale of cotton is the Infant Mystics emblem. A succession of floats with a common theme follows, bearing costumed krewe members who literally sling "throws" to the throngs waving to get attention. Grabbing for throws is not for the timid and a few stomped fingers is the price of participation.

The routes are slightly different from day to day. Most start near the Civic Center and follow Church, turning left between the Courthouse and City Hall to Royal. They wrap around Bienville Square, down to Government and reach Spring Hill Avenue and Broad to the west before winding back to disband near the Civic Center.

Participants range from the century-long inclusion of such groups as the Excelsior Band to the recent Resurrected Cowbellion de Rakin Society.

The reason to watch a parade is to grab for and collect souvenirs thrown from the floats, except for the marshmellow pies which are to be eaten. But, parade etiquette prohibits bystanders from throwing anything back at the floats. Mobile's is strictly a family affair; the bare-bottomed men in elaborate headdress who strut in the streets in New Orleans wouldn't be appeciated here. It's okay to sip beer from plastic cups, but police ban beer cans and bottles along the route. Steel barricades parallel to the curbs keep people safely away from the floats.

Be aware that parking along a parade route will get your car towed. Side streets along Government from Royal to Broad are closed an hour prior to start. Government is closed on the final Sunday and Tuesday of the celebration.

The best place to watch an evening parade is in front of the WALA-TV studio at the Government and Joachim intersection because of the bright lights set up to televise the event. Across Government, the best view is from the balcony of the Admiral Semmes reserved for hotel guests, although the crowded perch reduces your chances of catching beads. Avoid the Broad Street route through an inner city neighborhood. Police are everywhere to control traffic and maintain order to promote a good time for everybody.

Parades are sponsored by committees of mystic societies. Among those marching prior to the final weekend are Maids of Mirth, established in 1950; the Mystic Stripers, 1940; and the Crew of Columbus, 1922, which marches on Friday night.

Friday night: The **Crewe of Columbus**, which dates from 1922, parades behind an emblem float of the famous explorer standing atop a revolving world while Indians dance among clouds. Temporary bleachers set up in front of the Mobile Public Library at 701 Government are available for handicapped persons through Tuesday.

Saturday: The major events are the **Floral Parade** in early afternoon and the **Mystics of Time** in the early evening. Father Time is seated in front of a clock with lighted, moving hands on the Mystics of Time's emblem float. Maskers representing riders from the floats surround him. Next comes Vernadean, a 150-foot-long fire- and smoke-breathing dragon with riders, followed by the queen's float, trailed by two baby dragons bearing masked riders. The MOT, which paraded for the 126th time in 1993, is one of the longest parades.

Ships berthed at the State Docks are open in the afternoons through Tuesday for free tours. Go north on U.S. 43 and follow the signs.

If you purchase tickets by Friday, attend the **Mobile Carnival Association**'s elaborate Saturday night coronation of King Felix III, Emperor of Joy, and his consort. A series of tableaus and entertainment make it an event to be remembered.

The court is not a place for *nouveau* arrivals. The selections of the king and queen are the highest honors bestowed by Mobile society. A pedigree of several generations having been in court is an ironclad requirement. Debutantes are in the court and a dozen bachelor knights attend the king.

Sunday (Joe Cain Day): It celebrates the town clerk who in 1866 revived Mardi Gras and the spirits of demoralized Mobilians during Union occupation following defeat in the Civil War. In a recently revived tradition, a local figure personifies Joe Cain's caricature of a Choctaw Indian chief who was never defeated in battle. **Chief Slacabamorinico** from Wragg Swamp wears head feathers and rides in a charcoal wagon pulled by giant Belgian draft horses. He is followed by members of the Excelsior Band, which has been marching since 1883. Several limos carry Cain's "merry widows" who visit his grave just inside the wall of the Church Street Cemetery. A succession of "Cain raisers" throws beads and Moon Pies. Although the procession isn't until mid-afternoon, people come downtown early and enjoy the carnival atmosphere. Street vendors sell food, cotton candy and souvenirs. Party-goers bring their own beer.

Monday: **King Felix** arrives at the foot of Government Street in late morning, followed at noon by the **Floral Parade** and the **King and Knights Parade**. The **Infant Mystics**, which celebrated their 125th anniversary ball in 1993, follow at dusk. (Because Monday has a lighter parade schedule than Saturday and Tuesday, this is a good day to take a break and visit **Bellingrath Gardens** to see the huge beds of tulips, jonquils and other bulbs.)

THE BEST OF MARDI GRAS

Saturday night: Coronation of King Felix III and his queen
        Mystics of Time Parade
Sunday afternoon: Joe Cain Procession
Tuesday: Comic Cowboys Parade in afternoon
        Order of Myths Parade at night

Tuesday (Mardi Gras Day): It's the Big Day when locals pack a picnic basket and spend most of the day downtown. If the weather is favorable, most of the 200,000 celebrants arrive early, turning parking lots and even sidewalks into a bumper-to-bumper tailgate party. Some even park between Government and Church the night before to ensure a parking space as a base of operation. Picnickers cover Spanish Plaza with tablecloths and well-stocked coolers.

Even though the first parade isn't until late morning, you should attempt to arrive downtown before 8:30. Major arteries like I-10, Government, Dauphin and Old Shell are bumper-to-bumper after 9 a.m. and close-in parking spaces quickly become scarce.

The all-female Order of Athena begins the first parade at 11 a.m., followed by the Knights of Revelry, founded in 1874. The Knights' traditional leader, Folly, rides high on a champagne glass symbolically banishing tears and sorrow, leaving only merriment. King Felix III and his queen glide by under a giant crown, followed by the Comic Cowboys who satirize politicians with their raunchy humor.

The Mammoth Parade staged by the black Mobile Area Mardi Gras Association for King Elexis is in mid-afternoon. Fill the afternoon lull by "people watching" in Bienville Square and stop by the peanut store on Dauphin for a bag of roasted nuts or visit George's for candy.

The Order of Myths, Mobile's oldest parading society, has the honor of being the season finale. A team of mules pulls the emblem float of Folly Chasing Death around a broken column, a mystic symbolism which dates from 1868. A dozen or so themed floats follow, bearing cheerful krewe members who sling small Frisbees, candy and beads to the outstretched hands of parade-watchers and conclude the celebration for another year.

To anyone who has been to New Orleans and tried to get a hotel room during Carnival, the availability of rooms at West Mobile motels along I-65 is rather surprising. That's because this Mardi Gras is still primarily a local event.

To buy tickets to the coronation, call the Mobile Carnival Association at the Chamber of Commerce at 432-3324 or 432-3325. For additional information and schedules, phone the Department of Tourism at 1-800-252-3862.

Mid-March
Azalea Trail Festival - Spanish Plaza - Mobile's legendary azaleas are usually at their peak in late March and early April. A self-guided tour of the largest azaleas is marked by small signs along the streets. The Allied Arts Festival, which features performing and fine arts in Spanish Plaza the day of the road run, and a driving tour of homes are of special interest. Azalea Trail Maids pose at a selected house with beautiful azaleas each Saturday during the four-week event. Phone 1-800-252-3862.

Last Saturday in March
Azalea Trail Run - Downtown - Local runners go shoulder-to-shoulder with some of the world's best in the annual 10K Azalea Trail Run through downtown streets on Saturday morning. As many as 5,000 begin at Barton Academy at 8 a.m. and go west on Government, north on Fulton, east on Dauphin and south to Broad to end at the Civic Center. The certified course is accurate to within a yard a mile.

Up to 6,000 runners participate in the two-mile fun run which follows. The Expo opens Friday at noon and a seafood pasta dinner Friday night is the first major activity. Awards parties follow the races. Downtown hotels are usually booked solid because

6,000 out-of-towners come. Phone 473-RACE.

Second Friday and Saturday in March
Historic Mobile Homes Tour - Citywide - Mobile's stately historic residences generally date from the city's "golden ages, " especially the cotton kingdom era of 1820-65 and the timber era of 1880 -1910.

Tours showcase between 25 and 30 homes by categories (cottages, townhouses, etc.) with hours arranged for morning, afternoon and candlelight tours, so that visitors may choose from several routes over several days. It is possible to visit many homes in a day, but Mobile is a city where it's a shame not to stay at least two days or longer. Look for special coverage of the tour schedule in the March edition of *Mobile Bay Monthly* magazine or read the Sunday edition of the Mobile paper. For ticket information, write P.O. Box 66247 or phone 433-0259, 438-7281.

March 15-April 15 – Theodore
Azalea Masterpiece - Bellingrath Gardens - Millions of azalea blossoms and flowering bulbs transform this world-famous garden into a breathtaking wonderland of pink, red and white. Although beautiful any season of the year, Bellingrath is at its best in spring when azaleas blanket the landscape. The timing of color peaks vary from year to year because of the weather. Open daily, 7 a.m. until dusk. For a recorded message on what's blooming when, phone 973-2217.

Mid-April
Mobile Jazz Festival - Various locations - Local musicians perform with nationally known guest artists at different locations throughout the city. The University of South Alabama, Mobile Arts Council, county schools and local government support the festival committee. The series began in the mid-1960s.

Third Saturday in April
Dauphin Island Sailboat Regatta - Sailboats race 17 miles from Dog River on the Eastern Shore southwest across the bay to Dauphin Island. The race began in 1958 when the Dauphin Island Businessmen's Association invited local yacht clubs on Mobile Bay to race to their island. The Buccaneer, Fairhope, Lake Forest and Mobile clubs take turns hosting.

The first race begins near Fairhope in midmorning and continues past the historic Middle Bay Light House to Dauphin Island. The shore activities on the island begin mid-afternoon, with the trophy presentation Saturday night. Return races are the following day.

The event has grown from 54 boats the first year to more than 300. Ranked by the Gulf Yachting Association as the largest one-day sailing event in the nation, it attracts sailboats and crews from throughout North America and Europe. Take Hwy. 188 to Dauphin Island. Phone 344-5545 or 479-8190.

Thursday-Saturday before Father's Day
Choctaw Indian Pow Wow - Mt. Vernon - Members of the Mowa (Mobile-Washington) Band of Choctaw Indians stage a public spring festival with games, crafts and food on the Indian reservation. Follow signs off U.S. 43 north of Mobile. Locations for future pow wows are uncertain.

Fourth week of June

America's Young Woman of the Year - This is what Mobile used to call the **America's Junior Miss Pageant**. Fifty high-school senior girls, representing their home states, compete for scholarships and prizes. In this classy pageant, academics, creativity, fitness, performing arts, leadership, spirit and poise are the values personified by the contestants. Three nights of preliminaries are followed by the Saturday night finals when the winner receives a $30,000 scholarship from a $75,000 pool. Diane Sawyer and Deborah Norville are among the winners who have become successful in business and entertainment fields.

For nearly four decades, the scholarship program has survived even though contestants do not appear in bathing suits. Pageant attendance has declined in the past decade and the show has not been on network TV since 1985, causing concern for the future of the event. From a peak attendance of 7,500 in the 1960s and '70s, fewer than 2,000 have attended in recent years. Some blame the name change in 1989 and others point to the switch from April to June which eliminates contestants who would prefer to vacation with their families. Phone 438-3621.

Last weekend of June

Blessing of the Fleet - Seafood lovers flock to the Gulf Coast fishing village of Bayou La Batre for the colorful Blessing of the Fleet invoked by the Catholic Church to protect the shrimpers and fishing fleets. Fishing crews from along the coast paint their boats and dress them in brightly colored pennants, flags and other decorations for the festivities.

The tradition of the Blessing dates back centuries and has been held here since 1950. Preliminaries begin on Saturday as St. Margaret Church offers lots of fresh seafood, including boiled shrimp, gumbo, dipped fried fish and stuffed crab.

Underneath spreading live oaks a crowd gathers for the seafood contest. The onlookers cheer competitors, although perennial winner Diana Aikins can expect to repeat in oyster shucking (25 in three minutes is a good number) and shrimp deheading (300 in three minutes). Anyone who can pick and clean 12 crabs in three minutes is likely to win that category.

Sunday is the big day. At mid-morning, a Mass is celebrated at St. Margaret Church. In mid-afternoon, a land parade of bands, beauty contest winners and politicians in cars winds through the narrow streets from Alba High School to the bayou. When the land parade reaches the docks, the flotilla of flag-decked boats lined from deck-to-deck with people begins the water parade. The first boat leaving the dock carries Archbishop Oscar H. Lipscomb to the middle of the bayou where he says a brief prayer and lowers a wreath into the water in recognition for those who have lost their lives at sea.

As the archbishop's boat sails past the other boats, he offers his blessing and prayers for a safe and bountiful season. The boats then fall in line to form a spectacular procession down and back up the bayou. Because of the large crowds, arrive at the docks early and stake out your viewing spot. For exact times of major events, phone St. Margaret Church at 824-2415.

Fourth of July

Grand Bay Watermelon Festival - Farmers near this small town west of Mobile ship tons of red and yellow melons across the country each summer. To celebrate, they have invited visitors to join them to celebrate the harvest each year since 1974. Prior to the

Fourth, the Jaycees host such festivities as a street dance in the Sims Supermarket parking lot and a gospel singing at Festival Park. On the holiday, a full schedule allows you to shop arts and crafts, listen to live entertainment, try your hand at game booths and, of course, eat plenty of free watermelon. Since the festival wouldn't be complete without a watermelon queen and seed spitting, eating and biggest watermelon contests, you won't be disappointed. At best of all, it's free, though a small parking fee is charged.

Weekend in July

Living History - Fort Gaines - Scores of uniformed Confederate re-enactors set up camp for a weekend each summer to depict life at the fort in the year before it fell to the Union navy. You may watch re-enactors drill, fire muskets and perform guard duty during the day. On Saturday night, join a tour of the dark fort lighted only by lanterns and candles. Phone 861-6992.

Third weekend of July

Alabama Deep Sea Fishing Rodeo - Dauphin Island - More than 2,500 salt water fishermen head for open waters for trophy fish in the granddaddy of all Gulf Coast fishing contests. While competitors are plying in the gulf, landlubbers enjoy crafts, food booths and entertainment. A Liars Contest kicks off the rodeo on Thursday with a distinguished panel of judges. A major coastal event since 1929, the rodeo attracts 90,000 spectactors a year. Phone 476-8828.

Labor Day

Labor Day Parade and Rally - Fairgrounds - Thousands of union members and their families celebrate with speeches, a car show, charity displays, entertainment and city-sponsored fireworks in one of the state's largest Labor Day activities. A downtown parade winding from the Civic Center parking lot to Bienville Square precedes the event. Local and state politicians take turns at the microphone to extol the virtues of organized labor, especially on even-numbered years prior to elections. After 47 years, the event was moved from Saraland's Amelia Park in north Mobile County to the fairgrounds at Cody Road and Ziegler Boulevard to accommodate larger crowds. The United Labor Committee of South Alabama and other unions have been hosting the event since 1946.

Second half of September

September Celebration - Various bay locations - A celebration of graphic arts, performing arts and music involves dozens of mostly free events which attract some 40,000 people. After preliminary events, the Arts Explosion on Sunday afternoon in Bienville Square features music. A midday "brown bag" luncheon concert follows in Bienville each weekday. A highlight at the Fine Arts Museum of the South the concluding weekend is the annual **Outdoor Arts and Crafts Fair** in Langan Park staged since 1965. The $150,000 celebration overlaps National Arts Week. Some events are free. For exact dates and times, check the Arts and Leisure pages in *The Mobile Press* and *The Mobile Register*.

First Saturday in October
Fulton Sawmill Days - The town of 384 people attracts thousands who celebrate Clarke County's heritage as "the capital of Alabama forestry." Working teams of Belgian horses, mules, oxen and draft horses are hitched up for demonstrations. The pioneer logging show features antique Lindsey Log wagons and loaders hitched to working horse teams. Adults compete in crosscut sawing and broad ax chopping while kids watch puppet shows. Fiddlers, gospel singers, country musicians and western swing musicians provide live music during the day. A popular area is the logging camp food fair where the home cooking includes sawmill biscuits and gravy, chicken and dumplings, turnip greens and cracklin bread and other local foods. The celebration began as part of the Alabama Reunion in 1989 to celebrate the centennial of Scotch Lumber Co. and drew a crowd of 10,000. It gets bigger every year. Fulton is on U.S. 43 between Grove Hill and Thomasville.

Fourth weekend in October
Outdoor Arts and Crafts Fair - Langan Municipal Park - A family-oriented juried art show with entertainment, children's activities and refreshments, is presented by the Art Patrons League on the grounds of the Fine Arts Museum of the South. Artists display their works under colorful tents in a pine forest overlooking the lake. The event has been a major Mobile cultural activity since 1964. Phone 343-2667.

Early October
Gulf State Fair - Scores of thrill rides along the midway attract crowds by the thousands each night during the nine-day run. Major headliner entertainers, such as the band Alabama, appears at the fair's grandstand. The fair is the largest in the nation run by Jaycees and has been selected by the Association of Alabama Fairs as the best in the state. More than 250,000 attend. Advance tickets are sold in September.

November
Chrysanthemum Extravaganza - Bellingrath Gardens - Some 60,000 plants and millions of blooms create an explosion of gold, orange, white and other colors bordering and cascading over nearly everything in sight. Bellingrath is identified with azaleas, but as more people visit in late fall and see the mums show, they gain a new appreciation for this most remarkable gardens. The dramatic cascades flow from nearly every wall and bridge and from balconies of the 15-room home against a backdrop of antebellum brick and iron lace. Remember that the days are short. If you plan to photograph the gardens, you should arrive by 1 p.m. so that your tour is over by 3 p.m. or 3:30. Otherwise, the tall trees and bushes will be shading the vibrant mums and they will look dark in your pictures.

Saturday in early November
Theodore Pecan Festival - Middle School - Pecan growers celebrate the harvest with entertainment, antique cars, a cake walk, rides, crafts and food booths. It has been sponsored since 1989 by the Theodore Historic Foundation which is restoring the old Theodore-Dawes Building on the festival grounds as a museum. Phone 653-9528 or 653-7273.

Second weekend in November
Coden Heritage Days - Coden United Methodist Church - The ship-building and repairing heritage of this coastal community is celebrated by trawl board construction, net making, wood skiff building and demonstrations of seafood crafts. Antique boat engines and old cars are displayed. Seafood and barbecue dinners are served both days. The church location is 2 blocks south of Hwy. 188, off U.S. 90. Phone 824-4851.

Thanksgiving
Poarch Indian Thanksgiving Pow Wow - Atmore - The Poarch Band of Creek Indians celebrate Thanksgiving with visiting tribes and the event is open to the public. Costumed native Americans perform various dances and hold a princess contest. Indians display beadwork, baskets, quilts, jewelery worked in silver and other crafts. The pow wow has been held each Thanksgiving since 1971. Poarch, near I-65, is 8 miles north of Atmore on County Road 1. Phone 368-9136.

Thanksgiving night
Camellia Ball - Daughters of the city's most prominent families are presented at society's Camellia Ball, an event dating back four decades. Admission is by invitation.

First weekend in December
Candlelight Christmas at Oakleigh - 350 Oakleigh Place - Pathways leading to the 1833 mansion glow with hundreds of candles for two nights and the city's official Christmas tree stands on the front lawn. Inside, a massive tree in the first parlor is festooned with traditional decorations. The home is decorated by local designers using fresh garlands, pine, chinaberry, fruit, magnolia leaves and other native greenery.

You can enjoy Oakleigh's hot spiced tea, fruitcake, punch and other refreshments while listening to holiday music by local musicians. The gift shop offers inexpensive Christmas gifts and the Preservation Pantry in the archives building sells homemade candies, cakes and pastries, as well as small craft stocking stuffers.

A charming custom dating from Christmas 1855 is re-enacted one night when local boys, dressed as the Mobile Rifle Company, pay their respects to a girl dressed as "Miss Daisy," the young daughter of a former owner, Gen. T.K. Irwin. The program is sponsored by the Historic Mobile Preservation Society. Admission charged. Phone 432-6161 for hours.

First weekend in December
Christmas at Richards-DAR House - The 1860 house museum is decorated in Christmas finery by chapters of the Daughters of the American Revolution. Admission includes refreshments and a tour. On Saturday, bring your stamped Christmas cards to the carriage house for a holiday cancellation by the Postal Service. Phone 434-7320.

Mid-December
The Nutcracker - Civic Center Theater - Three performances of the traditional holiday story are performed by the Mobile Ballet on Saturday and Sunday. Children are invited to meet the cast following the matinees. For dates and tickets, phone 661-2244.

New Year's Eve
First Night Mobile - Thousands gather at downtown theaters, banks, churches and
Bienville Square for family-oriented entertainment and food to herald the new year.
Magicians, singers, theater groups, mimes, choirs, bands and dance groups perform
from the late afternoon for children and until 11:30 p.m. for adults. Many of the
activities and stages are set up on side streets flanking Dauphin, closed for the evening.
The area is bounded by Government, Lawrence, St. Francis and Water streets. The
alcohol-free, drug-free celebration climaxes with a fireworks extravaganza at midnight
over the Mobile River at the foot of Dauphin. Purchase a button at a Delchamps grocery
store for unlimited admission to the venues. The event, which attracted 15,000 the first
time it was held, is inspired by the First Night celebration in Boston. Phone 434-7304.

SIDE TRIP TO BAYOU LA BATRE

Bayou La Batre, the most attractive fishing village on the Mobile side of the bay,
is along the Gulf Coast, just a short drive from the I-10 state welcome center at the
Mississippi state line. Bayou La Batre was founded by Joseph Bosarge in 1786 as part
of a Spanish land grant. The main street is a bayou, where trawlers are often three or
four abreast on both sides of the tributary as it enters the Mississippi Sound.

Oyster reefs are harvested from Mobile to Dauphin Island. Prices are lowest during
peak spawning season between November and January.

Drive to Bayou La Batre to get a glimpse of the shrimp trawlers working out of the
bayou or the several hundred other smaller vessels which drag the waters for shrimp,
oysters, crabs and mullet. As befitting the seafood capital of the state, recipes for
seafood are prized in families and handed down through the generations. A specialty
is gumbo, a mixture of shrimp, crab, okra, spices and other ingredients boiled to
perfection.

Not surprisingly, the **Catalina** restaurant (phone 824-2104) and the **Lighthouse**
(824-2500) both serve the freshest fish you'll find anywhere.

Although it is a relatively small town, the seafood industry is riding a changing tide
of economic fortune. Bayou La Batre sometimes ranks among the top 30 ports in the
country, and Bon Secour, across the bay, is about 50th.

Seafood processing began more than a century ago in Alabama. The state's first
oyster cannery was built in Bayou La Batre. Because of the seasonality of seafood, some
early canneries relied on oysters in the winter, vegetables in the spring and early
summer and shrimp during fall and early winter harvests in order to stay in business
year round.

A drive around the town also shows that shipbuilding is a major industry,
although things are not as busy as a decade ago when nearly 30 boat builders employed
1,500 workers. Changing currency exchanges gave foreign shipbuilders a cost advantage. Nonetheless, an average of 100 vessels are constructed annually. The best time
to visit is in June for the Blessing of the Fleet.

SIDE TRIP TO DAUPHIN ISLAND

Early in the 1700s Frenchmen founded the first white settlement in the Louisiana
Territory on Dauphin Island, which they originally named "Massacre" because of the
many human skeletons found there. When the group realized the island's potential as
a defense post, the name was changed to Dauphin after the son of Louis XIV, and the
settlement was moved to the mainland.

The cigar-shaped, 15-mile long island 3 miles off the coast of Mobile County's mainland is shaped by the flow of the Mississippi Sound on its north and the open waters of the Gulf of Mexico along the south. It measures 2 miles across at its widest point, with Bienville Boulevard as the main east-west street.

A bridge spanning the Mississippi Sound in 1955 created the first permanent access. It was heavily damaged by Hurricane Frederic in 1979 and replaced several years later. It carries traffic on Hwy. 163 from Mobile to the island.

Tucked down below Mobile, Dauphin Island is not as convenient as other beaches. Therefore, many Alabamians have never been here, preferring instead to go to the Gulf Shores area or Florida for their sun and surf vacation. The relative isolation of the island's 850 permanent residents is broken in summer with the influx of tourists and a smaller group of Canadian and northern "snowbirds" in the winter. The head count soars to 70,000 who jam the island in July during the Deep Sea Fishing Rodeo.

If you think that a trip to Dauphin Island is the same as one to Gulf Shores, you may be surprised at the differences. Sand dunes reach as high as 35 feet near the Isle Dauphine Golf Club. Litter is a problem, especially on the long unpopulated west end, where volunteers haul off tons of trash each September during a national coastal cleanup project.

Dauphin Island's origin is unique in the state. It is Alabama's only true barrier island, built out of sedimentary sands originating in the Appalachian mountains and ultimately flowing out of Mobile Bay. The westerly drift of currents has edged Dauphin and sister islands in Mississippi to the west. The eastern edge has eroded and the western end is constantly being supplemented. An interesting example of this process is that most of Petit Bois in Mississippi was in Alabama only two centuries ago. However, environmentalists wonder if this shift will continue because dams on the rivers in Alabama could be slowing the process. The dredged channel in Mobile Bay may become the repository of the sands that Dauphin Island requires to keep building onto it.

Ultimately, the Mississippi barrier islands and Dauphin Island that form the Mississippi Sound could disappear, erasing the estuary that makes the northern Gulf Coast one of the nation's most productive fishing grounds.

Still relatively undeveloped, there are a few condos, restaurants, rental houses, small motels and a campground.

The best public beaches are at the eastern end and one near the middle with covered picnic areas, boardwalks, playgrounds and bathhouses. The tiny red, two-room schoolhouse near the middle beach educates about 60 students from kindergarten to sixth grade and is the smallest of the 700 elementary schools in Alabama.

Sunbathers at the beach on the eastern end, however, are warned not to enter the water. A short distance from the shore, the depth of the water drops sharply to about 14 feet into a virtual trough surrounding the island. The convergence of Mobile Bay and the Gulf of Mexico results in a strong, highly dangerous undertow.

If fishing is your goal, you've come to the right place. You can use two fishing piers, including one which stretches 850 feet into the sound. Rental fishing boats are available at Dauphin Isle Marina.

ATTRACTIONS

AUDUBON BIRD SANCTUARY is an excellent place for birdwatching. You can roam over 160 acres and expect to spot many of the nearly 200 species, which include yellow-headed blackbirds and ospreys. This is a stopover before or after a two-day migration to the Yucatan Peninsula in Mexico. The best viewing periods are during birds' departures in October and returns in April. The Audubon Sanctuary is near Fort Gaines.

FORT GAINES is a star-shaped brick fortress which has guarded the western approach to Mobile Bay since 1861. At least 46 Confederates were killed or wounded during a 114-hour barrage by Union Adm. Farragut's forces during the Battle of Mobile Bay in 1864. Gaines and its sister fort across the bay, Fort Morgan, then fell into enemy hands for the first time during the war.

Several of the nations which have claimed the coastal region of present-day Alabama have built fortifications here, beginning with a small wooden fort constructed by the French in 1717. Spanish and English navies later stationed men at this eastern tip of the island. After Americans captured Mobile from the Spanish in 1813, they made the first serious attempt to construct a permanent fortification.

Foundation work began in 1819 and was suspended several years later. U.S. Army Chief Engineer J.G. Totten designed a brick-walled pentagon, based on European forts which had shown successful defenses against attacks by land and invasions by water. Construction began in 1856. The Alabama militia seized the nearly completed fort just before the Civil War started and Confederate forces finished the work.

During the Battle of Mobile Bay, the fort sustained heavy damage which was repaired by the U.S. over the next decade. Additional buildings were added following the Spanish-American War.

Although Fort Morgan across the bay remained active as late as World War II, Fort Gaines stood abandoned for decades. Mobile County acquired and partially restored Fort Gaines before opening it as a museum in 1956. Its walls are 4.5 feet thick at the top and stand more than 22 feet high. (The fort is named for Gen. E. P. Gaines who, while commandant of Fort Stoddard in 1807, captured former Vice President Aaron Burr, who had conspired to create a new republic in Spanish America.) Allow 30 minutes to roam the parade grounds, investigate the vaulted tunnels, and walk out onto the bastions where the Civil War cannons still stand watch over the bay. Daily, 9-5. Closed Dec. 25 and Jan. 1. Admission. Phone 861-6992.

Go west on I-10 from Mobile and exit at Theodore Dawes. Take Hwy. 59 south and turn east on Hwy. 188, then south on 163 to the island. Turn left at the large water tank to reach Pelican Point. It is 2 miles east of the LeMoyne Drive intersection.

ISLE DAUPHINE GOLF CLUB has a challenging 18-hole course right on a private beach, swimming pool, tennis courts and restaurant. Formerly a private country club, it is open to the public. Phone 861-2433.

MOBILE BAY FERRY departs from Fort Gaines every 80 minutes or so during peak season to transport cars, trucks, boat trailers, travel homes and walk-on pedestrians to Fort Morgan. The 8-mile ride taking 30 minutes can save many miles of driving if you are headed to Gulf Shores. The fare for a car and all passengers is $12. Departures are about every 80 minutes. For times, phone 973-2251 or 1-800-634-4027.

Tuscaloosa	Troy	Talladega	Selma	Scottsboro	Phenix City	**Montgomery**	**Mobile**	**Huntsville**	Gulf Shores	Gadsden	Florence	Florala	Evergreen	Eufaula	Dothan	Decatur	Clanton	**Birmingham**	Auburn	Athens	Anniston	
119	167	24	127	89	127	108	277	103	299	28	152	230	186	175	204	105	84	62	97	120	0	Anniston
142	228	139	179	66	240	180	349	23	370	91	43	291	256	264	281	16	148	96	212	0	120	Athens
198	185	104	210	139	113	162	332	180	353	109	232	257	237	214	167	186	164	142	107	202	87	Atlanta, Ga.
163	79	84	104	190	32	56	226	197	247	126	233	151	131	68	122	195	90	118	0	212	97	Auburn
57	133	55	84	98	141	84	253	95	274	63	116	187	160	169	186	75	52	0	118	96	62	**Birmingham**
76	80	60	43	150	114	34	203	147	224	112	171	137	110	118	133	127	0	52	90	148	84	Clanton
96	182	94	133	65	193	133	303	55	323	54	69	236	211	218	233	28	101	49	167	46	82	Cullman
123	207	121	170	69	219	162	328	27	352	77	48	267	240	243	263	0	127	75	195	16	105	Decatur
63	145	150	49	212	180	99	162	209	209	178	231	195	117	180	198	186	92	114	153	203	174	Demopolis
208	55	180	142	286	101	103	203	278	178	231	298	67	103	54	0	263	133	186	122	281	204	Dothan
191	61	147	130	249	47	84	233	263	232	185	326	121	141	0	54	243	118	169	68	264	175	Eufaula
136	248	171	202	108	263	200	329	66	408	123	0	306	276	326	298	48	171	116	233	43	152	Florence
153	211	83	185	27	190	180	344	68	361	39	132	272	260	218	280	96	148	96	164	90	67	Fort Payne
120	176	50	147	64	152	147	305	75	328	0	123	239	225	185	231	77	112	63	126	91	28	Gadsden
273	184	278	203	372	279	191	48	369	0	328	408	112	115	232	178	352	224	274	247	370	299	Gulf Shores
126	202	76	152	29	187	178	322	39	343	35	106	265	257	211	257	51	121	69	161	63	64	Guntersville
151	227	116	178	43	227	179	348	0	369	75	66	282	257	263	278	27	147	95	200	23	103	**Huntsville**
190	286	294	200	339	331	250	188	309	236	310	258	303	256	335	360	315	240	241	304	298	303	Jackson, Miss.
225	172	253	180	351	246	169	0	348	48	305	329	115	93	233	203	328	203	253	226	349	277	**Mobile**
107	48	84	50	207	80	0	169	179	191	147	200	105	78	84	103	162	34	84	56	180	108	**Montgomery**
253	317	221	268	136	329	269	438	103	459	180	117	380	345	353	370	105	240	185	301	95	208	Nashville, Tenn.
294	313	292	298	437	387	348	141	440	189	414	418	234	256	433	464	421	338	345	400	435	401	New Orleans, La.
249	148	248	169	370	237	164	56	341	34	362	311	76	86	143	197	326	196	246	217	272	123	Pensacola, Fla.
190	90	113	130	215	0	80	246	227	279	152	263	162	141	47	101	219	114	141	32	240	127	Phenix City
155	230	105	181	0	215	207	351	43	372	64	108	294	286	249	286	69	150	98	190	66	89	Scottsboro
80	92	103	0	181	130	50	180	178	203	147	202	130	83	130	142	170	43	84	104	179	127	Selma
0	155	112	80	155	190	107	225	151	273	120	136	191	208	191	208	123	76	57	163	142	119	Tuscaloosa

WHAT TO DO
THIS WEEKEND

Each weekend offers a variety of family activities throughout Alabama. Review the listings after each city in the main text.

The following are just some of the better known events which merit an extra effort to attend. For a semi-annual, comprehensive Calendar of Events, contact the Alabama Bureau of Tourism & Travel at 1-800-ALABAMA.

† indicates that date may vary from year to year. Check the date with sponsors or local tourism agency before driving long distances.

◊ indicates that event is spread over a longer period of time than the indicated weekend.

JANUARY
First ◊ - Launch the year at Huntsville's **U.S. Space & Rocket Center.**
Second ◊ - See the nation's symbol soar at Guntersville's **Eagle Watch.**
Third - Watch future NFL rookies impress scouts in the **Senior Bowl.**
Fourth - Ducks and geese on Lake Eufaula are **Watchable Wildlife.**

FEBRUARY
First - Relive black history at the **Birmingham Civil Rights Institute.**
Second - Talk to the animals during the Montgomery **Zoo Weekend.**
Second/third † - Catch **Mardi Gras** beads in Mobile thru Tuesday.
Third/fourth † - See heroes at the **Sports Hall of Fame Banquet.**

MARCH
First - Count the rattlesnakes rounded up at Opp's **Rattlesnake Rodeo.**
Second - Be dazzled by **Bellingrath Gardens'** awesome azaleas.
Third - Shop Fairhope for great crafts at the **Arts and Crafts Festival.**
Fourth - Get real formal at the **Historic Selma Pilgrimage Ball.**

APRIL
First - Homes are on display for **Pilgrimage** in Tuscaloosa and Eufaula.
Second - Buy art at the **Calico Fort Arts and Crafts Fair** in Fort Deposit.
Easter - See the sun rise on the Moundville **Easter Sunrise Pageant.**
Third - Go global at the **International Festival of Arts** in Birmingham.
Fourth ◊ - Marvel at the talent at the **Alabama Shakespeare Festival.**

MAY
First - Cheer your favorites to the finish at Talladega's **Winston 500.**
Second - Appreciate art at Huntsville's spectacular **Panoply** festival.
Second/third † - Study beach at Gulf Shore's **Sea Oats Jamboree.**
Third - Clog dancing and music top Mentone's **Rhododendron Festival.**
Memorial Day - Hot-air balloons dazzle Decatur at **Alabama Jubilee.**

JUNE

First - Springville offers relaxed homespun fun at **Spring Fest.**
Second † - Fort Payne's "boys" throw a week-long party during **June Jam.**
Third - The heart of Birmingham loves all types of music during **City Stages.**
Fourth † - Clanton throws a peach of a party at the **Peach Festival.**
Last - Teach the kids about a great lady at the **Helen Keller Festival.**

JULY

First - Take the family to **"Looney's Tavern"** before summer slips by.
Fourth of July - Fireworks fill Alabama skies during **Independence Day.**
Second - Pros match the dots at Andalusia's **World Championship Domino Tournament.**
Third - Admire the chrome collection at Gadsden's **Antique Auto Meet.**
Fourth ◊ - Applaud local theatrical talent at Birmingham **Summerfest.**

AUGUST

First - "Soldiers" return to Gulf Shores for **Fort Morgan Civil War Weekend.**
Second - Spit seeds for distance at Greenville's **Watermelon Jubilee.**
Third - Watch cutters shinny up a tree at Lafayette's **East Alabama Pine Tree Festival.**
Last - Games, gags and great music put a "30" on summer at Birmingham's **Great Southern Kudzu Festival.**

SEPTEMBER

Labor Day - Concerts and tours fire up the **Tannehill Labor Day Celebration.**
Second - High-tech Huntsville goes country on **Old-Fashioned Trade Day.**
Third ◊ - Mobile harmonizes with the arts for **September Celebration.**
Fourth - Mules take back the streets in Winfield on **Mule Day.**

OCTOBER

First - Cullman, a real German town, cooks bratwurst for **Oktoberfest.**
Second - **National Shrimp Festival**: a good excuse to go to Gulf Shores.
Third - Invest in the South's folk art at Northport's **Kentuck Festival.**
Fourth - Florence welcomes knights at **Alabama Renaissance Faire.**
Last - Elberta smokes tons of pig for the **German Sausage Festival.**

NOVEMBER

First ◊- Dothan loves a big parade during the **National Peanut Festival.**
Second ◊- **Bellingrath** fall season is golden **Chrysanthemum Extravanganza.**
Third - Artists imitate life at Decatur's **Southern Wildlife Festival.**
Thanksgiving - Native Alabamians share the harvest at the **Poarch Indian Thanksgiving Pow Wow.**
Thanksgiving weekend - **Auburn-Alabama Game.** Nothing else matters.

DECEMBER

First - The Demopolis Santa gets wet feet at **Christmas on the River.**
Second - Huntsville museums deck the halls for **Christmas Open House.**
Third - Head to **Boaz** before the Christmas bargains are all gone.
Christmas - Football stars fall on Alabama in Montgomery's **Blue-Gray Classic.**
New Year's Eve - The family celebrates together at **First Night Mobile.**

INTERSTATE EXITS

Travelers know that rest opportunities along interstate highways are not in great abundance. Therefore, the following lists provide some advance notice of exits of special interest. They are listed by exit number or mile marker (M.M.) number.

I-65 from Mobile to Tennessee

Exit 3B	Airport Boulevard and motels
M.M. 25	Alabama River
Exit 37	To Gulf Shores via Hwys. 287 and 59
Exit 57	Poarch Bingo, exit to Monroeville
M.M. 85/88	**State Rest Area**, Evergreen
Exit 130	Bates Turkey Restaurant
M.M. 134	**State Rest Area**
Exit 142	Priester's Pecans
Exit 151	To Lowndesboro
Exit 167	U.S. 80 to Montgomery airport and Selma
Exit 168	Southern Bypass, Montgomery
Exit 171	**I-85** to Auburn, Atlanta
Exit 172	Exit to Herron St., State Capitol, downtown
Exit 173	Northern Bypass
Exit 186	Exit to Confederate Memorial Park
Exit 205	Clanton farmers' markets, peaches
M.M. 214	**State Rest Area**
Exit 246	Cracker Barrel, Oak Mountain State Park
Exit 250	**I-459** to Tuscaloosa or Gadsden, Chattanooga
Exit 252	Hoover, U.S. 31, to Galleria
Exit 256	Homewood, Green Springs
Exit 259	Birmingham Information Center, UAB
Exit 261	**I-59/20**, airport, downtown, Civic Center
Exit 287	Watch for hawks circling
M.M. 301	**State Rest Area**, Cullman
Exit 308	To Cullman, Ave Maria Grotto
Exit 310	Cracker Barrel, McDonald's
Exit 328	To Hartselle, antique mall
Exit 334	To Decatur, Point Mallard, wildlife refuge
Exit 340	**I-565**, Huntsville, Space & Rocket Center
Exit 351	Cracker Barrel. U.S. 72, Florence, Huntsville

I-20 from Mississippi to Georgia

Exit 45	Greentrack dog racing
MM 64	Black Warrior River
Exit 71	Tuscaloosa
Exit 100	Tannehill State Historical Park
Exit 168	Talladega Speedway, Talladega
Exit 185	Old Mill Antique Mall, Anniston
Exit 191	Cheaha State Park

I-10 from Florida to Mississippi

Exit 66	**Alabama Welcome Center**
Exit 53	Truck stops
Exit 44	Loxley/Hwy. 59 to Gulf Shores
Exit 38	To Malbis Church
Exit 35	Daphne, Spanish Fort, Malbis
Exits 27/30	Battleship Parkway, USS Alabama
Exit 26-A	Fort Conde, downtown Mobile
Exit 22-B	Hwy. 163, Dauphin Island, beaches
Exit 17	Tillman's Corner, 193 to Dauphin Island
Exit 15-A	To Bellingrath Gardens

U.S. 231 from Montgomery to Dothan

M.M. 97	Kohn jeans store
M.M. 95	**State Rest Area**
M.M. 79	Pike Pioneer Museum
M.M. 78	U.S. 29 to downtown Troy
M.M. 57	Pea River
M.M. 54	Hwy. 51 to Enterprise
M.M. 44	Ozark Holiday Inn/To Ft. Rucker
M.M. 38	**State Rest Area**
M.M. 23	Ross Clark Circle
M.M. 13	Wiregrass Commons
M.M. 12	Pecan shops
M.M. 12	Peanut Festival Fairgrounds
M.M. 8	Olympic Spa
M.M. 1	**Alabama Welcome Center**

U.S. 280 from Birmingham to Georgia

M.M. 32	Exit to DeSoto Caverns on Hwy. 76
M.M. 42	Sylacauga
M.M. 47	Russell Mills retail store, Alex City
M.M. 68	Hwy. 63 to Wind Creek Park
M.M. 81	Tallapoosa River
M.M. 89	Exit to Horseshoe Bend
M.M. 90	Exit to Still Waters Resort
M.M. 98	To Lyman Ward military school
M.M. 111	Hwy. 147 to Auburn

INDEX

Charles Winters

About the author

Lee Sentell is a fifth-generation Alabamian whose ancestors settled land ceded by Creek Indians after the Battle of Horsehoe Bend. His first travel series, a report on a Boy Scout jamboree, appeared in his hometown weekly, *The Ashland Progress*, at age 12. After graduating from Auburn, he edited newspapers in Birmingham and Decatur before his love of travel led to a career in the profession.

His work has appeared in *The New York Times* and *The Los Angeles Times*, as well as other national and international publications. His civic and professional activities have been recognized by Alabama Jaycees, Alabama Historical Commission, Alabama Travel Council, Alabama Associated Press Association and Sigma Delta Chi, professional journalism organization.

Sentell lives in a restored 120-year-old house within sight of the Tennessee River. This is his first book.

Back Cover:
U.S. Space & Rocket Center, Alabama's Constitution Village
Birmingham Civil Rights Institute, Riverchase Galleria
Alabama Shakespeare Festival, Alabama State Capitol
Gulf beaches, Bellingrath Gardens and Home